Colonial Maryland Soldiers and Sailors

1634-1734

Henry C. Peden, Jr., M.A.

HERITAGE BOOKS
2008

HERITAGE BOOKS
AN IMPRINT OF HERITAGE BOOKS, INC.

Books, CDs, and more—Worldwide

For our listing of thousands of titles see our website
at
www.HeritageBooks.com

Published 2008 by
HERITAGE BOOKS, INC.
Publishing Division
100 Railroad Ave. #104
Westminster, Maryland 21157

Copyright © 2001 Henry C. Peden, Jr.

All rights reserved. No part of this book may be reproduced or transmitted in any form or by any means, electronic or mechanical, including photocopying, recording or by any information storage and retrieval system without written permission from the author, except for the inclusion of brief quotations in a review.

International Standard Book Numbers
Paperbound: 978-1-58549-649-5
Clothbound: 978-0-7884-7307-4

FOREWORD

Many lists are extant for colonial soldiers of Maryland in the mid-18th century, most of which are muster rolls and records of payment for service during the 1740's and the French and Indian Wars in the late 1750's. One can simply consult Myrtie June Clark's *Colonial Soldiers of the South, 1732-1774*, plus articles in *Western Maryland Genealogy* and the *Maryland Historical Magazine*, to easily find those records.

There are, however, no such lists that are finger-tip available for colonial soldiers and sailors during the first hundred years of Maryland's history. While one may find references to militia lists being reported by captains at various times in the *Archives of Maryland*, a careful search of the holdings at the Maryland State Archives and the Maryland Historical Society has revealed that no such lists have survived from the early colonial period. This paucity in the records, therefore, enticed me to do the research which resulted in this compilation of *Colonial Maryland Soldiers and Sailors, 1634-1734*.

One shutters to think of all the brave Maryland men who fought at the Battle of the Severn in 1655, in Fendall's Rebellion of 1659, in the Revolution of 1689, in battles at sea, and in countless expeditions against the Indians, whose names have been lost forever. Actually, by Act of the Maryland Assembly in 1654, any person between the ages of 16 and 60 was considered eligible for military service (see *Archives of Maryland*, Volume I, page 347). Unfortunately, however, there are no extant lists to let us know who all of those citizen soldiers were.

Therefore, my book is intended to be a one-volume guide in identifying as many colonial soldiers and sailors of Maryland during its first hundred years as possible in order to assist those who want to join such patriotic organizations as the Colonial Dames of America, Colonial Dames of the 17th Century, and the Society of Colonial Wars, just to name a few.

It must be noted that this book is not intended to be a comprehensive genealogical study of every person named; that's left up to the individual researcher. In most cases, what one will find here is the names of the soldiers or sailors, places of residence, military and/or civil service information, dates of birth and death, and probate information (including widows names). In some cases, however, historians and genealogists will need to do additional resesearch before drawing conclusions.

Each entry is documented as to the source of the information. In brackets after each entry one will find codes to the references used, followed by the book number and/or page number for each source. The records cited are both primary and secondary sources; therefore, one should always consult the original records for accuracy and more complete information. The coded references are as follows:

AAGE = *Anne Arundel Gentry*, by Harry Wright Newman (Baltimore: Lord Baltimore Press, 1933)

AALR = Anne Arundel County Land Records

ARMD = *Archives of Maryland* (abstracts from 30 of the earliest published volumes of the Proceedings and Acts of the Assembly of Maryland and the Proceedings of the Council of Maryland between 1634 and 1734 (Baltimore: Maryland Historical Society, 1894-1972)

BALR = Baltimore County Land Records

BBCF = *Baltimore County Families, 1659-1759*, by Robert W. Barnes (Baltimore: Genealogical Publishing Company, 1989)

BCTL = *Baltimore County, Maryland, Tax List, 1699-1706*, by Raymond B. Clark, Jr. and Sara Seth Clark (Washington, DC: By the authors, 1964)

BDML = *A Biographical Dictionary of the Maryland Legislature, 1635-1789*. 2 vols. (Baltimore: The Johns Hopkins University Press, 1979, 1985)

CELR = Cecil County Land Records

CESM = *Citizens of the Eastern Shore of Maryland, 1659-1750*, by F. Edward Wright {Silver Spring, MD: Family Line Publications, 1986}

CFES = *Colonial Families of the Eastern Shore*. Volumes 1-3 by Robert W. Barnes and F. Edward Wright, 1996-1997; Volumes 4-5 by Christos Christou, Jr. and F. Edward Wright, 1998-1999; Volumes 6-9 by Henry C. Peden, Jr. and F. Edward Wright, 1999-2000 (Westminster, MD: Family Line Publications & Willow Bend Books)

CHLR = Charles County Land Records

CMSP = *Calendar of Maryland State Papers, The Black Books* (Publication of the Hall of Records Commission No. 1, 1943)

CVPR = *Calvert Papers: Colonial Ventures* (Maryland Historical Society, Microfilm Roll 12: Revenues of Lord Baltimore)

DOLR = Dorchester County Land Records

FAAH = *Founders of Anne Arundel and Howard Counties*, by J. D. Warfield (Baltimore: Kohn & Pollock, 1905; reprinted by Family Line Publications, Westminster, MD, 1990)

FDMP = *The Flowering of the Maryland Palatinate*, by Harry Wright Newman (Baltimore: Genealogical Publishing Company, 1985)

HBCC = *History of Baltimore City and County*, by J. Thomas Scharf (Philadelphia: Louis H. Everts, 1881; reprinted 1971)

HCCM = *A History of Calvert County, Maryland*, by Charles Francis Stein (Baltimore: Schneidereith & Sons, 1960; reprinted 1976)

INAC = *Abstracts of the Inventories & Accounts of the Prerogative Court of Maryland, 1674-1734*, by Vernon L. Skinner, Jr. (Westminster, MD: Family Line Publications, 1992-1996; 14 vols., original libers cited)

INBC = *Inhabitants of Baltimore County, 1692-1763*, by F. Edward Wright (Westminster, MD: Family Line Publications, 1987)

INCC = *Inhabitants of Cecil County, 1649-1774*, by Henry C. Peden, Jr. (Westminster, MD: Family Line Publications, 1993)

INKC = *Inhabitants of Kent County, 1637-1787*, by Henry C. Peden, Jr. (Westminster, MD: Family Line Publications, 1994)

KELR = Kent County Land Records

LMCL = *Lord Mayor's Court of London: Depositions Relating to Americans, 1641-1736*, by Peter Wilson Coldham (Washington, D.C.: National Genealogical Society, 1980)

MDAD = *Abstracts of the Administration Accounts of the Prerogative Court of Maryland*, by Vernon L. Skinner, Jr. (Westminster, MD: Family Line Publications and Willow Bend Books, 1995-1999; 11 vols., original libers cited)

MDHM = *Maryland Historical Magazine*

MDHR = Maryland Hall of Records, Colonial Wars Collection S962, Box 1, Folder 11 (Maryland State Archives Accession No. 4645)

MDCB = Maryland Commission Book No. 82 (Abstracts of the Records of the Council of Maryland, 1733-1773, published in the *Maryland Historical Magazine*, Vol. 26, in 1931)

MDEP = *Maryland Deponents, 1634-1799*, by Henry C. Peden, Jr. (Westminster, MD: Family Line Publications, 1991)

MDGZ = *The Maryland Gazette, 1727-1761*, by Karen Mauer Green (Galveston, TX: The Frontier Press, 1989)

MDWB = Maryland Will Books

MGSB = *Maryland Genealogical Society Bulletin*

MINV = *Abstracts of the Inventories of the Prerogative Court of Maryland, 1718-1734*, by Vernon L. Skinner, Jr. (Westminster, MD: Family Line Publications, 1990-1991; 6 vols., original libers cited)

OSES = *Old Somerset on the Eastern Shore of Maryland*, by Clayton Torrence (Richmond, VA: Whittet & Shepperson, 1935; reprinted by Family Line Publications, Westminster, MD, 1992)

PFMD = *Provincial Families of Maryland, Volume I*, compiled by the Genealogical Council of Maryland under the direction of Vernon L. Skinner, Jr. (Westminster, MD: Family Line Publications, 1998)

PGLR = Prince George's County Land Records

QALR = Queen Anne's County Land Records

RMHF = *Register of Maryland's Heraldic Families*, by Alice Norris Parran. 2 vols. (Baltimore: H. G. Roebuck & Son, 1935, 1938)

SCOT = *Scots on the Chesapeake, 1607-1830*, by David Dobson (Baltimore: Genealogical Publishing Company, 1992)

SHMD = *History of Maryland*, by J. Thomas Scharf (Hatsboro, PA: Tradition Press, 1879; reprinted 1967)

SOJR = *Somerset County Judicial Records*, by Frank V. Walczyk (Coram, NY: Peters Row, 1998) Volume I:1707-1711, Part 1, 1707-1708; Volume II:1707-1711, Part 2, 1709-1711; Volume III:1715-1717

SOTL = *Tax Lists of Somerset County, 1730-1740*, by J. Elliott Russo (Westminster, MD: Family Line Publications, 1992)

TALR = Talbot County Land Records

In the preparation of this book, the aforementioned primary and secondary sources were painstakingly scanned, page by page, line by line, to find the names of the soldiers and sailors of colonial Maryland from 1634 to 1734. While many of the approximately 5,000 men listed herein rendered military service either by land or on the sea, there will be those whose service could be questioned due to a lack of sufficient records to substantiate their service. This is especially true in the case of those styled "captain" and "mariner" or those "paid from the public good" since their service may have been of a commercial nature rather than a military one. Be that as it may, the information within these pages will hopefully be taken in the spirit intended and used accordingly by researchers.

Henry C. Peden, Jr.
Bel Air, Maryland
January 1, 2001

COLONIAL MARYLAND SOLDIERS AND SAILORS
1634-1734

ABBOTT, ---- (Talbot County), captain and owner of a ship (no name given) in 1697. {Ref: ARMD 25:600}
ABBOTT, ELLINOR, see "Samuell Abbott," q.v.
ABBOTT, JOHN (St. Mary's County), soldier (rank not stated) in 1642. {Ref: ARMD 4:130-131}
ABBOTT, NATHANIELL (Somerset County), Protestant and probable soldier in the Revolution of 1689; signed an address and took a loyalty oath supporting the King of England and "for enabling us to defend ourselves against all invaders" on Nov 28, 1689. {Ref: ARMD 8:140}
ABBOTT, SAMUELL (Talbot County), soldier (rank not stated) circa 1675; paid for his services in the late expedition against the Nanticoke Indians in 1678; "Samuel Abbott, Jr." died testate by Oct 29, 1702 (date of probate; his father Samuel was executor) and "Samuel Abbott" died testate by May 11, 1703 (date of probate; Ellinor Abbott, widow). Additional research will be necessary before drawing conclusions. {Ref: ARMD 7:89; MDWB 11:260, 11:320}
ABELL, ROBERT (St. Mary's County), captain by 1652. {Ref: ARMD 10:203}
ABELL, SAM (St. Mary's County), Protestant and probable soldier in the Revolution of 1689; signed an address and took a loyalty oath (made his "S" mark) supporting the King of England and the reestablishment of Lord Baltimore into power on Nov 28, 1689. {Ref: ARMD 8:147}
ABINGTON, ANDREW (Calvert County), Protestant, sheriff, and probable soldier in the Revolution of 1689; signed an address and took a loyalty oath supporting the King of England and the reestablishment of Lord Baltimore into power on Nov 28, 1689. {Ref: ARMD 8:145}
ABINGTON (ABBINGTON), JOHN (England and Calvert County), soldier (rank not stated) circa 1675; paid for his services in the late expedition against the Nanticoke Indians in 1678; a "John Abington, merchant, of London" died testate by November, 1694 (date of probate in Maryland) and he mentioned "kinsman John Abington" in his will. Additional research will be necessary before drawing conclusions. {Ref: ARMD 7:103; HCCM:233; INAC 13A:320; MDWB 16:64}
ABRAHAM, JOHN (Kent County), soldier (rank not stated) circa 1675; paid for his services in the late expedition against the Nanticoke Indians in 1678. {Ref: ARMD 7:94}
ACKWORTH (ACKWOORTH), RICHARD (Manokin Hundred, Somerset County), probable soldier (rank not stated) before 1682; paid for his services out of an assessment levied by the General Assembly for the public good in 1682; born circa 1634, died testate by Sep 9, 1676 (date of probate; Anne Ackwoorth, widow). {Ref: ARMD 7:443; OSES:280, 435; MDWB 5:76}

AD, PETER (Charles County), Protestant and probable soldier in the Revolution of 1689; signed an address and took a loyalty oath (made his "X" mark) supporting the King of England and the reestablishment of Lord Baltimore into power on Nov 28, 1689. {Ref: ARMD 8:138}

ADAMS, FRANCIS (Charles County), Protestant and probable soldier in the Revolution of 1689; signed an address and took a loyalty oath supporting the King of England and the reestablishment of Lord Baltimore into power on Nov 28, 1689. {Ref: ARMD 8:138}

ADAMS (ADAMES), HENRY (Port Tobacco, Charles County), soldier (rank not stated) by 1666; signed a petition to the governor to "displace Capt. William Boreman whom was lately constituted captain of the militia" on Sep 12, 1666; justice (quorum), 1674-1685; died testate by Jul 9, 1686 (date of probate). See "Humphrey Haggat," q.v. {Ref: ARMD 3:556, 3:560, 15:68, 15:327, 17:380; MDWB 4:204}

ADAMS (ADDAMS), JOHN (Calvert County), seaman on a ship (no name given) commanded by Capt. Ralph Story in 1662; born 1641 (aged 21 when deposed on Mar 15, 1662/3). {Ref: ARMD 49:13-15}

ADAMS, MARGARET, see "Richard Adams," q.v.

ADAMS, RICHARD (Baltimore County), Protestant and probable soldier in the Revolution of 1689; signed an address and took a loyalty oath (made his "R" mark) supporting the King of England and the reestablishment of Lord Baltimore into power on Nov 28, 1689; Richard Adams (Sr.) died testate by Mar 20, 1696/7 (date of probate; Margaret Adams, widow) and his son Richard Adams (Jr.) died by May 8, 1697 (date of administration bond). Additional research will be necessary before drawing conclusions. {Ref: ARMD 8:136; MDWB 7:255; BBCF:2}

ADAMS, SAMUELL (Calvert County), captain by 1720. {Ref: MDAD 3:101}

ADAMS, THOMAS (St. Mary's County), captain by 1653. {Ref: ARMD 3:300}

ADAMS, WILLIAM (England, and St. Mary's and Calvert Counties), captain by 1676; mariner, of Topsham, and master of the ship *Thomas and Mary* of London in 1677. {Ref: INAC 3:123, 155}

ADDISON, JOHN (Prince George's County), probable soldier in the 1730's; commissioned Ranger of Prince George's County "from Seneca Creek, downward" on Mar 23, 1738/9. {Ref: MDCB 82:72}

ADDISON, JOHN (England, and Charles and Prince George's Counties), captain "of foote in the upper parts of Charles County and New Scotland" in 1689; Protestant and soldier in the Revolution of 1689; signed an address and took a loyalty oath supporting the King of England and the reestablishment of Lord Baltimore into power on Nov 28, 1689; captain of horse troops in Charles County, 1689-1694; member of the Maryland Council, 1691-1698; he was ordered "to take care to raise 5 men and a captain to range from the falls of Potomock to the falls of Petuxant or in other places where it shall be needful to make quest after all skulking Indians" on Jun 14, 1694; colonel, commissioned

Jul 30, 1694; colonel, chief commander and military officer of Prince George's County, "And that the Colours for the said County be St. George's Cross, vizt., a Red cross in a White ffield" on Aug 17, 1695; colonel who swore allegiance to the King & Queen of England in 1696; the Maryland Council "recommended that the Honorable Colonel John Addison who lives convenient to the head of Potomock and has already been very serviceable in those parts, be appointed and have power to go & visit the Garrison & said men once a fortnight" on Oct 16, 1697 (noted that he and Mr. Hutchins were owners of the land where the Garrison was kept); died intestate circa March, 1705/6. See "Captain Bourne," q.v. {Ref: ARMD 8:138, 8:280, 8:404, 8:461, 13:243, 20:6, 20:68, 20:109, 20:130, 20:153, 20:281, 20:380, 20:546, 23:16, 23:105, 23:246-247, 38:73; BDML I:100; PGLR A:404; INAC 29:193, 229}

ADDISON, THOMAS (St. Mary's and Prince George's Counties), lieutenant colonel before 1712; colonel and member of the Maryland Council and Provincial Court, 1712-1727; born circa 1679 (aged about 45 when deposed in 1724), died testate by Jun 28, 1727 (date of probate; Eleanor Addison, widow). {Ref: ARMD 25:336, 25:377, 29:81, 30:170; BDML I:101; RMHF II:84; PGLR I:601; MDWB 19:188; MINV 12:295}

ADDISONE, JOHN (Kent County), soldier (rank not stated) circa 1675; paid for his services in the late expedition against the Nanticoke Indians in 1678. {Ref: ARMD 7:94}

AHERNE, PHILLIP (Dorchester County), soldier (rank not stated) circa 1675; paid for his services in the late expedition against the Nanticoke Indians in 1678. {Ref: ARMD 7:92}

AIKING (AKING, AIKINS), JAMES (England and Talbot County), captain, mariner, and commander of the ship *Alexander* of London riding in South River on Mar 7, 1725/6 and Feb 6, 1726/7 and Mar 13, 1727/8 and Mar 1, 1728/9 and Mar 31, 1730; died testate by Nov 8, 1732 (date of probate). {Ref: AALR SY#1:174, 254, 359; MDGZ, Mar 11, 1728/9 and Mar 31, 1730; MDWB 20:467; MINV 17:64}

AISQUITH (ASQUITH), WILLIAM (St. Mary's County), Protestant and soldier in the Revolution of 1689; signed an address and took a loyalty oath supporting the King of England and the reestablishment of Lord Baltimore into power on Nov 28, 1689; lieutenant by 1691; major by 1703; lieutenant colonel, 1706; colonel, 1708; member of the Lower House of the Maryland Legislature, 1704-1707; died testate by Apr 1, 1719 (date of probate; Elizabeth Aisquith, widow). {Ref: ARMD 8:147; BDML I:102; INAC 24:22; MDWB 15:55; MINV 2:161; MDAD 3:221}

AKERS, GEORGE (England and Queen Anne's County), captain by 1717. {Ref: INAC 37B:169}

ALCOCK, SAMUEL (Anne Arundel County), Quaker who was assigned to a foot company of Capt. John Norwood in 1662, but refused to serve for religious reasons and was fined accordingly. {Ref: AAGE:558}

ALCOCK, WILLIAM (Anne Arundel County), soldier (rank not stated) circa 1675; paid for his services in the late expedition against the Nanticoke Indians in 1678. {Ref: ARMD 7:96}

ALDERSON, WILLOBY (Virginia and Annapolis), colonel by 1702. {Ref: AALR WT#2:380}

ALDRIDGE, ELIZABETH, see "John Aldridge," q.v.

ALDRIDGE, JOHN (Talbot County), soldier (rank not stated) circa 1675; paid for his services in the late expedition against the Nanticoke Indians in 1678; died testate by Feb 25, 1702/3 (date of probate; Elizabeth Aldridge, widow). {Ref: ARMD 7:91; MDWB 11:264}

ALDRIDGE, NICHOLAS (Anne Arundel County), soldier (rank not stated) circa 1675; paid for his services in the late expedition against the Nanticoke Indians in 1678; military officer (rank not stated) who swore allegiance to the King & Queen of England in 1696 (name also listed as "Nicholas Aldridg" and "Nicholas Oldrudge"). {Ref: ARMD 7:97, 20:542}

ALDRIDGE, RICHARD (Somerset County), soldier (rank not stated) circa 1675; paid for his services in the late expedition against the Nanticoke Indians in 1678. {Ref: ARMD 7:98}

ALEXANDER, HENRY (Talbot County), soldier (rank not stated) circa 1675; paid for his services in the late expedition against the Nanticoke Indians in 1678; captain by 1684; captain "of a foot Company continued as formerly" in 1689; died testate by Apr 3, 1694 (date of probate; Margaret Alexander, widow, later m. Timothy Lane). {ARMD 7:89, 13:243; INAC 8:180, 13A:169; MDWB 7:36}

ALEXANDER, JAMES (Cecil County), captain and court commissioner in or before 1731. {Ref: Cecil County Judgments Liber SK#4}

ALEXANDER, THOMAS (Talbot County), lieutenant before 1678; paid for his services in the late expedition against the Nanticoke Indians in 1678. {Ref: ARMD 7:87, 7:89}

ALEXANDER, WILLIAM (Somerset County), Protestant and probable soldier in the Revolution of 1689; signed an address and took a loyalty oath supporting the King of England and "for enabling us to defend ourselves against all invaders" on Nov 28, 1689. {Ref: ARMD 8:139}

ALEXANDER, WILLIAM, JR. (Somerset County), Protestant and probable soldier in the Revolution of 1689; signed an address and took a loyalty oath supporting the King of England and "for enabling us to defend ourselves against all invaders" on Nov 28, 1689. {Ref: ARMD 8:140}

ALFORD (ALLFORD, OLFORD), JOHN (Dorchester County), soldier (rank not stated) circa 1675; paid for his services in the late expedition against the Nanticoke Indians in 1678; court justice, 1680-1685; died testate by Nov 11, 1702 (date of probate; Elizabeth Allford, widow; an administration account was filed on Nov 19, 1711 by Cecelie Bourk, wife of John Bourk). {Ref: ARMD 7:92, 15:326, 17:381; INAC 32C:112; MDWB 11:243}

ALLAN, ROBERT (England and Talbot County), captain and commander of the ship *Anne of Newcastle* by 1699. {Ref: TALR 9:109}

ALLANSON, JOHN (Charles County), captain by 1676. {Ref: CHLR G:23}

ALLANSON, THOMAS (Charles County), soldier (rank not stated) by 1666; signed a petition to the governor to "displace Capt. William Boreman whom was lately constituted captain of the militia" on Sep 12, 1666. {Ref: ARMD 3:556}

ALLEN, JOHN (England and Charles County), captain and master of a ship (no name given) in 1663 (his name was listed as "Jack Allen"); Maryland Council ordered that he "doe continue to range above Pascattaway and Over towards Petuxent with thirty horse till ordered to the Contrary" on Jun 16, 1676; captain on the Council of War in July, 1676; captain and delegate who was reported on Aug 29, 1678 as "lately deceased." {Ref: ARMD 2:553, 15:92, 15:99, 15:192; BDML I:106; CHLR G:68; MDEP:2}

ALLEN, THOMAS (St. Mary's County), captain and commander of the ketch *Quaker* "then lyeing in Pottuxen River being The Kings Mann of Warr" in 1684 and where it was reported that Mr. Christopher Rousby had been murdered by Col. George Talbott on Oct 31, 1684. {Ref: ARMD 17:299-307}

ALLEN, THOMAS (St. Mary's County), soldier (rank not stated) in 1642. {Ref: ARMD 4:130-131}

ALLEN, WILLIAM (Somerset County), soldier (rank not stated) circa 1675; paid for his services in the late expedition against the Nanticoke Indians in 1678. {Ref: ARMD 7:97}

ALLFORD, ELIZABETH, see "John Alford," q.v.

ALLMERRY (ALLMARRIE), JOHN (Coventry Parish, Somerset County), mariner, sailor, and slooper by 1709. {Ref: SOJR II:119, III:6}

ALLUMBY, GEORGE (Talbot County), soldier (rank not stated) circa 1675; paid for his services in the late expedition against the Nanticoke Indians in 1678; died testate by Nov 24, 1684 (date of probate). {Ref: ARMD 7:89; MDWB 4:102}

ALLWARD, JOHN (Charles County), Protestant and probable soldier in the Revolution of 1689; signed an address and took a loyalty oath supporting the King of England and the reestablishment of Lord Baltimore into power on Nov 28, 1689. {Ref: ARMD 8:138}

ALVEY, POPE (St. Mary's County), soldier (rank not stated) circa 1675; paid for his services in the late expedition against the Nanticoke Indians in 1678. {Ref: ARMD 7:101, 49:538-539}

AMOS, WILLIAM (Baltimore County), "was a member of the Anglican Church and an officer in the militia; according to tradition one day in 1738 a conversation with members of the Society of Friends convinced him of their religion and he helped to establish Little Falls Meeting" (in now Harford County); died testate by Mar 10, 1759 (date of probate; Ann Amos, widow). {Ref: BBCF:6; MDWB 30:645}

ANDERSON, ---- (St. Mary's County), colonel by 1678. {Ref: INAC 5:404}

ANDERSON, ANDREW (Kent County), soldier (rank not stated) on Isle of Kent who swore allegiance to the Commonwealth of England on Apr 5, 1652. {Ref: INKC:101}

ANDERSON (ANDERSONE), CORNELIUS (Somerset County), soldier (rank not stated) circa 1675; paid for his services in the late expedition against the Nanticoke Indians in 1678. {Ref: ARMD 7:97}

ANDERSON, DAVID (Barbadoes and Calvert County), captain and master of the frigate *Jane* in 1664-1665. {Ref: ARMD 49:445, 456}

ANDERSON, JAMES (England and Talbot County), captain and master of the ship *Ann* of New Castle in 1692; mariner of Old England and land owner in Talbot County by 1693; captain of the ship *Unity* of Maryland in 1694. {Ref: ARMD 8:445, 20:147; TALR 7:55}

ANDERSON, JOHN (Baltimore County), alias John Hancock, sailor by 1728; born circa 1701 (aged about 27 when reported to have been a runaway servant of Lloyd Harris in 1728). {Ref: MDGZ, Jan 14, 1728/9}

ANDERSON, JOHN (England and Talbot County), captain and master of the ship *Relief* of New Castle riding in Wye River on Jun 6, 1692. {Ref: ARMD 13:334-335}

ANDERSON, LANCELOT (Charles County), captain by 1664. {Ref: CHLR B:366}

ANDERSON, REBECCA, see "Thomas Anderson," q.v.

ANDERSON, ROBERT (England, and Kent and Cecil Counties), captain, mariner and master of the ship *Sarah* of London in 1729; master of the ship *Robert and Mary* in 1731; died testate by Mar 14, 1733/4 (date of probate). {Ref: MDGZ, Apr 15, 1729; CVPR:12; MDWB 21:74; MINV 18:359; CFES 3:24}

ANDERSON, THOMAS (Talbot County), doctor and probable soldier (rank not stated) by 1678; paid for his services in the late expedition against the Nanticoke Indians in 1678; died testate by Sep 20, 1692 (date of probate; Rebecca Anderson, widow). {Ref: ARMD 7:92; MDWB 6:5}

ANDERSON, WILLIAM (Talbot or Queen Anne's County), captain and commander of the ship *Lee* riding at anchor in Chester River on May 18, 1732 and Mar 21, 1733/4. {Ref: QALR RT#A:116, 262}

ANDERSON, WILLIAM (Kent County), soldier (rank not stated) circa 1675; paid for his services in the late expedition against the Nanticoke Indians in 1678. {Ref: ARMD 7:94}

ANDREW, PATRICK, see "Samuel Perrie," q.v.

ANDREWS, ANN, see "John Bigger," q.v.

ANDREWS, CHRISTOPHER (Baltimore County), soldier (rank not stated) circa 1675; paid for his services in the late expedition against the Nanticoke Indians in 1678. {Ref: ARMD 7:95}

ANDREWS, PATRICK, see "John Bigger," q.v.

ANDROS (ANDROSE), EDMUND (England, West Indies, New York, Virginia, but never a permanent resident of Maryland), military officer and colonial bureaucrat; governor of Virginia by 1697; born Dec 6, 1637 in Guernsey, died Feb 27, 1713/4 in London. See "Francis Nicholson," q.v. {Ref: BDML I:107; ARMD 23:294; PGLR A:121}

ANLLEY(?), ---- (Anne Arundel County), captain by 1698. {Ref: INAC 16:55}

ANNULLEN, MARKE (Somerset County), soldier (rank not stated) circa 1675; paid for his services in the late expedition against the Nanticoke Indians in 1678. {Ref: ARMD 7:99}

ANTE, JAMES (Calvert County), Protestant and probable soldier in the Revolution of 1689; signed an address and took a loyalty oath supporting the King of England and "to reestablish Lord Baltimore in his ancient power and government" on Nov 16, 1689. {Ref: ARMD 8:131}

ANTHONY, RICHARD (Somerset County), captain by 1700. {Ref: SOJR II:85}

ANTRUM, RICHARD (Somerset County), soldier (rank not stated) circa 1675; paid for his services in the late expedition against the Nanticoke Indians in 1678. {Ref: ARMD 7:99}

APPLEBY, WILLIAM (Potomac District), captain and master of the ship *3Blessing* in 1730-1731. {Ref: CVPR:12}

APPLEWHITE, THOMAS (England and Calvert County), captain and commander of the ship *Crown Malligo* in 1677. {Ref: ARMD 67:175}

APPS, THOMAS (Anne Arundel County), captain and commander of the ship *Colchester Adventure* riding at anchor in South River on Feb 4, 1717/8. {Ref: AALR IB#2:432}

ARBUTHNOTT, HUGH (England, and Anne Arundel and Prince George's Counties), captain and commander of the ship *Fortune* riding at anchor in the Chesapeake Bay on Jun 1, 1715; captain of a ship (no name given) in 1716; captain and commander of the ship *Owners Good Will* riding at anchor in Severn River on Nov 29, 1720; master of the ship *Unity* riding in the Patuxent River on Feb 24, 1723/4 and Jan 29, 1725/6; master of the ship *Betty* riding in the Patuxent River on Apr 11, 1726; captain and merchant in London by 1729 (name also listed as "Arbuthnot" and "Arbuthnol"); died by Dec 9, 1731 (date of letter of exemplification; George Buchanan, of Prince George's County, was his administrator in 1734). {Ref: AALR IB#2:216, CW#1:275; ARMD 25:351; MDGZ, May 24, 1734; PGLR M:148-150, M:426, Q:660}

ARCHER, AMBROSE (Somerset County), Protestant and probable soldier in the Revolution of 1689; signed an address and took a loyalty oath supporting the King of England and "for enabling us to defend ourselves against all invaders" on Nov 28, 1689. {Ref: ARMD 8:140}

ARDEN (ARDING), JOHN (Patapsco River, Baltimore County), soldier (rank not stated) circa 1675; paid for his services in the late expedition against the Nanticoke Indians in 1678; Protestant and probable soldier in the Revolution of 1689; signed an address and took a loyalty oath (made his "A" mark) supporting the King of England and the reestablishment of Lord Baltimore into power on Nov 28, 1689; died testate by Apr 20, 1694 (date of probate; Sarah Arden, widow). {Ref: ARMD 7:95, 8:137; BBCF:10; MDWB 7:23}

ARDICE, GEORGE (Kent County), soldier (rank not stated) circa 1675; paid for his services in the late expedition against the Nanticoke Indians in 1678. {Ref: ARMD 7:94}

ARMSTRONG, FRANCES, see "Francis Armstrong," q.v.

ARMSTRONG, FRANCIS (Calvert County), lieutenant by 1660; died testate by Oct 13, 1669 (date of probate; Frances Armstrong, widow). {Ref: ARMD 3:401; MDWB 1:334}

ARMSTRONG, RUSSELL (Talbot County), mariner in the 1730's and 1740's; "Russel Armstrong, planter" died testate by May 2, 1752 (nuncupative will given on Apr 12, 1752). {Ref: CFES 3:30; MDWB 28:306}

ARNOLD, BENJAMIN, see "James Phillips," q.v.

ARNOLD, THOMAS (St. Mary's and Calvert Counties), soldier (rank not stated) circa 1675; paid for his services in the late expedition against the Nanticoke Indians in 1678; died testate by Mar 21, 1710/1 (date of probate). {Ref: ARMD 7:103; MDWB 13:166}

ASH, BENJAMIN (England and St. Mary's County), captain and master of the ship *Success* of Plymouth in 1693. {Ref: ARMD 20:183}

ASHBROOKE, JAMES (Charles County), probable soldier (rank not stated) before 1682; paid for his services out of an assessment levied by the General Assembly for the public good in 1682; died testate by January, 1706/7 (date of probate; Elizabeth Ashbrooke, widow). {Ref: ARMD 7:440; MDWB 12:82}

ASHBY (ASHBIE), RICHARD (All Hallows Parish, Somerset County), mariner and sailor on the ship *Blessing* riding at anchor in Senepuxen Inlet on Apr 10, 1717. {Ref: MGSB 36:4, p. 645; SOJR III:190-191, 195-196}

ASHCOM (ASHCOMB), JOHN (St. Mary's and Calvert Counties), soldier (rank not stated) circa 1675; paid for his services in the late expedition against the Nanticoke Indians in 1678; died testate by Aug 31, 1684 (date of probate). {Ref: ARMD 7:103; HCCM:234; MDWB 4:65}

ASHFIELD, JOHN (Annapolis District), captain and master of the shallop *Saveall* in 1730-1731. {Ref: CVPR:12}

ASHLEY, ELIZABETH, see "Isaac Ashley," q.v.

ASHLEY, HENRY (Kent County), soldier (rank not stated) on Isle of Kent who swore allegiance to the Commonwealth of England on Apr 5, 1652. {Ref: INKC:101}

ASHLEY, ISAAC (Kent County), military officer (rank not stated) who swore allegiance to the King & Queen of England in 1696; died testate by Mar 29, 1709 (date of probate; Elizabeth Ashley, widow). {Ref: ARMD 20:541; MDWB 12:9, pt. 2}

ASHMAN, GEORGE (England and Baltimore County), lieutenant colonel before 1699; commissioner of Baltimore County, 1694; member of the Lower House of the Maryland Assembly, 1692-1699; he was injured when lightning struck the State House in the summer of 1699; died testate by Feb 23, 1699/1700 (date of probate; Elizabeth Ashman, widow). See "William Cromwell," q.v. {Ref: ARMD 25:96, BDML I:108; AAGE:567-571; BBCF:14; MDWB 6:339}

ASKEW, PHILIP (Somerset County), Protestant and probable soldier in the Revolution of 1689; signed an address and took a loyalty oath supporting the

King of England and "for enabling us to defend ourselves against all invaders" on Nov 28, 1689. {Ref: ARMD 8:141}

ASKEW, WILLIAM (Kent County), "seaman within the said county" and a "sailor belonging to the *Loves Increase* of Whitehaven" in 1697. {Ref: ARMD 25:600}

ASPINALL (ASPENALL), HENRY (Charles County), captain by 1676; court justice, 1680-1681; son-in-law of Walter Pake by 1665; died by Jul 10, 1686 (date of administration account). {Ref: ARMD 15:97, 15:327, 15:406, 49:540; CHLR H:273; INAC 2:353, 9:55}

ATHEY, GEORGE (Prince George's County), captain of foot troops in Piscattoway Parish, 1695/1696; died by Dec 21, 1710 (date of inventory). {Ref: ARMD 20:379; INAC 32B:12, 38A:112; RMHF I:54}

ATKINS, EDWARD (Prince George's County), captain by 1722; master and commander of the ship *Strong and Thomas* in 1722 and riding in the Patuxent River on Feb 24, 1723/4. {Ref: PGLR I:465, M:148}

ATKINS, JOHN (county or port not indicated), captain and master of the ship *Samuell* of London in 1691. {Ref: ARMD 8:239}

ATKINS, THOMAS (England and St. Mary's County), cook on the ship *Ruth* in 1676. {Ref: ARMD 51:474, 66:301}

ATKINSON, JOSEPH (Anne Arundel County), captain and commander of the ship *James* riding at anchor in South River on Apr 29, 1713; commander of the ship *Severn* riding at anchor in Severn River on May 10, 1720 and Apr 6, 1721 and Mar 7, 1721/2. {Ref: AALR IB#2:26, CW#1:167, 350, 479}

ATKINSON, SAMPSON (Somerset County), soldier (rank not stated) circa 1675; paid for his services in the late expedition against the Nanticoke Indians in 1678. {Ref: ARMD 7:97}

ATTAWAY (ATTOWAY), ANN, see "Thomas Attaway," q.v.

ATTAWAY (ATTOWAY), JOHN (St. Mary's County), captain before 1731; died testate by Nov 8, 1732 (date of probate). {Ref: MDWB 20:623; MINV 17:172; MDAD 11:326}

ATTAWAY (ATTOWAY, OTTAWAY), THOMAS (St. Mary's County), captain before 1689; empowered to command a troop of horse for St. Clements Hundred in 1689; Protestant and soldier in the Revolution of 1689; signed an address and took a loyalty oath supporting the King of England and the reestablishment of Lord Baltimore into power on Nov 28, 1689; captain and county coroner in 1694; military officer who swore allegiance to the King & Queen of England in 1696; died intestate by Dec 23, 1707 (date of inventory). {Ref: ARMD 8:147, 13:241, 20:106, 20:540; INAC 28:59}

ATTAWAY (ATTOWAY, OTTAWAY), THOMAS (St. Mary's County), soldier before 1708; petitioned the Maryland Council "praying Allowance for the Loss of his Thumb being one of the Guards" and was granted 2000 lbs. of tobacco on Dec 7, 1708; died testate by Jun 6, 1716 (date of probate; Ann Attaway, widow). {Ref: ARMD 27:290; MDWB 14:226; MDAD 1:48}

ATTERBURY, EDWARD (county or port not indicated), seaman on the ship *John Hopewell* of London under Capt. Henry Munday in 1699 who ran away to the pirate Capt. Henry King; reported by the Maryland Council that he "may happen to come into these American parts" in 1700. {Ref: ARMD 25:100}

ATTHEW, THOMAS (county not indicated), captain by 1696. {Ref: INAC 13B:143}

ATWOOD, RICHARD (St. Mary's County), soldier (rank not stated) by 1694 when paid for his services by the Maryland Assembly; military officer (rank not stated) who swore allegiance to the King & Queen of England in 1696. {Ref: ARMD 20:540, 38:35}

AUDLEY, EDWARD (county or port not indicated), captain and master of the ship *Jacob* of London in 1691. {Ref: ARMD 8:239}

AUGLYE, ---- (Calvert County), captain by Jul 8, 1686 when noted as "dead" on a list of debts due Capt. Charles Boteler. {Ref: INAC 9:29}

AUSTIN, JOHN (Calvert County), Protestant and probable soldier in the Revolution of 1689; signed an address and took a loyalty oath (made his "X" mark) supporting the King of England and "to reestablish Lord Baltimore in his ancient power and government" on Nov 16, 1689. {Ref: ARMD 8:132}

AUTUMM, RICHARD (Somerset County), soldier (rank not stated) circa 1675; paid for his services in the late expedition against the Nanticoke Indians in 1678. {Ref: ARMD 7:97-98}

AVENT, ROBERT (Prince George's County), captain and master of the ship *Anne* riding in the Patuxent River on Jan 4, 1723/4. {Ref: PGLR M:148}

AVERY, JOHN (Somerset County, and Sussex County, Delaware), mariner, 1667-1674; lieutenant of military forces and president of the Whorekill, 1675; captain, October, 1675; justice of the peace, 1672-1682. {Ref: ARMD 54:696; OSES:435; BDML II:516}

AYLER, GEORGE (county or port not indicated), captain and master of the brigantine *Hopewell* of Maryland in 1690. {Ref: ARMD 8:237}

AYLES, SAMUEL (county or port not indicated), captain and master of the ship *John and Thomas* of Maryland in 1691. {Ref: ARMD 8:240}

AYRES, EDWARD (Anne Arundel County), Quaker who was assigned to a foot company of Capt. John Norwood in 1662, but refused to serve for religious reasons and was fined accordingly. {Ref: AAGE:558}

AYRES, JOHN (Somerset County), mariner by the 1730's; captain and master of the schooner *Sarah* (built in Somerset County) in 1739. {Ref: MDCB 82:78}

AYRES, MR., see "Sampson Waring," q.v.

AYTON, H. (England and Annapolis), captain of the ship *Diligence* of London in 1734. {Ref: MDGZ, Jul 19, 1734}

BABB, ROBERT (England and Annapolis), captain of the ship *Grove* of London in 1729; master of the ship *Speedwell* in 1731. {Ref: MDGZ, Apr 1, 1729; CVPR:12}

BABBIDGE, JOHN (England and Talbot County), captain, mariner, master and commander of the ketch or vessel *Jacob* of Biddiford riding at anchor in Wye River on Feb 10, 1675/6. {Ref: ARMD 66:56}

BACHY, RICHARD (Talbot County), soldier (rank not stated) circa 1675; paid for his services in the late expedition against the Nanticoke Indians in 1678. {Ref: ARMD 7:92}

BACON, JOHN (Somerset County), mariner by 1715. {Ref: SOJR III:170}

BAGGS, THOMAS (Talbot County), soldier (rank not stated) circa 1675; paid for his services in the late expedition against the Nanticoke Indians in 1678. {Ref: ARMD 7:89}

BAILEY (BAILYE), JOHN, see "John Bayly," q.v.

BAILEY, JOSEPH (Pocomoke District), captain and master of the ship *Tryall* in 1730-1731. {Ref: CVPR:12}

BAILY, RICHARD (Talbot County), soldier (rank not stated) circa 1675; paid for his services in the late expedition against the Nanticoke Indians in 1678. {Ref: ARMD 7:87}

BAKER, ADAM (England and Annapolis), seaman on the ship *Hartwell* of London commanded by Capt. Nicholas Humphries in March, 1697/8. {Ref: ARMD 23:397}

BAKER, ANN, see "Col. John Baker," q.v.

BAKER, CHARLES, see "John Cockey," q.v.

BAKER, JOHN (St. Mary's and/or Charles County), soldier (rank not stated) circa 1675; paid for his services in the late expedition against the Nanticoke Indians in 1678; on Oct 13, 1697 the Maryland Council "ordered that the Commissary take no fees for any Administration granted out upon the Estate of John Baker, one of the Rangers lately kill'd at the Garrison, by reason the Estate is small, and that he was kill'd in the Kings Service" (on Sep 21, 1697); fellow soldier John Waples stated on Oct 12, 1697 "that on Tuesday the 21st of September last past, John Baker one of the Souldiers of the Garrison under the Conduct of Capt. Richard Brightwell went out of the Garrison to catch his horse being out of the Pasture, and being about three hundred yards from the fort; Wee immediately that were within heard him hollow and likewise supposed that he Shott of his Gunn and thereupon we immediately made towards the noise, and I being the first person that came up found the boddy with the head & his right arm cutt off to his Elbow and both carried away with his Musquett Powder and Shott bagg." See "James Waple," q.v. {Ref: ARMD 7:103, 23:224}

BAKER, JOHN (England and Anne Arundel County), captain and commander of the ship *Tower Hill* riding in South River on May 20, 1728; "John Baker, marriner, Dover, Kent County" died testate by Jan 7, 1729/30 (date of probate in London and later recorded in Anne Arundel County at the request of Thomas Gassaway). {Ref: AALR SY#1:411; MDWB 20:51}

BAKER, JOHN (St. Mary's County), captain by 1717; member of the Lower House of the Maryland Assembly between 1702 and 1721; colonel by 1726; died by Apr 22, 1730 (date of inventory; Mrs. Ann Baker, administratrix). {Ref: ARMD 34:203; BDML I:110; DOLR 8 Old 90; MINV 16:189}

BAKER, MARTHA, see "Thomas Baker," q.v.

BAKER, MICHAELL (Talbot County), soldier (rank not stated) circa 1675; paid for his services in the late expedition against the Nanticoke Indians in 1678. {Ref: ARMD 7:89}

BAKER, ROGER (St. Mary's County), captain by 1677; paid for his services in the late expedition against the Nanticoke Indians in 1678; colonel by 1685. {Ref: ARMD 7:103, 67:244; INAC 8:518}

BAKER, ROGER (England, Virginia, Maryland, "and other places"), captain by 1676; "Roger Baker, of Wapping, Middlesex" died testate by 1688 (wrote his will in England on Aug 15, 1676 and it was recorded in Maryland circa July, 1688 (date of inventory; county not indicated). {Ref: MDWB 6:41; INAC 10:32}

BAKER, THOMAS (Charles County), soldier (rank not stated) by 1664; Indian interpreter by 1678; died testate by Nov 18, 1684 (date of probate; Martha Baker, widow). {Ref: ARMD 15:232, 15:237; CHLR B:379; MDWB 4:57}

BAKER, THOMAS (Anne Arundel County), military officer (rank not stated) who swore allegiance to the King & Queen of England in 1696. {Ref: ARMD 20:542}

BALBERSTON, JAMES (Kent County), soldier (rank not stated) circa 1675; paid for his services in the late expedition against the Nanticoke Indians in 1678. {Ref: ARMD 7:94}

BALDING, JOHN, JR. (Anne Arundel County), soldier (rank not stated) circa 1675; paid for his services in the late expedition against the Nanticoke Indians in 1678. {Ref: ARMD 7:96}

BALDRIDGE, THOMAS (England, St. Mary's County, and Virginia), sergeant, 1637; attended the second General Assembly in 1637-1638; lieutenant, 1643; captain by 1648; major before 1655; died intestate in 1655. See "Henry Spinke," q.v. {Ref: ARMD 1:2, 3:132, 4:54, 4:453; BDML I:112; FMDP:169-172}

BALDWIN, HENRY (Annapolis District), captain of the sloop *Benedict* of Maryland in 1728-1729. {Ref: MDGZ, Feb 11, 1728/9}

BALDWIN, JOHN (Cecil County), captain circa 1734; county court justice, 1723-1752; colonel before 1752; died testate by Aug 15, 1752 (date of probate). {Ref: BDML I:112; MDWB 28:372}

BALE, THOMAS (England and Baltimore County), captain in the upper part of Patapsco Hundred in 1705; he was probably the "Capt. Bale" listed in the administration account filed on Aug 15, 1699 in the estate of William Burgess, deceased, Anne Arundel County; born circa 1664 (aged about 40 when deposed in 1704), died testate and was buried on Feb 5, 1707/8 (will probated on Mar 18, 1707/8; Sarah Bale, widow, was buried on the same date). {Ref: BCTL:55; INAC 19½B:153; MDWB 12:220; BBCF:24}

BALL, BENJAMIN (Dorchester County), captain of a sloop (no name given) in 1706; "Benjamin Ball, of Dorchester County, son of Benjamin Ball, of Calvert County" died testate by Jan 2, 1744/5 (date of probate; Elizabeth Ball, widow); inventory of the estate of "Capt. Benjamin Ball" was taken on Feb 11, 1744/5. {Ref: MDWB 12:99, 24:26; MINV 30:320}

BALL, ELIZABETH, see "Benjamin Ball," q.v.

BALL, JOHN (Charles County), captain by 1694 and to at least 1717 (mentioned in will of Robert Sanders in 1717). {Ref: INAC 12:150, 30:355; MDWB 14:445}

BALL, MARY, see "William Ball," q.v.

BALL, SUSANNAH, see "Thomas Ball," q.v.

BALL, THOMAS (Talbot County), lieutenant who swore allegiance to the King & Queen of England in 1696; "Thomas Ball, felt maker" died testate by Aug 9, 1722 (date of probate; Susannah Ball, widow), but he appears to have been a Quaker; therefore, additional research will be necessary before drawing conclusions about any military service. {Ref: ARMD 20:542; MDWB 18:29}

BALL, WILLIAM (England, and Anne Arundel and Baltimore Counties), soldier (rank not stated) circa 1675; paid for his services in the late expedition against the Nanticoke Indians in 1678; died testate by May 8, 1686 (date of probate; Mary Ball, widow). {Ref: ARMD 7:95; MDWB 4:205; BBCF:25}

BALLARD, CHARLES (England and Manokin Hundred, Somerset County), soldier (rank not stated) circa 1675; paid for his services in the late expedition against the Nanticoke Indians in 1678; county court justice, 1670-1682; died intestate in 1682. {Ref: ARMD 7:100, 15:175, 29:77; OSES:280, 435; INAC 8:1}

BALLARD, CHARLES (Somerset County), captain by 1701; justice of the peace, 1707; member of the Lower House of the Maryland Assembly in 1715; major by 1722; born circa 1670 (son of Charles Ballard, q.v.), died testate by Jan 21, 1724/5 (date of probate; Eleanor Ballard, widow). {Ref: BDML I:112; MDWB 18:363; SOJR I:1; CMSP 1:7 - The Black Books}

BALLARD, ELEANOR, see "Charles Ballard," q.v.

BALLARD, JOHN (Somerset County), captain by 1711. {Ref: ARMD 29:10}

BALLEY, WILLIAM (England and St. Mary's County), ship's carpenter on the *Sarah and Elizabeth* of Bristol in 1671. {Ref: ARMD 5:100}

BALLING, NICHOLAS (Potomac District), captain and master of the ship *America* in 1697. {Ref: ARMD 23:172}

BALTER, EDWARD (Anne Arundel County), captain of the brigantine *Susannah* in 1697. {Ref: ARMD 25:595}

BALTIMORE, CHARLES, LORD, see "Charles Calvert," q.v.

BANBURY, THOMAS (England and Queen Anne's County), seaman before 1727; "late of the town of Bidesford, Kingdom of Great Britain, gentleman, now residing in Queen Anne's County" in 1727. {Ref: TALR 13:364}

BAND, WILL (Kent County), soldier (rank not stated) on Isle of Kent who swore allegiance to the Commonwealth of England on Apr 5, 1652. {Ref: INKC:101}

BANKES, ANNE, see "Thomas Bankes," q.v.

BANKES, JOHN (Prince George's County), soldier (trooper) under the command of Capt. Richard Owen in June, 1699. {Ref: ARMD 24:121}

BANKES (BANKS, BANCKS), RICHARD (England, and Anne Arundel, St. Mary's, and Charles Counties), lieutenant, 1648-1656; member of the Maryland Assembly, 1647-1652; lieutenant and parliamentary commissioner of Anne Arundel County in 1652; lieutenant and commander of Newtowne Hundred in

1654-1655; captain, 1656-1663; born circa 1612, died circa 1667. {Ref: ARMD 4:492, 10:325, 10:355, 10:414, 10:470, 49:162, 53:281; FAAH:37; BDML I:113; CHLR A:140, B:34}

BANKES (BANKS), THOMAS (England and St. Mary's County), captain and master of the ship *Princess Ann* of London in 1691; captain of the ship *Ann and Hannah* which was taken by two French privateers while on a trip to London about May or June, 1693 "and Carryed into Ffrance whereby the said Ship and Cargoe was utterly lost" (affidavit signed Jul 8, 1695). {Ref: ARMD 8:239, 20:269}

BANKES, THOMAS (Calvert County), soldier (rank not stated) circa 1675; paid for his services in the late expedition against the Nanticoke Indians in 1678; died testate by Jul 23, 1685 (date of probate; Anne Bankes, widow). {Ref: ARMD 7:104, 17:375; MDWB 4:126}

BANKS, RICHARD (Prince George's County), captain and commander of the ship *Haddock* in 1722. {Ref: PGLR I:465}

BANNESTER, JOHN (Talbot County), soldier (rank not stated) circa 1675; paid for his services in the late expedition against the Nanticoke Indians in 1678. {Ref: ARMD 7:87}

BANNING, EDWARD (Talbot County), soldier (rank not stated) circa 1675; paid for his services in the late expedition against the Nanticoke Indians in 1678; died testate by Apr 16, 1712 (date of probate; Susannah Banning, widow). {Ref: ARMD 7:92; MDWB 13:465}

BANUM (BAINHAM, BENHAM), ALEXANDER (St. Mary's and Charles Counties, and Virginia), servant of Thomas Baldridge, and soldier (rank not stated) in 1642; paid for 3 weeks' service under Capt. William Brainthwaite in November, 1642; captain by 1657; court justice and sheriff of Westmoreland County, Virginia, by 1657. {Ref: ARMD 3:119; CHLR B:44}

BANY, RICHARD (Prince George's County), mariner before 1709; died by Nov 30, 1709 (date of inventory). {Ref: INAC 30:221}

BARBAR, ---- (England and Annapolis), captain by 1696. {Ref: ARMD 20:460}

BARBER, JAMES (Somerset County), Protestant and probable soldier in the Revolution of 1689; signed an address and took a loyalty oath supporting the King of England and "for enabling us to defend ourselves against all invaders" on Nov 28, 1689. {Ref: ARMD 8:140}

BARBER, JOHN (Somerset County), Protestant and probable soldier in the Revolution of 1689; signed an address and took a loyalty oath supporting the King of England and "for enabling us to defend ourselves against all invaders" on Nov 28, 1689. {Ref: ARMD 8:141}

BARBER, LUKE (England and St. Mary's County), physician and surgeon in the army of Oliver Cromwell before 1655; member of the Maryland Council, 1659-1660; captain by 1663; deputy governor, 1657-1658; died testate by November, 1668 (will written on Jul 31, 1664, but not probated until Jan 4, 1674/5; Elizabeth Barber, widow). {Ref: ARMD 41:291, 49:28; BDML I:114; RMHF I:65; MDWB 1:534}

BARBON, ---- (Prince George's County), major by 1701; sheriff, 1701. {Ref: ARMD 24:147}

BARCOCK, EDWARD (Dorchester County), captain by 1701. {Ref: INAC 21:143}

BARE (BEAR), THEODORE (Somerset County), captain before 1734; died intestate by Mar 19, 1734/5 (date of inventory). {Ref: MINV 21:102}

BARIFFE (BARRIFFE), JOHN (St. Mary's County), captain by 1654; died before Apr 25, 1659 (provincial court proceedings noted that Capt. William Evans was his administrator). {Ref: ARMD 10:366, 41:291}

BARKE, JOHN, see "John Lucas," q.v.

BARKER, JOHN (Talbot County), soldier (rank not stated) circa 1675; paid for his services in the late expedition against the Nanticoke Indians in 1678; Protestant and probable soldier in the Revolution of 1689; signed an address and took a loyalty oath supporting the King of England and the reestablishment of Lord Baltimore into power on Nov 28, 1689; died testate by Apr 19, 1709 (date of probate). {Ref: ARMD 7:89, 7:97; MDWB 12:80, pt. 2}

BARKER, JOHN (Somerset County), soldier (rank not stated) circa 1675; paid for his services in the late expedition against the Nanticoke Indians in 1678. {Ref: ARMD 7:97}

BARKSTEAD, JOSHUA (Somerset County), ranger by 1692. {Ref: ARMD 8:547}

BARNARD, CHARLES (Anne Arundel County), captain by the 1730's; died intestate before Jun 17, 1742 (date of inventory). {Ref: MINV 27:423}

BARNES, ABRAHAM (Virginia and Somerset County), major before 1731 (mentioned in the will of Robert King which was written in Accomack County, Virginia in 1731 and probated in Somerset County, Maryland in 1755). {Ref: MDWB 29:434}

BARNES, ANDREW (England and Talbot County), seaman and carpenter on the ship *Ann* of New Castle in 1692. {Ref: ARMD 8:447}

BARNES, FRANCIS (Kent County), soldier (rank not stated) on Isle of Kent who swore allegiance to the Commonwealth of England on Apr 5, 1652; died circa 1668 (will was written on Apr 30, 1667 at Kent Island, but no date of probate was given; Isabelle Barnes, widow). {Ref: INKC:101; MDWB 1:319}

BARNES, GODFREY (Prince George's County), soldier (rank not stated) under the command of Col. Ninian Beale from June, 1699 to May, 1700. {Ref: ARMD 24:121-122}

BARNES, ISABELLE, see "Francis Barnes," q.v.

BARNES, JOHN (St. Mary's County), soldier (rank not stated) circa 1675; paid for his services in the late expedition against the Nanticoke Indians in 1678. {Ref: ARMD 7:102}

BARNES, SAMUEL (Prince George's County), captain and master of the ship *Humes* riding in the Patuxent River on Mar 30, 1726. {Ref: PGLR M:150}

BARNES, THOMAS (Talbot County), soldier (rank not stated) circa 1675; paid for his services in the late expedition against the Nanticoke Indians in 1678. {Ref: ARMD 7:87}

BARNETT, FRANCIS (Cecil County), military officer (rank not stated) who swore allegiance to the King & Queen of England in 1696. {Ref: ARMD 20:546}

BARON, JOHN (Somerset County), Protestant and probable soldier in the Revolution of 1689; signed an address and took a loyalty oath supporting the King of England and "for enabling us to defend ourselves against all invaders" on Nov 28, 1689. {Ref: ARMD 8:139}

BARRES, RALPH (Anne Arundel County), captain and commander of the ship *Mayfield* riding in Severn River on Mar 13, 1721/2. {Ref: AALR CW#1:482}

BARRETT, THOMAS (county or port not indicated), sailor on the ship *Mayflower* under the command of Capt. Collard Groves before 1659 and "one of the company taken upon on the ship *St. George*" by 1659. {Ref: ARMD 41:306-309; MDEP:8}

BARRY, JAMES (New England and Somerset County), mariner and captain by 1707; noted as "being a foreigner and out of this province" in 1709. {Ref: SOJR I:39, II:151}

BARRY, JOHN (Barbadoes and Anne Arundel County), captain by 1705 (named as an overseer in the will of Marcus Brandt, late of the town of St. Michaells and Island of Barbadoes, which will was recorded in Anne Arundel County on Jul 23, 1705). {Ref: AALR C#2:34}

BARRY, RICHARD (county or port not indicated), carpenter's mate on the ship *Mary* of London commanded by Capt. Francis Wells in 1709; died testate circa July 26, 1709 (date of nuncupative will in Maryland, but place of probate was not indicated). {Ref: MDWB 12:148, pt. 2}

BARSLOE, THOMAS (Calvert County), captain before 1694; died by Jun 5, 1694 (date of inventory). {Ref: INAC 13A:178}

BARTDYNDALE, JOHN (St. Mary's County), Protestant and probable soldier in the Revolution of 1689; signed an address and took a loyalty oath supporting the King of England and the reestablishment of Lord Baltimore into power on Nov 28, 1689. {Ref: ARMD 8:147}

BARTLET, JAMES (St. Mary's County), captain by 1685. {Ref: INAC 9:14}

BARTLETT, NICHOLAS (Talbot County), ensign before 1678; paid for his services in the late expedition against the Nanticoke Indians in 1678. {Ref: ARMD 7:87, 89}

BARTON, JOAN, see "Lewis Barton," q.v.

BARTON, LEWIS (England and Baltimore County), soldier (rank not stated) circa 1675; paid for his services in the late expedition against the Nanticoke Indians in 1678; died intestate by Mar 4, 1692/3 (date of administration bond; Joan Barton, widow, later married William Farfarr, *q.v.*). {Ref: ARMD 7:96; BBCF:31}

BARTON, RODGAR (county not indicated), lieutenant in the Maryland troops "raised to strengthen Albany, New York and resist the French and Indian enemies" in 1690. {Ref: SHMD I:355}

BARTON, SARAH, see "William Barton," q.v.

BARTON, WILLIAM (Charles and Prince George's Counties), captain by 1676; court justice, 1680; paid for his services out of an assessment levied by the General Assembly for the public good in 1682; captain who was appointed justice of the peace in Charles County by the Maryland Council on Sep 22, 1687; captain of a foot company "as formerly" in 1689; major in the militia of Prince George's County, 1695-1696; died by Aug 4, 1697 (date of inventory). {Ref: ARMD 2:554, 5:565, 7:442, 7:611, 8:399, 13:243, 15:327, 15:406, 20:379, 20:546; INAC 15:54}

BARTON, WILLIAM (Calvert, Charles, and Prince George's Counties), major by 1695; military officer who swore allegiance to the King & Queen of England in 1696; member of the Lower House of the Maryland Assembly, 1696-1698, 1704-1705; high sheriff of Prince George's County, 1699-1702, and Charles County, 1704-1705; lieutenant colonel, 1703-1705; born Feb 27, 1667/8, died testate by Nov 6, 1705 (date of probate; Sarah Barton, widow). {Ref: ARMD 23:252, 24:28, 25:27; BDML I:117; CHLR S:284; MDWB 3:643, 25:397}

BARTON, WILLIAM (Annapolis District), captain and master of the brigantine *Hannah* of Dublin in 1730. {Ref: MDGZ, May 26, 1730}

BARTON, WILLIAM, SR. (England, and St. Mary's and Charles Counties), soldier (rank not stated) in the Battle of the Severn on Mar 25, 1655 who was rewarded by Lord Baltimore for his loyalty in 1656; captain and mariner before 1657 (deed of gift to his grandson William Thomas on Dec 29, 1657 and William Barton, Jr. was a witness); member of the Lower House of the Maryland Assembly, 1659-1660; born circa 1605 (aged about 52 when deposed in 1657), died in early 1680's (exact date was not indicated). {Ref: ARMD 10:568, 41:9; BDML I:116-117; MDEP:9}

BARTON, WILLIAM, SR. (Charles County), Protestant and probable soldier in the Revolution of 1689; signed an address and took a loyalty oath supporting the King of England and the reestablishment of Lord Baltimore into power on Nov 28, 1689; "Capt. William Barton" was born circa 1634 (aged about 64 when deposed in 1698). {Ref: ARMD 8:138; MDEP:8}

BARWICK (BARWYCK), DANIELL (St. Mary's County), captain by 1653. {Ref: ARMD 10:320-321}

BASHA, ANDREW (St. Mary's County), soldier (rank not stated) in 1642. {Ref: ARMD 4:130-131}

BASHA, GILES (St. Mary's County), soldier (rank not stated) in 1642. {Ref: ARMD 4:130-131}

BASILION, PETER, see "Captain Letort," q.v.

BASNETT, JOSEPH (Somerset County), soldier (rank not stated) circa 1675; paid for his services in the late expedition against the Nanticoke Indians in 1678. {Ref: ARMD 7:97}

BASS, GEORGE (county or port not indicated), captain and master of the sloop *Charles* of Topsham in 1691. {Ref: ARMD 8:238}

BASS, RICHARD (St. Mary's County), captain and master of a ship (no name given) riding at anchor at the mouth of Patuxent River on Jul 1, 1695 (date of petition). {Ref: ARMD 20:306}

BASSE, JOHN (county or port not indicated), captain and commander of the ship *John* of Topsham in 1670. {Ref: MDHM 5:340}

BATEMAN (BATMAN), ABIGAIL, see "William Bateman," q.v.

BATEMAN, CHRISTOPHER (Kent and Cecil Counties), soldier and probable officer by the 1730's; captain by 1739; born circa 1703 (aged about 29 when deposed in 1732). {Ref: CFES 3:76; MDEP:9}

BATEMAN, ELIZABETH, see "William Bateman," q.v.

BATEMAN, WILLIAM (Kent and Cecil Counties), military officer (rank not stated) who swore allegiance to the King & Queen of England in 1696; one "William Batman" died testate in Cecil County by Mar 31, 1709 (date of probate; Abigail Batman, widow) and a "William Bateman" died testate in Kent County by Apr 6, 1716 (date of probate; Elizabeth Bateman, widow). Additional research will be necessary before drawing conclusions. {Ref: ARMD 20:540; MDWB 12:39, pt. 2; MDWB 14:260}

BATEMAN (BAETMAN), WILLIAM (Charles County), soldier by 1665; "prest in the last indian March up the bay" and paid for his services on Dec 7, 1665. {Ref: ARMD 53:618-619}

BATES, THOMAS (Annapolis District), captain and master of the sloop *John* in 1731. {Ref: CVPR:12}

BATHEAD, JOHN (Kent County), "seaman within the said county" and a "sailor belonging to the *Factor* of Bediford" in 1697. {Ref: ARMD 25:599}

BATSON, E. (Calvert County), Protestant and probable soldier in the Revolution of 1689; signed an address and took a loyalty oath supporting the King of England and the reestablishment of Lord Baltimore into power on Nov 28, 1689. {Ref: ARMD 8:145}

BATSON, EDWARD (Annapolis District), appointed "Navall Officer of the Porte of Annapolis" on Jun 30, 1698. {Ref: ARMD 23:439}

BATTEE (BATTEY, BATTY), FERDINANDO (Anne Arundel County), soldier (rank not stated) circa 1675; paid for his services in the late expedition against the Nanticoke Indians in 1678; died testate by Apr 2, 1706 (date of probate; Elizabeth Battee, widow, later married Thomas Hood). {Ref: ARMD 7:96, 7:611; MDWB 3:744; INAC 29:226}

BATTIN, MARGERY, see "William Battin," q.v.

BATTIN, NICHOLAS (St. Mary's County), captain and master of the ship *Windmill* in 1693. {Ref: ARMD 20:183}

BATTIN (BATTEN), WILLIAM (Virginia, and Pickawaxon Hundred, Charles County), "captain who probably derived his title from his seafaring adventures" (Harry W. Newman's *The Smoots of Maryland and Virginia*, p. 50); born circa 1618 (aged about 43 when deposed in 1661), died by 1662 (Margery Battin or

Batten, widow and administratrix). {Ref: ARMD 41:387, 49:45, 53:65, 53:107, 53:207; CHLR B:26; MDEP:9}

BATTS, NATHANIELL (St. Mary's County), Indian interpreter by 1653. {Ref: ARMD 10:347}

BAWDEN, HUGH (Charles County), Protestant and probable soldier in the Revolution of 1689; signed an address and took a loyalty oath supporting the King of England and the reestablishment of Lord Baltimore into power on Nov 28, 1689. {Ref: ARMD 8:138}

BAXTER, WILLIAM (Talbot County), soldier (rank not stated) circa 1675; paid for his services in the late expedition against the Nanticoke Indians in 1678. {Ref: ARMD 7:88}

BAYARD, NICHOLAS (Cecil County), captain; petitioned the Maryland Council in May, 1697, "praying to be Excused from bearing any Military Command, Setting forth his being Appointed by the ffield Officers of Caecill County to be a Captain of one of the foot Companies there." {Ref: ARMD 23:99}

BAYARD (BYARD), PETER (Cecil County), military officer (rank not stated) who swore allegiance to the King & Queen of England in 1696. {Ref: ARMD 20:545}

BAYARD, PETER (Cecil County), captain and master of the ship *Bohemia Industry* in 1728-1729; militia captain by 1739; member of the Lower House of the Maryland Assembly, 1745-1749; colonel by 1756; born Jul 10, 1702, died testate by Nov 25, 1766 (date of probate; Susanna Bayard, widow). {Ref: BDML I:118; MDGZ, Mar 11, 1728/9; CELR 5:524; MINV 15:47; MDWB 35:29}

BAYARD, SUSANNA, see "Peter Bayard," q.v.

BAYLEY, CHARLES (county not indicated), probable soldier (rank not stated) before 1682; paid for his services out of an assessment levied by the General Assembly for the public good in 1682. {Ref: ARMD 7:439}

BAYLEY, GEORGE (Somerset County), Protestant and probable soldier in the Revolution of 1689; signed an address and took a loyalty oath supporting the King of England and "for enabling us to defend ourselves against all invaders" on Nov 28, 1689. {Ref: ARMD 8:141}

BAYLEY, NICHOLAS (county not indicated), probable soldier (rank not stated) before 1682; paid for his services out of an assessment levied by the General Assembly for the public good in 1682. {Ref: ARMD 7:439}

BAYLY, GEORGE (Talbot County), soldier (rank not stated) circa 1675; paid for his services in the late expedition against the Nanticoke Indians in 1678. {Ref: ARMD 7:92}

BAYLY, JOHN (St. Clements Bay, Charles County), soldier (rank not stated) who was issued a "gun or fowling piece" by Col. Warren on Sep 15, 1694; "John Bailye" died testate by Feb 16, 1712/3 (date of probate). {Ref: ARMD 20:206, 20:208; MDWB 13:582}

BAYNE, ANN, see "John Bayne," q.v.

BAYNE (BEANE, BANE), JOHN (Charles and St. Mary's Counties), captain of horse troops, 1694; member of the Lower House of the Maryland Assembly,

1694-1696; military officer who swore allegiance to the King & Queen of England in 1696; sheriff of St. Mary's County, 1694; sheriff of Charles County, 1696-1698; died testate by Oct 25, 1701 (date of probate; Ann Bayne, widow). {Ref: ARMD 20:73, 20:106 20:543, 23:468, 24:212, 25:20, 38:35, 38:74-75; BDML I:120; RMHF II:84; CHLR C#2:173; INAC 13B:108, 22:32; MDWB 11:217}

BEACH, RICHARD (England, and St. Mary's or Annapolis), captain and master of the ship *Providence* of Portsmouth riding at anchor in Patuxent River in 1705. {Ref: AALR WT#2:325}

BEACHEM, WILLIAM (Annapolis District), captain and master of the sloop *Mary* in 1731. {Ref: CVPR:12}

BEAKSTON, THOMAS (Cecil County), Protestant and probable soldier in the Revolution of 1689; signed an address and took a loyalty oath supporting the King of England and the reestablishment of Lord Baltimore into power on Nov 18, 1689. {Ref: ARMD 8:135}

BEAL, SHADRACH (Charles County), captain and merchant by 1704. {Ref: INAC 25:166}

BEALE, AUDREY, see "William Godwin," q.v.

BEALE, MARTIN (Calvert County), Protestant and probable soldier in the Revolution of 1689; signed an address and took a loyalty oath (made his "H" Mark) supporting the King of England and "to reestablish Lord Baltimore in his ancient power and government" on Nov 16, 1689. {Ref: ARMD 8:132}

BEALE, RICHARD (Prince George's County), captain by 1726. See "William Godwin," q.v. {Ref: PGLR M:68}

BEALE, THOMAS (England, and William & Mary Parish, St. Mary's County), captain by 1704; member of the Lower House of the Maryland Assembly, 1697-1707; major by 1706; died testate by May 25, 1713 (date of probate). {Ref: ARMD 23:17, BDML I:122; MDWB 13:500; INAC 34:201}

BEALL (BEALE), CHARLES (Prince George's County), lieutenant in 1705; captain by 1728; born circa 1672-1673 (aged about 53 when deposed on Aug 21, 1725 and Aug 28, 1726). {Ref: ARMD 25:186; MDAD 9:211; PGLR I:676, M:63, Q:704}

BEALL (BEALE), GEORGE (Prince George's County), soldier and probable officer by the 1720's; colonel before 1770; born circa 1695 (aged about 75 when deposed in 1770). {Ref: MDEP:10}

BEALL (BEALE), JOHN (Prince George's County), foot soldier (rank not stated) under the command of Capt. Richard Owen from June, 1699 to May, 1700. {Ref: ARMD 24:122}

BEALL (BEALE), NINIAN (Scotland, Barbadoes, and Calvert and Prince George's Counties), soldier who was taken prisoner by Oliver Cromwell at the Battle of Dunbar in 1650 and indentured to service in the American colonies; later enlisted in the Calvert County Rangers and was a lieutenant by 1668 and captain by 1676; ordered by the Maryland Council "to continue ranging at the head of Pottuxen River and guarding those parts and care taken for tending the Cropps of those that were employed in that Service by the previous order" in

1678; paid for his services in the late expedition against the Nanticoke Indians in 1678; captain, along with six men, "commanded out to continue Rangeing betweene the head of Pottuxen River and the branches thereabouts up to the Susquehannogh ffort for the discovery of any Indian enemy that may appeare" as ordered by the Maryland Council on Feb 27, 1681; paid for his services out of an assessment levied by the General Assembly for the public good in 1682; officer of Mount Calvert Town in 1686; "Major Bell liveing at the head of Patuxen River above thirty miles above him [Henry Norris] had discovered a fort of foreigne Indians being in number as he could guesse ten thousand" in 1689 (letter from John Courts to Capt. Lawrence Washington dated Mar 26, 1689); major and leader in the Revolution of 1689; commanded by the Maryland Council "to keep ten or twelve men in Armes to Range the woods between patuxen and patomack ... and upon any discovery of Indians appearing in Hostile manner to give notice thereof to the Council" on Mar 28, 1689; high sheriff of Calvert County in 1692; major and "commander in chief (under his Excellency the Captain Generall) of all their Majesty's forces or Militia of Horse and Foot in Calvert County" in 1692; lieutenant colonel, 1692, and colonel of Calvert County troops, 1694-1698; Presbyterian and member of the Lower House of the Maryland Assembly, 1696-1700; sent to treat with the Indians, 1697-1699; colonel of rangers "upon Potomack" in 1698; colonel of Prince George's County troops in 1699-1700; born circa 1625 (aged about 83 when deposed in 1708 and aged 90 odd years when deposed in 1715), died testate by Feb 28, 1717/8 (date of probate). See "Richard Brightwell" and the other "Ninian Beall," q.v. {Ref: ARMD 5:502, 7:103, 7:148, 7:441, 8:92-93, 8:410, 8:445, 13:242, 15:187, 17:72, 20:108, 20:130, 20:369, 23:406, 24:35, 24:121-122; BDML I:122; HCCM:27, 235; FAAH:101-102; CHLR N:329; CHLR R:543; PGLR A:156; MDWB 14:504; RMHF I:59-62, II:86-87, 318; MDEP:10}

BEALL, NINIAN (Prince George's County), colonel before 1727; born circa 1648 (aged about 79 when deposed on Jun 27, 1727). *Note:* Due to an identification problem, some of the information about the aforementioned Ninian Beall could pertain to this Ninian Beall. Additional research will be necessary before drawing conclusions. {Ref: PGLR M:221}

BEALL, RANDOLPH (Charles County), captain by 1689. {Ref: ARMD 13:243}

BEANE, CHARLES (Charles County), soldier (rank not stated) by 1666; signed a petition to the governor to "displace Capt. William Boreman whom was lately constituted captain of the militia" on Sep 12, 1666. {Ref: ARMD 3:556, 3:561}

BEANE, CHRISTOPHER (Calvert County), Protestant and probable soldier in the Revolution of 1689; signed an address and took a loyalty oath (made his "B" mark) supporting the King of England and "to reestablish Lord Baltimore in his ancient power and government" on Nov 16, 1689. {Ref: ARMD 8:132}

BEANE, JOHN, see "John Bayne," q.v.

BEANES, ELIZABETH, see "James Bigger," q.v.

BEANES, WILLIAM, see "James Bigger," q.v.

BEARD, LEWIS (Somerset County), soldier (rank not stated) circa 1675; paid for his services in the late expedition against the Nanticoke Indians in 1678. {Ref: ARMD 7:98}

BEARD, RICHARD, JR. (Annapolis, Anne Arundel County), probable soldier (rank not stated) circa 1675; paid for his services in the late expedition against the Nanticoke Indians in 1678; court justice, 1679-1685; credited with making the first map of Annapolis; born circa 1652 (aged about 44 when deposed in 1696), died intestate in 1703 (son of Richard Beard who died testate in 1681); administration account filed Nov 19, 1706 by Susanna Beard, widow. {Ref: ARMD 7:97, 7:611, 15:253, 17:379; BDML I:126; FAAH:106-107; ARMD 20:492; MDWB 2:143; INAC 26:88}

BEARD, SUSANNA, see "Richard Beard, Jr.," q.v.

BEARD, WILLIAM (Dorchester County), soldier (rank not stated) circa 1675; paid for his services in the late expedition against the Nanticoke Indians in 1678. {Ref: ARMD 7:93}

BEARTON, MEECK (Kent County), soldier (rank not stated) in Capt. William Leeds (Leeads) Company by May 23, 1662, at which time he signed a petition about the misuse of company money by Capt. Thomas Brednox (Bradnox), late of Isle of Kent, deceased. {Ref: ARMD 3:455}

BEAUCHAMP (BEACHAMP), EDMOND (Somerset County), Protestant and probable soldier in the Revolution of 1689; signed an address and took a loyalty oath supporting the King of England and "for enabling us to defend ourselves against all invaders" on Nov 28, 1689. {Ref: ARMD 8:141}

BEAVEN, MARY, see "Charles Bevin," q.v.

BECK, ANTHONY (London, England and Anne Arundel County), captain by the 1730's; member of the South River Club in 1742; died intestate before Apr 19, 1750 (date of inventory approval by Jane Beck, administratrix). {Ref: FAAH:201; MINV 43:72}

BECK, GEORGE AND FRANCES, see "Humphrey Howell" and "William Trego," q.v.

BECK, JANE, see "Anthony Beck," q.v.

BECK, SAMUEL (Queen Anne's County), captain of a ship (no name given) in 1728. {Ref: CESM:64}

BECKELLS, THOMAS (Kent County), military officer (rank not stated) who swore allegiance to the King & Queen of England in 1696; "Thomas Beckles, schoolmaster" died testate by Mar 1, 1708/9 (date of probate; Anne Beckles, widow). {Ref: ARMD 20:541; MDWB 12:7, pt. 2}

BECKETT, HUMPHREY (Prince George's County), soldier (trooper) under the command of Capt. Richard Owen in June, 1699; born circa 1674 (aged about 44 when deposed in 1719 and aged about 63 when deposed in 1737). {Ref: ARMD 24:121; MDEP:11}

BECKLES, ANNE, see "Thomas Beckells," q.v.

BECKLEY, JOHN (Anne Arundel County), captain before 1733; died by Apr 18, 1733 (date of inventory approval). {Ref: MINV 17:442}

BECKSLEY, WILLIAM (Talbot County), captain of a foot company, 1689. {Ref: ARMD 13:243}

BECKWITH, HENRY (Dorchester County), soldier (rank not stated) circa 1675; paid for his services in the late expedition against the Nanticoke Indians in 1678; "Henry Beckwith, Sr." died testate by Oct 27, 1717 (date of probate). {Ref: ARMD 7:93; MDWB 14:451}

BEDE, NICHOLAS, see "Thomas Clark," q.v.

BEDFORD, HUGH (St. Mary's County), captain by 1695. {Ref: INAC 18:166}

BEDWORTH, RICHARD (Anne Arundel County), soldier (rank not stated) circa 1675; paid for his services in the late expedition against the Nanticoke Indians in 1678; died testate by Jul 3, 1683 (date of probate; Sarah Bedworth, widow). {Ref: ARMD 7:96; MDWB 4:17}

BEEDLE (BEADLE, BEDELL), EDWARD (England, Virginia, and Baltimore County), soldier (rank not stated) circa 1675; paid for his services in the late expedition against the Nanticoke Indians in 1678; court justice, 1679-1685; Protestant and probable soldier in the Revolution of 1689; signed an address and took a loyalty oath supporting the King of England and the reestablishment of Lord Baltimore into power on Nov 28, 1689; died intestate by Oct 11, 1697 (date of administration account). {Ref: ARMD 7:95, 8:136, 15:253, 15:327, 17:380; BBCF:35}

BEESTONE, GEORGE (Cecil County), Protestant and probable soldier in the Revolution of 1689; signed an address and took a loyalty oath supporting the King of England and the reestablishment of Lord Baltimore into power on Nov 18, 1689. {Ref: ARMD 8:135}

BEETENSON, EDWARD (county not indicated), probable soldier (rank not stated) before 1682; paid for his services out of an assessment levied by the General Assembly for the public good in 1682. {Ref: ARMD 7:441}

BEEVIN, THOMAS (Calvert County), Protestant and probable soldier in the Revolution of 1689; signed an address and took a loyalty oath supporting the King of England and "to reestablish Lord Baltimore in his ancient power and government" on Nov 16, 1689. {Ref: ARMD 8:132}

BEEZLEY, JOSEPH, see "Joseph Bezely," q.v.

BEFORE, WILLIAM (Talbot County), soldier (rank not stated) circa 1675; paid for his services in the late expedition against the Nanticoke Indians in 1678. {Ref: ARMD 7:92}

BELCHER, HENRY, see "Henry Belsher," q.v.

BELL, ADAM (St. Mary's County), acting naval officer at Patuxent in 1718; died testate by Dec 30, 1718 (date of probate; Ann Bell, widow). {Ref: ARMD 33:180; MDWB 15:152; MDAD 2:426}

BELL, ANN, see "Adam Bell," q.v.

BELL, EDWARD (Talbot County), soldier (rank not stated) circa 1675; paid for his services in the late expedition against the Nanticoke Indians in 1678. {Ref: ARMD 7:92}

BELL, GEORGE (Somerset County), mariner by 1730; captain and master of the ship *Edward* in 1730-1731; captain and master of the sloop *Benedict* in 1734; born circa 1698 (aged about 32 when deposed in 1730). {Ref: MDGZ, Aug 9, 1734; CVPR:12; MDEP:11}

BELL, ISAAC (Somerset County), mariner by 1730; captain and master of the ship *Esther and Hannah* in 1731; born circa 1696 (aged about 34 when deposed in 1730). {Ref: CVPR:12; MDEP:11}

BELLARD, JOHN (England and Annapolis), seaman on the ship *Hartwell* of London commanded by Capt. Nicholas Humphries in March, 1697/8. {Ref: ARMD 23:397}

BELLIN, THOMAS (Pocomoke District), captain and master of the ship *Neptune* in 1731. {Ref: CVPR:12}

BELSHAW, THOMAS (Cecil County), soldier (rank not stated) circa 1675; paid for his services in the late expedition against the Nanticoke Indians in 1678. {Ref: ARMD 7:95}

BELSHER (BELCHER), HENRY (county not indicated), sergeant before 1682; paid for his services out of an assessment levied by the General Assembly for the public good in 1682; Protestant and soldier in the Revolution of 1689; signed an address and took a loyalty oath supporting the King of England and the reestablishment of Lord Baltimore into power on Nov 28, 1689. {Ref: ARMD 7:439, 7:442, 8:138}

BELT, JOSEPH (Anne Arundel and Prince George's Counties), lieutenant colonel by 1723; colonel by 1726; member of the Lower House of the Maryland Assembly, 1725-1737; born circa 1680 (aged about 35 when deposed in 1715), died testate on Jun 26, 1761 (will probated on Sep 14, 1761; Margery Belt, widow). {Ref: ARMD 34:742, 39:13, 39:55, 39:151; BDML I:128-129; PGLR M:211, Q:465; RMHF I:62-63, 318; MDEP:12; MDWB 31:414}

BENHAM, MATHEW (county or port not indicated), gunner on the ship *Mayflower* in 1659. {Ref: ARMD 41:309}

BENIAM, GEORGE (Somerset County), Protestant and probable soldier in the Revolution of 1689; signed an address and took a loyalty oath supporting the King of England and "for enabling us to defend ourselves against all invaders" on Nov 28, 1689. {Ref: ARMD 8:140}

BENN, JONATHAN (England and St. Mary's County), captain and commander of the ship *Rainbow* of Lancaster in 1694. {Ref: ARMD 20:147}

BENNETT, DOROTHY, see "Edward Bennett," q.v.

BENNETT, EDWARD (Quantico, Somerset County), soldier (rank not stated) circa 1675; paid for his services in the late expedition against the Nanticoke Indians in 1678; paid for his services out of an assessment levied by the General Assembly for the public good in 1682; died testate by Dec 28, 1706 (date of probate; Dorothy Bennett, widow). {Ref: ARMD 7:98, 7:443; MDWB 12:113}

BENNETT, ELIZABETH, see "Richard Bennett," q.v.

BENNETT, HENRY (Anne Arundel County), soldier (rank not stated) circa 1675; paid for his services in the late expedition against the Nanticoke Indians in 1678; died testate by Jun 8, 1686 (date of probate). {Ref: ARMD 7:96; MDWB 4:217}

BENNETT, JOHN (St. Mary's County), soldier (rank not stated) in 1642. {Ref: ARMD 4:130-131}

BENNETT, JOHN (Kent County), mariner by 1660. {Ref: ARMD 54:205; INKC:126}

BENNETT, JOHN (Anne Arundel County), probable soldier (rank not stated) before 1682; paid for his services out of an assessment levied by the General Assembly for the public good in 1682; died testate by Mar 1, 1698/9 (date of probate). {Ref: ARMD 7:440; MDWB 6:205}

BENNETT (BENNIT), JOHN (England and St. Mary's County), gunner and seaman on the ship *Ruth* in 1676-1677. {Ref: ARMD 51:474, 66:301, 67:36}

BENNETT, RICHARD (Virginia and Anne Arundel County), captain by 1656; major general of militia in 1666; born circa 1614 (aged about 44 when deposed in 1658), died testate in 1675 (nuncupative will probated on Jan 14, 1675/6; Elizabeth Bennett, widow). {Ref: ARMD 3:331; FAAH:41; MDEP:12; ARMD 41:86; MDWB 5:142}

BENNETT, WILLIAM (Charles County), soldier (rank not stated) circa 1675; paid for his services in the late expedition against the Nanticoke Indians in 1678. {Ref: ARMD 7:101}

BENOIT, THOMAS (Prince George's County), captain and master of the ship *Elizabeth and Francis* riding in the Patuxent River on Feb 24, 1723/4. {Ref: PGLR M:148}

BENSON, JAMES (Talbot County), soldier (rank not stated) circa 1675; paid for his services in the late expedition against the Nanticoke Indians in 1678; captain of a troop of horse by 1693; military officer who swore allegiance to the King & Queen of England in 1696 and who had arms and ammunition in his possession in 1697; Protestant and soldier in the Revolution of 1689; signed an address and took a loyalty oath supporting the King of England and the reestablishment of Lord Baltimore into power on Nov 28, 1689; major before 1709; died testate by Mar 23, 1709/10 (date of probate; Mary Benson, widow). {Ref: ARMD 7:88, 8:144, 8:560, 8:562, 20:542, 23:286; MDWB 13:87; INAC 21:123}

BENSTEAD (BENSET), WILLIAM, see "John Cooke," q.v.

BENTLY, JEREMIAH (England and Anne Arundel County), mariner, of Kingston upon Hull, who owned a plantation in Maryland by 1702. {Ref: AALR WT#1:307}

BENTLY, STEPHEN (Dorchester County), soldier (rank not stated) circa 1675; paid for his services in the late expedition against the Nanticoke Indians in 1678; one "Stephen Bentley" was born circa 1658 (aged about 57 when deposed in Baltimore County in 1715). Additional research will be necessary before drawing conclusions. {Ref: ARMD 7:93; MDEP:13}

BENTON, MARKE (Kent County), soldier (rank not stated) on Isle of Kent who swore allegiance to the Commonwealth of England on Apr 5, 1652. {Ref: INKC:101}

BERKELEY, WILLIAM, see "William Claiborne," q.v.

BERRY, ---- (England and St. Mary's), captain and commander of His Majesty's Ship (ketch) *Deptford* in 1688. {Ref: ARMD 8:53}

BERRY, GEORGE (St. Mary's County), captain and mariner by 1649. {Ref: ARMD 4:521}

BERRY, GILBERT (county or port not indicated), captain and master of the ship *James* of Bideford in 1690. {Ref: ARMD 8:238}

BERRY, JAMES (Virginia and Calvert County), Puritan leader by 1649; commissioner and judge of Patuxent (now Calvert) County; captain by 1676; died intestate circa 1685. {Ref: HCCM:236; INAC 2:107; RMHF I:64}

BERRY, WILLIAM (Dorchester County), soldier (rank not stated) circa 1675; paid for his services in the late expedition against the Nanticoke Indians in 1678. {Ref: ARMD 7:93}

BERRY, WILLIAM (Talbot County), soldier (rank not stated) circa 1675; paid for his services in the late expedition against the Nanticoke Indians in 1678. {Ref: ARMD 7:89}

BERTLEY, RALPH (Charles County), soldier (rank not stated) circa 1675; paid for his services in the late expedition against the Nanticoke Indians in 1678. {Ref: ARMD 7:101}

BESLEY, ---- (St. Mary's County), soldier before 1657 at which time 6000 lbs. of tobacco was "allowed widdow Besley for her Reliefe, her husband being Slain in the Publique Service Leaving behind him four Small Children" (by order of the Maryland Assembly in September, 1657). {Ref: ARMD 1:363-364}

BESSON (BEESON, BESSONE), THOMAS (England, Virginia, and Anne Arundel County), captain who served under Captain Fuller at the Battle of the Severn on Mar 25, 1655 and served on a Council of War after the battle; member of the Lower House of the Maryland Assembly in 1657 and 1666; commissioned and put in command of "all the forces on the south side of Anne Arrundell River up to the head thereof and the north side of South River up to the head thereof" on Dec 9, 1661; noted as "Captaine of the Trayned Band" in 1663; county commissioner in 1664; born circa 1616 (aged about 58 when deposed on Mar 10, 1674/5), died testate by Apr 29, 1679 (date of probate; Hester Besson, widow). {Ref: ARMD 1:359, 3:444, 49:81, 49:304, 51:155; FAAH:26-27; RMHF II:291; MDEP:13; BDML I:132; INAC 2:294; MDWB 10:42}

BEST, JONATHAN (Charles County), soldier (rank not stated) circa 1675; paid for his services in the late expedition against the Nanticoke Indians in 1678. {Ref: ARMD 7:101}

BETTELLEY, FRANCIS (Prince George's County), foot soldier (rank not stated) under the command of Capt. Richard Owen in June, 1699. {Ref: ARMD 24:122}

BETTS, BRIDGET, see "George Betts," q.v.

BETTS, GEORGE (Somerset County), quartermaster before 1682; paid for his services out of an assessment levied by the General Assembly for the public good in 1682; died testate by Dec 1, 1711 (date of probate; Bridget Betts, widow). {Ref: ARMD 7:442; OSES:153, 280, 437; MDWB 13:381}

BETTS, WILLIAM (Dorchester County), soldier (rank not stated) circa 1675; paid for his services in the late expedition against the Nanticoke Indians in 1678. {Ref: ARMD 7:92}

BETTS, WILLIAM (Somerset County), soldier (rank not stated) circa 1675; paid for his services in the late expedition against the Nanticoke Indians in 1678. {Ref: ARMD 7:98}

BETTY, JAMES (Kent County), "seaman within the said county" and a "sailor belonging to the *Factor* of Bediford" in 1697. {Ref: ARMD 25:599}

BEVAN, EVAN (Annapolis District), captain and master of the ship *Morning Star* of Philadelphia in 1729; master of the ship *Wilmore* in 1731. {Ref: MDGZ, Apr 15, 1729; CVPR:12}

BEVAN (BEVANS, BEVANES), JOHN (Gunpowder Hundred, Baltimore County), Protestant and probable soldier in the Revolution of 1689; signed an address and took a loyalty oath supporting the King of England and the reestablishment of Lord Baltimore into power on Nov 28, 1689; born circa 1640 (aged about 83 when deposed in 1723). {Ref: ARMD 8:137; BBCF:40}

BEVIN, CHARLES (Anne Arundel County), soldier (rank not stated) circa 1675; paid for his services in the late expedition against the Nanticoke Indians in 1678; one "Charles Beaven" died testate in Prince George's County by Jun 21, 1699 (date of probate; Mary Beaven, widow). {Ref: ARMD 7:96; MDWB 6:285}

BEZELY (BEEZLEY, BESELY), JOSEPH (Anne Arundel County), captain and commander of the ship *Baltemore* riding at anchor in Herring Bay on Mar 9, 1714; commander of the ship *Charles* riding at anchor in Herring Bay on Dec 17, 1715 and Jan 5, 1716/7 and Nov 19, 1717 and Jan 5, 1718/9 and Jan 26, 1719/20 and Mar 6, 1721/2 and Jan 1, 1722/3 and Jan 24, 1723/4. {Ref: AALR IB#2:196, 258, 325, 399, 524, AALR CW#1:119, 479, AALR CW#2:59, 219}

BIBBY, JOHN (Potomac District), captain and master of the ship *Scipio* in 1730-1731. {Ref: CVPR:12}

BICKFORD, HUGH (St. Mary's County), captain and master of a ship (no name given) in 1695. {Ref: INAC 10:403}

BICKFORD, JOHN (Annapolis District), captain and master of the ship *Elizabeth* in 1702. {Ref: AALR WT#2:330}

BICKFORD, PAUL (Charles County and Potomac District), captain by 1695 and master of the ship *James and Thomas* in 1697. {Ref: ARMD 20:234, 23:171}

BIGGER, ANN, see "John Bigger," q.v.

BIGGER, ELIZABETH, see "James Bigger," q.v.

BIGGER (BIGGOR, BIGGERS), JOHN (Calvert and Prince George's Counties), captain by 1689; member of the Lower House of the Maryland Assembly, 1692-1693; captain of rangers and county commissioner, 1694; major, commissioned Oct 9, 1694; lieutenant colonel of Calvert County, appointed Aug 17, 1695; colonel, 1696; military officer who swore allegiance to the King & Queen of England in 1696; colonel and commander-in-chief of Calvert County, 1705-1707; land owner in Prince George's County; born circa 1658 (aged about 56 when deposed in 1714), died testate by Nov 18, 1714 (date of probate; Ann Bigger, widow; administration account filed on May 30, 1717 by Ann Andrews, wife of Patrick Andrews); "John Biggor" might have been the "Col. Biggott" mentioned in an administration account of John Hutchins, deceased, of Calvert County, on Mar 20, 1716/7. See "James Bigger," q.v. {Ref: ARMD 8:399, 13:253, 20:63, 20:108, 20:153, 20:281, 20:543, 24:113, 24:290, 25:200, 25:596; BDML I:132; HCCM:237; PGLR F Old 5:453; MDEP:13; MDWB 14:14; INAC 37A:25, 38A:81, 38A:87}

BIGGER, JAMES (Calvert and Prince George's Counties), captain before 1689; commanded by the Maryland Council "to keep ten or twelve men in Armes to Range the woods betweene patuxen and patomack [and] upon any discovery of Indians appearing in Hostile manner to give speedy notice [and] have a Deligent Eye upon the motions of the Virginians and if they should attempt a landing on this side to use your Endeavour to prevent their Attempts" on Mar 28, 1689; captain, 1694; wrote his will on May 4, 1705 in Prince George's County and died by Feb 21, 1706/7 (date of inventory; Elizabeth Bigger, widow; administratrix on Nov 22, 1708 was Elizabeth Beanes, wife of William Beanes); will was not probated until Oct 1, 1711 (trustee was his brother John Bigger, q.v.). {Ref: ARMD 8:92, 20:108; HCCM:237; INAC 25:388, 29:31; MDWB 13:439}

BIGGOTT, COLONEL, see "John Bigger," q.v.

BIGLANDS, HENRY (Talbot County), captain and master of the brigantine *Ogle* in 1734-1735. {Ref: MDCB 82:26}

BIGNALL, NATHANIEL (Prince George's County), foot soldier (rank not stated) under the command of Capt. Richard Owen in June, 1699. {Ref: ARMD 24:122}

BILLINGS, JAMES (Dorchester County), mariner by 1734; captain and master of the ship *Rider* (built at Nanticoke River) in 1738. {Ref: MDCB 82:63}

BILLINGSLY, JOHN (St. Mary's or Calvert County), major by 1656. {Ref: ARMD 10:494, 10:509}

BILLTON, THOMAS (Cecil County), Protestant and probable soldier in the Revolution of 1689; signed an address and took a loyalty oath supporting the King of England and the reestablishment of Lord Baltimore into power on Nov 18, 1689. {Ref: ARMD 8:135}

BINNEY, THOMAS (Annapolis and Patuxent Districts), captain and master of the ship *Hopewell* at Patuxent in 1730; captain of the sloop *Endeavour* at Annapolis in 1734. {Ref: MDGZ, Jul 19, 1734; CVPR:12}

BIRCH, ---- (Talbot County), captain by 1718. {Ref: MDAD 1:186}

BIRD, HENRY (England and Annapolis), captain and master of the ship *William and Elizabeth* in 1697. {Ref: ARMD 23:340}

BIRD, PETER (England and Annapolis), captain and master of the ship *William and Elizabeth* in 1693. {Ref: ARMD 23:339}

BIRKETT (BIRKHEAD), CHRISTOPHER (Anne Arundel County), captain of the ship *Agreement* in 1664; "Christopher Birkhead, mariner" owned land on Herring Creek by Aug 20, 1665 (date of original land patent). {Ref: AALR RCW#2:1; MDHM 5:339}

BIRKETT, THOMAS (Talbot County), soldier (rank not stated) circa 1675; paid for his services in the late expedition against the Nanticoke Indians in 1678. {Ref: ARMD 7:88}

BIRKLAND, RICHARD (Somerset County), soldier (rank not stated) circa 1675; paid for his services in the late expedition against the Nanticoke Indians in 1678. {Ref: ARMD 7:99}

BISHOP (BISHOPP), ABRAHAM (Talbot County), soldier (rank not stated) circa 1675; paid for his services in the late expedition against the Nanticoke Indians in 1678. {Ref: ARMD 7:91}

BISHOP, HENRY (England and St. Mary's County), soldier (rank not stated) by 1642; member of the Maryland Assembly, 1638-1642; ordered by the Governor of Maryland on Aug 25, 1642 as follows: "You are notwithstanding any former Order or Instructions to the contrary to permitt all Inhabitants of your Division to tend their Cropps only upon any alarum they are to repair without any delay to your ffort and upon any alarum from Patuxent you are to repair with all your Strength to aid that ffort, and the English there whereof fail not, And this shall be your warrant;" paid in November, 1642 for one month's service under Capt. William Brainthwaite; died by 1645. {Ref: ARMD 3:107, 3:119, 3:122; BDML I:134}

BISHOP, JOHN (Somerset County), soldier (rank not stated) circa 1675; paid for his services in the late expedition against the Nanticoke Indians in 1678; died testate by May 1, 1697 (date of probate; Mary Bishop, widow). {Ref: ARMD 7:99; MDWB 7:265}

BISHOP, MARY, see "John Bishop," q.v.

BISHOP, THEOPHOLIS (Prince George's County), soldier (rank not stated) under the command of Col. Ninian Beale from June, 1699 to May, 1700. {Ref: ARMD 24:121-122}

BLACK, ROBERT (Somerset County), mariner by 1726. {Ref: MDAD 8:48}

BLACK, THOMAS (Kent County), "seaman within the said county" and a "sailor (mate) belonging to the *Factor* of Bediford" in 1697. {Ref: ARMD 25:599}

BLACK, WILLIAM (St. Mary's County), captain and master of the pink *Mary* of Maryland in 1693. {Ref: ARMD 20:182}

BLACKBURNE, EDWARD (Calvert County), Protestant and probable soldier in the Revolution of 1689; signed an address and took a loyalty oath (made his "E" mark) supporting the King of England and "to reestablish Lord Baltimore in his ancient power and government" on Nov 16, 1689. {Ref: ARMD 8:131}

BLACKBURNE, JOHN (Talbot County), soldier (rank not stated) circa 1675; paid for his services in the late expedition against the Nanticoke Indians in 1678. {Ref: ARMD 7:88}

BLACKISTON, EBENEZER, see "Ebenezer Blakiston," q.v.

BLACKISTON, ELIZABETH, see "Nehemiah Blakiston," q.v.

BLACKISTON, NATHANIEL (St. Mary's County), Protestant and probable soldier in the Revolution of 1689; signed an address and took a loyalty oath supporting the King of England and the reestablishment of Lord Baltimore into power on Nov 28, 1689. {Ref: ARMD 8:146}

BLACKMORE, JOHN (Anne Arundel County), military officer (rank not stated) who swore allegiance to the King & Queen of England in 1696; he was possibly the John Blackmore who served a seaman on a private man of war ship (no name given) out of Jamaica under the command of Capt. George Rainer in 1690 and which returned to Maryland in 1692; mariner by Aug 4, 1697 (date of deed); mariner of St. James Parish in 1700; mariner of Anne Arundel County on Aug 2, 1712 (appointment of attorney). {Ref: ARMD 20:541, 23:473; AALR WH#4:93, WT#1:143, IB#2:262, SY#1:226}

BLACKSTONE (BLAKESTONE, BLAKISTON), PETER (England and Talbot County), captain and master of the pink *Supply* in 1706; mariner and land owner in Maryland by 1712; "Peter Blakestone, the Elder, late of Parish of Stepney in County of Middlesex, mariner" died testate before Nov 28, 1724 (appointment of attorney). {Ref: AALR SY#1:124; TALR 9:380; INAC 33B:126}

BLACKSTONE (BLACKSTON), THOMAS (England and Calvert County), captain and master of the ship *Adventure* in 1731; captain and owner of the sloop *Dolphin* in the 1730's; captain of the ship *Annapolis Adventure* of Maryland in 1734; land owner in Maryland by the time he died testate at Southwork, Parish of St. John, County Surry, in May, 1741, leaving his land and sloop *Dolphin* "lying at Maryland in America" to his brother Richard Blackstone, mariner, of London; the inventory of Capt. Thomas Blackstone was taken in Calvert County on Jun 11, 1742. {Ref: MDWB 24:186; CFES 1:46; CVPR:12; MINV 27:110}

BLADEN, WILLIAM (England, and St. Mary's and Anne Arundel Counties), clerk of the Lower House, 1695-1698; naval officer of the Port of Annapolis, 1698-1718; Register of the Admiralty Court, 1698-1703; member of the Lower House of the Maryland Assembly from Annapolis, 1708; commissary general, 1708-1715; colonel before 1718; born circa 1670, died intestate on Aug 7, 1718 (Anne Bladen widow). {Ref: ARMD 25:107, 27:202, 29:12, 33:180; BDML I:136; MINV 1:324}

BLADES, ROBERT (Somerset County), probable soldier (rank not stated) before 1682; paid for his services out of an assessment levied by the General Assembly for the public good in 1682. {Ref: ARMD 7:442}

BLAIR, DAVID (Annapolis District), captain and master of the ship *Port Glascow* in 1730-1731. {Ref: CVPR:12}

BLAIR, WILLIAM (Prince George's County), captain, mariner, master and commander of the ship *Providence* in 1702; probably the "Capt. Blaire" mentioned in an administration account for the estate of Levin Covington, deceased, of Prince George's County in 1727. {Ref: ARMD 25:139; MDAD 8:439}

BLAKE, JOHN (Anne Arundel County), captain and commander of the galley *Queen Anne* riding at anchor in South River on Aug 23, 1708. {Ref: AALR WT#2:645}

BLAKE, THOMAS (Ireland and Calvert County), captain and county justice "who fought in the Indian wars with Col. Casparus Hermann" in the 1670's; military officer (rank not stated) who swore allegiance to the King & Queen of England in 1696; Protestant and soldier in the Revolution of 1689; signed an address and took a loyalty oath supporting the King of England and "to reestablish Lord Baltimore in his ancient power and government" on Nov 16, 1689; sheriff, 1700-1702; died by Jun 8, 1702 (date of inventory). {Ref: ARMD 8:132, 20:543; HCCM:238; INAC 23:125, 24:256, 25:136}

BLAKE, THOMAS (Calvert County), mariner and captain by 1703; died intestate before May 14, 1712 (date of administration account filed by Jane Rye, widow, who had married Charles Rye). {Ref: AALR WT#2:175; INAC 33A:172-173}

BLAKE, WILLIAM (Talbot County), mariner by the 1730's; died intestate before Mar 11, 1740/1 (date of inventory). {Ref: MINV 26:262}

BLAKISTON (BLACKISTON, BLACKSTONE), EBENEZER (England and Cecil County), captain of a foot company in Worton and South Sassafras Hundred, 1689; captain, 1698; court justice, 1702; born circa 1650 (aged about 47 when deposed in 1697), died intestate by Oct 25, 1709 (date of burial). {Ref: ARMD 13:244, 23:177, 25:26, 25:125; CFES 1:37; MDEP:14; INAC 32B:106}

BLAKISTON (BLACKISTON, BLACKSTONE), EBENEZER (Kent County), captain by 1724; member of the Lower House of the Maryland Assembly, 1724-1734; coroner, 1740; major by 1745; born circa 1684 (aged about 41 when deposed in 1726 and aged about 61 when deposed in 1745), died by Jan 19, 1746/7. {Ref: ARMD 39:55, 39:151; BDML I:134-135; MDEP:14; CFES 1:38; INKC:178}

BLAKISTON (BLACKISTON, BLACKSTONE), NATHANIEL (England and Anne Arundel County), colonel, of London, gentleman, by Dec 6, 1711; colonel recognized by the Upper and Lower Houses of the Maryland Assembly in October, 1714, stating that he "has served this province to his utmost as their Agent" and a salary of £120 per annum was authorized to be paid. {Ref: ARMD 29:458; AALR IB#2:3}

BLAKISTON (BLACKISTON), NEHEMIAH (St. Mary's County), captain of a troop of horse "for St. Georges, Poplar hill Newtowne and the other hundreds on the east side of St. Mary's river" in 1689; colonel, 1692; provincial court justice, 1691-1693; chancellor and commissary general, 1692-1693; member of the Maryland Council, 1691-1693; died in December, 1693 (Madam Elizabeth Blackiston, administratrix in 1697). {Ref: ARMD 8:280, 8:404, 13:241, 20:8, 23:103; BDML I:137; INAC 10:403; RMHF I:69}

BLAKISTON (BLACKISTON), NEHEMIAH (St. Mary's County), colonel by 1696; captain general and governor in chief of Maryland in 1700. {Ref: ARMD 23:18, 24:1}

BLAMPY (BLAMPEE), PHILLIP (Somerset County), mariner by 1715. {Ref: SOJR III:70-71}

BLANCKENSTEIN, WILLIAM (St. Mary's County), Protestant and probable soldier in the Revolution of 1689; signed an address and took a loyalty oath supporting the King of England and the reestablishment of Lord Baltimore into power on Nov 28, 1689. {Ref: ARMD 8:147}

BLAND, THOMAS (Anne Arundel County), soldier (rank not stated) circa 1675; paid for his services in the late expedition against the Nanticoke Indians in 1678; military officer (rank not stated) who swore allegiance to the King & Queen of England in 1696. {Ref: ARMD 7:96-97, 20:542}

BLANEY, DAVID (Wye River, Talbot County), soldier (rank not stated) who had arms and ammunition in his possession in 1697; died testate by May 26, 1699 (date of probate; Catherine Blaney, widow). {Ref: ARMD 23:286; MDWB 6:282}

BLAY, EDWARD (Anne Arundel, Cecil, and Kent Counties), court justice, 1685 (quorum, 1702); captain (Cecil County) by 1696; lieutenant colonel by 1703; colonel by 1704; member of the Lower House of the Maryland Assembly, representing Kent County, between 1697 and 1713; born circa 1653 (aged about 33 when deposed in 1686), died by Apr 26, 1714 (date of inventory). {Ref: ARMD 5:533, 17:381, 23:20, 24:151, 25:125, 29:204; BDML I:138; MDEP:15; INKC:156; INAC 35A:372}

BLEKE, ROBERT (county not indicated), probable soldier (rank not stated) before 1682; paid for his services out of an assessment levied by the General Assembly for the public good in 1682. {Ref: ARMD 7:440}

BLEVIN, RICHARD (St. Mary's County), captain by 1719. {Ref: MDAD 2:220}

BLEWS, ROBERT (county not indicated), probable soldier (rank not stated) before 1682; paid for his services out of an assessment levied by the General Assembly for the public good in 1682. {Ref: ARMD 7:439-440}

BLIKERN, ---- (St. Mary's County), captain by 1710. {Ref: INAC 32B:10}

BLISS, GEORGE (county or port not indicated), sailor on the ship *Samuel and John* commanded by Capt. Phillips in 1696. {Ref: ARMD 25:557; MDEP:15}

BLOMFIELD, JOHN (St. Mary's County), soldier (rank not stated) circa 1675; paid for his services in the late expedition against the Nanticoke Indians in 1678; Protestant and probable soldier in the Revolution of 1689; signed an address and took a loyalty oath supporting the King of England and the reestablishment of Lord Baltimore into power on Nov 28, 1689. {Ref: ARMD 7:102, 8:147}

BLORNCAY, DAVID (Talbot County), lieutenant who swore allegiance to the King & Queen of England in 1696. {Ref: ARMD 20:542}

BLOYSE (BLOYCE), THOMAS (Manokin Hundred, Somerset County), soldier (rank not stated) circa 1675; paid for his services in the late expedition against the Nanticoke Indians in 1678. {Ref: ARMD 7:98, 7:100; OSES:280, 437}

BLUNT, ANN, see "Richard Blunt (Blunte)," q.v.

BLUNT, RANDALL (Charles County), captain by 1679. {Ref: INAC 6:682}

BLUNT, RICHARD (Talbot County), corporal who swore allegiance to the King & Queen of England in 1696. {Ref: ARMD 20:542}

BLUNT (BLUNTE), RICHARD (Kent County), soldier (rank not stated) on Isle of Kent who swore allegiance to the Commonwealth of England on Apr 5, 1652; soldier (rank not stated) in Capt. William Leeds (Leeads) Company by May 23, 1662, at which time he signed a petition about the misuse of company money by Capt. Thomas Brednox (Bradnox), late of Isle of Kent, deceased; born between 1615 and 1621 (aged about 36 when deposed in 1651 and aged about 35 when deposed in 1656), died testate and was buried Sep 16, 1669 (will written on Aug 17, 1669, but no date of probate was indicated; Ann Blunt, widow). {Ref: ARMD 3:455, 10:133, 54:68, 54:188; BDML I:139; MDEP:15; INKC:101, 125; MDWB 1:340}

BLUNT (BLOUNT), WILLIAM (Kent and St. Mary's Counties), captain in 1642; appointed to command "the Souldiery of our County of St. Marie's to leavie, Muster and train all or any English able to bear arms" on Jun 23, 1642; member of the Maryland Council, 1642-1643; apparently left Maryland in 1643 and never returned. {Ref: ARMD 1:169, 3:103, 4:155; BDML I:139}

BOAGE, MARY, see "John Bogue," q.v.

BOARMAN (BOREMAN), WILLIAM (England, and St. Mary's and Charles Counties), soldier (rank not stated) fined in 1656 for supporting the Calverts at the Battle of Severn on Mar 25, 1655, but was later rewarded for his support with extensive patronage in the 1660's; captain by 1661; member of the Lower House of the Maryland Assembly, 1671-1675; major on the Council of War in July, 1676; paid for his services in the late expedition against the Nanticoke Indians in 1678; sheriff, 1678; court justice, 1679 (listed once as "William Boareman, Jr."); major, 1681; born circa 1627 (aged about 80 when deposed on Sep 15, 1707), died testate by Jun 17, 1709 (date of probate; Mary Boarman, widow). See "James Lindsey" and "William Godwin," q.v. {Ref: ARMD 3:435, 3:453, 3:503, 3:556, 5:35, 7:102, 7:252, 15:92, 15:99, 15:232, 15:256, 15:326, 49:516; BDML I:148; RMHF II:93; CHLR F:25, S:110, C#2:158, D#2:45; MDWB 12:108, pt. 2; INAC 30:60}

BODDY, NICHOLAS (Charles County), lieutenant by 1677. {Ref: INAC 4:312}

BODKIN, ---- (St. Mary's County), captain by 1675. {Ref: INAC 1:528}

BODWELL, OTTWELL (Talbot County), soldier (rank not stated) circa 1675; paid for his services in the late expedition against the Nanticoke Indians in 1678. {Ref: ARMD 7:88}

BOGUE, JOHN (St. Mary's and Calvert Counties), lieutenant, commissioned May 8, 1658; born circa 1628-1629 (aged about 30 when deposed on Jan 15, 1658/9); "John Boage, of Calvert County" died testate by Dec 16, 1667 (date of probate; Mary Boage, widow). {Ref: ARMD 3:344, 41:220, 49:17, 49:61; MDWB 1:301}

BOILS, JOSEPH (county not indicated), private in the Maryland troops "raised to strengthen Albany, New York and resist the French and Indian enemies" in 1690. {Ref: SHMD I:355}

BOLITHOE (BOLITHO), WILLIAM (Somerset County), captain and mariner before 1721; died testate by Mar 6, 1721/2 (date of probate; Mary Bolithoe, widow). See "William Planner," q.v. {Ref: MDWB 17:120; MINV 9:141}

BOLTER, ---- (Calvert County), captain by 1679. {Ref: INAC 6:631}

BONAK, CHARLES (St. Mary's County), seaman whose name appeared on "a list of men that goe by water when employed" in 1697. {Ref: ARMD 25:597}

BOND, ALICE, see "Peter Bond," q.v.

BOND, GILES (England and Anne Arundel County), mariner, of London, bound for Maryland in February, 1700/1. {Ref: AALR WT#1:262}

BOND, JOHN (Baltimore and/or Anne Arundel County), captain by 1718. {Ref: MDAD 1:281, 2:47}

BOND, PETER (England, and Anne Arundel and Baltimore Counties), soldier (rank not stated) circa 1675; paid for his services in the late expedition against the Nanticoke Indians in 1678; died testate by Apr 28, 1705 (date of probate; Alice Bond, widow). {Ref: ARMD 7:96; BDML I:141; MDWB 3:451; BBCF:47}

BOND, STEPHEN (Somerset County), soldier (rank not stated) circa 1675; paid for his services in the late expedition against the Nanticoke Indians in 1678. {Ref: ARMD 7:100}

BOND, WILLIAM (Baltimore County), probable soldier in the 1730's; captain by 1737 (at which time he received a bounty payment for squirrels heads). {Ref: INBC:28}

BONNER, WILLIAM (county or port not indicated), mate on the ship *John and Christian* of Bristol in 1668. {Ref: MDHM 5:340}

BONNICK (BONNETT), THOMAS (England and St. Mary's County), cooper on the ship *Ruth* in 1676. {Ref: ARMD 51:474, 66:301}

BOOGE, JOHN (England and Anne Arundel County), captain and commander of the ship *Daniel* riding at anchor in South River on Mar 11, 1707. {Ref: AALR WT#2:589}

BOONE, HUMPHREY (Anne Arundel and Baltimore Counties), probable soldier when he received payment "for acts of public service" in 1681; captain by 1692; captain of foot troops in 1693-1694; military officer who swore allegiance to the King & Queen of England in 1696; died testate on Nov 20, 1709 (will probated on Nov 30, 1709). {Ref: ARMD 20:108, 20:201, 20:541; AAGE:531-532; MDWB 12:205, pt. 2; BBCF:55; RMHF II:335}

BOOSH, JOHN (Wiccocomacoe, Somerset County), soldier (rank not stated) circa 1675; paid for his services in the late expedition against the Nanticoke Indians in 1678. {Ref: ARMD 7:98}

BOOTH, ISAAC (county not indicated), probable soldier by 1694 when paid for his services by the Maryland Assembly. {Ref: ARMD 38:55}

BOOTH, JOSIAS (Talbot County), corporal who swore allegiance to the King & Queen of England in 1696. {Ref: ARMD 20:542}

BOOTH, WILLIAM (Kent County), mariner by 1732. {Ref: CFES 7:20}

BOOTHBY, EDWARD (St. Mary's and Baltimore County), clerk to the Provincial Court at St. Mary's, 1686-1688; member of the Lower House of the Maryland Assembly (representing Baltimore County), 1692-1693; deputy commissary, 1693; paid for his services in 1695; agent to Pennsylvania on Indian affairs, 1697, but any record of military service or rank not found; court justice, 1694-1698; died Dec 12, 1698 (will probated on Jan 10, 1698/9; Elizabeth Boothby, widow). See "Henry Johnson," q.v. {Ref: BDML I:144; ARMD 23:428, 38:72; BBCF:55; MDWB 6:233}

BOOTHBY, ELIZABETH, see "Henry Johnson," q.v.

BORDLEY, ---- (Kent or Queen Anne's County), colonel by 1710. {Ref: INAC 32B:47}

BOREING, SARAH, see "John Boring," q.v.

BOREMAN, WILLIAM, see "William Boarman," q.v.

BORID, THOMAS (Talbot County), captain by 1710. {Ref: INAC 32B:33}

BORING, ANN, see "John Boring," q.v.

BORING (BOREING), JOHN (Baltimore County), captain by 1732; born circa 1682 (aged about 50 when deposed in 1732), died intestate by Nov 28, 1750 (date of inventory; Sarah Boreing, widow). {Ref: HBCC:55; BBCF:56; MINV 45:133}

BORING (BOREING, BOARING), JOHN (Baltimore County), lieutenant before 1678; paid for his services in the late expedition against the Nanticoke Indians in 1678; died testate by Aug 5, 1690 (date of probate; Ann Boring, widow). {Ref: ARMD 7:95, 15:253, 15:327; BBCF:56}

BOSTOCK (BOSTICK), NATHANIEL (Annapolis District), captain and commander of His Majesty's Advice Boat *Eagle* in 1701-1702. {Ref: ARMD 24:303, 25:117, 25:126}

BOSTOCK, WILLIAM (Annapolis District), captain and commander of His Majesty's Advice Boat *Swift* in 1697-1698. {Ref: ARMD 23:408-409}

BOSTON, SAMUEL (Baltimore County), sheriff, 1674; captain by 1675; died intestate by Mar 6, 1677/8 (date of administration bond; Mary Boston, widow). {Ref: BALR RR#HS; INAC 5:178; BBCF:58, 64}

BOSWORTH, JOHN (England and St. Mary's), captain and commander of the ship *Charity* of London in 1654. {Ref: ARMD 10:394}

BOTELER, CHARLES (Calvert County), captain by 1676; major and clerk of the court by 1678; paid for his services in the late expedition against the Nanticoke Indians in 1678 and 1681 (name listed once as "Charles Botler" and once as "Charles Butler"); died by Jul 8, 1686 (date of an administration account). See "Captain Auglye" and "Thomas Carleton," q.v. {Ref: ARMD 7:104, 7:252; HCCM:239; INAC 2:179, 9:29}

BOTELER, JOHN (England and Kent County), captain and leader of William Claiborne's forces on Kent Island in 1638; born circa 1601, died intestate in 1642. {Ref: ARMD 3:75, 4:128; BDML I:149}

BOTTS (BOTS), RICHARD (Charles County), mariner before 1659; served as a seaman on Daniel Hutt's bark for 7 or 8 months in 1659. {Ref: CHLR A:50}

BOTTWELL, ATTWELL (Talbot County), soldier (rank not stated) circa 1675; paid for his services in the late expedition against the Nanticoke Indians in 1678. {Ref: ARMD 7:89}

BOULTER, JOHN (England and St. Mary's), purser and steward on the ship *Ark* in 1633-1634; born circa 1593 (aged about 40 at the time of his sailing for Maryland in November, 1633). {Ref: FMDP:343}

BOULTLOT, WILLIAM (Kent County), military officer (rank not stated) who swore allegiance to the King & Queen of England in 1696. {Ref: ARMD 20:540}

BOULTON, ENOCH (Anne Arundel County), soldier (rank not stated) circa 1675; paid for his services in the late expedition against the Nanticoke Indians in 1678. {Ref: ARMD 7:97}

BOULTON, SARAH, see "William Boulton," q.v.

BOULTON, WILLIAM (Queen Anne's County), captain and commander of the pink *Betty* riding at anchor in Severn River on Jan 23, 1705/6; died testate by Apr 26, 1710 (date of probate; Sarah Boulton, widow). {Ref: AALR WT#2:293; MDWB 13:7}

BOUND (BOUNDS), JOHN (Wicomico, Somerset County), soldier (rank not stated) circa 1675; paid for his services in the late expedition against the Nanticoke Indians in 1678. {Ref: ARMD 7:98; OSES:153}

BOURK, CECELIE, see "John Alford," q.v.

BOURNE, ELIZABETH, see "Samuell Bourne," q.v.

BOURNE, ELKENATH (St. Mary's County), seaman on a ship (no name given) commanded by Capt. Richard Husbands in 1649. {Ref: ARMD 10:9}

BOURNE, SAMUEL (England and Calvert County), captain by 1689; letter from John Addison to John West on Mar 25, 1689 stated that "there is nine thousand French and Senecoes at Captain Bourne's upon the Cliffs in Anne Arundell" and a letter from John Courts to Capt. Lawrence Washington dated Mar 26, 1689 reported that Captain Bourne had been killed by Indians at the mouth of Patuxent River. {Ref: ARMD 8:93; HCCM:240}

BOURNE (BOURN), SAMUELL (Patuxent River, Calvert County), captain on the Council of War in July, 1676; quorum, 1675; justice of the peace, 1679; court justice, 1680; captain of "a troope of horse as formerly" in 1689; major and naval officer of Patuxent District before 1694; died testate by Jun 16, 1694 (date of inventory; will written on May 16, 1693; date of probate not indicated; Elizabeth Bourne, widow); on Nov 14, 1694 his widow filed a petition for the fees he was due as late naval officer. {Ref: ARMD 7:611, 8:93, 13:242, 15:68, 15:99, 15:268, 15:327, 17:71, 20:173; MDWB 2:302; INAC 13A:120}

BOUTFLOWER, JAMES (Prince George's County), captain and master of the ship *Seghorn and Moreti* riding in the Patuxent River on Apr 30, 1726. {Ref: PGLR M:149}

BOUYE, JOHN (St. Mary's County), probable soldier who was allowed 400 pounds of tobacco by the Maryland Council "for service per him done for the country" in 1692. {Ref: ARMD 8:404}

BOVILE, JAMES (Somerset County), seaman by 1716. {Ref: INAC 37A:82}

BOWDEN, WALTER (Cecil County), captain and master of the ship *Ann* riding at anchor in Sassafras River on Mar 9, 1707/8. {Ref: CELR 1:483}

BOWELL, GEORGE (Talbot County), soldier (rank not stated) circa 1675; paid for his services in the late expedition against the Nanticoke Indians in 1678; Protestant and probable soldier in the Revolution of 1689; signed an address and took a loyalty oath supporting the King of England and the reestablishment of Lord Baltimore into power on Nov 18, 1689. {Ref: ARMD 7:88, 8:134}

BOWEN, ---- (Calvert County), captain by 1695. {Ref: INAC 10:482}

BOWEN, HENRY (Talbot County), soldier (rank not stated) circa 1675; paid for his services in the late expedition against the Nanticoke Indians in 1678. {Ref: ARMD 7:89}

BOWEN (BOYNE), JONAS (Baltimore County), soldier (rank not stated) circa 1675; paid for his services in the late expedition against the Nanticoke Indians in 1678; died testate by Apr 13, 1699 (date of probate; Martha Bowen, widow). {Ref: ARMD 7:96; BBCF:61}

BOWEN, MARTHA, see "Jonas Bowen," q.v.

BOWEN, WALTER (St. Mary's County), soldier (rank not stated) circa 1675; paid for his services in the late expedition against the Nanticoke Indians in 1678. {Ref: ARMD 7:103}

BOWEN, WILLIAM (Somerset County), Protestant and probable soldier in the Revolution of 1689; signed an address and took a loyalty oath supporting the King of England and "for enabling us to defend ourselves against all invaders" on Nov 28, 1689. {Ref: ARMD 8:139}

BOWLES, ---- (St. Mary's or Calvert County), captain by 1698. {Ref: ARMD 23:466}

BOWLES, ANTHONY (county or port not indicated), captain and master of the ship *Success* of London in 1690. {Ref: ARMD 8:237}

BOWLING, JAMES (St. Mary's County), soldier (rank not stated) circa 1675; paid for his services in the late expedition against the Nanticoke Indians in 1678; court justice, 1680; captain by 1683; born circa 1636 (aged about 22 when deposed in 1658), died testate by Oct 10, 1693 (date of probate; Mary Bowling, widow, later married Capt. John Dent). {Ref: ARMD 7:102, 15:326, 17:181-183, 20:58, 41:175-180; MDEP:18; CHLR M:220; MDWB 2:272; INAC 8:246, 13A:176; RMHF I:81-82}

BOWMAN, CHARLES (Prince George's County), soldier and probable officer by the 1730's; colonel by 1742. {Ref: MDAD 19:179}

BOWMAN, JOHN (Charles County), captain and commander of the ship *Elizabeth and Mary* anchored at Wicomico River on May 9, 1683. {Ref: CHLR N:308}

BOWMAN, SAMUELL (Charles County), mariner and captain by 1717 (mentioned in will of Robert Sanders). {Ref: MDWB 14:445}

BOWMAN, THOMAS (Dorchester County), soldier (rank not stated) circa 1675; paid for his services in the late expedition against the Nanticoke Indians in 1678. {Ref: ARMD 7:92}

BOWYERS, FRANCIS (Charles County), soldier (rank not stated) who was issued a "gun or fowling piece" by Col. Warren on Sep 15, 1694. {Ref: ARMD 20:206, 20:208}

BOYD, JAMES, see "John Norwood," q.v.

BOYER, ROBERT (Somerset County), Protestant and probable soldier in the Revolution of 1689; signed an address and took a loyalty oath supporting the King of England and "for enabling us to defend ourselves against all invaders" on Nov 28, 1689. {Ref: ARMD 8:141}

BOYES, PHINES (Kent County), "seaman within the said county" and a "sailor belonging to the *Loves Increase* of Whitehaven" in 1697. {Ref: ARMD 25:600}

BOYLAIN, GEORGE (Prince George's County), captain and commander of the ship *Princess Amelia* in 1722. {Ref: PGLR I:465}

BOYMAN, GEORGE (Somerset County), Protestant and probable soldier in the Revolution of 1689; signed an address and took a loyalty oath supporting the King of England and "for enabling us to defend ourselves against all invaders" on Nov 28, 1689. {Ref: ARMD 8:140}

BOYMAN, GEORGE (Prince George's County), captain and master of the ship *Sampson* riding in the Patuxent River on Dec 28, 1723. {Ref: PGLR M:148}

BOYMAN, JOHN (Somerset County), Protestant and probable soldier in the Revolution of 1689; signed an address and took a loyalty oath supporting the King of England and "for enabling us to defend ourselves against all invaders" on Nov 28, 1689. {Ref: ARMD 8:141}

BOYMAN, WILLIAM (Somerset County), Protestant and probable soldier in the Revolution of 1689; signed an address and took a loyalty oath supporting the King of England and "for enabling us to defend ourselves against all invaders" on Nov 28, 1689. {Ref: ARMD 8:141}

BOYNE, JONAS, see "Jonas Bowen," q.v.

BOYS, ROBERT (Prince George's County), a seafaring man in 1697. {Ref: ARMD 25:596}

BOYS, THOMAS (St. Mary's County), captain and mariner by 1637. {Ref: ARMD 1:6, 4:225}

BOYS, WILLIAM (Prince George's County), a seafaring man in 1697. {Ref: ARMD 25:596}

BOZENE, SAMUEL (Calvert County), Protestant, justice of the peace, and probable soldier in the Revolution of 1689; signed an address and took a loyalty oath supporting the King of England and the reestablishment of Lord Baltimore into power on Nov 28, 1689. {Ref: ARMD 8:145}

BOZMAN (BOSMAN), THOMAS (Talbot County), officer by the 1720's; colonel by 1746; member of the Lower House of the Maryland Assembly, 1723-1724;

born circa 1693, died testate by Jul 21, 1752 (date of probate). {Ref: BDML I:157-158; MDWB 28:359}

BRABATCH (BAREBATCH), THOMAS (county or port not indicated), sailor and privateer in 1707, aged 14 years old. {Ref: ARMD 27:34, 27:116}

BRADBY, JAMES (Anne Arundel County), captain and commander of the ship *Ursula* riding at anchor in South River on Sep 17, 1705 and Jun 21, 1708, and riding at anchor in Severn River on May 6, 1713. {Ref: AALR WT#2:249, WT#2:636, IB#2:27}

BRADFORD, AMBROSE (Calvert County), captain and master of a small rum vessel (no name given) of Captain Bowles on Patuxent River. {Ref: ARMD 23:466-467}

BRADFORD, JOHN (England and Prince George's County), captain by 1708; major by 1714; member of the Lower House of the Maryland Assembly, 1708-1716; Maryland Council indicated that "a report being spread of some disturbance likely to arise from Indians about Rock Creek in Prince George's County ... his Excellency and the Council think it fit that Major Bradford repair thither in order to obviate any such disturbances" on May 17, 1715; colonel by 1722; died testate by May 11, 1726 (date of probate; Joyce Bradford, widow). {Ref: ARMD 30:107, 30:158, 30:184, 30:360, 34:742; BDML I:158; PGLR F Old 5:511; PGLR Q:334; MDWB 18:464; MINV 12:162}

BRADFORD, JOYCE, see "John Bradford," q.v.

BRADFORD, WILLIAM (England and Baltimore County), "may have come to Maryland in the early 18th century as a schoolmaster and officer in the colonial army; may be the same William who in 1722 petitioned the court that at the time of his levy, 1721, he was servant whose term expired in September, 1721;" commissioned coroner of Baltimore County as "Capt. William Bradford" in 1742; died intestate by Mar 21, 1757 (date of administration bond). {Ref: BBCF:65}

BRADLEY, ANDREW (St. Mary's County), soldier (rank not stated) circa 1675; paid for his services in the late expedition against the Nanticoke Indians in 1678. {Ref: ARMD 7:103}

BRADLEY, DANIELL (England and St. Mary's County), captain and master of a ship *Joseph* of London who was recommended for commodore on Jul 1, 1695 and commissioned by the governor on Jul 7, 1695. {Ref: ARMD 20:306-307, 23:28}

BRADLEY (BRADLY), HENRY (Dorchester County), soldier (rank not stated) circa 1675; paid for his services in the late expedition against the Nanticoke Indians in 1678; died testate by Jul 1, 1679 (date of probate; Mary Bradley, widow). {Ref: ARMD 7:93; MDWB 10:61}}

BRADLEY (BRADLEE), JOHN (Somerset County), mariner by 1734; captain, master and owner of the schooner *Mary and John* in 1737 built in Somerset County in 1734). {Ref: MDCB 82:51}

BRADLEY, MARY, see "Henry Bradley," q.v.

BRADLEY, ROBERT (England and Prince George's County), captain and master of the ship *Edward and Dudley* in 1696. {Ref: ARMD 23:72-73}

BRADNOX (BRADNOCKE, BRODNOX, BREDNOX, BROADNAX), THOMAS (Kent County), commander's mate, Kent Island, 1641; member of the Maryland Assembly between 1637 and 1647; soldier (rank not stated) on Isle of Kent who swore allegiance to the Commonwealth of England on Apr 5, 1652; sheriff, 1653; captain, commissioned Jul 20, 1658, to command all the forces on the Isle of Kent; captain and member of the Kent County Court, 1658-1661; born between 1599 and 1608 (aged about 40 when deposed twice in 1648, aged about 57 when deposed in 1656, and aged about 58 when deposed in 1658), died testate by Dec 25, 1661 (date of probate; Mary Bradnox, widow). See "John Emkson," q.v. {Ref: ARMD 3:349, 3:351, 3:455, 4:458, 54:106, 54:132, 54:142, 54:194, 54:220; BDML I:159; MDEP:19; INKC:101, 109; MDWB 1:154}

BRADSHAW, JOHN (Somerset County), soldier (rank not stated) circa 1675; paid for his services in the late expedition against the Nanticoke Indians in 1678. {Ref: ARMD 7:97}

BRADSHAW, JOHN (Charles County), soldier (rank not stated) circa 1675; paid for his services in the late expedition against the Nanticoke Indians in 1678. {Ref: ARMD 7:101}

BRADSHAW, THOMAS (Charles County), soldier (rank not stated) circa 1675; paid for his services in the late expedition against the Nanticoke Indians in 1678. {Ref: ARMD 7:101}

BRAINE (BRAINS), JAMES (Anne Arundel County), captain by 1696; commander of the ship *James and Benjamin* riding in South River in 1698. {Ref: ARMD 23:10, 23:28, 25:18; INAC 16:135}

BRAITHWAITE (BRAINTHWAIT), WILLIAM (England, Isle of Kent, and St. Mary's County), gentleman and member of the Maryland Assembly, 1637-1638; commander of the Isle of Kent, 1638-1639; captain by 1640; paid for one month's service in November, 1642; commander of St. Mary's County, 1643-1644; died by February, 1649/50. {Ref: ARMD 3:122, 4:91, 4:131; BDML I:159-160; MDEP:20; RMHF I:254; INKC:178}

BRAMHAM, RICHARD (England and Patuxent District), captain of the sloop *Judith and Elizabeth* in 1694-1695. {Ref: ARMD 23:317}

BRAN, ---- (Charles County), captain by 1699. {Ref: INAC 11B:46}

BRAND, JOHN (Patuxent District), sailor on the ship *Sea Horse* in 1729; noted as a Dutchman who speaks English, he had reportedly run away from the ship. {Ref: MDGZ, Jun 10, 1729}

BRANDT, MARCUS, see "John Barry," q.v.

BRANDT, RANDOLPH (Charles County), captain of a troop of horse by 1678; ordered by the Maryland Council "to range his troope no higher then the Pascattoway fort" in 1678; paid for his services in the late expedition against the Nanticoke Indians in 1678; member of the Lower House of the Maryland Assembly, 1681-1682; died testate by Feb 10, 1698/9 (date of probate); name sometimes listed as "Randolph Brendt" and "Rando. Brandt" and "Randall Brandt" and "Randolph Brant." {Ref: ARMD 7:100, 7:265, 15:186, 15:198, 15:317, 15:400, 17:72, 17:358; BDML I:160; CHLR Z:72; INAC 9:55, 20:50; MDWB 6:222}

BRATHERY, JOHN (Prince George's County), captain and master of the ship *John and Robert* riding in the Patuxent River on Jan 24, 1724/5. {Ref: PGLR M:149}

BRATHWAITE, GAWEN (Potomac District), captain and master of the ship *Goodwill* in 1730-1731. {Ref: CVPR:12}

BRAUGHTON, JOHN (Somerset County), Protestant and probable soldier in the Revolution of 1689; signed an address and took a loyalty oath supporting the King of England and "for enabling us to defend ourselves against all invaders" on Nov 28, 1689. {Ref: ARMD 8:141}

BRAY, RICHARD (Annapolis District), captain of the ship *Hopewell* of Fowey in 1728-1729. {Ref: MDGZ, Mar 11, 1728/9 and Jun 24, 1729}

BRAY, THOMAS, see "Edward Dorsey," q.v.

BREDNOX, THOMAS, see "Thomas Bradnox," q.v.

BREED, AMOS (Boston and Annapolis), captain and master of the sloop *Abigail* of Boston in 1729-1731; captain of the sloop *Hannah and Lydia* in 1734. {Ref: MDGZ, Jul 1, 1729 and Nov 29, 1734; CVPR:12}

BREMINGTON, JOHN (Talbot County), captain of foot soldiers in Chester and Wye Rivers, commissioned Jul 2, 1677. {Ref: ARMD 5:11}

BRENT, GEORGE (Virginia and Charles County), captain by 1696; a "George Breett" was a Protestant and probable soldier in the Revolution of 1689; signed an address and took a loyalty oath in Charles County supporting the King of England and the reestablishment of Lord Baltimore into power on Nov 28, 1689. See "William Chandler," q.v. {Ref: ARMD 8:138; INAC 13B:108, 14:127}

BRENT, GILES (England, Isle of Kent, Virginia, and St. Mary's and Charles Counties), captain by 1639; member of the Maryland Assembly (special writ), 1638-1648; member of the Maryland Council, 1638-1644; commander of Kent Island, 1639-1644; acting governor and lieutenant general, 1643-1644; captain, 1651-1663; born 1600, died by Feb 16, 1671/2 (he was the brother of Mistress Margaret Brent, spinster, land owner, businesswoman, agent and executrix of Gov. Leonard Calvert). {Ref: ARMD 3:104, 4:107, 4:357, 10:4, 10:150, 49:156; BDML I:161; INKC:178; CHLR B:44; RMHF I:84}

BRENT, HENRY, see "John Payne," q.v.

BRENT, MARGARET, see "Giles Brent," q.v.

BRENT, MARY, see "William Chandler," q.v.

BRENTS, WILLIAM (Kent County), soldier (rank not stated) circa 1675; paid for his services in the late expedition against the Nanticoke Indians in 1678. {Ref: ARMD 7:94}

BRERETON, THOMAS (Somerset County), major by 1675. {Ref: CESM:36}

BRERETON, THOMAS (Anne Arundel County), sailor on the sloop *Margrett's Industry* in 1707. {Ref: ARMD 27:31, 27:33-35}

BRERETON, WILLIAM (Somerset County), court justice, 1679-1680; probable soldier (rank not stated) before 1682; paid for his services out of an assessment levied by the General Assembly for the public good in 1682; Protestant and probable soldier in the Revolution of 1689; signed an address and took a loyalty oath supporting the King of England and "for enabling us to defend ourselves against all invaders" on Nov 28, 1689. {Ref: ARMD 7:442-443, 8:141, 15:275, 15:328}

BRESLY, PETER (St. Mary's County), colonel by 1716. {Ref: INAC 37A:160}

BRETTAINE, JOHN (Talbot County), soldier (rank not stated) circa 1675; paid for his services in the late expedition against the Nanticoke Indians in 1678. {Ref: ARMD 7:89}

BREWER, JAMES (St. Mary's County), soldier (rank not stated) circa 1675; paid for his services in the late expedition against the Nanticoke Indians in 1678. {Ref: ARMD 7:102}

BREWER, WILLIAM (St. Mary's County), soldier (rank not stated) circa 1675; paid for his services in the late expedition against the Nanticoke Indians in 1678. {Ref: ARMD 7:102}

BRICE, JOHN (England, and Severn Hundred, Anne Arundel County), captain before 1700; county court justice, 1702-1713; member of the Lower House of the Maryland Assembly in 1709; died intestate in December, 1713 (Sarah Worthington, widow). See "John Worthington," q.v. {Ref: BDML I:165; FAAH:75, 156-157; RMHF II:98-99}

BRIDGER, JOSEPH (county not indicated), colonel by 1688. {Ref: INAC 10:61}

BRIDGES, JOSIAS (Patapsco Hundred, Baltimore County), ranger in 1694/1695; appointed by Capt. John Oldton as a "well quallified person & good woods man & fit to be Imployed in Ranging for the Publick Service of this Province" on Mar 23, 1694/5 (name listed once as "Josiah Bridges"). {Ref: ARMD 20:205; BBCF:69}

BRIDGES, RICHARD (Talbot County), soldier (rank not stated) circa 1675; paid for his services in the late expedition against the Nanticoke Indians in 1678; died testate by Apr 19, 1713 (date of probate). {Ref: ARMD 7:92; MDWB 13:584}

BRIDGES, THOMAS (Talbot County), soldier (rank not stated) circa 1675; paid for his services in the late expedition against the Nanticoke Indians in 1678; "Thomas Briges" died testate by Apr 18, 1696 (date of probate). {Ref: ARMD 7:92; MDWB 7:167; INAC 14:1}

BRIGGS, THOMAS (Prince George's County), colonel by 1715. {Ref: PGLR F Old 5:552}

BRIGHT, FRANCIS (Kent Island), soldier (rank not stated) on Isle of Kent who swore allegiance to the Commonwealth of England on Apr 5, 1652; "Francis Bright of Kent Island in Talbot County" died testate by May 25, 1705 (date of probate). {Ref: INKC:101; MDWB 3:667}

BRIGHT, THOMAS (Kent County), corporal before 1682; paid for his services out of an assessment levied by the General Assembly for the public good in 1682. {Ref: ARMD 7:440}

BRIGHTWELL, RICHARD (Charles, Calvert, and Prince George's Counties), ranger, 1675; captain of a party of rangers in Calvert County "from the Falls of Pottomuck to the Branches of Pottuxen" in 1692; captain of horse troops, 1694; captain of horse troops in Prince George's County and commander of the party of Rangers upon Potomock River 1695-1697; military officer (rank not stated) who swore allegiance to the King & Queen of England in 1696; died testate by Aug 29, 1698 (date of probate). See "Thomas Orton," q.v. {Ref: ARMD 8:398, 8:445, 15:56, 20:108, 20:379, 20:396, 20:423, 20:546, 23:75, 23:224, 38:74; PGLR A:63A; MDWB 6:182}

BRIMINGTON, JACOB (Talbot County), captain by 1668; land owner in Kent County in 1669. {Ref: ARMD 54:437; INKC:136}

BRINDLEY, LAURENCE (Somerset County), soldier (rank not stated) circa 1675; paid for his services in the late expedition against the Nanticoke Indians in 1678. {Ref: ARMD 7:98}

BRISCOE, ELEANOR, see "John Briscoe," q.v.

BRISCOE, JOHN (Charles County), captain before 1720; born circa 1678 (aged about 47 when deposed in 1725), died testate by Apr 8, 1734 (date of probate; Eleanor Briscoe, widow). {Ref: CHLR H#2:334; MDEP:21; MDWB 21:59; MINV 18:275}

BRISCOE, JOHN (Charles County), soldier and probable officer in the 1730's; captain before 1741; died testate by Feb 15, 1741/2 (date of probate; Mary Briscoe, widow). {Ref: MDWB 22:424; MINV 27:299}

BRISCOE, MARY, see "John Briscoe," q.v.

BRISCOE, PHILIP, SR. (St. Mary's and Charles Counties), captain before 1702; member of the Lower House of the Maryland Assembly, 1699-1700; court justice in St. Mary's County by 1691 and Charles County in 1696-1709; styled "colonel" by the time of his death; died testate by Jan 29, 1724/5 (date of probate; Susannah Briscoe, widow). {Ref: ARMD 23:18; BDML I:167; RMHF I:317; INAC 22:32; CHLR C#2:26-28; MDWB 18:339; MDAD 7:216}

BRISCOE, SUSANNAH, see "Philip Briscoe," q.v.

BRISCOE (BRISCO), THOMAS (Calvert County), naval officer for Patuxent District, commissioned Nov 10, 1694. {Ref: ARMD 20:186}

BRITTEN, RICHARD (Somerset County), Protestant and probable soldier in the Revolution of 1689; signed an address and took a loyalty oath supporting the King of England and "for enabling us to defend ourselves against all invaders" on Nov 28, 1689. {Ref: ARMD 8:141}

BRITTINGHAM, WILLIAM, see "Francis Martin," q.v.

BRITTON, THOMAS (England and Annapolis), captain, mariner and commander of the ship *Resothecon* of Bristol in 1699; captain of a ship (no name given) in 1702. {Ref: ARMD 24:303; AALR WT#1:108}

BRITTON, WILLIAM (England and Talbot County), mariner of Bitheford, County Devon in Old England before 1685; land owner in Talbot County by 1685; died intestate by Sep 10, 1733. {Ref: TALR 5:47; QALR RT#A:283}

BROADED, WILLIAM (Potomac District), captain and master of the ship *James and Thomas* in 1697. {Ref: ARMD 23:172}

BROADHURST, ---- (Somerset County), captain by 1734. {Ref: MDAD 12:271}

BROADWATER, CHARLES (Anne Arundel County), captain and commander of the ship *Robert and John* riding at anchor in Herring Bay on Jun 17, 1711 and May 2, 1713. {Ref: AALR PK:380, IB#2:27}

BROADWAY (BRODWAY), NICHOLAS (Talbot County), soldier (rank not stated) circa 1675; paid for his services in the late expedition against the Nanticoke Indians in 1678; born circa 1630-1632 (aged about 24 when deposed in 1656 and aged about 30 when deposed in 1660). {Ref: ARMD 7:90, 54:191; INKC:125; MDEP:21}

BROCK (BROCKE), EDWARD (Calvert and Prince George's Counties), captain by 1681; died testate by Jun 19, 1714 (date of probate). {Ref: ARMD 7:221; MDWB 13:723; INAC 35A:342; MDEP:50}

BROCK, JAMES (Calvert and Prince George's Counties), mate on the ship *Adventure* commanded by Capt. Francis Harbin in 1698; captain by 1700 and to at least 1730. {Ref: ARMD 23:467; PGLR A:211, Q:225}

BROCK, PETER (Annapolis District), captain and master of the galley *Prosperous* in 1731. {Ref: CVPR:12}

BROCKENDON, JAMES (Somerset County), soldier (rank not stated) circa 1675; paid for his services in the late expedition against the Nanticoke Indians in 1678. {Ref: ARMD 7:98}

BRODGAT, THOMAS (county not indicated), private in the Maryland troops "raised to strengthen Albany, New York and resist the French and Indian enemies" in 1690. {Ref: SHMD I:355}

BROME, ANN, see "John Broome, III," q.v.

BROMLEY, THOMAS (Somerset County), Protestant and probable soldier in the Revolution of 1689; signed an address and took a loyalty oath supporting the King of England and "for enabling us to defend ourselves against all invaders" on Nov 28, 1689. {Ref: ARMD 8:140}

BROMWELL, ISAAC (England and Calvert County), captain and master of the ship *Assurance* in 1635. See "Caleb Pusey," q.v. {Ref: RMHF II:100}

BROOK, MARTIN (Potomac District), captain and master of the ship *Kent* in 1730-1731. {Ref: CVPR:12}

BROOKE, ANNE, see "Baker Brooke," q.v.

BROOKE, BAKER (England and Calvert County), member of the Maryland Council, 1658-1679; one of the most powerful men in the colony due to his marriage in 1664 to Ann Calvert, daughter of the proprietor Gov. Leonard Calvert; styled "colonel" by 1671; surveyor general, 1671-1679; deputy governor, 1669-1670; born in 1628, died testate by Mar 26, 1679 (date of probate; Anne Brooke, widow). {Ref: BDML I:168; HCCM:239; RMHF I:90-91, II:102; MDWB 10:1}

BROOKE (BROOKES), CLEMENT (Prince George's County), captain by 1722; commander of the ship *Experiment* riding in Severn River on Nov 20, 1722; captain of the ship *Baltemore* of London in 1729; mariner and master of the ship *Preston* at Patuxent in 1730-1731; commander of the ship *Tristan* riding at anchor in Chester River on Jul 3, 1732; "Clement Brooke, Jr., gentleman, Prince George's County, des. as of London, mariner, bound on voyage for City of London" wrote his will on Aug 31, 1731; died in Prince George's County by

Nov 28, 1732 (date of probate; Mary Brooke, widow). {Ref: AALR CW#1:534; PGLR Q:196; QALR RT#A:129; MDGZ, Apr 15, 1729; CVPR:12; MDWB 20:436; MDAD 12:148}

BROOKE, ELLINOR, see "Thomas Brooke," q.v.

BROOKE (BROOKS), FRANCIS (Kent and Talbot Counties), soldier (rank not stated) circa 1675; paid for his services in the late expedition against the Nanticoke Indians in 1678; born circa 1634 (aged about 24 when deposed in 1658). {Ref: ARMD 7:91, 54:159; MDEP:23; INKC:119}

BROOKE, JOHN (Charles County), soldier (rank not stated) circa 1675; paid for his services in the late expedition against the Nanticoke Indians in 1678. {Ref: ARMD 7:101}

BROOKE, JOHN (Dorchester and Talbot Counties), soldier (rank not stated) circa 1675; paid for his services in the late expedition against the Nanticoke Indians in 1678; court justice, 1680-1685; member of the Lower House of the Maryland Assembly, 1681-1688; paid for his services out of an assessment levied by the General Assembly for the public good in 1682; town officer of Yarmouth, 1686; deputy commissary, 1692; born circa 1646, died testate by Mar 21, 1692/3 (date of probate; Judah Brooke, widow). {Ref: ARMD 7:92, 7:440, 15:326, 17:381; BDML I:169; MDWB 7:26, 13:142}

BROOKE, MARY, see "Clement Brooke," q.v.

BROOKE, ROBERT (England, and Charles and Calvert Counties), commander of Charles County in 1650; commander of Patuxent (now Calvert) County in 1654; member of the Maryland Council, 1650; provincial court justice, 1650-1654; born 1602, died intestate on Jul 20, 1655. See "Thomas Brooke," q.v. {Ref: BDML I:171; HCCM:243; RMHF I:90-91}

BROOKE, THOMAS (Calvert and Prince George's Counties), colonel by 1692; member of the Maryland Council, 1692-1707, 1715-1724; provincial court justice, 1694; deputy secretary, 1694-1696; acting governor, 1720; born circa 1659/1660 (son of Thomas Brooke, q.v.), died testate on Jan 7, 1730/1 (will probated on Jan 25, 1730/1). {Ref: BDML I:172; HCCM:28; MDWB 20:125}

BROOKE (BROOKES), THOMAS (England and Calvert County), captain, commissioned May 8, 1658 to command all the forces from George Reade's on the south side and St. Leonard's Creek on the north side to the head of Patuxent River; major, commissioned Feb 11, 1660; sheriff, 1668; member of the Lower House of the Maryland Assembly, 1663-1676; major, court justice (quorum), and justice of the peace in 1674; colonel on the Council of War in July, 1676; born circa 1638 (son of Robert Brooke, q.v.), died testate by Dec 29, 1676 (date of probate; Ellinor Brooke, widow, and niece of Thomas Hatton, q.v.). {Ref: ARMD 2:239, 3:344, 3:402, 3:522, 5:28, 15:37, 15:99, 49:212, 49:353, 51:146, 51:321; BDML I:171; INAC 4:328; HCCM:27-28, 243-244; FAAH:47; RMHF I:91, I:342, II:162; MDWB 5:123}

BROOKE, THOMAS (Kent County), soldier (rank not stated) in Capt. William Leeds (Leeads) Company by May 23, 1662, at which time he signed a petition about the misuse of company money by Capt. Thomas Brednox (Bradnox), late of Isle of Kent, deceased. {Ref: ARMD 3:455}

BROOKES (BROOKS), FRANCIS (England, and Kent and St. Mary's Counties), soldier (rank not stated) in 1642; member of the Lower House of the Maryland Assembly, 1647-1650; born circa 1608 (aged about 40 when deposed in 1648), died intestate by January, 1658/9. {Ref: ARMD 4:130-131, 4:440; BDML I:173}

BROOKES, JOHN (St. Mary's County), soldier (rank not stated), 1679, lost a bridle and saddle at the Susquehannah Fort. {Ref: ARMD 7:148}

BROOKES (BROOKS), JOHN (Charles County), soldier (rank not stated) circa 1675; paid for his services in the late expedition against the Nanticoke Indians in 1678; trumpeter in 1680; died testate by Mar 30, 1714 (date of probate). {Ref: ARMD 7:101; INAC 7A:197; MDWB 13:690}

BROOKES, WILL (Calvert County), Protestant and probable soldier in the Revolution of 1689; signed an address and took a loyalty oath supporting the King of England and "to reestablish Lord Baltimore in his ancient power and government" on Nov 16, 1689. {Ref: ARMD 8:131}

BROOME, JOHN, I (England and Calvert County), commander of the colonial militia "in the days of Gov. Leonard Calvert" (i.e., before 1647). {Ref: HCCM:245}

BROOME, JOHN, II (Calvert County), colonel and commander of the county infantry; born circa 1656, died in 1689 on shipboard as he was about to return from England. {Ref: HCCM:245}

BROOME, JOHN, III (Calvert County), colonel and burgess in 1712; sheriff, 1714; justice, 1731-1738; born circa 1676 (aged about 44 when deposed in 1720), died testate by Jan 26, 1738/9 (date of probate; Ann Brome *[sic]*, widow). {Ref: HCCM:246; MDEP:23}

BROOMSKILL (BRUMSKILL), JOHN (Anne Arundel or Calvert County), captain and commander of the ship *Ruth* in 1694. {Ref: INAC 13A:239, 15:230}

BROTHERS, HOWEL (England and Annapolis), seaman on the ship *Hartwell* of London commanded by Capt. Nicholas Humphries in March, 1697/8. {Ref: ARMD 23:397}

BROUGHTON, ROBERT (Oxford District), captain and master of the ship *Ann* in 1731. {Ref: CVPR:12}

BROWN, ABRAIM (county not indicated), private in the Maryland troops "raised to strengthen Albany, New York and resist the French and Indian enemies" in 1690. {Ref: SHMD I:355}

BROWN (BROWNE), DAVID (Scotland and Somerset County), captain before 1678; paid for his services in the late expedition against the Nanticoke Indians in 1678; captain and court justice (quorum), 1679-1680; president of the Somerset County Court, 1687-1688; captain of a company of foot in 1689; Protestant and soldier in the Revolution of 1689; signed an address and took a loyalty oath supporting the King of England and "for enabling us to defend ourselves against all invaders" on Nov 28, 1689; colonel in 1690; member of the Maryland Council, 1691-1697; colonel who swore allegiance to the King & Queen of England in 1696; died testate by Sep 17, 1697 (date of probate).

{Ref: ARMD 5:569, 7:97, 7:100, 7:611, 8:141, 8:280, 13:244, 15:275, 15:328, 20:6, 20:110, 20:153, 20:202, 20:544, 23:15, 23:285, 38:73; BDML I:176; CESM:37; MDWB 6:150; INAC 16:221}

BROWN, ELIZABETH, see "John Brown (Browne)," q.v.

BROWN, FRANCIS (county or port not indicated), negro seaman on the ship *John Hopewell* of London under Capt. Henry Munday in 1699 who ran away to the pirate Capt. Henry King; reported by the Maryland Council that he "may happen to come into these American parts" in 1700. {Ref: ARMD 25:100}

BROWN, GEORGE (county not indicated), ship's surgeon who settled in Maryland in 1708 and died in 1762. {Ref: SCOT:15}

BROWN, GEORGE (Anne Arundel County), captain and mariner before 1720; died by Sep 13, 1720 (date of inventory). {Ref: MINV 4:258}

BROWN (BROWNE), HENRY (England and Potomac District), captain and master of the ship *Loyalty* of Liverpool in 1697. {Ref: ARMD 23:138, 23:171-172}

BROWN, JAMES (Queen Anne's County), ensign of the militia in the Upper Chester and Choptank Rivers area on Jun 30, 1732; captain before 1755; born circa 1695 (aged about 60 in March, 1755). {Ref: MDHR 1:11; CFES 3:75}

BROWN, JANE, see "John Brown (Kent County)," q.v.

BROWN, JETHRO (Anne Arundel County), captain and commander of the galley *Henrietta* riding at anchor in Herring Bay on Apr 7, 1720. {Ref: AALR CW#1:150}

BROWN, JOHN (Kent County), major by 1733; born 1699, died intestate by Aug 11, 1747 (date of inventory; Jane Brown, widow). {Ref: CFES 2:33; INKC:178; MINV 35:540}

BROWN, JOHN (Anne Arundel County), captain and commander of the ship *King George* riding in Severn River on May 15, 1721. {Ref: AALR CW#1:371}

BROWN, JOHN (England and Annapolis), mariner by 1690; captain and commander of a ship (no name given) in 1692 and 1698. {Ref: ARMD 13:289, 23:466; AALR IH#2:69}

BROWN (BROWNE), JOHN (Talbot County), soldier (rank not stated) circa 1675; paid for his services in the late expedition against the Nanticoke Indians in 1678; died testate by Sep 27, 1698 (date of probate; Elizabeth Brown, widow). {Ref: ARMD 7:88; MDWB 6:165}

BROWN, JOHN, JR. (county or port not indicated), captain of a ship (no name given) in 1696. {Ref: ARMD 25:588}

BROWN, JOHN ELLIOT (Annapolis District), captain of the sloop *Bonaventure* in 1729. {Ref: MDGZ, May 20, 1729}

BROWN, MARY, see "Samuel Browne (Brown)," q.v.

BROWN, PEREGRINE (Kent County), captain by 1733; appeared in Kent County debt books, 1733-1769; captain of militia company in 1748. {Ref: INKC:179}

BROWN, SAMUEL (Annapolis District), captain of the ship *Phoenix* in 1734. {Ref: MDGZ, Nov 29, 1734}

BROWN (BROWNE), THOMAS (Anne Arundel County), soldier (rank not stated) circa 1675; paid for his services in the late expedition against the Nanticoke Indians in 1678; appointed Ranger "from Mr. Snowden's plantation upwards to the extent of the county" in 1692; military officer (rank not stated) who swore allegiance to the King & Queen of England in 1696; "Thomas Browne, Sr." died testate by Jun 4, 1715 (date of probate). {Ref: ARMD 7:96, 8:339, 20:541; FAAH:166; MDWB 14:54}

BROWN (BROWNE), THOMAS (Talbot County), soldier (rank not stated) circa 1675; paid for his services in the late expedition against the Nanticoke Indians in 1678; died testate by Feb 12, 1693/4 (date of probate). {Ref: ARMD 7:88; MDWB 2:258}

BROWN, WILLIAM (Somerset County), soldier (rank not stated) circa 1675; paid for his services in the late expedition against the Nanticoke Indians in 1678. {Ref: ARMD 7:99}

BROWNE, ADDAM (Talbot County), soldier (rank not stated) circa 1675; paid for his services in the late expedition against the Nanticoke Indians in 1678. {Ref: ARMD 7:88}

BROWNE (BROWN), DANIEL (Calvert County), Protestant and probable soldier in the Revolution of 1689; signed an address and took a loyalty oath supporting the King of England and "to reestablish Lord Baltimore in his ancient power and government" on Nov 16, 1689; "Daniel Brown, carpenter" was born circa 1656 (aged about 58 when deposed in 1714). {Ref: ARMD 8:132; MDEP:23}

BROWNE, DANIELL (Charles County), soldier (rank not stated) in Capt. James Langworth's Company before 1661 (year of the captain's death, but his ammunition report was not filed until 1664 by Henry Adames). {Ref: CHLR B:379}

BROWNE, ELIZABETH, see "John Browne (Brown)," q.v.

BROWNE, GEORGE (Kent County), soldier (rank not stated) circa 1675; paid for his services in the late expedition against the Nanticoke Indians in 1678. {Ref: ARMD 7:94}

BROWNE, GILES (Kent County), "seaman within the said county" and a "sailor belonging to the *Loves Increase* of Whitehaven" in 1697. {Ref: ARMD 25:600}

BROWNE, JOHN (Anne Arundel County), soldier (rank not stated) who served under Captain Fuller at the Battle of the Severn on Mar 25, 1655 and served on a Council of War after the battle; died circa 1673. {Ref: FAAH:26, 165}

BROWNE (BROWN), JOHN (England and Anne Arundel County), captain and mariner of London in 1673; he and brother Peregrine Browne were active in the Revolution of 1689 in Maryland. {Ref: FAAH:164-165; RMHF II:342}

BROWNE (BROWN), JOHN (Somerset County), Protestant and probable soldier in the Revolution of 1689; signed an address and took a loyalty oath supporting the King of England and "for enabling us to defend ourselves against all invaders" on Nov 28, 1689 (name was listed twice); one John Brown died intestate in Somerset County by Feb 1, 1724/5 (date of administration account). {Ref: ARMD 8:139-140; MDAD 6:335}

BROWNE, JOHN (England, and St. Mary's and Calvert Counties), captain by 1688; commander of the ship *Ann* of London in 1694; one John Browne died testate in St. Mary's County by Feb 24, 1701/2 (date of probate). {Ref: ARMD 20:146; INAC 10:39; MDWB 11:178}

BROWNE, JOHN (New England, and Kent and Anne Arundel Counties), mariner "of Salam in New Ingland" by 1660; mariner in 1676. {Ref: ARMD 51:480; INKC:127}

BROWNE (BROWN), JOHN (Baltimore County), soldier (rank not stated) in Capt. Anthony Drew's Company in 1711; "John Browne of St. George's Parish, Spesutie Hundred" died testate by May 16, 1716 (date of probate; Elizabeth Browne, widow). {Ref: ARMD 29:13; MDWB 15:111; BBCF:74}

BROWNE, MARGARETT, see "Thomas Browne," q.v.

BROWNE (BROUNE), NICHOLAS (Kent County), soldier (rank not stated) on Isle of Kent who swore allegiance to the Commonwealth of England on Apr 5, 1652; died by Feb 1, 1655/6. {Ref: INKC:101, 107}

BROWNE (BROWN), PEREGRINE (England, and Anne Arundel, Talbot, and Cecil Counties), captain by 1670; master of a ship (no name given) in 1692; captain and merchant of London on Jun 8, 1699 (date of bill of exchange which was recorded in Cecil County on Aug 7, 1703); died by Dec 14, 1713 (date of inventory); brother of "John Browne (Brown)," *q.v.* {Ref: ARMD 13:289; FAAH:83, 165; TALR 9:103; CELR 1:323; INAC 36A:138}

BROWNE, PETER (Somerset County), mariner by 1726. {Ref: MDAD 8:48}

BROWNE, SAMUEL (England, and Anne Arundel and Baltimore Counties), captain before 1734; mariner, late of London, but now of Anne Arundel County, purchased land on the west side of the great falls of the Gunpowder River in Baltimore County on Sep 9, 1734. {Ref: BALR HWS#M}

BROWNE (BROWN), SAMUEL (Baltimore County), probable soldier (rank not stated) before 1682; paid for his services out of an assessment levied by the General Assembly for the public good in 1682; Protestant and probable soldier in the Revolution of 1689; signed an address and took a loyalty oath supporting the King of England and the reestablishment of Lord Baltimore into power on Nov 28, 1689; died testate on Oct 5, 1712 (will probated on Jun 2, 1713; Mary Brown, widow). {Ref: ARMD 7:441, 8:137; BBCF:73}

BROWNE (BROWN), SAMUEL (Anne Arundel County and Patuxent District), captain by 1692; naval officer before 1692; captain in 1696. {Ref: ARMD 13:262; INAC 13B:139; FAAH:490}

BROWNE (BROWN), THOMAS (Baltimore County), soldier (rank not stated) circa 1675; paid for his services in the late expedition against the Nanticoke Indians in 1678; one "Thomas Brown" died testate by Apr 14, 1680 (date of probate; no family mentioned in his will) and a "Thomas Browne" died testate by Nov 29, 1708 (date of probate; Margarett Browne, widow). Additional research will be necessary before drawing conclusions. {Ref: ARMD 7:95; MDWB 2:86, 12:300; BBCF:74}

BROWNE, WILLIAM (Somerset County), sergeant before 1682; paid for his services out of an assessment levied by the General Assembly for the public good in 1682; Protestant and soldier (rank not stated) in the Revolution of 1689; signed an address and took a loyalty oath supporting the King of England and "for enabling us to defend ourselves against all invaders" on Nov 28, 1689. {Ref: ARMD 7:440, 8:140}

BROWNING (BROWING), JACOB (Baltimore County), soldier (rank not stated) circa 1675; paid for his services in the late expedition against the Nanticoke Indians in 1678; died intestate by Apr 7, 1679 (date of administration bond). {Ref: ARMD 7:95; BBCF:78}

BROWNING (BROWING), WILLIAM (county or port not indicated), captain and master of the ship *Chester Merchant* of Bydeford or Bidyford in 1690. {Ref: ARMD 8:237-238}

BROWNLOW, ISRAELL (Patuxent District), captain and master of the ship *Samuell* in 1730-1731. {Ref: CVPR:12}

BRUMSKILL, JOHN, see "John Broomskell," q.v.

BRYANT, HUMPHREY (county or port not indicated), captain and master of the ship *Expediticon* (or *Expedition*) of Biddeford in 1690. {Ref: ARMD 8:238}

BRYERS, RICHARD (England and Annapolis), seaman on the ship *Hartwell* of London commanded by Capt. Nicholas Humphries in March, 1697/8. {Ref: ARMD 23:397}

BUCHANAN, GEORGE, see "Hugh Arbuthnott," q.v.

BUCKER, JOHN (Kent County), soldier (rank not stated) circa 1675; paid for his services in the late expedition against the Nanticoke Indians in 1678. {Ref: ARMD 7:94}

BUFLIN, NATHANIEL (England, and St. Mary's or Talbot County), youngest mate on the ship *Ruth* in 1676. {Ref: ARMD 51:474}

BUFORD, THOMAS, see "Humphrey Warren, Jr.," q.v.

BULL, STEPHEN (Anne Arundel County), captain and commander of the ship *Elizabeth* riding at anchor in South River on Jul 16, 1719. {Ref: AALR CW#1:41}

BULLOCK, JOHN (Calvert County), Protestant and probable soldier in the Revolution of 1689; signed an address and took a loyalty oath supporting the King of England and "to reestablish Lord Baltimore in his ancient power and government" on Nov 16, 1689. {Ref: ARMD 8:132}

BULLOX, JOSEPH (Charles County), Protestant and probable soldier in the Revolution of 1689; signed an address and took a loyalty oath supporting the King of England and the reestablishment of Lord Baltimore into power on Nov 28, 1689. {Ref: ARMD 8:138}

BUNTIN, JOHN (England and Somerset County), mate on the ship *Katherine* of Londonderry in 1692. {Ref: ARMD 13:337}

BURBAGE, ---- (St. Mary's County), captain of a sloop (no name given) in 1652. {Ref: ARMD 10:239}

BURBAGE, THOMAS (St. Mary's County), colonel by 1653; died by 1656 (his widow later married Capt. Edward Streeter, *q.v.*). {Ref: ARMD 10:323, 10:381, 10:469, 41:126}

BURBIDGE (BURBYDGE), RICHARD (England, and Anne Arundel and Prince George's Counties), captain and master of the ship *Johannah* of London in 1700; captain and merchant of St. Dunstan in Stepney, County Middlesex, died testate by 1730. {Ref: AALR WT#1:75; INAC 32A:32; PGLR Q:230}

BURCH, WILLIAM (Somerset County), Protestant and probable soldier in the Revolution of 1689; signed an address and took a loyalty oath supporting the King of England and "for enabling us to defend ourselves against all invaders" on Nov 28, 1689. {Ref: ARMD 8:140}

BURFORD, EDWARD (England and Anne Arundel County), captain by 1688; master of the ship *Abraham and Francis* in 1692; commander of the ship *James* in 1698; commander of the ship *Unity* (name misinterpreted once as *Vinty*) on Jun 23, 1708 when he reported "I must goe into ye freshes of patapscoe for fer of the worm and there take part of my loading." {Ref: ARMD 8:371, 23:434; AALR WT#2:636, 638; INAC 10:312}

BURGESS, BENJAMIN (Anne Arundel County), a seafaring apprentice in 1697, "borne and belonging to this county, son of Col. William Burgess," *q.v.*; mariner by 1704. {Ref: ARMD 25:596; AALR WT#2:243, 255}

BURGESS, CHARLES (Anne Arundel County), a seafaring apprentice in 1697, "borne and belonging to this county, son of Col. William Burgess," *q.v.* {Ref: ARMD 25:596}

BURGESS (BURGES), EDWARD (Anne Arundel County), captain by 1678; paid for his services in the late expedition against the Nanticoke Indians in 1678; court justice, 1679 (quorum, 1685); officer of the town of London in 1686; Protestant and captain of foot troops in the Revolution of 1689; died testate by Mar 14, 1722/3 (date of probate; Sarah Burgess, widow). {Ref: ARMD 5:462, 5:502, 7:96, 13:242, 15:253, 20:200-201; FAAH:40, 53, 190; MDWB 18:144; MINV 8:107; MDAD 7:83}

BURGESS (BURGES), PHILLIP (St. Mary's County), soldier (rank not stated) circa 1675; paid for his services in the late expedition against the Nanticoke Indians in 1678. {Ref: ARMD 7:103}

BURGESS (BURGES), RICHARD (England and Patuxent District), captain of the flyboat *Maryland Merchant* of Bristol in 1695. {Ref: ARMD 23:317}

BURGESS, SARAH, see "Edward Burgess," *q.v.*

BURGESS, URSULA, see "William Burgess," *q.v.*

BURGESS (BURGES, BURGIS), WILLIAM (England, Virginia, and Anne Arundel County), lieutenant who served under Captain Fuller at the Battle of the Severn on Mar 25, 1655 and served on a Council of War after the battle; member of the Lower House of the Maryland Assembly in 1659, 1669-1686; captain by 1661 when placed in command of the South River Rangers; high sheriff in 1664; commissioned "commander-in-chief of all the forces in Anne Arundel County" on Jun 6, 1665; burgess (member of the General Assembly), 1671; court justice (quorum), 1674-1685; major by 1675; colonel on the Council of War in July, 1676; paid for his services in the late expedition against the Nanticoke Indians in 1678; colonel and Protestant in command of the foot forces of Anne Arundel County in 1681 ("Colonel of a regiment of Trained Bands and sometimes General of all ye Military Forces of this Province"); born circa 1622, died testate on Jan 24, 1686/7 (will probated Feb 19, 1686/7; Ursula Burgess, widow). See "Benjamin Burgess" and "Charles Burgess" and "Robert Franklin" and "Nicholas Painter," q.v. {Ref: ARMD 1:382, 2:239, 3:523, 5:309, 5:527, 7:97, 15:37, 15:59, 15:67, 15:99, 15:251, 15:253, 17:76, 17:379, 49:313; FAAH:26, 49-52; BDML I:182; AALR WT#1:45; INAC 19½B:153; MDWB 4:242}

BURGHWAY, JACOB (county not indicated), Indian interpreter and probable soldier in 1697-1698. {Ref: ARMD 23:429}

BURKE, JEREMIAH (England and Annapolis), seaman on the ship *Hartwell* of London commanded by Capt. Nicholas Humphries in March, 1697/8. {Ref: ARMD 23:397}

BURKHAM, ROGER (Somerset County), Protestant and probable soldier in the Revolution of 1689; signed an address and took a loyalty oath supporting the King of England and "for enabling us to defend ourselves against all invaders" on Nov 28, 1689. {Ref: ARMD 8:141}

BURNAM, ALICE, see "William Burnham," q.v.

BURNHAM, WILLIAM (St. Mary's and/or Charles County), captain and commander of the ship *Constant* in 1689; one "William Burnam" died testate in Charles County by Apr 20, 1695 (date of probate; Alice Burnam, widow). {Ref: ARMD 8:151, 8:170; MDWB 7:71}

BURROUGHS (BURROWS), JOHN (St. Mary's County), ranger by 1675; soldier (rank not stated) circa 1675; paid for his services in the late expedition against the Nanticoke Indians in 1678; died testate by Dec 5, 1717 (date of probate; Mary Burroughs, widow). {Ref: ARMD 7:103, 15:56; MDWB 14:641; MDAD 2:417}

BURT, EDWARD (Anne Arundel County), captain and commander of the ship *Gowon* (or *Gawin*) riding in South River on Mar 2, 1721/2 and Mar 13, 1722/3. {Ref: AALR CW#1:479, RCW#2:103}

BURTON, EDWARD (Kent County), soldier (rank not stated) on Isle of Kent who swore allegiance to the Commonwealth of England on Apr 5, 1652. {Ref: INKC:101}

BURTON, EDWARD (county not indicated), probable soldier (rank not stated) before 1682; paid for his services out of an assessment levied by the General Assembly for the public good in 1682. {Ref: ARMD 7:441}

BURTON, FRANCIS (St. Mary's County), soldier (rank not stated) circa 1675; paid for his services in the late expedition against the Nanticoke Indians in 1678; one Francis Burton died testate in Calvert County by Feb 15, 1694/5 (date of probate; Mary Burton, widow). {Ref: ARMD 7:104; MDWB 7:47}

BURTON, JOHN (Anne Arundel County), seaman on the ship *John Hopewell* of London under Capt. Henry Munday in 1699 who ran away to the pirate Capt. Henry King; reported by the Maryland Council that he "may happen to come into these American parts" in 1700. {Ref: ARMD 25:100}

BURTON, JOHN (Anne Arundel County), captain by 1717; commander of the ship *Henry* riding at anchor in Herring Bay on Mar 27, 1717 and Feb 28, 1717/8 and Apr 18, 1721, riding in Chesapeake Bay on Apr 17, 1722, and riding in the Patuxent River on Dec 28, 1723; captain, 1733. {Ref: ARMD 25:100; AALR IB#2:345, AALR IB#2:438, AALR CW#1:354, 483; PGLR M:148; MDAD 12:60}

BURTON, LEWIS (county not indicated), probable soldier (rank not stated) before 1682; paid for his services out of an assessment levied by the General Assembly for the public good in 1682. {Ref: ARMD 7:441}

BURTON, MARY, see "Francis Burton," q.v.

BURTON, WILLIAM (England and Talbot County), mariner in the 1730's and 1740's; captain before 1745 (date of power of attorney). {Ref: CFES 3:130}

BURTT, THOMAS (Talbot County), Protestant and probable soldier in the Revolution of 1689; signed an address and took a loyalty oath supporting the King of England and the reestablishment of Lord Baltimore into power on Nov 28, 1689. {Ref: ARMD 8:144}

BUSHELL, ---- (Anne Arundel County), captain by 1721. {Ref: MDAD 4:32}

BUSHELL, ADAM (county not indicated), probable soldier (rank not stated) before 1682; paid for his services out of an assessment levied by the General Assembly for the public good in 1682. {Ref: ARMD 7:441}

BUSKILL, CHRISTOPHER (Potomac District), captain and master of the ship *Thomas* in 1697. {Ref: ARMD 23:172}

BUSKILL (BUSKELL), NATHAN (England and St. Mary's County), second mate on the ship *Ruth* in 1676 and mate on the same ship in 1677. {Ref: ARMD 66:301, 67:36}

BUSKIN, LEAVIN (St. Mary's County), major by 1652. {Ref: ARMD 10:210}

BUSSE, ANN, see "George Bussey," q.v.

BUSSEY (BUSSEE, BUSSE), GEORGE (Baltimore and Calvert Counties), Protestant and probable soldier in the Revolution of 1689; signed an address and took a loyalty oath supporting the King of England and "to reestablish Lord Baltimore in his ancient power and government" on Nov 16, 1689; died testate by Apr 3, 1693 (date of probate; Ann Busse, widow). {Ref: ARMD 8:132; BBCF:87; MDWB 6:46}

BUSSEY (BUSSEE), HEZEKIAH (Baltimore and Calvert Counties), Protestant and probable soldier in the Revolution of 1689; signed an address and took a loyalty oath supporting the King of England and "to reestablish Lord Baltimore in his ancient power and government" on Nov 16, 1689; brother of "George Bussey," q.v. (sons of George Bussey of Baltimore County). {Ref: ARMD 8:132; BBCF:87}

BUTLER, CHARLES (Calvert County), major by 1685. See "Charles Boteler," q.v. {Ref: INAC 8:487}

BUTLER, EDWARD (Anne Arundel County), chaplin of the ship *Nightingale* commanded by Capt. Ezekiell Wright before 1720; died intestate by Feb 16, 1720/1 (date of administration account). {Ref: MDAD 3:278}

BUTLER, JOHN (St. Mary's County), military officer (rank not stated) who swore allegiance to the King & Queen of England in 1696. {Ref: ARMD 20:540}

BUTLER, PHILLIP (Pocomoke District), captain and master of the ship *Pine Apple* in October, 1730. {Ref: CVPR:12}

BUTLER, SAMUEL (Oxford District), captain and master of the ship *Fish Hawk* in March, 1730/1. {Ref: CVPR:12}

BUTLER, THOMAS (Somerset County), a seafaring man in 1697. {Ref: ARMD 25:598}

BUTLER, WILLIAM (Talbot County), soldier (rank not stated) circa 1675; paid for his services in the late expedition against the Nanticoke Indians in 1678. {Ref: ARMD 7:88}

BUXTON, FRANCIS (Calvert County), Protestant and probable soldier in the Revolution of 1689; signed an address and took a loyalty oath supporting the King of England and "to reestablish Lord Baltimore in his ancient power and government" on Nov 16, 1689. {Ref: ARMD 8:131}

CABLE, JOHN (Charles County), soldier (rank not stated) before 1682; paid for his services out of an assessment levied by the General Assembly for the public good in 1682; private in the Maryland troops "raised to strengthen Albany, New York and resist the French and Indian enemies" in 1690. {Ref: ARMD 7:440; SHMD I:355}

CABLE, JOSEPH (Charles County), private in the Maryland troops "raised to strengthen Albany, New York and resist the French and Indian enemies" in 1690. {Ref: SHMD I:355}

CABNALL, EDWARD (St. Mary's County), soldier (rank not stated) circa 1675; paid for his services in the late expedition against the Nanticoke Indians in 1678. {Ref: ARMD 7:103}

CADE, ROBERT (Somerset County), Protestant and probable soldier in the Revolution of 1689; signed an address and took a loyalty oath supporting the King of England and "for enabling us to defend ourselves against all invaders" on Nov 28, 1689. {Ref: ARMD 8:139}

CADY, RICHARD (county or port not indicated), mariner by 1693. {Ref: INAC 10:332}

CAGE, JOHN (Charles County), probable soldier circa 1643; [quote] "Mar 7, 1650/1 a patent to John Cage has 100 acres of land due by assignment from Richard Lawrence as appears on record has 50 acres more due for his service performed to Capt. Thomas Cornwallis in the Province many years since" [unquote] was entered in court records on Oct 13, 1663; died testate by Jul 9, 1676 (date of probate; Susannah Cage, widow, married Thomas Clipsham, *q.v.*, immediately after John Cage's death). See "Thomas Cornwallis," q.v. {Ref: CHLR B:184-185, M:190; MDWB 5:289; INCA 7A:151}

CAGE, JOHN (Charles County), Protestant and probable soldier in the Revolution of 1689; signed an address and took a loyalty oath supporting the King of

England and the reestablishment of Lord Baltimore into power on Nov 28, 1689. {Ref: ARMD 8:138}

CAHAN, BENJAMIN (Annapolis District), captain and master of the sloop *Dolphin* in 1730. {Ref: CVPR:12}

CAIN, JOHN (Charles County), soldier (rank not stated) in Capt. James Langworth's Company before 1661 (year of the captain's death, but his ammunition report was not filed until 1664 by Henry Adames); "John Caine" was born circa 1618-1620 (aged about 40 when deposed in 1658 and 1660). {Ref: CHLR B:379; ARMD 53:85; MDEP:27}

CALLAWAY (CALLOWAY, CALLIWAY), ANTHONY (Kent County), soldier (rank not stated) on Isle of Kent who swore allegiance to the Commonwealth of England on Apr 5, 1652; soldier (rank not stated) in Capt. William Leeds (Leeads) Company by May 23, 1662, at which time he signed a petition about the misuse of company money by Capt. Thomas Brednox (Bradnox), late of Isle of Kent, deceased; born circa 1629 (aged about 26 when deposed twice in 1655). {Ref: ARMD 3:455, 54:52-56; INKC:101, 107}

CALLOCK, JOHN (Charles County), Protestant and probable soldier in the Revolution of 1689; signed an address and took a loyalty oath supporting the King of England and the reestablishment of Lord Baltimore into power on Nov 28, 1689. {Ref: ARMD 8:138}

CALTHROP, WILLIAM (Talbot County), soldier (rank not stated) circa 1675; paid for his services in the late expedition against the Nanticoke Indians in 1678. {Ref: ARMD 7:89}

CALVERT, BENEDICT LEONARD (England and Anne Arundel County), captain general, commander-in-chief, and governor of Maryland, 1726-1731; born Sep 20, 1700, died Jun 1, 1732 at sea on his way back to England. {Ref: BDML I:185-186; QALR IK#C:271}

CALVERT, CECILIUS (St. Mary's County), commissioned lieutenant general and governor of Maryland on Jun 16, 1676 when he was only nine years old "during the absence of his Lordship [who was his father, Gov. Charles Calvert] out of this province" (and served through 1679); born 1667, died 1681. {Ref: ARMD 15:92, 15:112; BDML I:187}

CALVERT, CHARLES (England and Anne Arundel County), probably an ensign, First Grenadier Guards, by 1709; captain by 1720; member of the Maryland Council, 1727-1733; commissary general, 1727-1728; died Feb 2, 1733/4. {Ref: BDML I:188}

CALVERT, CHARLES (England and St. Mary's County), lieutenant general and governor of Maryland, 1661-1675; proprietor of Maryland, 1675-1714; born Aug 27, 1637, died Feb 20, 1714/5 in England (Charles, Lord Baltimore; Lady Margaret, widow). {Ref: ARMD 3:439, 15:59; BDML I:187-188; RMHF II:107; MDWB 13:741}

CALVERT, CHARLES (England and Anne Arundel County), proprietor of Maryland, 1715-1751; governor, 1732-1733; Lord of the Admiralty (in

England), 1741; born Sep 29, 1699, died Apr 24, 1751 in England. {Ref: BDML I:188-189; RMHF II:107}

CALVERT, LEONARD (England and St. Mary's County), leader of the first settlers who came to Maryland on the ships *Ark* and *Dove* and arrived at St. Mary's on Mar 25, 1634; lieutenant general and first governor of Maryland, 1634-1647; born circa 1606, died testate on Jun 11, 1647 (nuncupative will probated on Jun 14, 1647). See "Giles Brent" and "Francis Trafford" and "Thomas Greene" and "Baker Brooke," q.v. {Ref: ARMD 1:2, 4:15; BDML I:190; FMDP:180-184; RMHF I:100-101; MDWB 1:9}

CALVERT, MARY, see "William Chapline," q.v.

CALVERT, PHILIP (England and St. Mary's County), lieutenant general and governor of Maryland, 1660-1661; commissary general, 1672-1682; born 1626, died 1682. {Ref: ARMD 3:323; BDML I:190-191}

CALVERT, WILLIAM (England and St. Mary's County), member of the Lower House of the Maryland Assembly, 1663-1666; attorney general, 1666-1669; member of the Maryland Council, 1669-1682; colonel by 1678; colonel and Roman Catholic in command of the foot forces of St. Mary's County, 1679-1681; born circa 1642, died May 26, 1682. {Ref: ARMD 5:309; BDML I:191; INAC 5:404}

CAMIOLL, JAMES (county not indicated), private in the Maryland troops "raised to strengthen Albany, New York and resist the French and Indian enemies" in 1690. {Ref: SHMD I:355}

CAMPBELL (CAMBELL), AEGN. (St. Mary's County), Protestant and probable soldier in the Revolution of 1689; signed an address and took a loyalty oath supporting the King of England and the reestablishment of Lord Baltimore into power on Nov 28, 1689. {Ref: ARMD 8:147}

CAMPBELL, CATHERINE, see "John Campbell (Cambell)," q.v.

CAMPBELL, ELIZABETH, see "Walter Campbell," q.v.

CAMPBELL (CAMBELL), HUGH (England and Maryland, port not indicated), captain by 1695; master of the ship *James* in 1695. {Ref: ARMD 20:340}

CAMPBELL (CAMBELL), JOHN (England and William & Mary Parish, St. Mary's County), captain, St. Mary's Guard, 1679; major, empowered to command a troop of horse "for St. Georges Poplar Hill, Newtowne St. Clements Bay Hundred" in 1689; member of the Lower House of the Maryland Assembly, 1692-1693; major, commissioned again on Oct 9, 1694; born 1634, died testate by Nov 4, 1695 (date of probate; Catherine Campbell, widow). {Ref: ARMD 7:148, 13:241, 20:106, 20:130, 20:152, 23:17, 51:270; BDML I:191; INAC 6:512, 13B:28; MDWB 7:190}

CAMPBELL, JOHN (Potomac District), captain and master of the ship *Edward* in 1730-1731. {Ref: CVPR:12}

CAMPBELL, WALTER (Scotland and Dorchester County), military officer (rank not stated) in 1696; member of the Lower House of the Maryland Assembly, 1697-1700; sheriff, 1695-1698; born circa 1666 (aged about 40 when deposed in 1706), died testate by Apr 13, 1738 (date of probate; Elizabeth Campbell, widow). {Ref: BDML I:191-192; MDEP:28; MDWB 21:870}

CAMPLIN, WILLIAM (Patuxent District), captain and master of the ship *Ann* in 1731. {Ref: CVPR:12}

CANE, TIMOTHY (St. Mary's County), military officer (rank not stated) who swore allegiance to the King & Queen of England in 1696. {Ref: ARMD 20:540}

CANNON, SAMUEL (Charles County), mariner by 1734; captain and master of the sloop *William* in 1735 (built at the Potomac River). {Ref: MDCB 82:42; MINV 60:696}

CANNON, STEPHEN (Virginia and Somerset County), soldier (rank not stated) circa 1675; paid for his services in the late expedition against the Nanticoke Indians in 1678; died by Nov 27, 1701 (date of inventory). {Ref: ARMD 7:98; INAC 21:227}

CAREW, HENRY (St. Mary's County), soldier (rank not stated) circa 1675; paid for his services in the late expedition against the Nanticoke Indians in 1678; "Henry Carewe" was born circa 1642 (aged about 36 when deposed in 1678). {Ref: ARMD 7:102; MDEP:28}

CAREY, THOMAS, see "Thomas Cary (Carey)," q.v.

CARLETON, THOMAS (Calvert County), captain by 1674 (noted as "dead" on a list of debts due Capt. Charles Boteler in 1674). {Ref: INAC 1:91, 9:29}

CARLETON, WILLIAM (Charles County), captain and sloopmaster by 1719 (name appeared on a list of payments from the estate of Thomas Waple, deceased, in August, 1719). {Ref: MDAD 2:128}

CARLINE, HENRY (Kent County), soldier (rank not stated) on Isle of Kent who swore allegiance to the Commonwealth of England on Apr 5, 1652; assistant commander (commissioner) of Kent County in 1654 (name also listed as "Henry Carlyen" and "Henery Carlin"); born circa 1608 (aged about 47 when deposed in 1656 and aged about 48 when deposed in 1655). {Ref: ARMD 54:61, 54:73; INKC:101, 103, 108}

CARLYLE, ALEXANDER, see "Edward North," q.v.

CARNABY, ROGER (St. Mary's County), captain of the ship *Dolphin* at Patuxent in 1708. {Ref: ARMD 27:240}

CARNE, JOHN (England and St. Mary's County), captain and master of the ship *George* of Plymouth in 1693. {Ref: ARMD 20:182}

CARPENTER, CHARLES (Charles County), soldier (rank not stated) who was issued a "gun or fowling piece" by Col. Warren on Sep 15, 1694. {Ref: ARMD 20:206, 20:208}

CARPENTER (CARPHENTER), EDMOND (Kent County), soldier (rank not stated) in Capt. William Leeds (Leeads) Company by May 23, 1662, at which time he signed a petition about the misuse of company money by Capt. Thomas Brednox (Bradnox), late of Isle of Kent, deceased. {Ref: ARMD 3:455}

CARPENTER, JOHN (England and Anne Arundel County), captain and commander of the brigantine *Grundy* riding at anchor in South River on May

28, 1712; commander of the ship *Collchester Adventure* (or *Colechester Adventure*) riding at anchor in South River on May 22, 1719 and Jun 16, 1721; mariner and land owner in Anne Arundel County on May 21, 1722 (appointment of attorney and date of conveyance) and lot owner in Annapolis by 1723; captain and commander of the ship *Severn* of London riding in Severn River on Feb 14, 1723/4 and Mar 18, 1724/5 and Apr 10, 1728 and Jun 21, 1729; captain of the ship *Duke* in 1734; died intestate by Sep 9, 1749 (date of inventory). See "Charles Dickinson," q.v. {Ref: AALR PK:454; AALR CW#1:1, 372; AALR RCW#2:39, 222; AALR SY#1:2, 78, 371; PGLR M:509; MDGZ, Jun 24, 1729 and Nov 1, 1734; MINV 41:152}

CARPENTER, NICHOLAS (Somerset County), Protestant and probable soldier in the Revolution of 1689; signed an address and took a loyalty oath supporting the King of England and "for enabling us to defend ourselves against all invaders" on Nov 28, 1689. {Ref: ARMD 8:140}

CARPENTER, THOMAS (Somerset County), captain and commander of the ship *Jonathan and Mary* "which foundered at sea" in 1708. {Ref: ARMD 27:304}

CARR (CARRE), JOHN (Delaware, and Baltimore and Cecil Counties), captain before 1673; sheriff, 1675; died testate by Oct 2, 1676 (date of probate; Petronella or Peternella Carre, widow). {Ref: ARMD 15:47; INAC 1:321, 2:280; BBCF:97; MDWB 5:86}

CARR, JULIATHA, see "Walter Carr," q.v.

CARR, PETER (Patuxent District), captain and master of the ship *John and Margarett* in 1731. {Ref: CVPR:12}

CARR (CARRE), PETRONELLA, see "John Carr," q.v.

CARR, WALTER (Anne Arundel County), soldier (rank not stated) circa 1675; paid for his services in the late expedition against the Nanticoke Indians in 1678; born circa 1633 (aged 52 and upwards when deposed on Feb 27, 1685), died in 1699 (date of inventory; Juliatha Carr, widow). {Ref: ARMD 7:96, 17:447; BBCF:95-96; ARMD 17:447; MDEP:29}

CARRE, PETERNELLA, see "John Carr (Carre)," q.v.

CARRINGTON, JOHN (Patapsco Hundred, Baltimore County), soldier (rank not stated) circa 1675; paid for his services in the late expedition against the Nanticoke Indians in 1678; died testate by Apr 9, 1696 (date of probate; Catherine Carrington, widow). {Ref: ARMD 7:95; BBCF:97; MDWB 7:168}

CARSS, ROBERT (St. Mary's County), Protestant and probable soldier in the Revolution of 1689; signed an address and took a loyalty oath supporting the King of England and the reestablishment of Lord Baltimore into power on Nov 28, 1689. {Ref: ARMD 8:147}

CARTER, ---- (St. Mary's County), captain by 1655. See "Sampson Waring," q.v. {Ref: ARMD 10:413}

CARTER, EDWARD (Virginia and Baltimore County), colonel in Nansemond County, Virginia before 1660; land owner in Baltimore County by 1661. {Ref: BALR RR#HS; BBCF:98}

CARTER, EDWARD (Anne Arundel County), captain by 1664 (date of deed in which he was mentioned); colonel by 1702 (formerly owned land on Herring Creek). {Ref: AALR IT#5:79-80, WT#1:250}

CARTER, JOHN (Somerset County), soldier (rank not stated) circa 1675; paid for his services in the late expedition against the Nanticoke Indians in 1678. {Ref: ARMD 7:100}

CARTER, VALENTINE (Queen Anne's County), captain by 1722. {Ref: MDAD 5:154}

CARTWRIGHT, CHARLES (Talbot County), Protestant and probable soldier in the Revolution of 1689; signed an address and took a loyalty oath supporting the King of England and the reestablishment of Lord Baltimore into power on Nov 18, 1689. {Ref: ARMD 8:134}

CARVILE (CARVELL), JOHN (St. Mary's County), major by 1692 and member of the Lower House of the Maryland Assembly in 1692; paid for his services in 1695. *Identification problem:* "John Carvell" was born circa 1634 (aged about 23 when deposed in 1657) and may be the aforementioned John Carvell (Carvile), but he is not listed in *A Biographical Dictionary of the Maryland Legislature, 1635-1789*. "John Carvile" was born circa 1670 in St. Mary's County, served in the Lower House of the Maryland Assembly from Cecil County in 1697 and from Kent County in 1708, died testate in Kent County by Sep 6, 1709 (date of probate; Mary Carvill *[sic]*, widow, later married Richard Smithers before 1718) and is listed in the aforementioned *Dictionary*; however, no military service is indicated. Additional research will be necessary before drawing conclusions. {Ref: ARMD 13:350, 38:72, 41:71; BDML I:202; MDEP:29; Admin. Accounts 1:147; MDWB 12:253, pt. 2}

CARVILE (CARVILL), THOMAS (Virginia and St. Mary's County), Protestant and soldier in the Revolution of 1689 who sided with John Coode, *q.v.*; signed an address and took a loyalty oath supporting the King of England and the reestablishment of Lord Baltimore into power on Nov 28, 1689; died in 1717 (father of John Carvile, *q.v.*). {Ref: ARMD 8:147; BDML I:202}

CARVILL, MARY, see "John Carvile (Carvell)," q.v.

CARVILLE, JOHN (Kent County), soldier in the 1730's and 1740's; captain by 1756; born circa 1706 (aged about 40 when deposed in 1747, aged about 50 when deposed in 1756, and aged about 61 when deposed in 1767), died intestate in 1771. {Ref: CFES 2:50; KELR JS#28:294; MDEP:30}

CARWEN, GEORGE (St. Mary's County), captain by 1669. {Ref: ARMD 51:338}

CARY (CAREY), EDWARD (Somerset County, and Sussex County, Delaware), soldier (rank not stated) circa 1675; paid for his services in the late expedition against the Nanticoke Indians in 1678; died intestate by May 3, 1704 (Lidia Carey, widow). {Ref: ARMD 7:98; Sussex County Court Records}

CARY (CAREY), LIDIA, see "Edward Cary," q.v.

CARY (CAREY), RACHEL, see "Thomas Cary," q.v.

CARY (CAREY), THOMAS (Monie Hundred, Somerset County), soldier (rank not stated) circa 1675; paid for his services in the late expedition against the Nanticoke Indians in 1678; died testate by Dec 17, 1723 (date of probate; Rachel Carey, widow). {Ref: ARMD 7:100; MDWB 18:231}

CARZEY, JAMES (Talbot County), soldier (rank not stated) circa 1675; paid for his services in the late expedition against the Nanticoke Indians in 1678. {Ref: ARMD 7:87}

CASEY (COSEY, KEYSEY, KERSEY), THOMAS (Charles County), soldier (rank not stated) circa 1675; paid for his services in the late expedition against the Nanticoke Indians in 1678; soldier (rank not stated) in 1679, crippled in the Susquehannah War; soldier "being Lamed at the Susquehannah Fort Petitions for Allowance of his Pension formerly granted him" on Nov 10, 1682; he petitioned the Upper House of the Maryland Assembly "for his Pension, being wounded and disabled in the Country service at the ffort" and his petition was endorsed "This house doe thinke the peticoner an Object of Charity, And that hee ought to bee allowed his yearly pention and arreares" on Apr 21, 1684. {Ref: ARMD 7:101, 7:148, 7:376, 7:442, 13:29, 13:90}

CASTEEN, JOSEPH (Dorchester County), soldier (rank not stated) circa 1675; paid for his services in the late expedition against the Nanticoke Indians in 1678. {Ref: ARMD 7:93}

CASTLE, ROBERT (Baltimore County), soldier (rank not stated) circa 1675; paid for his services in the late expedition against the Nanticoke Indians in 1678. {Ref: ARMD 7:96}

CASWELL, RICHARD (England, Baltimore County, and North Carolina), deputy sheriff, 1724; member of the Lower House of the Maryland Assembly, 1738-1744; probable officer by 1734 since he qualified as captain of a troop of horse in Gunpowder Hundred in 1735; born 1685 in London, resided at Joppa in Baltimore (now Harford) County by 1712, and died Apr 24, 1755 in Johnston (now Lenoir) County, North Carolina. {Ref: BDML I:203-204; BBCF:100}

CATTLIN (CATTLEN, CATTLYN, CATELYNE), ROBERT, JR. (Virginia and Annamessex, Somerset County), soldier (rank not stated) circa 1675; paid for his services in the late expedition against the Nanticoke Indians in 1678; paid for his services out of an assessment levied by the General Assembly for the public good in 1682; died testate by Jun 15, 1699 (date of probate). {Ref: ARMD 7:99, 7:441; OSES:279, 438; MDWB 6:350; INAC 19½B:82}

CATTLIN (CATTLEN, CATTLYN, CATELYNE), ROBERT, SR. (Virginia and Annamessex, Somerset County), soldier (rank not stated) circa 1675; paid for his services in the late expedition against the Nanticoke Indians in 1678. {Ref: ARMD 7:99; OSES:279, 438}

CAUFT, EDWARD (Dorchester County), captain by 1725. {Ref: MDAD 7:126}

CAULK, ISAAC (Cecil County), Protestant and probable soldier in the Revolution of 1689; signed an address and took a loyalty oath supporting the King of

England and the reestablishment of Lord Baltimore into power on Nov 18, 1689. {Ref: ARMD 8:135}

CAUSEY, JOHN (Dorchester County), soldier (rank not stated) circa 1675; paid for his services in the late expedition against the Nanticoke Indians in 1678; died intestate by Mar 11, 1724/5 (date of administration account). {Ref: ARMD 7:92; MDAD 6:303}

CAUSINE (CAUSEEN), IGNATIUS (Port Tobacco, Charles County), soldier (rank not stated) by 1666; signed a petition to the governor to "displace Capt. William Boreman whom was lately constituted captain of the militia" on Sep 12, 1666; member of the Lower House of the Maryland Assembly, 1671-1675; captain by 1676; court justice, 1680 (quorum, 1685); "Capt. Causeen" was appointed justice of the peace in Charles County by the Maryland Council on Sep 22, 1687, but lost all of his offices after the Revolution of 1689; born circa 1642, died testate by Jun 11, 1695 (date of probate; Jane Causine, widow). {Ref: ARMD 3:556, 5:565, 15:327, 17:380; BDML I:204; CHLR S:211; MDWB 7:93}

CAUTHER, JAMES (St. Mary's County), captain by 1643. {Ref: ARMD 3:137}

CAVE, WILLIAM (county not indicated), probable soldier (rank not stated) before 1682; paid for his services out of an assessment levied by the General Assembly for the public good in 1682. {Ref: ARMD 7:442-443}

CERSTON, EDWARD (Charles County), Protestant and probable soldier in the Revolution of 1689; signed an address and took a loyalty oath supporting the King of England and the reestablishment of Lord Baltimore into power on Nov 28, 1689. {Ref: ARMD 8:138}

CHADWORTH, ---- (Charles County), captain by 1661. {Ref: CHLR A:176}

CHAILLE, MOSES (Pocomoke District), captain and master of the ship *Mary* in October, 1730. {Ref: CVPR:12}

CHAILLE, PETER (Pocomoke District), captain and master of the ship *Mary* in March, 1730/1. {Ref: CVPR:12}

CHAIRES (CHAIERS), JOHN (Talbot County), Protestant and probable soldier in the Revolution of 1689; signed an address and took a loyalty oath supporting the King of England and the reestablishment of Lord Baltimore into power on Nov 18, 1689. {Ref: ARMD 8:134}

CHAMBERLAINE, WILLIAM (Cecil County), Protestant and probable soldier in the Revolution of 1689; signed an address and took a loyalty oath supporting the King of England and the reestablishment of Lord Baltimore into power on Nov 18, 1689. {Ref: ARMD 8:135}

CHAMBERS, NICHOLAS (England, Prince George's County and Patuxent District), captain and master of the ship *Ruby* of London in 1729-1733. {Ref: MDGZ, Apr 1, 1729; PGLR Q:652; CVPR:12}

CHAMBERS, RICHARD (Manokin Hundred, Somerset County), soldier (rank not stated) circa 1675; paid for his services in the late expedition against the Nanticoke Indians in 1678; Protestant and probable soldier in the Revolution of 1689; signed an address and took a loyalty oath supporting the King of

England and "for enabling us to defend ourselves against all invaders" on Nov 28, 1689. {Ref: ARMD 7:100, 8:141; OSES:153}

CHAMBERS, RICHARD (county or port not indicated), mariner in the 1730's; captain and master of the snow *Prince of Orange* (built at Sunderland, Great Britain) in 1739. {Ref: MDCB 82:72}

CHAMP, ROBERT (Baltimore County), soldier (rank not stated) circa 1675; paid for his services in the late expedition against the Nanticoke Indians in 1678. {Ref: ARMD 7:96}

CHAMPLIN, WILLIAM (Oxford District), captain and master of the ship *Swallow* in March, 1730/1. {Ref: CVPR:12}

CHANCELEER, JOHN (Somerset County), Protestant and probable soldier in the Revolution of 1689; signed an address and took a loyalty oath supporting the King of England and "for enabling us to defend ourselves against all invaders" on Nov 28, 1689. {Ref: ARMD 8:139}

CHANDLER, ELIAS (Calvert County), seaman on a ship commanded by Capt. Ralph Story in 1662; born circa 1640 (aged about 22 when deposed on Mar 15, 1662/3). {Ref: ARMD 49:12-15; MDEP:31}

CHANDLER, JOB (Anne Arundel County), major who served under Governor Stone at the Battle of the Severn on Mar 25, 1655. {Ref: FAAH:25-26; ARMD 41:205}

CHANDLER, JOHN (Kent County), soldier (rank not stated) circa 1675; paid for his services in the late expedition against the Nanticoke Indians in 1678; military officer (rank not stated) who swore allegiance to the King & Queen of England in 1696. {Ref: ARMD 7:94, 20:541}

CHANDLER, MARY, see "William Chandler," q.v.

CHANDLER, WILLIAM (Charles County), colonel and Protestant in command of the foot forces of Charles County in 1681; colonel and high sheriff, 1681-1683; served at the Garrison at Zachaja and was paid for his services out of an assessment levied by the General Assembly for the public good in 1682; died testate by May 18, 1685 (date of probate; Mary Chandler, widow; by May 21, 1697 Mary Brent (relict) was the wife of Capt. George Brent, of Virginia (date of administration account). {Ref: ARMD 7:339, 7:440, 15:356, 17:72, 17:76, 17:142, 17:390; CHLR I:184; MDWB 4:112; INAC 9:306, 14:127}

CHAPLINE (CHAPLAINE), WILLIAM (Calvert County), Puritan and probable soldier in the Revolution of 1689; signed an address and took a loyalty oath supporting the King of England and "to reestablish Lord Baltimore in his ancient power and government" on Nov 16, 1689; he was the son of William Chapline, a Puritan, who died in 1669 (and was a grandson of Capt. Isaac Chapline of the Royal Navy and Mary Calvert, a sister of the first Lord Baltimore). {Ref: ARMD 8:131; HCCM:248}

CHAPMAN, RICHARD (Charles County), soldier (rank not stated) circa 1675; paid for his services in the late expedition against the Nanticoke Indians in

1678; died testate after Mar 16, 1718/9 (date of nuncupative will; Ann Chapman, widow). {Ref: ARMD 7:101; MDWB 17:9}

CHAPPELL, ANDREW (St. Mary's County), captain and mariner before 1639; died intestate by Feb 28, 1639/40 (date of inventory). {Ref: ARMD 4:59, 4:90}

CHAPTON, WILLIAM (Talbot County), soldier (rank not stated) circa 1675; paid for his services in the late expedition against the Nanticoke Indians in 1678. {Ref: ARMD 7:87}

CHARLETON, THOMAS (Calvert County), captain by 1671. {Ref: Land Patent, Aug 15, 1671}

CHEAGER, PHILIP, see "Philip Holedger," q.v.

CHEATH, WILLIAM (Calvert County), Protestant and probable soldier in the Revolution of 1689; signed an address and took a loyalty oath (made his "W" mark) supporting the King of England and "to reestablish Lord Baltimore in his ancient power and government" on Nov 16, 1689. {Ref: ARMD 8:132}

CHEEKE, EDWARD (Dorchester County), soldier (rank not stated) circa 1675; paid for his services in the late expedition against the Nanticoke Indians in 1678. {Ref: ARMD 7:93}

CHEFEY, SAMUEL (Charles County), mariner by 1714. {Ref: CHLR F#2:33}

CHENEY (CHEYNEY), RICHARD (All Hallows Parish, Anne Arundel County), soldier (rank not stated) circa 1675; paid for his services in the late expedition against the Nanticoke Indians in 1678; paid again in 1681; born circa 1649, died intestate and buried Dec 6, 1704. {Ref: ARMD 7:96, 7:208; AAGE:349-350}

CHERALD, JOHN (county not indicated), probable soldier (rank not stated) before 1682; paid for his services out of an assessment levied by the General Assembly for the public good in 1682. {Ref: ARMD 7:440}

CHESELDYNE, KENELM (Lincolnshire, England and St. Mary's County), Protestant and leader in the Revolution of 1689; signed an address and took a loyalty oath supporting the King of England and the reestablishment of Lord Baltimore into power on Nov 28, 1689; attorney general, 1676-1681; member of the Lower House of the Maryland Assembly, 1676-1682, 1686-1690; commissary general, 1693-1699; member of the Maryland Council, 1704-1708; born in 1640, died testate by Dec 18, 1708 (date of probate). {Ref: ARMD 8:146; BDML I:216-217; RMHF I:106-108; MDWB 12:307}

CHESEMAN, WILLIAM (Dorchester County), soldier (rank not stated) circa 1675; paid for his services in the late expedition against the Nanticoke Indians in 1678; a "William Chisum" died testate after Oct 21, 1697 (date he wrote his will; Ann Chisum, widow). Additional research will be necessary before drawing conclusions. {Ref: ARMD 7:93; MDCW 7:355}

CHESHIRE, RICHARD (Talbot County), captain of a ship (no name given) in 1694; captain of a ship (no name given) riding at the Port of Williamstadt on the Eastern Shore, in 1696. {Ref: ARMD 20:120, 20:426}

CHESHIRE, WILLIAM (Talbot County), probable soldier (rank not stated) before 1682; paid for his services out of an assessment levied by the General Assembly for the public good in 1682. {Ref: ARMD 7:441}

CHEVERILL, JOHN (St. Mary's County), Protestant and probable soldier in the Revolution of 1689; signed an address and took a loyalty oath supporting the King of England and the reestablishment of Lord Baltimore into power on Nov 28, 1689. {Ref: ARMD 8:146}

CHEW, ANNE, see "Samuel Chew," q.v.

CHEW, BENJAMIN (Annapolis District), captain and master of the sloop *Lloyd* in 1729. {Ref: MDGZ, May 20, 1729}

CHEW, JOHN (England, Virginia, and Calvert County), Puritan and colonel before 1650; died on the West River circa 1658. {Ref: HCCM:248}

CHEW, SAMUEL (Virginia, and Herring Bay, Anne Arundel County), colonel, 1675-1677; member of the Lower House of the Maryland Assembly, 1661; member of the Maryland Council, 1671-1676; colonel on the Council of War in July, 1676; born circa 1630, died testate on Mar 15, 1676/7 (will probated on Jun 12, 1677; Anne Chew, widow). {Ref: ARMD 2:507, 15:59, 15:99; FAAH:109-110; BDML I:218; HCCM:248-249; RMHF II:297; MDWB 5:241}

CHILD, ABRAHAM (Anne Arundel County), probable soldier (rank not stated) before 1682; paid for his services out of an assessment levied by the General Assembly for the public good in 1682. {Ref: ARMD 7:443}

CHILMAN, RICHARD (St. Mary's County), soldier (rank not stated) circa 1675; paid for his services in the late expedition against the Nanticoke Indians in 1678. {Ref: ARMD 7:102}

CHILTON, EDWARD (county not indicated), appointed advocate of the Vice Admiralty of the Colony of Maryland on Apr 29, 1697. {Ref: ARMD 23:321}

CHINTON, HUGH (Calvert County), Protestant and probable soldier in the Revolution of 1689; signed an address and took a loyalty oath supporting the King of England and "to reestablish Lord Baltimore in his ancient power and government" on Nov 16, 1689. {Ref: ARMD 8:131}

CHISUM, WILLIAM, see "William Cheseman," q.v.

CHITTLE, WILLIAM (St. Mary's County), soldier (rank not stated) circa 1675; paid for his services in the late expedition against the Nanticoke Indians in 1678. {Ref: ARMD 7:103}

CHIVERS, MICHAELL (county not indicated), probable soldier by 1694 when paid for his services by the Maryland Assembly. {Ref: ARMD 38:55}

CHRISTIAN, JOHN (Charles County), captain and master of the ship *Hope* riding in Patuxent River on Apr 8, 1707. {Ref: CHLR Z:271}

CHRISTIAN, JOHN (England and Somerset County), sailor on the ship *Betty Gally* of Liverpool riding at anchor in Monocan River on Jan 16, 1716/7. {Ref: SOJR III:185-186}

CHRISTOPHER, JOHN (Calvert, Somerset, and Worcester Counties), Protestant and probable soldier in the Revolution of 1689; signed an address and took a loyalty oath supporting the King of England and "for enabling us to defend ourselves against all invaders" on Nov 28, 1689; born Jan 15, 1669 in Calvert County (aged about 63 when deposed in Somerset County in 1733), died testate by Mar 8, 1748/9 in Worcester County (date of probate; Mary Christopher, widow). {Ref: ARMD 8:141; MDEP:32; MDWB 26:24; F. Edward Wright's *Maryland Eastern Shore Vital Records, 1648-1725*, p. 102}

CHUBB, JACOB (St. Mary's County), captain and master of the ship *Portsmouth* in 1693. {Ref: ARMD 20:182-183}

CHUMLEY, FRANCIS (Charles County), soldier (rank not stated) circa 1675; paid for his services in the late expedition against the Nanticoke Indians in 1678. {Ref: ARMD 7:101}

CLAGETT, MARY, see "Thomas Clagett," q.v.

CLAGETT (CLAGGETT, CLEGETT), THOMAS (England, and Christ Church Parish, Calvert County), officer in the British Navy before 1670; captain and naval officer in Maryland by 1678; Protestant and probable soldier in the Revolution of 1689; signed an address and took a loyalty oath supporting the King of England and "to reestablish Lord Baltimore in his ancient power and government" on Nov 16, 1689; died by Nov 16, 1703 (date of probate; Sarah Clegett, widow). {Ref: ARMD 5:569, 7:611, 8:131; 8:473, 17:71, 23:18; RMHF I:325; HCCM:250; INAC 5:404, 24:212}

CLAGETT, THOMAS (Prince George's County), captain, appointed Nov 10, 1709 by the Maryland Council to replace Capt. Henry Ridgely who had removed to Anne Arundel County; member of the Lower House of the Maryland Assembly, 1712; sheriff between 1713 and 1722; born in 1678 (aged about 40 when deposed in 1718, aged about 49 when deposed in 1727, and aged about 50 when deposed in 1728), died testate by Mar 27, 1733 (date of probate; Mary Clagett, widow). {Ref: ARMD 27:403; BDML I:220; PGLR I:49, M:294, M:479; MDWB 20:670; MINV 17:277; MDEP:33}

CLAGETT, THOMAS, JR., see "Thomas Fogg," q.v.

CLAGG, WALTER (Kent County), "seaman within the said county" and a "sailor belonging to Mr. Powers ship in the stocks" in 1697. {Ref: ARMD 25:599}

CLAIBORNE (CLAYBORNE, CLEYBORNE), WILLIAM (England, Virginia, and Isle of Kent, but never settled permanently in Maryland), arrived in Virginia in 1621 as a provincial officer and began acquiring land in 1624; he led an expedition up the Chesapeake Bay in 1627 and established a trading post on Kent Island, which he actively developed; captain and commander of Kent Island in 1631; he was the most persistent opponent of Lord Baltimore's claims in the area of the Chesapeake Bay and battled with the proprietory forces from 1634 to the 1660's; he was represented by George Scovell, of Nancimmim [Nansemond], Virginia, when he left his estate undisposed upon his departure from Maryland on Mar 24, 1637 for Kecoughtan, Virginia; he became general and chief commander of Virginia forces in 1644; returned to Maryland by 1646 and claimed he had a commission from Sir William Berkeley (of Virginia) to take the Isle of Kent and such estate that formerly belonged to him therein; however, he apparently could not muster enough support to assault and overthrow the Maryland government; he again embarked for Virginia; colonel, 1652; born 1600, died circa 1677. See "John Boteler" and "John Fullwood" and "Robert Vaughan," q.v. {Ref: ARMD 3:93, 3:264, 4:458-459, 5:172, 10:186; BDML I:221-222}

CLAIR, THOMAS (Oxford District), captain and master of the ship *Betty* in 1731. {Ref: CVPR:12}

CLARK, JOHN (Magothy River, Anne Arundel County), lieutenant by 1692; submitted an "Account for himself and Eleven Men with their Horses severall days in Service" on Oct 14, 1692; died testate by May 16, 1709 (date of probate; Sarah Clark, widow). {Ref: ARMD 8:391, 8:404; MDWB 12:32, pt. 2}

CLARK, JOHN (England and Annapolis), captain and commander of the ship *John and Margarett* in 1698. {Ref: ARMD 23:434}

CLARK, JULIAN, see "Thomas Clark," q.v.

CLARK, MARY, see "Thomas Clark," q.v.

CLARK, NATHANIEL (Somerset County), Protestant and probable soldier in the Revolution of 1689; signed an address and took a loyalty oath supporting the King of England and "for enabling us to defend ourselves against all invaders" on Nov 28, 1689. {Ref: ARMD 8:140}

CLARK, RICHARD (Prince George's County), captain and master of the ship *Strong and Thomas* riding in the Patuxent River on Feb 5, 1725/6. {Ref: PGLR M:149; MDAD 8:439}

CLARK, ROBERT (Potomac District), captain and master of the ship *Walpoole* in 1730-1731. {Ref: CVPR:12}

CLARK, ROBERT (Anne Arundel County), soldier (rank not stated) who served under Governor Stone at the Battle of the Severn on Mar 25, 1655. {Ref: FAAH:26}

CLARK, THOMAS (St. Mary's County), soldier (rank not stated) by 1682; petitioned the General Assembly and "prays that he may be Allowed out of the publick Levy for Twelve days attendance with horse and Arms in Guarding Daniel Mathena, Nicholas Bede, and Jackanapes the Indian" on Nov 15, 1682; one Thomas Clark died testate by Dec 4, 1711 (date of probate; Julian Clark, widow) and another Thomas Clark died testate by Nov 10, 1719 (date of probate of nuncupative will; Mary Clark, widow). Additional research will be necessary before drawing conclusions. {Ref: ARMD 7:392; MDWB 13:375, 15:280}

CLARKE, DANIELL (Anne Arundel County), military officer (rank not stated) who swore allegiance to the King & Queen of England in 1696; died testate after Oct 2, 1696 (date will was written, but date of probate was not given; Elizabeth Clarke, widow). {Ref: ARMD 20:542; MDWB 6:97}

CLARKE, ELIZABETH, see "Daniell Clarke," q.v.

CLARKE, GEORGE (St. Mary's County), captain by 1729. {Ref: MDAD 10:229}

CLARKE, GILBERT (St. Mary's and Charles Counties), Protestant and probable soldier in the Revolution of 1689; signed an address and took a loyalty oath supporting the King of England and the reestablishment of Lord Baltimore into power on Nov 28, 1689; born circa 1657 (aged about 27 when deposed in 1684). {Ref: ARMD 8:138, 17:306, 23:441}

CLARKE, JOHN (Dorchester County), soldier (rank not stated) circa 1675; paid for his services in the late expedition against the Nanticoke Indians in 1678. {Ref: ARMD 7:93}

CLARKE, JOHN (Charles County), soldier (rank not stated) circa 1675; paid for his services in the late expedition against the Nanticoke Indians in 1678; born circa 1653 (adjudged to be 12 years old in 1665), died testate by Aug 12, 1698 (date of probate). See "William Randford," q.v. {Ref: ARMD 7:101, 53:601; MDWB 6:177}

CLARKE, MARY, see "Robert Clarke," q.v.

CLARKE, NEAL (Anne Arundel County), military officer (rank not stated) who swore allegiance to the King & Queen of England in 1696; born in 1664 (aged about 49 when deposed in 1713, aged about 60 when deposed in 1724, and aged about 62 when deposed in 1726). {Ref: ARMD 20:542; PGLR I:590; MDEP:34}

CLARKE, PHILIP (St. Mary's County), commissioned naval officer "from Point look out to Portobacco in Potomock River" on Nov 19, 1694; member of the Lower House of the Maryland Assembly, 1692-1698; naval officer of the Potomock District in 1697; died testate by Aug 11, 1699 (date of probate). {Ref: ARMD 20:186, 23:117, 23:171, 24:40; BDML I:224; MDWB 6:270}

CLARKE, RICHARD (Calvert County), Protestant and probable soldier in the Revolution of 1689; signed an address and took a loyalty oath supporting the King of England and "to reestablish Lord Baltimore in his ancient power and government" on Nov 16, 1689. {Ref: ARMD 8:131}

CLARKE, RICHARD (Anne Arundel County), military officer (rank not stated) who swore allegiance to the King & Queen of England in 1696. {Ref: ARMD 20:541}

CLARKE, RICHARD (St. Mary's County), soldier (rank not stated) circa 1675; paid for his services in the late expedition against the Nanticoke Indians in 1678. {Ref: ARMD 7:103}

CLARKE, ROBERT (Talbot County), probable soldier (rank not stated) circa 1675; paid for his services in the late expedition against the Nanticoke Indians in 1678; died testate by Aug 23, 1703 (date of probate; Mary Clarke, widow). {Ref: ARMD 7:87; MDWB 11:375}

CLARKE, ROBERT (Charles County), soldier (rank not stated) in Capt. James Langworth's Company before 1661 (year of the captain's death, but his ammunition report was not filed until 1664 by Henry Adames). See "Bryan Orson," q.v. {Ref: CHLR B:379}

CLARKE, SAMPSON (England and St. Mary's County), captain and master of the ship *Rogers* of Plymouth in 1693. {Ref: ARMD 20:182}

CLARKE, THOMAS (Somerset County), soldier (rank not stated) circa 1675; paid for his services in the late expedition against the Nanticoke Indians in 1678. {Ref: ARMD 7:98}

CLASH, NICHOLAS (Talbot County), soldier (rank not stated) circa 1675; paid for his services in the late expedition against the Nanticoke Indians in 1678. {Ref: ARMD 7:91}

CLASTONE, ROBERT (Anne Arundel County), soldier (rank not stated) circa 1675; paid for his services in the late expedition against the Nanticoke Indians in 1678. {Ref: ARMD 7:96}

CLAY, HENRY (Kent and Talbot Counties), soldier (rank not stated) on Isle of Kent who swore allegiance to the Commonwealth of England on Apr 5, 1652; soldier (rank not stated) circa 1675; paid for his services in the late expedition against the Nanticoke Indians in 1678; born circa 1619-1621 (aged about 27 when deposed in 1648 and aged about 40 when deposed in 1659). {Ref: ARMD 4:451, 7:91; INKC:101, 120}

CLAY, ROBERT (Calvert County), captain by 1717. {Ref: INAC 37B:43}

CLAYTON, MARY, see "Solomon Clayton" and "William Clayton," q.v.

CLAYTON, SOLOMON (Cecil, Talbot and Queen Anne's Counties), cornet in a troop of horse on Jun 30, 1732; member of the Lower House of the Maryland Assembly in 1715 and between 1732 and 1739; part owner of the shallop *Bohemia* in 1739 (built at Bohemia River in 1737); born 1684-1685 (aged about 46 when deposed in 1731 and aged between 42 and 43 when deposed in 1727), died testate on Sep 13, 1739 (will probated on Oct 20, 1739; Mary Clayton, widow). {Ref: BDML I:225-226; MDHR 1:11; MDCB 82:73; MDWB 22:109; MDEP:35}

CLAYTON, WILLIAM (Cecil and Talbot Counties), mariner in the 1720's and 1730's; captain and part owner of the shallop *Bohemia* in 1739 (built at Bohemia River in 1737); born circa 1692 (aged about 41 in 1733), died testate by Jan 23, 1740/1 (date of probate; Mary Clayton, widow, later married Thomas Lane). {Ref: MDCB 82:73; MDEP:35; MDWB 22:304}

CLEARE (CLARE), HENRY (England, and Anne Arundel, Charles, and Prince George's Counties), captain and mariner of London, "now bound for Maryland" on Oct 17, 1716; mentioned in an administration account in Prince George's County in 1727. {Ref: AALR CW#1:38; CHLR H#2:189; MDAD 8:337}

CLEEVES, THOMAS (Anne Arundel County), captain and commander of the ship *Panther* riding at anchor in Herring Bay on Nov 21, 1705; captain of the ship *Golden Lyon* riding at anchor in Herring Bay on Jun 21, 1708; captain to at least 1716. {Ref: AALR W#2:264, 636; INAC 37A:115}

CLEGETT, SARAH, see "Thomas Clagett," q.v.

CLEMENTS, JOHN (Talbot County), soldier (rank not stated) before 1676; died testate by Aug 3, 1676 (date of probate; Mary Clements, widow, later married James Derumple); Mary Clements was paid 600 pounds of tobacco in 1678 for her husband's services in the late expedition against the Nanticoke Indians. {Ref: ARMD 7:88; MDAD 4:296; MDWB 1:174}

CLERKE, JOHN (county not indicated), probable soldier (rank not stated) before 1682; paid for his services out of an assessment levied by the General Assembly for the public good in 1682. {Ref: ARMD 7:440}

CLEVERS, JOHN (Baltimore County), soldier (rank not stated) circa 1675; paid for his services in the late expedition against the Nanticoke Indians in 1678. {Ref: ARMD 7:95}

CLIFT, JOHN (Talbot County), sergeant who swore allegiance to the King & Queen of England in 1696. {Ref: ARMD 20:542}

CLIFTON, JOSIAH (county or port not indicated), captain and master of the ship *Eagle* of London in 1691; captain, 1696. {Ref: ARMD 8:239, 23:28}

CLIPSHAM, THOMAS (Charles County), probable soldier (rank not stated) circa 1675; paid for his services in the late expedition against the Nanticoke Indians in 1678 (name listed once as "Thomas Clipshane"); court justice, 1680; died intestate by Oct 30, 1684 (date of inventory; Susanna Clipsham, widow). See "John Cage," q.v. {Ref: ARMD 7:102-103, 15:327; INAC 8:414, 8:414}

CLIVE, NATHANIEL (Queen Anne's County), proposed for ensign in the Third Company of Foot on Jun 30, 1732. {Ref: MDHR 1:11}

CLOCKER, DANIEL (St. Mary's County), soldier (rank not stated) in 1642; paid for 3 weeks' service under Capt. William Brainthwaite in November, 1642; died testate by Feb 12, 1675/6 (date of probate). {Ref: ARMD 3:119, 3:122, 10:148; MDEP:35; MDWB 2:390; INAC 8:223}

CLOFTON (CLOUGHTON), JAMES (St. Mary's County), captain and mariner by 1637. {Ref: ARMD 4:17-20}

CLOUDS, RICHARD (St. Mary's County), Protestant and soldier in the Revolution of 1689; signed an address and took a loyalty oath supporting the King of England and the reestablishment of Lord Baltimore into power on Nov 28, 1689; soldier (rank not stated) who was issued a "gun or fowling piece" by Col. Warren on Sep 15, 1694; "Richard Cloud" was "one of the persons appointed for deciding differences with the Choptico Indians" in 1697; "Richard Clouds" was a captain by 1698. {Ref: ARMD 8:146; 20:206, 20:208, 23:18, 23:226, 23:442-444; INAC 19½A:156}

CLOUGHTANE, THOMAS (Dorchester County), soldier (rank not stated) circa 1675; paid for his services in the late expedition against the Nanticoke Indians in 1678. {Ref: ARMD 7:93}

CLOWBELLS, STEPHEN (Talbot County), soldier (rank not stated) circa 1675; paid for his services in the late expedition against the Nanticoke Indians in 1678. {Ref: ARMD 7:91}

CLOWDY, PETER (county not indicated), probable soldier (rank not stated) before 1682; paid for his services out of an assessment levied by the General Assembly for the public good in 1682. {Ref: ARMD 7:442}

CLOWTER, RICHARD (Charles County), soldier (rank not stated) circa 1675; paid for his services in the late expedition against the Nanticoke Indians in 1678; paid for his services out of an assessment levied by the General Assembly for the public good in 1682. {Ref: ARMD 7:101, 7:440}

CLUGSTONE, MICHAEL (Somerset County), Protestant and probable soldier in the Revolution of 1689; signed an address and took a loyalty oath supporting the King of England and "for enabling us to defend ourselves against all invaders" on Nov 28, 1689. {Ref: ARMD 8:141}

COARD, WILLIAM (Somerset County), Protestant and probable soldier in the Revolution of 1689; signed an address and took a loyalty oath supporting the King of England and "for enabling us to defend ourselves against all invaders" on Nov 28, 1689. {Ref: ARMD 8:140}

COATS, JOHN, see "John Courts," q.v.

COBB, JAMES (St. Mary's County), soldier (rank not stated) circa 1675; paid for his services in the late expedition against the Nanticoke Indians in 1678. {Ref: ARMD 7:103}

COBREATH (COLBREATH, COBRETH), JOHN (Calvert County), captain, commissioned "to command all the forces on the Clifts" on Jun 6, 1665; Major Henry Jowles was ordered to take under his command the company formerly belonging to Capt. John Cobreath on Aug 17, 1676; born circa 1620-1621 (aged about 34 when deposed in 1656 and aged about 48 when deposed in 1678), died testate by Mar 6, 1688/9 (date of probate). {Ref: ARMD 3:523, 15:125; INAC 6:259, 10:214; HCCM:251; MDEP:36; MDWB 6:50}

COCK, AMBROSE (Annapolis and Potomac Districts), captain and commander of the ship *Merry Christmas* riding in South River on Feb 25, 1722/3; master and commander of the ship *Calvert* riding in West River on Feb 4, 1724/5 and riding in the Eastern Branch of the Patuxent River on Jan 31, 1725/6; master of the ship *Monmouth* in 1730-1731. {Ref: AALR RCW#2:103, SY#1:70; PGLR M:149-150; CVPR:12}

COCK, DEAN (England, and Anne Arundel and Cecil Counties), captain and commander of a ship (no name given) in 1695-1696; captain, of Cecil County, 1696; captain, of London, 1697-1702 (name also listed as "Deane Cock" and "Dean: Cock" and misspelled once as "Capt. Deane Cook"). {Ref: ARMD 23:28, 23:290, 25:588, 25:595; CELR 1:214; INCC:134; INAC 23:105}

COCK, JOHN (Prince George's and/or Anne Arundel County), captain and commander of the ship *Mary* in 1722-1728, riding in the Eastern Branch of Patuxent River on Feb 24, 1723/4 and Jan 24, 1724/5, and riding in South River on Jun 30, 1728. {Ref: AALR SY#1:423; PGLR I:465, M:148-149}

COCK, MICHAELL (Oxford District), captain and master of the ship *Peach Blossom* in 1730. {Ref: CVPR:12}

COCK, WILLIAM (Anne Arundel County), military officer (rank not stated) who swore allegiance to the King & Queen of England in 1696. {Ref: ARMD 20:541}

COCKEY, EDWARD (Baltimore County and Kent Island, Queen Anne's County), captain circa 1720; born circa 1685, died testate by May 23, 1751 (date of probate; Mary Cockey, widow). {Ref: BBCF:118; MDWB 28:92}
COCKEY, ELIZABETH, see "John Cockey," q.v.
COCKEY, JOHN (Anne Arundel and Baltimore Counties), captain circa 1720; listed on tax list for Back River Upper Hundred in 1737; born circa 1680-1681, died testate on Aug 15, 1746 (will probated on May 11, 1746; Elizabeth Cockey, widow, later married Charles Baker). {Ref: BBCF:118; INBC:20; MDWB 24:473; MINV 36:6; PFMD:17-18}
COCKEY, MARY, see "Edward Cockey," q.v.
COCKEY, THOMAS (Anne Arundel and Baltimore Counties), captain by 1720; born circa 1677 (aged about 57 when deposed in 1734), died testate by Oct 22, 1737 (date of probate). {Ref: BBCF:117-118; MDEP:36; AALR CW#1:320}
CODD, ST. LEGER (Virginia, and Cecil and Kent Counties), captain, 1709-1730; member of the Lower House of the Maryland Assembly, 1712-1722; provincial court justice, 1722-1730; born circa 1675 (son of Col. St. Leger Codd, *q.v.*), died intestate by Jun 25, 1730 (date of inventory). {Ref: ARMD 29:391, 29:396, 30:129, 30:359, 33:365, 34:61; BDML I:227; INKC:150; MINV 16:528-535; MDAD 12:80}
CODD, ST. LEGER (England, Virginia, and Kent and Cecil Counties), colonel, Virginia militia, 1671; court justice in Cecil County in 1687; colonel, Maryland militia, 1688-1689, 1694-1707; Protestant and leader in the Revolution of 1689; signed an address and took a loyalty oath supporting the King of England and the reestablishment of Lord Baltimore into power on Nov 18, 1689; colonel and member of the Maryland Assembly from Cecil County, 1692; colonel of militia in Kent County in 1694; colonel and member of the General Assembly from Cecil County, 1701; born circa 1634, died testate by Feb 9, 1707/8 (date of probate). {Ref: ARMD 8:23, 8:135, 13:252, 13:351, 20:107, 24:129; BDML I:227; MDWB 12:195}
CODINERA, ---- (St. Mary's County), captain by 1719. {Ref: MDAD 2:313}
CODNER, JOHN (St. Mary's County), captain by 1719. {Ref: MDAD 1:419}
COHOONE, DARBY (Dorchester County), soldier (rank not stated) circa 1675; paid for his services in the late expedition against the Nanticoke Indians in 1678. {Ref: ARMD 7:93}
COLCLOUGH, GEORGE (county not indicated), major by 1660. {Ref: ARMD 41:441}
COLE, CHARLES (Calvert County), Protestant and probable soldier in the Revolution of 1689; signed an address and took a loyalty oath (made his "C" mark) supporting the King of England and "to reestablish Lord Baltimore in his ancient power and government" on Nov 16, 1689. {Ref: ARMD 8:132}
COLE, GEORGE (Kent County), "seaman within the said county" and a "sailor belonging to the *Factor* of Bediford" in 1697. {Ref: ARMD 25:599}

COLE, PETER (Cecil County), soldier (rank not stated) circa 1675; paid for his services in the late expedition against the Nanticoke Indians in 1678. {Ref: ARMD 7:95}

COLE, REBECCA, see "Robert Cole," q.v.

COLE, RICHARD (Somerset County), Protestant and probable soldier in the Revolution of 1689; signed an address and took a loyalty oath supporting the King of England and "for enabling us to defend ourselves against all invaders" on Nov 28, 1689. {Ref: ARMD 8:140}

COLE, ROBERT (St. Mary's County), ensign before 1663; he and wife Rebecca were both deceased by 1663 (as noted in the deposition of William Bretton). {Ref: ARMD 49:3}

COLE, STEPHEN (England and Anne Arundel County), captain by 1699; master of the ship *Hope* of London riding at anchor in South River on Jul 2, 1702. {Ref: AALR WT#2:264; INAC 19½B:75}

COLEBORNE, THOMAS (Charles County), "corporall to Major Wheeler" in August, 1681. {Ref: ARMD 15:401}

COLEBOURNE, WILLIAM, see "William Coulbourne," q.v.

COLEGATE, RICHARD (England and Baltimore County), captain by 1706; extensive land owner on the north side of Patapsco before 1706; member of the Lower House of the Maryland Assembly, 1707-1721; major by 1716; colonel by 1721; "Richard Colegate, Petapsicoe River, merchant" died testate by Feb 16, 1721/2 (date of probate; Rebecca Colegate, widow, later married James Powell before May 23, 1722). {Ref: ARMD 29:282, 29:321, 29:384, 33:365; BCTL:61; HBCC:55; BDML I:228; MDWB 17:230; MINV 9:102; MDAD 6:184; BBCF:124}

COLEMAN, ELIAS (Somerset County), soldier (rank not stated) circa 1675; paid for his services in the late expedition against the Nanticoke Indians in 1678. {Ref: ARMD 7:99}

COLEMAN (COLLMAN), JOSEPH (England and Annapolis), captain of the ship *Dover Merchant* of London in 1696-1698. {Ref: ARMD 23:340, 23:393, 23:466, 25:588}

COLHIL, ASHD. (Calvert County), Protestant and probable soldier in the Revolution of 1689; signed an address and took a loyalty oath supporting the King of England and "to reestablish Lord Baltimore in his ancient power and government" on Nov 16, 1689. {Ref: ARMD 8:132}

COLHOON (COLHOUNE), JOHN (Somerset County), soldier (rank not stated) circa 1675; paid for his services in the late expedition against the Nanticoke Indians in 1678; Protestant and probable soldier in the Revolution of 1689; signed an address and took a loyalty oath supporting the King of England and "for enabling us to defend ourselves against all invaders" on Nov 28, 1689. {Ref: ARMD 7:99, 8:141}

COLLETT, RICHARD (St. Mary's County), possible captain by 1660; commissioned by the lieutenant general of this province in 1663 to seize a certain vessel called the *Content* of Boston in New England riding then at anchor in Patuxent River and under command of Capt. Joseph Winslow, master; born circa 1621 (aged about 44 when deposed in 1665), died testate by Apr 28, 1668 (date of probate; Elizabeth Collett, widow). {Ref: ARMD 3:394, 49:23, 49:500; MDWB 1:314}

COLLIER (COLLYER), CHARLES (Prince George's County), captain of the ship *Charles* in 1682; brother of Thomas Collier or Collyer, q.v. (who was aged about 46 in 1696 and was a riding surveyor of the province of Maryland); died intestate by May 27, 1718 (date of administration account). {Ref: ARMD 23:7-8; MDAD 1:4}

COLLIER, ELIZABETH, see "Robert Collier," q.v.

COLLIER (COLYER), FRANCIS (Calvert and Prince George's Counties), Protestant and probable soldier in the Revolution of 1689; signed an address and took a loyalty oath supporting the King of England and the reestablishment of Lord Baltimore into power on Nov 28, 1689; died intestate by Jul 8, 1724 (date of administration account). {Ref: ARMD 8:145; MDAD 6:22}

COLLIER, JAMES (Baltimore County), probable soldier (rank not stated) before 1682; paid for his services out of an assessment levied by the General Assembly for the public good in 1682. {Ref: ARMD 7:441, 7:611}

COLLIER, JOHN (Anne Arundel and Baltimore Counties), lieutenant, commissioned Jul 20, 1658; captain by 1661; one John Collier died intestate by Jul 5, 1676 (date of inventory) and another John Collier died intestate by 1688 (date of administration account). Additional research will be necessary before drawing conclusions. {Ref: ARMD 3:349, 3:351, 3:435; BBCF:126}

COLLIER (COLLYER), ROBERT (Virginia and Somerset County), soldier (rank not stated) circa 1675; paid for his services in the late expedition against the Nanticoke Indians in 1678; died testate by Feb 8, 1702/3 (date of probate; Elizabeth Collier, widow). {Ref: ARMD 7:98; MDWB 11:290}

COLLIER, THOMAS (Calvert County), Protestant and probable soldier in the Revolution of 1689; signed an address and took a loyalty oath supporting the King of England and the reestablishment of Lord Baltimore into power on Nov 28, 1689. {Ref: ARMD 8:145}

COLLIER (COLLYER), THOMAS (Talbot County), marshall of the vice admiralty for Maryland's Eastern Shore, appointed Apr 29, 1697; captain and naval officer of the port of Williamstadt, 1697-1711; born circa 1650 (aged about 46 when deposed in 1696), died intestate by Oct 16, 1719 (date of inventory). See "Charles Collier," q.v. {Ref: ARMD 23:116, 23:321, 25:20, 29:21; TALR 9:52; MDEP:38; MINV 5:132}

COLLIN, THOMAS (England and St. Mary's County), captain and master of the ship *Ebenezar* of Plymouth in 1693. {Ref: ARMD 20:182}

COLLINGS, EDWARD (Annapolis District), captain of the ship *Enterprise* in 1734. {Ref: MDGZ, Aug 2, 1734}

COLLINS, BARBARA, see "Thomas Collins," q.v.

COLLINS, EDWARD (Kent County), "seaman within the said county" and a "sailor (mate) belonging to the *Factor* of Bediford" in 1697; possibly the "Capt.

Edward Collins" who received payment on Jul 22, 1726 from the estate of John Hackett, deceased, of Queen Anne's County. {Ref: ARMD 25:599; MDAD 7:451}

COLLINS (COLLINGS), GEORGE (Somerset County), soldier (rank not stated) circa 1675; paid for his services in the late expedition against the Nanticoke Indians in 1678; died testate by Feb 10, 1702/3 (date of probate). {Ref: ARMD 7:98; MDWB 11:290}

COLLINS (COLLINGS), JOHN (Queen Anne's County), proposed for lieutenant in the Third Company of Foot on Jun 30, 1732; captain before 1749; died by Apr 3, 1749 (date of inventory). {Ref: MDHR 1:11; MINV 39:89}

COLLINS (COLLENS), RICHARD (Talbot County), soldier (rank not stated) circa 1675; paid for his services in the late expedition against the Nanticoke Indians in 1678. {Ref: ARMD 7:90}

COLLINS (COLLENS), THOMAS (Talbot County), soldier (rank not stated) circa 1675; paid for his services in the late expedition against the Nanticoke Indians in 1678; died intestate by March, 1687. {Ref: ARMD 7:87; Talbot County Judgments NN:6}

COLLINS, THOMAS (Talbot County), soldier (rank not stated) circa 1675; paid for his services in the late expedition against the Nanticoke Indians in 1678; died testate by Jun 29, 1698 (date of probate; Barbara Collins, widow). {Ref: ARMD 7:91; MDWB 6:118}

COLLINS (COLLENS), THOMAS (Dorchester County), soldier (rank not stated) circa 1675; paid for his services in the late expedition against the Nanticoke Indians in 1678. {Ref: ARMD 7:93}

COLLINS (COLLENS), WILLIAM (Kent County), soldier (rank not stated) circa 1675; paid for his services in the late expedition against the Nanticoke Indians in 1678. {Ref: ARMD 7:94}

COLLISON, GEORGE (Kent County), soldier (rank not stated) in Capt. William Leeds (Leeads) Company by May 23, 1662, at which time he signed a petition about the misuse of company money by Capt. Thomas Brednox (Bradnox), late of Isle of Kent, deceased. {Ref: ARMD 3:455}

COLLSON, ---- (Charles County), captain by 1706; he might have been the "Robert Collson, gentleman" who died testate by Apr 20, 1715 (date of probate; Ann Collson, widow). Additional research will be necessary before drawing conclusions. {Ref: CHLR C#2:18; MDWB 14:50}

COLLYER, CHARLES, see "Charles Collier," q.v.

COLTSTON, JOHN (Somerset County), Protestant and probable soldier in the Revolution of 1689; signed an address and took a loyalty oath supporting the King of England and "for enabling us to defend ourselves against all invaders" on Nov 28, 1689. {Ref: ARMD 8:139}

COLVERT, THOMAS (England and St. Mary's County), seaman on the ship *Ruth* in 1676. {Ref: ARMD 66:301}

COLVILL, JOHN (Anne Arundel and Calvert Counties), captain and commander of the ship *Molly* riding in Severn River on Mar 18, 1722/3; master of the ship

Pankerville at Patuxent in 1730-1731; master of the brigantine *Giles* in 1734 (built in Maryland in 1733). {Ref: AALR RCW#2:104; CVPR:12; MDCB 82:19}

COLVILL, THOMAS (England, Cecil County, and Virginia), captain by 1730; colonel by 1739; member of the Lower House of the Maryland Assembly, 1738-1751; born circa 1688, died near Alexandria, Virginia in 1766. See "John Copson," q.v. {Ref: BDML I:228; MDGZ, Apr 26, 1745}

COMBES, GEORGE (St. Mary's County), captain of a ship (no name given) in 1690. {Ref: ARMD 8:178}

COMBES (COOMBES), WILLIAM (Talbot County), lieutenant before 1678; paid for his services in the late expedition against the Nanticoke Indians in 1678; court justice, 1680-1689; major of horse troops in 1689; Protestant and soldier in the Revolution of 1689; signed an address and took a loyalty oath supporting the King of England and the reestablishment of Lord Baltimore into power on Nov 28, 1689; Peter Sayer wrote, in part, that "because Will: Combes was to muster by Coade's order on Thursday, I stay'd with him, to see how my old soudliers would look upon me being cashier'd" on Dec 31, 1689. {Ref: ARMD 7:88-89, 8:144, 8:159, 13:243, 15:327, 17:380}

COMBS, ---- (Prince George's County), captain and commander of the ship *Shereman* in 1722. {Ref: PGLR I:465}

COMEGYS (COMIGYS, COMEGIS, COMMAGIS), CORNELIUS (Kent and Cecil Counties), soldier (rank not stated) circa 1675; paid for his services in the late expedition against the Nanticoke Indians in 1678; court justice, 1676-1687 (quorum, 1687); captain of a company of foot "in Chester & Langford bay hundred" in 1689; one person by this name was charged along with Amos Nichols in Cecil County as "persons living upon the ffrontiers of this province & driving a secret trade with the fforaign Indians" in 1696; Indian interpreter, 1697-1698; "Cornelius Comigys of Kent County" died testate by Jun 22, 1708 (date of probate; Rebecka Comegys, widow) and "Cornelius Comegys (Comegoes) of Cecil County" died testate by Mar 7, 1711/2 (date of probate). Additional research will be necessary before drawing conclusions. {Ref: ARMD 7:94, 7:610, 8:23, 13:241, 15:93, 15:328, 17:379, 20:405, 20:415, 23:428; MDWB 12:235}

COMEGYS, REBECKA, see "Cornelius Comegys," q.v.

COMEGYS, WILLIAM (Kent County), military officer (rank not stated) who swore allegiance to the King & Queen of England in 1696; born circa 1664 (aged about 52 when deposed in 1716 and aged about 70 when deposed in 1734). {Ref: ARMD 8:193, 20:540; MDEP:38}

COMES, ENOCK (Calvert County), Protestant and probable soldier in the Revolution of 1689; signed an address and took a loyalty oath supporting the King of England and "to reestablish Lord Baltimore in his ancient power and government" on Nov 16, 1689. {Ref: ARMD 8:131}

COMINS, ALEXANDER (St. Mary's County), soldier (rank not stated) in 1642; paid for 3 weeks' service under Capt. William Brainthwaite in November, 1642. {Ref: ARMD 3:122}

COMMINGS, FRANCIS (Kent County), soldier (rank not stated) circa 1675; paid for his services in the late expedition against the Nanticoke Indians in 1678. {Ref: ARMD 7:94}

COMMINS, PHILLIP (Kent County), soldier (rank not stated) on Isle of Kent who swore allegiance to the Commonwealth of England on Apr 5, 1652. {Ref: INKC:101}

COMPSTON, CHARLES (county or port not indicated), captain and master of the ship *William and Mary* of Maryland in 1690. {Ref: ARMD 8:236}

CONNAWAY (CONAWAY), JAMES (England and Anne Arundel County), mariner by 1678; land owner by Mar 5, 1682/3 (date of deed). {Ref: AALR IH#1:18; INAC 5:288}

CONNAWAY, JOHN (county not indicated), probable soldier (rank not stated) before 1682; paid for his services out of an assessment levied by the General Assembly for the public good in 1682. {Ref: ARMD 7:442}

CONNER, JAMES (Somerset County), Protestant and probable soldier in the Revolution of 1689; signed an address and took a loyalty oath supporting the King of England and "for enabling us to defend ourselves against all invaders" on Nov 28, 1689. {Ref: ARMD 8:139}

CONNERS, WILLIAM (Talbot County), Protestant and probable soldier in the Revolution of 1689; signed an address and took a loyalty oath supporting the King of England and the reestablishment of Lord Baltimore into power on Nov 18, 1689. {Ref: ARMD 8:134}

CONNIER (CONNER), PHILIP (England, and St. Mary's and Kent Counties), soldier (rank not stated) in St. Mary's County in 1642; chief commander of Kent County, 1652-1658; apparently cooperated with the Parliamentary Commissioners and continued as a justice, but was removed from his military post after the proprietory party regained control of the Maryland government in 1658; born circa 1615, died intestate in 1660. {Ref: ARMD 4:130-131, BDML I:229; INKC:103, 178}

CONTEE, JOHN (England, and Charles and Somerset Counties), major by 1704; judge for probate of wills and granting administrations in 1704; lieutenant colonel by 1705; member of the Lower House of the Maryland Assembly, 1705-1707; naval officer at Pocomoke, 1705-1708; colonel, 1705-1708; member of the Maryland Council, 1708; died testate by Aug 16, 1708 (date of council meeting; his will was probated on Aug 21, 1708; Mary Contee, widow). {Ref: ARMD 25:183, 25:245, 25:251, 27:402; BDML I:230; CHLR Z:192; MDWB 12:276, 31:6}

CONTEE, THOMAS (Anne Arundel County), colonel circa 1700. {Ref: FAAH:47}

CONTEN, CHRISTOPHER (Prince George's County), captain and commander of the ship *Bridlington* in 1722. {Ref: PGLR I:465}

CONWAY, JAMES (Anne Arundel County), captain by 1674. {Ref: INAC 1:158}

COODE, ANN, see "John Coode," q.v.

COODE, ELIZABETH, see "John Coode," q.v.

COODE (COOD), JOHN (England and St. Mary's County), captain by 1676; paid for his services in the late expedition against the Nanticoke Indians in 1678; commander of the governor's yacht by 1681; captain and court justice (quorum), 1679; first a Catholic and then a Protestant, he was the leading spirit and head of the militia in the Revolution of 1689; signed an address and took a loyalty oath supporting the King of England and the reestablishment of Lord Baltimore into power on Nov 28, 1689; commander-in-chief and acting governor of Maryland, 1689-1690 (a letter was addressed "To the Honorable John Coode, Commander in Chiefe at his House near Potomack River in Maryland" on May 30, 1690); lieutenant colonel, commissioned Jul 30, 1694; sheriff, 1695-1696; military officer who swore allegiance to the King & Queen of England in 1696; colonel by 1696; member of the Lower House of the Maryland Assembly, between 1676 and 1708; member of the Maryland Council, 1691; one John Cood, born circa 1648, died testate by Mar 28, 1709 (date of probate; Elizabeth Coode, widow), and another John Coode died testate by Apr 29, 1718 (date of probate; Ann Coode, widow); also, John Cood was referred to as "Col. John Cood" and "Capt. John Cood (alias Code), late High Sheriff" in two depositions taken on Sep 22, 1696. Additional research will be necessary before drawing conclusions. See "Richard Sewall" and "George Talbott" and "Nicholas Gassaway," q.v. {Ref: ARMD 7:102, 7:137, 8:146, 8:181, 8:280, 13:241, 15:255, 20:130, 20:152, 20:491, 20:540, 23:18, 23:36, 25:140, 27:202, 27:410; HCCM:27; FAAH:190; SHMD I:355; BDML I:233; MDWB 12:341, 14:646}

COODE (COOD), PETER (St. Mary's and Cecil Counties), captain and commander of His Majesty's Advice Boat *Messenger* in 1700-1702. {Ref: ARMD 24:19, 24:303, 25:95; CELR 1:215}

COOK, BABINGTON (Anne Arundel County), captain and commander of the ship *Henry and Jane* riding in Rhode River on May 26, 1726. {Ref: AALR SY#1:197}

COOK, CHARLES (Prince George's County), captain by 1699. {Ref: INAC 19½B:24}

COOK, JOHN (Oxford District), captain and master of the ship *Leopard* in 1731. {Ref: CVPR:12}

COOKE, JOHN (Talbot County), soldier (rank not stated) circa 1675; paid for his services in the late expedition against the Nanticoke Indians in 1678; died intestate before Mar 16, 1708 (date of deed from John Valliant to William Benstead which mentioned Cooke's orphaned sons; Mary Cooke, widow, had married William Benstead or Benset). {Ref: ARMD 7:88; TALR 11:71; Land Commissions 6:170}

COOKE, JOHN (Baltimore County), soldier (rank not stated) circa 1675; paid for his services in the late expedition against the Nanticoke Indians in 1678. {Ref: ARMD 7:95}

COOKE, MARY, see "John Cooke," q.v.

COOKE, MILES (England and St. Mary's County), captain and mariner by 1653; mariner of London in 1660; mariner of Reddriffe in 1661; captain and master of the ship *Maryland Merchant* in 1663; born circa 1624 (aged about 36 when deposed in 1660). {Ref: ARMD 3:387, 10:272, 41:277, 41:302, 49:41-42, 53:175; CHLR A:181}

COOKERY, HENRY (St. Mary's County), captain and master of the sloop *Providence* in 1693. {Ref: ARMD 20:183}

COOKNEY, JOHN (England and St. Mary's County), seaman on the ship *Ruth* in 1676-1677. {Ref: ARMD 66:301, 67:36}

COOKSEY, SAMUELL (St. Mary's and Charles Counties), Protestant and probable soldier in the Revolution of 1689; signed an address and took a loyalty oath supporting the King of England and the reestablishment of Lord Baltimore into power on Nov 28, 1689; naval officer of the Potomock District before 1695; died testate by Feb 7, 1708/9 (date of probate; Christian Cooksey, widow). {Ref: ARMD 8:146, 20:250; MDWB 12:330}

COOPER, JANE, see "Samuel Cooper," q.v.

COOPER, RALPH (England and Baltimore County), mariner, of Stepbunheath Parish, County Middlesex, before 1680; land owner in Baltimore County by 1681; captain and master of the ship *Jonathon and Margaret* in 1692. {Ref: ARMD 8:371; BALR RR#HS}

COOPER, SAMUEL (Somerset County), soldier (rank not stated) circa 1675; paid for his services in the late expedition against the Nanticoke Indians in 1678; deputy surveyor, 1685; died testate by Jul 26, 1688 (date of probate; Jane Cooper, widow). {Ref: ARMD 7:99, 17:390; MDWB 6:26}

COOPER, WILLIAM (England and Annapolis), captain by 1696; commander of the ship *Jeoffryes* "riding in Seavorn River" on Feb 23, 1697/8; master of the ship *Jeffereys* "now riding at anchor in the River of Seaverne and by God's grace bound for London" on Apr 30, 1700; captain, 1702. See "Isaac Hammerton" and "Walter Needham," q.v. {Ref: ARMD 23:387, 23:466, 24:303, 25:588; TALR 9:74}

COOPER, WILLIAM (Kent County), sailor by 1723. {Ref: MDAD 5:148}

COPLEY, LIONEL (England and St. Mary's County), captain in the King's Regiment, 1676; lieutenant governor of Hull, England, 1681-1690; captain general and governor of Maryland, 1691-1693; born in 1648, died testate on Sep 12, 1693 (will probated on Sep 23, 1693). {Ref: ARMD 13:321, 20:105, 20:202; BDML I:234; MDWB 6:51; INAC 12:45}

COPPEDGE, EDWARD (Kent County), soldier (rank not stated) on Isle of Kent who swore allegiance to the Commonwealth of England on Apr 5, 1652; mariner by 1659 when "prest to assist the Sheriffe of Kent County in a Boate uppon the Country service, for making, or concluding a Peace with the Eastern Shoare Indians ... which he denyed to doe ... The said Coppage sayth that he did not refuse to goe with him, But only willed him to goe & gett his other Company ready; & then hee would satisfy him, whither hee would obey his Command, & goe along with him, or noe. As to those Contumelious words wherewith he is now taxed, hee doth not deny the same." For his contempt

Coppage received twenty lashes on his bare back as ordered by the Provincial Court on Aug 2, 1659. {Ref: ARMD 315-316; INKC:101}

COPPEDGE (COPEDGE, COPPAGE, COPPIGE), JOHN (Kent, Talbot, and Queen Anne's Counties), captain of foot troops on Isle of Kent, commissioned Jul 30, 1694; captain who swore allegiance to the King & Queen of England in Talbot County in 1696; justice of the peace before 1709 in Queen Anne's County who "being lame desires to be excused & It is granted him" on Nov 1, 1709; "John Copedge of Kent Island in Queen Anne's County" wrote his will on Oct 30, 1709 and died by Jul 29, 1713 (date of administration account filed by Mrs. Jane Copedge); yet, his will was not probated until Dec 12, 1715. Additional research will be necessary before drawing conclusions. {Ref: ARMD 20:107, 20:131, 20:542; CESM:31; INAC 34:62; MDWB 14:76}

COPPEDGE (COPEDGE), JANE, see "John Coppedge," q.v.

COPPER, GEORGE, see "John Derricutt," q.v.

COPPING (COPPIN), EDMUND (England and St. Mary's County), boatswain on the ship *Ruth* in 1676-1677. {Ref: ARMD 51:474, 66:301, 67:36}

COPPISTONE, BARTHOLOMEW (St. Mary's County), soldier (rank not stated) circa 1675; paid for his services in the late expedition against the Nanticoke Indians in 1678. {Ref: ARMD 7:103}

COPSON, JOHN (England and Cecil County), soldier and officer by the 1730's; major before 1740; John Copson, alias John Weaver, formerly of Bedford, Parish of St. Paul, England, died intestate by Apr 20, 1740 (left no will *per se*, but orally requested Col. Thomas Colvill to be his executor). {Ref: MDWB 22:192; MINV 26:179; CELR 4:419}

CORAM, WILLIAM (Baltimore County), soldier (rank not stated) circa 1675; paid for his services in the late expedition against the Nanticoke Indians in 1678. {Ref: ARMD 7:95}

CORD, THOMAS (Baltimore County), probable soldier (rank not stated) before 1682; paid for his services out of an assessment levied by the General Assembly for the public good in 1682; died testate by Jun 7, 1721 (date of probate). {Ref: ARMD 7:441; MDWB 16:476; MDAD 4:200; BBCF:135}

CORNELIUS, ANDREW (Kent County), soldier (rank not stated) circa 1675; paid for his services in the late expedition against the Nanticoke Indians in 1678. {Ref: ARMD 7:94}

CORNELIUS, WILLIAM (St. Mary's County), mariner before 1654; served on a sloop (not named) of Symon Overzee (a merchant of Virginia) which was "then lying in St. George's River in the province of Maryland" in February, 1654; born circa 1620 (aged about 34 when deposed on Jun 16, 1654). {Ref: ARMD 41:147}

CORNEY, JOHN (New England and Talbot County), mariner "of Boston in New England" in 1718; resident and land owner on Tuckahoe Creek in Talbot County by 1719. {Ref: CFES 2:231; TALR 12:344, 12:398}

CORNISH, JOHN (Charles County), Protestant and probable soldier in the Revolution of 1689; signed an address and took a loyalty oath supporting the King of England and the reestablishment of Lord Baltimore into power on Nov 28, 1689. {Ref: ARMD 8:138}

CORNISH, JOHN (England and Pocomoke, Somerset County), major by 1703; sheriff, 1703; "John Cornish, major, son of Robert, yeoman, Somersett County, Thurleston, Devon" died testate by Sep 30, 1707 (date of probate). {Ref: ARMD 25:150; SOJR I:19; OSES:153; MDWB 12:201; INAC 24:207, 28:193}

CORNISH, ROBERT, see "John Cornish," q.v.

CORNWALLIS (CORNWALLIES, CORNWALLEYS), THOMAS (England, and St. Mary's and Charles Counties), captain and Roman Catholic who arrived in Maryland on the ship *Ark* on March 25, 1634; member of the Maryland Council, 1637-1642; chief military officer in Maryland in the 1630's and 1640's; captain of an expedition against the Indians in 1643; land owner in Charles County in 1654; captain, 1652-1675; land owner in Cecil County before 1675; born circa 1605, died testate in England in 1676. See "John Cage," q.v. {Ref: ARMD 1:2, 1:6, 10:191, 41:39, 49:17; FMDP:188-189; BDML I:235; CELR 1:98; RMHF I:120-121; Land Patent, Jul 14, 1654}

CORNWELL, NICHOLAS (Somerset County), Protestant and probable soldier in the Revolution of 1689; signed an address and took a loyalty oath supporting the King of England and "for enabling us to defend ourselves against all invaders" on Nov 28, 1689. {Ref: ARMD 8:139}

CORRALL, GEORGE (Talbot County), soldier (rank not stated) circa 1675; paid for his services in the late expedition against the Nanticoke Indians in 1678. {Ref: ARMD 7:88}

CORWAINE (CORWIN), TEAGUE (England and St. Mary's), mariner on the ship *Golden Fortune* "now ryding in St. George's River" on Jan 29, 1659/60. {Ref: ARMD 41:362}

COSEY, THOMAS, see "Thomas Casey," q.v.

COSH, WILLIAM (Calvert County), mariner, 1665. {Ref: ARMD 49:445}

COSTIN (COSTYN), HENRY (Talbot County), soldier (rank not stated) circa 1675; paid for his services in the late expedition against the Nanticoke Indians in 1678; born in 1644 (aged about 60 when deposed in 1704 and aged about 71 when deposed in 1715; name listed once as "Henry Custin"). {Ref: ARMD 7:88; MDEP:41, 46}

COTTER, WILLIAM (Rhode River, Anne Arundel County), seamen on a ship (a private man-of-war, no name given) out of Jamaica in 1690 under the command of Capt. George Rainer and which returned to Maryland in 1692; died testate by Apr 21, 1702 (date of probate). {Ref: ARMD 23:473; MDWB 11:206}

COTTERELL (COTTERAL), JOHN (England and Annapolis), captain and commander of the ship *Hope* of London in 1696-1698. {Ref: ARMD 23:290, 23:393, 23:466, 25:588}

COTTINGHAM (COTTINGTON), THOMAS (Annamessex, Somerset County), soldier (rank not stated) circa 1675; paid for his services in the late expedition against the Nanticoke Indians in 1678. {Ref: ARMD 7:99-100; OSES:279, 438}

COTTON, ANTHONY (St. Mary's County), captain and mariner, 1639. {Ref: ARMD 4:59}

COUCH, SAMUEL (county not indicated), private in the Maryland troops "raised to strengthen Albany, New York and resist the French and Indian enemies" in 1690. {Ref: SHMD I:355}

COUGHLAN, WILLIAM (Anne Arundel County), captain and master of the sloop *Biddy* (built at South River) in 1733. {Ref: MDCB 82:8}

COULBOURNE, ANN, see "William Coulbourne, Jr.," q.v.

COULBOURNE (COLEBOURN, COLEBORNE), WILLIAM (England, Virginia, and Annamessex, Somerset County), "captain of foot from Monoakin to Pocomoke," commissioned Feb 9, 1669; sheriff by 1673; commissioned "captain and commander of a troop of horse" on Oct 25, 1673; colonel by 1678 when paid for his services in the late expedition against the Nanticoke Indians in 1678; colonel and court justice (quorum), 1679; colonel and court justice, 1680; colonel and Protestant in command of the foot forces in Dorchester and Somerset Counties in 1681; colonel in command of the militia and horse troops in Somerset County in 1687; colonel of foot troops in 1689; Protestant and soldier in the Revolution of 1689; signed an address and took a loyalty oath supporting the King of England and "for enabling us to defend ourselves against all invaders" on Nov 28, 1689; born circa 1630, died testate by Mar 11, 1689/90 (date of probate). {Ref: ARMD 5:61, 5:120-122, 5:309, 5:554, 5:568, 7:97, 7:611, 8:140, 13:244, 15:275, 15:328, 17:68, 17:76; OSES:279, 438-439; INAC 1:520}

COULBOURNE (COLEBOURN, COULBORN), WILLIAM, JR. (Virginia and Annamessex, Somerset County), captain by 1683; captain lieutenant in the foot troops of Somerset County, commissioned Dec 2, 1687, under the command of Col. William Coulbourn; Protestant and soldier in the Revolution of 1689; signed an address and took a loyalty oath supporting the King of England and "for enabling us to defend ourselves against all invaders" on Nov 28, 1689; captain, 1694; born circa 1650, died testate by Jun 9, 1701 (date of probate; Ann Coulbourne, widow). {Ref: ARMD 5:568, 7:611, 8:139, 20:110; CESM:38; OSES:153, 438; MDWB 11:110}

COULTON, THOMAS (Talbot County), lieutenant before 1678; paid for his services in the late expedition against the Nanticoke Indians in 1678. {Ref: ARMD 7:92}

COURBY, JOHN (Charles County), Protestant and probable soldier in the Revolution of 1689; signed an address and took a loyalty oath supporting the King of England and the reestablishment of Lord Baltimore into power on Nov 28, 1689. {Ref: ARMD 8:138}

COURSEY, ANN, see "Thomas Coursey," q.v.

COURSEY, ELIZABETH, see "William Coursey," q.v.

COURSEY, HENRY (Ireland, Virginia, and St. Mary's, Calvert, Kent, and Talbot Counties), soldier (rank not stated) who served as a messenger under Governor Stone at the Battle of the Severn on Mar 25, 1655; member of the Maryland Council, 1661-1686; colonel by 1677; paid for his services in expeditions against the Nanticoke Indians in 1678 and 1682; court justice (quorum), 1679; colonel and Protestant in command of the foot forces in Cecil and Kent Counties in 1681; colonel and Indian Agent for the Province of Maryland at the peace talks at Fort Albany in 1681; colonel in command of the militia in Kent County, 1687-1694; member of the Lower House of the Maryland Assembly, representing Talbot County, 1694-1695; colonel, paid for his services in 1695; born circa 1629 (aged about 29 when deposed in 1657 and 1658; name listed once as "Cowrsey"), died testate by Oct 30, 1695 (date of probate). See "Josias Lanham" and "John Strong" and "William Pearce" and "Nathaniell Evetts" and "Jacob Young" and "Thomas Coursey," q.v. {Ref: ARMD 5:309, 5:527, 5:554, 7:92, 7:112, 7:363, 7:443, 15:254, 17:68, 17:75, 17:85, 20:205, 38:74; MDEP"41; FAAH:26; HCCM:251; BDML I:236; INKC:116; MDWB 7:184}

COURSEY, JAMES (Talbot County), soldier (rank not stated) circa 1675; paid for his services in the late expedition against the Nanticoke Indians in 1678; died testate by May 5, 1714 (date of probate). {Ref: ARMD 7:92; BDML I:236; MDWB 13:717}

COURSEY, JOHN (Kent County), soldier (rank not stated) on Isle of Kent who swore allegiance to the Commonwealth of England on Apr 5, 1652. {Ref: INKC:101}

COURSEY, THOMAS (Kent County), military officer (rank not stated) who swore allegiance to the King & Queen of England in 1696; captain before 1701; born circa 1655 (son of Col. Henry Coursey, *q.v.*), died testate by Jul 31, 1701 (date of probate; Ann Coursey, widow). {Ref: ARMD 20:541; INAC 21:277, 24:261, 26:223; MDWB 11:140}

COURSEY, WILLIAM (Ireland, Virginia and St. Mary's, Calvert, Kent, and Talbot Counties), acting sheriff, Calvert County, 1658; major by 1659; county surveyor, 1659; member of the Lower House of the Maryland Assembly, representing Talbot County, 1666; sheriff, 1667; court justice, 1661-1685 (quorum, 1679-1685); major, paid for his services in the late expedition against the Nanticoke Indians in 1678; major and court justice, 1680-1681; died by Aug 12, 1685 (date of inventory). {Ref: ARMD 5:4, 5:28, 7:88, 15:68, 15:226, 15:327, 15:346; BDML I:237; INAC 8:410, 10:155}

COURSEY, WILLIAM (Talbot and Queen Anne's Counties), Protestant and probable soldier in the Revolution of 1689; signed an address and took a loyalty oath supporting the King of England and the reestablishment of Lord Baltimore into power on Nov 18, 1689; major before 1706; colonel, 1707; member of the Lower House of the Maryland Assembly, 1696-1697; member of the Maryland Council, 1704-1716; died testate by Feb 3, 1717/8 (date of probate; Elizabeth Coursey, widow). {Ref: ARMD 8:134, 25:245, 25:336, 27:377, 29:347, 30:129; BDML I:237; QALR ET#A:68; MDWB 14:472}

COURSEY, WILLIAM (Queen Anne's County), proposed for ensign in the Second Company of Foot on Jun 30, 1732; born in 1703, died testate by Mar 28, 1769 (date of probate). {Ref: MDHR 1:11; BDML I:236; MDWB 37:125}
COURSEY, WILLIAM (Kent County), colonel by 1733. {Ref: INKC:178}
COURTNEY, JOHN (England, and St. Mary's or Talbot County), seaman on the ship *Ruth* in 1676. {Ref: ARMD 51:474}
COURTNEY, THOMAS (St. Mary's County), lieutenant, 1678; captain lieutenant, 1681; captain by 1696; died by Jun 26, 1706 (date of probate). {Ref: ARMD 15:220, 17:64; MDWB 12:54; INAC 14:78, 26:166}
COURTS (COATS), JOHN (Charles County), soldier (rank not stated) circa 1675; paid for his services in the late expedition against the Nanticoke Indians in 1678; captain of horse troops in 1689; very active in the Revolution of 1689; member of the Maryland Council, 1691-1702; justice of a special Court of Oyer & Terminer, 1692; paid for 10 days horse service in 1692; captain of horse troops, 1694; lieutenant colonel, commissioned Jul 30, 1694; colonel of Charles County, appointed Aug 17, 1695; military officer who swore allegiance to the King & Queen of England in 1696; colonel, 1696-1697; born circa 1655/6, died testate by Dec 15, 1702 (date of probate); his son John was deposed on Nov 6, 1712 regarding arms and ammunition in his deceased father John Courts' house (name listed once as "John Courte, Sr."). See "Ninian Beale" and "Captain Bourne," q.v. {Ref: ARMD 7:101, 8:414, 8:424, 13:243, 17:380, 20:16, 20:63, 20:109, 20:130, 20:543, 23:19, 23:252, 24:11, 25:597, 29:96, 29:110, 38:73; BDML I:237; INAC 22:106; MDWB 11:246}
COUTIS, MARSCH. (St. Mary's County), Protestant and probable soldier in the Revolution of 1689; signed an address and took a loyalty oath supporting the King of England and the reestablishment of Lord Baltimore into power on Nov 28, 1689. {Ref: ARMD 8:147}
COVANT (COVENT), ABSOLON (Charles or Calvert County), captain by 1662; captain, mariner, and commander of the ship *Jacob* in 1664-1665. {Ref: CHLR B:26; ARMD 49:422, 521}
COVENTON, MARY, see "John Covington," q.v.
COVERT, THOMAS (England, and St. Mary's or Talbot County), seaman on the ship *Ruth* in 1676. {Ref: ARMD 51:474}
COVILL, RICHARD (England and St. Mary's), mariner, captain and commander of the ship *Frances* of London, 1677-1678. {Ref: ARMD 15:233}
COVINGTON, ELENOR, see "Philip Covington," q.v.
COVINGTON (COVENTON), JOHN (Somerset County), soldier (rank not stated) circa 1675; paid for his services in the late expedition against the Nanticoke Indians in 1678; paid for his services out of an assessment levied by the General Assembly for the public good in 1682; died testate by Mar 12, 1693/4 (date of probate; Mary Coventon, widow). {Ref: ARMD 7:97, 7:98, 7:100, 7:443; MDWB 2:317}
COVINGTON, LEONARD, see "William Blair," q.v.

COVINGTON, NEHEMIAH (Virginia and Monie, Somerset County), soldier (rank not stated) circa 1675; paid for his services in the late expedition against the Nanticoke Indians in 1678; paid for his services out of an assessment levied by the General Assembly for the public good in 1682; commissioned by the Maryland Council and "empowered to be General Interpreter for this Government upon any treaty to be made with the Indians of the Eastern Shore" on Oct 20, 1697; died testate by Aug 5, 1713 (date of probate; Rebecca Covington, widow). {Ref: ARMD 7:100, 7:442, 23:251; OSES:280, 439; MDWB 13:549}

COVINGTON, PHILIP (Somerset County), captain before 1732; died testate by Mar 17, 1732/3 (date of probate; Elenor Covington, widow). {Ref: MDWB 20:287; MINV 17:698}

COVINGTON, REBECCA, see "Nehemiah Covington," q.v.

COVINGTON, THOMAS (Monie, Somerset County), soldier (rank not stated) circa 1675; paid for his services in the late expedition against the Nanticoke Indians in 1678; died testate by Sep 11, 1704 (date of probate). {Ref: ARMD 7:100; OSES:280, 440; MDWB 12:50}

COVINGTON, THOMAS (Kent County), military officer (rank not stated) who swore allegiance to the King & Queen of England in 1696; member of the Lower House of the Maryland Assembly, 1708; died before Oct 25, 1709 (date of assembly meeting). {Ref: ARMD 20:540, 27:202, 27:410}

COWARD, JOHN (Kent or Queen Anne's County), captain by 1716; master of the schooner *Charming Betty* (built in Choptank River) in 1735; master of the schooner *Hopewell* (built in Talbot County) in 1736. {Ref: INAC 37C:148; MDCB 82:30, 46}

COWARD, RICHARD (England and Talbot County), captain before 1721; "Richard Coward, late of Bristol, England, merchant" died testate in Talbot County by Jun 11, 1722 (date of probate; Sibilla or Sybilla Coward, widow). {Ref: MDWB 17:225; MDAD 4:32, 6:384}

COWARD, SIBILLA, see "Richard Coward," q.v.

COWLEY, GEORGE (Talbot County), captain by 1676; paid for his services in the late expedition against the Nanticoke Indians in 1678; court justice, 1679-1689. {Ref: ARMD 7:89, 7:148, 13:243, 15:254, 15:327; TALR 6:28; INAC 4:109}

COWLEY, JAMES (Potomac District), captain and master of the ship *Alice* in 1730-1731. {Ref: CVPR:12}

COWMAN, JOSEPH (County Cumberland, England and West River, Anne Arundel County), captain and commander of the ship *Champion* of London riding in West River on Mar 5, 1721/2 and Jan 31, 1722/3 and Feb 12, 1723/4 and Jan 18, 1724/5 and Feb 12, 1725/6 and Mar 15, 1726/7 and Mar 19, 1727/8 and Feb 4, 1728/9; captain and member of the South River Club in 1742; born circa 1696 (aged about 45 when deposed in 1741), died testate by Nov 5, 1753 (date of probate; Sarah Cowman, widow). {Ref: AALR CW#1:479, AALR RCW#2:87, 222, AALR SY#1:60, 164, 265, 363; MDGZ, Feb 11, 1728/9; FAAH:201; MDEP:42; MDWB 28:553}

COWS, GEORGE (Dorchester County), captain by 1699. {Ref: INAC 19½A:1}

COX, ---- (St. Mary's County), soldier (rank not stated) in 1642. {Ref: ARMD 4:130-131}
COX, AMBROSE (Talbot County), soldier (rank not stated) circa 1675; paid for his services in the late expedition against the Nanticoke Indians in 1678. {Ref: ARMD 7:87}
COX (COXE), EDWARD (Kent County), soldier (rank not stated) on Isle of Kent who swore allegiance to the Commonwealth of England on Apr 5, 1652. {Ref: INKC:101}
COX, HENRY (St. Mary's County), captain, commissioned Mar 23, 1656/7. {Ref: ARMD 3:320}
COX, HENRY (Calvert County), Protestant and probable soldier in the Revolution of 1689; signed an address and took a loyalty oath supporting the King of England and "to reestablish Lord Baltimore in his ancient power and government" on Nov 16, 1689. {Ref: ARMD 8:132}
COX, HENRY (Calvert County), major by 1714; colonel before 1721; born circa 1673 (aged about 41 when deposed in 1714), died intestate by Nov 21, 1721 (date of administration account). {Ref: MDEP:43; MDAD 4:60, 10:540, 12:314}
COX, JAMES (Charles County), soldier (rank not stated) circa 1675; paid for his services in the late expedition against the Nanticoke Indians in 1678; sergeant before 1682; paid for his services out of an assessment levied by the General Assembly for the public good in 1682. {Ref: ARMD 7:101, 7:440}
COX, JOHN (Pocomoke District), captain and master of the ship *Trueman* in 1730-1731. {Ref: CVPR:12}
COX, THOMAS (Anne Arundel County), soldier (rank not stated) circa 1675; paid for his services in the late expedition against the Nanticoke Indians in 1678; paid for his services out of an assessment levied by the General Assembly for the public good in 1682. {Ref: ARMD 7:97, 7:442}
COXALL, WILLIAM (Talbot County), soldier (rank not stated) circa 1675; paid for his services in the late expedition against the Nanticoke Indians in 1678. {Ref: ARMD 7:92}
COZENS, RICHARD (county not indicated), private in the Maryland troops "raised to strengthen Albany, New York and resist the French and Indian enemies" in 1690. {Ref: SHMD I:355}
CRABB, ELIZABETH, see "Thomas Crabb," q.v.
CRABB, HENRY (Kent County), soldier (rank not stated) circa 1675; paid for his services in the late expedition against the Nanticoke Indians in 1678. {Ref: ARMD 7:94}
CRABB, THOMAS (Charles County), captain by 1705; member of the Lower House of the Maryland Assembly, 1708-1711; major by 1717; colonel by 1719; died testate by Mar 8, 1719/20 (date of probate; Elizabeth Crabb, widow). {Ref: ARMD 27:410, 27:495; BDML I:241; CHLR Z:181-185; MDWB 16:20; MINV 4:83}
CRACKSON (CRAKSON, CRAXON, CRAXTONE), THOMAS (Charles County), soldier by 1665 who was "prest in the last indian March up the bay" and paid for his services on Dec 7, 1665; soldier again (rank not stated) before

1678 and was paid for his services in the late expedition against the Nanticoke Indians in 1678; born circa 1639 (aged about 22 when deposed in 1661), died testate by Dec 31, 1702 (date of probate; Ann Craxon, widow). {Ref: ARMD 7:101, 53:147, 53:618-619; MDWB 11:387}

CRADDOCK, ---- (St. Mary's County), captain by 1719. {Ref: MDAD 2:50}

CRAGG, HENRY (Kent County), "seaman within the said county" and a "sailor (mate) belonging to the *Loves Increase* of Whitehaven" in 1697. {Ref: ARMD 25:600}

CRANE, ROBERT (St. Mary's County), Protestant and probable soldier in the Revolution of 1689; signed an address and took a loyalty oath supporting the King of England and the reestablishment of Lord Baltimore into power on Nov 28, 1689. {Ref: ARMD 8:147}

CRAWFFORD, JA. (Calvert County), Protestant and probable soldier in the Revolution of 1689; signed an address and took a loyalty oath supporting the King of England and "to reestablish Lord Baltimore in his ancient power and government" on Nov 16, 1689. {Ref: ARMD 8:132}

CRAWFORD, LAURENCE (Somerset County), Protestant and probable soldier in the Revolution of 1689; signed an address and took a loyalty oath supporting the King of England and "for enabling us to defend ourselves against all invaders" on Nov 28, 1689. See "John White," q.v. {Ref: ARMD 8:141}

CRAWFORD, M. (Potomac District), captain and master of the ship *Butterfly Fancy* in 1730-1731. {Ref: CVPR:12}

CRAWLEY, JOHN (Somerset County), soldier (rank not stated) circa 1675; paid for his services in the late expedition against the Nanticoke Indians in 1678; Protestant and soldier in the Revolution of 1689; signed an address and took a loyalty oath supporting the King of England and "for enabling us to defend ourselves against all invaders" on Nov 28, 1689. {Ref: ARMD 7:98, 8:141}

CRAWLEY, JOHN (Calvert County), captain before 1730; died by Dec 9, 1730 (mentioned as being deceased in the accounts paid from the estate of Thomas Holdsworth, deceased). {Ref: MDAD 10:567}

CRAXON, ANN, see "Thomas Crackson," q.v.

CREED, THOMAS (Anne Arundel County), captain and commander of the ship *Forward Falley* riding at anchor in South River on Jul 14, 1716. {Ref: AALR IB#2:286}

CRESAP, THOMAS (England, and Baltimore, Prince George's, Frederick, and Washington Counties), ferryman on the Susquehanna River circa 1727; captain of militia and local magistrate circa 1729 by which time he had established a farm in Baltimore (now Harford) County on Maryland's disputed northern border with Pennsylvania; supported by Lord Baltimore, his aggressive defiance of Pennsylvania authority escalated the controversy into armed conflict (Conojacular War); he earned the respect of Maryland officials, but was referred to as "The Maryland Monster" by Pennsylvanians who burned his home in 1737; court justice in Prince George's County, 1739-1748, and

Frederick County, 1748-1775; colonel, 1749; member of the Lower House of the Maryland Assembly, representing Frederick County, 1757-1775; served on the Committee of Observation early in the Revolutionary War, 1774-1775; his home and trading post at Old Town in Western Maryland was on the trail that the Iroquois followed in their wars with the Southern Indians; acted as agent in dealing with the Cherokees and Iroquois in western Maryland and often advised Gov. Dinwiddie of Virginia on Indian affairs; born circa 1702 (aged about 30 when deposed on Dec 13, 1732, aged about 31 when deposed on Feb 19, 1733/4, and aged about 32 when deposed on Mar 26, 1735), died testate in Washington (now Allegany) County in 1788. {Ref: ARMD 28:20-21, 28:60, 28:68; BDML I:244-245; INCC:134; MDEP:44}

CREVIN, EDWARD (St. Mary's County), Protestant and probable soldier in the Revolution of 1689; signed an address and took a loyalty oath supporting the King of England and the reestablishment of Lord Baltimore into power on Nov 28, 1689. {Ref: ARMD 8:147}

CREW, ANTO. (Baltimore County), Protestant and probable soldier in the Revolution of 1689; signed an address and took a loyalty oath supporting the King of England and the reestablishment of Lord Baltimore into power on Nov 28, 1689. *Note:* This "Anto. Crew" may actually be "Anthony Drew," *q.v.*, who appeared in the Baltimore County tax list for 1692, was a captain by 1711, and died testate in 1720. Additional research will be necessary before drawing conclusions. {Ref: ARMD 8:136; BBCF:185}

CREW, DANELL (St. Mary's County), Protestant and probable soldier in the Revolution of 1689; signed an address and took a loyalty oath supporting the King of England and the reestablishment of Lord Baltimore into power on Nov 28, 1689. {Ref: ARMD 8:146}

CRIBB, NICHOLAS (England and Somerset County), captain, commander and master of the ship *Betty Gally* of Liverpool riding at anchor in Monocan River on Jan 16, 1716/7. {Ref: SOJR III:185-186}

CRISOPE, WILLIAM (Calvert County), captain by 1706. {Ref: INAC 26:113}

CROCHEE, WILLIAM (Kent County), soldier (rank not stated) circa 1675; paid for his services in the late expedition against the Nanticoke Indians in 1678. {Ref: ARMD 7:94}

CROCKER, ROBERT (Cecil County), captain of the sloop *Ruby* in 1734. {Ref: CELR 5:144; MDGZ, Nov 29, 1734}

CROCKETT, RICHARD (Somerset County), corporal before 1682; paid for his services out of an assessment levied by the General Assembly for the public good in 1682. {Ref: ARMD 7:442-443}

CROMPTON, THOMAS (Calvert County), soldier and probable officer in the 1730's; major at the time of his death in December, 1744 (estate inventory taken on Feb 5, 1744/5; Mary Crompton, widow). {Ref: MDGZ, Jan 17, 1745; MINV 31:19}

CROMWELL, ELIZABETH, see "William Cromwell," q.v.

CROMWELL, HANNAH, see "John Cromwell," q.v.

CROMWELL, JOHN (Prince George's and Anne Arundel Counties), captain of militia before 1733; died testate by May 9, 1734 (date of probate; Hannah Cromwell, widow, later married William Worthington). {Ref: MDWB 21:35; MINV 23:415, 24:317; HBCC:55; RMHF I:236}

CROMWELL, OLIVER, see "Richard Snowden" and "Ninian Beall" and "Luke Barber," q.v.

CROMWELL, WILLIAM (Baltimore County), soldier (rank not stated) circa 1675; paid for his services in the late expedition against the Nanticoke Indians in 1678; died testate by Mar 3, 1684/5 (date of probate; Elizabeth Cromwell, widow, later married George Ashman). {Ref: ARMD 7:96; AAGE:582-583; MDWB 4:26; BBCF:146}

CROOK (CROOKE), ROBERT (England and Cecil County), Protestant and probable soldier in the Revolution of 1689; signed an address and took a loyalty oath supporting the King of England and the reestablishment of Lord Baltimore into power on Nov 18, 1689; military officer (rank not stated) who swore allegiance to the King & Queen of England in 1696; member of the Lower House of the Maryland Assembly, 1692-1693; died testate by Aug 28, 1693 (date of probate). {Ref: ARMD 8:135, 20:545; BDML I:245; MDWB 7:309}

CROOKSHANK, ---- (Calvert County), captain by 1719. {Ref: MDAD 2:66}

CROOKSHANK, ANDREW (England and Somerset County), captain and late master of the ship *Katherine* of Londonderry who was charged with murder in 1692. {Ref: ARMD 13:337-339}

CROSBY, BURDON (England and Patuxent District), captain by 1731; master of the ship *Adventure* riding at anchor in the Patuxent River on Jul 17, 1731. {Ref: PGLR Q:316; CVPR:12; MDAD 11:15}

CROSCOMBE, EZEKIELL (England and Kent County), captain and commander of the ship *King Solomon* in 1669 (listed as "Capt. Crosscombe" in 1678). {Ref: INKC:134; INAC 5:444}

CROSFEILD, STEPHEN (Anne Arundel County), captain by 1721. {Ref: MDAD 4:32}

CROSSE, WILLIAM (Talbot County), soldier (rank not stated) circa 1675; paid for his services in the late expedition against the Nanticoke Indians in 1678. {Ref: ARMD 7:88-89}

CROSSMAN (CROSMAN), ROBERT (England and St. Mary's County), captain of the ship *Antilope* of Liverpool in 1674; commander of the ship *Vine* in 1678; captain to at least 1684 (name mistakenly listed once as "Richard Crosman"). {Ref: ARMD 17:312, 67:420; INAC 6:319, 6:330, 8:517}

CROSTON, EDM. (county not indicated), captain by 1687. {Ref: INAC 10:115}

CROUCH, EDWARD (Charles County), soldier (rank not stated) circa 1675; paid for his services in the late expedition against the Nanticoke Indians in 1678. {Ref: ARMD 7:101}

CROUCH, GEORGE (Talbot County), soldier (rank not stated) circa 1675; paid for his services in the late expedition against the Nanticoke Indians in 1678. {Ref: ARMD 7:87}

CROUCH, GEORGE (Kent County), soldier (rank not stated) on Isle of Kent who swore allegiance to the Commonwealth of England on Apr 5, 1652; "George Croutch" died intestate circa 1655 (Marye or Marie Croutch, widow). {Ref: INKC:101, 106}

CROUCH, JOSIAH (Talbot County), soldier (rank not stated) circa 1675; paid for his services in the late expedition against the Nanticoke Indians in 1678; died testate by Nov 14, 1692 (date of probate; name listed as "Josias Crouch"). {Ref: ARMD 7:91; MDWB 2:281}

CROUCH, MARY, see "Robert Crouch," q.v.

CROUCH, ROBERT (Virginia and Somerset County), Protestant and probable soldier in the Revolution of 1689; signed an address and took a loyalty oath supporting the King of England and "for enabling us to defend ourselves against all invaders" on Nov 28, 1689; born circa 1640, died testate by Nov 28, 1711 (date of probate; Mary Crouch, widow). {Ref: ARMD 8:141; MDWB 13:362}

CROUCH, WILLIAM (Anne Arundel County), soldier (rank not stated) who served under Captain Fuller at the Battle of the Severn on Mar 25, 1655 and served on a Council of War after the battle. {Ref: FAAH: 26, 38}

CROUCHEE (CRUCHEE), JOHN (county or port not indicated), captain and commander of the brigantine *Happy Return* of New York in 1689 and the bark *Ann and Catharine* of New York in 1690. {Ref: ARMD 8:151, 8:170, 8:238}

CROUDER, THOMAS (St. Mary's County), soldier (rank not stated) circa 1675; paid for his services in the late expedition against the Nanticoke Indians in 1678. {Ref: ARMD 7:103}

CROUTCH, MARYE, see "George Crouch," q.v.

CRUCKSHANK, ROBERT (Kent County), captain by 1722. {Ref: MINV 7:93}

CRUMP, WILLIAM (Talbot County), captain before 1689; "captain of a foot Company continued as formerly" in 1689. {Ref: ARMD 13:243}

CUFF, JOHN (Talbot County), soldier (rank not stated) circa 1675; paid for his services in the late expedition against the Nanticoke Indians in 1678. {Ref: ARMD 7:92}

CULER, WILLIAM (Prince George's County), foot soldier (rank not stated) under the command of Capt. Richard Owen in June, 1699. {Ref: ARMD 24:122}

CUMBER, JOHN (St. Mary's County), captain by 1657; commissioned captain lieutenant on Jul 20, 1658. {Ref: FAAH:29; ARMD 3:349, 3:351}

CUMPTON, JAMES (St. Mary's County), soldier (rank not stated) circa 1675; paid for his services in the late expedition against the Nanticoke Indians in 1678. {Ref: ARMD 7:102}

CUNNEY (CUNNEE), JOHN (Charles County), soldier (rank not stated) circa 1675; paid for his services in the late expedition against the Nanticoke Indians in 1678. {Ref: ARMD 7:101}

CUNNINGHAM (CONNINGHAM), DANIELL (St. Mary's County), soldier (rank not stated) circa 1675; for whom payment was made to his estate for his services in the late expedition against the Nanticoke Indians in 1678. {Ref: ARMD 7:103}

CURDY, WILLIAM (Talbot County), colonel by 1715. {Ref: MDEP:45}

CURKE, JOHN (England and St. Mary's), helper on the ship *Dove* in 1633-1634. {Ref: FMDP:343}

CURLING, GEORGE (Anne Arundel County), captain and commander of the ship *Fortune* riding at anchor in South River on Jan 10, 1716. {Ref: AALR IB#2:325}

CURREY, ROBERT (Calvert County), military officer (rank not stated) who swore allegiance to the King & Queen of England in 1696. {Ref: ARMD 20:543}

CURTIS (CURTICE), DANIEL (Virginia and Annamessex, Somerset County), captain lieutenant by 1678; paid for his services in the late expedition against the Nanticoke Indians in 1678; captain by 1680; died testate by Mar 9, 1681 (date of probate; Mary Curtis, widow). {Ref: ARMD 7:97; OSES:279, 440; INAC 7B:113; MDWB 2:154}

CURTIS, EDMUND (Kent County), captain and commander of the frigate *Ginny* in 1654. {Ref: INKC:103}

CURTIS (CURTICE), JOHN (Dorchester County), soldier (rank not stated) circa 1675; paid for his services in the late expedition against the Nanticoke Indians in 1678; one John Curtis died testate in Somerset County by Mar 11, 1706/7 (date of probate). {Ref: ARMD 7:92; MDWB 12:120}

CURTIS, MARTIN (Somerset County), Protestant and probable soldier in the Revolution of 1689; signed an address and took a loyalty oath supporting the King of England and "for enabling us to defend ourselves against all invaders" on Nov 28, 1689. {Ref: ARMD 8:139}

CURTIS, MARY, see "Daniel Curtis," q.v.

CURTIS, MICHAEL, see "Justinian Gerrard," q.v.

CURTIS, WILLIAM (England and Patuxent District), captain of the ship *America* of Bideford in 1697. See "John Dalling," q.v. {Ref: ARMD 23:137}

CUT (CUTS), JOHN (New England and Anne Arundel County), captain of a ship (no name given) commandeered by Captain Fuller at the Battle of the Severn on Mar 25, 1655; also served on a Council of War after the battle. {Ref: FAAH:23-26}

CUTCHIN, ROBERT, see "Moses Groom," q.v.

CUTLER, WILLIAM (Prince George's County), soldier (trooper) under the command of Capt. Richard Owen in June, 1699. {Ref: ARMD 24:121}

CUTTERBROOKE, WILLIAM (county or port not indicated), captain and master of the pink *Hope* in 1686. {Ref: ARMD 23:57}

CYVILE, THOMAS (Talbot County), soldier (rank not stated) circa 1675; paid for his services in the late expedition against the Nanticoke Indians in 1678. {Ref: ARMD 7:87}

DAILL, PETER (Anne Arundel County), captain and commander of the ship *William*, lying in West River on Jun 30, 1707. {Ref: AALR WT#2:510}

DALLAHIDE (DOLLAHIDE, DOLLAHYDE), FRANCIS (England, and Anne Arundel and Baltimore Counties), captain by 1714; member of the Lower House of the Maryland Assembly, representing Baltimore County, 1704-1707, 1715-1720; sheriff, 1707-1709; court justice, 1715-1718; died by May, 1721 (date of administration bond; Sarah Dallahide, widow, later married William Graves). {Ref: ARMD 30:107, 30:160, 30:360, 33:365, 34:61, 34:204; BBCF:155; BDML I:273}

DALLING, JOHN (Patuxent District), late mate to Capt. Curtis of the ship *America* in 1696, petitioned the Maryland Council on Dec 3, 1696 "setting forth that being grievously afflicted with a timpany, and that whereas no Doctor will undertake to looke after him, therefore humbly prayes that some doctor may be assign'd to tend him & to endeavour the Recovery of his health." {Ref: ARMD 23:338}

DALLY, JOHN (Talbot County), Protestant and probable soldier in the Revolution of 1689; signed an address and took a loyalty oath supporting the King of England and the reestablishment of Lord Baltimore into power on Nov 28, 1689. {Ref: ARMD 8:144}

DALTON, EDWARD (Talbot County), soldier (rank not stated) circa 1675; paid for his services in the late expedition against the Nanticoke Indians in 1678. {Ref: ARMD 7:88}

DALTON, JAMES (Dorchester County), soldier (rank not stated) circa 1675; paid for his services in the late expedition against the Nanticoke Indians in 1678. {Ref: ARMD 7:92}

DAMES, JOHN (Talbot County), soldier (rank not stated) circa 1675; paid for his services in the late expedition against the Nanticoke Indians in 1678. {Ref: ARMD 7:91}

DANDY, MITCH. (Calvert County), Protestant and probable soldier in the Revolution of 1689; signed an address and took a loyalty oath supporting the King of England and "to reestablish Lord Baltimore in his ancient power and government" on Nov 16, 1689. {Ref: ARMD 8:131}

DANFORD, WILLIAM (county not indicated), private in the Maryland troops "raised to strengthen Albany, New York and resist the French and Indian enemies" in 1690. {Ref: SHMD I:355}

DANIELL, JOSIAH (England and Potomac District), captain before 1696; commander of His Majesty's Hired Ship the *Prince of Orange* in 1696 (name also listed as "Josias Daniell"). {Ref: ARMD 20:489, 20:514, 23:4, 23:10, 23:27}

DANIELL, LEONARD (Talbot County), soldier (rank not stated) circa 1675; paid for his services in the late expedition against the Nanticoke Indians in 1678. {Ref: ARMD 7:91}

DANIELSON, ---- (Dorchester County), major by 1696. {Ref: ARMD 25:559-560}

DANNHON(?), ---- (Cecil County), major by 1705. {Ref: INAC 25:119}

DANT, THOMAS (St. Mary's County), soldier (rank not stated) circa 1675; paid for his services in the late expedition against the Nanticoke Indians in 1678. {Ref: ARMD 7:102}

DARBY, ---- (Kent County), captain by 1706; possibly the William Darby who died intestate in Kent County by Oct 5, 1717 (date of inventory). {Ref: ARMD 34:195; MINV 39A:5; MDAD 3:1}

DARBY, JOHN (Cecil County), Protestant and probable soldier in the Revolution of 1689; signed an address and took a loyalty oath supporting the King of England and the reestablishment of Lord Baltimore into power on Nov 18, 1689. {Ref: ARMD 8:135}

DARE, WILLIAM, SR. (England and Cecil County), soldier and probable officer by 1689 (opposed the Revolution of 1689); military officer (rank not stated) who swore allegiance to the King & Queen of England in 1696; member of the Lower House of the Maryland Assembly between 1686 and 1714; died testate by Aug 13, 1719 (date of probate). {Ref: ARMD 8:23, 17:381, 20:545; BDML I:250; MDWB 15:203; MDAD 5:312}

DARNALL (DARNELL), HENRY (England, and Calvert, Prince George's and Anne Arundel Counties), captain on the Council of War, 1676-1677; sheriff, 1674-1679; lieutenant colonel, justice of the peace, and member of the Maryland Council, 1679-1689; member of the Lower House of the Maryland Assembly, 1674; colonel and Roman Catholic in command of the horse troops in Charles, St. Mary's, and part of Calvert County in 1681; member of the Maryland Council, 1681-1688; keeper of the Great Seal of this province, 1684; receiver general, 1684-1711; principal keeper of the forest and chief ranger, 1684; colonel, 1698; died testate by Jul 17, 1711 (date of probate). {Ref: ARMD 5:309, 5:310, 5:527, 7:112, 7:611, 15:99, 15:118, 15:253, 15:268, 17:75, 17:196, 25:27, 51:533; BDML I:250-251; AALR WT#2:408; PGLR A:43; INAC 4:154; MDWB 13:223-232}

DARROLL, JOSEPH (Pocomoke District), captain and master of the ship *Two Brothers* in 1731. {Ref: CVPR:12}

DASHIELL (DASHIELS), ARTHUR (Pocomoke District), captain and master of the ship *Monaic* in June, 1731; master of the brigantine *Martha* in 1736 (built at Clognakilly in the Kingdom of Ireland in 1722). {Ref: CVPR:12; MDCB 82:47}

DASHIELL (DASHIELS), CHARLES (Pocomoke District), captain and master of the ship *Monaic* in October, 1730. {Ref: CVPR:12}

DASHIELL, ELIZABETH, see "George Dashiell," q.v.

DASHIELL (DASHIELDS), GEORGE (Somerset County), deputy ranger by 1715; captain by 1725; major by 1733; member of the Lower House of the Maryland Assembly, 1719-1737; colonel by 1736; court justice, 1734-1748 (quorum, 1740-1748); born Jan 31, 1690/1, died testate on Nov 7, 1748 (will probated on Nov 14, 1748; Elizabeth Dashiell, widow). {Ref: SOJR III:10; ARMD 39:151; BDML I:252; MDWB 25:516}

DASHIELL, HESTER (ESTHER), see "Robert Dashiell," q.v.

DASHIELL, JAMES (Somerset County), Protestant and probable soldier in the Revolution of 1689; signed an address and took a loyalty oath supporting the King of England and "for enabling us to defend ourselves against all invaders" on Nov 28, 1689. {Ref: ARMD 8:141}

DASHIELL (DASHIELE, DASHIELDS), JAMES (Scotland, Virginia, and Wicomico, Somerset County), soldier (rank not stated) circa 1675; paid for his services in the late expedition against the Nanticoke Indians in 1678; member of the Lower House of the Maryland Assembly, 1676-1682; paid for his services out of an assessment levied by the General Assembly for the public good in 1682; court justice, 1679-1680; military officer (rank not stated) who swore allegiance to the King & Queen of England in 1696; born circa 1634, died testate by Aug 31, 1697 (date of probate). {Ref: ARMD 7:98, 7:442, 15:175, 15:328, 20:544; BDML I:253; OSES:283, 440; MDWB 7:328; RMHF I:131}

DASHIELL (DASHIELE), JAMES, JR. (Scotland, Virginia, and Somerset County), probable soldier (rank not stated) before 1682; paid for his services from an assessment levied by the General Assembly for the public good in 1682; court justice, 1699-1708; born circa 1660, died testate by Mar 14, 1708/9 (date of probate; Isabell Dashiell, widow). {Ref: ARMD 7:443; BDML I:253; MDWB 12:332; INAC 30:423}

DASHIELL (DASHIEL), ROBERT (Somerset County), possible soldier in the 1730's and 1740's; captain before 1745; died testate by Apr 1, 1745 (date of inventory; will was written on May 11, 1744, but no date of probate was given; Hester or Esther Dashiell, widow). *Note:* Since his name does not appear on any extant militia lists between 1732 and 1745, his service was either prior to 1732 or he was a sea captain. Additional research will be necessary before drawing conclusions. {Ref: MDWB 23:673; MINV 30:440}

DATTOLEG, PATTRICK (Talbot County), sergeant who swore allegiance to the King & Queen of England in 1696. {Ref: ARMD 20:542}

DAVENPORT (DEVENPORT), RANDALL (Talbot County), captain before 1678; paid for his services in the late expedition against the Nanticoke Indians in 1678; paid for his services out of an assessment levied by the General Assembly for the public good in 1682. {Ref: ARMD 7:91, 7:440}

DAVICE, JOHN (Kent County), soldier (rank not stated) circa 1675; paid for his services in the late expedition against the Nanticoke Indians in 1678. {Ref: ARMD 7:94}

DAVIDGE, JOHN (Anne Arundel County), captain by 1729; major by 1745; born circa 1698 (aged about 77 when deposed in 1745 and aged about 80 when deposed in 1748). {Ref: MINV 15:58; MDEP:47}

DAVIES, HUMPHREY (Talbot County), soldier (rank not stated) circa 1675; paid for his services in the late expedition against the Nanticoke Indians in 1678. {Ref: ARMD 7:88}

DAVIES, JOHN (Dorchester County), soldier (rank not stated) circa 1675; paid for his services in the late expedition against the Nanticoke Indians in 1678. {Ref: ARMD 7:94}

DAVIES, JOHN (St. Mary's County), Protestant and probable soldier in the Revolution of 1689; signed an address and took a loyalty oath supporting the

King of England and the reestablishment of Lord Baltimore into power on Nov 28, 1689. {Ref: ARMD 8:146}

DAVIES, JONAS (Talbot County), soldier (rank not stated) circa 1675; paid for his services in the late expedition against the Nanticoke Indians in 1678. {Ref: ARMD 7:91}

DAVIES, SAMUELL (Somerset County), soldier (rank not stated) circa 1675; paid for his services in the late expedition against the Nanticoke Indians in 1678. {Ref: ARMD 7:98}

DAVIES, THOMAS (Charles County), soldier (rank not stated) circa 1675; paid for his services in the late expedition against the Nanticoke Indians in 1678. {Ref: ARMD 7:101}

DAVIES, WILLIAM (Cecil County), soldier (rank not stated) circa 1675; paid for his services in the late expedition against the Nanticoke Indians in 1678. {Ref: ARMD 7:95}

DAVIES, WILLIAM (Baltimore County), soldier (rank not stated) circa 1675; paid for his services in the late expedition against the Nanticoke Indians in 1678. {Ref: ARMD 7:96}

DAVIS, DAVID (Kent County), "seaman within the said county" and a "sailor (mate) belonging to the *Loves Increase* of Whitehaven" in 1697. {Ref: ARMD 25:600}

DAVIS, ELIZABETH, see "John Davis," q.v.

DAVIS, GRIFFITH (county not indicated), probable soldier (rank not stated) before 1682; paid for his services out of an assessment levied by the General Assembly for the public good in 1682. {Ref: ARMD 7:440}

DAVIS, HANNAH, see "Tamberlaine Davis," q.v.

DAVIS, HOPKIN (Talbot County), commissioned "captain of foot soldiers in Choptanck and St. Miles Rivers" on Jul 2, 1677; captain, 1702. {Ref: ARMD 5:11; CESM:44}

DAVIS, JOHN (Somerset County), Protestant and probable soldier in the Revolution of 1689; signed an address and took a loyalty oath supporting the King of England and "for enabling us to defend ourselves against all invaders" on Nov 28, 1689. {Ref: ARMD 8:141}

DAVIS, JOHN (England and Annapolis), seaman on the ship *Hartwell* of London commanded by Capt. Nicholas Humphries in March, 1697/8. {Ref: ARMD 23:397}

DAVIS, JOHN (Anne Arundel County), military officer (rank not stated) who swore allegiance to the King & Queen of England in 1696. {Ref: ARMD 20:542}

DAVIS, JOHN (St. Michael's Parish, Talbot County), captain by 1689; military officer who swore allegiance to the King & Queen of England in 1696 (name listed once as "John Davies"); born circa 1654 (aged about 50 when deposed in 1704), died by Jan 15, 1712/3 (date of probate; Elizabeth Davis, widow). {Ref: ARMD 8:504, 13:243, 20:542, 23:22; INAC 12:125, 13A:304, 35B:50; TALR 7:9; MDWB 13:497; MDEP:47}

DAVIS, JOHN (Pocomoke District), mariner in the 1730's; captain and owner of the sloop *Greyhound* in 1739 (built at Pocomoke River in 1738). {Ref: MDCB 82:74}

DAVIS, MEREDITH (Prince George's County), probable soldier by the 1730's; commissioned Ranger for Prince George's County "from Seneca Creek upwards to the Limits of the said county" on Jun 30, 1738. {Ref: MDCB 82:60}

DAVIS, MORRIS (Calvert County), Protestant and probable soldier in the Revolution of 1689; signed an address and took a loyalty oath supporting the King of England and "to reestablish Lord Baltimore in his ancient power and government" on Nov 16, 1689. {Ref: ARMD 8:132}

DAVIS, NATHANIEL (England and Annapolis), captain and commander of the ship *Sarah and Susannah* in 1696-1698 (name listed once as "Nathaniel Davies"). {Ref: ARMD 23:393, 23:466, 25:588}

DAVIS, ROBERT (England and Annapolis), seaman on the ship *Hartwell* of London commanded by Capt. Nicholas Humphries in March, 1697/8. {Ref: ARMD 23:397}

DAVIS, PHIL. (Queen Anne's County), captain by 1725. {Ref: MDAD 7:1}

DAVIS, SAMUEL (Somerset County), Protestant and probable soldier in the Revolution of 1689; signed an address and took a loyalty oath supporting the King of England and "for enabling us to defend ourselves against all invaders" on Nov 28, 1689. {Ref: ARMD 8:141}

DAVIS, TAMBERLAINE (Talbot County), captain and mariner before 1734; died testate by May 17, 1735 (date of probate; Hannah Davis, widow). {Ref: MDWB 21:433; MINV 21:196; TALR 14:417}

DAVIS, WILLIAM (Somerset County), Protestant and probable soldier in the Revolution of 1689; signed an address and took a loyalty oath supporting the King of England and "for enabling us to defend ourselves against all invaders" on Nov 28, 1689. {Ref: ARMD 8:140}

DAVIS, WILLIAM (Anne Arundel County), Quaker who was assigned to a foot company of Capt. John Norwood in 1662, but refused to serve for religious reasons and was fined accordingly. {Ref: AAGE:558}

DAVISE, WILLIAM (Kent County), soldier (rank not stated) in Capt. William Leeds (Leeads) Company by May 23, 1662, at which time he signed a petition about the misuse of company money by Capt. Thomas Brednox (Bradnox), late of Isle of Kent, deceased; born circa 1635 (aged about 25 when deposed on Dec 20, 1660). {Ref: ARMD 3:455, 54:190; INKC:125}

DAVISON, ALEXANDER (Talbot County), sailor by 1720. {Ref: MDAD 2:518}

DAVISON, THOMAS (Prince George's County), captain and master of the galley *Patuxent* riding in the Patuxent River on Feb 2, 1725/6. {Ref: PGLR M:149-150}

DAVY, ROBERT (Calvert County), Protestant and probable soldier in the Revolution of 1689; signed an address and took a loyalty oath supporting the King of England and "to reestablish Lord Baltimore in his ancient power and government" on Nov 16, 1689. {Ref: ARMD 8:131}

DAWBURNE, THOMAS (Anne Arundel County), soldier (rank not stated) circa 1675; paid for his services in the late expedition against the Nanticoke Indians in 1678. {Ref: ARMD 7:96}

DAWKINS, SIMON, see "---- Dockings," q.v.

DAWKINS, WILLIAM (Calvert County), Protestant and probable soldier in the Revolution of 1689; signed an address and took a loyalty oath supporting the King of England and "to reestablish Lord Baltimore in his ancient power and government" on Nov 16, 1689. {Ref: ARMD 8:131}

DAWSEY, JOHN (Dorchester County), ensign before 1678; paid for his services in the late expedition against the Nanticoke Indians in 1678. {Ref: ARMD 7:93}

DAWSON, ANTHONY (Dorchester County), captain by 1676; paid for his services in the late expedition against the Nanticoke Indians in 1678; captain of a foot company before 1689. {Ref: ARMD 7:93, 13:244, 15:124; INAC 3:7}

DAWSON, JOHN (Annapolis District), captain and master of the ship *John and Mary* in 1730-1731. {Ref: CVPR:12}

DAWSON, MARY, see "Ralph Dawson, Jr. and Sr.," q.v.

DAWSON (DARSON), RALPH, JR. (Talbot County), Protestant and soldier in the Revolution of 1689; signed an address and took a loyalty oath supporting the King of England and the reestablishment of Lord Baltimore into power on Nov 18, 1689; "Ralph Dawson, planter" died testate by Feb 7, 1708/9 (date of probate; Mary Dawson, widow). {Ref: ARMD 8:134; MDWB 12:11, pt. 2}

DAWSON (DARSON), RALPH, SR. (Talbot County), soldier (rank not stated) circa 1675; paid for his services in the late expedition against the Nanticoke Indians in 1678; Protestant and soldier in the Revolution of 1689; signed an address and took a loyalty oath supporting the King of England and the reestablishment of Lord Baltimore into power on Nov 18, 1689; captain before 1706; died testate by Jul 8, 1706 (date of probate; Mary Dawson, widow). {Ref: ARMD 7:91, 8:134; BDML II:860; MDWB 12:31}

DAY, ---- (county or port not indicated), captain of the brigantine *Josiah* in 1696; mentioned as being either a pirate or privateer in the 1696 deposition of James White, *q.v.* {Ref: ARMD 25:556-557; MDEP:15}

DAY, EDWARD (Somerset County), lieutenant before 1682; paid for his services out of an assessment levied by the General Assembly for the public good in 1682; possibly a captain by 1696. {Ref: ARMD 7:442-443, 25:559-560}

DAY, WILLIAM (Talbot County), soldier (rank not stated) circa 1675; paid for his services in the late expedition against the Nanticoke Indians in 1678. {Ref: ARMD 7:92}

DAYSONE, WILLIAM (Dorchester County), soldier (rank not stated) circa 1675; paid for his services in the late expedition against the Nanticoke Indians in 1678. {Ref: ARMD 7:94}

DEAKINS, JOHN (Calvert County), ranger under the command of Capt. Richard Brightwell in 1692. {Ref: ARMD 8:445}

DEALE, JOHN (Somerset County), Protestant and probable soldier in the Revolution of 1689; signed an address and took a loyalty oath supporting the King of England and "for enabling us to defend ourselves against all invaders" on Nov 28, 1689. {Ref: ARMD 8:139}

DEALE, JOHN (Somerset County), seaman by 1716. {Ref: INAC 37A:82}

DEAN, JOHN (Kent County), soldier (rank not stated) on Isle of Kent who swore allegiance to the Commonwealth of England on Apr 5, 1652. {Ref: INKC:101}

DEAN, THOMAS (St. Mary's County), captain and master of the ketch *Endeavour* of Salem in 1693. {Ref: ARMD 20:182}

DEANE, EDWARD (Charles County), soldier (rank not stated) in Capt. James Langworth's Company before 1661 (year of the captain's death, but his ammunition report was not filed until 1664 by Henry Adames); born circa 1620 (aged about 43 when deposed in 1663), died testate by Sep 8, 1671 (date of probate). {Ref: ARMD 53:493; CHLR B:379; MDWB 1:416; MDEP:49}

DEANE, GABRIELL (St. Mary's County), captain by 1679. {Ref: INAC 6:256}

DEANE, THOMAS (St. Mary's County), soldier (rank not stated) circa 1675; paid for his services in the late expedition against the Nanticoke Indians in 1678. {Ref: ARMD 7:103}

DEANE, WILLIAM (Anne Arundel County), captain and commander of the ship *Katherine* riding in Severn River on Apr 13, 1728. {Ref: AALR SY#1:375}

DE BORALE, PETER (Talbot County), soldier (rank not stated) circa 1675; paid for his services in the late expedition against the Nanticoke Indians in 1678. {Ref: ARMD 7:88}

DE COLLARY, ISAAC (Somerset County), soldier (rank not stated) circa 1675; paid for his services in the late expedition against the Nanticoke Indians in 1678. {Ref: ARMD 7:97}

DEEBLE, JEREMIAH (St. Mary's County), captain and master of a ship (no name given) riding at anchor at the mouth of the Patuxent River on Jul 1, 1695 (date of petition). {Ref: ARMD 20:306, 23:28}

DEERING, SAMUELL (St. Mary's County), soldier (rank not stated) circa 1675; paid for his services in the late expedition against the Nanticoke Indians in 1678. {Ref: ARMD 7:103}

DELAHAY, THOMAS (Talbot County), soldier (rank not stated) circa 1675; paid for his services in the late expedition against the Nanticoke Indians in 1678; Protestant and probable soldier in the Revolution of 1689; signed an address and took a loyalty oath supporting the King of England and the reestablishment of Lord Baltimore into power on Nov 28, 1689 (signature misinterpreted once as "V. Delahay" when it was most likely "T. Delahay"); died intestate on Feb 29, 1699/1700 (Eve Delahay, widow, later married Richard Holmes). {Ref: ARMD 7:88, 8:144; TALR 9:215; St. Peter's P. E. Church Records}

DELAHIDE, THOMAS (Somerset County), Protestant and probable soldier in the Revolution of 1689; signed an address and took a loyalty oath supporting the

King of England and "for enabling us to defend ourselves against all invaders" on Nov 28, 1689. {Ref: ARMD 8:141}

DELAMONTANY, JESSE (Annapolis District), captain and master of the ship *Bohemia* in 1731. {Ref: CVPR:12}

DELAPLAINE, JAMES (county or port not indicated), captain and master of the sloop *Hopewell* of New York in 1689. {Ref: ARMD 8:236}

DELAROCHE, CHARLES (St. Mary's County), soldier (rank not stated) in 1668; died testate by Jan 22, 1675/6 (date of probate; Elizabeth Delaroche, widow, was paid for his services in the late expedition against the Nanticoke Indians in 1678). {Ref: ARMD 5:35, 7:102; MDWB 2:378}

DELASATIAS, SEBASTIAN (Somerset County), soldier (rank not stated) circa 1675; paid for his services in the late expedition against the Nanticoke Indians in 1678. {Ref: ARMD 7:99}

DEMBOE, JOHN (Cecil County), soldier (rank not stated) circa 1675; paid for his services in the late expedition against the Nanticoke Indians in 1678. {Ref: ARMD 7:95}

DENAHOE (DENNEHO), DANIELL (Somerset County), soldier (rank not stated) circa 1675; paid for his services in the late expedition against the Nanticoke Indians in 1678; "Daniel Denneho, Sr." died testate by Jan 10, 1704/5 (date of probate; Martha Denneho, widow). {Ref: ARMD 7:99, 7:100; MDWB 12:8}

DENAIRE, JOHN (Dorchester County), soldier (rank not stated) circa 1675; paid for his services in the late expedition against the Nanticoke Indians in 1678. {Ref: ARMD 7:93}

DENICE, WILLIAM (Somerset County), captain and master of the ship *Mary* in 1698. {Ref: ARMD 23:281}

DENNARD, SAMUELL (county or port not indicated), captain and master of the ship *Loyalty* of Biddeford in 1691. {Ref: ARMD 8:240}

DENNEHO, MARTHA, see "Daniell Denahoe," q.v.

DENNIS, DONNOCK (Virginia and Pocomoke, Somerset County), soldier (rank not stated) circa 1675; paid for his services in the late expedition against the Nanticoke Indians in 1678; died testate by Mar 23, 1716/7 (date of probate; Elizabeth Dennis, widow); his first name was spelled four different ways: Donagh, Donnock, Donnack, and Dennack. {Ref: ARMD 7:100; OSES:280, 441; MDWB 14:278}

DENNIS, ELIZABETH, see "Donnock Dennis," q.v.

DENNIS, JOHN (Annapolis District and Somerset County), captain and master of the snow *Samuel* of Maryland in 1734; master and owner of the sloop *Pocomoke* in 1734-1735; master and owner of the sloop *Molly and Betty* (built in Somerset County) in 1736. {Ref: MDGZ, Jul 19, 1734; MDCB 82:25, 45}

DENNIS, LEVIN (Somerset County), colonel before 1715. {Ref: SOJR III:1}

DENNIS, RICHARD (Somerset County), Protestant and probable soldier in the Revolution of 1689; signed an address and took a loyalty oath supporting the

King of England and "for enabling us to defend ourselves against all invaders" on Nov 28, 1689. {Ref: ARMD 8:141}

DENNIS, ROBERT (St. Mary's County), captain by 1651. {Ref: ARMD 3:265}

DENNY, CHRISTOPHER (Talbot County), soldier (rank not stated) circa 1675; paid for his services in the late expedition against the Nanticoke Indians in 1678. {Ref: ARMD 7:88}

DENNY, PHILLIP (Talbot County), soldier (rank not stated) circa 1675; paid for his services in the late expedition against the Nanticoke Indians in 1678. {Ref: ARMD 7:88}

DENT, ANN, see "George Dent," q.v.

DENT, ELIZABETH, see "William Dent," q.v.

DENT, GEORGE (Charles County), captain by 1726; member of the Lower House of the Maryland Assembly, 1719-1727; colonel by 1734; provincial court justice, 1728-1754; born Sep 27, 1690 (aged about 45 when deposed in 1736 and aged about 46 when deposed in April, 1737), died testate on May 12, 1754 (will probated Jun 15, 1754; Ann Dent, widow). {Ref: ARMD 38:368; CHLR T#2:368; BDML I:262; MDWB 29:193; MDEP:50}

DENT, JANE PITTMAN GRAY, see "Peter Dent," q.v.

DENT, JOHN (St. Mary's County), soldier (rank not stated) who "rendered military servuce during the Indian wars of the colony" before 1679; soldier who lost a bridle and saddle at the Susquehannah Fort in 1679; captain by 1689; Protestant and soldier in the Revolution of 1689, empowered to command a troop of horse for Chaptico Hundred; signed an address and took a loyalty oath supporting the King of England and the reestablishment of Lord Baltimore into power on Nov 28, 1689; captain of foot troops in St. Mary's County in 1694; died testate by May 5, 1712 (date of probate; brother of "Thomas Dent," *q.v.*). See "James Bowling," q.v. {Ref: ARMD 7:148, 8:146, 13:241, 15:326, 15:256, 20:58, 20:106, 23:18; RMHF I:139, II:273; MDWB 13:442}

DENT, PETER (St. Mary's and Somerset Counties), Protestant and soldier in the Revolution of 1689; signed an address and took a loyalty oath supporting the King of England and "for enabling us to defend ourselves against all invaders" on Nov 28, 1689; military officer (rank not stated) who swore allegiance to the King & Queen of England in 1696; member of the Lower House of the Maryland Assembly, 1701-1704; deputy commissary, 1700-1708; born circa 1665, son of Col. Thomas Dent, *q.v.*, died testate by Mar 7, 1710/1 (date of probate; Jane Pittman Gray Dent, widow). {Ref: ARMD 8:141, 20:544; BDML I:264-265; MDWB 13:207}

DENT, REBECCA, see "Thomas Dent," q.v.

DENT, THOMAS (England and St. Mary's County), colonel circa 1650; sheriff, 1654; court justice, 1659; died testate by Apr 21, 1676 (date of probate; Rebecca Dent, widow). {Ref: RMHF II:273; MDWB 5:19}

DENT, THOMAS (Charles County), captain by 1708; sheriff, 1711-1714; member of the Lower House of the Maryland Assembly, 1715-1718; born circa 1685-

1686 (aged about 39 when deposed in 1725); committed to debtor's prison (due to gambling) in 1722; died penniless in 1725. {Ref: ARMD 30:107, 30:359, 33:175; BDML I:265-266; CHLR #2:190; MDEP:50}

DENT, WILLIAM (St. Mary's and Charles Counties), soldier before 1689 who served in the early Indian wars and subsequently rose to the rank of colonel; captain of foot troops by 1694; coroner and clerk of the indictments in 1694; commissioned "naval officer for the upper parts of Charles County, beginning at Portobacco and upwards to the head of the county" on Nov 19, 1694 (serving to 1704); major, 1695; military officer who swore allegiance to the King & Queen of England in 1696; member of the Lower House of the Maryland Assembly, 1694-1704; in May, 1702, "finding his health much impaired and living very remote from the Seat of Government" he requested to be discharged from service as Attorney General of this Province; born circa 1660 (aged about 37 when deposed in 1697), eldest son of Col. Thomas Dent, *q.v.*; died testate by Feb 17, 1704/5 (date of probate; Elizabeth Dent, widow). {Ref: ARMD 20:109, 20:130, 20:186, 20:543, 24:128, 25:14, 25:597, 38:75; BDML I:266; RMHF II:273; CHLR C#2:143, H#2:303; INAC 25:390; MDWB 3:475; MDEP:51}

DENTON, HENRY (Anne Arundel County), naval officer for the port of Annapolis in 1697; appointed register of the Vice Admiralty of the Colony of Maryland on Apr 29, 1697. {Ref: ARMD 23:109, 23:321}

DENTON, JAMES (St. Mary's County), ensign before 1682; paid for his services out of an assessment levied by the General Assembly for the public good in 1682. {Ref: ARMD 7:441}

DERD, BENJAMIN (Somerset County), soldier (rank not stated) circa 1675; paid for his services in the late expedition against the Nanticoke Indians in 1678. {Ref: ARMD 7:97}

DERRICUTT, JOHN (Kent County), captain before 1690; captain and master of the ship *Sunflower* of Barnstaple (or Barnstable) in 1690 (name misinterpreted once as "John Donicott"); on Mar 3, 1725/6 he was mentioned in the deposition of George Copper, aged about 56, who was a former servant of Col. Hance Hanson, *q.v.* {Ref: ARMD 8:238; CFES 2:83; KELR JS#W:543}

DERUMPLE, JAMES, see "John Clements," q.v.

DE SOUSA, MATHIAS (St. Mary's County), captain and skipper of a ship (no name given) in 1642. See "John Prettiman," q.v. {Ref: ARMD 4:138; FMDP:261}

DEVALL, JOHN (Anne Arundel County), military officer (rank not stated) who swore allegiance to the King & Queen of England in 1696. {Ref: ARMD 20:541}

DEVONISH, ROBERT (Talbot County), soldier (rank not stated) circa 1675; paid for his services in the late expedition against the Nanticoke Indians in 1678; one "Robert Deonish" (Devonish?) died testate in Kent County by Sep 9, 1701 (date of probate). {Ref: ARMD 7:92; MDWB 11:115}

DEYZER, S. (Charles County), Protestant and probable soldier in the Revolution of 1689; signed an address and took a loyalty oath supporting the King of

England and the reestablishment of Lord Baltimore into power on Nov 28, 1689. {Ref: ARMD 8:138}

DIAMOND, JOHN (Baltimore County), soldier (rank not stated) circa 1675; paid for his services in the late expedition against the Nanticoke Indians in 1678. {Ref: ARMD 7:95}

DICKENSON, ---- (Dorchester County), captain of a sloop (no name given) damaged by ice in the Nanticoke River in 1728. {Ref: MDGZ, Jan 7, 1728/9}

DICKENSON, REBECCA, see "John Dickinson," q.v.

DICKINSON, CHARLES (Prince George's County), seaman "belonging to the ship *Severn*" under Capt. John Carpenter in 1729. {Ref: PGLR M:509}

DICKINSON, EDWARD (Calvert County), Protestant and probable soldier in the Revolution of 1689; signed an address and took a loyalty oath supporting the King of England and "to reestablish Lord Baltimore in his ancient power and government" on Nov 16, 1689. {Ref: ARMD 8:131}

DICKINSON, HANNAH, see "James Dickinson," q.v.

DICKINSON, JAMES (Bullenbrook Hundred, Talbot County), captain by 1722; commander of the ship *William and Hannah* in 1722 and captain of the same ship riding in South River on Jan 30, 1723/4; listed as a taxable in Talbot County in 1733; captain and merchant; died testate by Jan 1, 1738/9 (date of probate; Hannah Dickinson, widow). {Ref: AALR RCW#2:221; PGLR I:465; CESM:25; MDWB 22:12}

DICKINSON, JOHN (Talbot County), soldier (rank not stated) circa 1675; paid for his services in the late expedition against the Nanticoke Indians in 1678 (name also listed as "John Dickyson" and "John Dickison" and "John Dickienson"); born circa 1633-1634 (aged about 79 or 80 when deposed in 1713), died testate by Apr 28, 1718 (date of probate; Rebecca Dickenson, widow). {Ref: ARMD 7:89; MDEP:52; MDWB 14:582}

DICKINSON, WALTER (Talbot County), soldier (rank not stated) circa 1675; paid for his services in the late expedition against the Nanticoke Indians in 1678 (name also listed as "Walter Dickison" and "Walter Dickysone" and "Walter Dickenson"); died testate by Apr 4, 1681 (date of probate). {Ref: ARMD 7:90, 15:254; MDWB 2:136}

DICKINSON, WILLIAM (Talbot County), soldier (rank not stated) circa 1675; paid for his services in the late expedition against the Nanticoke Indians in 1678 (name also listed as "William Dickison" and "William Dickysone"); died intestate by Apr 28, 1718 (date of administration account). {Ref: ARMD 7:87; MDAD 6:26}

DIEGAS, DEVORAUX, see "Devorex Dregors," q.v.

DIGGES (DIGGS), WILLIAM (England, Virginia, and St. Mary's and Charles Counties), captain of horse in Virginia in 1674; served in Bacon's Rebellion, 1676; sheriff of York County, 1679; captain of St. Mary's County militia by 1680; colonel and member of the Maryland Council, 1681-1688; keeper of the Great Seal of this province in 1684; officer of the City of St. Mary's in 1686;

commander of the Catholic forces during the Revolution of 1689; born circa 1650, died testate by Jul 24, 1697 (date of probate; Elizabeth Digges, widow). {Ref: ARMD 5:309, 5:462, 5:527, 7:123, 15:269, 17:74, 17:196; BDML I:271-272; CHLR Q:31; INAC 15:318; RMHF I:146-147, II:137; MDWB 7:292}

DIGGES, WILLIAM (Baltimore County), Protestant and probable soldier in the Revolution of 1689; signed an address and took a loyalty oath supporting the King of England and the reestablishment of Lord Baltimore into power on Nov 28, 1689. {Ref: ARMD 8:137}

DIMMIT (DEMMITT, DAMMIT), WILLIAM (Baltimore County), soldier (rank not stated) circa 1675; paid for his services in the late expedition against the Nanticoke Indians in 1678; died intestate by Mar 31, 1711 (date of administration bond). {Ref: ARMD 7:96; BBCF:172}

DINE, JOSHUA, see "Joshua Doyne," q.v.

DISHAROON, LEWIS (Wicomico Hundred, Somerset County), constable by 1709; Indian interpreter circa 1721-1725 (name also listed as "Luoss Disharun" and "Lewis Dishroon"); born circa 1678 (aged about 55 when deposed in 1733), died testate by Jun 7, 1745 (date of probate). {Ref: SOJR II:60; CESM:49, 61; MDEP:52; MDWB 24:182}

DISINGTON, JOHN (St. Mary's County), captain of a ship (no name given) in 1696. {Ref: INAC 13B:96}

DISNEY, WILLIAM (Anne Arundel County), military officer (rank not stated) who swore allegiance to the King & Queen of England in 1696; died testate by Jun 20, 1721 (date of probate). {Ref: ARMD 20:542; MDWB 16:460}

DIXON, AMBROSE (England, Virginia, and Annamessex, Somerset County), member of the Lower House of the Maryland Assembly in 1671; soldier (rank not stated) circa 1675; paid for his services in the late expedition against the Nanticoke Indians in 1678; born circa 1620, died testate and buried on Apr 12, 1687 (will written on Apr 7, 1686, but not probated until Aug 10, 1688; Mary Dixon, widow). *Note:* Ambrose was a soldier, an innkeeper, and an elected official in spite of the fact that he was a Quaker (their tenets did not tolerate bearing arms, fighting, drinking, and taking oaths). See "Thomas Dixon," q.v. {Ref: ARMD 7:99, 7:100; BDML I:272; OSES:279, 442; MDWB 6:22}

DIXON, DANIEL (England and Talbot County), mariner by 1726; captain, of Whitehaven, St. Bees Parish, County Cumberland, by Feb 25, 1730/1 when he was granted power of attorney to manage the lands of Margaret Wilson, widow, in Maryland; captain and master of the ship *Dilligence* in 1731; mariner, of Talbot County, on Feb 17, 1735 (date of deed); probably died in England after 1745. {Ref: TALR 13:643, 14:142; CVPR:12; CFES 3:130}

DIXON, MARY, see "Ambrose Dixon," q.v.

DIXON, SUSANNA, see "Thomas Dixon," q.v.

DIXON, THOMAS (Virginia and Annamessex, Somerset County), soldier (rank not stated) circa 1675; paid for his services in the late expedition against the Nanticoke Indians in 1678; Protestant and soldier in the Revolution of 1689;

signed an address and took a loyalty oath supporting the King of England and "for enabling us to defend ourselves against all invaders" on Nov 28, 1689; member of the Lower House of the Maryland Assembly, 1694-1697; military officer (rank not stated) who swore allegiance to the King & Queen of England in 1696; captain by 1697; court justice, 1694-1704; name listed as "Capt. Thomas Dickson" in 1709; born circa 1655 (son of Ambrose Dixon, *q.v.*), died testate by May 5, 1720 (date of probate; Susanna Dixon, widow). {Ref: ARMD 7:100, 8:141; 20:544; SOJR I:95, II:175; BDML I:273; MDWB 16:100}

DOAKES, HENRY (Calvert County), Protestant and probable soldier in the Revolution of 1689; signed an address and took a loyalty oath supporting the King of England and "to reestablish Lord Baltimore in his ancient power and government" on Nov 16, 1689. {Ref: ARMD 8:132}

DOBBINS, EDWARD (England and Anne Arundel County), captain and master of the ship *Mary* of London riding at anchor in South River on Sep 30, 1701. {Ref: AALR WT#2:330}

DOBBS (DOBES), JOHN (Kent and Queen Anne's Counties), soldier (rank not stated) in Capt. William Leeds (Leeads) Company by May 23, 1662, at which time he signed a petition about the misuse of company money by Capt. Thomas Brednox (Bradnox), late of Isle of Kent, deceased; soldier (rank not stated) circa 1675; paid for his services in the late expedition against the Nanticoke Indians in 1678; "John Dobs" died testate in Queen Anne's County by Apr 14, 1720 (date of probate of his nuncupative will). {Ref: ARMD 3:455, 7:94; MDWB 16:286}

DOCKINGS, ---- (Baltimore County), sergeant before 1682; paid for his services out of an assessment levied by the General Assembly for the public good in 1682. *Note:* This could be "Simon Dawkins (Dockings)" who died intestate by Jun 1, 1686 at which time an administration bond was posted by Col. George Wells, *q.v.* {Ref: ARMD 7:441; BBCF:161}

DOCWRA (DOCKWRA), THOMAS (Anne Arundel County), captain by 1712; member of the Lower House of the Maryland Assembly, representing Annapolis in 1712-1714; died intestate by September, 1719. {Ref: ARMD 29:49, 29:105, 29:125, 29:391, 29:415; BDML I:273}

DODD, RICHARD (Charles County), Protestant and probable soldier in the Revolution of 1689; signed an address and took a loyalty oath supporting the King of England and the reestablishment of Lord Baltimore into power on Nov 28, 1689. {Ref: ARMD 8:138}

DODSON, SAMUELL (Potomac District), captain and master of the ship *Robert and Samuell* in 1696-1697. {Ref: ARMD 23:172, 23:290}

DODSTONE, RICHARD (county not indicated), probable soldier (rank not stated) before 1682; paid for his services out of an assessment levied by the General Assembly for the public good in 1682. {Ref: ARMD 7:439}

DOLBERY, WILLIAM (England and St. Mary's County), captain and master of the ship *Sarum Merchant* of Poole in 1684; born circa 1644 (aged about 40 when deposed in 1684). {Ref: ARMD 17:304}

DOLTEN (DOLLEN?), BENJAMIN (England and Cecil County), mariner and merchant of London; captain of the ship *Anne* of London before 1702; died testate by Mar 3, 1700/1 (date of inventory in Cecil County). {Ref: CELR 1:316; INAC 21:38}

DOLTY, GEORGE (St. Mary's County), sergeant, 1652. {Ref: ARMD 10:134}

DONALDSON (DONNILSON), JOHN (Somerset County), captain by 1733; master of the sloop *Success* (built at Hunting Creek in Accomack County, Virginia in 1727) in 1734. {Ref: MDCB 82:19; MDAD 11:721}

DONICOTT, JOHN, see "John Derricutt," q.v.

DONOVAN, ---- (Calvert County), colonel by 1686 (name appeared on a list of debts due Dr. Patrick Innis, deceased). {Ref: INAC 9:306}

DORMAN, JOHN (Somerset County), soldier (rank not stated) circa 1675; paid for his services in the late expedition against the Nanticoke Indians in 1678; died intestate by Apr 2, 1725 (date of administration account). {Ref: ARMD 7:97; MDAD 6:340}

DORMAN, JOHN (Calvert County), captain before 1702; died testate by Apr 28, 1702 (date of probate; Mary Dorman, widow). {Ref: MDWB 11:194; INAC 21:398}

DORMAN, MATTHEW (Virginia and Somerset County), soldier (rank not stated) circa 1675; paid for his services in the late expedition against the Nanticoke Indians in 1678 (name misinterpreted once as "Mathew Dormer"); paid for his services out of an assessment levied by the General Assembly for the public good in 1682; Protestant and probable soldier in the Revolution of 1689; signed an address and took a loyalty oath supporting the King of England and "for enabling us to defend ourselves against all invaders" on Nov 28, 1689; died testate by Jan 16, 1692/3 (date of probate; Phillipa Dorman, widow). {Ref: ARMD 7:99-100, 7:442, 8:141; MDWB 6:39}

DORMAN, PHILLIPA, see "Mathew Dorman," q.v.

DORR, JOHN (Somerset County), soldier (rank not stated) circa 1675; paid for his services in the late expedition against the Nanticoke Indians in 1678. {Ref: ARMD 7:99}

DORRELL, JOHN (Talbot County), captain and master of the ship *Sea Flower* in 1680. {Ref: ARMD 69:310-311}

DORRINGTON, ELIZABETH, see "William Dorrington," q.v.

DORRINGTON, RICHARD (Calvert and St. Mary's Counties), soldier (rank not stated) circa 1675; paid for his services in the late expedition against the Nanticoke Indians in 1678. {Ref: ARMD 7:103}

DORRINGTON, WILLIAM (Calvert and Dorchester Counties), soldier (rank not stated) circa 1675; paid for his services in the late expedition against the Nanticoke Indians in 1678; court justice (quorum), 1679; died testate by Jun 23,

1697 (date of probate; Elizabeth Dorrington, widow). {Ref: ARMD 7:94, 15:254, 15:326; LMCL:22; MDWB 7:290}

DORSEY, ANNE, see "Joshua Dorsey," q.v.

DORSEY, COMFORT, see "John Dorsey," q.v.

DORSEY (DARCEY, D'ARCY), EDWARD (Virginia, and Anne Arundel and Baltimore Counties), captain by 1678; paid for service of 15 days (and 12 days for two men, not named) in the late expedition against the Nanticoke Indians in 1678; major in command of the militia of Anne Arundel County in 1687; major of horse troops in 1689; Protestant and major in the Revolution of 1689; signed an address and took a loyalty oath supporting the King of England and the reestablishment of Lord Baltimore into power on Nov 28, 1689; member of the Lower House of the Maryland Assembly, representing Anne Arundel County, 1694-1697; major, commissioned again on Oct 9, 1694; military officer who swore allegiance to the King & Queen of England in 1696; major who "has a great Charge of a Wife & twelve Children the most of them being very small" (part of statement by Rev. Dr. Thomas Bray to the Maryland Assembly on May 4, 1700); member of the Lower House of the Maryland Assembly, representing Baltimore County, 1701-1705; colonel on the south side of the Patapsco in 1701-1703, in Elk Ridge Hundred in 1703, and on the upper part of the north side of Patapsco in 1704; born circa 1645, died testate by Dec 31, 1705 (date of probate; Margaret Dorsey, widow, who later married John Israel). See "Joshua Dorsey" and "Samuel Dorsey," q.v. {Ref: ARMD 5:462, 5:554, 7:96, 7:149, 7:611, 8:137, 13:242, 20:153, 20:541, 23:15, 24:19, 24:129, 25:596, 38:72; BCTL:21, 33, 45; BBCF:178; FAAH:40, 55-59, 190, 345; BDML I:274; AALR IB#2:252; HCCM:464-469; RMHF I:148; MDWB 3:725; Dorsey and Nimmo's *The Dorsey Family* (1947), pp. 8-25}

DORSEY, EDWARD (Anne Arundel County), a seafaring apprentice in 1697, "borne and belonging to this county, son of Capt. John Dorsey," *q.v.* {Ref: ARMD 25:596}

DORSEY, JANE, see "Samuel Dorsey," q.v.

DORSEY, JOHN (Virginia, and Anne Arundel and Baltimore Counties), captain by 1695; military officer (rank not stated) who swore allegiance to the King & Queen of England in 1696; captain and member of the Lower House of the Maryland Assembly, 1692-1693, 1701-1704; member of the Maryland Council, 1710-1714; captain on the south side of the Patapsco, 1701; captain, 1711-1714; born circa 1645, died testate by Mar 22, 1714/5 (date of probate; Pleasance Dorsey, widow). See "Edward Dorsey," q.v. {Ref: ARMD 20:541, 24:128, 25:294, 29:4; BDML I:275; BCTL:21; MDWB 14:26}

DORSEY, JOHN (Anne Arundel and Baltimore Counties), captain of militia by 1717; sheriff, 1713-1715; colonel and member of the Lower House of the Maryland Assembly, representing Baltimore County, 1721-1722; county commissioner by 1724; heavily in debt, he left his family in Maryland in 1726 to avoid imprisonment (possibly headed for the Carolinas); born circa 1682, died after 1736 (Comfort Dorsey, widow, was an inkeeper in Baltimore County in 1745). {Ref: ARMD 34:278; BDML I:275-276; BALR IS#G; BBCF:179; Dorsey and Nimmo's *The Dorsey Family* (1947), pp. 123-126}

DORSEY, JOSHUA (Anne Arundel County), a seafaring apprentice in 1697, "borne and belonging to this county, son of Major Edward Dorsey," *q.v.*; justice, 1714-1715; captain of the Elk Ridge militia in 1742; born circa 1686, died testate by Feb 6, 1747/8 (date of probate; Anne Dorsey, widow). {Ref: ARMD 25:596, 39:42, 39:125; FAAH:345-346; MDWB 25:315-318}

DORSEY, PLEASANCE, see "John Dorsey," q.v.

DORSEY, SAMUEL (Anne Arundel County), a seafaring apprentice in 1697, "borne and belonging to this county, son of Major Edward Dorsey," *q.v.*; born circa 1682, died testate on Feb 13, 1724/5 (nuncupative will probated on Feb 14, 1724/5; Jane Dorsey, widow). {Ref: ARMD 25:596; MDWB 18:342}

DOSON, THOMAS (Anne Arundel County), military officer (rank not stated) who swore allegiance to the King & Queen of England in 1696. {Ref: ARMD 20:542}

DOUGLAS, JOHN (Scotland and Charles County), lieutenant by 1665; captain by 1675; captain of a party of rangers ordered "to Range the woods about Pascattoway & the Susquahanough ffort, to take upp all such horses as they shall finde that were lost by the Souldiers in the late Expedition against the Susquahanough Indians" on Nov 3, 1675; major on the Council of War in July, 1676; colonel of militia of Charles and St. Mary's Counties, 1677-1678; member of the Lower House of the Maryland Assembly, 1676-1678 (name also listed as "John Duglas" and "John Douglass" and "John Dougles"); born in 1636 (aged about 21 when deposed in 1657 and aged about 25 when deposed in 1661), died testate by Jan 27, 1678/9 (date of probate; Sarah Douglas, widow, later married Ralph Smith). {Ref: ARMD 7:134, 15:56, 15:59, 15:99, 15:101, 41:28, 51:223, 53:60, 53:621; BDML I:280; RMHF II:325; CHLR F:216, H:1, 291; INAC 1:394, 4:191; MDWB 9:97}

DOUGLAS, JOSEPH (Charles County), colonel circa 1730; born circa 1671-1676 (aged about 65 when deposed in 1736, aged about 63 when deposed in 1737, and aged about 66 when deposed in 1742), died testate by Nov 23, 1756 (date of probate: Katherine Douglas, widow). {Ref: RMHF II:325-326; MDWB 30:274; MDEP:54}

DOUGLAS, KATHERINE, see "Joseph Douglas," q.v.

DOUGLAS, SARAH, see "John Douglas," q.v.

DOUNKAN (DOWNKEN), ANDREW (Anne Arundel County), captain and commander of the ship *Severn* riding in South River on Feb 16, 1722/3; commander of the ship *William* riding in Severn River on Sep 12, 1727. {Ref: AALR RCW#2:98, SY#1:297}

DOUTY (DOWTY), PETER (France and Somerset County), soldier (rank not stated) circa 1675; paid for his services in the late expedition against the Nanticoke Indians in 1678; died testate by May 6, 1710 (date of probate). {Ref: ARMD 7:98; MDWB 13:128}

DOVERIGNE, JOHN (St. Mary's County), captain by 1720. {Ref: MDAD 3:76}

DOWDALL, JOHN (Back Creek, Cecil County), major by 1723; died testate by Jan 1, 1728/9 (date of probate). {Ref: BDML II:815; CFES 2:145; INCC:135; MDWB 19:592; MINV 16:118}

DOWELL, ALEXANDER (Dorchester County), soldier (rank not stated) circa 1675; paid for his services in the late expedition against the Nanticoke Indians in 1678. {Ref: ARMD 7:93}

DOWLIN, WILLIAM (Talbot County), corporal who swore allegiance to the King & Queen of England in 1696. {Ref: ARMD 20:542}

DOWLING, RICHARD (Potomac District), captain and master of the ship *George* in 1697. {Ref: ARMD 23:172}

DOWNALL, JAMES (Calvert County), Protestant and probable soldier in the Revolution of 1689; signed an address and took a loyalty oath supporting the King of England and "to reestablish Lord Baltimore in his ancient power and government" on Nov 16, 1689. {Ref: ARMD 8:132}

DOWNES, JAMES (Talbot County), Protestant and probable soldier in the Revolution of 1689; signed an address and took a loyalty oath supporting the King of England and the reestablishment of Lord Baltimore into power on Nov 28, 1689. {Ref: ARMD 8:144}

DOWNING, HUGH (Talbot County), soldier (rank not stated) circa 1675; paid for his services in the late expedition against the Nanticoke Indians in 1678. {Ref: ARMD 7:92}

DOYNE, JOSHUA (St. Mary's County), captain by 1676; justice of the peace, 1677; court justice, 1679 (quorum, 1685); he was probably the "Joshua Dine" who was paid for his services out of an assessment levied by the General Assembly for the public good in 1682; sheriff, 1683; captain, 1687; died testate by Aug 16, 1698 (date of probate; Jane Doyne, widow). {Ref: ARMD 7:441, 15:66, 15:124, 15:153, 15:256, 15:326, 17:142, 17:181-182, 17:379; INAC 8:364, 9:324, 17:97; MDWB 6:169}

DRAPER, ALEXANDER (Virginia, and Annamessex, Somerset County, and Sussex County, Delaware), soldier (rank not stated) circa 1675; paid for his services in the late expedition against the Nanticoke Indians in 1678; located in Whorekill, Delaware in 1677. {Ref: ARMD 7:97; OSES:279, 443}

DRAPER, ELIZABETH, see "Lawrence Draper," q.v.

DRAPER, LAWRENCE (county not indicated), mariner by 1734; captain and master of the brigantine *Sea Nymph* (built in Dorchester County) in 1735. {Ref: MDCB 82:31}

DRAPER (DRYPER), LAWRENCE (England, and Anne Arundel and Baltimore Counties), soldier (rank not stated) circa 1675; paid for his services in the late expedition against the Nanticoke Indians in 1678; military officer (rank not stated) who swore allegiance to the King & Queen of England in 1696; captain by 1701; member of the Lower House of the Maryland Assembly, representing Anne Arundel County, 1701-1704; captain in Spesutie Hundred, Baltimore County, 1704; died testate by Aug 5, 1713 (date of probate; Elizabeth Draper, widow). {Ref: ARMD 7:96, 20:541, 24:224; BCTL:48; BBCF:184; BDML I:282; MDWB 13:559; INAC 35A:76}

DRAPER, NATHANIELL (Patuxent District), captain and master of the ship *Mary and Abigail* in 1730-1731. {Ref: CVPR:12}

DREGORS (DREGHOS, DREGAS), DEVOREX (Somerset County), Protestant and probable soldier in the Revolution of 1689; signed an address and took a loyalty oath supporting the King of England and "for enabling us to defend ourselves against all invaders" on Nov 28, 1689 (name misinterpreted once as "Devoraux Diegas"); died by 1709. {Ref: ARMD 8:139; SOJR II:20-23, 52-53}

DRESDAN, DAVID (Somerset County), Protestant and probable soldier in the Revolution of 1689; signed an address and took a loyalty oath supporting the King of England and "for enabling us to defend ourselves against all invaders" on Nov 28, 1689. {Ref: ARMD 8:141}

DREW, ANTHONY (Baltimore County), captain by 1711; died testate by May 17, 1720 (date of probate; Margaret Drew, widow). See "Anto. Crew," q.v. {Ref: ARMD 29:13; MDWB 16:73; BBCF:185}

DRINCK, JOHN, see "John Dunch," q.v.

DRISFEILD, NATHANIELL (Kent County), soldier (rank not stated) circa 1675; paid for his services in the late expedition against the Nanticoke Indians in 1678. {Ref: ARMD 7:94}

DRIVER, MATTHEW (England and Talbot County), captain and master of the brigantine *Mary* riding in Great Choptank River on Apr 2, 1706. {Ref: TALR 9:380}

DRIVER (DRYVER), ROBERT (England and Talbot County), mariner and sailor on the ship *Relief* of New Castle commanded by Capt. John Anderson in 1692. {Ref: ARMD 13:334-335}

DRUETT, ROBERT (county not indicated), probable soldier (rank not stated) before 1682; paid for his services out of an assessment levied by the General Assembly for the public good in 1682. {Ref: ARMD 7:441}

DRUMOND, RICHARD (Somerset County), captain by 1716. {Ref: SOJR III:180}

DUCK, ROBERT (St. Mary's County), captain and master of a ship (no name given) riding at anchor at the mouth of the Patuxent River on Jul 1, 1695 (date of petition). {Ref: ARMD 20:306}

DUDLEY, RICHARD (Talbot County), soldier (rank not stated) circa 1675; paid for his services in the late expedition against the Nanticoke Indians in 1678; died testate by May 5, 1702 (date of probate). {Ref: ARMD 7:89; MDWB 11:250}

DUDSON, RICHARD (Dorchester County), soldier (rank not stated) circa 1675; paid for his services in the late expedition against the Nanticoke Indians in 1678. {Ref: ARMD 7:93}

DUE, PATRICK, see "Richard Morton," q.v.

DUEBERRY, THOMAS (St. Mary's County), soldier (rank not stated) circa 1675; paid for his services in the late expedition against the Nanticoke Indians in 1678. {Ref: ARMD 7:102}

DUELL, JAMES (Dorchester County), soldier (rank not stated) circa 1675; paid for his services in the late expedition against the Nanticoke Indians in 1678. {Ref: ARMD 7:93}

DUFFILL, DANIEL (St. Mary's County), soldier (rank not stated) in 1642; paid for 3 weeks' service under Capt. William Brainthwaite in November, 1642. {Ref: ARMD 3:119, 3:122}

DUGGINS, MICHAEL (St. Mary's County), captain and mariner, 1644. {Ref: ARMD 4:300}

DUING, JOHN (Cecil County), military officer (rank not stated) who swore allegiance to the King & Queen of England in 1696. {Ref: ARMD 20:546}

DUKE, JAMES (Calvert County), "was known as Captain James Duke and was a staunch supporter of Lord Baltimore at the time of his Protestant Revolution" in 1689; died intestate circa 1692. {Ref: HCCM:258; RMHF I:152}

DULAP, NINIAN (Somerset County), Protestant and probable soldier in the Revolution of 1689; signed an address and took a loyalty oath supporting the King of England and "for enabling us to defend ourselves against all invaders" on Nov 28, 1689. {Ref: ARMD 8:141}

DUMARESQ, NICHOLAS (Annapolis District), captain of a ship (no name given) in 1698. {Ref: ARMD 23:404}

DUNCAN (DUNKAN), JAMES (Somerset County), Protestant and probable soldier in the Revolution of 1689; signed an address and took a loyalty oath supporting the King of England and "for enabling us to defend ourselves against all invaders" on Nov 28, 1689; died testate by Sep 12, 1696 (date of probate; Elizabeth Dunkan, widow). {Ref: ARMD 8:141; MDWB 7:241}

DUNCH, JOHN (England and Anne Arundel County), mariner of London before 1668; captain and master of the ship *Baltamore* of London in 1668-1673; land owner in Maryland by 1678 (name misinterpreted once as "John Drinck" and once as "John Dunck"). {Ref: ARMD 65:148-149; AALR PK:178; INAC 2:224}

DUNCH, WALTER (England and Anne Arundel County), mariner of London by 1666; land owner in Maryland by 1678 (name misinterpreted once as "Walter Dunck"). {Ref: AALR PK:178; LMCL:22}

DUNKAN, ELIZABETH, see "John Duncan," q.v.

DUNKIN, JOHN (England, and Kent and Queen Anne's Counties), captain and commander of the ship *Chester River* riding at anchor in the Chester River on Apr 14, 1726 and May 17, 1727. {Ref: QALR IK#C:47, 118; MDAD 12:613}

DUNKIN, TOBIAS (Calvert County), seaman on a ship commanded by Capt. Ralph Story in 1662; born circa 1630 (aged about 32 when deposed on Mar 15, 1662/3). {Ref: ARMD 49:12-15}

DUNN, HENRY (England and St. Mary's County), carpenter on the ship *Ruth* in 1676. {Ref: ARMD 51:474, 66:302}

DUNN, JOSEPH (Anne Arundel County), captain and commander of the galley *Bird* riding at anchor in South River on Apr 10, 1717 and Feb 1, 1717/8; died intestate by Jun 13, 1718 (date of inventory). {Ref: AALR IB#2:347, 426; MINV 1:15; MDAD 1:17}

DUNN (DUN), ROBERT (Kent County), captain before 1732; "Robert Dun, Sr." was born circa 1674 (aged about 52 when deposed in 1726) and "Robert Dunn, son of Robert" was born circa 1693 (aged about 39 when deposed in 1732). Additional research will be necessary before drawing conclusions. {Ref: INKC:179; MDEP:56}

DUNN (DUNNE), ROBERT (Kent County), soldier (rank not stated) on Isle of Kent who swore allegiance to the Commonwealth of England on Apr 5, 1652; born circa 1630 (aged about 26 when deposed on Jul 1, 1656). {Ref: ARMD 54:65; INKC:101, 108}

DUNSCOMB, JONATHAN (Pocomoke District), captain and master of the ship *St. Andrew* in 1730. {Ref: CVPR:12}

DUNSCOMB (DUNSCOMBE), PETER (England and Annapolis), captain and commander of the ship *Union*, of Topsham, riding in Severn River on Apr 19, 1728 and Apr 21, 1729 and Jun 11, 1730 and Nov 30, 1730. {Ref: AALR SY#1:382; MDGZ, Apr 22, 1729 and Jun 16, 1730; CVPR:12}

DUNSTONE, ---- (Charles County), captain by 1714. {Ref: INAC 36B:30}

DUPARE, JOHN (Potomac District), captain and master of the ship *Esther* in 1730-1731. {Ref: CVPR:12}

DUPE, JAMES (St. Mary's County), soldier (rank not stated) circa 1675; paid for his services in the late expedition against the Nanticoke Indians in 1678. {Ref: ARMD 7:103}

DURAND, WILLIAM (Virginia and Anne Arundel County), soldier (rank not stated) who served under Captain Fuller at the Battle of the Severn on Mar 25, 1655 and served on a Council of War after the battle. {Ref: FAAH:26, 42}

DURASS, NICHOLAS (St. Mary's County), soldier (rank not stated) circa 1675; paid for his services in the late expedition against the Nanticoke Indians in 1678. {Ref: ARMD 7:102}

DURDEN (DURDIN), STEPHEN (Talbot County), soldier (rank not stated) circa 1675; paid for his services in the late expedition against the Nanticoke Indians in 1678; died testate by Apr 1, 1710 (date of probate; Rebecca Durdin, widow). {Ref: ARMD 7:89; MDWB 13:20}

DUVALL, JOHN (Anne Arundel County), captain by 1700. {Ref: FAAH:90; PFMD:43}

DUVALL, MAREEN (France and Anne Arundel County), soldier (rank not stated) circa 1675; paid for his services in the late expedition against the Nanticoke Indians in 1678; died testate by Aug 13, 1694 (date of probate; Mary Duvall, widow). {Ref: ARMD 7:96; FAAH:104; RMHF I:154; MDWB 2:327}

DUVALL, MAREEN (Prince George's County), soldier by 1700; payment was made by the General Assembly "to Mareen Dovall & the men with him for Bringing the prisoners that made their Escape and other Charges" in 1700; one Mareen Duvall was the father of another Mareen Duvall and the grandfather of Mareen Duvall, Jr., all of age, in 1721. One Mareen Duvall was aged about 55 when deposed in 1718 and Mareen Duvall, Sr. was aged about 59 when deposed in 1746. Additional research will be necessary before drawing conclusions. {Ref: ARMD 7:96, 24:119; PGLR I:89, 125; MDEP:57}

DUVALL, MARY, see "Mareen Duvall," q.v.

DYAS, THOMAS (Somerset County), soldier (rank not stated) circa 1675; paid for his services in the late expedition against the Nanticoke Indians in 1678. {Ref: ARMD 7:97}

DYKE, MATHEW (Charles County), Protestant and probable soldier in the Revolution of 1689; signed an address and took a loyalty oath supporting the King of England and the reestablishment of Lord Baltimore into power on Nov 28, 1689. {Ref: ARMD 8:138}

DYNAM, JAMES (Talbot County), a seafaring man in 1697. {Ref: ARMD 25:601}

EAGER, GEORGE (Anne Arundel County), military officer (rank not stated) who swore allegiance to the King & Queen of England in 1696; died testate by Jan 23, 1706/7 (date of probate). {Ref: ARMD 20:541; MDWB 12:78}

EAGLE, WILLIAM (Talbot County), soldier (rank not stated) circa 1675; paid for his services in the late expedition against the Nanticoke Indians in 1678. {Ref: ARMD 7:89, 92}

EARLE, JAMES (Talbot and Queen Anne's Counties), sea captain before 1737 (son of James Earle, Sr.). {Ref: BDML I:292}

EARLE, JAMES, JR. (Talbot and Queen Anne's Counties), member of the Lower House of the Maryland Assembly, 1721-1722; sheriff, 1730-1733; captain lieutenant in a troop of horse on Jun 30, 1732; born circa 1694 (son of Michael Earle and nephew of James Earle, Sr.), died testate by Jul 9, 1739 (date of probate; Sarah Earle, widow). {Ref: MDHR 1:11; BDML I:292-294; MDWB 22:72}

EARLE, MICHAEL, see "James Earle, Jr.," q.v.

EARLE, SARAH, see "James Earle, Jr.," q.v.

EARLE, THOMAS (Talbot County), sergeant who swore allegiance to the King & Queen of England in 1696. {Ref: ARMD 20:542}

EASTERSON, WILLIAM, SR. (England and Talbot County), mariner of County Middlesex and land owner in Talbot County before 1694. {Ref: TALR 7:120}

EATHEY, ARTHUR (Charles County), Protestant and probable soldier in the Revolution of 1689; signed an address and took a loyalty oath supporting the King of England and the reestablishment of Lord Baltimore into power on Nov 28, 1689. {Ref: ARMD 8:138}

EATON, JOSEPH (St. Mary's County), captain and mariner, 1678-1682. See "William Godwin," q.v. {Ref: ARMD 5:421, 51:243}

EATON, RANDOLPH (county not indicated), captain of the ship *Neptune* in 1716. {Ref: ARMD 30:393}

EBES, EDWARD (Kent County), soldier (rank not stated) on Isle of Kent who swore allegiance to the Commonwealth of England on Apr 5, 1652. {Ref: INKC:101}

EDELL (EDALL), THOMAS (Anne Arundel County), captain by 1700. {Ref: INAC 20:92}

EDGECOMB, ROBERT (England and St. Mary's County), captain and master of the ship *Jane* of Plymouth in 1693. {Ref: ARMD 20:183}

EDLOE, JOSEPH (St. Mary's County), soldier (rank not stated) circa 1675; paid for his services in the late expedition against the Nanticoke Indians in 1678. {Ref: ARMD 7:103}

EDMONDS, RICHARD (Cecil and Baltimore Counties), captain before 1678; paid for his services in the late expedition against the Nanticoke Indians in 1678; "Richard Edmunds" died testate by Jan 7, 1688/9 (date of probate; Eliza or Elizabeth Edmunds, widow, later married a Gibson). {Ref: ARMD 7:95; MDWB 6:41; BBCF:197}

EDMONDSON (EDMONSTON), ARCHIBALD (Prince George's County), captain circa 1700; born circa 1671 (aged about 60 when deposed on May 31, 1731), died by Jun 28, 1734 (date of probate; Jane Edmonston, widow). {Ref: PGLR Q:606; MDWB 21:159; MINV 20:70}

EDMONDSON, JAMES (Talbot County), Protestant and probable soldier in the Revolution of 1689; signed an address and took a loyalty oath supporting the King of England and the reestablishment of Lord Baltimore into power on Nov 28, 1689. {Ref: ARMD 8:144}

EDMONDSON (EDMONSTON), JANE, see "Archibald Edmondson," q.v.

EDMONDSON (EDMUNDSON), JOHN (Ireland, Barbadoes, and Calvert and Talbot Counties), soldier (rank not stated) circa 1675; paid for his services in the late expedition against the Nanticoke Indians in 1678; coroner, 1678; court justice by 1689; supporter of the Revolution of 1689; signed an address and took a loyalty oath supporting the King of England, the Protestant government, and the reestablishment of Lord Baltimore into power on Nov 28, 1689; member of the Lower House of the Maryland Assembly, 1676-1692 (yet, he was a soldier and elected official in spite of the fact that he was a Quaker and their tenets did not tolerate bearing arms, fighting, and taking oaths); died testate by Apr 8, 1698 (date of probate; Sarah Edmondson, widow). {Ref: ARMD 7:90, 8:144, 8:159, 51:223; BDML I:303; MDWB 6:95}

EDMONDSON, SARAH, see "John Edmondson" and "William Johnson," q.v.

EDMONSON, JOHN (St. Mary's County), captain and commander of the ship *Elisabeth Burwick* in 1696. {Ref: INAC 13B:96}

EDMUNDS, ELIZABETH, see "Richard Edmonds," q.v.

EDWARD, DAVID (Charles County), captain by 1682. {Ref: INAC 7C:131}

EDWARDS, ---- (Patuxent River), captain of a ship (no name given) in 1729. {Ref: MDGZ, Apr 29, 1729}

EDWARDS, HUMPHREY (county not indicated), probable soldier (rank not stated) before 1682; paid for his services out of an assessment levied by the General Assembly for the public good in 1682. {Ref: ARMD 7:439}

EDWARDS, JOSEPH (Calvert County), Protestant and probable soldier in the Revolution of 1689; signed an address and took a loyalty oath supporting the

King of England and "to reestablish Lord Baltimore in his ancient power and government" on Nov 16, 1689. {Ref: ARMD 8:131}

EDWARDS, MOSSES (Baltimore County), ranger, appointed Mar 23, 1694/5 by Capt. John Oldton as a "well quallified person & good woods man & fit to be Imployed in Ranging for the Publick Service of this Province;" died intestate on Aug 6, 1727. {Ref: ARMD 20:205; BBCF:197}

EDWARDS, PHILIP (England and Calvert County), mariner by 1677. {Ref: INAC 4:570}

EDWARDS, THOMAS (Somerset County), Protestant and probable soldier in the Revolution of 1689; signed an address and took a loyalty oath supporting the King of England and "for enabling us to defend ourselves against all invaders" on Nov 28, 1689. {Ref: ARMD 8:140}

EDWARDS, WILLIAM (Cecil County), military officer (rank not stated) who swore allegiance to the King & Queen of England in 1696. {Ref: ARMD 20:546}

EDWARDSON, EDWARD (Kent County), soldier (rank not stated) circa 1675; paid for his services in the late expedition against the Nanticoke Indians in 1678. {Ref: ARMD 7:94}

EGG, JAMES (Dorchester County), soldier (rank not stated) circa 1675; paid for his services in the late expedition against the Nanticoke Indians in 1678. {Ref: ARMD 7:92}

ELDAYERLY, HENRY (Cecil County), military officer (rank not stated) who swore allegiance to the King & Queen of England in 1696. {Ref: ARMD 20:546}

ELDEST, HENRY (Cecil County), Protestant and probable soldier in the Revolution of 1689; signed an address and took a loyalty oath supporting the King of England and the reestablishment of Lord Baltimore into power on Nov 18, 1689. {Ref: ARMD 8:135}

ELETT, WILLIAM (Talbot County), lieutenant who swore allegiance to the King & Queen of England in 1696. {Ref: ARMD 20:542}

ELEY, THOMAS (Charles County), captain by 1707. {Ref: INAC 27:35}

ELGATE, WILLIAM, JR. (Somerset County), soldier (rank not stated) circa 1675; paid for his services in the late expedition against the Nanticoke Indians in 1678. {Ref: ARMD 7:98}

ELGATE, WILLIAM, SR. (Wicomico, Somerset County), soldier (rank not stated) circa 1675; paid for his services in the late expedition against the Nanticoke Indians in 1678; paid for his services out of an assessment levied by the General Assembly for the public good in 1682. {Ref: ARMD 7:98, 7:442-443; OSES:153}

ELLICE, ROBERT (Talbot County), ensign before 1678; paid for his services in the late expedition against the Nanticoke Indians in 1678. {Ref: ARMD 7:88}

ELLICOTT, WILLIAM (Queen Anne's County), lieutenant in the First Company of Foot on Jun 30, 1732. {Ref: MDHR 1:11}

ELLINGSWORTH, RICHARD (Somerset County), soldier (rank not stated) circa 1675; paid for his services in the late expedition against the Nanticoke Indians in 1678. {Ref: ARMD 7:98}

ELLIOTT, BROWNING (Baltimore and Anne Arundel Counties), captain before 1720; master of the frigate *Hart* in 1720; captain to at least 1730. {Ref: AALR CW#1:167; MDAD 10:299}

ELLIOTT, JOHN (Kent Island, Queen Anne's County), probable soldier and officer in the 1730's; captain before 1744; died testate by Aug 1, 1744 (date of probate; Susanna Elliott, widow). {Ref: MDWB 23:558; MINV 30:101}

ELLIOTT, MARY, see "William Elliott," q.v.

ELLIOTT, SUSANNA, see "John Elliott," q.v.

ELLIOTT, WILLIAM (Queen Anne's County), captain by 1727; member of the Lower House of the Maryland Assembly, 1722-1737; land owner on Kent Island in 1732; died testate by Apr 22, 1756 (date of probate; Mary Elliott, widow). {Ref: ARMD 39:151, 39:220; BDML I:304; MDWB 30:70; QALR RT#A:157}

ELLIOTT (ELLIOT), WILLIAM (Kent County), soldier (rank not stated) on Isle of Kent who swore allegiance to the Commonwealth of England on Apr 5, 1652; assistant commander (commissioner) of Kent County, 1654; born circa 1621 (aged about 34 when deposed on Oct 29, 1655); a "William Elleyeot" died testate by Sep 2, 1668 (date of probate). {Ref: INKC:101-104; MDWB 1:339}

ELLIS, HUGH (Calvert County), military officer (rank not stated) who swore allegiance to the King & Queen of England in 1696; died testate by Mar 15, 1697/8 (date of probate; Ruth Ellis, widow). {Ref: ARMD 20:543; MDWB 6:148}

ELLIS, JOHN (St. Mary's County), captain and master of a ship (no name given) in 1695. {Ref: INAC 10:403}

ELLIS, JOHN (Somerset County), Protestant and probable soldier in the Revolution of 1689; signed an address and took a loyalty oath supporting the King of England and "for enabling us to defend ourselves against all invaders" on Nov 28, 1689. {Ref: ARMD 8:141}

ELLIS, MERRICK (Somerset County), probable soldier and possible drummer before 1725; received payment for a drum head in 1725. {Ref: CESM:61}

ELLIS, PATRICK (England and Anne Arundel County), mariner before 1715; belonged to His Majesty's Sloop *Nightingale* when he wrote his will on Aug 24, 1715 in Anne Arundel County; died testate by Sep 16, 1715 (date of probate). {Ref: MDWB 14:69}

ELLIS, RUTH, see "Hugh Ellis," q.v.

ELLIS, SAMUELL (St. Mary's County), captain and commander of the bark *Mary* of Maryland in 1689. {Ref: ARMD 8:151, 8:170}

ELLIS, THOMAS (Somerset County), Protestant and probable soldier in the Revolution of 1689; signed an address and took a loyalty oath supporting the King of England and "for enabling us to defend ourselves against all invaders" on Nov 28, 1689. {Ref: ARMD 8:141}

ELLIS, THOMAS (St. Mary's County), soldier (rank not stated) circa 1675; paid for his services in the late expedition against the Nanticoke Indians in 1678. {Ref: ARMD 7:103}

ELLIS, WILLIAM (Ann Arundel and Prince George's Counties), captain and commander of the ship *William and John* riding at anchor in West River on Feb 9, 1711 riding at anchor in South River on Oct 29, 1714 riding at anchor in West River on Apr 12, 1716, and riding at anchor in South River on May 20, 1717 and May 21, 1718; master of the ship *Ruby* riding in the Patuxent River on Jan 24, 1724/5 and Jan 29, 1725/6. {Ref: AALR PK:427, IB#2:179, 271, 359, 460; PGLR M:148-149}

ELSEGETH, JOHN (Calvert County), military officer (rank not stated) who swore allegiance to the King & Queen of England in 1696. {Ref: ARMD 20:543}

ELTON, RALPH (Talbot County), soldier (rank not stated) circa 1675; paid for his services in the late expedition against the Nanticoke Indians in 1678. {Ref: ARMD 7:90}

ELTONHEAD, WILLIAM (England and Calvert County), member of the Maryland Council, 1649-1655; soldier (rank not stated) who served under Governor Stone and was captured and executed (shot) at the Battle of the Severn on Mar 25, 1655 (born circa 1616). {Ref: BDML I:304; FAAH:26-27; HCCM:24; RMHF I:165}

ELVES, HENRY (Cecil County), soldier and probable officer in the 1730's; captain by 1744. {Ref: INCC:134}

ELWELL, JONATHAN (Potomac District), captain and master of the ship *Two Brothers* in 1730-1731. {Ref: CVPR:12}

ELY, ---- (county not indicated), captain of a ship (no name given) in 1696. {Ref: ARMD 20:488}

ELY, JOHN (England and Calvert County), captain and master of the ship *Heron* of London in 1769. {Ref: INAC 6:631}

ELZEY, ARNOLD (Virginia and Manokin Hundred, Somerset County), probable soldier (rank not stated) before 1682; paid for his services out of an assessment levied by the General Assembly for the public good in 1682; Protestant and soldier in the Revolution of 1689; signed an address and took a loyalty oath supporting the King of England and "for enabling us to defend ourselves against all invaders" on Nov 28, 1689; captain of foot troops in 1694; military officer who swore allegiance to the King & Queen of England in 1696; captain before 1703; major (no date given); colonel before 1723; born circa 1661 (aged about 60 when deposed in 1721), died testate by Jun 13, 1733 (date of probate). {Ref: ARMD 7:442, 8:140, 20:110, 20:544, 24:318, 24:422; CESM:61; SOJR II:145, III:41; OSES:153, 444; MDAD 5:326; MDEP:59; MDWB 20:684}

ELZEY, PETER (Somerset County), Protestant and probable soldier in the Revolution of 1689; signed an address and took a loyalty oath supporting the King of England and "for enabling us to defend ourselves against all invaders" on Nov 28, 1689; (name also listed as "Peter Elzery" and "Petter Elzey"); born circa 1639 (aged about 71 when deposed in 1710), died intestate by Aug 17, 1720 (date of administration account). {Ref: ARMD 8:139; MDEP:59; MDAD 3:240}

EMBALY, SYOM (county or port not indicated), captain and master of the ship *James* of London in 1691. {Ref: ARMD 8:239}

EMERSON (EMMERSON), JOHN (Talbot County), soldier (rank not stated) circa 1675; paid for his services in the late expedition against the Nanticoke Indians in 1678; died testate by Jul 3, 1707 (date of probate). {Ref: ARMD 7:91; MDWB 12:141}

EMERSON, HENRY (Prince George's County), soldier (trooper) under the command of Capt. Richard Owen in June, 1699. {Ref: ARMD 24:121}

EMERSON, KATERN, see "Thomas Emerson," q.v.

EMERSON, THOMAS (Talbot County), major by 1716; member of the Lower House of the Maryland Assembly, 1716-1719; died testate by Apr 19, 1720 (date of probate). {Ref: ARMD 33:161, 33:566; BDML I:305; MDWB 16:24; MINV 6:118}

EMERSON (EMMERSON), THOMAS (Wye River, Talbot County), soldier (rank not stated) circa 1675; paid for his services in the late expedition against the Nanticoke Indians in 1678; died testate by Oct 16, 1686 (date of probate; Katern Emerson, widow). {Ref: ARMD 7:88, 7:91; MDWB 4:261}

EMIRS, RICHARD (Calvert County), Protestant and probable soldier in the Revolution of 1689; signed an address and took a loyalty oath (made his "R E" mark) supporting the King of England and "to reestablish Lord Baltimore in his ancient power and government" on Nov 16, 1689. {Ref: ARMD 8:132}

EMKSON, JOHN (Kent County), soldier (rank not stated) in Capt. William Leeds (Leeads) Company by May 23, 1662, at which time he signed a petition about the misuse of company money by Capt. Thomas Brednox (Bradnox), late of Isle of Kent, deceased. {Ref: ARMD 3:455}

EMMERY, WILLIAM (Talbot County), soldier (rank not stated) circa 1675; paid for his services in the late expedition against the Nanticoke Indians in 1678. {Ref: ARMD 7:90}

EMMES (EMMS), THOMAS (England, and Calvert and St. Mary's Counties), captain and master of the ship *John and Joseph* of Yarmouth in 1691; captain and master of a ship (no name given) riding at anchor at the mouth of the Patuxent River on Jul 1, 1695; mariner, of London, 1696; captain, 1698-1719; died between Apr 4, 1719 and Dec 25, 1720. {Ref: ARMD 8:239, 20:306, 23:466, 29:253; SOJR I:212; PGLR A:65; MDAD 1:401, 3:143, 5:348}

EMMIT, JOHN (Somerset County), Protestant and probable soldier in the Revolution of 1689; signed an address and took a loyalty oath supporting the King of England and "for enabling us to defend ourselves against all invaders" on Nov 28, 1689. {Ref: ARMD 8:141}

EMORY, JOHN (Queen Anne's County), captain before 1729; paid by the court "for cleaning the arms of this county" in 1729; born circa 1687 (depositions indicate he was aged about 42 in 1729, about 62 in 1749, about 56 in 1743, and about 76 in 1761). {Ref: CESM:67; MDEP:60}

ENGLAND, JOHN (England and St. Mary's County), captain and master of the ship *Society* of Bristol in 1665; captain, 1685. {Ref: MDHM 5:340; INAC 8:486}
ENGLISH, EDWARD, see "Edward Inglish," q.v.
ENINS, BENJAMIN (Calvert County), Protestant and probable soldier in the Revolution of 1689; signed an address and took a loyalty oath (made his "E" mark) supporting the King of England and "to reestablish Lord Baltimore in his ancient power and government" on Nov 16, 1689. {Ref: ARMD 8:132}
ENNALLS, BARTHOLOMEW (Virginia and Dorchester County), soldier (rank not stated) circa 1675; paid for his services in the late expedition against the Nanticoke Indians in 1678; member of the Lower House of the Maryland Assembly, 1676-1674; court justice, 1679-1685; died testate by Jun 20, 1688 (date of probate; Mary Ennalls, widow). {Ref: ARMD 7:93, 15:254, 15:326, 17:381; BDML I:306; MDWB 6:56}
ENNALLS, BARTHOLOMEW (Talbot County and Pocomoke District), captain and commander of the brigantine *Thomas and Elizabeth* of Maryland in 1720 (endorsement mentioned Capt. Thomas Hannah, shipmaster, in Glasgow); captain and master of the ship *Mary and Ann* in 1730-1731. {Ref: TALR 13:129; CVPR:12}
ENNALLS, ELIZABETH, see "Thomas Ennalls" and "Henry Ennalls," q.v.
ENNALLS, HENRY (Dorchester County), captain by 1702; member of the Lower House of the Maryland Assembly, 1712-1714; major by 1723; colonel by 1731; born circa 1674 (aged about 54 when deposed in 1728), died testate by Aug 16, 1734 (date of probate; Elizabeth Ennalls, widow). {Ref: ARMD 29:467; BDML I:307-308; DOLR 8 Old 247; SOJR III:66; MDWB 21:184; MDEP:60}
ENNALLS, JOHN (Dorchester County), captain before 1694; major, commissioned Oct 9, 1694. {Ref: ARMD 20:153}
ENNALLS, JOSEPH (Dorchester County), soldier and probable officer in the 1730's; major (no date given); colonel at the time of his death; born 1702, died testate by Jan 30, 1760 (date of probate; Mary Ennalls, widow). {Ref: BDML I:309, 455; MDWB 30:831}
ENNALLS, MARY, see "Joseph Ennalls" and "Bartholomew Ennalls," q.v.
ENNALLS (ENOLDS), THOMAS (Dorchester County), captain of a foot company, 1689; major, 1694; lieutenant colonel by Jul 11, 1698 at which time he was appointed to decide differences between the English colonists and the Nanticoke Indians in 1678; lieutenant colonel and King's Surveyor of Dorchester County, 1700; colonel by 1701/2; member of the Lower House of the Maryland Assembly, 1692-1702; member of the Maryland Council, 1703-1718; died testate by Aug 13, 1718 (date of probate; Elizabeth Ennalls, widow). {Ref: ARMD 13:244, 20:205, 23:457, 24:29, 24:194, 25:245, 27:377, 29:351, 33:156; BDML I:311; MDWB 14:631}
ENNALLS, WILLIAM (Kent County), colonel by 1733. {Ref: INKC:178}
ENNALLS, WILLIAM (Dorchester County), lieutenant colonel by 1723; colonel by 1728; member of the Lower House of the Maryland Assembly, 1728-1731;

died testate by Dec 5, 1731 (date of probate). {Ref: BDML I:312; MDWB 20:301; MINV 16:666}

ENNEXSON, JOHN (Talbot County), military officer (rank not stated) who swore allegiance to the King & Queen of England in 1696. {Ref: ARMD 20:542}

ENNIS, THOMAS (Prince George's County), captain by 1697. {Ref: ARMD 25:596}

ENNIS, THOMAS (England and Anne Arundel County), mariner, of London, by 1700. {Ref: AALR WT#1:332}

ERVIN (ERVING), JOHN (Somerset County), mariner by 1709. {Ref: SOJR II:151}

ESKBRIDGE, GEORGE (Scotland and Potomac River), captain and burgess of Glasgow before 1718; came to Maryland in 1718. {Ref: SCOT:46}

ESTES, JOHN (England and St. Mary's), captain and commander of the ship *Providence* of Deale in 1685. {Ref: ARMD 17:382-383}

ESTES, MATTHEW (St. Mary's County), captain and master of the ship brigantine *Dolpin* (or *Dolphin*) of Pennsylvania in 1694. {Ref: ARMD 20:147}

EVANS, EDWARD (Somerset County), Protestant and probable soldier in the Revolution of 1689; signed an address and took a loyalty oath supporting the King of England and "for enabling us to defend ourselves against all invaders" on Nov 28, 1689. {Ref: ARMD 8:139}

EVANS (EVENS), EDWARD (St. Mary's County), soldier (rank not stated) by 1679; served 14 days at the Susquehannah Fort under Captain Slye in 1679; died testate by Feb 28, 1694/5 (date of probate; Mary Evans, widow). {Ref: ARMD 7:148; MDWB 7:53}

EVANS, ELIZABETH, see "William Evans," q.v.

EVANS, JOB (Anne Arundel County), appointed Ranger "from Mr. Snowden's plantation downwards the rest of the county" in 1692. {Ref: ARMD 8:339}

EVANS, JOHN (St. Mary's County), soldier (rank not stated) circa 1675; paid for his services in the late expedition against the Nanticoke Indians in 1678; died testate by May 25, 1688 (date of probate). {Ref: ARMD 7:104; MDWB 4:302}

EVANS, JOHN (Somerset County), soldier (rank not stated) circa 1675; paid for his services in the late expedition against the Nanticoke Indians in 1678; paid for his services out of an assessment levied by the General Assembly for the public good in 1682; died testate by Jun 8, 1686 (date of probate; Mary Evans, widow). {Ref: ARMD 7:98, 7:442; MDWB 4:216}

EVANS, JOHN (county or port not indicated), captain, commodore and commander of Her Majesty's Ship *Dreadnaught* in 1704. {Ref: ARMD 24:398}

EVANS, JOHN (Baltimore County), soldier (rank not stated) circa 1675; paid for his services in the late expedition against the Nanticoke Indians in 1678. {Ref: ARMD 7:95}

EVANS, MARY, see "John Evans" and "Edward Evans," q.v.

EVANS, MORGAN (Somerset County), soldier (rank not stated) circa 1675; paid for his services in the late expedition against the Nanticoke Indians in 1678. {Ref: ARMD 7:98}

EVANS, NICHOLAS (Stepney Parish, Somerset County), military officer (rank not stated) who swore allegiance to the King & Queen of England in 1696; captain by 1697 and to at least 1715; colonel before 1722; died testate by May 20, 1723 (date of probate; Rachel Evans, widow). {Ref: ARMD 20:544; SOJR III:172-173; BDML I:470; INAC 21:194; MDWB 18:140, 6:150; MINV 9:275}

EVANS, RACHEL, see "Nicholas Evans," q.v.

EVANS, ROBERT (St. Mary's County), soldier (rank not stated) circa 1675; paid for his services in the late expedition against the Nanticoke Indians in 1678. {Ref: ARMD 7:103}

EVANS, ROBERT (Dorchester County), soldier (rank not stated) circa 1675; paid for his services in the late expedition against the Nanticoke Indians in 1678. {Ref: ARMD 7:92}

EVANS, ROGER (county not indicated), probable soldier (rank not stated) before 1682; paid for his services out of an assessment levied by the General Assembly for the public good in 1682. {Ref: ARMD 7:440}

EVANS, THOMAS (Talbot County), Protestant and soldier in the Revolution of 1689; signed an address and took a loyalty oath supporting the King of England and the reestablishment of Lord Baltimore into power on Nov 18, 1689; ensign by 1696; swore allegiance to the King & Queen of England in 1696; died testate by Jun 2, 1705 (date of probate). {Ref: ARMD 8:134, 20:542; MDWB 3:670}

EVANS, THOMAS (Calvert and/or Prince George's County), captain by 1700 and to at least 1714. {Ref: INAC 11B:60, 35A:298}

EVANS, THOMAS (Somerset County), ship's carpenter by 1709. {Ref: SOJR II:174-175}

EVANS, WALTER (Calvert and Prince George's Counties), ranger under the command of Capt. Richard Brightwell in 1692 (name listed as "Waller Evans"); born circa 1645-1648 (aged about 60 when deposed in 1708, aged about 80 or 81 when deposed on Mar 29, 1729 and May 1, 1729 and Jun 23, 1730, and aged about 85 when deposed again in 1730). {Ref: ARMD 8:445; PGLR M:403, M:443, Q:1; MDEP:6}

EVANS, WILLIAM (St. Mary's County), lieutenant by 1646; lieutenant of the fort at St. Inigos in 1648; captain who served under Governor Stone at the Battle of the Severn on Mar 25, 1655; commissioned Jul 20, 1658 to command all the forces from Poplar Hill exclusively to Wicocomaco River; colonel, 1659; burgess (member of the General Assembly), 1658-1662; sheriff, 1663-1664; member of the Maryland Council, 1664-1668; died testate in March, 1668/9 (death noted in a Chancery Court inquisition on May 13, 1669; Elizabeth Evans, widow). See "John Jordaine" and "John Bariffe," q.v. {Ref: ARMD 1:227, 1:382, 1:426, 3:344, 3:351, 4:375, 10:4, 10:465, 41:51, 49:54, 49:190, 51:282-285; FAAH:26; BDML I:314; MDWB 1:331}

EVANS, WILLIAM (Dorchester County), soldier (rank not stated) circa 1675; paid for his services in the late expedition against the Nanticoke Indians in 1678. {Ref: ARMD 7:93}

EVATTS, NATHANIEL, see "Nathaniell Evetts," q.v.

EVELIN (EVELYN), GEORGE (England and St. Mary's County), captain and commander of the Isle of Kent, 1637; member of the Maryland Assembly 1637; died after Oct 11, 1649 (date of indenture). {Ref: ARMD 1:2-6, 4:27-28, 4:34-35, 41:344-344; BDML I:314; INKC:178}

EVELIN (EVELYN), ROBERT (England and St. Mary's County), lieutenant, 1637; captain by 1642; died circa 1649. {Ref: ARMD 4:34; BDML I:314}

EVERARD, FRANCIS (Anne Arundel County), probable soldier (rank not stated) before 1682; paid for his services out of an assessment levied by the General Assembly for the public good in 1682. {Ref: ARMD 7:439}

EVERARD, THOMAS (St. Mary's and Anne Arundel Counties), captain and commander of the ship *Thomas and Susanna* in 1687-1691. {Ref: ARMD 8:151, 8:178, 8:236, 8:240; INAC 18:89}

EVERETT, JOHN (St. Mary's County), soldier (rank not stated), 1661, under Capt. John Collier, he was called before the Maryland Council on Oct 12, 1661 "to answere for his Contempt in Running from his Collors [and] Pleades that he could not beare Armes against the Indians for Conscience sake." It was then ordered that Everett be retained in custody and tried by a court-martial. At the Council meeting on November 28, 1661 when called "to answer his Contempt in running from his Collors when prest to goe to the Sasquehannough Forte" Everett repeated he could not bear arms for conscience sake. The Council ordered that he be tried at the next Provincial Court and "in the interim be Committed into the Sherriff's hands and ... kept in chaynes and beate his owne Bread." {Ref: ARMD 3:435, 3:441}

EVERETT, JOSEPH (Kent County), soldier (rank not stated) circa 1675; paid for his services in the late expedition against the Nanticoke Indians in 1678. {Ref: ARMD 7:94}

EVERS, WILLIAM (Prince George's County), captain and master of the ship *Sarah* riding in the Patuxent River on Feb 24, 1723/4 and Dec 29, 1725 and Jan 28, 1725/6 (name mistakenly listed once as "William Ewin"); master of the ship *Mary* on Dec 9, 1730 in the Patuxent District. {Ref: PGLR M:148-150; CVPR:12; MDAD 8:439}

EVETT (EVETTS, EVATTS), NATHANIELL (Kent County), ensign before 1678; paid for his services in the late expedition against the Nanticoke Indians in 1678; "Mr. Nathaniel Evelt" was a court justice in Kent County in 1680; Col. Henry Coursey mentioned in a letter to the Maryland Council that "My Ensigne whose name is Nathaniel Evatts is soe crippled with the gripeing of the Gutts that he is Quite disabled" in 1681; born circa 1639 (aged about 25 when deposed in 1664). {Ref: ARMD 7:94, 15:93, 15:328, 17:77, 54:372}

EWEN, ANN, see "William Ewen," q.v.

EWEN, JOHN (Anne Arundel County), ensign, commissioned Apr 6, 1664. {Ref: ARMD 3:492}

EWEN, RICHARD (Anne Arundel County), lieutenant, commissioned Apr 6, 1664; gentleman and justice of the peace, 1674. {Ref: ARMD 3:492, 15:38}

EWEN (EWENS), RICHARD (Anne Arundel County), Puritan and captain by 1654; participated in the Battle of the Severn on Mar 25, 1655 and served on a Council of War after the battle; member of the Maryland Council in 1655; speaker of the Maryland Assembly in 1657; major by 1657; commissioned "to command as his own company all the forces from the south side of South River up to the head thereof and Mr. Anthony Salway's house in the Herring Creek exclusively" on Jul 20, 1658; burgess (member of the General Assembly) in 1659; died in 1660. {Ref: ARMD 1:359, 1:382, 3:316, 3:349, 3:351, 10:419; FAAH:26, 29; HCCM:259; BDML I:315}

EWEN (EWENS), WILLIAM (England and Cliffs, Calvert County), captain by 1658; member of the Maryland Assembly, representing Patuxent (Calvert) County, 1654; provincial court justice, 1656-1658; born circa 1608 (aged about 45 when deposed in 1653), died testate by Feb 15, 1675/6 (date of probate; Ann Ewen, widow). {Ref: BDML I:315; ARMD 10:305; MDWB 2:393}

EXON (EXTON), HENRY (St. Mary's County), soldier (rank not stated) circa 1675; paid for his services in the late expedition against the Nanticoke Indians in 1678; paid again in 1682; born circa 1635 (aged about 49 when deposed in 1684). {Ref: ARMD 7:102, 7:443, 17:322}

FAIRBANK (FAIRBANCK), DAVID (Second Creek, Talbot County), soldier (rank not stated) circa 1675; paid for his services in the late expedition against the Nanticoke Indians in 1678; "David Fairbanck, Sr." died testate by Jan 28, 1713/4 (date of probate; Ann Fairbanck, widow). {Ref: ARMD 7:92; MDWB 13:672}

FAIRBROTHER (FFARBROTHER), JOHN (Anne Arundel County), military officer (rank not stated) who swore allegiance to the King & Queen of England in 1696; died testate by Oct 14, 1702 (date of probate; Jane Fairbrother, widow). {Ref: ARMD 20:542; MDWB 11:227}

FANEY, JOHN (Calvert County), Protestant and probable soldier in the Revolution of 1689; signed an address and took a loyalty oath supporting the King of England and "to reestablish Lord Baltimore in his ancient power and government" on Nov 16, 1689. {Ref: ARMD 8:131}

FARE, ---- (county not indicated), captain by 1698. {Ref: INAC 13B:33}

FARFARR (FARFAR, FARFER), WILLIAM (Baltimore County), captain by the late 1600's; born circa 1649 (aged about 69 in 1718), died testate by Mar 27, 1721 (date of probate). See "Lewis Barton," q.v. {Ref: MDWB 17:233; MINV 9:96; BBCF:212}

FARGESON, ROBERT (St. Mary's County), Protestant and probable soldier in the Revolution of 1689; signed an address and took a loyalty oath supporting the King of England and the reestablishment of Lord Baltimore into power on Nov 28, 1689. {Ref: ARMD 8:147}

FARMER, JOHN (England and St. Mary's County), captain and master of the ketch *Tryall* of Bytheford in 1690; captain of a ship (no name given) in 1694. {Ref: ARMD 8:237, 20:139}

FARROW, EDMUND (England and St. Mary's County), captain and master of the ship *Returne* of London in 1694. {Ref: ARMD 20:147}

FARWELL, RICHARD (Somerset County), Protestant and probable soldier in the Revolution of 1689; signed an address and took a loyalty oath supporting the King of England and "for enabling us to defend ourselves against all invaders" on Nov 28, 1689. {Ref: ARMD 8:140}

FASSIT (FASSITT, FASSETT), WILLIAM (Baltimore Hundred, Somerset County), captain before 1726; died testate by May 30, 1735 (date of probate; Mary Fassit, widow). {Ref: MDWB 19:286, 21:385; SOTL:1730-1734; MINV 21:111}

FELOO, RICHARD, see "Richard Fido (Fedo)," q.v.

FELTON, EDWARD (Kent County), soldier (rank not stated) circa 1675; paid for his services in the late expedition against the Nanticoke Indians in 1678. {Ref: ARMD 7:94}

FENDALL, ELIZABETH, see "John Fendall," q.v.

FENDALL, JAMES (Sussex, England and Baltimore County), captain and mariner by 1683; died before May 14, 1694 (date of administration account). {Ref: BCCF:215; INAC 12:139}

FENDALL, JOHN (North Carolina and Charles County), captain by 1711; member of the Lower House of the Maryland Assembly, 1712-1729; colonel by 1721; born circa 1673 (aged about 46 when deposed in 1719 and aged about 56 when deposed in 1730), son of Josias Fendall, *q.v.*; spent his childhood in North Carolina and returned to Maryland by 1702; died testate by Oct 28, 1734 (date of probate; Elizabeth Fendall, widow). {Ref: ARMD 30:107, 30:359, 33:365, 34:61, 34:199; CHLR M#2:59; BDML I:317-318; CHLR H#2:461; INAC 33A:71; FAAH:47; MDWB 21:219; MINV 20:361; MDEP:63}

FENDALL, JOSIAS (England, North Carolina, and St. Mary's and Charles Counties), captain by 1654; served in Gov. William Stone's forces at the Battle of the Severn on Mar 25, 1655; led the proprietary soldiers in recapturing Maryland's government from the commissioners in 1657; captain general and governor of Maryland in 1658; in 1659 he joined with a majority of the Lower House members in a rebellion that resulted in the colony's becoming a commonwealth; he was permanently barred from holding office in 1661; in 1678 he was accused of making scandalous speeches against the government; in 1681 he was arrested for an alleged conspiracy against the government and was "banished from this province by due course of law" in 1684; he migrated to North Carolina and died circa 1688. See "John Fendall," q.v. {Ref: ARMD 1:369, 3:347, 5:312, 17:64, 17:272, 53:330; FAAH:25; BDML I:318; CHLR B:26-30}

FENTON, MOSES (Somerset County), Protestant and soldier in the Revolution of 1689; signed an address and took a loyalty oath supporting the King of England and "for enabling us to defend ourselves against all invaders" on Nov 28, 1689; captain by 1707 (when mentioned in the will of John Cornish) and to at least 1715. {Ref: ARMD 8:141; MDWB 12:201; SOJR I:102, III:11}

FERGESON, JOHN (county not indicated), private in the Maryland troops "raised to strengthen Albany, New York and resist the French and Indian enemies" in 1690. {Ref: SHMD I:355}

FERNELEY (FIRNELEY), HENRY (Calvert County), Protestant and soldier in the Revolution of 1689; signed an address and took a loyalty oath supporting the King of England and the reestablishment of Lord Baltimore into power on Nov 28, 1689; military officer (rank not stated) who swore allegiance to the King & Queen of England in 1696. {Ref: ARMD 8:145, 20:543}

FERRY, JOHN (Back River, Baltimore County), captain by 1696; swore allegiance to the King & Queen of England in 1696; member of the Lower House of the Maryland Assembly, 1694-1698; died testate by Mar 11, 1698/9 (date of probate). {Ref: ARMD 20:544; BDML I:320; INAC 19½A:61; MDWB 6:227; BBCF:216}

FERRYS, WILLIAM (county or port not indicated), captain and master of the ship *Martin* of White Haven in 1691. {Ref: ARMD 8:238}

FETHERSON, NATHANIEL (England and St. Mary's County), captain and master of the ship *Adventure* of Lancaster in 1693. {Ref: ARMD 20:182}

FIDO (FEDO), RICHARD (Calvert County), private in the Maryland troops "raised to strengthen Albany, New York and resist the French and Indian enemies" in 1690 (name listed once as "Richard Feloo"); died testate by Nov 8, 1703 (date of probate). {Ref: SHMD I:355; MDWB 11:391}

FIELDING, JAMES (Dorchester County), soldier (rank not stated) circa 1675; paid for his services in the late expedition against the Nanticoke Indians in 1678. {Ref: ARMD 7:92}

FILKINS, HENRY (county or port not indicated), mariner by 1734; captain and master of the sloop *Mercury* in 1736 (built in the colony of Virginia in 1733). {Ref: MDCB 82:46}

FILLMORE, WILLIAM (county not indicated), probable soldier (rank not stated) before 1682; paid for his services out of an assessment levied by the General Assembly for the public good in 1682. {Ref: ARMD 7:440}

FINCH, FRANCIS (Kent County), soldier (rank not stated) in Capt. William Leeds (Leeads) Company by May 23, 1662, at which time he signed a petition about the misuse of company money by Capt. Thomas Brednox (Bradnox), late of Isle of Kent, deceased. {Ref: ARMD 3:455}

FINCH, PRISCILLA, see "William Finch," q.v.

FINCH, SAMUELL (Dorchester County), soldier (rank not stated) circa 1675; paid for his services in the late expedition against the Nanticoke Indians in 1678. {Ref: ARMD 7:93}

FINCH (FFINCH), WILLIAM (Prince George's County), captain and master of the ship *Bradley* (or *Bradly*) riding in the Patuxent River on Jan 24, 1724/5 and Mar 30, 1726; master of the ship *Gould* in 1731; "Capt. William Finch, Jr." died intestate by Nov 15, 1742 (date of probate; Priscilla Finch, widow). {Ref: PGLR M:148, 150; CVPR:12; MINV 27:270}

FINLEY, ROBERT (Charles County), colonel by 1707; Commissary of Arms by Aug 16, 1708 when ordered by the governor "to inspect into the Arms, Ammunition and other warlike Stores of this Province of Maryland" and petitioned the Maryland Council for proper payment for his services on Nov 8, 1709; Commissary of Arms to at least 1712; colonel, 1729. {Ref: ARMD 27:396, 27:402, 29:154; INAC 28:19; MINV 15:46}

FINNEY, RACHEL, see "William Finney," q.v.

FINNEY, WILLIAM (Talbot County), soldier (rank not stated) circa 1675; paid for his services in the late expedition against the Nanticoke Indians in 1678; Protestant and soldier in the Revolution of 1689; signed an address and took a loyalty oath supporting the King of England and the reestablishment of Lord Baltimore into power on Nov 28, 1689; member of the Lower House of the Maryland Assembly, 1692-1693; he was listed as "Major Wm. Ffinney" in 1692 and "Major Ffiny of Talbot County" in 1694 and commissioned lieutenant colonel on Oct 9, 1694, yet he was called "Major Wm. Ffinney" in 1696 when he was a vestryman for St. Paul's Parish; died in April, 1696. {Ref: ARMD 7:91, 8:144, 20:151, 20:153, 20:202, 23:21; BDML I:320}

FINNEY, WILLIAM (Talbot County), captain before 1723; died by Nov 18, 1723 (date of inventory; Mrs. Rachel Finney, administratrix). {Ref: MINV 10:48}

FIRST, DANIELL (county not indicated), probable soldier (rank not stated) before 1682; paid for his services out of an assessment levied by the General Assembly for the public good in 1682. {Ref: ARMD 7:439}

FISH, JOHN (Dorchester County), soldier (rank not stated) circa 1675; paid for his services in the late expedition against the Nanticoke Indians in 1678. {Ref: ARMD 7:92}

FISHBOURNE (FISHBORNE), RALPH (Talbot County), soldier (rank not stated) circa 1675; paid for his services in the late expedition against the Nanticoke Indians in 1678; court justice, 1685; born circa 1642 (aged about 22 when deposed in 1664). {Ref: ARMD 7:90, 17:380, 54:373}

FISHER, ALEXANDER (Dorchester County), soldier (rank not stated) circa 1675; paid for his services in the late expedition against the Nanticoke Indians in 1678; died testate by Mar 4, 1698/9 (date of probate; Elizabeth Fisher, widow). {Ref: ARMD 7:93; MDWB 6:308}

FISHER, ELIZABETH, see "Alexander Fisher," q.v.

FISHER, HENRY (Somerset County), seaman by 1716. {Ref: INAC 37A:82}

FISHER, JOHN (Baltimore County), probable soldier (rank not stated) before 1682; paid for his services out of an assessment levied by the General Assembly for the public good in 1682. {Ref: ARMD 7:441}

FISHER, SARAH, see "Thomas Fisher," q.v.

FISHER, THOMAS (Talbot and Queen Anne's Counties), captain by 1719; member of the Lower House of the Maryland Assembly, 1719-1721; died testate by Mar 1, 1721/2 (date of probate; Sarah Fisher, widow). {Ref: BDML I:321; MDWB 17:130; MINV 8:40}

FISHLY, ROBERT (county or port not indicated), captain and master of the ship *Samdebigg* of Barnstaple (Barnstable) in 1691. {Ref: ARMD 8:238}

FITCH, ADAM (Somerset County), Protestant and probable soldier in the Revolution of 1689; signed an address and took a loyalty oath supporting the King of England and "for enabling us to defend ourselves against all invaders" on Nov 28, 1689. {Ref: ARMD 8:140}

FITZHERBERT, EDWARD (England and St. Mary's County), major by 1671; member of the Maryland Council, 1671-1673; an early land owner in what is now Prince George's County, he probably returned to England in 1673. {Ref: ARMD 2:239, 2:253; BDML I:321; PGLR A:43}

FLEET (FFLEETE), HENRY (Virginia and St. Mary's County), captain and trader in Virginia by 1623; Indian interpreter after 1627; gentleman and captain in Maryland after 1633; "It was Captain Fleet who guided Leonard Calvert to this spot on the Potomac. He was busy about his fur trade in the River of the Patowomecke when the *Ark* and the *Dove* reached St. Clement's Isle" on Mar 25, 1634; died by 1660. {Ref: ARMD 1:2, 10:221; FMDP:204-209}

FLETCHER (FFLETCHER), HENRY (Potomac District), captain and master of the ship *George* in 1730-1731. {Ref: CVPR:12}

FLETCHER, RICHARD (Talbot County), captain by 1718. {Ref: MDAD 1:187}

FLETCHER, ROBERT (St. Mary's County), Protestant and probable soldier in the Revolution of 1689; signed an address and took a loyalty oath supporting the King of England and the reestablishment of Lord Baltimore into power on Nov 28, 1689. {Ref: ARMD 8:146}

FLETCHER, WILLIAM (London and Annapolis), captain and master of the pinke *Rebecca* of Liverpool in 1691. {Ref: ARMD 8:239}

FLETCHER (FFLETCHER), WILLIAM (Annapolis District), captain and master of the ship *Elizabeth* of Boston in 1730-1731. {Ref: CVPR:12}

FLORANCE, CHARLES (Oxford District), captain and master of the ship *Rebecca* in 1731. {Ref: CVPR:12}

FLOWERS, WILLIAM (Dorchester County), soldier (rank not stated) circa 1675; paid for his services in the late expedition against the Nanticoke Indians in 1678. {Ref: ARMD 7:94}

FLOYD, FRANCIS (Dorchester County), soldier (rank not stated) circa 1675; paid for his services in the late expedition against the Nanticoke Indians in 1678. {Ref: ARMD 7:93}

FLOYD, THOMAS (St. Mary's County), soldier (rank not stated) circa 1675; paid for his services in the late expedition against the Nanticoke Indians in 1678. {Ref: ARMD 7:103}

FLOYD, WILLIAM (St. Mary's County), soldier (rank not stated) circa 1675; paid for his services in the late expedition against the Nanticoke Indians in 1678. {Ref: ARMD 7:103}

FOGG, THOMAS (England, and Calvert and Talbot Counties), captain and master of the ship *Colchester Adventure* riding in the Patuxent River on Feb 5, 1724/5;

captain and master of the ship *Edeleford Adventure* riding in the Patuxent River on Apr 15, 1726; captain and master of the ship *Colchester Adventure* riding at anchor in the Patuxent River on Jul 12, 1728 (name misinterpreted once as "Thomas Frogg" and once as "Thomas Hogg"); wrote his will as "Thomas Fogg, marriner, of London" on Jun 29, 1727 (probated in Talbot County on Jun 11, 1730; Ann Fogg, widow, later married Thomas Clagett, Jr.). {Ref: MDWB 20:42; PGLR M:149-150, M:412; MDAD 10:719}

FOLD, JOHN (Baltimore County), Protestant and probable soldier in the Revolution of 1689; signed an address and took a loyalty oath supporting the King of England and the reestablishment of Lord Baltimore into power on Nov 28, 1689. {Ref: ARMD 8:137}

FOOD (FORD?), ---- (Cecil County), captain by 1676. {Ref: INAC 4:302}

FORBY, BENJAMIN (Talbot County), soldier (rank not stated) circa 1675; paid for his services in the late expedition against the Nanticoke Indians in 1678. {Ref: ARMD 7:92}

FORD, ANN, see "Thomas Ford (Fford)," q.v.

FORD, DIANA, see "John Ford," q.v.

FORD, EDWARD (Charles County), soldier (rank not stated) circa 1675; paid for his services in the late expedition against the Nanticoke Indians in 1678 (name listed once as "Edward Foord"); died testate by Jan 19, 1693/4 (date of probate; Elizabeth Ford, widow). {Ref: ARMD 7:101; RMHF II:324; MDWB 2:246}

FORD, ELIZABETH, see "Edward Ford," q.v.

FORD, JOHN (St. Mary's and/or Calvert County), captain by 1696; died testate by Aug 14, 1707 (date of probate; Diana Ford, widow). {Ref: INAC 14:80; MDWB 12:146}

FORD (FOORD), JOHN (Dorchester County), soldier (rank not stated) circa 1675; paid for his services in the late expedition against the Nanticoke Indians in 1678. {Ref: ARMD 7:93}

FORD (FOORD), THOMAS (Anne Arundel County), soldier (rank not stated) circa 1675; paid for his services in the late expedition against the Nanticoke Indians in 1678. {Ref: ARMD 7:96}

FORD (FFORD), THOMAS (Kent and Queen Anne's Counties), military officer (rank not stated) who swore allegiance to the King & Queen of England in 1696; died testate by Jul 18, 1709 (date of probate; Ann Ford, widow). {Ref: ARMD 20:540; MDWB 12:197, pt. 2}

FOREMAN, GEORGE (Annapolis District), captain and master of the snow *Samuel* of Maryland in 1733. {Ref: MDCB 82:2}

FOREMAN, MARGARET, see "Robert Foreman," q.v.

FOREMAN, ROBERT (Kent County), soldier (rank not stated) circa 1675; paid for his services in the late expedition against the Nanticoke Indians in 1678; died testate by Mar 15, 1719/20 (date of probate; Margaret Foreman, widow). {Ref: ARMD 7:94; MDWB 15:341}

FORRESTER, EDWARD (Anne Arundel County), captain by 1721. {Ref: MDAD 4:32}

FORSTER, MATTHEW (England and Annapolis), captain by 1703. {Ref: AALR WT#2:70}
FORSUCH, CHARLES, see "Charles Gorsuch," q.v.
FORTUNE, DAVID (Dorchester County), soldier (rank not stated) circa 1675; paid for his services in the late expedition against the Nanticoke Indians in 1678. {Ref: ARMD 7:93}
FORTUNE, ROBERT (Talbot County), soldier (rank not stated) circa 1675; paid for his services in the late expedition against the Nanticoke Indians in 1678; a "Robert Fortine" died testate by Jun 11, 1703 (date of probate; nuncupative will was given in March, 1703) and a "Robert Fortune" died testate by May 30, 1713 (date of probate). Additional research will be necessary before drawing conclusions. {Ref: ARMD 7:92; MDWB 11:326, 13:560}
FOSSETT, JOHN (Cecil County), soldier (rank not stated) circa 1675; paid for his services in the late expedition against the Nanticoke Indians in 1678. {Ref: ARMD 7:95}
FOSSIT, WILLIAM (Somerset County), Protestant and probable soldier in the Revolution of 1689; signed an address and took a loyalty oath supporting the King of England and "for enabling us to defend ourselves against all invaders" on Nov 28, 1689. {Ref: ARMD 8:141}
FOSTER, ---- (St. Mary's County), captain by 1689. {Ref: INAC 10:201}
FOSTER, JAMES (Anne Arundel County), military officer (rank not stated) who swore allegiance to the King & Queen of England in 1696. {Ref: ARMD 20:541}
FOSTER, RALPH (St. Mary's County), Protestant and probable soldier in the Revolution of 1689; signed an address and took a loyalty oath supporting the King of England and the reestablishment of Lord Baltimore into power on Nov 28, 1689. {Ref: ARMD 8:146}
FOSTER, RUBT. (St. Mary's County), Protestant and probable soldier in the Revolution of 1689; signed an address and took a loyalty oath supporting the King of England and the reestablishment of Lord Baltimore into power on Nov 28, 1689. {Ref: ARMD 8:147}
FOUNTAIN (FOUNTAINE), NICHOLAS (France and Manokin Hundred, Somerset County), soldier (rank not stated) circa 1675; paid for his services in the late expedition against the Nanticoke Indians in 1678; born circa 1640, died testate by Oct 1, 1708 (date of probate; Joanna Fountain, widow). {Ref: ARMD 2:282, 7:99; OSES:444; MDWB 12:336}
FOWKE (FOUKE), GERARD (Staffordshire, England, and Westmoreland County, Virginia, and Charles County, Maryland), captain by 1658 and colonel by 1662 in Virginia; colonel and member of the Lower House of the Maryland Assembly, 1666; born un 1625, died by Oct 12, 1669. {Ref: ARMD 2:63; BDML I:326; CHLR B:361}
FOWKE, JOHN (county not indicated), officer or mate belonging to His Majesty's Advice Boat *Messenger* commanded by Capt. Peter Coode on Mar 7, 1701/2. {Ref: CELR 1:215}

FOWKE, ROGER (Charles County), soldier (rank not stated) circa 1675; paid for his services in the late expedition against the Nanticoke Indians in 1678. {Ref: ARMD 7:101}

FOWLER, EDWARD (Somerset County), soldier (rank not stated) circa 1675; paid for his services in the late expedition against the Nanticoke Indians in 1678. {Ref: ARMD 7:97}

FOWLER, HENRY (Prince George's County), colonel before 1712. {Ref: PGLR F Old 5:258}

FOWLER, JOSEPH (Charles County), soldier (rank not stated) who was issued a "gun or fowling piece" by Col. Warren on Sep 15, 1694; a "Joseph Fowller" died testate in St. Mary's County by Nov 8, 1706 (date of probate). {Ref: ARMD 20:206, 20:208; MDWB 12:101}

FOWLER (FOULER), PETER (Calvert County), Protestant and probable soldier in the Revolution of 1689; signed an address and took a loyalty oath supporting the King of England and "to reestablish Lord Baltimore in his ancient power and government" on Nov 16, 1689. {Ref: ARMD 8:132}

FOWLER (FOULLER), SM. (Calvert County), Protestant and probable soldier in the Revolution of 1689; signed an address and took a loyalty oath (made his "S F" mark) supporting the King of England and "to reestablish Lord Baltimore in his ancient power and government" on Nov 16, 1689. {Ref: ARMD 8:132}

FOWLER, TOBIAS (Somerset County), soldier (rank not stated) circa 1675; paid for his services in the late expedition against the Nanticoke Indians in 1678. {Ref: ARMD 7:97}

FOX, WILLIAM (Talbot County), mariner and land owner by 1667. {Ref: TALR 1:28}

FOYE, FRANCIS (Baltimore County), probable soldier (rank not stated) before 1682; paid for his services out of an assessment levied by the General Assembly for the public good in 1682. {Ref: ARMD 7:441}

FRANCIER, THOMAS (Anne Arundel County), captain by 1682. {Ref: INAC 8:283}

FRANCIS, JACOB (Talbot County), soldier (rank not stated) circa 1675; paid for his services in the late expedition against the Nanticoke Indians in 1678. {Ref: ARMD 7:88-89}

FRANCIS, JONATHON (Anne Arundel County), captain by 1687. {Ref: INAC 18:89}

FRANCIS, MARY, see "Thomas Francis (Ffrancis)," q.v.

FRANCIS, STEPHEN (Annapolis, Anne Arundel County), mariner before 1699; died by Jul 18, 1699 (date of probate). {Ref: MDWB 6:275; INAC 19:86}

FRANCIS, THOMAS (Rhode River, Anne Arundel County), soldier (rank not stated) circa 1675; paid for his services in the late expedition against the Nanticoke Indians in 1678; court justice (quorum), 1679-1685; captain by 1683; major by 1685; died intestate by May 13, 1686 (date of inventory). {Ref: ARMD 7:96, 7:611, 15:253, 17:379; FAAH:196; INAC 9:3}

FRANCIS (FFRANCIS), THOMAS (Anne Arundel County), captain and master of the brigantine *Fisher* of Maryland in 1695; captain of the ship *Adventure* and a "seafaring man borne and belonging to this county" in 1697; died testate by Oct 26, 1698 (date of probate; Mary Francis, widow). {Ref: ARMD 20:338, 25:595-596; MDWB 6:173}

FRAND, NICHOLAS (Kent County), "seaman within the said county" and a "sailor belonging to Mr. Powers ship in the stocks" in 1697. {Ref: ARMD 25:599}

FRANKLAND, JOHN (Somerset County), Protestant and probable soldier in the Revolution of 1689; signed an address and took a loyalty oath supporting the King of England and "for enabling us to defend ourselves against all invaders" on Nov 28, 1689. {Ref: ARMD 8:141}

FRANKLIN (FRANKLING), HENRY (Charles County), Protestant and probable soldier in the Revolution of 1689; signed an address and took a loyalty oath supporting the King of England and the reestablishment of Lord Baltimore into power on Nov 28, 1689; died intestate by Apr 27, 1721 (date of administration account). {Ref: ARMD 8:138; MDAD 3:418}

FRANKLIN (FRANKLYN), JOHN (England, and All Hallows Parish, Somerset County), captain by 1701; justice of the peace by 1707; member of the Lower House of Maryland Assembly, 1701-1711; major by 1711; lieutenant colonel by 1715; died testate by Nov 24, 1727 (date of probate; referred to as "Col. John Frankling" when his inventory was taken on May 29, 1728). {Ref: ARMD 24:129, 27:202; BDML I:329; CMSP 1:7 - The Black Books; SOJR I:1, II:33, III:128; MDWB 19:286; MINV 13:268}

FRANKLIN (FRANCKLIN), ROBERT (St. Mary's County), soldier (rank not stated) by 1657; wounded (lame) and paid for his services in September, 1657. {Ref: ARMD 1:364}

FRANKLIN (FRANCKLIN, FRANCKLYN), ROBERT (England and Anne Arundel County), soldier (rank not stated) circa 1675; paid for his services in the late expedition against the Nanticoke Indians in 1678; member of the Lower House of the Maryland Assembly, 1671-1675; gentleman and justice of the peace, 1674; sheriff, 1678-1682; born circa 1635, died before Nov 7, 1682 (date of inventory; his widow Sarah was deposed on Feb 27, 1685, aged 47, the now wife of John Willowby, and also mentioned her father Col. Burgess). {Ref: ARMD 7:96, 15:38, 15:231, 17:446-447; BDML I:328; INAC 8:27}

FRANKLIN, SARAH, see "Robert Franklin," q.v.

FRANKLIN, THOMAS (St. Mary's County), soldier (rank not stated) in 1642; "Tho: Franclin" was paid for 3 weeks' service under Capt. William Brainthwait in November, 1642. {Ref: ARMD 3:119, 3:122}

FRANKLIN, THOMAS, see "Peasly Ingram," q.v.

FRAWNER, EDWARD (Charles County), soldier (rank not stated) circa 1675; paid for his services in the late expedition against the Nanticoke Indians in 1678. {Ref: ARMD 7:101}

FRAY, EDWARD (Somerset County), soldier (rank not stated) circa 1675; paid for his services in the late expedition against the Nanticoke Indians in 1678. {Ref: ARMD 7:97}

FRAZER, MARY, see "Peter Frazer," q.v.

FRAZER (FRAZIER), PETER (Calvert and Prince George's Counties), captain and master of the ship *Molly* in 1731; died intestate by Jun 12, 1740 (date of inventory; Mary Frazer, widow). {Ref: CVPR:12; MINV 15:561, 26:173}

FRAZER, ROBERT (St. Mary's County), Protestant and probable soldier in the Revolution of 1689; signed an address and took a loyalty oath supporting the King of England and the reestablishment of Lord Baltimore into power on Nov 28, 1689. {Ref: ARMD 8:146}

FRAZER (FRAZIER), WILLIAM (Dorchester County), mariner by 1734; captain and master of the sloop *Boneta* (built at Wye River) in 1735; died intestate by Aug 13, 1752 (date of inventory approval). {Ref: MDCB 82:32; MINV 50:24}

FREELAND, WILLIAM (Talbot County), soldier (rank not stated) circa 1675; paid for his services in the late expedition against the Nanticoke Indians in 1678. {Ref: ARMD 7:92}

FREEMAN, FRAN. (Calvert County), Protestant and probable soldier in the Revolution of 1689; signed an address and took a loyalty oath supporting the King of England and "to reestablish Lord Baltimore in his ancient power and government" on Nov 16, 1689. {Ref: ARMD 8:132}

FREEMAN, JOHN (Annapolis, Anne Arundel County), captain before 1707; major by 1708; died testate by Jan 12, 1708/9 (date of probate; Margaret Freeman, widow). {Ref: ARMD 25:238; INAC 28:122; MDWB 12:311}

FREEMAN, MARGARET, see "John Freeman," q.v.

FREEMAN, WILLIAM (Cecil County), military officer (rank not stated) who swore allegiance to the King & Queen of England in 1696. {Ref: ARMD 20:545}

FRENCH, FRANCIS (England and St. Mary's), chirurgeon on the ship *Globe* of London commanded by Capt. Bartholomew Watts in 1682. {Ref: ARMD 7:281}

FRIEND, EDWARD (Prince George's County), captain and master of the ship *Matthew and Samuel* riding in the Patuxent River on Jan 7, 1723/4. {Ref: PGLR M:148}

FRISBY, ANN, see "William Frisby," q.v.

FRISBY, ARIANA, see "James Frisby," q.v.

FRISBY, JAMES (England, Virginia, and Baltimore and Cecil Counties), gentleman, 1672, Baltimore County; member of the Lower House of the Maryland Assembly, representing Cecil County, 1676-1684; soldier (rank not stated) circa 1675; paid for his services in the late expedition against the Nanticoke Indians in 1678; coroner, Cecil County, 1678; court justice, 1679 (quorum, 1687); captain by 1683; he was noted as "The Honorable James Ffrisby, Esq." at a meeting of the General Assembly on Apr 29, 1700; born circa 1651, died testate by Jun 19, 1704 (date of probate). {Ref: ARMD 7:95, 8:23, 15:255, 15:326, 24:40; BDML I:331; MDWB 3:268}

FRISBY, JAMES (Cecil County), captain by 1713; member of the Lower House of the Maryland Assembly, 1712-1720; born in 1684, died testate by Dec 30, 1719 (date of probate; Ariana Frisby, widow). {Ref: ARMD 29:204, 30:360, 33:165, 33:566, 34:64, 51:102, 51:223; BDML I:331-332; CELR 3:229; MDWB 16:4; MINV 4:1}

FRISBY, JANE, see "William Frisby," q.v.
FRISBY, WILLIAM (Kent County), soldier and officer in the 1730's; major before 1738; died intestate by Aug 28, 1738 (date of inventory approval; Jane Frisby, widow). {Ref: MINV 23:394}
FRISBY, WILLIAM, SR. (Virginia, and Baltimore and Kent Counties), opposed the Revolution of 1689; major of militia, commissioned Jul 30, 1694; member of the Lower House of the Maryland Assembly, 1694-1697, 1704-1708; born before 1664, died testate in December, 1713 (will probated Jan 4, 1713/4; Ann Frisby, widow). {Ref: ARMD 27:202, 30:131; BDML I:333; MDWB 13:654}
FRITH, HENRY (Talbot County), Protestant and probable soldier in the Revolution of 1689; signed an address and took a loyalty oath supporting the King of England and the reestablishment of Lord Baltimore into power on Nov 18, 1689. {Ref: ARMD 8:134}
FROST, LEWIS (England and Cecil County), captain and mariner, of London, by 1698; master of the ship *John and Samuel* riding at anchor in Sassafras River on Mar 19, 1698/9. {Ref: CELR 1:156, 165}
FROST, WILLIAM (Charles County), Protestant and probable soldier in the Revolution of 1689; signed an address and took a loyalty oath supporting the King of England and the reestablishment of Lord Baltimore into power on Nov 28, 1689. {Ref: ARMD 8:138}
FRY, DAVID (Somerset County), soldier (rank not stated) circa 1675; paid for his services in the late expedition against the Nanticoke Indians in 1678; died testate by Feb 19, 1680/1 (date of probate). {Ref: ARMD 7:100; MDWB 2:129}
FULLER, EDWARD (Talbot County), soldier (rank not stated) circa 1675; paid for his services in the late expedition against the Nanticoke Indians in 1678; born circa 1638 (aged about 27 when deposed in 1663, aged about 25 when deposed in 1665, and aged about 28 when deposed in 1666). {Ref: ARMD 7:92; MDEP:67}
FULLER, ROBERT (Talbot County), soldier (rank not stated) circa 1675; paid for his services in the late expedition against the Nanticoke Indians in 1678. {Ref: ARMD 7:90}
FULLER, THOMAS (Talbot County), soldier (rank not stated) circa 1675; paid for his services in the late expedition against the Nanticoke Indians in 1678. {Ref: ARMD 7:87}
FULLER, WILLIAM (Virginia, Anne Arundel and Kent Counties, Barbadoes, and South Carolina), captain by 1652; commander of an expedition against the Eastern Shore Indians in 1652-1654; county justice in 1654-1656; captain in command of Anne Arundel forces (at least 170 men whose names are not extant) at the Battle of the Severn on Mar 25, 1655; served on a Council of War after the battle; governor, 1655-1658, paid for defraying the cost of his guard in September, 1657; supported Fendall's Rebellion in 1659-1660 and left Maryland thereafter for Barbadoes to avoid arrest; served on the South Carolina Council, 1679-1682; died by 1695. See "Roger Heamans" and "Captain Cut,"

q.v. {Ref: ARMD 1:364-365, 3:316-317, 10:419, 10:429, 41:163; BDML I:333-334; FAAH:23-26, 37-38; INKC:103}

FULLWOOD, JOHN (Isle of Kent), interpreter for William Claiborne as early as 1636; lived among the Susquehannough Indians (named listed as "John Fullwood, alias Sands"). {Ref: ARMD 5:231-232}

FURBUSH, NATHANIEL (county not indicated), private in the Maryland troops "raised to strengthen Albany, New York and resist the French and Indian enemies" in 1690. {Ref: SHMD I:355}

FURBY, THOMAS (Talbot County), soldier (rank not stated) circa 1675; paid for his services in the late expedition against the Nanticoke Indians in 1678. {Ref: ARMD 7:91}

FURLAND, EDWARD (Somerset County), soldier (rank not stated) circa 1675; paid for his services in the late expedition against the Nanticoke Indians in 1678. {Ref: ARMD 7:100}

FURNIS (FURNESSE), WILLIAM (Manokin Hundred, Somerset County), soldier (rank not stated) circa 1675; paid for his services in the late expedition against the Nanticoke Indians in 1678; died circa 1689. {Ref: ARMD 7:100; OSES:280, 445}

FYFIELD, ---- (St. Mary's County), captain and commander of the ship *Abraham and James* in 1690. {Ref: ARMD 8:171}

GADSBY, JOHN, see "Christopher Randall," q.v.

GAINES, FRANCIS (Annapolis District), captain and master of the ship *Fancey* of Virginia in 1729. {Ref: MDGZ, Apr 22, 1729}

GAITHER, EDWARD (Anne Arundel County), probable officer in the 1730's; captain before 1741; died intestate by May 21, 1741 (date of inventory; Margarett Gaither, widow). {Ref: MINV 26:168}

GAITHER (GATHER), JOHN (Anne Arundel County), soldier (rank not stated) circa 1675; paid for his services in the late expedition against the Nanticoke Indians in 1678; military officer (rank not stated) who swore allegiance to the King & Queen of England in 1696 (name misinterpreted once as "John Gaitheso"); died by Jun 9, 1707 (date of inventory; Ruth Gaither, widow). {Ref: ARMD 7:96, 20:541, 26:336; FAAH:107-108; RMHF II:293, 342, 345}

GAITHER, MARGARETT, see "Edward Gaither," q.v.

GAITHER, RUTH, see "John Gaither," q.v.

GAITS, JOSEPH (county or port not indicated), captain and master of the ship *Sun--- [sic]* of London in 1690. {Ref: ARMD 8:237}

GALE, BETTY, see "George Gale," q.v.

GALE, GEORGE (Cumberland, England, and Gloucester, Virginia, and Monie, Somerset County), major by 1707; member of the Lower House of the Maryland Assembly, 1708-1711; lieutenant colonel by 1711 (styled "colonel" in a 1713 inventory and a 1715 administration account); born circa 1671, died testate by Aug 20, 1712 (date of probate; Betty Gale, widow). {Ref: ARMD 27:202, 29:4, 29:77; SOJR I:87; BDML I:334-335; MDWB 13:438; INAC 34:131, 36B:237}

GALE, GEORGE (Monie Hundred, Somerset County), soldier and probable officer in the 1730's; captain by 1735; major by 1739; member of the Lower House of the Maryland Assembly, 1742-1744; colonel by 1744; born circa 1706, died testate by Jan 11, 1772 (date of probate). {Ref: SOTL:1735, 1739; BDML I:335; MDWB 38:614}

GALE, LEVIN (Wicomico Hundred, Somerset County), lieutenant colonel before 1727; member of the Lower House of the Maryland Assembly, 1725-1738; provincial court justice, 1726-1744; colonel by 1728; member of the Upper House (Maryland Council), 1738-1742; naval officer for the Pocomoke District, 1733-1740; major general of the Eastern Shore in 1742; born circa 1704 (aged about 29 when deposed in 1733), died testate by Apr 24, 1744 (date of probate). {Ref: ARMD 39:151, 39:220; BDML I:337-338; SOTL:1731; MDWB 23:455; MDCB 82:2; MDEP:67}

GALLEHAUGH, RICHARD (Dorchester County), soldier (rank not stated) circa 1675; paid for his services in the late expedition against the Nanticoke Indians in 1678. {Ref: ARMD 7:92}

GALLON, JOHN (England and Talbot County), captain and mariner of Stepney in London before 1703; master and commander of the ship *Westmoreland Indiaman* by 1703; land owner in Talbot County by Feb 12, 1703 (date he wrote his will). {Ref: TALR 12:14}

GALPIN, PHILIP (county not indicated), private in the Maryland troops "raised to strengthen Albany, New York and resist the French and Indian enemies" in 1690. {Ref: SHMD I:355}

GAMES, JOHN (Talbot County), soldier (rank not stated) circa 1675; paid for his services in the late expedition against the Nanticoke Indians in 1678. {Ref: ARMD 7:92}

GAMES, JOHN (England and St. Mary's), crew member on the ship *Dove* in 1633-1634. {Ref: FMDP:343}

GANDY, JOHN (England, and Talbot and Queen Anne's Counties), mariner and captain, of London, before 1692; land owner in Talbot County by 1692 and land owner in Queen Anne's County by 1715 (name misinterpreted once as "Capt. Jno. Gaudy"). {Ref: TALR 6:10; INAC 25:208; MDWB 14:77}

GANTT (GAUNT), THOMAS (Calvert County), soldier (rank not stated) circa 1675; paid for his services in the late expedition against the Nanticoke Indians in 1678; Protestant, justice of the peace, and probable soldier in the Revolution of 1689; signed an address and took a loyalty oath supporting the King of England and the reestablishment of Lord Baltimore into power on Nov 28, 1689. {Ref: ARMD 7:104, 8:145; HCCM:262}

GARDINER, JOHN (St. Mary's County), captain before 1717 (mentioned in the will of Robert Sanders); died testate by Dec 9, 1717 (date of probate; Mary Gardiner, widow). {Ref: MDWB 14:445, 14:470}

GARDINER, JOHN (St. Mary's County), probable soldier and officer in the 1730's; captain before 1744; died intestate by Jun 7, 1744 (date of inventory approval). {Ref: MINV 29:241}

GARDINER (GARDNER), LUKE (England, Virginia, and St. Mary's and Charles Counties), lieutenant by 1660; member of the Lower House of the Maryland Assembly, 1659-1662, 1671; captain by 1664; sheriff, 1672-1674; born circa 1622 (aged about 50 when deposed in 1672), died testate by Aug 12, 1674 (date of probate; Elizabeth Gardner, widow). {Ref: ARMD 3:503, 49:498; BDML I:344-345; MDWB 1:631; PFMD:31; MDEP:68}

GARDINER, MARY, see "John Gardiner," q.v.

GARDINER, RICHARD (St. Mary's County), captain before 1692; died by Mar 20, 1692/3 (date of inventory). {Ref: INAC 12:92}

GARDNER, ANDREW (Oxford District), captain and master of the ship *Pearle* in 1730. {Ref: CVPR:12}

GARDNER, ELIZABETH, see "Luke Gardiner," q.v.

GARDNER, HABBAKUCK (Patuxent District), captain and master of the ship *Greyhound* in 1730-1731. {Ref: CVPR:12}

GARDNER, JOHN (Talbot County), soldier (rank not stated) circa 1675; paid for his services in the late expedition against the Nanticoke Indians in 1678. {Ref: ARMD 7:92}

GARDNER, RICHARD (Calvert County), captain by 1696. {Ref: ARMD 23:18}

GARFOOTH, JOHN (Potomac District), captain and master of the ship *Mutuall Consent* in 1697. {Ref: ARMD 23:172}

GARLING, SYMON (Calvert and St. Mary's Counties), Protestant and probable soldier in the Revolution of 1689; signed an address and took a loyalty oath (made his "G V" mark) supporting the King of England and "to reestablish Lord Baltimore in his ancient power and government" on Nov 16, 1689; born circa 1665 (aged about 50 when deposed in 1715; name listed as "Simon Gerling"). {Ref: ARMD 8:131; MDEP:69}

GARNISH, JOHN (St. Mary's County), soldier (rank not stated) circa 1675; paid for his services in the late expedition against the Nanticoke Indians in 1678. {Ref: ARMD 7:102}

GARRARD, JAMES (St. Mary's County), soldier (rank not stated) circa 1675; paid for his services in the late expedition against the Nanticoke Indians in 1678. {Ref: ARMD 7:102}

GARRARD, JOHN (Prince George's County), captain and master of the ship *Murdock* riding at anchor in the Patuxent River on Jul 24, 1719. {Ref: PGLR F Old 5:374}

GARY, CLARE, see "Stephen Gary," q.v.

GARY, OLIVER (Dorchester County), soldier (rank not stated) circa 1675; paid for his services in the late expedition against the Nanticoke Indians in 1678. {Ref: ARMD 7:93}

GARY, STEPHEN (Dorchester County), court justice, 1675; soldier (rank not stated) circa 1675; paid for his services in the late expedition against the

Nanticoke Indians in 1678; sheriff, 1678-1681; died testate by Apr 6, 1686 (date of probate; Clare Gary, widow). {Ref: ARMD 7:93, 15:69, 15:232; MDWB 4:202; RMHF I:181}

GARY, STEPHEN (county or port not indicated), mariner by 1658. {Ref: ARMD 41:137}

GARY (GAREY), WILLIAM (Talbot County), soldier (rank not stated) circa 1675; paid for his services in the late expedition against the Nanticoke Indians in 1678; died testate by Feb 3, 1698/9 (date of probate). {Ref: ARMD 7:87, 7:91; MDWB 6:243}

GASCOYNE (GASCOIGNE), WILLIAM (Talbot County), soldier (rank not stated) circa 1675; paid for his services in the late expedition against the Nanticoke Indians in 1678. {Ref: ARMD 7:90-91}

GASIER, ---- (St. Mary's County), captain by 1695. {Ref: INAC 10:403}

GASKILL, WILLIAM (Kent County), captain in the 1730's; appeared in Kent County debt books, 1736-1742. {Ref: INKC:179}

GASKIN, JOHN, see "William Greenwood," q.v.

GASKING, ANNE, see "William Greenwood," q.v.

GASS (GOSS), JOHN (Annapolis District), captain of the sloop *Biddy* of Maryland in 1734. {Ref: MDGZ, Jul 19, 1734}

GASSAWAY, JOHN (Anne Arundel County), captain by 1696; born circa 1672, died intestate on Sep 2, 1697. {Ref: FAAH:171; PFMD:37}

GASSAWAY, NICHOLAS (England and Anne Arundel County), captain before 1678; paid for his services in the late expedition against the Nanticoke Indians in 1678; court justice, 1679-1692; captain of militia by 1681; paid again for his services in 1681; major by 1685; justice (quorum), 1685-1691; major of foot troops in 1689; Protestant and major in the Revolution of 1689; colonel by 1690; assistant commander of rangers and "also a lieutenant *[sic]* under Col. John Coode" in 1691; born Mar 11, 1634/5, died testate by Jan 27, 1691/2 (date of probate). See "Nicholas Gassaway, Jr.," q.v. {Ref: ARMD 5:554, 7:97, 7:248, 7:611, 8:324, 13:242, 15:253, 17:379; FAAH:40, 170, 190; BDML I:347; RMHF I:325; AALR WT#2:64; MDWB 2:228; INAC 11A:36; PFMD:36}

GASSAWAY, NICHOLAS, JR. (Anne Arundel County), captain of foot troops in 1694; military officer who swore allegiance to the King & Queen of England in 1696; born circa 1668, died intestate on Mar 10, 1699/1700. *Note:* One source mistakenly stated that he had died in his 81st year; however, he actually died in his 31st year; born circa 1668, son of Col. Nicholas Gassaway, q.v. {Ref: ARMD 20:108, 20:541; FAAH:171; INAC 19:98, 20:103; PFMD:36}

GASSAWAY, SUSANNA, see "Thomas Gassaway," q.v.

GASSAWAY, THOMAS (Anne Arundel County), captain by 1720; sheriff, 1715-1716; court justice, 1716-1720; member of the Lower House of the Maryland Assembly, 1739; born Feb 20, 1683/4, died testate on Sep 12, 1739 (will probated on Oct 25, 1739; Susanna Gassaway, widow). {Ref: BDML I:347; AALR CW#1:412; FAAH:172; MDWB 22:97}

GATCHELL, BENJAMIN (Annapolis District), captain of the sloop *Dove* of Maryland in 1728-1731. {Ref: MDGZ, Dec 17, 1728; CVPR:12}

GATCHELL, WILLIAM (Cecil County), mariner before 1734; captain of the sloop *Bohemia Industry* in 1734; master of the schooner *Sarah* (built at the Wiccocomoco River in 1731) in 1736 (name listed once as "William Gaitshall" and misinterpreted once as "William Gaitskell"). {Ref: MDGZ, Sep 27, 1734; MDCB 82:43}

GAUNT, THOMAS, see "Thomas Gantt," q.v.

GELDERSON, DAVID (Kent County), soldier (rank not stated) on Isle of Kent who swore allegiance to the Commonwealth of England on Apr 5, 1652. {Ref: INKC:101}

GELLY, THOMAS (Somerset County), soldier (rank not stated) circa 1675; paid for his services in the late expedition against the Nanticoke Indians in 1678. {Ref: ARMD 7:98-99}

GENALLES (GENALLIS), JOHN (St. Mary's County), soldier (rank not stated in 1642; paid for 3 weeks' service under Capt. William Brainthwaite in November, 1642. {Ref: ARMD 3:119, 3:122}

GENID, JOSEPH (Talbot County), lieutenant who swore allegiance to the King & Queen of England in 1696. {Ref: ARMD 20:542}

GERARD, MR., see "Captain Hinfield," q.v.

GERARD, SARAH, see "Justinian Gerrard," q.v.

GERLING, SIMON, see "Symon Garling," q.v.

GERRARD, ---- (Anne Arundel County), captain at the Battle of the Severn on Mar 25, 1655. {Ref: FAAH:25}

GERRARD (GERARD), JUSTINIAN (St. Clement's Manor, St. Mary's County), captain before 1678; paid for his services in the late expedition against the Nanticoke Indians in 1678; captain of a militia company in 1682; died testate by Jan 22, 1688/9 (date of probate; Sarah Gerard, widow, later married Michael Curtis). {Ref: ARMD 7:102, 17:88; RMHF II:155; MDWB 6:43; INAC 5:400, 10:223, 13A:220}

GIBBONS, ---- (New England and St. Mary's County), major or sergeant major in 1659-1660 (both ranks were indicated). {Ref: ARMD 41:395; MDEP:99}

GIBBONS, EDWARD (St. Mary's County), major, 1653; major general, 1658. {Ref: ARMD 3:326, 10:324}

GIBBONS, HENRY (Somerset County), soldier (rank not stated) circa 1675; paid for his services in the late expedition against the Nanticoke Indians in 1678. {Ref: ARMD 7:97}

GIBBONS (GIBBINS), WILLIAM (Anne Arundel County), military officer (rank not stated) who swore allegiance to the King & Queen of England in 1696. {Ref: ARMD 20:541}

GIBBS, EDWARD (Somerset County), soldier (rank not stated) circa 1675; paid for his services in the late expedition against the Nanticoke Indians in 1678; paid for his services out of an assessment levied by the General Assembly for the public good in 1682. {Ref: ARMD 7:100, 7:443}

GIBBS, JOHN (Charles County), Protestant and probable soldier in the Revolution of 1689; signed an address and took a loyalty oath supporting the King of England and the reestablishment of Lord Baltimore into power on Nov 28, 1689. {Ref: ARMD 8:138}

GIBBS, ROBERT (Annamessex Hundred, Somerset County), captain by 1717. {Ref: SOJR III:188-189}

GIBBS, SAMUELL (England and St. Mary's), captain and master of the ship *Adventuror* (or *Adventurer*) of London in 1690; captain and commander of the ship *Patuxent Merchant* of London in 1694. {Ref: ARMD 8:238, 20:147}

GIBSON, ELIZA, see "Richard Edmonds," q.v.

GIBSON, ELIZABETH, see "Miles Gibson," q.v.

GIBSON, ISAAC (Kent County), soldier (rank not stated) circa 1675; paid for his services in the late expedition against the Nanticoke Indians in 1678 (name listed as "Isaack Gibsone"). {Ref: ARMD 7:94}

GIBSON, JACOB (Island Hundred, Talbot County), colonel by 1733; died testate by Jun 10, 1741 (date of probate). {Ref: CESM:18; MDWB 22:362; MINV 27:336}

GIBSON, JAMES (Potomac District), captain and master of the ship *Goodwill* in 1730-1731. {Ref: CVPR:12}

GIBSON, JOHN (Kent County), soldier (rank not stated) on Isle of Kent who swore allegiance to the Commonwealth of England on Apr 5, 1652; soldier (rank not stated) in Capt. William Leeds (Leeads) Company by May 23, 1662, at which time he signed a petition about the misuse of company money by Capt. Thomas Brednox (Bradnox), late of Isle of Kent, deceased. {Ref: ARMD 3:455; INKC:101}

GIBSON, MARY, see "Robert Gibson," q.v.

GIBSON, MICHAEL (Baltimore County), probable soldier (rank not stated) before 1682; paid for his services out of an assessment levied by the General Assembly for the public good in 1682. {Ref: ARMD 7:441}

GIBSON, MILES (Baltimore County), Protestant and probable soldier in the Revolution of 1689; signed an address and took a loyalty oath supporting the King of England and the reestablishment of Lord Baltimore into power on Nov 28, 1689; born circa 1644 (aged about 29 when deposed in 1673), died intestate by May 26, 1692 (date of inventory; Elizabeth Gibson, widow). {Ref: ARMD 8:136, 65:201; BBCF:249-250}

GIBSON, ROBERT (Baltimore County), probable soldier (rank not stated) before 1682; paid for his services out of an assessment levied by the General Assembly for the public good in 1682; died testate by Jun 12, 1704 (date of probate; Mary Gibson, widow). {Ref: ARMD 7:441; MDWB 3:236}

GIBSON, WILLIAM (Talbot County), soldier (rank not stated) circa 1675; paid for his services in the late expedition against the Nanticoke Indians in 1678. {Ref: ARMD 7:88}

GILBERTE, JOHN, see "John Guilbert," q.v.

GILDAR (GILDART), RICHARD (England and Charles County), merchant, mariner and master of the ship *Iverson* of Liverpool in 1714-1716. {Ref: CHLR H#2:10, 19}

GILES, ALLEN (England and Annapolis), captain and master of the ship *Esther* of Newcastle in 1730. {Ref: MDGZ, Jun 16, 1730}

GILES, CLEMENT (Somerset County), Protestant and probable soldier in the Revolution of 1689; signed an address and took a loyalty oath supporting the King of England and "for enabling us to defend ourselves against all invaders" on Nov 28, 1689. {Ref: ARMD 8:139}

GILES, JOHN (Baltimore and Annapolis), captain by 1724; master of the sloop *Tryal* in 1734 (built on the Ware River in Mockjack Bay in Virginia in 1733). {Ref: MDAD 6:179; MDCB 82:19; MDGZ, Jul 19, 1734}

GILES (GYLES), WILLIAM (Somerset County), soldier (rank not stated) circa 1675; paid for his services in the late expedition against the Nanticoke Indians in 1678; trumpeter before 1682; paid for his services out of an assessment levied by the General Assembly for the public good in 1682. {Ref: ARMD 7:98, 7:442-443}

GILL, JOHN (Anne Arundel County), captain and commander of the ship *William and Mary* riding at anchor in South River on Feb 25, 1707/8. {Ref: AALR WT#2:586}

GILL, ROGER (Kent County), soldier (rank not stated) circa 1675; paid for his services in the late expedition against the Nanticoke Indians in 1678. {Ref: ARMD 7:94}

GILLAM (GILHAM, GILHAIN), SAMUELL (St. Mary's County), captain and commander of the ketch *Crane* or *Crain* in 1689. {Ref: ARMD 8:151, 8:170, 8:236}

GILLEBRAND, NICHOLAS (county or port not stated), seaman on the ship *John Hopewell* of London under Capt. Henry Munday in 1699 who ran away to the pirate Capt. Henry King; reported by the Maryland Council that he "may happen to come into these American parts" in 1700. {Ref: ARMD 25:100}

GILLIS, ADAM (county or port not indicated), captain and master of the ship *William and Mary* of Londonderry in 1691. {Ref: ARMD 8:240}

GILSON, JOHN (county or port not indicated), captain and master of the ship *Hopewell* of Kingsail (or Kingsale) in 1665. {Ref: ARMD 49:561; MDHM 5:340}

GINNIS (GENNES), WILLIAM (St. Mary's County), captain of a ship (no name given) in 1690-1696. {Ref: ARMD 8:178; INAC 14:80}

GIRLING, RICHARD (Talbot County), soldier (rank not stated) circa 1675; paid for his services in the late expedition against the Nanticoke Indians in 1678. {Ref: ARMD 7:89; 54:384}

GIRTH, RALPH (Baltimore County), soldier (rank not stated) circa 1675; paid for his services in the late expedition against the Nanticoke Indians in 1678. {Ref: ARMD 7:95}

GIST, RICHARD (Baltimore County), soldier and officer by the 1730's; captain before 1737 (appeared on tax list for Patapsco Upper Hundred; he also had quarters in Soldier's Delight Hundred in 1737); born circa 1683 (aged about 54 when deposed in 1737), died intestate on Dec 28, 1740 (name listed once as "Richard Geist"). {Ref: BBCF:257; INAC 28:54; INBC:22, 26; MDEP:71}

GIVAN, JAMES (Rowastico, Somerset County), captain before 1723; died testate by May 11, 1724 (date of probate; Martha Givan, widow). {Ref: MDWB 18:251; MINV 10:246}

GIVAN, MARTHA, see "James Givan," q.v.

GIVAN, ROBERT, SR. (Stepney Parish, Somerset County), captain before 1734; died testate by Oct 4, 1735 (date of probate). {Ref: MDWB 21:451; MINV 21:219}

GIVAN, WILLIAM (Pocomoke District), captain and master of the ship *Ann* in 1731; captain and master of the brigantine *Nanticoke* (built in Somerset County) in 1733. {Ref: CVPR:12; MDCB 82:7}

GLANDVILL, ROBERT (county or port not indicated), captain and master of the ship *K to S--- Hollow [sic]* of Salsen in 1690. {Ref: ARMD 8:236}

GLANNITT, JOHN (Kent County), "seaman within the said county" and a "sailor belonging to the *Factor* of Bediford" in 1697. {Ref: ARMD 25:599}

GLANVELL (GLANVILL), WILLIAM (Kent County), military officer (rank not stated) who swore allegiance to the King & Queen of England in 1696; died testate by Oct 17, 1719 (date of probate; Mary Glanvill, widow). {Ref: ARMD 20:541; MDWB 15:257}

GLEAR, SAMUEL (Kent County), "seaman within the said county" and a "sailor belonging to the *Factor* of Bediford" in 1697. {Ref: ARMD 25:599}

GLEW, ROBERT (county not indicated), probable soldier (rank not stated) before 1682; paid for his services out of an assessment levied by the General Assembly for the public good in 1682. {Ref: ARMD 7:439}

GLOACE, GEORGE (county not indicated), probable soldier (rank not stated) before 1682; paid for his services out of an assessment levied by the General Assembly for the public good in 1682. {Ref: ARMD 7:440}

GLOVER, DANIEL (Talbot County), Protestant and probable soldier in the Revolution of 1689; signed an address and took a loyalty oath supporting the King of England and the reestablishment of Lord Baltimore into power on Nov 18, 1689. {Ref: ARMD 8:134}

GLOVER, GILS (Charles County), soldier (rank not stated) in Capt. James Langworth's Company before 1661 (year of the captain's death, but his ammunition report was not filed until 1664 by Henry Adames). {Ref: CHLR B:379}

GLOVER, JOHN (Talbot County), soldier (rank not stated) circa 1675; paid for his services in the late expedition against the Nanticoke Indians in 1678. {Ref: ARMD 7:89}

GLOVER, JOSEPH (county or port not indicated), captain and master of the ketch *Ann* of Boston in 1691. {Ref: ARMD 8:240}

GLOVER, THOMAS (Patuxent District), captain and master of the ship *Allexander* in 1731. {Ref: CVPR:12}

GOAD, JAMES (Pocomoke District), captain and master of the ship *Poulton Merchant* in 1731. {Ref: CVPR:12}

GOASBY, JOHN (Charles County), Protestant and probable soldier in the Revolution of 1689; signed an address and took a loyalty oath supporting the King of England and the reestablishment of Lord Baltimore into power on Nov 28, 1689. {Ref: ARMD 8:138}

GODDARD, GEORGE (Somerset County), soldier (rank not stated) circa 1675; paid for his services in the late expedition against the Nanticoke Indians in 1678. {Ref: ARMD 7:97, 7:98}

GODFREY, GEORGE (Charles County), soldier (rank not stated) circa 1675; paid for his services in the late expedition against the Nanticoke Indians in 1678; court justice, 1680; lieutenant of a troop of horse in 1681; born circa 1644 (aged about 70 when deposed in 1714), died testate by Aug 15, 1722 (date of probate). See "James Smallwood," q.v. {Ref: ARMD 5:312, 5:334, 7:101, 15:327, 15:400, 15:404; BDML II:740; MDWB 18:8; MDAD 5:293; MDEP:72}

GODLAD, WILLIAM (county or port not indicated), captain and commander of the ship *Susanne* of London in 1664. {Ref: MDHM 5:340}

GODSGRACE, JOHN (Calvert County), military officer (rank not stated) and civil officer who swore allegiance to the King & Queen of England in 1696 (name listed once as "John Godscross"); John Godsgrace, Sr. *[sic]*, probable son of the first John Godsgrace who settled on the Patuxent River in 1652, died testate by Oct 18, 1722 (date of probate; Rebecca Godsgrace, widow, later married Benjamin Sedwick). {Ref: ARMD 20:543; HCCM:264; MDWB 18:25; MDAD 5:305}

GODSHALL, JOHN (county not indicated), probable soldier (rank not stated) before 1682; paid for his services out of an assessment levied by the General Assembly for the public good in 1682. {Ref: ARMD 7:441}

GODWIN, WILLIAM (England and St. Mary's County), seaman who was apprenticed to Capt. Joseph Eaton, mariner, in 1682, but was later sold to Thomas Gerard in Maryland; born 1668 (aged 16 according to a petition filed at Whitehall, England on Dec 9, 1684 by Godwin's sister, Mrs. Audrey Beale, wife of Capt. Richard Beale, one of His Majesty's Brigandiers; also stated that Godwin was Sir William Boreman's nephew). {Ref: ARMD 5:421-424}

GOLD, RICHARD (Talbot County), soldier (rank not stated) circa 1675; paid for his services in the late expedition against the Nanticoke Indians in 1678. {Ref: ARMD 7:90}

GOLDSBOROUGH (GOULSBOROUGH), ROBERT (Talbot County), soldier (rank not stated) circa 1675; paid for his services in the late expedition against the Nanticoke Indians in 1678; Protestant and probable soldier in the Revolution of 1689; signed an address and took a loyalty oath supporting the King of England and the reestablishment of Lord Baltimore into power on Nov 18, 1689. {Ref: ARMD 7:90, 8:134; RMHF I:173-174}

GOLDSMITH, GEORGE (Baltimore County), Protestant and probable soldier in the Revolution of 1689; signed an address and took a loyalty oath supporting the King of England and the reestablishment of Lord Baltimore into power on Nov 28, 1689; born after 1658, died testate by Apr 8, 1692 (date of probate; Martha Goldsmith, widow). {Ref: ARMD 8:137; BBCF:261; MDWB 2:97}

GOLDSMITH (GOLDSMYTH, GOULDSMITH), GEORGE (England, and Baltimore and Cecil Counties), captain by 1664; member of the Lower House of the Maryland Legislature, 1659-1660; sheriff, 1664-1665; land owner on the south side of Bohemia River in Cecil County; died testate by Jul 20, 1666 (date of probate; Mary Gouldsmith, widow). {Ref: ARMD 5:10; BDML I:367; BBCF:261; CELR 2:299-302; MDWB 1:254}

GOLDSMITH, JOHANNA, see "Samuel Goldsmith," q.v.

GOLDSMITH (GOOLDSMITH), JOHN (Virginia and Manokin Hundred, Somerset County), soldier (rank not stated) circa 1675; paid for his services in the late expedition against the Nanticoke Indians in 1678; Protestant and probable soldier in the Revolution of 1689; signed an address and took a loyalty oath supporting the King of England and "for enabling us to defend ourselves against all invaders" on Nov 28, 1689. {Ref: ARMD 7:100, 8:140; OSES:280, 445}

GOLDSMITH, MARTHA, see "George Goldsmith," q.v.

GOLDSMITH, MARY, see "George Goldsmith," q.v.

GOLDSMITH, MATHEW (Baltimore County), Protestant and probable soldier in the Revolution of 1689; signed an address and took a loyalty oath supporting the King of England and the reestablishment of Lord Baltimore into power on Nov 28, 1689. {Ref: ARMD 8:136}

GOLDSMITH (GOULDSMITH), SAMUEL (England and Baltimore County), major by 1658; burgess (member of the General Assembly), 1659-1664; died testate by Oct 6, 1671 (date of probate; Johanna Gouldsmith, widow). See "George Wells," q.v. {Ref: ARMD 1:382, 49:341; BDML I:367; BBCF:261; MDWB 1:442}

GOODDAY, EDWARD (Charles County), soldier (rank not stated) who was issued a "gun or fowling piece" by Col. Warren on Sep 15, 1694. {Ref: ARMD 20:206, 20:208}

GOODERICKE, GEORGE, see "William Lewis," q.v.

GOODERICKE, ROBERT, see "Robert Goodrick," q.v.

GOODHAND, CHRISTOPHER (Talbot and/or Kent County), soldier (rank not stated) circa 1675; paid for his services in the late expedition against the Nanticoke Indians (name listed once as "Christopher Goodstand" when paid in Talbot County); court justice, 1685 (quorum, 1687); appointed one of the new commissioners for Kent County in 1687; died testate by Oct 4, 1704 (date of probate). {Ref: ARMD 7:88, 8:23, 17:379; MDWB 3:654}

GOODINGE, ROBERT (St. Mary's County), captain of a ship (no name given) in 1690. {Ref: ARMD 8:178}

GOODMAN, RICHARD (Annapolis District), seaman and carpenter on the ship *Hume* commanded by Capt. James Aiking in 1729; he and his brother Samuel Goodman were reported to have run away from the ship while lying in South River in March, 1730. {Ref: MDGZ, Mar 31, 1730}

GOODMAN, SAMUEL (Annapolis District), seaman and sawyer on the ship *Hume* in 1730. See "Richard Goodman," q.v. {Ref: MDGZ, Mar 31, 1730}

GOODRICK (GOODERICKE), ROBERT (Charles County), soldier (rank not stated) in Capt. James Langworth's Company before 1661 (year of the captain's death, but his ammunition report was not filed until 1664 by Henry Adames); born circa 1632-1635 (aged about 70 when deposed in 1702 and 1705). {Ref: CHLR B:379, Z:226; MDEP:73}

GOODRIDGE, NICHOLAS (England and Cecil County), mariner, of London, before 1675; land owner on Sassafras River and Hoving Creek in Cecil County in 1675. {Ref: CELR 1:46}

GOODRIDGE, TIMOTHY (Talbot County), soldier (rank not stated) circa 1675; paid for his services in the late expedition against the Nanticoke Indians in 1678; born circa 1631 (aged about 27 when deposed in 1658), died testate by May 27, 1685 (date of probate). {Ref: ARMD 7:89, 41:85; MDWB 4:134}

GOODWIN, THOMAS (Anne Arundel County), captain of a ship (no name given) in 1697. {Ref: ARMD 25:595}

GOOKINS, DANIEL (South River, Anne Arundel County), captain by 1653. {Ref: ARMD 10:293-294}

GORDING, LOTT (county or port not indicated), captain and master of the ship *Amity* of Boston in 1691. {Ref: ARMD 8:239}

GORDON, AGNES, see "Robert Gordon," q.v.

GORDON (GOURDON), ALEXANDER (Anne Arundel County), lieutenant, commissioned Jul 20, 1658. {Ref: ARMD 3:349, 3:351}

GORDON, RICHARD (Somerset County), captain by 1730. {Ref: MDAD 10:443}

GORDON, ROBERT (Scotland and Annapolis), captain by 1723; member of the Lower House of the Maryland Assembly, 1725-1752; provincial court justice, 1732-1752; born circa 1676, died intestate on Sep 9, 1753 (inventory taken on Nov 7, 1753; Agnes Gordon, widow). {Ref: ARMD 39:55, 39:151, 30:220; BDML I:367; MDGZ, Apr 1, 1729}

GORDON, THOMAS (Somerset County), Protestant and probable soldier in the Revolution of 1689; signed an address and took a loyalty oath supporting the King of England and "for enabling us to defend ourselves against all invaders" on Nov 28, 1689. {Ref: ARMD 8:140}

GORI, DANIEL (county not indicated), private in the Maryland troops "raised to strengthen Albany, New York and resist the French and Indian enemies" in 1690. {Ref: SHMD I:355}

GORSUCH, CHARLES (England, and Talbot and Baltimore Counties), soldier (rank not stated) circa 1675; paid for his services in the late expedition against the Nanticoke Indians in 1678; Protestant and probable soldier in the Revolution of 1689; signed an address and took a loyalty oath supporting the King of England and the reestablishment of Lord Baltimore into power on Nov 28, 1689 (name mistakenly listed once as "Charles Forsuch"); born before Aug 25, 1642 (date of baptism in England; stated he was aged 60 or more when deposed in 1714), died by Jun 25, 1716 (date of administration bond). {Ref: ARMD 7:89, 7:611, 8:137; BBCF:266; MDEP:73}

GORSUCH, HANNAH, see "Lovelace Gorsuch," q.v.

GORSUCH, LOVELACE (Baltimore and Dorchester Counties), soldier (rank not stated) circa 1675; paid for his services in the late expedition against the Nanticoke Indians (in Talbot County) in 1678; Lovelace Gorsuch died testate in Dorchester County by Mar 3, 1703/4 (date of probate; Hannah Gorsuch, widow) and his son Lovelace Gorsuch died testate by Jun 14, 1709 (date of probate). Additional research will be necessary before drawing conclusions. {Ref: ARMD 7:89; MDWB 11:284; MDWB 12:135, pt. 2}

GOSLING, THOMAS (Potomac District), captain and master of the ship *Rogers* in 1697. {Ref: ARMD 23:172}

GOSS, JOHN (St. Mary's County), soldier (rank not stated) circa 1675; paid for his services in the late expedition against the Nanticoke Indians in 1678. {Ref: ARMD 7:103}

GOSS, ROBERT (Ireland and Somerset County), captain and master of the ship *Marygold* of Belfast in 1692. {Ref: ARMD 8:504}

GOUGH, CHARLES (St. Mary's County), Protestant and probable soldier in the Revolution of 1689; signed an address and took a loyalty oath supporting the King of England and the reestablishment of Lord Baltimore into power on Nov 28, 1689. {Ref: ARMD 8:147}

GOULD, JAMES (Queen Anne's County), lieutenant of militia in the Upper Chester and Choptank Rivers area in 1732; born circa 1675 (aged about 49 when deposed in 1724 and aged about 59 when deposed in 1735). {Ref: MDHR 1:11; MDEP:74}

GOULD, JOHN (Kent County), soldier (rank not stated) on Isle of Kent who swore allegiance to the Commonwealth of England on Apr 5, 1652; born circa 1612 (aged about 40 when deposed in 1652). {Ref: ARMD 54:6; INKC:101; MDEP:74}

GOULD, RICHARD, see "Richard Gold," q.v.

GOULDING, JAMES (Queen Anne's County), sailor by 1728 on a ship (no name given) commanded by Capt. Samuel Beck; died in 1728. {Ref: CESM:64}

GOULDING, MATHEW (Oxford District), captain and master of the ship *Laverpoole Merchant* (or *Liverpool Merchant*) in 1731. {Ref: CVPR:12}

GOULDSMITH, SAMUEL, see "George Wells," q.v.

GOUTE, ---- (Dorchester County), captain by 1699; prob. John Goutee (Gootee, Gotee) who was in Maryland before 1679. {Ref: INAC 19½A:125; Land Patents}

GOVER, EPHRAIM (Annapolis and Patuxent Districts), captain and master of the ship *Rachell* riding in Lyons Creek on May 9, 1726 and at Patuxent on Oct 19, 1730. {Ref: AALR SY#1:191; CVPR:12}

GOWLAND, ROBERT (county or port not indicated), captain and commander of the ship *Rappahanock Merchant* of London in 1677. {Ref: MDHM 5:340}

GOYEDER, ---- (Pocomoke, Somerset County), captain by 1666. {Ref: OSES:73}

GRAHAM, WILLIAM (North Britain and Potomac District), mariner by 1734; captain, master and part owner of the ship *Caledonia* (built at Potomac River) in 1738. {Ref: MDCB 82:52}

GRAIMS, ROBERT (county not indicated), private in the Maryland troops "raised to strengthen Albany, New York and resist the French and Indian enemies" in 1690. {Ref: SHMD I:355}

GRAINGE, GEORGE (England, and St. Mary's or Talbot County), cabin boy on the ship *Ruth* in 1676. {Ref: ARMD 51:474}

GRANDY, ---- (Anne Arundel County), captain by 1698. {Ref: INAC 16:24}

GRANGER, CHRISTOPHER (Kent County), soldier (rank not stated) circa 1675; paid for his services in the late expedition against the Nanticoke Indians in 1678. {Ref: ARMD 7:94}

GRANGER, EDWARD (Talbot County), soldier (rank not stated) circa 1675; paid for his services in the late expedition against the Nanticoke Indians in 1678. {Ref: ARMD 7:90}

GRANT, THOMAS (England and Annapolis), captain and master of the ship *Swan* of Bristoll in 1696. {Ref: ARMD 23:318}

GRAVENOR (GRAVENER), HENRY (Annapolis District), captain and commander of the ship *James and Elizabeth* riding at anchor in Severn River on Mar 18, 1707. {Ref: AALR WT#2:598; INAC 31:264}

GRAVES, JOHN (Charles County), soldier (rank not stated) who was issued a "gun or fowling piece" by Col. Warren on Sep 15, 1694. {Ref: ARMD 20:206, 20:208}

GRAVES, THOMAS (county or port not indicated), captain and master of the ship *Richard and Sarah* in 1690. {Ref: ARMD 8:237}

GRAVES, WILLIAM, see "Francis Dallahide," q.v.

GRAY, ELISABETH, see "John Gray" and "Joseph Gray," q.v.

GRAY, FRANCIS (Talbot County), mate on a ship (no name given) in 1720. {Ref: MDAD 2:518}

GRAY, JANE PITTMAN, see "Peter Dent," q.v.

GRAY, JOHN (Somerset County), Protestant and probable soldier in the Revolution of 1689; signed an address and took a loyalty oath supporting the King of England and "for enabling us to defend ourselves against all invaders" on Nov 28, 1689; born circa 1655, died testate by Jun 18, 1732 (date of probate; Elisabeth Gray, widow). {Ref: ARMD 8:140; MDWB 17:416}

GRAY (GREY), JOHN (Charles County), mariner before 1700; one "John Gray (Grey)" died by Apr 16, 1709 (date of administration account), another "John Grey" died testate by Dec 20, 1716 (date of probate), and one "John Gray" was born circa 1645 (aged about 50 when deposed in 1695). Additional research will be necessary before drawing conclusions. {Ref: INAC 29:238, 32B:256; MDWB 14:276; MDEP:75}

GRAY, JONATHAN (Somerset County), captain and mariner by 1714. {Ref: SOJR III:64}

GRAY, JOSEPH (England and Somerset County), probable soldier (rank not stated) before 1682; paid for his services out of an assessment levied by the General Assembly for the public good in 1682; member of the Lower House of the Maryland Assembly, 1704-1707; born circa 1664, died intestate by November, 1724 (inventory taken on Jan 23, 1724/5; Elisabeth Gray, widow). {Ref: ARMD 7:439; BDML I:371; MINV 11:649}

GRAY, MICHAEL (Somerset County), probable soldier (rank not stated) before 1682; paid for his services out of an assessment levied by the General Assembly for the public good in 1682. {Ref: ARMD 7:441}

GRAY, THOMAS (Somerset County), captain, master and owner of the sloop *Betty* (built in Somerset County) in 1734. {Ref: MDCB 82:21}

GRAY, THOMAS (Calvert County), captain and master of the ship *Primrose* of London in 1691; captain by 1691 and to at least 1705. {Ref: ARMD 8:239; INAC 25:138}

GREAVES, JOHN (St. Mary's County), Protestant and probable soldier in the Revolution of 1689; signed an address and took a loyalty oath supporting the King of England and the reestablishment of Lord Baltimore into power on Nov 28, 1689; born circa 1666 (aged about 53 when deposed in 1719). {Ref: ARMD 8:146; MDEP:75}

GREEN (GREENE), ANN, see "Leonard Green," q.v.

GREEN, ELIZABETH, see "John Green," q.v.

GREEN, HENRY (Kent County), military officer (rank not stated) who swore allegiance to the King & Queen of England in 1696; died testate by May 11, 1709 (date of probate; Lucy Green, widow). {Ref: ARMD 20:541; MDWB 12:25, pt. 2}

GREEN, JOHN (Talbot County), soldier (rank not stated) circa 1675; paid for his services in the late expedition against the Nanticoke Indians in 1678. {Ref: ARMD 7:91}

GREEN, JOHN (St. Mary's County), soldier (rank not stated) circa 1675; paid for his services in the late expedition against the Nanticoke Indians in 1678; Protestant and probable soldier in the Revolution of 1689; signed an address and took a loyalty oath supporting the King of England and the reestablishment of Lord Baltimore into power on Nov 28, 1689; died testate by Feb 1, 1706/7 (date of probate; Elizabeth Green, widow). {Ref: ARMD 7:102, 8:146; MDWB 12:87}

GREEN, JOHN (county or port not indicated), captain and master of the ship *Kent* of London in 1691. {Ref: ARMD 8:238}

GREEN, JOHN (county not indicated), private in the Maryland troops "raised to strengthen Albany, New York and resist the French and Indian enemies" in 1690. {Ref: SHMD I:355}

GREEN, JOSEPH (county or port not indicated), captain and master of the sloop *Quaker* of Maryland in 1690. {Ref: ARMD 8:237}

GREEN, JOSEPH (Talbot County), Protestant and probable soldier in the Revolution of 1689; signed an address and took a loyalty oath supporting the

King of England and the reestablishment of Lord Baltimore into power on Nov 18, 1689. {Ref: ARMD 8:134}

GREEN (GREENE), LEONARD (St. Mary's County), constable, 1676; soldier (rank not stated) circa 1675; paid for his services in the late expedition against the Nanticoke Indians in 1678; member of the Lower House of the Maryland Assembly, 1682-1684; died testate by Jul 4, 1688 (date of probate; Ann Greene, widow). {Ref: ARMD 7:102; BDML I:373; MDWB 4:313}

GREEN, THOMAS (Kent County), military officer (rank not stated) who swore allegiance to the King & Queen of England in 1696. {Ref: ARMD 20:540}

GREEN, THOMAS (Anne Arundel County), military officer (rank not stated) who swore allegiance to the King & Queen of England in 1696. {Ref: ARMD 20:542}

GREEN, THOMAS (St. Mary's County), Protestant and probable soldier in the Revolution of 1689; signed an address and took a loyalty oath supporting the King of England and the reestablishment of Lord Baltimore into power on Nov 28, 1689. {Ref: ARMD 8:147}

GREEN, WILLIAM (Somerset County), soldier (rank not stated) circa 1675; paid for his services in the late expedition against the Nanticoke Indians in 1678. {Ref: ARMD 7:99}

GREEN, WILLIAM (Anne Arundel County), military officer (rank not stated) who swore allegiance to the King & Queen of England in 1696. {Ref: ARMD 20:542}

GREENAWAY, JAMES (Anne Arundel County), soldier (rank not stated) circa 1675; paid for his services in the late expedition against the Nanticoke Indians in 1678. {Ref: ARMD 7:96}

GREENBERRY, CHARLES (England and Anne Arundel County), military officer (rank not stated) who swore allegiance to the King & Queen of England in 1696; major, 1698 (son of the late Col. Nicholas Greenberry, deceased); member of the Lower House of the Maryland Assembly, 1701-1708; lieutenant colonel, 1708-1713; member of the Upper House (Maryland Council), 1709-1713; born circa 1672, died testate on Nov 19, 1713 (will probated on Dec 8, 1713; Rachel Greenberry, widow). See "Charles Greenbury," q.v. {Ref: ARMD 20:541, 23:419, 24:224, 27:202, 27:377, 27:410, 29:268; BDML I:372-373; MDWB 13:542; INAC 35A:347}

GREENBERRY (GREENBURY), NICHOLAS (England and Anne Arundel County), captain before 1678; paid for his services in the late expedition against the Nanticoke Indians in 1678; captain of foot troops in 1689; major by 1690; member of the Maryland Council in 1691 (president, 1693-1694); colonel of horse troops, 1692-1694; authorized to erect three forts against invading Indian in 1692; acting governor of the province in 1693 following the death of Lionel Copley; ordered "to raise 12 men, vizt. 6 in Anne Arundel and 6 in Baltimore County, to be imployed to Range as he shall see it needful" on Jun 14, 1694; appointed Judge of the Court of Admiralty for the Western Shore on Oct 18, 1694; military officer who swore allegiance to the King & Queen of England in 1696 (name listed once as "Greenebury"); born 1627, died testate on Dec 17,

1697 (will probated on Mar 5, 1697/8; Ann Greenbury, widow). See "Charles Greenberry" and "Richard Hill, Sr.," q.v. {Ref: ARMD 5:462, 7:96, 8:280, 20:6, 20:68, 20:110, 20:153, 20:161, 20:201, 20:541, 23:29, 23:419, 38:73; FAAH:40, 162-163, 190; BDML I:373; RMHF I:325; MDWB 7:314; INAC 21:327}

GREENBERRY, RACHEL, see "Charles Greenberry," q.v.

GREENBURY, ANN, see "Nicholas Greenberry," q.v.

GREENBURY, CHARLES (Anne Arundel County), colonel by 1720 (received payment from the estate of Michaell Sinklar, deceased, on Feb 10, 1720/1). See "Charles Greenberry," q.v. {Ref: MDAD 3:295}

GREENE, EDWARD (Somerset County), ranger by 1692. {Ref: ARMD 8:547}

GREENE, JAMES (Charles County), probable soldier (rank not stated) before 1682; paid for his services out of an assessment levied by the General Assembly for the public good in 1682; born circa 1659 (aged about 15 in 1674). {Ref: ARMD 7:439; 60:552}

GREENE, THOMAS (St. Mary's County), boatswain by 1643. {Ref: ARMD 4:221}

GREENE (GREEN), THOMAS (England and St. Mary's County), Catholic and close friend of Leonard Calvert; appointed captain general and governor of Maryland on Jun 9, 1647, but never commissioned (superseded by William Stone on Aug 6, 1648); acting governor in 1649 (discharged from all offices on Aug 6, 1650 for usurping his authority); died by Jan 23, 1651/2 (date of probate). {Ref: ARMD 1:213; BDML I:373-374; RMHF II:175}

GREENFIELD, ANNE, see "Thomas Truman Greenfield," q.v.

GREENFIELD, ELEANOR, see "James Greenfield," q.v.

GREENFIELD, JAMES (Prince George's County), captain by 1721; born circa 1685 (aged about 46 when deposed in 1731), died testate by March, 1733/4 (will probated on Mar 26, 1734; Eleanor Greenfield, widow). {Ref: PGLR I:183, Q:397, 525; MDWB 21:20; MINV 20:39; MDEP:76}

GREENFIELD, MARTHA, see "Thomas Greenfield," q.v.

GREENFIELD, THOMAS (England, and Calvert and Prince George's Counties), major, commissioned Jul 30, 1694; sheriff of Prince George's County, 1696-1699; provincial court justice, 1699-1707; colonel, 1707; member of the Maryland Council, 1708-1715; born circa 1649, died testate by Nov 7, 1715 (date of probate; Martha Greenfield, widow). {Ref: ARMD 20:130, 20:379, 25:245, 25:277, 27:377, 29:4, 30:158; BDML I:374; CHLR F#2:50; PGLR F Old 5:460; MDWB 14:89; INAC 36C:222, 290; MDAD 3:231}

GREENFIELD, THOMAS TRUEMAN (Calvert, Prince George's and St. Mary's Counties), captain by 1708; member of the Lower House of the Maryland Assembly, representing St. Mary's County, 1708-1721 (name listed once as "Capt. Truman Greenfield" and once as "Capt. Thomas Greenfield"); colonel by 1723; born circa 1682 (aged about 47 when deposed on Sep 13, 1729 and aged about 49 when deposed on July 7, 1731), died Dec 10, 1733 (will probated on Mar 11, 1733/4; Anne Greenfield, widow). {Ref: ARMD 27:202, 29:51, 29:391, 30:129, 30:359, 33:156, 34:199; BDML I:375; PGLR I:183, M:520, Q:526; MDWB 20:892; MINV 20:83; MDEP:76}

GREENHALGH (GREENEHAGH, GREENHALCH, GREENHALD), EDWARD (St. Mary's County), captain by 1689; empowered to command a troop of horse "for St. Marys, St. James, St. Inegoes and St. Michaels hundreds" in 1689; Protestant and soldier in the Revolution of 1689; signed an address and took a loyalty oath supporting the King of England and the reestablishment of Lord Baltimore into power on Nov 28, 1689; captain of foot troops in 1694 (paid for his services); military officer who swore allegiance to the King & Queen of England in 1696; died by May 28, 1699 (date of first inventory). {Ref: ARMD 8:146, 13:241, 20:72, 20:106, 20:540, 38:55; INAC 19:122, 20:199, 24:22}

GREENOLD (GREENEHOLD), JOHN (Isle of Kent), soldier by 1648 who was "prisoner at Mr. Sturman's after the taking of St. Thomas fort" (no date given); born circa 1625 (aged about 25 when deposed in 1650). {Ref: ARMD 4:381, 10:29; MDEP:76}

GREENSLADE, PHILLIP (England and Baltimore County), mariner of Barnstaple (Barnstable), in Devon, before 1684; land owner in Baltimore County on May 2, 1684; died by Aug 25, 1720 (Jean Greenslade, widow). {Ref: BALR RR#HS; BALR IS#G; BBCF:280}

GREENWOOD, SAMUELL (Baltimore County), soldier (rank not stated) circa 1675; paid for his services in the late expedition against the Nanticoke Indians in 1678; died by Jun 27, 1696 (date of administration bond). {Ref: ARMD 7:95; BBCF:280}

GREENWOOD, WILLIAM (England, and Talbot and Queen Anne's Counties), mariner, of London, and land owner in Talbot County by Sep 18, 1718 (date of power of attorney to his sister and brother-in-law Anne and John Gasking or Gaskin, of Talbot County); captain and commander of the ship *Margaret* riding at anchor in Severn River on Sep 4, 1719; captain and master of the ship *Content* of Maryland in 1727; mariner and land owner in Queen Anne's County in 1734. {Ref: TALR 12:362, 12:394; AALR CW#1:53; QALR IK#C:118, 148; QALR RT#A:321; MDAD 3:252}

GRESHAM, JOHN (St. Mary's County), soldier (rank not stated) in 1642. {Ref: ARMD 4:130-131}

GREY, JOHN, see "John Gray," q.v.

GRIBBLE (GRIBLE), PHILLIP (England, and Talbot and Queen Anne's Counties), captain and mariner of Northam, County Devon, before 1717; land owner in Talbot County (now Queen Anne's) by 1718-1719. {Ref: QALR IK#B:11; INAC 37B:62; MDAD 1:273, 2:160}

GRIFFIN, JOHN (Baltimore County), captain of the ship *Prince* in 1724. {Ref: BALR IS#G; BBCF:282}

GRIFFIN, THOMAS (county or port not indicated), captain of the ship *Industry* in 1692. {Ref: ARMD 13:308}

GRIFFITH, CHARLES (Anne Arundel County), captain circa 1720. {Ref: FAAH:158}

GRIFFITH, LEWIS (Dorchester County), soldier (rank not stated) circa 1675; paid for his services in the late expedition against the Nanticoke Indians in 1678. {Ref: ARMD 7:92}
GRIFFITH, ROBERT (Kent County), soldier (rank not stated) circa 1675; paid for his services in the late expedition against the Nanticoke Indians in 1678. {Ref: ARMD 7:94}
GRIFFITH (GRIFFEN), THOMAS (Cecil County), mariner before 1705; land owner on Back Creek and Elk River in 1705. {Ref: CELR 2:74-75}
GRIGGS, FRANCIS (Calvert County), ranger under the command of Capt. Richard Brightwell in 1692. {Ref: ARMD 8:445}
GRIGGS, JOHN (Calvert County), Protestant, justice of the peace, and probable soldier in the Revolution of 1689; signed an address and took a loyalty oath supporting the King of England and the reestablishment of Lord Baltimore into power on Nov 28, 1689. {Ref: ARMD 8:145}
GRINDALL, ANN, see "Christopher Grindall," q.v.
GRINDALL (GRINDAL), FRANCIS (Kent County), "seaman within the said county" by 1697; "sailor (master) belonging to the *Loves Increase* of Whitehaven" and being within the District of Patuxent in Maryland and bound for Europe in June, 1697. {Ref: ARMD 23:137, 25:600}
GRINDALL (GRENDALL), CHRISTOPHER (England, and Anne Arundel and Baltimore Counties), captain and master of the ship *Three Sisters* in 1731-1733; master and part owner of the ship *Frederick* in 1737 (built at South River in 1733); member of the South River Club in 1742; "Christopher Grindall, late of London, now of Maryland, mariner" died testate by May 18, 1749 (date of probate; Ann Grindall, widow). {Ref: MDGZ, Mar 16, 1732/3; CVPR:12; MDCB 82:49; FAAH:201; BBCF:283; MDWB 26:36; MINV 41:314}
GRINDINGSTONE, CAPTAIN, see "John Jenkins," q.v.
GRINDY, CHARLES (Talbot County), soldier (rank not stated) circa 1675; paid for his services in the late expedition against the Nanticoke Indians in 1678. {Ref: ARMD 7:92}
GRINLAW, JOHN (Charles County), soldier (rank not stated) in Capt. James Langworth's Company before 1661 (year of the captain's death, but his ammunition report was not filed until 1664 by Henry Adames). {Ref: CHLR B:379}
GROOM, DANIEL (Anne Arundel County), captain and commander of the ship *Hester* riding in Herring Bay on Jul 2, 1708. {Ref: AALR WT#2:637}
GROOM, DOROTHY, see "Moses Groom," q.v.
GROOM, MOSES (Anne Arundel and Baltimore Counties), Protestant and probable soldier in the Revolution of 1689; signed an address and took a loyalty oath supporting the King of England and the reestablishment of Lord Baltimore into power on Nov 28, 1689; born circa 1645-1649 (aged about 18 when deposed in 1663 and aged about 19 when deposed in 1668), died by Jan 21,

1698/9 (date of administration bond; Dorothy Groom, widow, later married Robert Cutchin). {Ref: ARMD 8:137; BBCF:284; MDEP:77}

GROOME, SAMUEL (England, and St. Mary's and/or Cecil County), captain and mariner, of London, before 1664; he recorded his cattle mark on Mar 13, 1664 in St. Mary's County, paid a debt he owed to the estate of Edward Keene in Calvert County on Jul 5, 1677, and recorded an indenture in Cecil County on Nov 7, 1677; commander of the ship *William and Mary* in 1668-1669; "Samuel Groome, the Younger" was commander of the ship *Globe* of London in 1679. {Ref: ARMD 49:422, 426; CELR 1:115; INAC 4:154; MDHM 5:339, 341}

GROSS, ROGER (Talbot County), soldier (rank not stated) circa 1675; paid for his services in the late expedition against the Nanticoke Indians in 1678. {Ref: ARMD 7:88}

GROTIER, FRANCIS (Annapolis District), captain and master of the ship *Endeavour* in 1731. {Ref: CVPR:12}

GROVES, COLLARD (county or port not indicated), captain of the ship *Mayflower* in 1659. See "Thomas Barrett," q.v. {Ref: ARMD 41:306; MDEP:8}

GROVES, GEORGE (Charles County), soldier (rank not stated) circa 1675; paid for his services in the late expedition against the Nanticoke Indians in 1678; died testate by Jan 3, 1713/4 (date of probate). {Ref: ARMD 7:101; MDWB 13:630}

GROVES, JOHN (Talbot County), soldier (rank not stated) circa 1675; paid for his services in the late expedition against the Nanticoke Indians in 1678. {Ref: ARMD 7:89}

GROW, JOS. (Anne Arundel County), captain by 1729. {Ref: MINV 15:57}

GRUMBELL, THOMAS (county not indicated), probable soldier (rank not stated) before 1682; paid for his services out of an assessment levied by the General Assembly for the public good in 1682. {Ref: ARMD 7:439}

GRUNDY, ROBERT (Talbot County), mariner, merchant and land owner before 1695; captain by 1695 and to at least 1709; major by 1713; colonel by 1719; died testate by Nov 29, 1720 (date of probate). {Ref: TALR 7:141; CESM:47; MDAD 2:223; INAC 31:95; MDWB 16:227; MINV 11:192; MDAD 7:260}

GRUSHY, THOMAS (Talbot County), captain by 1720. {Ref: MDAD 3:252}

GUGNIS, ---- (Kent County), captain and mariner, 1652. {Ref: ARMD 3:279}

GUILBERT (GILBERTE), JOHN (Talbot County), captain by 1678; soldier (rank not stated) circa 1675; paid for his services in the late expedition against the Nanticoke Indians in 1678; died by Oct 12, 1678 (date of administration account). {Ref: ARMD 7:87; INAC 5:305}

GULICK, WILLIAM (Somerset County), soldier (rank not stated) circa 1675; paid for his services in the late expedition against the Nanticoke Indians in 1678. {Ref: ARMD 7:99}

GUMEY, JOHN (Charles County), Protestant and probable soldier in the Revolution of 1689; signed an address and took a loyalty oath supporting the King of England and the reestablishment of Lord Baltimore into power on Nov 28, 1689. {Ref: ARMD 8:138}

GUMM, ROGER (Somerset County), soldier (rank not stated) circa 1675; paid for his services in the late expedition against the Nanticoke Indians in 1678. {Ref: ARMD 7:97}

GUNDRY, GIDEON (Cecil County), Protestant and probable soldier in the Revolution of 1689; signed an address and took a loyalty oath supporting the King of England and the reestablishment of Lord Baltimore into power on Nov 18, 1689. {Ref: ARMD 8:135}

GUNION, JOHN (Kent County), "seaman within the said county" and a "sailor belonging to the *Factor* of Bediford" in 1697. {Ref: ARMD 25:599}

GUNNELL, GEORGE (Baltimore and Cecil Counties), soldier (rank not stated) circa 1675; paid for his services in the late expedition against the Nanticoke Indians in 1678; died after 1694. {Ref: ARMD 7:95; BBCF:287}

GUNNEY, JOHN (county or port not indicated), captain and master of the ship *Constant Mary* in 1692. {Ref: ARMD 8:371}

GUNTER, PHILLIP (Dorchester County), soldier (rank not stated) circa 1675; paid for his services in the late expedition against the Nanticoke Indians in 1678. {Ref: ARMD 7:93}

GURNALL, THOMAS (county not indicated), captain by 1695. {Ref: ARMD 23:290}

GUTHRIDGE, TIMOTHY (Talbot County), soldier (rank not stated) circa 1675; paid for his services in the late expedition against the Nanticoke Indians in 1678. {Ref: ARMD 7:89}

GUYTHER, NICHOLAS, see "Nicholas Gwither," q.v.

GWEAST, WALTER (St. Mary's County), soldier at St. Inego's fort in 1647. {Ref: ARMD 4:311}

GWITHER (GWYTHER, GUYTHER), NICHOLAS (St. Mary's and Charles Counties), lieutenant by 1650; sheriff of St. Mary's County, 1650-1657; captain who served under Governor Stone at the Battle of the Severn on Mar 25, 1655; sheriff of Charles County, 1658-1661; captain "of St. Hieroms in the province of Maryland" in 1658; member of the Lower House of the Maryland Assembly in 1663; born circa 1625-1626 (aged about 28 when deposed in 1654 and aged about 39 when deposed in 1664), died intestate by March, 1665/6. {Ref: ARMD 1:532, 10:32, 10:321, 10:362, 41:137, 41:254, 49:145, 49:176; FAAH:25-26; BDML I:379}

GWITHER (GWYTHER, GUITHER), RICHARD (St. Mary's County), lieutenant by 1649. {Ref: ARMD 10:9}

GYLLEY (GILLEY, GILLET?), THOMAS (Somerset County), probable soldier (rank not stated) before 1682; paid for his services out of an assessment levied by the General Assembly for the public good in 1682. {Ref: ARMD 7:443}

HACALAND, WILLIAM (Somerset County), Protestant and probable soldier in the Revolution of 1689; signed an address and took a loyalty oath supporting the King of England and "for enabling us to defend ourselves against all invaders" on Nov 28, 1689. {Ref: ARMD 8:140}

HACKETT, HESTER, see "William Hackett," q.v.

HACKETT, JOHN (Talbot and Queen Anne's Counties), soldier (rank not stated) circa 1675; paid for his services in the late expedition against the Nanticoke Indians in 1678; died testate by March 25, 1725 (date of probate; Katherine Hackett, widow). {Ref: ARMD 7:88; MDWB 18:360; MINV 11:41}

HACKETT, KATHERINE, see "John Hackett," q.v.

HACKETT, NICHOLAS (Talbot County), soldier (rank not stated) circa 1675; paid for his services in the late expedition against the Nanticoke Indians in 1678; Indian interpreter by 1684. {Ref: ARMD 7:88, 17:229}

HACKETT, WILLIAM (Kent, Talbot, and Queen Anne's Counties), Protestant and soldier in the Revolution of 1689; signed an address and took a loyalty oath supporting the King of England and the reestablishment of Lord Baltimore into power on Nov 18, 1689 (name spelled "Hackit"); military officer (rank not stated) who swore allegiance to the King & Queen of England in 1696; he was probably the "Capt. Hackett" mentioned in the administration account of Nicholas Hudson, deceased, in Cecil County on Oct 14, 1695, and the "Capt. Haccket" mentioned in the inventory of Capt. Benjamin Bolten, deceased, in Cecil County on Mar 3, 1700/1; "William Hackett, major of train band of Queen Anne's County" died testate by Mar 21, 1719/20 (date of probate; Hester Hackett, widow). {Ref: ARMD 8:134, 20:540; INAC 13B:94, 21:38, 34:38; MDWB 16:148}

HADDAWAY (HADAWAY), GEORGE (Talbot County), soldier (rank not stated) circa 1675; paid for his services in the late expedition against the Nanticoke Indians in 1678; "George Hadaway, Sr." was born circa 1658 (aged about 53 when deposed in 1711), died testate by May 22, 1722 (date of probate; Sarah Hadaway, widow). {Ref: ARMD 7:92; MDWB 17:160; MDEP:79}

HADDAWAY (HADAWAY), PETER (Talbot County), soldier (rank not stated) circa 1675; paid for his services in the late expedition against the Nanticoke Indians in 1678; born circa 1652 (aged about 29 when deposed in 1681). {Ref: ARMD 7:91, 15:412-413}

HADDAWAY, ROBERT (Talbot County), soldier (rank not stated) circa 1675; paid for his services in the late expedition against the Nanticoke Indians in 1678. {Ref: ARMD 7:91}

HADDAWAY (HADAWAY), SARAH, see "George Haddaway," q.v.

HADDEN, JOHN (Anne Arundel County), mariner by 1726; captain and commander of the brigantine *London Town* riding in South River on Jan 23, 1726/7; died intestate by Dec 26, 1729 (date of inventory). {Ref: AALR SY#1:236; MINV 16:331; MDAD 11:265}

HADDOCK (HADDICK), BENJAMIN (England and Prince George's County), mariner of England and land owner in Prince George's County by 1700; died testate by Jun 4, 1703 (date of probate). {Ref: PGLR A:309; MDWB 11:335}

HADDOCK, JAMES (Prince George's County), captain before 1717; colonel by 1720; died testate by May 2, 1731 (date of probate; Sarah Haddock, widow). {Ref: PGLR M:210; INAC 39C:86; MDWB 20:197; MINV 16:227; MDAD 3:150}

HADDOCK, SARAH, see "James Haddock," q.v.

HADDOCK, THOMAS (Prince George's County), captain by 1730 (date of deposition). {Ref: MDEP:79}

HAGGAT (HAGGETT), HUMPHREY (Charles County), soldier (rank not stated) in Capt. James Langworth's Company before 1661 (year of the captain's death, but his ammunition report was not filed until 1664 by Henry Adames); born circa 1628 (aged about 33 when deposed in 1661), died testate by Jul 30, 1663 (date of probate; Anne Haggett, widow). {Ref: ARMD 53:208; CHLR B:379; MDWB 1:177}

HAGGETT, ANNE, see "Humphrey Haggat," q.v.

HAGRUP, CAPTAIN (county not indicated), Indian interpreter by 1700. {Ref: ARMD 25:104}

HAIE, EDWARD (St. Mary's County), Protestant and probable soldier in the Revolution of 1689; signed an address and took a loyalty oath supporting the King of England and the reestablishment of Lord Baltimore into power on Nov 28, 1689. {Ref: ARMD 8:147}

HAIES, JOHN, see "John Hayes," q.v.

HAIMES, WILLIAM (Calvert County), Protestant and probable soldier in the Revolution of 1689; signed an address and took a loyalty oath supporting the King of England and the reestablishment of Lord Baltimore into power on Nov 28, 1689. {Ref: ARMD 8:145}

HAIMON, THOMAS (county or port not indicated), captain and master of the ship (no name given) of Maryland in 1690. {Ref: ARMD 8:237}

HALEY, JOHN (Annapolis District), captain and master of the ship *Batchelours Hall* in 1730-1731. {Ref: CVPR:12}

HALFORD, GILES (Somerset County), soldier (rank not stated) circa 1675; paid for his services in the late expedition against the Nanticoke Indians in 1678. {Ref: ARMD 7:97}

HALL, ALEXANDER (Talbot County), captain before Jul 3, 1709 (date of marriage to Mrs. Mabel Knowles). {Ref: Robert W. Barnes' *Maryland Marriages, 1634-1777*, p. 76}

HALL, ALICE, see "Charles Hall," q.v.

HALL, AMBROSE (county not indicated), probable soldier (rank not stated) before 1682; paid for his services out of an assessment levied by the General Assembly for the public good in 1682. {Ref: ARMD 7:439}

HALL, AQUILA, see "James Phillips," q.v.

HALL, AVARILLA, see "Edward Hall," q.v.

HALL, BENJAMIN (Calvert County), Protestant and probable soldier in the Revolution of 1689; signed an address and took a loyalty oath supporting the King of England and "to reestablish Lord Baltimore in his ancient power and government" on Nov 16, 1689. {Ref: ARMD 8:132}

HALL, BENJAMIN (Calvert, St. Mary's, Charles, and Prince George's Counties), captain by 1700; member of the Lower House of the Maryland Assembly,

1697-1704; born circa 1667, died testate by Mar 29, 1721 (date of probate; Mary Hall, widow). {Ref: ARMD 24:128; BDML I:381-382; MDWB 16:354}

HALL, CHARLES (Annamessex, Somerset County), soldier (rank not stated) circa 1675; paid for his services in the late expedition against the Nanticoke Indians in 1678; one Charles Hall died testate by Aug 13, 1695 (date of probate; Alice Hall, widow) and another Charles Hall, planter, died testate by Jul 22, 1709 (date of probate; Martha Hall, widow). Additional research will be necessary before drawing conclusions. {Ref: ARMD 7:100; OSES:153; MDWB 7:129; MDWB 12:183, pt. 2}

HALL, EDWARD (Baltimore County), soldier and probable officer prior to 1730; styled "colonel" by the time of his death in 1742; born circa 1696 (aged about 43 when deposed in 1739), died testate by Aug 23, 1742 (date of probate; Avarilla Hall, widow). {Ref: BBCF:292; MDWB 23:117; MINV 30:417; MDEP:80}

HALL, ELISHA (Calvert County), Protestant and probable soldier in the Revolution of 1689; signed an address and took a loyalty oath supporting the King of England and "to reestablish Lord Baltimore in his ancient power and government" on Nov 16, 1689; born circa 1663 (aged about 51 when deposed in 1714). {Ref: ARMD 8:131; MDEP:80}

HALL, ELIZABETH, see "Henry Hall," q.v.

HALL, FAYRES (Baltimore County), captain and master of the ship *John and Mary* riding in Patapsco River on Jan 16, 1724/5. {Ref: BALR IS#G}

HALL, HANNAH, see "John Hall," q.v.

HALL, HENRY (Somerset County), Protestant and probable soldier in the Revolution of 1689; signed an address and took a loyalty oath supporting the King of England and "for enabling us to defend ourselves against all invaders" on Nov 28, 1689. {Ref: ARMD 8:140}

HALL, HENRY (Anne Arundel County), soldier and probable officer in the 1730's; member of the Lower House of the Maryland Assembly, 1740-1754; major by 1745; born Mar 2, 1702/3, died intestate on May 18, 1756 (Elizabeth Hall, widow). {Ref: BDML I:384; FAAH:99; MDGZ, Apr 26, 1745; MINV 64:226, 233, 240}

HALL, JEANE, see "Richard Hall," q.v.

HALL, JOHN (Spesutia Hundred, Baltimore County), captain by 1695; sheriff, Baltimore County, 1691-1694; military officer who swore allegiance to the King & Queen of England in 1696; member of the Lower House of the Maryland Assembly, 1696-1707; member of the Upper House (Maryland Council), 1709-1737; born circa 1657-1658 (aged about 51 when deposed in 1709 and aged about 79 when deposed in 1736), died testate by Aug 27, 1737 (date of probate). {Ref: ARMD 20:544; BCTL:1; BDML I:385-386; MDWB 12:792; BBCF:292; MDEP:80}

HALL, JOHN (Baltimore County), soldier and probable officer in the 1730's; major by 1737; member of the Lower House of the Maryland Assembly, 1745-1748; colonel by 1750; born Dec 3, 1701, died testate by May 11, 1774 (date of probate; Hannah Hall, widow). {Ref: BDML I:386; MDGZ, Apr 26, 1745; MDWB 39:712; BBCF:293}

HALL, JOHN (Somerset County), soldier (rank not stated) circa 1675; paid for his services in the late expedition against the Nanticoke Indians in 1678. {Ref: ARMD 7:98}

HALL, JOSEPH (Calvert County), Protestant and probable soldier in the Revolution of 1689; signed an address and took a loyalty oath supporting the King of England and "to reestablish Lord Baltimore in his ancient power and government" on Nov 16, 1689. {Ref: ARMD 8:131}

HALL, JOSEPH (St. Mary's County), soldier (rank not stated) circa 1675; paid for his services in the late expedition against the Nanticoke Indians in 1678. {Ref: ARMD 7:103}

HALL, MARGARET, see "Walter Hall," q.v.

HALL, MARTHA, see "Charles Hall," q.v.

HALL, MARY, see "Benjamin Hall," q.v.

HALL, NATHANIELL (Pocomoke District), captain and master of the ship *Lewis* in 1731. {Ref: CVPR:12}

HALL, RICHARD (Talbot County), soldier (rank not stated) circa 1675; paid for his services in the late expedition against the Nanticoke Indians in 1678; died testate by Jul 4, 1704 (date of probate; Jeane Hall, widow). {Ref: ARMD 7:89; MDWB 3:244}

HALL, ROBERT (Somerset County), Protestant and probable soldier in the Revolution of 1689; signed an address and took a loyalty oath supporting the King of England and "for enabling us to defend ourselves against all invaders" on Nov 28, 1689. {Ref: ARMD 8:141}

HALL, STEPHEN (Somerset County), ship's carpenter in 1707. {Ref: SOJR I:39}

HALL, THOMAS (England and St. Mary's County), master's mate on the ship *Sarah and Elizabeth* of Bristol in 1671. {Ref: ARMD 5:100}

HALL, WALTER (Cross Manor, St. Mary's County), lieutenant colonel, 1663; member of the Lower House of the Maryland Legislature, 1676-1678; died testate by Dec 5, 1678 (date of probate; Margaret Hall, widow). {Ref: ARMD 49:176; BDML I:389; MDWB 9:64}

HALL, WILLIAM (Somerset County), Protestant and probable soldier in the Revolution of 1689; signed an address and took a loyalty oath supporting the King of England and "for enabling us to defend ourselves against all invaders" on Nov 28, 1689. {Ref: ARMD 8:140}

HALLET, THOMAS (England and Anne Arundel County), captain and commander of the ship *Saint Mary's* of Bristol in 1682. {Ref: INAC 7C:151}

HALLOWES (HOLLOWES, HOLLIS), JOHN (England, St. Mary's County, and Westmoreland County, Virginia), captain by 1653; major, 1655; born circa 1613-1616 (aged about 40 when deposed in 1653 and aged about 41 when deposed in 1657). {Ref: ARMD 3:174, 10:265, 10:279, 10:541, 10:547; FMDP:220-222; MDEP:95}

HALTERS, ROBERT (Kent County), soldier (rank not stated) on Isle of Kent who swore allegiance to the Commonwealth of England on Apr 5, 1652. {Ref: INKC:101}

HAMBLETON, JOHN (Talbot County), Protestant and probable soldier in the Revolution of 1689; signed an address and took a loyalty oath supporting the King of England and the reestablishment of Lord Baltimore into power on Nov 18, 1689. {Ref: ARMD 8:134}

HAMBLETON, W. (Talbot County), Protestant and probable soldier in the Revolution of 1689; signed an address and took a loyalty oath supporting the King of England and the reestablishment of Lord Baltimore into power on Nov 18, 1689. {Ref: ARMD 8:134}

HAMER, JOHN (Kent County), military officer (rank not stated) who swore allegiance to the King & Queen of England in 1696; a "John Hamour" died testate in Queen Anne's County by Jun 7, 1722 (date of probate; Elizabeth Hamour, widow). {Ref: ARMD 20:540; MDWB 17:193}

HAMILTON (HAMBLETON), ANDREW (Talbot County), soldier (rank not stated) circa 1675; paid for his services in the late expedition against the Nanticoke Indians in 1678; Protestant and probable soldier in the Revolution of 1689; signed an address and took a loyalty oath supporting the King of England and the reestablishment of Lord Baltimore into power on Nov 18, 1689. {Ref: ARMD 7:91, 8:134}

HAMILTON, JOSEPH (Pocomoke District), captain and master of the ship *Elizabeth* in 1730. {Ref: CVPR:12}

HAMILTON, SARAH, see "William Hamilton," q.v.

HAMILTON, WILLIAM (Baltimore County), colonel by 1734; member of the Lower House of the Maryland Assembly, 1722-1737; county commissioner, 1729; born circa 1682 (aged about 60 when deposed in 1742), died testate by Nov 7, 1759 (date of probate; Sarah Hamilton, widow). {Ref: BDML I:391; MDWB 30:737; MDEP:81}

HAMMERTON, ISAAC (England and Annapolis), seaman on the ship *Jefferyes* commanded by Capt. William Cooper on Feb 23, 1697/8 and who was "employed to bring John Sheffield's shallop from Patuxent to West River about a fortnight or three weeks ago." {Ref: ARMD 23:387}

HAMMON (HAMON, HAMMAN), HENRY (Somerset County), soldier (rank not stated) circa 1675; paid for his services in the late expedition against the Nanticoke Indians in 1678; Protestant and probable soldier in the Revolution of 1689; signed an address and took a loyalty oath supporting the King of England and "for enabling us to defend ourselves against all invaders" on Nov 28, 1689. {Ref: ARMD 7:100, 8:141}

HAMMON, JOHN (Talbot County), soldier (rank not stated) circa 1675; paid for his services in the late expedition against the Nanticoke Indians in 1678. {Ref: ARMD 7:89}

HAMMON, PHILLIP (Somerset County), soldier (rank not stated) circa 1675; paid for his services in the late expedition against the Nanticoke Indians in 1678. {Ref: ARMD 7:97}

HAMMOND, CHARLES (Anne Arundel County), military officer (rank not stated) who swore allegiance to the King & Queen of England in 1696; major by 1708 (referred to as "colonel" in 1710, but he called himself "major" when he wrote his will in 1713); member of the Lower House of the Maryland legislature, 1710-1713; born circa 1670, died testate on Nov 23, 1713 (will probated on Jan 19, 1713/4; Hannah Hammond, widow). {Ref: ARMD 20:541, 29:468; AALR WH#4:49, 109; BDML I:391-392; MDWB 13:608; INAC 35A:114}

HAMMOND, CHARLES (Anne Arundel County), provincial court justice, 1732-1735; commissioned Commissioner for Emitting Bills of Credit on Jan 29, 1733/4; member of the Maryland Council, 1735-1771; probable soldier and officer by 1720; colonel by 1761; born circa 1693 (aged about 68 when deposed in 1761), died testate on Sep 13, 1772 (will probated on Oct 13, 1772). {Ref: BDML I:392; MDCB 82:3; MDWB 38:815; MDEP:82}

HAMMOND (HAMOND), EDWARD (All Hallows Parish, Somerset County), military officer (rank not stated) who swore allegiance to the King & Queen of England in 1696; captain by 1702; in the will of Thomas Purnall written on Feb 27, 1720/1 he stated that he held land previously owned by Capt. Edward Hammond on Copoinco Neck; "Edward Hammond, Sr." died testate by Sep 4, 1718 (date of probate). {Ref: ARMD 20:544; SOJR I:6, 14, II:79, III:2, 62; MDWB 14:674, 18:91}

HAMMOND, ELIZABETH, see "William Hammond," q.v.

HAMMOND, HANNAH, see "Charles Hammond," q.v.

HAMMOND, JOHN (Anne Arundel County), colonel before 1682 (date of deed). {Ref: AALR IH#1:22}

HAMMOND, JOHN (England and Anne Arundel County), captain by 1691; court justice (quorum), 1692; captain of horse troops in 1694; major, 1695; military officer who swore allegiance to the King & Queen of England in 1696; Maryland Council proceedings state that "Major John Hammond be constituted Lieutenant Colonel" on Apr 15, 1698; referred to as "colonel" in 1699; member of the Maryland Council, 1702-1705; commissioned major general and chief military officer of the Western Shore on Jul 6, 1707; born 1643, died testate on Nov 24, 1707 (will probated on Dec 4, 1707; Mary Hammond, widow). {Ref: ARMD 8:324, 13:252, 20:107-108, 20:541, 23:278, 24:11, 24:135, 25:25, 25:80, 25:130, 25:185, 25:251, 38:72; FAAH:40, 179; BDML I:393; INAC 29:144; MDWB 12:184; RMHF I:196-197, II:171, 335}

HAMMOND, JOHN (Anne Arundel County), soldier and probable officer by 1730; captain before 1740; born circa 1701 (aged about 39 when deposed in 1740). {Ref: MDEP:82}

HAMMOND, MARY, see "John Hammond" and "Thomas Hammond," q.v.

HAMMOND, MORDECAI (Anne Arundel County), captain by 1726. {Ref: MINV 11:620}

HAMMOND, SARAH, see "William Hammond," q.v.

HAMMOND (HAMOND), THOMAS (Baltimore County), captain of horse troops in 1694; captain who swore allegiance to the King & Queen of England in 1696; major by 1701; member of the Lower House of the Maryland Assembly, 1701-1714, 1722-1724; major on the north side of the Patapsco, 1703; colonel by 1712; died testate by Feb 2, 1724/5 (date of probate; Mary Hammond, widow). {Ref: ARMD 20:110, 20:544, 29:97, 29:392; BCTL:35; BDML I:399; MDWB 18:350}

HAMMOND, WILLIAM (Baltimore County), probable officer in the 1730's; colonel by 1737 (listed on tax list for Patapsco Upper Hundred; he also had quarters in Soldier's Delight Hundred); born 1702, died by Jan 16, 1752 of smallpox (will probated on Feb 11, 1752; Sarah Hammond, widow). {Ref: BBCF:298; INBC:22, 25; MDWB 28:240}

HAMMOND, WILLIAM (Anne Arundel County), military officer (rank not stated) who swore allegiance to the King & Queen of England in 1696; died testate by Feb 28, 1710/1 (date of probate; Elizabeth Hammond, widow). {Ref: ARMD 20:542; MDWB 13:181}

HAMOUR, JOHN, see "John Hamer," q.v.

HAMSON, GILBERT (St. Mary's County), captain by 1727. {Ref: MDAD 8:226}

HAMTON (HAMPTON), JOHN (St. Mary's County), captain by 1646. {Ref: ARMD 3:177, 10:99}

HANCOCK, JOHN (Patuxent, Calvert County and Pocomoke, Somerset County), soldier (rank not stated) circa 1675; paid for his services in the late expedition against the Nanticoke Indians in 1678. See "John Anderson," q.v. {Ref: ARMD 7:99; OSES:434}

HANDCOCK, STEPHEN (Anne Arundel County), military officer (rank not stated) who swore allegiance to the King & Queen of England in 1696. {Ref: ARMD 20:542}

HANDY, ISAAC (Somerset County and Pocomoke District), mariner by 1726; captain and part owner of the sloop *Samuel and Mary* (with his brothers Stephen and Thomas Handy) in 1726; master of the ship *James and Ann* in 1731; master of the sloop *Ann* in 1738 (built in Somerset County in 1737) militia captain by 1744; colonel by 1755; died Nov 12, 1762. {Ref: BDML I:402; CVPR:12; MDCB 82:52}

HANDY, JANE, see "John Handy," q.v.

HANDY, JOHN (Somerset County), soldier and probable officer by the 1720's; captain by 1742; born circa 1694-1695 (aged about 38 when deposed in 1733 and aged 49 when deposed in 1743), died testate by May 28, 1745 (date of probate; Jane Handy, widow). {Ref: DOLR 12 Old 157; MDWB 24:105-107; MDEP:83}

HANDY, SAMUELL (Somerset County), soldier (rank not stated) circa 1675; paid for his services in the late expedition against the Nanticoke Indians in 1678; deputy ranger in 1716; "Samuel Handy, Sr." died testate by Sep 13, 1721 (date of probate). {Ref: ARMD 7:97; SOJR III:36; MDWB 17:24}

HANDY, STEPHEN, see "Isaac Handy," q.v.

HANDY, THOMAS, see "Isaac Handy," q.v.

HANLEY, ARTHUR (Somerset County), Protestant and probable soldier in the Revolution of 1689; signed an address and took a loyalty oath supporting the King of England and "for enabling us to defend ourselves against all invaders" on Nov 28, 1689. {Ref: ARMD 8:141}

HANLEY, DANIEL (St. Mary's County), Protestant and probable soldier in the Revolution of 1689; signed an address and took a loyalty oath supporting the King of England and the reestablishment of Lord Baltimore into power on Nov 28, 1689. {Ref: ARMD 8:146}

HANMAN, EDWARD (Kent County), soldier (rank not stated) circa 1675; paid for his services in the late expedition against the Nanticoke Indians in 1678. {Ref: ARMD 7:94}

HANNAH, MICHAEL (Somerset County), Protestant and probable soldier in the Revolution of 1689; signed an address and took a loyalty oath supporting the King of England and "for enabling us to defend ourselves against all invaders" on Nov 28, 1689. {Ref: ARMD 8:140}

HANNAH, THOMAS, see "Bartholomew Ennalls," q.v.

HANS (HANSE, HANCE) ---- (Cecil and St. Mary's Counties), soldier (rank not stated) by 1678; a certificate from the Commissioners of St. Mary's County Court was read at the General Assembly on May 13, 1682 "concerning Wadden Hanse the Daughter of One Hanse a Sweed who was killed at the Susquehannah fort, and thereupon Vote that four thousand Pounds be raised this year out of the Publick and Ordered to be paid in St. Marie's County, that one thousand pounds thereof be paid to William Wherritt for his keeping the child hitherto, that the other three thousand be paid to the Commissioners of St. Marie's County to be by them paid to Such person as Shall take the Child as an Apprentice or Orphan Child, till she shall come to Eighteen Years of Age, the Person that takes her to Oblige to teach the Girle to read and Sowe." {Ref: ARMD 7:312}

HANS (HANSE, HANCE), JOHN (Cecil County), captain by 1696; Indian interpreter before 1700. See "John Hans Tilman," q.v. {Ref: ARMD 23:94, 25:104}

HANSE, WADDEN, see "---- Hanse" and "Hance Jordaine," q.v.

HANSLAP (HANSLAPP, HANSLOPE, HENSLAPE), HENRY (Anne Arundel County), soldier (rank not stated) circa 1675; paid for his services in the late expedition against the Nanticoke Indians in 1678; captain by 1683; clerk of the county court by 1683; sheriff, 1686; captain of foot troops in the Revolution of 1689; born circa 1635 (aged about 59 when deposed in 1694), died testate by Oct 23, 1698 (date of probate; Elizabeth Hanslap, widow). {Ref: ARMD 5:470, 7:97, 7:450, 7:611, 13:242, 23:19; FAAH:190; MDWB 6:163; MDEP:83}

HANSON, ANDREW (Kent County), soldier (rank not stated) on Isle of Kent who swore allegiance to the Commonwealth of England on Apr 5, 1652. {Ref: INKC:101}

HANSON, ELIZABETH, see "Samuel Hanson," q.v.

HANSON (HANCESON), HANS (Delaware Bay, New Sweden, and Kent and Cecil Counties), court justice, 1685-1687 (quorum, 1702); captain by 1693; captain of horse troops, commissioned Jul 30, 1694; lieutenant colonel, commissioned Oct 9, 1694; paid for his services in 1695; military officer who swore allegiance to the King & Queen of England in 1696; member of the Commission of the Peace in Kent County, 1697; colonel and member of the General Assembly in 1700 (name listed also as "Hanse Hanson" and "Coll. Hance Hanson" and "Coll. Hance Hanceson" and "Mr. Hans Hanson"); born circa 1646-1647 (aged about 28 when deposed in 1674 and aged about 37 when deposed in 1684), died testate by Apr 27, 1704 (date of probate; Martha Hanson, widow; account filed on Jul 7, 1708 by Martha Pott, wife of William Pott). See "John Derricutt," q.v. {Ref: ARMD 8:23, 17:293, 17:379, 20:107, 20:131, 20:152, 20:541, 23:198, 24:40, 23:21, 24:112, 25:125, 25:169, 38:75; BDML I:404-405; KELR JS#W:543; INKC:150; MDWB 3:264; INAC 25:86, 28:163; MDEP:83}

HANSON, JOHN (Charles County), soldier (rank not stated) circa 1675; paid for his services in the late expedition against the Nanticoke Indians in 1678; paid for his services out of an assessment levied by the General Assembly for the public good in 1682; died testate by Jul 5, 1714 (date of probate). {Ref: ARMD 7:101, 7:440; MDWB 13:719}

HANSON, JOHN (Cecil County), captain before 1717; died by Jun 14, 1717 (date of administration account). {Ref: INAC 39B:64}

HANSON, MARTHA, see "Hans Hanson," q.v.

HANSON, RANDALL (St. Mary's and Charles County), lieutenant, 1660; court justice in Charles County, 1685. {Ref: ARMD 3:401, 17:380}

HANSON, ROBERT (Charles County), soldier and probable officer before 1710; sheriff, 1715; member of the Lower House of the Maryland Assembly, 1719-1741; major by 1730; colonel by 1732; born in 1680 (aged 57 when deposed in 1737, aged 61 when deposed in 1741, aged 63 when deposed in 1763, aged 65 when deposed in 1745, and aged 67 when deposed in 1747), died testate by Sep 27, 1748 (date of probate). {Ref: ARMD 39:13, 39:55, 39:151, 39:220; BDML I:406; MDWB 25:412; MDEP:83; MINV 41:217}

HANSON, SAMUEL (Charles County), soldier and probable officer by the 1730's; major before 1744; born circa 1705 (aged about 39 when deposed in 1744). {Ref: ARMD 40:83}

HANSON, SAMUEL (Charles County), captain circa 1716; member of the Lower House of the Maryland Assembly, 1716-1717, 1728-1731; sheriff, 1717-1720; born circa 1685 (aged about 54 when deposed in 1739), "Samuel Hanson, Sr." died on Oct 26, 1740 (will written on Oct 22, 1740 and probated on Mar 5, 1740/1; Elizabeth Hanson, widow). {Ref: BDML I:407; MDWB 22:296; MDEP:84}

HANSTED, WILLIAM (Talbot County), soldier (rank not stated) circa 1675; paid for his services in the late expedition against the Nanticoke Indians in 1678. {Ref: ARMD 7:88}

HANSTILMAN, ---- (county not indicated), captain who was "appointed to go to the Indians at the head of the bay by an order of the last Assembly" on Oct 15, 1697. {Ref: ARMD 23:234}

HANTON, W. (Annapolis District), captain of the ship *William and Sarah* in 1734. {Ref: MDGZ, Aug 2, 1734}

HARBERT (HERBERT), WILLIAM (Charles County), soldier (rank not stated) before 1682; paid for his services out of an assessment levied by the General Assembly for the public good in 1682; captain by 1705; member of the Lower House of the Maryland Assembly, 1708; died testate by Jul 26, 1718 (date of probate; the will of his widow Sarah Harbert was probated on the same day). {Ref: ARMD 7:440, 27:202; BDML I:410; MDWB 14:661-662; MINV 1:281-288; MDAD 3:31, 3:224}

HARBET, MICHAEL (Talbot County), Protestant and probable soldier in the Revolution of 1689; signed an address and took a loyalty oath supporting the King of England and the reestablishment of Lord Baltimore into power on Nov 18, 1689. {Ref: ARMD 8:134}

HARBIN, FRANCIS (Calvert County), captain by 1691; master of a ship (no name given) riding at anchor at the mouth of the Patuxent River on Jul 1, 1695; captain and commander of the ship *Adventure* in 1698. See "James Brock," q.v. {Ref: ARMD 20:306, 23:435, 23:467; INAC 10:403; MDWB 16:29}

HARD, GEORGE (Talbot County), soldier (rank not stated) circa 1675; paid for his services in the late expedition against the Nanticoke Indians in 1678. {Ref: ARMD 7:92}

HARDIDGE, WILLIAM (St. Mary's County), captain by 1696. {Ref: INAC 14:81}

HARDIGE (HARDICH), WILLIAM (Virginia and St. Mary's County), soldier (rank not stated) in 1642; paid for 3 weeks' service under Capt. William Brainthwaite in November, 1642; born circa 1618 (aged about 37 when deposed in 1655). {Ref: ARMD 3:120, 3:122; MDEP:84}

HARDIN (HARDING), ROBERT (Talbot County), soldier (rank not stated) circa 1675; paid for his services in the late expedition against the Nanticoke Indians in 1678; died testate by Mar 18, 1706/7 (date of probate; Elizabeth Hardin, widow). {Ref: ARMD 7:88-89; MDWB 12:103}

HARDING, JOHN (St. Mary's County), Protestant and probable soldier in the Revolution of 1689; signed an address and took a loyalty oath supporting the King of England and the reestablishment of Lord Baltimore into power on Nov 28, 1689. {Ref: ARMD 8:147}

HARDY (HARDYE), ANNE, see "Robert Hardy," q.v.

HARDY, HENRY (Charles County), Protestant and soldier in the Revolution of 1689; signed an address and took a loyalty oath supporting the King of England and the reestablishment of Lord Baltimore into power on Nov 28, 1689; military officer (rank not stated) who swore allegiance to the King & Queen of England in 1696; captain by 1697; died intestate by September, 1722 (date of administration account). {Ref: ARMD 8:138, 20:543, 23:234, 33:158; INAC 21:167; MDAD 4:229}

HARDY, JAMES (county or port not indicated), captain and master of the ship *William and Sarah* of Maryland in 1691. {Ref: ARMD 8:239}

HARDY, ROBERT (Virginia and Somerset County), soldier (rank not stated) circa 1675; paid for his services in the late expedition against the Nanticoke Indians in 1678 (name also listed as "Robert Hardie" and "Robert Hardye"); died testate by Aug 25, 1679 (date of probate; Anne Hardye, widow). {Ref: ARMD 7:98; MDWB 10:55}

HARDY, WILLIAM (St. Mary's County), Protestant and probable soldier in the Revolution of 1689; signed an address and took a loyalty oath supporting the King of England and the reestablishment of Lord Baltimore into power on Nov 28, 1689. {Ref: ARMD 8:147}

HARE, HENRY (Kent County), soldier (rank not stated) in Capt. William Leeds (Leeads) Company by May 23, 1662, at which time he signed a petition about the misuse of company money by Capt. Thomas Brednox (Bradnox), late of Isle of Kent, deceased. {Ref: ARMD 3:455}

HARES, WILLIAM (Dorchester County), soldier (rank not stated) circa 1675; paid for his services in the late expedition against the Nanticoke Indians in 1678. {Ref: ARMD 7:93}

HARGISSONE, GEORGE (Dorchester County), soldier (rank not stated) circa 1675; paid for his services in the late expedition against the Nanticoke Indians in 1678. {Ref: ARMD 7:93}

HARLE, JAMES (Dorchester County), soldier (rank not stated) circa 1675; paid for his services in the late expedition against the Nanticoke Indians in 1678. {Ref: ARMD 7:93}

HARMAN, THOMAS (Talbot and/or Kent County), captain of horse troops in 1689; died by May 10, 1695 (date of inventory). {Ref: ARMD 13:243; INAC 13A:388, 19:85}

HARMER, GODEFRID (New Sweden and Baltimore County), Indian interpreter in 1661 (name listed as "Gothofrid Harmer"); "Godfrey Harmer, of Gunpowder River" died testate by May 20, 1674 (date of probate; Mary Harmer, widow, later married John Stansby, *q.v.*). {Ref: ARMD 3:411; MDWB 1:613; BDML II:769; BBCF:303}

HARNESONE, ARON (Kent County), soldier (rank not stated) circa 1675; paid for his services in the late expedition against the Nanticoke Indians in 1678. {Ref: ARMD 7:94}

HARNESS, JACOB (Anne Arundel County), soldier (rank not stated) circa 1675; paid for his services in the late expedition against the Nanticoke Indians in 1678; died testate by Mar 26, 1705 (date of probate). {Ref: ARMD 7:96; MDWB 3:450}

HARRIS, AUGUSTINA, see "James Harris," q.v.

HARRIS, ELEANOR, see "Lloyd Harris," q.v.

HARRIS, ELIZABETH, see "Thomas Harris," q.v.

HARRIS, GEORGE (Somerset County), soldier (rank not stated) circa 1675; paid for his services in the late expedition against the Nanticoke Indians in 1678; captain by 1705. {Ref: ARMD 7:98; SOJR I:120}

HARRIS, GEORGE (Prince George's County), captain by 1696. {Ref: ARMD 23:247; PGLR Q:525}

HARRIS, JAMES (Kent and Cecil Counties), captain by 1709; member of the Lower House of the Maryland Assembly, 1710-1737; sheriff, Kent County, 1711-1713; provincial court justice, 1716-1726; captain who brought a bill before the Lower House of the Maryland Assembly "for ascertaining the manner of Takeing the Evidences of Seafareing men" on May 3, 1718; major by 1726; member of the Maryland Council, 1739-1742; colonel by 1742; born circa 1682 (aged about 48 when deposed in 1730), died testate by Nov 17, 1743 (date of probate; Augustina Harris, widow). {Ref: ARMD 30:137, 30:359, 30:389, 33:165; BDML I:413; INKC:150; MDWB 23:416; MDEP:85}

HARRIS, JOHN (Somerset County), probable soldier (rank not stated) before 1682; paid for his services out of an assessment levied by the General Assembly for the public good in 1682. {Ref: ARMD 7:441-442}

HARRIS, JOHN (Prince George's County), foot soldier (rank not stated) under the command of Capt. Richard Owen from June, 1699 to May, 1700. {Ref: ARMD 24:122}

HARRIS, JOHN (St. Mary's County), captain by 1692. {Ref: INAC 10LC:22}

HARRIS, JOHN (county or port not indicated), seaman on the ship *John Hopewell* of London under Capt. Henry Munday in 1699 who ran away to the pirate Capt. Henry King; reported by the Maryland Council that he "may happen to come into these American parts" in 1700. {Ref: ARMD 25:100}

HARRIS, JOHN (Charles County), a seafaring man "belonging to Mr. Lyne" in 1697. {Ref: ARMD 25:597}

HARRIS, JOHN (England, Charles County and Patuxent District), captain and commander of the ship *Dover* of London in 1678-1679; captain and master of the ship *Gerard* riding in Wicocomoco River in 1682; captain and master of the ship *Mary* (or *Mary and Ann*) in 1684; commander of the ship *James and Benjamin* in 1694; captain and commander of the ship *Globe* of London in 1697. See "Patrick Innes," q.v. {Ref: ARMD 7:286, 15:245, 23:137; CHLR K:219; INAC 13A:239}

HARRIS, JOHN (Pocomoke District), captain and master of the ship *Pine Apple* in March, 1730/1. {Ref: CVPR:12}

HARRIS, LLOYD (Baltimore County), probable soldier in the 1730's; coroner, 1735; commissioned Ranger on Oct 27, 1737; died by Jun 28, 1743 (date of administration bond; Eleanor Harris, widow). {Ref: MDCB 82:51; BBCF:305}

HARRIS, MARY, see "William Johnson," q.v.

HARRIS, MOSES (Talbot County), soldier (rank not stated) circa 1675; paid for his services in the late expedition against the Nanticoke Indians in 1678; died testate after Feb 16, 1711/2 (date will was written; date of probate not given). {Ref: ARMD 7:91; MDWB 13:455}

HARRIS, THOMAS (county or port not indicated), mariner by 1734; captain and master of the brigantine *Charming Molly* in 1736 (built in Talbot County in 1732). {Ref: MDCB 82:44}

HARRIS, THOMAS (Charles County), captain by 1706; died intestate by Jul 27, 1734 (date of inventory; Elizabeth Harris, widow). {Ref: CHLR C#2:31; MINV 18:468}

HARRIS, WILLIAM (Prince George's County), captain and commander of the ship *Tobias* in 1722. {Ref: PGLR I:465}

HARRIS, WILLIAM (England, and Kent and Cecil Counties), supported the Revolution of 1689; military officer (rank not stated) who swore allegiance to the King & Queen of England in 1696; justice, Kent County, 1686-1692, and Cecil County, 1692-1704; captain by 1699; major by 1701; colonel of Cecil County in 1703; born circa 1644-1649 (aged about 40 when deposed in 1684 and aged about 50 when deposed in 1699), died testate by Nov 21, 1712 (date of probate). {Ref: ARMD 8:23, 20:545, 17:291, 25:169; BDML I:415; INAC 18:194; MDWB 13:488; MDEP:85}

HARRIS, WILLIAM (England and St. Mary's County), captain and master of the ship *Sarah and Elizabeth* of Bristol in 1671. {Ref: ARMD 5:100}

HARRIS, WILLIAM (England and St. Mary's County), seaman on the ship *Ruth* in 1676-1677. {Ref: ARMD 67:36}

HARRISON, CHARLES (Anne Arundel County), military officer (rank not stated) who swore allegiance to the King & Queen of England in 1696. {Ref: ARMD 20:541}

HARRISON, ELIZABETH, see "Joseph Harrison," q.v.

HARRISON, FRANCIS (Talbot County), soldier (rank not stated) circa 1675; paid for his services in the late expedition against the Nanticoke Indians in 1678; died testate by May 31, 1711 (date of probate). {Ref: ARMD 7:88; MDWB 13:241}

HARRISON, FRANCIS (Charles County), soldier (rank not stated) circa 1675; paid for his services in the late expedition against the Nanticoke Indians in 1678; captain by 1710. {Ref: ARMD 7:101; INAC 31:344}

HARRISON (HARRISOS?), GEORGE (Charles County), sailor by 1719. {Ref: MDAD 2:128}

HARRISON, GILBERT (St. Mary's County), captain by 1727; master of the ship *Henrietta* in 1730-1731. {Ref: CVPR:12; MDAD 8:288}

HARRISON, HANS (Charles or St. Mary's County), lieutenant colonel by 1699; injured when lightning struck the State House in the summer of 1699. {Ref: ARMD 25:96}

HARRISON, JAMES (St. Mary's County), soldier (rank not stated) circa 1675; paid for his services in the late expedition against the Nanticoke Indians in 1678. {Ref: ARMD 7:103}

HARRISON, JOHN (Annapolis District), captain and master of the brigantine *London Town* of Maryland in 1728-1729. {Ref: MDGZ, Feb 11, 1728/9}

HARRISON, JOSEPH (England and Charles County), soldier (rank not stated) by 1664; signed a petition to the governor to "displace Capt. William Boreman whom was lately constituted captain of the militia" on Sep 12, 1666 (name listed once as "Joseph Harryson"); member of the Lower House of the Maryland Assembly, 1661-1664; born circa 1623 (aged about 36 when deposed in 1659), died testate by Dec 26, 1673 (date of probate; Elizabeth Harrison, widow). {Ref: ARMD 3:556, 3:560, 41:312, 49:241; BDML I:416-417; CHLR B:379; MDWB 1:589}

HARRISON, JOSEPH (Charles County), captain by 1722; member of the Lower House of the Maryland Assembly, 1715, 1722-1727; born on Oct 27, 1687, died testate by May 5, 1727 (date of probate; Verlinda Harrison, widow). *Note:* He was "captain" when he wrote his will on Dec 24, 1726, but was called "colonel" when his inventory was taken on Jul 5, 1727 and then as "captain" in an administration account filed on Oct 9, 1729. {Ref: ARMD 34:401; BDML I:417; MDWB 19:151; MINV 12:207; MDAD 10:3}

HARRISON, JOSEPH (Charles County), captain before 1719; died by May 4, 1719 (date of inventory). {Ref: MINV 2:110}

HARRISON, MILES (Somerset County), soldier (rank not stated) circa 1675; paid for his services in the late expedition against the Nanticoke Indians in 1678; Protestant and soldier in the Revolution of 1689; signed an address and took a loyalty oath supporting the King of England and "for enabling us to defend ourselves against all invaders" on Nov 28, 1689 (name listed once as "Miles Harrisone"). {Ref: ARMD 7:97, 8:141}

HARRISON, ROBERT (Talbot County), Protestant and probable soldier in the Revolution of 1689; signed an address and took a loyalty oath supporting the King of England and the reestablishment of Lord Baltimore into power on Nov 18, 1689. {Ref: ARMD 8:134}

HARRISON, VERLINDA, see "Joseph Harrison," q.v.

HARRISON, WILLIAM (England and St. Mary's County), seaman on the ship *Ruth* in 1676. {Ref: ARMD 51:474, 66:301}

HART, ABRAHAM (Talbot County), soldier (rank not stated) circa 1675; paid for his services in the late expedition against the Nanticoke Indians in 1678. {Ref: ARMD 7:92}

HART, JOHN (Ireland, England, Spain, Portugal, Anne Arundel County, and Leeward Islands), colonial bureaucrat who served as a military officer (captain) in Spain and Portugal before coming to Maryland; captain general and governor of Maryland, 1713-1720; governor of Leeward Islands, 1721-1727. {Ref: ARMD 25:277, 25:338, 29:354; BDML I:420}

HART, THOMAS (St. Mary's County), captain and mariner by 1642. {Ref: ARMD 4:127}

HARVEY (HARVY), HENRY (Dorchester County), soldier (rank not stated) circa 1675; paid for his services in the late expedition against the Nanticoke Indians in 1678. {Ref: ARMD 7:93}

HARVEY (HARVY), JOHN (Charles County), soldier (rank not stated) circa 1675; paid for his services in the late expedition against the Nanticoke Indians in 1678. {Ref: ARMD 7:101}

HARVEY (HARVY), RICHARD (Somerset County), soldier (rank not stated) circa 1675; paid for his services in the late expedition against the Nanticoke Indians in 1678. {Ref: ARMD 7:98}

HARVIE, JOHN (England and Annapolis), captain and master of the ship *Industry* of Biddeford in 1728-1734. {Ref: MDGZ, Mar 11, 1728/9 and Jul 19, 1734; CVPR:12}

HARWOOD, ---- (Anne Arundel County), captain by 1680. {Ref: INAC 7A:34}

HARWOOD, PATRICK (Dorchester County), soldier (rank not stated) circa 1675; paid for his services in the late expedition against the Nanticoke Indians in 1678. {Ref: ARMD 7:93}

HARWOOD, PETER (Talbot County), mariner by 1734. {Ref: CFES 3:130}

HARWOOD, PHINEAS (Potomac District), captain and master of the ship *Virginia Merchant* in 1697. {Ref: ARMD 23:171-172}

HARWOOD, THOMAS (England, and Talbot and Cecil Counties), captain and mariner, of London, before 1664; master of the ship *Thomas and Mary* in 1667 land owner in Talbot County, 1664-1672, and Cecil County, 1674. {Ref: ARMD 49:293, 54:522; TALR 5:15; CELR 1:8; MDHM 5:341}

HASCALL, WILLIAM (county or port not indicated), captain and master of the ketch *Retone* in 1691. {Ref: ARMD 8:239}

HASCULA, DENNIS, see "Dennis Huscula," q.v.

HASFURT (HOSFOORD), GEORGE (Virginia, and Annamessex, Somerset County), chirurgeon and schoolmaster by 1665; under sheriff, 1669; soldier (rank not stated) circa 1675; paid for his services in the late expedition against the Nanticoke Indians in 1678; born circa 1640 (aged about 24 in 1664), died in 1686 or 1687. {Ref: OSES:286, 446; ARMD 7:99}

HASLEDONE, RICHARD (Talbot County), soldier (rank not stated) circa 1675; paid for his services in the late expedition against the Nanticoke Indians in 1678. {Ref: ARMD 7:88}

HASLEWOOD, ELIZABETH, see "Henry Haslewood," q.v.

HASLEWOOD (HAZLEWOOD), HENRY (Baltimore County), court justice, 1674 (quorum, 1679); captain by 1678; paid for his services in the late expedition against the Nanticoke Indians in 1678; "Henry Haslewood" died testate by Nov 4, 1680 (date of probate; Elizabeth Haslewood, widow) and his son "Henry Hazellwood" died testate by Jun 9, 1699 (date of burial). Additional research will be necessary before drawing conclusions. {Ref: ARMD 7:95, 15:38, 15:253; MDWB 2:122, 6:264; INAC 6:462, 12:150; BBCF:308}

HASLEWOOD, WILLIAM (Dorchester County), soldier (rank not stated) circa 1675; paid for his services in the late expedition against the Nanticoke Indians in 1678. {Ref: ARMD 7:92}

HASLING, JEREMIAH, see "Philip Holedger," q.v.

HASLING, MARY, see "Philip Holedger," q.v.

HAST (HASTE), DANIELL (Wicomico, Somerset County), soldier (rank not stated) circa 1675; paid for his services in the late expedition against the Nanticoke Indians in 1678; paid for his services out of an assessment levied by the General Assembly for the public good in 1682; died testate by Feb 9, 1701/2 (date of inventory; will was written on Nov 21, 1701, but no date of probate was given). {Ref: ARMD 7:98, 7:443; OSES:153, 284, 446; INAC 25:395; MDWB 11:287}

HASTINGS, JOHN (Calvert County), captain before 1706; died by Aug 14, 1706 (date of inventory). {Ref: INAC 25:352, 28:350}

HATCH, WILLIAM (Charles County), soldier (rank not stated) circa 1675; paid for his services in the late expedition against the Nanticoke Indians in 1678. {Ref: ARMD 7:101}

HATCHMAN, THOMAS (Baltimore County), colonel by 1724; "Thomas Hatchman, innholder" died testate by Feb 20, 1734/5 (date of probate; Sarah Hatchman, widow). {Ref: BALR IS#G; BBCF:309; MDWB 21:320}

HATFIELD, ---- (Talbot County), captain by 1689 (probably William Hatfield who immigrated to Talbot County by 1676 with his wife and daughter, both named Elizabeth). {Ref: ARMD 8:159; Land Patent WC#2:331, 358}

HATTON, SAMUEL (Talbot County), soldier (rank not stated) circa 1675; paid for his services in the late expedition against the Nanticoke Indians in 1678. {Ref: ARMD 7:88-89}

HATTON, THOMAS (Anne Arundel County), officer and late secretary of Maryland who was slain at the Battle of the Severn on March 25, 1655. See "Thomas Brooke (Brookes)," q.v. {Ref: FAAH:25, 27, 47}

HAW, CHRISTOPHER (Baltimore County), soldier (rank not stated) circa 1675; paid for his services in the late expedition against the Nanticoke Indians in 1678. {Ref: ARMD 7:95}

HAWKINS, ARNAULT (Kent County), colonel by 1725. {Ref: MDAD 7:131}

HAWKINS, ELIZABETH, see "Henry Hawkins" and "John Hawkins," q.v.

HAWKINS, ERNEST (Queen Anne's County), lieutenant colonel in the First Company of Foot on Jun 30, 1732. {Ref: MDHR 1:11}

HAWKINS, HENRY (Charles County), soldier (rank not stated) circa 1675; paid for his services in the late expedition against the Nanticoke Indians in 1678; paid for his services out of an assessment levied by the General Assembly for the public good in 1682; died testate by Jan 12, 1702/3 (date of probate; Sarah Hawkins, widow). {Ref: ARMD 7:101, 7:440; MDWB 11:371}

HAWKINS, HENRY (Charles County), Protestant and probable soldier in the Revolution of 1689; signed an address and took a loyalty oath supporting the King of England and the reestablishment of Lord Baltimore into power on Nov 28, 1689; captain, commissioned Jul 30, 1694; member of the Lower House of the Maryland Assembly, 1688-1699; court justice, 1680-1699; died testate by May 12, 1699 (date of probate; Elizabeth Hawkins, widow). {Ref: ARMD 8:138, 15:327, 17:380, 20:130; BDML I:424; MDWB 6:310}

HAWKINS, JOHN (Talbot, Kent and Queen Anne's Counties), Protestant and soldier in the Revolution of 1689; signed an address and took a loyalty oath supporting the King of England and the reestablishment of Lord Baltimore into power on Nov 18, 1689; cornet before 1692; captain by 1692; paid for 10 days horse service on Nov 18, 1692; military officer who swore allegiance to the King & Queen of England in 1696; captain and owner of a deck sloop (no name given) in 1697; sheriff, 1703; major by 1708; member of the Maryland Assembly from Queen Anne's County, 1714-1717; born circa 1657, died testate by Sep 26, 1717 (date of probate; Elizabeth Hawkins, widow). {Ref: ARMD 8:134, 8:424, 20:540, 24:113, 25:150, 25:337, 25:599, 29:452; BDML I:424; MDWB 14:535}

HAWKINS, JOHN (New England and Baltimore County), captain and mariner of Boston before 1651; came to Baltimore (now Cecil) County in 1651; murdered by servants at his plantation on Elk River on Feb 16, 1670/1 (Sarah Hawkins, widow, moved to New York City by 1672). {Ref: LMCL:23; ARMD 15:20, 65:1-8; BCLR IS#IK:42-44}

HAWKINS, MARGARET, see "Ralph Hawkins," q.v.

HAWKINS, RALPH (Magothy River, Anne Arundel County), Quaker who was assigned to a foot company of Capt. John Norwood in 1662, but refused to serve for religious reasons and was fined accordingly; "Ralph Hawkins, Sr." died testate after Sep 19, 1669 (date his will was written) and he had a son Ralph (date of probate not indicated; Margaret Hawkins, widow). Additional research will be necessary before drawing conclusions. {Ref: AAGE:558; FAAH:43; MDWB 1:351}

HAWKINS, ROBERT (St. Mary's County), soldier (rank not stated) circa 1675; paid for his services in the late expedition against the Nanticoke Indians in 1678. {Ref: ARMD 7:103}

HAWKINS, SARAH, see "Henry Hawkins" and "John Hawkins," q.v.

HAWLEY, WILLIAM (St. Mary's County), captain by 1649; died in 1654. {Ref: ARMD 4:503, 10:321, 51:496-503; 57:184}

HAWTAN, WILLIAM (Charles County), Protestant and probable soldier in the Revolution of 1689; signed an address and took a loyalty oath supporting the King of England and the reestablishment of Lord Baltimore into power on Nov 28, 1689. {Ref: ARMD 8:138}

HAWTON, MANNAH (Charles County), soldier by 1675 and ranger referred to as "Mannah Hawton the Indian" in 1675. {Ref: ARMD 15:56}

HAYDEN, M. V., see "Mathias Vanderheyden," q.v.

HAYES (HAIES), JOHN (Baltimore County), Protestant and probable soldier in the Revolution of 1689; signed an address and took a loyalty oath supporting the King of England and the reestablishment of Lord Baltimore into power on Nov 28, 1689 (name listed as "John Haies"); he may have been the "Col. Hayes" who was an administrator of the estate of Edward Beedle in 1697; he was probably the John Hayes who was born circa 1663 (aged about 60 when deposed in 1723) and died testate by Jan 30, 1726/7 (date of probate).

Additional research will be necessary before drawing conclusions. {Ref: ARMD 8:137; BBCF:35, 314-315; MDWB 19:70; MDEP:88}

HAYNES, JOHN (England and Charles County), captain and commander of the ship *Sarah and Frances* of London in 1708. {Ref: CHLR C#2:71}

HAZLEWOOD, HENRY, see "Henry Haslewood," q.v.

HEA, CHARLES (Charles County), soldier (rank not stated) circa 1675; paid for his services in the late expedition against the Nanticoke Indians in 1678. {Ref: ARMD 7:101}

HEAMANS, ROGER (Anne Arundel County), captain and master of the ship *Golden Lyon* who offered the services of his ship and men to Capt. Fuller at the Battle of the Severn on Mar 25, 1655; also served on a Council of War after the battle. {Ref: FAAH:23, 26}

HEAP, FRANCIS (Somerset County), Protestant and probable soldier in the Revolution of 1689; signed an address and took a loyalty oath supporting the King of England and "for enabling us to defend ourselves against all invaders" on Nov 28, 1689. {Ref: ARMD 8:140}

HEARNE, WILLIAM (Somerset County), Protestant and probable soldier in the Revolution of 1689; signed an address and took a loyalty oath supporting the King of England and "for enabling us to defend ourselves against all invaders" on Nov 28, 1689. {Ref: ARMD 8:140}

HEATH, JOHN (Somerset County), soldier (rank not stated) circa 1675; paid for his services in the late expedition against the Nanticoke Indians in 1678; died intestate by Nov 20, 1719 (date of administration account). {Ref: ARMD 7:97; MDAD 2:387}

HEATH, SIMON (Kent County), "seaman within the said county" and a "sailor belonging to the *Factor* of Bediford" in 1697. {Ref: ARMD 25:599}

HEATHRED, THOMAS (Talbot County), soldier (rank not stated) circa 1675; paid for his services in the late expedition against the Nanticoke Indians in 1678. {Ref: ARMD 7:90}

HEAYS, ROBERT (Cecil County), mariner by 1726. {Ref: TALR 13:375}

HEBB, THOMAS (St. Mary's County), seaman whose name appeared on "a list of men that goe by water when employed" in 1697. {Ref: ARMD 25:597}

HEDGE, THOMAS, see "Thomas Jones," q.v.

HEDLY, ---- (county or port not indicated), mate (ship not named) in 1696. {Ref: INAC 13B:139}

HEIGHE, JAMES (All Saint's Parish, Calvert County), captain before 1689; "was known as Captain James Heighe and took the side of King William in the Revolution of 1689 ... his son was also known as Captain James Heighe" (son was a minor under age 18 in 1725); died testate by Nov 12, 1725 (date of probate; Ann Heighe, widow). {Ref: HCCM:271; MDWB 18:410}

HELY, CLEMENT (St. Mary's County), Protestant and probable soldier in the Revolution of 1689; signed an address and took a loyalty oath supporting the

King of England and the reestablishment of Lord Baltimore into power on Nov 28, 1689. {Ref: ARMD 8:146}

HEMPSONE, NICHOLAS (Baltimore County), soldier (rank not stated) circa 1675; paid for his services in the late expedition against the Nanticoke Indians in 1678. {Ref: ARMD 7:95}

HEMSLEY, JUDITH, see "William Hemsley, Sr.," q.v.

HEMSLEY, WILLIAM (Queen Anne's County), proposed for lieutenant in the Second Company of Foot on Jun 30, 1732; member of the Lower House of the Maryland Assembly, 1728-1736; born in 1703, died Oct 2, 1736. {Ref: BDML I:431-432; MDHR 1:11}

HEMSLEY (HELMSLEY), WILLIAM, SR. (Kent and Talbot Counties), captain before 1678; paid for his services in the late expedition against the Nanticoke Indians in 1678; court justice, 1681-1685; born circa 1634 (aged about 26 when deposed on Dec 20, 1660), died testate after Feb 26, 1684/5 (date his will was written, but date of probate not stated; Judith Hemsley, widow). {Ref: ARMD 7:87, 7:611, 15:346, 24:40; BDML I:431; INKC:125; MDWB 4:121; MDEP:89}

HENDERSON, JAMES (Somerset County), Protestant and probable soldier in the Revolution of 1689; signed an address and took a loyalty oath supporting the King of England and "for enabling us to defend ourselves against all invaders" on Nov 28, 1689. {Ref: ARMD 8:141}

HENDERSON, JOHN (Somerset County), Protestant and probable soldier in the Revolution of 1689; signed an address and took a loyalty oath supporting the King of England and "for enabling us to defend ourselves against all invaders" on Nov 28, 1689. {Ref: ARMD 8:140}

HENFEILD, ROBERT, see "Robert Hinfield," q.v.

HENLEY (HENLY), EDWARD (St. Mary's County), Protestant and probable soldier in the Revolution of 1689; signed an address and took a loyalty oath supporting the King of England and the reestablishment of Lord Baltimore into power on Nov 28, 1689. {Ref: ARMD 8:146}

HENLEY (HENLY), LAURENCE (Somerset County), soldier (rank not stated) circa 1675; paid for his services in the late expedition against the Nanticoke Indians in 1678. {Ref: ARMD 7:97}

HENLEY (HENLY), ROBERT (England and Charles County), captain by 1676; court justice, 1658-1660, 1672-1684; member of the Lower House of the Maryland Assembly, 1659-1660, 1676-1682; born circa 1617, died testate by Mar 31, 1684 (date of probate). {Ref: ARMD 2:553, 15:327, 60:46; BDML I:434; MDWB 4:31}

HENRY, ROBERT JENCKINS (Somerset and Dorchester Counties), captain by 1734; major by 1745; colonel by 1752; member of the Lower House of the Maryland Assembly, 1738-1766; born circa 1712, died testate by Nov 14, 1766 (date of probate; Gertrude Henry, widow). {Ref: BDML I:437-438; MDWB 34:323}

HEPENELL, HUGH (Calvert County), Protestant and probable soldier in the Revolution of 1689; signed an address and took a loyalty oath supporting the

King of England and "to reestablish Lord Baltimore in his ancient power and government" on Nov 16, 1689. {Ref: ARMD 8:131}

HERBERT, PHILLIP (Talbot County), soldier (rank not stated) circa 1675; paid for his services in the late expedition against the Nanticoke Indians in 1678. {Ref: ARMD 7:88}

HERBERT, WILLIAM, see "William Harbert," q.v.

HERMAN, AUGUSTINE (Prague, and New Amsterdam, New York, and Baltimore and Cecil Counties), member of the Maryland Council and colonel of militia after 1659; justice of Baltimore County, 1668, and Cecil County, 1674; served on commission to treat with the Indians in 1678; born 1605, died 1686. {Ref: RMHF II:84, 164-165}

HERMAN, CASPARUS AUGUSTINE (New Amsterdam, New York, New Castle, Pennsylvania, and Cecil County, Maryland), Protestant and leader in the Revolution of 1689; signed an address and took a loyalty oath supporting the King of England and the reestablishment of Lord Baltimore into power on Nov 18, 1689; colonel by 1692 (name also listed as "Gasparus Harman" and "Col. Casparus Harman" and "Col. Casparus Augustus Herman" and "Col. Casparus Hermen" and "Col. Casparus Hearman" and misinterpreted once as "Collonel Cuspany Herman"); court justice, 1687 (quorum, 1688); member of the Lower House of the Maryland Assembly, 1694-1697; military officer who swore allegiance to the King & Queen of England in 1696; born circa 1657 (aged about 38 when deposed in 1695), died intestate by June, 1697. See "Thomas Blake," q.v. {Ref: ARMD 8:23, 8:49, 8:135, 8:399, 8:474, 20:111, 20:153, 20:203-204, 20:370, 20:405, 20:545, 23:15, 38:73; BDML I:438-439; CELR 2:252; INCC:135; INAC 17:37, 25:167, 34:142; MDEP:90}

HERMAN, EPHRAIM AUGUSTINE (New Castle, Pennsylvania, and Cecil County, Maryland), lieutenant colonel by 1714; member of the Lower House of the Maryland Assembly, 1715-1734; colonel by 1717; born 1683, died intestate by Jun 4, 1735 (date of inventory); name also listed as "Ephraim Augustus Herman" and "Col. Ephraim Augt. Herrman." {Ref: ARMD 30:107, 30:360, 33:565, 34:5, 34:61; BDML I:439; CELR 3:215, 224, 247; INCC:134; MINV 20:520}

HERON, WILLIAM (England and Talbot County), mariner, of Stockton, before 1694; died by Sep 28, 1694 (date of inventory in Talbot County). {Ref: INAC 13A:168}

HERRON, MATHIAS (county or port not indicated), captain and master of the ship *Resolution* of Hull in 1690. {Ref: ARMD 8:237}

HETSON, ISAAC (Talbot County), captain before 1721 (received payment from the estate of Thomas Martin, deceased, on Jul 3, 1721). {Ref: MDAD 3:473}

HEWETT, BENJAMIN (Patuxent District), captain and master of the ship *Anna Maria* in 1731. {Ref: CVPR:12}

HEWETT, JOHN (county not indicated), mariner before 1702; died by May 1, 1702 (date of administration account). {Ref: INAC 21:347}

HEWIT, HENRY (Anne Arundel County), military officer (rank not stated) who swore allegiance to the King & Queen of England in 1696. {Ref: ARMD 20:541}

HEWIT (HEWETT, HUETT), THOMAS (England and Annapolis), captain, master, and commander of the ship *Speedwell* of London riding in West River on Feb 1, 1725/6 and Mar 15, 1727/8 and Feb 4, 1728/9; master of the ship *Dilligence* in 1731. {Ref: AALR SY#1:159, 359; MDGZ, Feb 4, 1728/9 and Jul 1, 1729; CVPR:12}

HEYDEN, CHARLES (county or port not indicated), captain and master of the ship *Alath* of Bristol in 1690. {Ref: ARMD 8:237}

HEYDON, SAMUELL (Somerset County), soldier (rank not stated) circa 1675; paid for his services in the late expedition against the Nanticoke Indians in 1678. {Ref: ARMD 7:98}

HEYLINS, THOMAS (Talbot County), soldier (rank not stated) circa 1675; paid for his services in the late expedition against the Nanticoke Indians in 1678. {Ref: ARMD 7:88}

HICKERSONE, ---- (county not indicated), captain by 1696. {Ref: INAC 13B:136}

HICKMAN, SAMUELL (St. Mary's County), soldier (rank not stated) circa 1675; paid for his services in the late expedition against the Nanticoke Indians in 1678. {Ref: ARMD 7:103}

HICKS, JASPER (county or port not indicated), captain and commander of the ship *Kingfisher* in 1694. {Ref: ARMD 20:119}

HICKS, JOHN (Somerset County), Protestant and probable soldier in the Revolution of 1689; signed an address and took a loyalty oath supporting the King of England and "for enabling us to defend ourselves against all invaders" on Nov 28, 1689. {Ref: ARMD 8:141}

HICKS, LEVIN (Great Choptank Parish, Dorchester County), captain by 1715; major before 1730 (name listed as "Maj. Liv: Hicks"); died testate by Mar 16, 1731/2 (date of probate which listed his name as "Liven Hicks" although an inventory of his estate in 1732 listed his name as "Capt. Levin Hicks"). {Ref: ARMD 25:529; SOJR III:66; MDWB 20:331; MINV 16:599}

HICKS, SARAH, see "Thomas Hicks," q.v.

HICKS, THOMAS (England and Dorchester County), major by Jul 11, 1698 at which time he was appointed to decide differences between the English colonists and the Nanticoke Indians; member of the Lower House of the Maryland Assembly, 1694-1711; born circa 1659, died testate by Aug 6, 1722 (date of probate; Sarah Hicks, widow). {Ref: ARMD 23:457; BDML I:439-440; RMHF II:178; MDWB 17:310; MINV 8:2; MDAD 5:286}

HICKS, THOMAS (Great Choptank Parish, Dorchester County), captain before 1729; born circa 1687-1688 (aged about 42 when deposed in 1729 and aged about 47 when deposed in 1735). {Ref: ARMD 25:529; DOLR 9 Old 293; MDEP:91}

HICKS, WILLIAM (Annapolis District), captain of the sloop *Molly* of Maryland in 1732-1733. {Ref: MDGZ, Mar 16, 1732/3}

173

HIDE, EDWARD (Dorchester County), soldier (rank not stated) circa 1675; paid for his services in the late expedition against the Nanticoke Indians in 1678. {Ref: ARMD 7:93}

HIGGENBOTHAM, RICHARD (Somerset County), soldier (rank not stated) circa 1675; paid for his services in the late expedition against the Nanticoke Indians in 1678. {Ref: ARMD 7:97}

HIGGS, GILES (Talbot County), soldier (rank not stated) circa 1675; paid for his services in the late expedition against the Nanticoke Indians in 1678. {Ref: ARMD 7:88}

HIGGS, JOHN (Talbot County), soldier (rank not stated) circa 1675; paid for his services in the late expedition against the Nanticoke Indians in 1678. {Ref: ARMD 7:88}

HIGGS, WILLIAM (Pocomoke District), captain and master of the ship *St. Andrew* in 1731. {Ref: CVPR:12}

HIGHIGBOTHAM, MATTH. (Annapolis District), captain of the sloop *Johns* in 1734. {Ref: MDGZ, Nov 1, 1734}

HILL, ABELL (Anne Arundel County), soldier (rank not stated) circa 1675; paid for his services in the late expedition against the Nanticoke Indians in 1678. {Ref: ARMD 7:96}

HILL, CLEMENT (England and St. Mary's County), soldier (rank not stated) circa 1675; paid for his services in the late expedition against the Nanticoke Indians in 1678; sheriff, 1674-1677; member of the Lower House of the Maryland Assembly, 1678-1686; member of the Upper House (Maryland Council), 1686-1688; justice, 1679 (quorum, 1685); "Clement Hill, Sr." died testate by Apr 26, 1708 (date of probate). {Ref: ARMD 7:102, 15:256, 15:326, 17:379; BDML I:440-441; RMHF I:371; MDWB 12:252}

HILL, CRISPIN (Annapolis District), captain and master of the ship *Sarah and Frances* in 1731. {Ref: CVPR:12}

HILL, EDWARD (St. Mary's County), captain by 1648. {Ref: ARMD 4:389, 4:494, 10:129}

HILL, GEORGE (Baltimore County and Patuxent District), captain and commander of the ship *Robert and Mary* in 1729; master of the ship *Sarah* in 1731. {Ref: MDGZ, Apr 29, 1729; CVPR:12; MDAD 11:641}

HILL, GEORGE (Somerset County), soldier (rank not stated) circa 1675; paid for his services in the late expedition against the Nanticoke Indians in 1678. {Ref: ARMD 7:98}

HILL, GYLES (St. Mary's County), lieutenant, 1697. See "Richard Owen," q.v. {Ref: ARMD 23:246}

HILL, HENRY (Anne Arundel and Dorchester Counties), mariner, captain and master of the brigantine *Friendship* in 1693; captain of the brigantine *Betty* in 1697; a seafaring man of Anne Arundel County, "borne and belonging to this county" in 1697; mariner of Dorchester County by Mar 29, 1701 (date of deed). {Ref: ARMD 20:182, 25:595-596; BDML I:336; AALR WT#1:259}

HILL, HUTTON (Pocomoke District), captain and master of the ship *Sommersett* in 1730. {Ref: CVPR:12}

HILL, JOHN (England and St. Mary's), captain by 1633 who arrived in Maryland with the first colonists on March 25, 1634. {Ref: FMDP:229, 344}

HILL, RICHARD (Kent County), soldier (rank not stated) circa 1675; paid for his services in the late expedition against the Nanticoke Indians in 1678. {Ref: ARMD 7:94}

HILL, RICHARD (Somerset County), Protestant and probable soldier in the Revolution of 1689; signed an address and took a loyalty oath supporting the King of England and "for enabling us to defend ourselves against all invaders" on Nov 28, 1689. {Ref: ARMD 8:139}

HILL, RICHARD (Kent County), captain by 1733. {Ref: INKC:179}

HILL, RICHARD (Charles County), captain by 1676; paid for his services in 1681 and 1682. {Ref: ARMD 2:552, 7:251, 7:442, 17:86}

HILL, RICHARD (Annapolis and Philadelphia), captain and master of the ship *Ann Arundell* of Maryland in 1691; captain and master of the ship *Hope* of Maryland in 1694-1695; a seafaring man in 1697, "borne and belonging to this county" (named listed once as "Capt. Richard Hill, Jr."); captain and land owner near Annapolis before 1701; mariner, of Philadelphia, by 1705, and eldest son of Capt. Richard Hill, late of Anne Arundel County, deceased. {Ref: ARMD 8:240, 20:117, 20:338, 25:596; AALR WT#1:259, WT#2:216}

HILL, RICHARD, SR. (England, Virginia, and Baltimore and Anne Arundel Counties), captain by 1675; justice, 1679 (quorum, 1685); captain and officer of the town of Seavern (Severn) in 1686; Protestant and captain who opposed the Revolution of 1689 ("a Scotchman, bold in speech, who spoke what others only dared to think") and was replaced by Nicholas Greenberry; signed an address and took a loyalty oath in Baltimore County supporting the King of England and the reestablishment of Lord Baltimore into power on Nov 28, 1689; appointed naval officer at "An-Arundell Town" on Oct 18, 1694; appointed naval officer of the Port of Annapolis on Nov 17, 1694; served on a commission to set the boundary between Baltimore County and Anne Arundel County in 1696; Maryland Council proceedings state that "Captain Hill by reason of his being an Antient Officer be Constituted Colonel" on Apr 15, 1698; born circa 1640, died testate by Nov 30, 1700 (date of inventory). {Ref: ARMD 5:462, 5:470, 8:136, 15:38, 15:59, 15:253, 17:379, 20:160, 20:200, 20:260, 23:419, 24:35, 25:25, 38:73; FAAH:39-40, 165, 190; BDML I:441-442; BBCF:326; BALR IS#IK:91-92; INAC 20:94}

HILL, THOMAS (Kent County), soldier (rank not stated) on Isle of Kent who swore allegiance to the Commonwealth of England on Apr 5, 1652; born circa 1603-1604 (aged about 50 when deposed in 1653 and aged about 52 when deposed in 1656). {Ref: ARMD 54:21; INKC:101, 108}

HILL, THOMAS (Oxford District), captain and master of the ship *Succession* in 1731. {Ref: CVPR:12}

HILL, THOMAS (county not indicated), captain by 1695. {Ref: ARMD 20:228}
HILL, VALENTINE (Charles County), Protestant and probable soldier in the Revolution of 1689; signed an address and took a loyalty oath supporting the King of England and the reestablishment of Lord Baltimore into power on Nov 28, 1689. {Ref: ARMD 8:138}
HILL, WILLIAM (England and Cecil County), captain and master of the ship *Ann* of London in 1691; captain of a brigantine (no name given) in 1697. {Ref: ARMD 8:239, 25:598}
HILLIARD, EDWARD (St. Mary's County), seaman whose name appeared on "a list of men that goe by water when employed" in 1697. {Ref: ARMD 25:597}
HILLING, NATHANIELL (Cecil County), military officer (rank not stated) who swore allegiance to the King & Queen of England in 1696. {Ref: ARMD 20:545}
HILLS, THOMAS (Calvert County), Protestant and probable soldier in the Revolution of 1689; signed an address and took a loyalty oath supporting the King of England and "to reestablish Lord Baltimore in his ancient power and government" on Nov 16, 1689. {Ref: ARMD 8:132}
HILLS, THOMAS (Kent County), soldier (rank not stated) in Capt. William Leeds (Leeads) Company by May 23, 1662, at which time he signed a petition about the misuse of company money by Capt. Thomas Brednox (Bradnox), late of Isle of Kent, deceased. {Ref: ARMD 3:455}
HILLS, WILLIAM (Anne Arundel County), lieutenant, commissioned Dec 9, 1661. {Ref: ARMD 3:444}
HILLSTON, GEORGE (Talbot County), captain by 1672. {Ref: ARMD 54:560}
HILTON, JOHN (St. Mary's County), Protestant and probable soldier in the Revolution of 1689; signed an address and took a loyalty oath supporting the King of England and the reestablishment of Lord Baltimore into power on Nov 28, 1689. {Ref: ARMD 8:146}
HINDER, WILLIAM (Anne Arundel County), captain and commander of the ship *Amity* riding in South River on May 16, 1726. {Ref: AALR SY#1:196}
HINFIELD (HENFEILD), ROBERT (St. Mary's County), captain of a ship (no name given) in 1656; he brought Irish servants to sell at Mr. Gerard's quartering house at Mattapany in 1661-1662. {Ref: ARMD 10:468, 41:477, 49:123}
HINSEY, WILLIAM (Charles County), soldier (rank not stated) circa 1675; paid for his services in the late expedition against the Nanticoke Indians in 1678. {Ref: ARMD 7:101}
HINSON, ANN, see "John Hynson," q.v.
HINSON, JOHN, see "John Hynson," q.v.
HINSON, RANDOLPH (Charles County), Protestant and probable soldier in the Revolution of 1689; signed an address and took a loyalty oath supporting the King of England and the reestablishment of Lord Baltimore into power on Nov 28, 1689. {Ref: ARMD 8:138}

HINTON, RICHARD (Anne Arundel County), captain and commander of the galley *Anne* riding at anchor in South River on Aug 22, 1718. {Ref: AALR IB#2:504}

HINTON, THOMAS (St. Mary's County), soldier (rank not stated) circa 1675; paid for his services in the late expedition against the Nanticoke Indians in 1678. {Ref: ARMD 7:102}

HINWOOD, ROBERT (Anne Arundel County), military officer (rank not stated) who swore allegiance to the King & Queen of England in 1696. {Ref: ARMD 20:542}

HITCH, ABRAHAM (Talbot County), soldier (rank not stated) circa 1675; paid for his services in the late expedition against the Nanticoke Indians in 1678. {Ref: ARMD 7:88}

HITCHINS, DANIEL (Prince George's County), captain and commander of the ship *Loyall Friend* in 1722-1725 and riding in the Patuxent River on Jan 24, 1724/5 (name misspelled once as "Daniell Hitchory"). {Ref: PGLR I:465, M:148-149}

HIXON, THOMAS (St. Mary's County), Protestant and probable soldier in the Revolution of 1689; signed an address and took a loyalty oath supporting the King of England and the reestablishment of Lord Baltimore into power on Nov 28, 1689. {Ref: ARMD 8:147}

HOCKADAY, JOHN (county or port not indicated), captain and master of the ship *Nephew* of Bydeford in 1690. {Ref: ARMD 8:238}

HODGES, JOHN (Queen Anne's County), captain by 1717. {Ref: INAC 39B:33}

HODGES, THOMAS (Baltimore County), Protestant and probable soldier in the Revolution of 1689; signed an address and took a loyalty oath supporting the King of England and the reestablishment of Lord Baltimore into power on Nov 28, 1689. {Ref: ARMD 8:137}

HODGETT, CHARLES (county not indicated), probable soldier (rank not stated) before 1682; paid for his services out of an assessment levied by the General Assembly for the public good in 1682. {Ref: ARMD 7:439}

HODGSON, JONATHAN (Kent County), "seaman within the said county" and a "sailor belonging to the *Loves Increase* of Whitehaven" in 1697. {Ref: ARMD 25:600}

HODGSON, NICHOLAS (Annapolis District), captain and master of the ship *Monokin* in 1731. {Ref: CVPR:12}

HODGSON, WILLIAM (St. Mary's County), Protestant and probable soldier in the Revolution of 1689; signed an address and took a loyalty oath supporting the King of England and the reestablishment of Lord Baltimore into power on Nov 28, 1689. {Ref: ARMD 8:146}

HODSKEYS, RICHARD (St. Mary's County), captain by 1654; commissioned captain of militia "in St. Maries and Patomock River from Clements Bay downwards to Point Lookout including all St. Maries and the forces therein" on Apr 24, 1655. {Ref: ARMD 10:413}

HODSON, JOHN, see "John Hudson," q.v.

HODSON, JOHN (England, and Annapolis and Patuxent Districts), captain of the ship *Malley* of Newcastle in 1728; master of the ship *Adventure* in 1731. {Ref: CVPR:12; MDGZ, Feb 11, 1728/9}
HODSON (HODSONE), RICHARD (Charles County), soldier (rank not stated) circa 1675; paid for his services in the late expedition against the Nanticoke Indians in 1678. {Ref: ARMD 7:101}
HOG, DANIELL (Calvert County), captain by 1687. {Ref: INAC 9:410}
HOGG, THOMAS, see "Thomas Frogg," q.v.
HOLBRONE, CHARLES (Kent County), soldier (rank not stated) circa 1675; paid for his services in the late expedition against the Nanticoke Indians in 1678. {Ref: ARMD 7:94}
HOLBROOKE, THOMAS (Somerset County), probable soldier (rank not stated) before 1682; paid for his services out of an assessment levied by the General Assembly for the public good in 1682; "Thomas Holbrock (Holbrook)" died testate by Nov 24, 1718 (date of probate). {Ref: ARMD 7:443; MDWB 15:15}
HOLDSWORTH (HOLDEWORTH), JOHN (Calvert County), Protestant and probable soldier in the Revolution of 1689; signed an address and took a loyalty oath supporting the King of England and "to reestablish Lord Baltimore in his ancient power and government" on Nov 16, 1689. {Ref: ARMD 8:131; HCCM:274}
HOLDSWORTH (HOWLDSWORTH), JOSHUA (St. Mary's County), Protestant and probable soldier in the Revolution of 1689; signed an address and took a loyalty oath supporting the King of England and the reestablishment of Lord Baltimore into power on Nov 28, 1689; died intestate by Apr 28, 1719 (date of administration account). {Ref: ARMD 8:146; MDAD 1:416}
HOLDSWORTH (HOLDEWORTHY), SAMUEL (Calvert County), Protestant and probable soldier in the Revolution of 1689; signed an address and took a loyalty oath supporting the King of England and "to reestablish Lord Baltimore in his ancient power and government" on Nov 16, 1689. {Ref: ARMD 8:131; HCCM:274}
HOLDSWORTH, THOMAS, see "Richard Smith" and "John Crawley," q.v.
HOLEADGER (HOLEDGER), PHILIP (Cecil and Kent Counties), military officer (rank not stated) who swore allegiance to the King & Queen of England in 1696; noted as "lately married to Mary Hasling, daughter of Jeremiah Hasling, late of South River in this province, deceased" in 1665 (name also listed as "Phillip Holedger" and "Phillip Holeager" and "Philip Holleger" and misinterpreted once as "Philip Cheager"); died testate in Kent County by Jun 16, 1725 (date of probate; Jane Holeadger, widow). {Ref: ARMD 20:545, 49:441-442, 49:564; CELR 1:173; MDWB 18:386; MINV 12:104; MDAD 8:463}
HOLEMAN (HOLLMAN, HOULDMAN), ABRAHAM (Kent and Baltimore Counties), soldier (rank not stated) on Isle of Kent who swore allegiance to the Commonwealth of England on Apr 5, 1652; "Abraham Houldman" died testate in Baltimore County after Dec 23, 1663 (date he wrote his will, but no date of probate was given; Isabell Houldman, widow) and his son "Abraham Holman"

died testate by Jun 1, 1686 (date of probate). {Ref: ARMD 54:136; INKC:101; BBCF:335; MDWB 1:213, 4:219}

HOLEMAN (HOLMAN), WILLIAM (Anne Arundel County), captain and commander of the ship *Globe* riding at anchor in Herring Bay on Jan 23, 1705/6 and May 5, 1712 riding at anchor in the Chesapeake Bay on May 31, 1714, and riding at anchor in the Severn River on Feb 1, 1715/6. {Ref: AALR WT#2:293, AALR PK:448, AALR IB#2:139, 265}

HOLLAND, ANTHONY (Herring Creek, Anne Arundel County), soldier (rank not stated) circa 1675; paid for his services in the late expedition against the Nanticoke Indians in 1678; died testate by Aug 1, 1703 (date of probate). {Ref: ARMD 7:96; MDWB 11:316}

HOLLAND, ELIZABETH, see "William Holland," q.v.

HOLLAND, FRANCES, see "Richard Holland," q.v.

HOLLAND, FRANCIS (Anne Arundel County), soldier (rank not stated) circa 1675; paid for his services in the late expedition against the Nanticoke Indians in 1678; one Francis Holland died testate by Aug 12, 1684 (date of probate; Margaret Holland, widow) and another Francis Holland, of Herring Creek, died testate by Jan 19, 1687/8 (date of probate; Sarah Holland, widow). Additional research will be necessary before drawing conclusions. {Ref: ARMD 7:96; MDWB 4:134, 4:293}

HOLLAND, GEORGE (Anne Arundel County), soldier (rank not stated) circa 1675; paid for his services in the late expedition against the Nanticoke Indians in 1678; died testate by Jun 22, 1685 (date of probate). {Ref: ARMD 7:96; MDWB 4:139}

HOLLAND, JOHN (Anne Arundel County), probable soldier (rank not stated) before 1682; paid for his services out of an assessment levied by the General Assembly for the public good in 1682; died testate by Aug 2, 1710 (date of probate). {Ref: ARMD 7:442-443; MDWB 13:72}

HOLLAND, MARGARET, see "Francis Holland," q.v.

HOLLAND, MICHAEL (Somerset County), a seafaring man in 1697; captain and mariner by 1715 (name listed once as "Mica. Holland"). {Ref: ARMD 25:598; SOJR III:69-71}

HOLLAND, RICHARD (Dorchester County), soldier (rank not stated) circa 1675; paid for his services in the late expedition against the Nanticoke Indians in 1678; one Richard Holland died testate in Somerset County by Jun 16, 1696 (date of probate; Frances Holland, widow). {Ref: ARMD 7:93; MDWB 7:148}

HOLLAND, SARAH, see "Francis Holland," q.v.

HOLLAND, WILLIAM (Anne Arundel County), captain by 1691; captain of foot troops, 1694; sheriff, 1694; military officer who swore allegiance to the King & Queen of England in 1696; lieutenant colonel by 1701; member of the Lower House of the Maryland Assembly, 1701-1731; colonel by 1706; member of the Maryland Council, 1708-1729; died testate by Oct 25, 1732 (date of probate; Elizabeth Holland, widow). {Ref: ARMD 8:324, 20:77, 20:108, 20:541, 23:19, 23:292,

24:128, 24:224, 25:185, 25:245, 25:512, 27:377, 29:83, 29:204, 38:72; HCCM:273; AALR WH#4:49, WT#2:451; BDML I:447; MDWB 20:458; MINV 17:454-459}

HOLLINGSWORTH (HOLLINSWORTH), CHARLES (Talbot County), Protestant and probable soldier in the Revolution of 1689; signed an address and took a loyalty oath supporting the King of England and the reestablishment of Lord Baltimore into power on Nov 18, 1689; born circa 1638-1639 (aged about 21 when deposed in 1660 and aged about 60 when deposed in 1698). {Ref: ARMD 8:134, 41:504; MDEP:94}

HOLLINGSWORTH (HOLLINSWORTH), JOHN (Talbot County), soldier (rank not stated) circa 1675; paid for his services in the late expedition against the Nanticoke Indians in 1678; born circa 1638-1639 (aged about 19 or 20 when deposed twice in 1658), "John Hollingsworth, Sr." died testate by Jun 29, 1698 (date of probate). {Ref: ARMD 7:90, 41:167, 41:252; MDWB 6:119; MDEP:94}

HOLLIS (HOLLICE), HENRY (St. Mary's and Calvert Counties), soldier (rank not stated) circa 1675; paid for his services in the late expedition against the Nanticoke Indians in 1678; born circa 1653 (aged about 25 when deposed in 1678), died testate by Apr 23, 1688 (date of probate). {Ref: ARMD 7:103; MDWB 6:10; MDEP:94}

HOLLIS, JOHN (Somerset County), probable soldier (rank not stated) before 1682; paid for his services out of an assessment levied by the General Assembly for the public good in 1682. {Ref: ARMD 7:441}

HOLLIS, WILLIAM (Baltimore County), Protestant and probable soldier in the Revolution of 1689; signed an address and took a loyalty oath supporting the King of England and the reestablishment of Lord Baltimore into power on Nov 28, 1689; died testate by Feb 8, 1704/5 (date of probate). {Ref: ARMD 8:136; MDWB 3:452}

HOLLYDAY, ELEANOR, see "Leonard Hollyday," q.v.

HOLLYDAY (HOLLIDAY), JAMES (England, and Prince George's, Talbot and Queen Anne's Counties), naval officer of the Port of Oxford, commissioned Aug 23, 1737; styled "colonel" by the time of his death; member of the Lower House of the Maryland Assembly, 1725-1727; member of the Upper House (Maryland Council), 1735-1747; Treasurer of the Eastern Shore, 1727-1747; born Jun 18, 1696, died Oct 8, 1747. {Ref: BDML I:450-451; MDCB 82:50; RMHF I:208}

HOLLYDAY (HOLLIDAY), LEONARD (Calvert and Prince George's Counties), captain by 1720; colonel by 1733; county court justice, 1721-1733; born circa 1691-1692 (aged nearly 40 when deposed in 1731 and aged about 40 when deposed in 1732), died testate by Jun 26, 1741 (date of probate; Eleanor Hollyday, widow). {Ref: BDML I:453; CHLR H#2:384; PGLR F Old 5:267; PGLR Q:523; MDWB 22:359; MINV 27:268; MDEP:95}

HOLLYDAY (HOLLIDAY), THOMAS (England, and Calvert and Prince George's Counties), opposed the Revolution of 1689; captain before 1694; captain lieutenant in 1694; lieutenant colonel of militia in Prince George's County on Mar 3, 1695/6; military officer who swore allegiance to the King &

Queen of England in 1696; born circa 1661, died by Feb 20, 1702/3 (date of probate). {Ref: ARMD 20:78, 20:108, 20:379, 20:546; BDML I:453; RMHF II:335; MDWB 11:279}

HOLLYDAY, THOMAS (Prince George's County), a seafaring man in 1697. {Ref: ARMD 25:596}

HOLMES, RICHARD, see "Thomas Delahay," q.v.

HOLMES, THOMAS (St. Mary's County), soldier (rank not stated) in 1642; paid for 3 weeks' service under Capt. William Brainthwaite in November, 1642. {Ref: ARMD 3:119, 3:122}

HOLT, DAVID (St. Mary's County), Protestant and probable soldier in the Revolution of 1689; signed an address and took a loyalty oath supporting the King of England and the reestablishment of Lord Baltimore into power on Nov 28, 1689. {Ref: ARMD 8:147}

HOLT, JOHN (Talbot County), soldier (rank not stated) circa 1675; paid for his services in the late expedition against the Nanticoke Indians in 1678. {Ref: ARMD 7:88}

HOMEWOOD, ANN, see "Thomas Homewood," q.v.

HOMEWOOD, JAMES (Magothy River, Anne Arundel County), military officer (rank not stated) who swore allegiance to the King & Queen of England in 1696; captain before 1703; died testate by Mar 18, 1703/4 (date of probate; Mary Homewood, widow). {Ref: ARMD 20:541; AAGE:561-562; MDWB 11:401}

HOMEWOOD, JOHN (Magothy River, Anne Arundel County), Quaker who was fined for refusing to bear arms in 1658; assigned to a foot company of Capt. John Norwood in 1662, but refused to serve for religious reasons and was fined accordingly; yet, he held public office as a member of the Lower House of the Maryland Assembly, 1663-1664, 1676-1682, and as a court justice (quorum), 1674-1679; also paid in 1678 for his services in the late expedition against the Nanticoke Indians; born circa 1635, died testate by Sep 28, 1682 (date of probate; Sarah Homewood, widow, daughter of Thomas Meeres, *q.v.*). {Ref: ARMD 7:97, 15:37, 51:223; AAGE:558-559; FAAH:45; BDML I:454; MDWB 4:70}

HOMEWOOD, MARY, see "John Homewood," q.v.

HOMEWOOD, SARAH, see "John Homewood," q.v.

HOMEWOOD, THOMAS (Magothy River, Anne Arundel County), captain by the 1730's; born 1704 (aged about 31 when deposed in 1735), died intestate on May 19, 1739 (inventory taken on Oct 6, 1739; Ann Homewood, widow). {Ref: AAGE:562-563; INAC 18:284; MINV 24:206, 25:274; MDEP:95}

HOOD, ELIZABETH, see "Ferdinando Battee," q.v.

HOOD, MATHEW (Dorchester County), soldier (rank not stated) circa 1675; paid for his services in the late expedition against the Nanticoke Indians in 1678. {Ref: ARMD 7:93}

HOOD, ROBERT (Annapolis District), captain and master of the schooner *Lamb* of Maryland in 1728-1729. {Ref: MDGZ, Dec 31, 1728 and Jul 8, 1729}

HOOD, THOMAS, see "Ferdinando Battee," q.v.

HOOKE, JEREMIAH (Somerset County), corporal before 1682; paid for his services out of an assessment levied by the General Assembly for the public good in 1682. {Ref: ARMD 7:442-443}

HOOKE, THOMAS (Anne Arundel County), soldier (rank not stated) circa 1675; paid for his services in the late expedition against the Nanticoke Indians in 1678; one "Thomas Hook" died testate in Prince George's County by May 26, 1698 (date of probate). Additional research will be necessary before drawing conclusions. {Ref: ARMD 7:97; MDWB 6:104}

HOOKEN, JOSEPH (Cecil County), captain by 1683. {Ref: ARMD 7:612}

HOOKER, THOMAS (Baltimore County), Quaker who was appointed Ranger "from the falls of Back River downward the extent of the county" in 1692; born 13th day of 6th month, 1660; still living in 1701. {Ref: ARMD 8:339; BBCF:336-337}

HOOPER, ENNALLS (Dorchester County), soldier and probable officer in the 1730's; major by 1746; colonel by 1751; member of the Lower House of the Maryland Assembly, 1751-1752; died intestate in 1763. {Ref: BDML I:455}

HOOPER, GEORGE (Somerset and Dorchester County), probable soldier (rank not stated) before 1682; paid for his services out of an assessment levied by the General Assembly for the public good in 1682; died testate by Nov 25, 1695 (date of probate). {Ref: ARMD 7:441; MDWB 7:175}

HOOPER, HENRY (Calvert County), captain who was commissioned "to command all the forces from George Reade's on the south side of Patuxent River to Cedar Point and from St. Leonard's Creek on the north side to the Cove" on May 8, 1658; county court justice, 1658-1661; died intestate circa 1676. {Ref: ARMD 3:344; BDML I:455; HCCM:274-275}

HOOPER, HENRY (Dorchester County), captain by 1723; member of the Lower House of the Maryland Assembly, 1732-1766; colonel by 1734; born circa 1687, died Apr 20, 1767 (will probated on May 4, 1767). {Ref: ARMD 34:742, 39:220; BDML I:456; MDGZ, Apr 26, 1745; MDWB 35:382}

HOOPER, JOHN (Patuxent District), captain and master of the ship *Snowden's Dispatch* in 1731. {Ref: CVPR:12}

HOOPER, JOSEPH (St. Mary's County), mariner, 1665. {Ref: ARMD 49:438}

HOPE, GEORGE (Anne Arundel and Baltimore Counties), sailor before 1683; presented a petition to the General Assembly "for being exempt from Publick and County Levys The Petitioner having lost one of his legs at Sea by a Shot with a Bullett" which was endorsed Oct 20, 1683; died testate by Jul 22, 1721 (date of probate; Judith Hope, widow). See "William Slade," q.v. {Ref: ARMD 7:477; MDWB 16:480; BBCF:338}

HOPEWELL, HUGH (St. Mary's County), soldier (rank not stated) circa 1675; paid for his services in the late expedition against the Nanticoke Indians in 1678; one "Hugh Hopewell, Sr." died testate in Calvert County by Feb 20, 1688 (date of probate; Ann Hopewell, widow) and he had a son named Hugh; also, "Hugh Hopewell of Sackawit in Patuxent, St. Mary's County, planter" was born circa 1618 (aged about 50 when deposed in 1668). Additional research will be necessary before drawing conclusions. {Ref: ARMD 7:103, 51:400; MDWB 16:7}

HOPEWELL, RICHARD (St. Mary's County), captain before 1720; colonel by 1732; member of the Lower House of the Maryland Assembly, 1732-1734; died testate by Jan 6, 1745/6 (date of probate). {Ref: ARMD 39:151; BDML I:459; MDWB 24:272; MDAD 3:229}

HOPKINS, ANDREW (county or port not stated), mariner before 1725; born circa 1691 (aged about 34 when deposed in 1725). {Ref: MDEP:96}

HOPKINS, DENIS (Talbot County), soldier (rank not stated) circa 1675; paid for his services in the late expedition against the Nanticoke Indians in 1678. {Ref: ARMD 7:88}

HOPKINS, JOHANNAH, see "Philip Hopkins," q.v.

HOPKINS, JOSEPH (Cecil County), captain and court justice (quorum), 1679-1685; died testate by May 21, 1686 (date of probate; wife mentioned, but not named; administration account filed by Sarah Kennard, relict, on Apr 11, 1688). {Ref: ARMD 15:255, 15:326, 17:381; CFES 2:209; INAC 9:508; MDWB 4:188}

HOPKINS, NATHANIEL (Somerset County), captain by 1724; member of the Lower House of the Maryland Assembly, 1722-1724; died testate by Mar 20, 1739/40 (date of probate). {Ref: BDML I:459; MDWB 22:152}

HOPKINS, PHILIP (Kent County), military officer (rank not stated) who swore allegiance to the King & Queen of England in 1696; died testate by Aug 5, 1712 (date of probate; Johannah Hopkins, widow). {Ref: ARMD 20:540; MDWB 13:449}

HOPKINS, PHILIP (Charles County), captain of foot troops in 1689. {Ref: ARMD 13:243}

HOPKINS, SAMUELL (Somerset County), Protestant and probable soldier in the Revolution of 1689; signed an address and took a loyalty oath supporting the King of England and "for enabling us to defend ourselves against all invaders" on Nov 28, 1689. {Ref: ARMD 8:141}

HOPKINS, SAMUEL, JR. (Somerset County), Protestant and probable soldier in the Revolution of 1689; signed an address and took a loyalty oath supporting the King of England and "for enabling us to defend ourselves against all invaders" on Nov 28, 1689. {Ref: ARMD 8:140}

HOPKINS, THOMAS (St. Mary's County), captain by 1675; died testate by Apr 18, 1709 (date of probate; Ann Hopkins, widow). {Ref: INAC 3:35, 6:380; MDWB 12:96, pt. 2}

HOPKINS, THOMAS (Talbot County), Protestant and probable soldier in the Revolution of 1689; signed an address and took a loyalty oath supporting the King of England and the reestablishment of Lord Baltimore into power on Nov 18, 1689; born circa 1667 (aged about 74 when deposed in 1741). {Ref: ARMD 8:134; MDEP:96}

HOPKINS, WILLIAM (England, and Anne Arundel and Kent Counties), captain and mariner of Bitheford in Great Britain in the 1720's and 1730's; master of the ship *Unity* of Biddiford in 1730-1731; owner of a water lot in Chestertown in 1735 and appeared in Kent County debt books between 1736-1769. {Ref: BDML II:750; CFES 1:350; KELR JS#18:155; MDGZ, Jun 16, 1730; INKC:179; CVPR:12}

HOPPER, CHRISTOPHER (county or port not indicated), mariner by 1693. {Ref: INAC 10:332}

HOPPER, ROBERT (England and Cecil County), mariner, of Scarborough, before 1682; land owner in Cecil County by 1682. {Ref: TALR 4:179}

HOPSON, THOMAS (Prince George's County), captain and commander of the ship *Mary* riding in the Patuxent River on Feb 24, 1723/4 and Jan 24, 1724/5. {Ref: PGLR I:465, M:148-149}

HORNE, JOHN (Calvert County), captain by 1663. {Ref: ARMD 49:31}

HORNE, JOSEPH (Talbot County), soldier (rank not stated) circa 1675; paid for his services in the late expedition against the Nanticoke Indians in 1678. {Ref: ARMD 7:90}

HORNE, MARGARATT, see "William Horne," q.v.

HORNE, WILLIAM (Anne Arundel County), soldier (rank not stated) before 1682; paid for his services out of an assessment levied by the General Assembly for the public good in 1682; military officer (rank not stated) who swore allegiance to the King & Queen of England in 1696; died testate by Oct 19, 1719 (date of probate; Margaratt Horne, widow). {Ref: ARMD 7:441, 20:541; MDWB 14:119}

HORNSLY, JAMES (county not indicated), captain by 1698. {Ref: INAC 13A:41}

HORSEY, ISAAC (Coventry Parish, Somerset County), captain by 1707; colonel by 1733; born circa 1665, died testate by Jul 11, 1752 (date of probate). {Ref: SOJR I:37, III:47-48; MDWB 21:226, 28:355}

HORSEY, NATHANIELL (Somerset County), Protestant and probable soldier in the Revolution of 1689; signed an address and took a loyalty oath supporting the King of England and "for enabling us to defend ourselves against all invaders" on Nov 28, 1689; born circa 1660, died testate by Nov 9, 1721 (date of probate; Sarah Horsey, widow). {Ref: ARMD 8:141; MDWB 17:86, 23:549}

HORSEY, SARAH, see "Nathaniell Horsey," q.v.

HORSEY, STEPHEN (England, Virginia, and Somerset County), possible soldier (rank not stated) circa 1675; paid for his services in the late expedition against the Nanticoke Indians (since he was a shipwright his services may have been non-military); born circa 1651, died testate by Oct 3, 1722 (date of probate; Hannah Horsey, widow); "Stephen Horsey, Sr., of Monnocan Parish, shipwright" was the son of "Stephen Horsey, Sr." *[sic]* who died in 1672. {Ref: ARMD 5:4, 7:100; OSES:300, 446; BDML I:462; MDWB 1:458; MDWB 17:315}

HORST, Samuell (Patuxent District), captain and master of the ship *Content* in 1730-1731. {Ref: CVPR:12}

HORTON, JONATHAN (county not indicated), sergeant in the Maryland troops "raised to strengthen Albany, New York and resist the French and Indian enemies" in 1690. {Ref: SHMD I:355}

HORTON, JOSEPH (St. Mary's or Charles County), ranger in 1675. {Ref: ARMD 15:56}

HORTROP, RICHARD (St. Mary's County), seaman whose name appeared on "a list of men that goe by water when employed" in 1697. {Ref: ARMD 25:597}
HOSKINS, ANN, see "Philip Hoskins," q.v.
HOSKINS, JOHN (Charles County), soldier (rank not stated) who was issued a "gun or fowling piece" by Col. Warren on Sep 15, 1694. {Ref: ARMD 20:206, 20:208}
HOSKINS, PHILIP (England and Charles County), soldier (rank not stated) circa 1675; paid for his services in the late expedition against the Nanticoke Indians in 1678; captain by 1690; member of the Lower House of the Maryland Assembly, 1692-1717; captain of foot troops and county commissioner, 1694; military officer who swore allegiance to the King & Queen of England in 1696; captain in 1703, colonel by 1706; appointed president of Charles County Court on Oct 26, 1710; born circa 1650, died testate by Apr 3, 1718 (date of probate; Anne Hoskins, widow). {Ref: ARMD 7:101, 8:404, 13:253, 20:109, 20:234, 20:543, 24:36, 25:101, 27:494, 29:125, 29:391, 30:359; BDML I:463-464; CHLR C#2:190; INAC 5:360; MDWB 14:475, 16:218; MDAD 2:22-24}
HOSTER, JOSEPH (Potomac District), captain and master of the ship *Endeavour* in 1730-1731. {Ref: CVPR:12}
HOULDEN, JOHN (St. Mary's County), soldier (rank not stated) circa 1675; paid for his services in the late expedition against the Nanticoke Indians in 1678. {Ref: ARMD 7:102}
HOULDMAN, ISABELL, see "Abraham Holeman," q.v.
HOUSWIFE, GILES (Baltimore County), soldier (rank not stated) circa 1675; paid for his services in the late expedition against the Nanticoke Indians in 1678. {Ref: ARMD 7:96}
HOWARD, ---- (Kent County), sergeant by 1638. {Ref: ARMD 3:77}
HOWARD, CORNELIUS (Virginia and Anne Arundel County), ensign, commissioned Dec 9, 1661; paid for his services in the late expedition against the Nanticoke Indians in 1678; member of the Lower House of the Maryland Assembly, 1671-1675; captain by 1679; died testate by Oct 15, 1680 (date of probate; Elizabeth Howard, widow). {Ref: ARMD 3:444, 7:96, 15:253; BDML I:465; AALR WT#2:71; FAAH:71; MDWB 2:107; INAC 38B:121}
HOWARD, CORNELIUS, JR. (Anne Arundel County), military officer (rank not stated) who swore allegiance to the King & Queen of England in 1696; captain, mariner, and boatwright; born circa 1670, died testate by Mar 19, 1716/7 (date of probate). {Ref: ARMD 20:541; BDML I:465; FAAH:76; MDWB 14:275; MDAD 1:15}
HOWARD, EDMOND (Somerset County), Protestant and probable soldier in the Revolution of 1689; signed an address and took a loyalty oath supporting the King of England and "for enabling us to defend ourselves against all invaders" on Nov 28, 1689. {Ref: ARMD 8:141}
HOWARD, ELIZABETH, see "Cornelius Howard," q.v.
HOWARD, JOHN (Anne Arundel County), captain before 1703; born circa 1667, died testate by Feb 23, 1703/4 (date of probate). {Ref: BDML II:862; MDWB 11:420}

HOWARD, JOHN (Charles County), captain by the 1730's (possibly a sea captain since he requested in his will that his youngest son become an apprentice at sea); died testate by Mar 22, 1742/3 (date of probate; Rebecca Brooke Howard, widow). {Ref: MDWB 23:51; MINV 27:441}

HOWARD, MARY, see "Nathaniel Howard" and "William Howard," q.v.

HOWARD, MATTHEW (Magothy River, Anne Arundel County), military officer (rank not stated) who swore allegiance to the King & Queen of England in 1696. {Ref: FAAH:75; ARMD 20:541}

HOWARD, MICHAEL (Oxford District, Talbot County), naval officer for the port of Oxford, commissioned Jul 25, 1733; born circa 1696 (aged about 40 when deposed in 1736). {Ref: ARMD 28:88; MDCB 82:1; MDEP:98}

HOWARD, NATHANIEL (St. Mary's County), captain before 1721; died intestate by Mar 23, 1721/2 (date of administration account; Mrs. Mary Howard, administratrix). {Ref: MDAD 4:189}

HOWARD, PHILIP (Severn River, Anne Arundel County), captain by 1700; died testate by Feb 24, 1701/2 (date of probate); land claim filed by his widow Ruth Howard in 1706 (name listed once as "Capt. Phill. Howard"). {Ref: AALR IH#1:220; FAAH:74; INAC 19½B:73, 21:259; MDWB 11:153}

HOWARD, REBECCA BROOKE, see "John Howard," q.v.

HOWARD, RUTH, see "Philip Howard," q.v.

HOWARD, WILLIAM (St. Mary's County), captain and master of the ship *John* of London in 1691; died by March, 1720 (date of inventory; Mrs. Mary Howard, administratrix). {Ref: ARMD 8:239; MINV 5:53}

HOWARD, WILLIAM (Baltimore County), colonel by 1710; one William Howard died testate by Mar 5, 1717/8 (date of probate; Martha Howard, widow) and another William Howard died on Jan 29, 1718. Additional research will be necessary before drawing conclusions {Ref: INAC 32A:82; MDWB 14:543; BBCF:344}

HOWE, JOSEPH (Calvert County), Protestant and probable soldier in the Revolution of 1689; signed an address and took a loyalty oath supporting the King of England and the reestablishment of Lord Baltimore into power on Nov 28, 1689. {Ref: ARMD 8:145}

HOWELL, ELIZABETH, see "Thomas Howell," q.v.

HOWELL, GEORGE (Somerset County), soldier (rank not stated) circa 1675; paid for his services in the late expedition against the Nanticoke Indians in 1678. {Ref: ARMD 7:99}

HOWELL, HUMPHREY (England, and St. Mary's and/or Calvert County), mariner before 1645; "skipper of Mr. Rosier's vessel" in 1645; born circa 1613 (aged about 35 when deposed in 1648); possibly the "Capt. Howell" who appeared on a list of debts in the estates of George and Frances Beckwith, deceased, in Calvert County in 1676. {Ref: ARMD 4:465; INAC 2:319}

HOWELL, JOHN (England and Talbot County), captain by 1689; master of the ship *Sheild* of Straton in 1689-1691; died by May 1, 1703 (date of inventory in Talbot County). {Ref: ARMD 8:236, 8:238, 27:242; INAC 23:42}

HOWELL, JOHN (Queen Anne's County), mariner by 1733. {Ref: QALR RT#A:283}
HOWELL, PAUL (Talbot County), soldier (rank not stated) circa 1675; paid for his services in the late expedition against the Nanticoke Indians in 1678. {Ref: ARMD 7:87}
HOWELL, THOMAS (Anne Arundel, Baltimore, and Cecil Counties), captain by 1657; commissioned "to command all the forces on the south side of Seaverne River up to the head thereof and the north side of South River up the head thereof" on Jul 20, 1658; burgess (member of the Lower House of the Maryland Assembly) from Anne Arundel County, 1659-1660, and Baltimore County, 1666, 1671-1674; captain and gentleman, Baltimore County, 1660-1672; captain and justice (quorum) for Cecil County, 1674-1675; born circa 1610-1611 (aged about 50 when deposed on Jan 21, 1660/1 in Kent County), died testate by Nov 28, 1675 (date of probate; Elizabeth Howell, widow). {Ref: ARMD 1:382, 2:63, 2:239, 3:349, 3:351, 15:38, 15:41, 51:102, 51:118, 54:194; FAAH:28-29; HBCC:44; BDML I:469; BALR RR#HS; BBCF:344; TALR 1:68; MDWB 2:367; CFES 1:203; INAC 5:121; MDEP:98}
HOWES, GEORGE (county or port not stated), servant (cabin boy) for Capt. William Mitchell, *q.v.*, on board the ship *Thomas and John* at Debtford in 1652; born cirea 1629 (aged about 23 when deposed in 1652). {Ref: ARMD 10:226}
HOWSE, HAWTON (Anne Arundel County), soldier (rank not stated) circa 1675; paid for his services in the late expedition against the Nanticoke Indians in 1678. {Ref: ARMD 7:97}
HOWSEN, LEANARD (Potomac District), captain and master of the brigantine *Resolution* in 1697. {Ref: ARMD 23:172}
HOXTON, WALTER (Anne Arundel, Prince George's, and Charles Counties), captain by 1706; commander of the ship *Rame* riding in South River on Nov 1, 1708; commander of the ship *Anne* in 1722; master of the ship *Globe* riding in the Potomac River on Feb 24, 1723/4; master of the ship *Tristann* or *Tristan* riding in the Patuxent River on Jan 24, 1724/5 and Jan 29, 1725/6 (name mistakenly listed once as "Walter Bopton"); master of the ship *Baltimore* in 1731. {Ref: AALR WT#2:376, 663; CHLR H#2:40; PGLR I:465, M:148-150, 282; CVPR:12}
HOXWITH, BENJAMIN (Prince George's County), captain and commander of the ship *Mary* in 1722. {Ref: PGLR I:465}
HUBBARD, RICHARD (England, and Cecil and Anne Arundel Counties), captain and master of the ship *Dover* of London riding at anchor in Sassafras River on Apr 19, 1703; captain, 1729. {Ref: CELR 1:324, 355; MINV 15:68}
HUBBERT (HUBBARD), HENRY (Anne Arundel County), captain and commander of the ship *Dove* riding at anchor in South River on Jul 8, 1708; captain, 1729. {Ref: AALR WT#2:637-638; MINV 15:68}
HUD, JOHN (Kent County), soldier (rank not stated) on Isle of Kent who swore allegiance to the Commonwealth of England on Apr 5, 1652. {Ref: INKC:101}
HUDSON, HENRY (Port Tobacco, Charles County), mariner by 1663. {Ref: ARMD 49:110}

HUDSON, JEFFRY (St. Mary's County), soldier (rank not stated) circa 1675; paid for his services in the late expedition against the Nanticoke Indians in 1678. {Ref: ARMD 7:102}

HUDSON (HODSON, HUDSONE), JOHN (Virginia and Dorchester County), gentleman and justice (quorum), 1674; soldier (rank not stated) circa 1675; paid for his services in the late expedition against the Nanticoke Indians in 1678; captain by 1696; member of the Lower House of the Maryland Assembly, 1704-1711; born circa 1652-1653 (aged about 26 when deposed in 1678 and aged about 66 when deposed in 1719; name listed as "John Hudson, Sr." in 1719), died testate by Apr 21, 1730 (date of probate). {Ref: ARMD 7:92-93, 10:375, 27:203; BDML I:469; DOLR 8 Old 201; MDEP:99; MDWB 19:899}

HUDSON (HODSON), JOHN, SECUNDUS (Virginia and Great Choptank Parish, Dorchester County), captain by 1723; member of the Lower House of the Maryland Assembly, 1722-1724; justice, 1729-1733; born circa 1688-1695 (aged between 43 and 50 when deposed twice in 1738; name listed as "John Hudson, Jr.") and "Capt. John Hodson 2nd" died intestate by Mar 8, 1745/6 (date of inventory approval). {Ref: ARMD 25:529, 34:742; BDML I:470; MDEP:99; MINV 32:119}

HUES, ROBERT, see "Robert Hughes," q.v.

HUETT, JOHN (Somerset County), Protestant and probable soldier in the Revolution of 1689; signed an address and took a loyalty oath supporting the King of England and "for enabling us to defend ourselves against all invaders" on Nov 28, 1689. {Ref: ARMD 8:139}

HUETT, ROBERT (St. Mary's County), soldier (rank not stated) in 1642. {Ref: ARMD 4:130-131}

HUGHES (HEWES), EVAN (Charles County), probable soldier (rank not stated) before 1682; paid for his services out of an assessment levied by the General Assembly for the public good in 1682; "Even Hugh" died testate by Dec 6, 1717 (date of probate). {Ref: ARMD 7:439; MDWB 14:426}

HUGHES (HUGHS), LUKE (Potomac District), captain and master of the ship *Cockermouth* in 1730-1731. {Ref: CVPR:12}

HUGHES (HEWES), MATHIAS (St. James Parish, Anne Arundel County), soldier (rank not stated) circa 1675; paid for his services in the late expedition against the Nanticoke Indians in 1678; military officer (rank not stated) who swore allegiance to the King & Queen of England in 1696; died testate after Jan 21, 1702/3 (date will was written, but date of probate was not given). {Ref: ARMD 7:96, 20:541; MDWB 11:329}

HUGHES, PETER (St. Mary's County), "boatswine of Capt. Partis' ship" in 1677. {Ref: INAC 5:345}

HUGHES (HUES), ROBERT (Cecil County), military officer (rank not stated) who swore allegiance to the King & Queen of England in 1696. {Ref: ARMD 20:545}

HUGHES (HUGHS), THOMAS (London and Charles County), captain and master of the ship *Truelove* of Liverpool riding at anchor in the Potomac River on Jun 6, 1707. {Ref: CHLR Z:272}

HUGHES (HUGHS), THOMAS (Anne Arundel County), military officer (rank not stated) who swore allegiance to the King & Queen of England in 1696. {Ref: ARMD 20:541}

HUILE, JOHN (county not indicated), captain by 1698. {Ref: ARMD 25:35}

HULTHAUS, STEPHAN (Prince George's County), captain and master of the ship *Young's Goodwill* riding in the Eastern Branch of Patuxent River on Feb 24, 1723/4. {Ref: PGLR M:148}

HUME, JAMES (Potomac District), captain and master of the ship *Fame* in 1730-1731. {Ref: CVPR:12}

HUME, JOHN (Oxford and Patuxent Districts), captain and master of the ship *Content* in 1730; master of the ship *Clapham* in 1731. {Ref: CVPR:12}

HUMPHREYS, ALEXANDER (Anne Arundel County), probable soldier (rank not stated) before 1682; paid for his services out of an assessment levied by the General Assembly for the public good in 1682. {Ref: ARMD 7:442}

HUMPHREYS, MARY, see "Thomas Humphreys (Humphries)," q.v.

HUMPHREYS (HUMPHRIES), NICHOLAS (England and Annapolis), captain and commander of the ship *Hartwell* of London between 1696 and 1702. {Ref: ARMD 23:397, 23:466, 24:303, 25:588}

HUMPHREYS, THOMAS (Anne Arundel County), probable soldier (rank not stated) before 1682; paid for his services out of an assessment levied by the General Assembly for the public good in 1682. {Ref: ARMD 7:443}

HUMPHREYS, THOMAS (Anne Arundel County), naval officer for the Patuxent District, 1722-1726; died by Nov 15, 1726 near New York. {Ref: BDML I:472}

HUMPHREYS (HUMPHRIES), THOMAS (Somerset County), captain before 1734; died testate by Mar 7, 1734/5 (date of probate; Mary Humphreys, widow). {Ref: MDWB 21:304; MINV 20:494}

HUNE, ---- (Anne Arundel County), captain by 1687. {Ref: INAC 18:89}

HUNGERFORD, WILLIAM (St. Mary's County), soldier (rank not stated) in 1647. {Ref: ARMD 1:226}

HUNKING, JOHN (Annapolis District), captain and commander of the brigantine *Owners Adventure* in 1706. {Ref: AALR WT#2:329}

HUNT, BENJAMIN (Dorchester County), captain before 1698; died by Apr 26, 1698 (date of inventory). {Ref: INAC 16:115}

HUNT, CHRISTIAN, see "John Hunt," q.v.

HUNT, ELIZABETH, see "John Hunt," q.v.

HUNT, HENRY (county or port not indicated), captain of a ship (no name given) in 1729. {Ref: MDGZ, Jun 3, 1729}

HUNT, JOHN (Pennsylvania, Virginia, and Talbot County), captain before 1706; "John Hunt, merchant of Philadelphia in the province of Pennsylvania and at present in Virginia" wrote his will on Oct 7, 1706 and died by Dec 24, 1706 (date of probate; mentioned his mother Elizabeth Hunt in Barbadoes); an inventory of his estate taken on Sep 4, 1707 in Talbot County indicated "John Hunt, of Pennsylvania, died in Virginia"). {Ref: ARMD 7:92; MDWB 12:99; INAC 27:77}

HUNT, JOHN (Harris Creek, Talbot County), soldier (rank not stated) circa 1675; paid for his services in the late expedition against the Nanticoke Indians in 1678; died testate by Jan 1, 1704/5 (date of probate; Christian Hunt, widow). {Ref: MDWB 3:468}

HUNT, JOSIAH (Charles County), private in the Maryland troops "raised to strengthen Albany, New York and resist the French and Indian enemies" in 1690. {Ref: SHMD I:355}

HUNT, THOMAS (Charles County), private in the Maryland troops "raised to strengthen Albany, New York and resist the French and Indian enemies" in 1690; born circa 1667-1669 (aged about 45 when deposed in 1714 and aged about 53 when deposed in 1720). {Ref: SHMD I:355}

HUNT (HUNTT), THOMAS (Prince George's County), captain and master of the ship *Prince William* riding in the Patuxent River on Aug 12, 1726; captain of the ship *Molly* in 1727-1728, riding at anchor in the Potomac River on Apr 26, 1728. {Ref: PGLR M:150, 235, 412}

HUNT, WORNELL (Ireland, West Indies, and Anne Arundel County), captain of the City Company of Annapolis, appointed Oct 27, 1711; member of the Lower House of the Maryland Assembly, 1708-1711; died by March, 1728/9. {Ref: ARMD 29:12, 29:33, 29:37; BDML I:472-473}

HUNTER, JOHN (Kent County), military officer (rank not stated) who swore allegiance to the King & Queen of England in 1696. {Ref: ARMD 20:540}

HUNTINGTON (HUNTONTON), JOHN (Kent County and Pocomoke District), captain before 1730; master of the ship *Little John* in 1730-1731. {Ref: CVPR:12; MDAD 11:617}

HURLE, JOHN (England, and St. Mary's and Calvert Counties), captain by 1687; commander of the ship *Providence* of London in 1694-1695. {Ref: ARMD 20:72, 20:146, 20:150, 20:338; INAC 9:410}

HURSE, HENRY (Pocomoke District), captain and master of the ship *Richard* in 1731. {Ref: CVPR:12}

HURST, THOMAS (Prince George's County), captain by 1699. {Ref: INAC 19½B:24}

HURT, GEORGE (Annapolis District), captain of the frigate *Hart* in 1729-1734. {Ref: MDGZ, Jun 3, 1729 and Nov 29, 1734; CVPR:12}

HURT, JOHN (Kent County), military officer (rank not stated) who swore allegiance to the King & Queen of England in 1696. {Ref: ARMD 20:540}

HURT, NICHOLAS (Kent County), military officer (rank not stated) who swore allegiance to the King & Queen of England in 1696. {Ref: ARMD 20:540}

HUSBANDS, EDWARD (St. Mary's County), soldier (rank not stated) circa 1675; paid for his services in the late expedition against the Nanticoke Indians in 1678. {Ref: ARMD 7:103}

HUSBANDS, RICHARD (St. Mary's County), captain and mariner by 1649; master of the ship *Hopefull Adventure* in 1652; captain, 1659. See "Elkenath Bourne" and "Thomas Munnes," q.v. {Ref: ARMD 4:523, 4:546, 10:9, 10:197, 10:202, 41:277, 41:302}

HUSBANDS, ROBERT (Baltimore County), soldier (rank not stated) circa 1675; paid for his services in the late expedition against the Nanticoke Indians in 1678. {Ref: ARMD 7:95}

HUSBANDS (HUSBAND), WILLIAM (Annapolis District), captain and master of the sloop *Sarah* in 1734-1735 (built at Free Town in New England in 1729). {Ref: MDCB 82:21, 33; MDGZ, Nov 29, 1734}

HUSCULA (HUSCULAW, HASCULA), DENNIS (St. Mary's County), soldier (rank not stated) circa 1675; paid for his services in the late expedition against the Nanticoke Indians in 1678; died testate by Mar 18, 1687/8 (date of probate; Elizabeth Husculaw, widow). {Ref: ARMD 7:102, 17:94; MDWB 4:304}

HUSSEY, JOHN (Kent County), soldier (rank not stated) circa 1675; paid for his services in the late expedition against the Nanticoke Indians in 1678. {Ref: ARMD 7:94}

HUSSEY, THOMAS (Kent County), probable soldier (rank not stated) before 1682; paid for his services out of an assessment levied by the General Assembly for the public good in 1682. {Ref: ARMD 7:440}

HUTCHENS, JAMES (Queen Anne's County), ensign in the First Company of Foot on Jun 30, 1732. {Ref: MDHR 1:11}

HUTCHINGS, RICHARD (St. Mary's County), soldier (rank not stated) circa 1675; paid for his services in the late expedition against the Nanticoke Indians in 1678. {Ref: ARMD 7:103}

HUTCHINGS, WILLIAM (Calvert County), Protestant and probable soldier in the Revolution of 1689; signed an address and took a loyalty oath supporting the King of England and "to reestablish Lord Baltimore in his ancient power and government" on Nov 16, 1689. {Ref: ARMD 8:131}

HUTCHINS, ANN, see "Charles Hutchins," q.v.

HUTCHINS, CHARLES (England and Dorchester County), court justice, 1674-1685; colonel by 1690; member of the Maryland Council, 1692-1700; died testate by Oct 23, 1700 (date of probate; Ann Hutchins, widow). {Ref: ARMD 15:38, 15:326, 17:381, 20:6, 20:151, 20:153, 20:209, 23:251, 24:6, 24:29, 38:35; BDML I:473; DOLR 6 Old 187; MDWB 11:127}

HUTCHINS, ELIZABETH, see "Francis Hutchins," q.v.

HUTCHINS, FRANCIS (England, and Hunting Creek, Calvert County), Protestant and possible soldier who opposed the Revolution of 1689; signed an address and took a loyalty oath (made his "F H" mark) supporting the King of England and "to reestablish Lord Baltimore in his ancient power and government" on Nov 16, 1689; member of the Lower House of the Maryland Assembly, 1682-1684, 1694-1697; died testate by Jul 14, 1698 (date of probate; Elizabeth Hutchins, widow). {Ref: ARMD 8:131; HCCM:275; BDML I:473; MDWB 6:104}

HUTCHINS, MR., see "John Addison," q.v.

HUTCHINSON, WILLIAM (England and St. Mary's County), seaman on the ship *Ruth* in 1676. {Ref: ARMD 51:474, 66:301}

HUTCHINSON (HUTCHISON), WILLIAM (Scotland, and Charles and Prince George's Counties), Protestant and soldier in the Revolution of 1689; signed an address and took a loyalty oath supporting the King of England and the reestablishment of Lord Baltimore into power on Nov 28, 1689; captain, commissioned Jul 30, 1694; member of the Lower House of the Maryland Assembly from Charles County, 1694-1696, and Prince George's County, 1696-1697; died testate by Apr 23, 1711 (date of probate; Sarah Hutchison, widow). {Ref: ARMD 8:138, 20:130, 25:103; BDML I:473-474; MDWB 13:317; MDAD 2:1}

HUTCHISON (HUTCHESON), JOEL (Anne Arundel County), captain in the 1730's and 1740's; died intestate by Jan 3, 1746/7 (date of inventory). *Note:* Since his name does not appear on any extant militia lists between 1732 and 1746, his service was either prior to 1732 or he was a sea captain. Additional research will be necessary before drawing conclusions. {Ref: MINV 35:81}

HUTCHISON, SARAH, see "William Hutchinson," q.v.

HUTCHYSON, CHARLES (Dorchester County), soldier (rank not stated) circa 1675; paid for his services in the late expedition against the Nanticoke Indians in 1678. {Ref: ARMD 7:92}

HUTCHYSON, FRANCIS (Somerset County), soldier (rank not stated) circa 1675; paid for his services in the late expedition against the Nanticoke Indians in 1678. {Ref: ARMD 7:97}

HUTT, DANIEL (Charles County), captain and master of the bark *Mayflower* in 1659, but at the time "not being an inhabitant of this province, did without lycense upon the 29th day of March last, att Pamaunkey in Pascatoway River" unlawfully trade with the Indians; shipping, trading, or otherwise involved with the militia in 1664. See "Thomas Mitchell" and "Thomas Payne" and "Robert Maphyes" and "Richard Botts," q.v. {Ref: ARMD 41:287-288; CHLR A:50, B:379}

HUTTON, FRANCIS (England and St. Mary's County), seaman on the ship *Ruth* in 1676; probable soldier (rank not stated) by 1682; paid for his services out of an assessment levied by the General Assembly for the public good in 1682. {Ref: ARMD 7:440, 51:474, 66:301}

HYATT, JOHN (Calvert County), Protestant and possible soldier in the Revolution of 1689; signed an address and took a loyalty oath (made his "X" mark) supporting the King of England and "to reestablish Lord Baltimore in his ancient power and government" on Nov 16, 1689. {Ref: ARMD 8:132}

HYDE (HIDE), JOHN (England and Anne Arundel County), captain and merchant of London and Annapolis circa 1690; captain and master of the ship *Elizabeth and Katherine* in 1692; born circa 1665, died 1760. {Ref: ARMD 8:371; INAC 20:205, 22:2; RMHF I:216, II:166, 184}

HYEMS, FRANCIS (St. Mary's County), soldier (rank not stated) circa 1675; paid for his services in the late expedition against the Nanticoke Indians in 1678. {Ref: ARMD 7:103}

HYFIELD, RICHARD (Calvert County), ranger under the command of Capt. Richard Brightwell in 1692. {Ref: ARMD 8:445}

HYLAND, JOHN (England and Cecil County), colonel in the English Army who "resigned his commission owing to some difficulty about his coat-of-arms" and emigrated to Maryland; born circa 1638 (aged about 57 when deposed in 1695), died by May 1, 1696 (date of inventory). {Ref: RMHF II:290; INAC 13B:106; MDEP:101; Johnston's *History of Cecil County*, p. 522}

HYNSON (HINSON), CHARLES (Kent County), colonel by 1733; born Aug 27, 1692 (stated his age was about 37 when deposed in 1730 and about 50 when deposed in 1742), died testate by Apr 11, 1748 (date of probate; Francina Hynson, widow; her name was misinterpreted as "Teruncina Hynson" in one account). {Ref: CFES 2:171; KELR JS#20:159; INKC:178; MDEP:101; MDWB 25:294; MINV 41:9}

HYNSON (HINSON), FRANCINA, see "Charles Hynson," q.v.

HYNSON (HINSON), JOHN (Virginia, and Kent and Cecil Counties), soldier (rank not stated) circa 1675; paid for his services in the late expedition against the Nanticoke Indians in 1678; captain lieutenant of a company of foot, commissioned Feb 28, 1681; court justice (quorum), 1676-1687; captain of a company of foot "in Easterneck and Swann Creeke hundred" in 1689; major of militia before 1694; member of the Commission of the Peace in Kent County, 1697; colonel, commissioned Oct 9, 1694; colonel of Kent County, appointed Aug 17, 1695; military officer who swore allegiance to the King & Queen of England in 1696; member of the Lower House of the Maryland Assembly at various times between 1681 and 1704; born circa 1645, died testate before May 10, 1705 (date of burial; will probated on Jun 5, 1705; Ann Hinson, widow). {Ref: ARMD 7:94, 8:23, 13:241, 15:93, 17:77-78, 17:379, 20:107, 20:152, 20:281, 20:541, 23:198, 24:128, 38:73; BDML I:475-476; CFES 2:165; MDWB 3:656}

HYNSON (HINSON), JOHN (Cecil County), captain by 1703; sheriff, 1703; born circa 1670, died testate by Oct 9, 1708 (date of probate; Mary Hynson, widow). {Ref: ARMD 25:150; BDML I:476; MDWB 12:30, pt. 2}

HYNSON (HINSON), MARY, see "Nathaniel Hynson" and "John Hynson," q.v.

HYNSON (HINSON), NATHANIEL (Kent County), colonel by 1709; member of the Lower House of the Maryland Assembly, 1716-1721; sheriff of Cecil County in 1707 (colonel of Kent County when deposed on Nov 4, 1721 and stated that he was high sheriff of Cecil County about 14 years ago); born circa 1679, died testate by Jan 26, 1721/2 (date of probate; Mary Hynson, widow). {Ref: ARMD 25:378, 30:359, 33:175, 34:61, 34:199; BDML I:476; CFES 2:168; MDWB 17:68; INKC:150, 178; MINV 7:93}

HYNSON (HINSON), THOMAS (Cecil County), soldier and probable officer in the 1730's; captain by 1740; born Oct 10, 1702 (stated his age was about 35 when deposed in 1740), died testate by Mar 4, 1748/9 (date of probate). {Ref: CFES 2:173; KELR JS#23:135; MDEP:101; MDWB 26:81}

HYNSON (HINSON), THOMAS (Kent County), assistant commander (commissioner) of Kent County in 1654; member of the Lower House of the Maryland Assembly in 1654; referred to as "Lieut. Hinson" in 1655; high sheriff, 1655-1656; supported Fendall's Rebellion, 1659/1660; born circa 1619-1620 (aged about 36 when deposed on Oct 29, 1655 and aged about 35 when deposed on Feb 1, 1655/6), died intestate by Jan 25, 1667/8 (date of administration bond). {Ref: BDML I:477; RMHF I:264; MDEP:101; INKC:103-107}

HYNSON (HINSON), WILLIAM (Kent County), probable soldier in the 1730's and officer in the 1740's and 1750's; called "major" by the time of his death; member of the Lower House of the Maryland Assembly, 1754-1766; born Dec 23, 1708 (stated he was aged about 40 when deposed in 1750, aged about 53 when deposed in 1761, and aged between 58 and 59 when deposed in 1767), died intestate by Oct 17, 1767 (date of administration bond). {Ref: BDML I:477; MDEP:101}

IDLE, EDWARD (Talbot County), sailor by 1720. {Ref: MDAD 2:518}

ILIVE, ISAAC (Kent County), soldier (rank not stated) on Isle of Kent who swore allegiance to the Commonwealth of England on Apr 5, 1652. {Ref: INKC:101, 106}

INDIAN ANATCHCOMO, see "John Odber," q.v.

INDIAN JACKANAPES, see "Thomas Clark," q.v.

INGLE, HUGH (Somerset County), soldier (rank not stated) circa 1675; paid for his services in the late expedition against the Nanticoke Indians in 1678. {Ref: ARMD 7:97}

INGLE, RICHARD (St. Mary's County), captain and mariner by 1642; captain and master of the ship *Reformation* in 1650; mariner "of Wapping in the County of Middlesex" in 1652. {Ref: ARMD 3:179, 4:189, 4:513, 10:12, 10:103, 10:211, 10:372}

INGLE, WILLIAM (Somerset County), soldier (rank not stated) circa 1675; paid for his services in the late expedition against the Nanticoke Indians in 1678. {Ref: ARMD 7:98}

INGLISH (ENGLISH), EDWARD (Cecil County), court justice (quorum), 1679-1685; high sheriff, 1682-1683; major, 1686-1687; during the Maryland-Pennsylvania border troubles in 1686 he invaded New Castle County with 40 armed horsemen; died intestate by May 8, 1694 (date of administration account). See "Nathaniell Utie," q.v. {Ref: ARMD 5:460, 5:554, 15:255, 15:326, 17:115, 17:142, 17:381; HBCC:65; INAC 12:158}

INGOLDSBY, ROBERT (Charles County), soldier (rank not stated) circa 1675; paid for his services in the late expedition against the Nanticoke Indians in 1678. {Ref: ARMD 7:101}

INGRAM, JAMES (Somerset County), soldier (rank not stated) circa 1675; paid for his services in the late expedition against the Nanticoke Indians in 1678. {Ref: ARMD 7:98}

INGRAM, MARY, see "Thomas Ingram," q.v.

INGRAM, PEASLY (Baltimore County), probable officer by the 1730's; captain before 1740; born circa 1708, died intestate by Jun 18, 1740 (date of inventory; Ruth Ingram, widow, later married Thomas Franklin). {Ref: MINV 26:1; BBCF:352}

INGRAM, ROBERT (Kent County), military officer (rank not stated) who swore allegiance to the King & Queen of England in 1696; died testate by Aug 25, 1708 (date of probate). {Ref: ARMD 20:541; MDWB 12:272}

INGRAM, RUTH, see "Peasly Ingram," q.v.

INGRAM, SAMUEL (Patuxent and Potomac Districts), captain, master, and commander of the ship *Margrett* (or *Margaret*) in 1722-1726, riding in the Patuxent River on Jan 24, 1724/5 (ship's name was listed once as *Mary*), riding in the Potomac River on Dec 29, 1725, and riding in the Patuxent River on Mar 30, 1726; master of the ship *Potomack* in 1730-1731. {Ref: PGLR I:465, M:149-150; CVPR:12}

INGRAM, THOMAS (Kent County), major by 1667; sheriff, 1668; died testate by Jul 27, 1671 (date of probate; Mary Ingram, widow). {Ref: ARMD 5:21, 5:28, 51:321, 54:460; INKC:133; MDWB 1:406}

INNES, PATRICK (St. Mary's County), chirurgeon on the ship *Gerard* commanded by Capt. Harris in 1682, now lying in Wicocomoco River. {Ref: ARMD 7:286, 17:94}

INNES, WILLIAM (Queen Anne's County), lieutenant in the Fourth Company of Foot on Jun 30, 1732. {Ref: MDHR 1:11}

IRELAND, GILBERT (England and St. Mary's County), mariner, of Liverpool, by 1734; captain, master and owner of the ship *Hamilton* in 1735 (built at the Potomac River). {Ref: MDCB 82:42; MDAD 12:473}

ISAAC, EDWARD (England and Calvert County), captain before 1663; it is said that the brothers Edward and Joseph Isaac were officers in the English Army and were sent to America in charge of Scottish prisoners of war; Edward died in 1689 (Jane Isaac, widow) and Joseph died testate by Feb 23, 1688/9 (date of probate; Margaret Isaac, widow). {Ref: HCCM:277; MDWB 6:53}

ISAAC, JANE, see "Edward Isaac," q.v.

ISAAC, JOSEPH, see "Edward Isaac," q.v.

ISAAC, MARGARET, see "Edward Isaac," q.v.

ISAAC, SUTTON (Calvert County), captain by 1733. {Ref: HCCM:277}

IVARY, THEOPHILUS (New England and Cecil County), mariner by 1733; land owner on Pate's Creek and Elk River in 1733. {Ref: CELR 4:343}

IVRITT, JOHN (England and Talbot County), mariner of the Parish of Stephenheath in County Middlesex and land owner in Talbot County by 1688. {Ref: TALR 5:168}

JACK, PATRICK (Pocomoke District), captain and master of the ship *Jane* in 1730. {Ref: CVPR:12}

JACKSON, ANN, see "Samuel Jackson," q.v.

JACKSON, EDWARD (Heart's Desire, Cecil County), captain and court commissioner by 1731; died testate by Jun 30, 1740 (probate; Elizabeth Jackson, widow). {Ref: MDWB 22:189; MINV 26:471; Judgments Liber SK#4}

JACKSON, ELIZABETH, see "Edward Jackson," q.v.

JACKSON, FRANCIS, see "Edmond Lister," q.v.

JACKSON, HENRY (Talbot County), a seafaring man in 1697. {Ref: ARMD 25:601}

JACKSON, JAMES (Baltimore County), ensign before 1696; swore allegiance to the King & Queen of England in 1696; one James Jackson died testate by May 21, 1698 (date of probate; Martha Jackson, widow) and his son James Jackson died testate by Oct 31, 1718 (date of probate; Sarah Jackson, widow). Additional research will be necessary before drawing conclusions. {Ref: ARMD 20:544; MDWB 6:78, 14:719}

JACKSON, MARGARET, see "Thomas Jackson," q.v.

JACKSON, MARTHA, see "James Jackson," q.v.

JACKSON, RICHARD (Talbot County), soldier (rank not stated) circa 1675; paid for his services in the late expedition against the Nanticoke Indians in 1678. {Ref: ARMD 7:88}

JACKSON, SAMUEL (Somerset County), probable soldier (rank not stated) before 1682; paid for his services out of an assessment levied by the General Assembly for the public good in 1682 (name listed once as "Samuel Jacson"); died testate by Oct 30, 1688 (date of probate; Ann Jackson, widow). {Ref: ARMD 7:442-443; MDWB 6:38}

JACKSON, SARAH, see "James Jackson," q.v.

JACKSON, THOMAS (St. Mary's County), soldier (rank not stated) in 1642; paid for 3 weeks' service under Capt. William Brainthwaite in November, 1642; died testate by Jul 16, 1687 (date of probate; Margaret Jackson, widow). {Ref: ARMD 3:119, 3:122; MDWB 4:255}

JACKSON, THOMAS (Anne Arundel County), soldier (rank not stated) circa 1675; paid for his services in the late expedition against the Nanticoke Indians in 1678. {Ref: ARMD 7:96}

JACKSON, WILLIAM (Charles County), soldier (rank not stated) circa 1675; paid for his services in the late expedition against the Nanticoke Indians in 1678. {Ref: ARMD 7:101}

JACOB, ---- (Kent Island and Talbot County), captain by 1652 (mentioned in the will of William Jones of Kent Island); possibly the "Col. Jacob" who appeared on a list of payments in the estate of Madam Henrietta Maria Lloyd, deceased, in Talbot County on May 2, 1702. {Ref: MDWB 1:42; INAC 21:339}

JADWIN (JADWYN), JOHN (Talbot County), soldier (rank not stated) circa 1675; paid for his services in the late expedition against the Nanticoke Indians in 1678; died testate by Apr 24, 1707 (date of probate). {Ref: ARMD 7:89; MDWB 12:136}

JAGOE (JAGO), RICHARD (Kent and Queen Anne's Counties), military officer (rank not stated) who swore allegiance to the King & Queen of England in

1696; died intestate by Sep 29, 1728 (date of administration account). {Ref: ARMD 20:540; MDAD 9:208}

JAMES, CHARLES (England, and Baltimore and Cecil Counties), captain of a troop of horse, 1689; justice and county commissioner, 1692-1694; died intestate in 1698. {Ref: ARMD 8:458-459, 8:474, 13:244, 20:111; BDML II:481; INCC:135; INAC 23:98}

JAMES, EDWARD (England, and Kent and Talbot Counties), soldier (rank not stated) circa 1675; paid for his services in the late expedition against the Nanticoke Indians in 1678; requested to be a ranger and was appointed on Oct 14, 1692; died testate in Talbot County by May 30, 1704 (date of probate). {Ref: ARMD 7:94, 8:392; MDWB 3:272}

JAMES, ELISHER (Talbot County), captain and owner of a ship (no name given) in 1697. {Ref: ARMD 25:601}

JAMES, JAMES (England and Somerset County), cabin boy on the ship *Betty Gally* of Liverpool riding at anchor in Monocan River on Jan 16, 1716/7. {Ref: SOJR III:185-186}

JAMES, JOHN (Cecil County), captain and master of the ship *Bohemia Brothers* in 1689; military officer (rank not stated) who swore allegiance to the King & Queen of England in 1696; died testate by Jan 21, 1698/9 (date of probate). {Ref: ARMD 8:236, 15:255, 15:326, 20:545; MDWB 6:247}

JAMES, JOHN (Annapolis and Oxford Districts), captain and commander of the ship *Speedwell* riding in Herring Bay on Apr 21, 1724; master of the ship *Benedict Leonard* in 1731. {Ref: AALR RCW#2:235; CVPR:12}

JAMES, MARY, see "Thomas James," q.v.

JAMES, RICE (Talbot County), soldier (rank not stated) circa 1675; paid for his services in the late expedition against the Nanticoke Indians in 1678. {Ref: ARMD 7:92}

JAMES, THOMAS (Baltimore County and Pennsylvania-Delaware), soldier (rank not stated) circa 1675; paid for his services in the late expedition against the Nanticoke Indians in 1678; died by Jun 6, 1705 (date of administration bond in New Castle County; Mary James, widow). {Ref: ARMD 7:95; BBCF:358}

JANSON, PETER (county or port not stated), seaman and "one of the company taken upon the ship *St. George*" in 1659. {Ref: ARMD 41:308}

JARBOE (JARBO), JOHN (France, Virginia, and St. Mary's County), lieutenant, commissioned May 8, 1658; lieutenant colonel, 1660; sheriff, 1667-1672; member of the Lower House of the Maryland Assembly, 1671-1675; colonel by the time of his death; born circa 1619 (aged about 40 when deposed on Jun 21, 1659), died testate by Mar 9, 1674/5 (date of probate; Mary Jarboe, widow). {Ref: ARMD 3:344, 3:401, 5:4, 41:341, 49:176, 51:321, 53:484; BDML II:482; RMHF I:302; INAC 1:372; MDEP:104; MDWB 2:66}

JARMON, JOHN (St. Mary's County), captain by 1719. {Ref: MDAD 2:290}

JARRETT, JOHN (Somerset County), soldier (rank not stated) circa 1675; paid for his services in the late expedition against the Nanticoke Indians in 1678. {Ref: ARMD 7:100}

JARRETT, RICHARD (Somerset County), Protestant and probable soldier in the Revolution of 1689; signed an address and took a loyalty oath supporting the King of England and "for enabling us to defend ourselves against all invaders" on Nov 28, 1689. {Ref: ARMD 8:140}

JARVIS, HUMPHRY (Somerset County), soldier (rank not stated) circa 1675; paid for his services in the late expedition against the Nanticoke Indians in 1678. {Ref: ARMD 7:98}

JEFFRIES, ABELL (county or port not indicated), captain and master of the ketch *America* of Topsham in 1690. {Ref: ARMD 8:237}

JENIFER, DANIEL (England, Virginia, and St. Mary's and Calvert Counties), lieutenant by 1666; captain, 1667; captain lieutenant, commissioned Apr 1, 1668; member of the Lower House of the Maryland Assembly, 1671; captain, 1674-1675; sheriff, Accomack County, 1680; colonel by 1683; born circa 1637 (aged about 27 when deposed in 1664), died by Feb 21, 1692/3 (date of administration request). {Ref: ARMD 1:532, 2:239, 3:557, 5:28, 15:47; BDML II:483-484; INAC 1:525}

JENIFER, DANIEL OF ST. THOMAS (Virginia and St. Mary's County), captain before 1718; born circa 1672, died by Jul 2, 1730 (date of probate; Elizabeth Jenifer, widow). {Ref: BDML II:483; MDWB 20:17; MDAD 1:199}

JENIFER, ELIZABETH, see "Daniel of St. Thomas Jenifer," q.v.

JENIFER, MARY, see "Michael Jenifer," q.v.

JENIFER, MICHAEL (St. Mary's County), captain before 1728; died testate by Sep 2, 1728 (date of probate; Mary Jenifer, widow, later married James Smith). {Ref: MDWB 19:488; MDAD 10:177}

JENKINS (JENCKINS), FRANCIS (England and Somerset County), soldier (rank not stated) circa 1675; paid for his services in the late expedition against the Nanticoke Indians in 1678; court justice (quorum), 1679-1680; sheriff, 1683; captain of the horse troops of Somerset County, commissioned Dec 2, 1687; Protestant and leader in the Revolution of 1689; signed an address and took a loyalty oath supporting the King of England and "for enabling us to defend ourselves against all invaders" on Nov 28, 1689; colonel by 1699; he was noted in the proceedings of the Maryland Council as "very aged and lives at a great distance [in] Sommersett County" in 1707; member of the Maryland Council, 1709; born circa 1650, died testate by Jun 7, 1710 (date of probate; Mary Jenkins, widow). See "Robert King," q.v. {Ref: ARMD 5:568, 7:99, 7:612, 8:141, 15:275, 15:328, 17:142, 24:135, 25:251, 27:377; BDML II:486-487; MDWB 12:201, 13:65; INAC 32B:70}

JENKINS (JENCKINS), JOHN (St. Mary's County), captain and master of the ship *Golden Fleece* in 1693. {Ref: ARMD 20:182}

JENKINS, JOHN (Charles County and North Carolina), captain and burgess (member of the Maryland Assembly), 1658-1660; referred to as "Capt. Grindingstone" in 1658; supported Fendall's Rebellion in 1659/1660 and was dismissed from office in 1661; migrated to North Carolina, served in the "Rebel

Parliament" and was acting governor, 1672-1676, 1679-1681; died Dec 17, 1681. {Ref: ARMD 1:382, 3:402, 41:450, 53:49; BDML II:487; CHLR A:61}

JENKINS (JENCKINS), LEWIS (England and Potomac District), captain and master of the ship *Amity* in 1697. {Ref: ARMD 23:171-172}

JENKINS, MARY, see "Francis Jenkins," q.v.

JENKINS, THOMAS (county or port not indicated), captain and master of the ship *Success* of Maryland (built in Boston) in 1733. {Ref: MDCB 82:5}

JENKINS, THOMAS (Talbot County), probable soldier (rank not stated) before 1682; paid for his services out of an assessment levied by the General Assembly for the public good in 1682; "Thomas Jenkins, wheelwright" died testate by May 19, 1719 (date of probate). {Ref: ARMD 7:441; MDWB 15:106}

JENNINGS, DANIELL (Potomac District), captain and master of the ship *Nymphet* in 1730-1731. {Ref: CVPR:12}

JEROME (JERAM), BENJAMIN (Anne Arundel County), captain and commander of the ship *Thomas* riding at anchor in South River on Mar 25, 1712; commander of the ship *Success* riding in West River on Mar 16, 1721/2. {Ref: AALR PK:446, CW#1:482}

JEWITT, ROBERT (Anne Arundel County), captain and commander of the ship *Catherine* riding in South River on May 24, 1722. {Ref: AALR CW#1:495}

JINGLE, HUGH (Somerset County), Protestant and probable soldier in the Revolution of 1689; signed an address and took a loyalty oath supporting the King of England and "for enabling us to defend ourselves against all invaders" on Nov 28, 1689. {Ref: ARMD 8:139}

JOAD, ANDREW (Anne Arundel County), captain by 1722. See "Andrew Joud," q.v. {Ref: MDAD 5:13}

JODVIN, NICHOLAS (Somerset County), Protestant and probable soldier in the Revolution of 1689; signed an address and took a loyalty oath supporting the King of England and "for enabling us to defend ourselves against all invaders" on Nov 28, 1689. {Ref: ARMD 8:141}

JOHN, HENRY (county not indicated), captain by 1684. {Ref: ARMD 13:64}

JOHNS, ROBERT (Kent County), soldier (rank not stated) circa 1675; paid for his services in the late expedition against the Nanticoke Indians in 1678. {Ref: ARMD 7:94}

JOHNSON, ---- (Dorchester County), captain of a ship (no named given) in 1723. {Ref: MDAD 5:279}

JOHNSON, ABRAHAM (St. Mary's County), captain, mariner and skipper by 1649. {Ref: ARMD 4:493, 10:53}

JOHNSON, ANNE, see "Peter Johnson," q.v.

JOHNSON, CHRISTOPHER (Baltimore County), probable soldier (rank not stated) before 1682; paid for his services out of an assessment levied by the General Assembly for the public good in 1682. {Ref: ARMD 7:441}

JOHNSON, CORNELIUS (Charles County), soldier (rank not stated) circa 1675; paid for his services in the late expedition against the Nanticoke Indians in 1678. {Ref: ARMD 7:101}

JOHNSON, CORNELIUS (Somerset County), soldier (rank not stated) circa 1675; paid for his services in the late expedition against the Nanticoke Indians in 1678 (name listed once as "Cornelius Johnsone"); died testate by Jun 17, 1687 (date of probate). {Ref: ARMD 7:99; MDWB 4:273}

JOHNSON, DAVID (Talbot County), soldier (rank not stated) circa 1675; paid for his services in the late expedition against the Nanticoke Indians in 1678; died testate by Jun 15, 1686 (date of probate; Elizabeth Johnson, widow). {Ref: ARMD 7:91; MDWB 4:219}

JOHNSON, EDWARD (Talbot County), soldier (rank not stated) circa 1675; paid for his services in the late expedition against the Nanticoke Indians in 1678. {Ref: ARMD 7:92}

JOHNSON, ELIZABETH, see "David Johnson" and "Henry Johnson" and "Robert Johnson," q.v.

JOHNSON, FRANCIS (Somerset County), soldier (rank not stated) circa 1675; paid for his services in the late expedition against the Nanticoke Indians in 1678. {Ref: ARMD 7:98}

JOHNSON, GEORGE (Virginia and Annamessex, Somerset County), sheriff, 1668; soldier (rank not stated) circa 1675; paid for his services in the late expedition against the Nanticoke Indians in 1678; court justice (quorum), 1679; died testate by Dec 23, 1681 (date of probate; Katherine Johnson, widow). {Ref: ARMD 7:99, 15:275, 51:321; OSES:284, 316, 448; MDWB 2:189}

JOHNSON, GEORGE (England and St. Mary's County), seaman on the ship *Ruth* in 1676. {Ref: ARMD 51:474, 66:301}

JOHNSON, HENRY (Baltimore County), captain by 1680; paid for his services out of an assessment levied by the General Assembly for the public good in 1682; member of the Lower House of the Maryland Assembly, 1682-1684; justice (quorum), 1680-1690; captain of a foot company in 1689; died testate by Jun 13, 1689 (date of probate; Elizabeth Johnson, widow; administration account filed on May 8, 1700 by Elizabeth Boothby, administratrix, and wife of Edward Boothby). See "Nathaniell Utie," q.v. {Ref: ARMD 7:441, 7:611, 13:243, 15:327, 17:380; BDML II:492-493; INAC 12:147, 19½B:67; BALR HS#1:328}

JOHNSON, HENRY (Dorchester County), soldier (rank not stated) circa 1675; paid for his services in the late expedition against the Nanticoke Indians in 1678. {Ref: ARMD 7:92}

JOHNSON, HENRY (Anne Arundel County), captain by 1722. {Ref: MDAD 5:24}

JOHNSON, JACOB, see "Hance Jordaine," q.v.

JOHNSON, JANE, see "Thomas Johnson," q.v.

JOHNSON, JEAFFREY (St. Mary's County), seaman whose name appeared on "a list of men that goe by water when employed" in 1697. {Ref: ARMD 25:597}

JOHNSON, JOHN, see "John Johnston," q.v.

JOHNSON, JOHN (Somerset County), soldier (rank not stated) circa 1675; paid for his services in the late expedition against the Nanticoke Indians in 1678; Protestant and probable soldier in the Revolution of 1689; signed an address and took a loyalty oath supporting the King of England and "for enabling us to defend ourselves against all invaders" on Nov 28, 1689. {Ref: ARMD 7:100, 8:140}

JOHNSON, KATHERINE, see "George Johnson," q.v.

JOHNSON, MILES (Talbot County), soldier (rank not stated) circa 1675; paid for his services in the late expedition against the Nanticoke Indians in 1678. {Ref: ARMD 7:87}

JOHNSON, PEETER (Kent County), soldier (rank not stated) in Capt. William Leeds (Leeads) Company by May 23, 1662, at which time he signed a petition about the misuse of company money by Capt. Thomas Brednox (Bradnox), late of Isle of Kent, deceased. {Ref: ARMD 3:455}

JOHNSON, PETER (St. Mary's and Calvert Counties), Puritan leader and captain by 1654; commissioned captain of militia "in Putuxent County downwards on both sides of the river" on Apr 23, 1655; born circa 1611 (aged about 42 when deposed in 1653), died intestate before May 27, 1656 (date that his widow Anne Johnson, of Patuxent, wrote her will). See "James Veitch," q.v. {Ref: ARMD 3:315, 10:287, 10:412; HCCM:35, 279; MDWB 1:64}

JOHNSON, PETER (St. Mary's County), Protestant and probable soldier in the Revolution of 1689; signed an address and took a loyalty oath supporting the King of England and the reestablishment of Lord Baltimore into power on Nov 28, 1689. {Ref: ARMD 8:146}

JOHNSON, RICHARD (England and Anne Arundel County), captain and mariner by 1704; commander of the ship *Providence Gally* of Maryland in 1705; commander of the ship *Richard and James* riding at anchor in South River on Jun 16, 1708. {Ref: ARMD 25:183; AALR WT#2:247, 631}

JOHNSON, ROBERT (Calvert County), Protestant and probable soldier in the Revolution of 1689; signed an address and took a loyalty oath (made his "R I" mark) supporting the King of England and "to reestablish Lord Baltimore in his ancient power and government" on Nov 16, 1689. {Ref: ARMD 8:131}

JOHNSON, ROBERT (St. Mary's County), captain and master of the ship *Alexander* of Greenoake in 1696. {Ref: ARMD 23:11}

JOHNSON, ROBERT (Somerset County), soldier (rank not stated) circa 1675; paid for his services in the late expedition against the Nanticoke Indians in 1678; Protestant and probable soldier in the Revolution of 1689; signed an address and took a loyalty oath supporting the King of England and "for enabling us to defend ourselves against all invaders" on Nov 28, 1689; "Robert Johnson, Jr." died testate by Feb 28, 1717/8 (date of probate) and "Robert Johnson, planter" died testate by Mar 9, 1720/1 (date of probate; Elizabeth Johnson, widow). Additional research will be necessary before drawing conclusions. {Ref: ARMD 7:99, 8:139; MDWB 14:550; MDWB 16:292; MDAD 4:87}

JOHNSON, SAMUEL (England and Prince George's County), captain in the 1730's; mariner, of London, and captain of the ship *Charles* riding in the Potomac River on Jun 14, 1741; died testate by Sep 14, 1741 (date of probate). {Ref: MDWB 22:401}

JOHNSON, THOMAS (Cecil County), ranger, 1724; justice, 1732-1738; captain (date not stated); born by 1700, died intestate by Mar 8, 1738/9 (date of inventory; Jane Johnson, widow). {Ref: BDML II:495; INCC:134; MINV 25:56}

JOHNSON, THOMAS (Calvert County), Protestant and probable soldier in the Revolution of 1689; signed an address and took a loyalty oath supporting the King of England and "to reestablish Lord Baltimore in his ancient power and government" on Nov 16, 1689. {Ref: ARMD 8:131}

JOHNSON, WILLIAM (St. Mary's County), soldier at St. Inego's fort in 1647. {Ref: ARMD 4:311}

JOHNSON, WILLIAM (England and Talbot County), mariner of London before 1682; land owner in Talbot County by 1682 (wrote his will on Feb 9, 1688/9); captain by 1689; commander of the ship *Content* in 1689; William Johnson, of Ratclife, Old England, mariner, married Sarah Edmondson of Talbot County; she died childless in London and he married second to Mary Harris; depositions in London on Feb 1, 1719/20 stated William Johnson, deceased, had "traded to Maryland and 37 or 38 years ago bought an estate on Chesapeake Bay." {Ref: ARMD 8:151, 8:170; TALR 4:181, 12:392; INAC 10:212; LMCL:39-40}

JOHNSTON, JOHN (Talbot County), soldier (rank not stated) circa 1675; paid for his services in the late expedition against the Nanticoke Indians in 1678 (name listed once as "John Johnson"); Protestant and probable soldier in the Revolution of 1689; signed an address and took a loyalty oath supporting the King of England and the reestablishment of Lord Baltimore into power on Nov 18, 1689; died testate by Sep 15, 1701 (date of probate; Ann Johnston, widow). {Ref: ARMD 7:90, 7:92, 8:134; MDWB 11:145}

JONES, ANDREW (Somerset County), soldier (rank not stated) circa 1675; paid for his services in the late expedition against the Nanticoke Indians in 1678; cornet before 1682; paid again for his services in 1682. {Ref: ARMD 7:99, 7:442}

JONES, ANN, see "David Jones" and "Richard Jones, Jr.," q.v.

JONES, DANIELL (Dorchester County), soldier (rank not stated) circa 1675; paid for his services in the late expedition against the Nanticoke Indians in 1678. {Ref: ARMD 7:93-94}

JONES, DAVID (Baltimore County), soldier (rank not stated) circa 1675; paid for his services in the late expedition against the Nanticoke Indians in 1678; died testate by Mar 14, 1686/7 (date of probate; Ann Jones, widow). {Ref: ARMD 7:95; BBCF:375; MDWB 4:240}

JONES (JOANES), EDWARD (Kent County), soldier (rank not stated) in Capt. William Leeds (Leeads) Company by May 23, 1662, at which time he signed a petition about the misuse of company money by Capt. Thomas Brednox (Bradnox), late of Isle of Kent, deceased. {Ref: ARMD 3:455}

JONES, EDWARD (Somerset County), Protestant and probable soldier in the Revolution of 1689; signed an address and took a loyalty oath supporting the King of England and "for enabling us to defend ourselves against all invaders" on Nov 28, 1689. {Ref: ARMD 8:141}

JONES, EMANUELL (Talbot County), sergeant who swore allegiance to the King & Queen of England in 1696. {Ref: ARMD 20:542}

JONES, EVAN (Charles County), soldier (rank not stated) circa 1675; paid for his services in the late expedition against the Nanticoke Indians in 1678 (noted in 1679 as having been crippled in the Susquehannah War). {Ref: ARMD 7:101, 7:148}

JONES, GEORGE (Prince George's County), captain by 1721; died intestate by Jan 13, 1720/30 (date of administration account). {Ref: PGLR I:202; MDAD 10:185, 384}

JONES, GRIFFITH (Kent County), military officer (rank not stated) who swore allegiance to the King & Queen of England in 1696; died testate by Jun 30, 1701 (date of probate; Lucy Jones, widow). {Ref: ARMD 20:541; MDWB 11:113}

JONES, HUGH (England and St. Mary's County), captain and master of the ship *George* of Plymouth in 1694. {Ref: ARMD 20:147}

JONES, ISAACK (St. Mary's County), captain and master of the ship *John and Mary* in 1693. {Ref: ARMD 20:183}

JONES, JANE, see "Morgan Jones," q.v.

JONES, JANEVARA, see "John Jones," q.v.

JONES, JOHN (Somerset County), Protestant and soldier in the Revolution of 1689; signed an address and took a loyalty oath supporting the King of England and "for enabling us to defend ourselves against all invaders" on Nov 28, 1689; member of the Lower House of the Maryland Assembly, 1704-1707, 1719-1722; captain before 1720; born Sep 24, 1668, died intestate by Dec 15, 1731 (date of inventory). {Ref: ARMD 8:140, 34:61; 34:199; BDML II:497; MDWB 16:382}

JONES, JOHN (Talbot County), soldier (rank not stated) circa 1675; paid for his services in the late expedition against the Nanticoke Indians in 1678; died testate by Feb 9, 1701/2 (date of probate; Janevara Jones, widow). {Ref: ARMD 7:87; MDWB 11:163}

JONES, JOHN (county or port not indicated), captain of the ship *Abraham and Isaac* in 1675. {Ref: MDHM 5:339}

JONES, JOHN (Prince George's County), soldier (rank not stated) under the command of Col. Ninian Beale from June, 1699 to May, 1700. {Ref: ARMD 24:121-122}

JONES, JOHN (England and Anne Arundel County), captain and commander of the ship *Speedwell* riding in Herring Bay on Apr 18, 1723; master of the ship *Ann* in Annapolis in 1730. {Ref: AALR RCW#2:136; CVPR:12}

JONES, JOHN (England and Anne Arundel, Baltimore and Kent Counties), mariner by 1720; captain and commander of the ship *John and William* lying at anchor in the Patapsco River on Sep 29, 1720; commander of the ship *Duke of London* riding in South River on May 24, 1722 and May 3, 1723 and Jun 27,

1724 and Jan 10, 1725/6 and Mar 23, 1726/7 and Nov 19, 1730; died by Jun 15, 1734 (date of inventory). {Ref: AALR CW#1:256, 495; AALR RCW#2:147, 255; AALR SY#1:154, 265; MDGZ, May 27, 1729 and Jun 16, 1730; CVPR:12; MINV 20:245}

JONES, LUCY, see "Griffith Jones," q.v.

JONES, MARY, see "William Jones," q.v.

JONES, MATHEW (Somerset County), Protestant and probable soldier in the Revolution of 1689; signed an address and took a loyalty oath supporting the King of England and "for enabling us to defend ourselves against all invaders" on Nov 28, 1689. {Ref: ARMD 8:139}

JONES, MORGAN (England and Talbot County), captain before 1699; master of the ship *Blew Bird's Delight* "riding at anchor in Fyall Road and bound by God's permission to Choptank River in Maryland" in September, 1699. {Ref: TALR 7:218}

JONES, MORGAN (Kent, Cecil, and Dorchester Counties), soldier (rank not stated) circa 1675; paid for his services in the late expedition against the Nanticoke Indians in 1678; born circa 1652 (aged about 24 when deposed on Aug 22, 1676 in Kent County; named listed as "Morgon Joanes"), died testate in Dorchester County by Jul 29, 1695 (date of probate; Jane Jones, widow; mentioned land in Dorchester and Cecil Counties). {Ref: ARMD 7:94; INKC:149; MDEP:108; MDWB 7:95}

JONES, PETER (Kent County), "seaman within the said county" and a "sailor belonging to Mr. Powers ship in the stocks" in 1697. {Ref: ARMD 25:599}

JONES, PHIL. (Anne Arundel County), captain by 1719. {Ref: MDAD 2:34}

JONES, PHILLIP (Talbot County), probable soldier (rank not stated) before 1682; paid for his services out of an assessment levied by the General Assembly for the public good in 1682. {Ref: ARMD 7:440, 54:512}

JONES, RICE (Kent County), soldier (rank not stated) circa 1675; paid for his services in the late expedition against the Nanticoke Indians in 1678; military officer (rank not stated) who swore allegiance to the King & Queen of England in 1696. {Ref: ARMD 7:94, 20:541}

JONES, RICHARD (Talbot County), soldier (rank not stated) circa 1675; paid for his services in the late expedition against the Nanticoke Indians in 1678; Protestant and probable soldier in the Revolution of 1689; signed an address and took a loyalty oath supporting the King of England and the reestablishment of Lord Baltimore into power on Nov 18, 1689; Richard Jones witnessed the will of Richard Jones, Jr. on Oct 15, 1704. {Ref: ARMD 7:88, 8:134; MDWB 3:463}

JONES, RICHARD, JR. (Anne Arundel County), captain by 1700; member of the Lower House of the Maryland Assembly, 1704-1714; chief justice of Anne Arundel County, 1709-1714; born circa 1671 (aged about 27 when deposed in 1698), died testate by May 4, 1714 (date of probate; Ann Jones, widow). {Ref: ARMD 27:202, 29:26, 29:33, 29:125, 29:468; AALR WH#4:49, WH#4:134, WT#1:97; MDEP:108; BDML II:498-499; MDWB 13:684}

JONES, ROBERT (St. Mary's County), captain by 1677; master of the ship *Yarmouth* of Biddeford in 1690; died testate by Jul 29, 1692 (date of probate). {Ref: ARMD 8:238; MDWB 6:3; INAC 4:1}

JONES, ROBERT (Baltimore County), soldier (rank not stated) circa 1675; paid for his services in the late expedition against the Nanticoke Indians in 1678; paid for his services out of an assessment levied by the General Assembly for the public good in 1682; died testate by Jan 6, 1690/1 (date of probate). {Ref: ARMD 7:95, 7:441; MDWB 7:128}

JONES, ROBERT, JR. (Baltimore County), soldier (rank not stated) circa 1675; paid for his services in the late expedition against the Nanticoke Indians in 1678. {Ref: ARMD 7:95}

JONES, SAMUELL (Somerset County), soldier (rank not stated) circa 1675; paid for his services in the late expedition against the Nanticoke Indians in 1678; died testate by Mar 1, 1719/20 (date of probate). {Ref: ARMD 7:98-99; MDWB 15:321}

JONES, THOMAS (Talbot County), soldier (rank not stated) circa 1675; paid for his services in the late expedition against the Nanticoke Indians in 1678. {Ref: ARMD 7:90, 7:92}

JONES, THOMAS (St. Mary's County), sloopman by 1678. {Ref: INAC 5:229}

JONES, THOMAS (Somerset and Worcester Counties), captain by 1672; "captain of Somerset County and commander of the forces in Worcester County" in 1672; paid for his services in the late expedition against the Nanticoke Indians in 1678; Protestant and probable soldier in the Revolution of 1689; signed an address and took a loyalty oath supporting the King of England and "for enabling us to defend ourselves against all invaders" on Nov 28, 1689; born circa 1641 (aged about 43 when deposed in 1684), died testate by Apr 25, 1701 (date of probate). {Ref: ARMD 5:111, 7:99, 8:141, 17:334; 65:41; CESM:36; INAC 5:382; MDWB 11:164}

JONES, THOMAS (Baltimore County), piper before 1699; he was noted in an administration account filed on Jan 10, 1699/1700 in the estate of Thomas Hedge, deceased, as "Thomas Jones, piper, runaway." {Ref: ARMD 20:424; INAC 19½A:142}

JONES, WILLIAM (Kent and Talbot Counties), soldier (rank not stated) on Isle of Kent who swore allegiance to the Commonwealth of England on Apr 5, 1652; soldier (rank not stated) circa 1675; paid for his services in the late expedition against the Nanticoke Indians in 1678; died testate by Jan 1, 1684/5 (date of probate; Mary Jones, widow). {Ref: ARMD 7:90-91; INKC:101; MDWB 4:171}

JONES, WILLIAM (Monie, Somerset County), soldier (rank not stated) circa 1675; paid for his services in the late expedition against the Nanticoke Indians in 1678; court justice, 1679-1680; paid for his services out of an assessment levied by the General Assembly for the public good in 1682. {Ref: ARMD 7:98, 7:442, 15:275; OSES:284}

JONES, WILLIAM (England and Kent, Talbot, and Queen Anne's Counties), mariner, of Bristol, before 1723; extensive land owner in Maryland who died intestate by 1724 (William Jones was his son and heir apparent). {Ref: QALR IK#B:273}

JORDAIN (JOURDAIN), JOHN (St. Mary's County), captain by 1669; a statement by his widow Elizabeth Scott on May 13, 1679 indicated she married first to Col. William Evans (who died in March, 1669), second to John Jordain in May, 1669 (who died about Sep 8, 1678), and third to Cuthbert Scott on Oct 28, 1678. {Ref: ARMD 51:282-285; INAC 1:519}

JORDAINE, HANCE (St. Mary's County), soldier (rank not stated) by 1678; a petition was submitted to the General Assembly on Sep 14, 1681 "by Jacob Johnson of St. Mary's County having married the widdow of Hance Jordaine who was killed at the Fort leaving his Wife big with Child in a Miserable Poor Condition who soon after was Delivered of two Children the one whereof Dyed the other still living. Hance Jordaine Died in Debt which the Petitioner hath paid and hath ever Since Maintained the other Orphan by his own hard Labour, and prays Consideration for what is Past & for the future Maintenance of the Said Orphan" in 1681. See "---- Hanse," q.v. {Ref: ARMD 7:171-172}

JORDAN, JOHN (Kent County), military officer (rank not stated) who swore allegiance to the King & Queen of England in 1696. {Ref: ARMD 20:541}

JORDAN, JUSTINIAN (St. Mary's County), captain by 1722; member of the Lower House of the Maryland Assembly, 1722-1737; major by 1733; lieutenant colonel in a troop of horse by 1748; born circa 1685-1686 (aged about 37 when deposed in 1722, aged about 43 when deposed in 1728, and aged about 52 when deposed in 1738), died between Feb 10, 1748/9 and May 3, 1749 (inventory approved on Aug 1, 1749). {Ref: ARMD 34:401, 39:55, 39:151; MDAD 5:106; MDEP:109; BDML II:500; MINV 40:345}

JORDAN, ROBERT (St. Mary's County), captain by 1688. {Ref: MDWB 6:48}

JORDAN, THOMAS (St. Mary's County), Protestant and possible soldier in the Revolution of 1689; signed an address and took a loyalty oath supporting the King of England and the reestablishment of Lord Baltimore into power on Nov 28, 1689. {Ref: ARMD 8:146}

JORDANE, WILLIAM (Talbot County), soldier (rank not stated) circa 1675; paid for his services in the late expedition against the Nanticoke Indians in 1678. {Ref: ARMD 7:87}

JOSEPH, WILLIAM (Ireland, England, and St. Mary's County), gentleman who arrived in the province by 1688 with a commission as chief executive; possible soldier (rank not stated) involved in the Revolution of 1689; he filed a "petition for allowance for a Horse & some Arms taken from him upon the late Revolution whilst himself sick at Mattapany" on May 31, 1692; returned to Ireland by 1701 and died by 1729. {Ref: ARMD 13:323; BDML II:500-501}

JOUD, ANDREW (Baltimore County), captain by 1723. See "Andrew Joad," q.v. {Ref: MDAD 5:182}

JOURDAIN, JOHN, see "John Jordain," q.v.

JOWLES, DRYDEN, see "Henry Peregrine Jowles," q.v.

JOWLES (JOULES, JOLES), HENRY (England, and Calvert and St. Mary's Counties), came to this province in 1670 and soon became an officer in the militia; commanded a company of foot and suppressed an insurrection at the Cliffs (no date given); major on the Council of War in July, 1676; colonel, 1679; colonel and Protestant in command of the foot forces of Calvert County, 1681-1694; sheriff, 1683; justice, 1680 (quorum), 1685; member of the Lower House of the Maryland Assembly, 1686-1691; Protestant, justice of the peace, and leader in the Revolution of 1689; signed an address and took a loyalty oath supporting the King of England and the reestablishment of Lord Baltimore into power on Nov 28, 1689; colonel of Calvert County, commissioned Jul 30, 1694, and colonel of St. Mary's County, appointed Aug 17, 1695; member of the Maryland Council, 1692-1700; born circa 1640, died testate by Feb 17, 1700/1 (date of probate; Sybill Jowles, widow). See "John Cobreth" and "Thomas Tasker," q.v. {Ref: ARMD 5:309, 5:554, 8:145, 8:280, 13:242, 15:99, 15:268, 15:327, 17:72, 17:76, 17:142, 17:379, 20:15, 20:111, 20:130, 20:153, 20:281, 23:29, 24:1, 25:1; BDML II:501; HCCM:27, 281-282; PGLR A:320; INAC 20:214; MDWB 6:399}

JOWLES, HENRY PEREGRINE (Calvert and St. Mary's Counties), captain by 1708; member of the Lower House of the Maryland Assembly, 1708-1719; colonel by 1719; born in 1681 (son of Henry Jowles, *q.v.*), died Mar 31, 1720 (will probated on Jun 9, 1720; Dryden Jowles, widow). {Ref: ARMD 27:202, 29:391, 30:359, 33:156; BDML II:501; MDWB 16:89}

JOWLES, SYBILL, see "Henry Jowles," q.v.

JOYCE, FRANCIS (Somerset County), Protestant and probable soldier in the Revolution of 1689; signed an address and took a loyalty oath supporting the King of England and "for enabling us to defend ourselves against all invaders" on Nov 28, 1689. {Ref: ARMD 8:141}

JUDE, MILES (Baltimore County), soldier (rank not stated) circa 1675; paid for his services in the late expedition against the Nanticoke Indians in 1678. {Ref: ARMD 7:95}

JUMP (JUMPE), WILLIAM (Talbot and Queen Anne's Counties), sergeant before 1696; swore allegiance to the King & Queen of England in 1696; died testate in Queen Anne's County after Mar 1, 1709/10 (date will was written; date of probate was not indicated). {Ref: ARMD 20:542; MDWB 13:414}

JUNIPER, DANIELL (Charles or Calvert County), captain by 1698. {Ref: ARMD 23:468; INAC 13A:46}

JURVILL, WILLIAM (Somerset County), Protestant and probable soldier in the Revolution of 1689; signed an address and took a loyalty oath supporting the King of England and "for enabling us to defend ourselves against all invaders" on Nov 28, 1689. {Ref: ARMD 8:140}

KEAT (KEATE), SAMUEL (Anne Arundel County), captain and commander of the ship *Elizabeth* riding at anchor in Herring Bay on Jun 11, 1720 and Apr 22, 1721. {Ref: AALR CW#1:172, 353}

KEEBLE, GEORGE (England and Prince George's County), captain and master of the ship *Providence* in 1696. {Ref: ARMD 23:72-73, 23:168}

KEECH (KEETCH), JAMES (England, and Calvert and St. Mary's Counties), ensign by 1689; supported the Revolution of 1689; captain by 1692; provincial court justice, 1698-1704; born circa 1651 (aged about 42 when deposed on Aug 24, 1693), died testate by Mar 25, 1708 (date of probate; Elizabeth Keech, widow). {Ref: ARMD 8:474, 8:558, 20:108, 23:432; BDML II:502; CHLR C#2:219; INAC 28:281; MDWB 12:215}

KEENE, ---- (Somerset County), soldier (rank not stated) circa 1675; "Mrs. Keene" was paid for his services in the late expedition against the Nanticoke Indians in 1678. {Ref: ARMD 7:100}

KEENE, EDWARD, see "Samuel Groome," q.v.

KEENE (KEEN, KEINE), HENRY (St. Mary's and Calvert Counties), lieutenant, 1655; captain, commissioned on Mar 23, 1656 in part of what was then Patuxent County; paid for his services in September, 1657; lieutenant, commissioned again on May 8, 1658; born circa 1625 (aged about 33 when deposed in October, 1658). {Ref: ARMD 1:364, 3:320, 3:344, 41:166; MDEP:110}

KEENE (KEEN), JOHN (Calvert and Dorchester Counties), captain before 1714, possibly as early as 1687; born 1657, died testate by Nov 14, 1723 (date of probate). {Ref: RMHF I:361, II:195; MDWB 14:683, 18:184; MINV 9:314; SOJR III:66}

KEENE, MARY, see "Richard Keene," q.v.

KEENE, RICHARD (England and Patuxent River, Calvert County), Quaker upon "refusing to be trained as a soldier, had taken from him sixty-seven pounds fifteen shillings, and was abused by the sheriff (Coursey), who drew his cutlass and therewith made a pass at the breast of the said Richard and struck him on the shoulder" in 1658; born circa 1628, died testate by Feb 7, 1675/6 (date of probate; Mary Keene, widow). {Ref: RMHF II:193; MDWB 2:384}

KEENE (KEEN), RICHARD (St. Mary's and Calvert Counties), soldier (rank not stated) circa 1675; paid for his services in the late expedition against the Nanticoke Indians in 1678; Protestant and soldier in the Revolution of 1689; signed an address and took a loyalty oath supporting the King of England and "to reestablish Lord Baltimore in his ancient power and government" on Nov 16, 1689; military officer (rank not stated) who swore allegiance to the King & Queen of England in 1696. {Ref: ARMD 7:103, 8:131, 20:543; HCCM:282}

KELLAM (KILLAM), JOHN (Somerset County), Protestant and probable soldier in the Revolution of 1689; signed an address and took a loyalty oath supporting the King of England and "for enabling us to defend ourselves against all invaders" on Nov 28, 1689; died testate by Mar 15, 1719/20 (date of probate). {Ref: ARMD 8:140; MDWB 15:306}

KELLET, ROGER (county or port not indicated), mariner by 1734; captain and part owner of the sloop *Betty and Ann* (built in Maryland) in 1738. {Ref: MDCB 82:67}

KELSALL, JOHN (Annapolis District), captain and master of the sloop *William and John* in 1730. {Ref: CVPR:12}

KELSEY, EDWARD (St. Mary's County), seaman whose name appeared on "a list of men that goe by water when employed" in 1697. {Ref: ARMD 25:597}

KEMBLE, JOHN (Talbot County), mariner by 1720 and land owner in Queen Anne's County by 1734. {Ref: TALR 12:407, 14:19}

KEMP, JOHN (Baltimore County), soldier (rank not stated) circa 1675; paid for his services in the late expedition against the Nanticoke Indians in 1678; died testate by Mar 15, 1686/7 (date of probate; Sarah Kemp, widow). {Ref: ARMD 7:96; MDWB 4:239; BBCF:383}

KEMP, SARAH, see "John Kemp," q.v.

KEMP, THOMAS (Talbot or Queen Anne's County), mariner by the 1730's; captain and master of the sloop *Rachel* (built at Wye River) in 1738. {Ref: MDCB 82:61}

KENNARD, JOHN (Annapolis District), captain of the sloop *Sea Flower* of New Hampshire in 1732-1733. {Ref: MDGZ, Mar 16, 1732/3}

KENNARD, SARAH, see "Joseph Hopkins," q.v.

KENNER, GODHAM (Virginia and/or St. Mary's County), colonel by 1706. {Ref: INAC 26:288}

KENNEY (KENNY), THOMAS (England, and Anne Arundel and Queen Anne's Counties), captain and commander of the ship *Globe* in 1728; captain of the ship *Raven* of Biddeford in 1734 (name misinterpreted once as "J. Kenney"); captain, master and owner of the ship *Juliana* in 1739 (built in Maryland in 1738). {Ref: MDGZ, Jul 19, 1734; MDCB 82:72; QALR IK#C:210-211}

KENNISTON, THOMAS (Calvert County), ranger under the command of Capt. Richard Brightwell in 1692. {Ref: ARMD 8:445}

KENT, JOHN (Calvert County), Protestant and probable soldier in the Revolution of 1689; signed an address and took a loyalty oath (made his "X" mark) supporting the King of England and "to reestablish Lord Baltimore in his ancient power and government" on Nov 16, 1689. {Ref: ARMD 8:132}

KENT, ROBERT (Talbot County), Protestant and probable soldier in the Revolution of 1689; signed an address and took a loyalty oath supporting the King of England and the reestablishment of Lord Baltimore into power on Nov 18, 1689. {Ref: ARMD 8:134}

KENTON, RICHARD (England and St. Mary's), boatswain on the ship *Dove* in 1633-1634. {Ref: FMDP:343}

KERNSTON, RICHARD (Talbot County), sergeant who swore allegiance to the King & Queen of England in 1696. {Ref: ARMD 20:542}

KEROYD, W. A. (Calvert County), Protestant and probable soldier in the Revolution of 1689; signed an address and took a loyalty oath supporting the King of England and "to reestablish Lord Baltimore in his ancient power and government" on Nov 16, 1689. {Ref: ARMD 8:131}

KERSEY, THOMAS, see "Thomas Casey," q.v.

KERSTEAD, LUCAS (New York and Pocomoke District), captain and commander of the sloop *Rachell* of New York in 1697. {Ref: ARMD 23:138}

KEY, HENRY (St. Mary's County), soldier (rank not stated) circa 1675; paid for his services in the late expedition against the Nanticoke Indians in 1678. {Ref: ARMD 7:103}

KEYAR, BENJAMIN (Somerset County), Protestant and probable soldier in the Revolution of 1689; signed an address and took a loyalty oath supporting the King of England and "for enabling us to defend ourselves against all invaders" on Nov 28, 1689. {Ref: ARMD 8:140}

KEYSER, TIMOTHY (Calvert County), captain by 1687. {Ref: INAC 9:421}

KEYSEY, THOMAS, see "Thomas Casey," q.v.

KIDD, ---- (county or port not indicated), captain and master of the ship *Adventure Gally* of New York in 1699. {Ref: ARMD 25:97}

KIDD, MARGARET, see "William Kidd," q.v.

KIDD, WILLIAM (Virginia and Calvert County), Protestant and probable soldier in the Revolution of 1689; signed an address and took a loyalty oath (made his "X" mark) supporting the King of England and "to reestablish Lord Baltimore in his ancient power and government" on Nov 16, 1689; died testate by Apr 20, 1693 (date of probate; Margaret Kidd, widow). {Ref: ARMD 8:132; HCCM:284; MDWB 6:47}

KIESFILD, JOCHEN (Calvert County), military officer (rank not stated) who swore allegiance to the King & Queen of England in 1696. {Ref: ARMD 20:543}

KILBOURNE (KILBOURN, KILBURN), CHARLES (Anne Arundel County), captain by 1709; "late captain of the City Company of Annapolis has sold his Interest there and removed into the Country" as noted by the Maryland Council on Oct 27, 1711; born circa 1659 (aged about 55 when deposed in 1714). See "Andrew Norwood," q.v. {Ref: ARMD 27:451, 29:12; MDEP:111}

KILLAM, JOHN, see "John Kellam," q.v.

KILLBURY, ---- (Anne Arundel County), captain by 1717. {Ref: INAC 38A:55}

KILLSHA, EDWARD (St. Mary's County), Protestant and probable soldier in the Revolution of 1689; signed an address and took a loyalty oath (made his "E" mark) supporting the King of England and the reestablishment of Lord Baltimore into power on Nov 28, 1689. {Ref: ARMD 8:147}

KILSON, ISAAC (Talbot County), captain before 1721 (received payment from the estate of James Taylor, deceased, on Jul 18, 1721). {Ref: MDAD 3:493}

KIMBALL (KEMBALL, KEMBELL), RICHARD (Somerset County), soldier (rank not stated) circa 1675; paid for his services in the late expedition against the Nanticoke Indians in 1678; corporal before 1682; paid for his services out of an assessment levied by the General Assembly for the public good in 1682; died testate by May 20, 1704 (date of probate). {Ref: ARMD 7:98, 7:442-443; MDWB 3:260}

KING, ANNE, see "Robert King," q.v.

KING, EDWARD (Somerset County), soldier (rank not stated) circa 1675; paid for his services in the late expedition against the Nanticoke Indians in 1678. {Ref: ARMD 7:97}

KING, ELIAS (England and Kent County), military officer (rank not stated) who swore allegiance to the King & Queen of England in 1696; member of the Lower House of the Maryland Assembly, 1692-1693, 1704-1706; colonel by 1703; died testate by Feb 21, 1706/7 (date of probate). {Ref: ARMD 20:540; BDML II:510; INKC:150; MDWB 12:83}

KING, ELIZABETH, see "John King," q.v.

KING, HENRY (Patapsco Hundred, Baltimore County), ranger, appointed by Capt. John Oldton as a "well quallified person & good woods man & fit to be Imployed in Ranging for the Publick Service of this Province" on Mar 23, 1694/5; died testate by Apr 30, 1718 (date of probate). {Ref: ARMD 20:205; BBCF:386; MDWB 14:600}

KING, HENRY (captain), see "Henry Munday," q.v.

KING, JOHN (Virginia and Morumsco, Somerset County), soldier (rank not stated) circa 1675; paid for his services in the late expedition against the Nanticoke Indians in 1678; quartermaster by 1682; paid for his services out of an assessment levied by the General Assembly for the public good in 1682; cornet in the horse troops of Somerset County, commissioned Dec 2, 1687; Protestant and soldier in the Revolution of 1689; signed an address and took a loyalty oath supporting the King of England and "for enabling us to defend ourselves against all invaders" on Nov 28, 1689; captain by 1692; died testate by Jul 28, 1696 (date of probate; Elizabeth King, widow). {Ref: ARMD 5:568, 7:100, 7:441, 8:141, 8:548, 20:110; CESM:39; MDWB 8:284; INAC 16:223, 32C:172}

KING, JOHN (Manokin Hundred, Somerset County), captain and master of the sloop *Philadelphia* in 1690; died intestate by May 1, 1727 (date of probate). {Ref: ARMD 8:237; CESM:10; MDWB 19:201; MINV 12:155, 16:713}

KING, JOSEPH (Prince George's County), foot soldier (rank not stated) under the command of Capt. Richard Owen in June, 1699. {Ref: ARMD 24:122}

KING, ROBERT (Annamessex, Somerset County), captain by 1724; major by 1727; colonel by 1734; member of the Lower House of the Maryland Assembly, 1722-1751; agent appointed to disburse currency out of the Loan Office for an expedition against the Spanish Indies (Supply Act of 1740); member of the commission appointed by the governor in 1744 to treat with the Indians of the Six Nations claiming land on the Susquehanna and Potomac Rivers; agent appointed to disburse currency out of the Loan Office for an attack on Canada (Supply Act of 1746); born Aug 29, 1689, died testate by Jun 26, 1755 (date of probate; Anne King, widow). See "Abraham Barnes," q.v. {Ref: ARMD 39:220; BDML II:512-513; CESM:40; SOTL:1731; MDWB 29:434}

KING, ROBERT (England and St. Mary's), mariner by 1663. {Ref: ARMD 49:44}

KING, ROBERT (England and Manokin Hundred, Somerset County), captain of a company of foot in 1689; Protestant and soldier in the Revolution of 1689; signed an address and took a loyalty oath supporting the King of England and "for enabling us to defend ourselves against all invaders" on Nov 28, 1689; major, 1691; provincial court justice, 1691-1697; called "a Scotch Irish Man" in 1692; naval officer for Somerset County, appointed Jun 14, 1694; died before Jun 24, 1697 (correspondence to the Maryland Council stated he was deceased and also mentioned his son-in-law Francis Jenckins). {Ref: ARMD 8:141, 13:244, 20:70, 20:110, 23:142, 23:289, 38:73; BDML II:511-512; INAC 32C:172}

KINGSBURY, JAMES (Charles County), Protestant and probable soldier in the Revolution of 1689; signed an address and took a loyalty oath supporting the King of England and the reestablishment of Lord Baltimore into power on Nov 28, 1689. {Ref: ARMD 8:138}

KINNAMONT, FRANCES, see "John Kinnimont," q.v.

KINNEY, THOMAS (Anne Arundel County), captain by 1729. {Ref: MINV 15:62}

KINNIMONT (KENNIMON, KENEMON), JOHN (Queen Anne's and Talbot Counties), soldier (rank not stated) circa 1675; paid for his services in the late expedition against the Nanticoke Indians in 1678; captain of a foot company before 1688; died testate by Sep 18, 1688 (date of probate; Frances Kinnamont, widow). {Ref: ARMD 7:87, 7:91, 13:243; TALR 13:283; MDWB 6:35}

KINNIS, EDMOND (England and Somerset County), sailor on the ship *Betty Gally* of Liverpool riding at anchor in Monocan River on Jan 16, 1716/7. {Ref: SOJR III:185-186}

KINWORD, RICHARD (Cecil County), military officer (rank not stated) who swore allegiance to the King & Queen of England in 1696. {Ref: ARMD 20:546}

KIPPS, FRANCIS (Baltimore County), mariner by 1734; captain and master of the sloop *Crump* (built at Patapsco River) in 1735. {Ref: HBCC:54; MDCB 82:41}

KIRBY (KERBY), JOHN (England and Talbot County), carpenter's mate on the ship *Ruth* in 1676-1677; mariner, of County Durham, by 1699; mariner on the pink *Anne* of Newcastle in 1700. {Ref: ARMD 51:474, 66:301, 67:36; TALR 9:8, 9:109}

KIRCOVEN, HENRY (St. Mary's County), soldier (rank not stated) before 1668; paid for his services in the last expedition against the Indians in 1668 {Ref: ARMD 5:35}

KIRK, BRIDGET, see "John Kirke (Kirk)," q.v.

KIRK, JOHN (St. Mary's County), captain by 1734. {Ref: MDAD 12:464}

KIRKE, JAMES (Potomac District), captain and master of the ship *Tower* in 1697. {Ref: ARMD 23:172}

KIRKE, JOHN (Dorchester County), soldier (rank not stated) circa 1675; paid for his services in the late expedition against the Nanticoke Indians in 1678; died circa 1687. {Ref: ARMD 7:93; BDML II:514}

KIRKE, JOHN (Charles County), soldier (rank not stated) who was issued a "gun or fowling piece" by Col. Warren on Sep 15, 1694. {Ref: ARMD 20:206, 20:208}

KIRKE (KIRK), JOHN (Somerset County), soldier (rank not stated) circa 1675; paid for his services in the late expedition against the Nanticoke Indians in 1678; "John Kirk, planter, Annamessex Hundred" died testate by Mar 15, 1719/20 (date of probate; Bridget Kirk, widow). {Ref: ARMD 7:100; MDWB 15:308}

KIRKLAND, RICHARD (Anne Arundel County), military officer (rank not stated) who swore allegiance to the King & Queen of England in 1696. {Ref: ARMD 20:541}

KISBE, PAUL (Calvert County), Protestant and probable soldier in the Revolution of 1689; signed an address and took a loyalty oath supporting the King of England and "to reestablish Lord Baltimore in his ancient power and government" on Nov 16, 1689. {Ref: ARMD 8:132}

KITCHENNER, EDWARD (Talbot County), soldier (rank not stated) circa 1675; paid for his services in the late expedition against the Nanticoke Indians in 1678. {Ref: ARMD 7:92}

KITSON, ISAAC (England and Talbot County), captain and land owner on Choptank River in Talbot County before 1724 and mariner, late of Rotherhithing, County of Surry, died by Dec 12, 1724 (appointment of attorney by Elizabeth Kitson, widow). {Ref: AALR SY#1:133}

KNAPP, ELIZABETH, see "Robert Knapp," q.v.

KNAPP (KNAP), JOHN (county not indicated), private in the Maryland troops "raised to strengthen Albany, New York and resist the French and Indian enemies" in 1690. {Ref: SHMD I:355}

KNAPP (KNAP), ROBERT (Talbot County), probable soldier (rank not stated) circa 1675; paid for his services in the late expedition against the Nanticoke Indians in 1678; died testate by Apr 22, 1682 (date of probate; Elizabeth Knapp, widow). {Ref: ARMD 7:90-91; MDWB 2:188}

KNIGHT, JOHN (England and Dorchester County), captain and commander of the ship *Encrease* of Youghall in 1688. {Ref: ARMD 8:54-55}

KNIGHT, PETER (Kent Island), "captain of the rebels on the Isle of Kent" by 1648. {Ref: 4:455-456}

KNIGHT, STEPHEN (Cecil County), naval officer "at the Head of the Bay" by 1711. {Ref: ARMD 29:12}

KNIGHTON, THOMAS (Anne Arundel County), a seafaring apprentice in 1697, "borne and belonging to this county, son of Thomas Knighton." {Ref: ARMD 25:596, 67:345; MDWB 6:12}

KNOLEWATER, JOHN (Charles County), Protestant and probable soldier in the Revolution of 1689; signed an address and took a loyalty oath supporting the King of England and the reestablishment of Lord Baltimore into power on Nov 28, 1689. {Ref: ARMD 8:138}

KNOTT, LUKE (Oxford District), captain and master of the ship *Bennett* in 1730. {Ref: CVPR:12}

KNOWLES, JOHN (Oxford District), captain and master of the ship *Peggy* in 1730-1731; mariner and land owner in Queen Anne's County in 1731. {Ref: QALR RT#A:93; CVPR:12}

KNOWLES, MABEL, see "Alexander Hall," q.v.

KNOX, ALEXANDER (Somerset County), Protestant and probable soldier in the Revolution of 1689; signed an address and took a loyalty oath supporting the

King of England and "for enabling us to defend ourselves against all invaders" on Nov 28, 1689. {Ref: ARMD 8:139}
KNOX, JAMES (Somerset County), Protestant and probable soldier in the Revolution of 1689; signed an address and took a loyalty oath supporting the King of England and "for enabling us to defend ourselves against all invaders" on Nov 28, 1689. {Ref: ARMD 8:139}
KNOX, JOHN (Somerset County), Protestant and probable soldier in the Revolution of 1689; signed an address and took a loyalty oath supporting the King of England and "for enabling us to defend ourselves against all invaders" on Nov 28, 1689. {Ref: ARMD 8:139}
KNOX, MALCOM (Somerset County), Protestant and probable soldier in the Revolution of 1689; signed an address and took a loyalty oath supporting the King of England and "for enabling us to defend ourselves against all invaders" on Nov 28, 1689. {Ref: ARMD 8:140}
KNOX, WILLIAM (Somerset County), Protestant and probable soldier in the Revolution of 1689; signed an address and took a loyalty oath supporting the King of England and "for enabling us to defend ourselves against all invaders" on Nov 28, 1689. {Ref: ARMD 8:140}
KOLLEY, NICHOLAS (Talbot County), sergeant who swore allegiance to the King & Queen of England in 1696. {Ref: ARMD 20:542}
KOTRELL, JOHN (Anne Arundel County), military officer (rank not stated) who swore allegiance to the King & Queen of England in 1696. {Ref: ARMD 20:542}
KYLL, ALEXANDER (Somerset County), Protestant and probable soldier in the Revolution of 1689; signed an address and took a loyalty oath supporting the King of England and "for enabling us to defend ourselves against all invaders" on Nov 28, 1689. {Ref: ARMD 8:140}
KYTE, JOHN (county or port not indicated), captain and master of the ship *James* in 1696. {Ref: ARMD 23:12}
LACE, JOSHUA (Oxford District), captain and master of the ship *Blackbourn* in 1731. {Ref: CVPR:12}
LADD, RICHARD (England and Calvert County), captain by 1674; justice of the peace, 1674-1681; sheriff, 1678; member of the Lower House of the Maryland Assembly, 1676-1684; justice (quorum), 1685; captain of a company of foot troops by 1689; died testate by Feb 10, 1691/2 (date of probate). {Ref: ARMD 7:265, 7:611, 13:242, 15:37, 15:231, 15:395, 17:71, 17:379, 24:18; BDML II:515-516; HCCM:285; MDWB 16:32}
LAHANNE, ARNAUT (France and Annapolis), Frenchman, chirurgeon and ship's doctor in 1695; served on the pink *John* of Bordeaux commanded by Capt. Peter Rivier, and on the ship *Hope* of Maryland commanded by Capt. Richard Hill, which went to Guinea and then returned to Maryland, and on the brigantine *Fisher* of Maryland commanded by Capt. Thomas Francis, bound for Barbadoes and "with design to get to Martinico in order to procure his passage for France." {Ref: ARMD 20:338}

LAKE, ROBERT (Isle of Kent), soldier (rank not stated) in 1642; born circa 1619 (aged about 21 when deposed in 1640). {Ref: ARMD 4:62, 4:130-131}

LAMASTER, JOSEPH (Potomac District), captain and master of the ship *George and Francis* in 1730-1731. {Ref: CVPR:12}

LAMB, JOHN (Talbot County), Protestant and probable soldier in the Revolution of 1689; signed an address and took a loyalty oath supporting the King of England and the reestablishment of Lord Baltimore into power on Nov 18, 1689. {Ref: ARMD 8:134}

LAMBER, SAMUELL (Charles County), soldier (rank not stated) in Capt. James Langworth's Company before 1661 (year of the captain's death, but his ammunition report was not filed until 1664 by Henry Adames). {Ref: CHLR B:379}

LAMBERT, JOHN (Charles County), soldier (rank not stated) circa 1675; paid for his services in the late expedition against the Nanticoke Indians in 1678; died testate by Feb 7, 1693/4 (date of probate). {Ref: ARMD 7:101; MDWB 2:246}

LAMING, ROGER (Anne Arundel County), captain and commander of the frigate *Chesapeake* riding in South River on May 6, 1712. {Ref: AALR PK:448}

LANCASTER, HENRY (Kent and Cecil Counties), soldier (rank not stated) circa 1675; paid for his services in the late expedition against the Nanticoke Indians in 1678; died testate by May 13, 1717 (date of probate). {Ref: ARMD 7:94; MDWB 14:346; MDAD 1:143}

LANCASTER, JOHN (St. Mary's County and Potomac District), captain and master of the brigantine *Planter* in 1693 and master of the ship *Loves Increase* in 1697; listed as "Capt. John Lancester" in 1706; John Lancaster and Joseph Lancaster owned the schooner *Catherine* (built at the Potomac River) in 1734. {Ref: ARMD 20:182, 23:172; INAC 26:288; MDCB 82:17}

LANCASTER, JOSEPH, see "John Lancaster," q.v.

LANCTHORN, ---- (St. Mary's County), captain by 1719. {Ref: MDAD 2:50}

LAND, RICHARD (Charles County), Protestant and soldier in the Revolution of 1689; signed an address and took a loyalty oath supporting the King of England and the reestablishment of Lord Baltimore into power on Nov 28, 1689; lieutenant by 1692; paid for 10 days horse service on Nov 18, 1692. {Ref: ARMD 8:138, 8:424}

LANDMANS, ROBERT (Talbot County), soldier (rank not stated) circa 1675; paid for his services in the late expedition against the Nanticoke Indians in 1678. {Ref: ARMD 7:90}

LANDOW, JAMES (Somerset County), captain by 1724. {Ref: CESM:62}

LANE, FRANCIS (Somerset County), mariner by 1726. {Ref: MDAD 8:48}

LANE, GEORGE (Virginia and Somerset County), Protestant and probable soldier in the Revolution of 1689; signed an address and took a loyalty oath supporting the King of England and "for enabling us to defend ourselves against all invaders" on Nov 28, 1689; died intestate before 1723 (Dennis Lane, widow). {Ref: ARMD 8:141; Rent Rolls}

LANE, JOHN (Talbot County), soldier (rank not stated) circa 1675; paid for his services in the late expedition against the Nanticoke Indians in 1678; a "John Lane (Lann) of Tuckhow in Queen Anne's County" died testate by Nov 23, 1714 (date of probate; Judith Lane, widow). {Ref: ARMD 7:88; MDWB 14:10}

LANE (LANN), JUDITH, see "John Lane," q.v.

LANE (LAINE), SAMUEL (Anne Arundel County), major by 1674; colonel by 1676; died testate before Apr 14, 1682 (date of inventory; wrote his will on Jan 18, 1681/2, but no date of probate was given). {Ref: FAAH:39; INAC 6:259, 7A:258, 8:283; MDWB 2:185}

LANE, THOMAS (county or port not indicated), captain and master of the snow *Henrietta* of Maryland (built at Wye River) in 1733. See "William Clayton," q.v. {Ref: MDCB 82:6}

LANE, TIMOTHY (Talbot County), sergeant by 1696; swore allegiance to the King & Queen of England in 1696. See "Henry Alexander," q.v. {Ref: ARMD 20:542}

LANE, WALTER (England, Virginia, and Somerset County), seaman in 1674; soldier (rank not stated) by 1678; paid for his services in the late expedition against the Nanticoke Indians in 1678; sub-sheriff, 1680; paid for his services out of an assessment levied by the General Assembly for the public good in 1682; member of the Lower House of the Maryland Assembly, 1697-1700; died testate by Mar 21, 1716/7 (date of probate). {Ref: ARMD 7:97, 7:441; BDML II:516; MDWB 14:282}

LANGLEY, RICHARD (Annapolis District and Calvert County), captain by 1698; commander of a ship (no name given) in 1698-1699. {Ref: ARMD 23:466; INAC 19:174}

LANGREENE, JAMES (Somerset County), Protestant and probable soldier in the Revolution of 1689; signed an address and took a loyalty oath supporting the King of England and "for enabling us to defend ourselves against all invaders" on Nov 28, 1689. {Ref: ARMD 8:141}

LANGSTON, JOHN (Charles County), major by 1698. {Ref: ARMD 23:442}

LANGWORTH, JAMES (England, and St. Mary's and Charles Counties), captain by 1659 and to at least 1664; member of the Lower House of the Maryland Assembly, 1658-1660; court justice, 1658-1660; born circa 1629-1630 (aged about 20 when deposed in 1650 and aged about 22 when deposed in 1651), died testate after Aug 18, 1660 (date he wrote his will which was probated circa February, 1660/1 by Agatha Langworth, widow). See "John Wheeler," q.v. {Ref: ARMD 3:411, 10:29, 10:141, 53:107; BDML II:517; CHLR A:121, B:379; MDWB 1:133}

LANHAM, JOSIAS (Kent County), ensign in a company of foot, commissioned Feb 28, 1681; he was noted as "my Major's Sonn in Law" by Col. Henry Coursey in his letter to the Maryland Council in 1681 (name misspelled once as "Josias Lankam"); constable, 1684; born circa 1649 (aged about 35 when deposed in 1684). {Ref: ARMD 17:77-79, 17:291-294}

LARKE, JOHN (Cecil County), soldier (rank not stated) circa 1675; paid for his services in the late expedition against the Nanticoke Indians in 1678. {Ref: ARMD 7:95}

LARKIN, THOMAS (Anne Arundel and Baltimore Counties), captain of South River in 1713 and gentleman of Annapolis in 1725; county court justice, 1717-1718; extensive land owner in Baltimore and Anne Arundel Counties; born circa 1673 (aged about 47 when deposed in 1720 and aged about 58 at the time of his death in 1731), died testate by May 19, 1731 (date of probate; Elizabeth Larkin, widow). {Ref: MDWB 20:274; MINV 16:373; AALR SY#1:188; CHLR D#2:80; MDGZ, Apr 13, 1733}

LARKIN (LARKINS), THOMAS (Anne Arundel County), captain by 1684 and to at least 1708; born circa 1637 (aged about 47 when deposed in 1684). {Ref: ARMD 25:240; AALR IT#5:30, WH#4:171, 179}

LARRAMORE, EDWARD (England and Cecil County), military officer (rank not stated) who swore allegiance to the King & Queen of England in 1696; member of the Lower House of the Maryland Assembly, 1708-1710 (name also listed as "Edward Larremore" and "Edward Larmoore"; born circa 1657, died intestate and buried on Feb 1, 1710/1 (inventory taken on May 11, 1711). {Ref: ARMD 20:545; INAC 32B:170; BDML II:518}

LARTIN, ROBERT (county or port not indicated), captain and master of the ship *William* of London in 1690. {Ref: ARMD 8:237}

LATER, WILLIAM (Kent County), soldier (rank not stated) circa 1675; paid for his services in the late expedition against the Nanticoke Indians in 1678. {Ref: ARMD 7:94}

LATHAM, GEORGE (Somerset County), Protestant and probable soldier in the Revolution of 1689; signed an address and took a loyalty oath supporting the King of England and "for enabling us to defend ourselves against all invaders" on Nov 28, 1689. {Ref: ARMD 8:140}

LAUDMER, HENRY (Kent County), "seaman within the said county" and a "sailor belonging to the *Factor* of Bediford" in 1697. {Ref: ARMD 25:599}

LAW, JOHN (Queen Anne's County), captain by 1718. {Ref: QALR IK#A:208}

LAW, WILLIAM (Dorchester and Somerset Counties), soldier (rank not stated) circa 1675; paid for his services in the late expedition against the Nanticoke Indians in 1678; Protestant and probable soldier in the Revolution of 1689; signed an address and took a loyalty oath supporting the King of England and "for enabling us to defend ourselves against all invaders" on Nov 28, 1689; died testate by Jul 2, 1703 (date of probate). {Ref: ARMD 7:93, 8:140; MDWB 11:349}

LAWRENCE, FRANCES, see "Henry Lawrence," q.v.

LAWRENCE, FRANCIS (St. Mary's County), colonel by 1685. {Ref: INAC 8:520}

LAWRENCE, HENRY (St. Mary's County), probable soldier (rank not stated) before 1682; paid for his services out of an assessment levied by the General Assembly for the public good in 1682; Protestant and probable soldier in the Revolution of 1689; signed an address and took a loyalty oath supporting the

King of England and the reestablishment of Lord Baltimore into power on Nov 28, 1689; died testate by Jul 29, 1694 (date of probate; Frances Lawrence, widow). {Ref: ARMD 7:441, 8:146; MDWB 2:324}

LAWRENCE, JAMES (Somerset County), soldier (rank not stated) circa 1675; paid for his services in the late expedition against the Nanticoke Indians in 1678. {Ref: ARMD 7:97}

LAWRENCE, JOHN (Dorchester County), soldier (rank not stated) circa 1675; paid for his services in the late expedition against the Nanticoke Indians in 1678. {Ref: ARMD 7:93}

LAWRENCE, RICHARD, see "John Cage," q.v.

LAWRENCE, SAMUELL (Annapolis District), captain and master of the ship *Josias* in 1731. {Ref: CVPR:12}

LAWRENCE (LAURENCE), SIR THOMAS (England, and St. Mary's and Anne Arundel Counties), baronet, 1681; royal placeman and "His Majesty's Secretary of this Province" in 1692-1714 (but he ruled from London after 1705); commissioned colonel of a regiment of foot soldiers on Jul 30, 1694; appointed judge of the Vice Admiralty of the Colony of Maryland on Apr 29, 1697; born circa 1645, died Apr 25, 1714 in London. {Ref: ARMD 8:402, 8:417, 20:130, 20:152, 20:209, 23:234, 23:321, 38:73; BDML II:519}

LAWRENCE (LAURENCE), WILLIAM (Kent County), lieutenant before 1681; captain of a company of foot, commissioned Feb 28, 1681; he was reported in 1687 to be "a person now grown aged and deaf and seldom helpfull to us, and himself desirous to be out" as a commissioner of Kent County (a replacement was requested); captain of a company of foot upon Kent Island in 1689; colonel and vestryman for Kent Island Parish in 1696. {Ref: ARMD 8:22, 13:241, 17:76-78, 23:21; TALR 7:47}

LAWRENCE, WILLIAM (Somerset County), Protestant and probable soldier in the Revolution of 1689; signed an address and took a loyalty oath supporting the King of England and "for enabling us to defend ourselves against all invaders" on Nov 28, 1689. {Ref: ARMD 8:140}

LAWS (LAWES), WILLIAM (Talbot County), soldier (rank not stated) circa 1675; paid for his services in the late expedition against the Nanticoke Indians in 1678; paid for his services out of an assessment levied by the General Assembly for the public good in 1682. {Ref: ARMD 7:88, 7:91, 7:440}

LAWSON, SAMUEL (England and St. Mary's), mate on the ship *Dove* in 1633-1634. {Ref: FMDP:343}

LAX, WILLIAM (England and Annapolis), captain before 1719; master and commander of the ship *Concord* of London riding in South River at various times between 1719 and 1731. See "William Lux," q.v. {Ref: AALR CW#1:33, 101, 276, 479; AALR RCW#2:219, 221; AALR SY#1:167, 148; MDGZ, May 20, 1729; CVPR:12}

LAYFIELD, GEORGE (England and Pocomoke, Somerset County), Customs Officer of the Crown in the Province of Maryland circa 1685; Protestant and probable soldier in the Revolution of 1689; signed an address and took a loyalty oath supporting the King of England and "for enabling us to defend ourselves against all invaders" on Nov 28, 1689; died testate by May 26, 1703 (date of probate; Priscilla Layfield, widow). {Ref: ARMD 8:141; OSES:375; MDWB 3:497}

LAYTON, WILLIAM (Somerset County), Protestant and probable soldier in the Revolution of 1689; signed an address and took a loyalty oath supporting the King of England and "for enabling us to defend ourselves against all invaders" on Nov 28, 1689. {Ref: ARMD 8:141}

LEACH, AMBROSE (Calvert County), Protestant and probable soldier in the Revolution of 1689; signed an address and took a loyalty oath supporting the King of England and "to reestablish Lord Baltimore in his ancient power and government" on Nov 16, 1689. {Ref: ARMD 8:132}

LEACH, JOHN (Calvert County), Protestant and probable soldier in the Revolution of 1689; signed an address and took a loyalty oath supporting the King of England and "to reestablish Lord Baltimore in his ancient power and government" on Nov 16, 1689 (name listed once as "John Leach, Jr."); born circa 1662 (aged about 50 when deposed in 1712), died intestate by Jun 14, 1714 (date of inventory). {Ref: ARMD 8:131; INAC 36A:4; HCCM:289; MDEP:115}

LECOMPTE, PHILEMON (Dorchester County), land commissioner and styled "captain" by 1728; member of the Lower House of the Maryland Assembly at various times between 1742 and 1768; born circa 1690 (aged about 40 when deposed in 1730), died testate by Aug 28, 1769 (date of probate; Mary Lecompte, widow). {Ref: BDML II:521-522; MDWB 37:400; MDEP:115}

LEE, ---- (North West Fork, Dorchester County), colonel by 1714. {Ref: SOJR III:69}

LEE, ELIZABETH, see "Philip Lee," q.v.

LEE, JOHN (St. Mary's County), captain by 1727. {Ref: MDAD 8:448}

LEE, PETER (Annapolis District), captain and master of the sloop *Ann* in 1731. {Ref: CVPR:12}

LEE, PHILIP (Virginia and Prince George's County), captain by 1708; member of the Lower House of the Maryland Assembly, 1708-1742; sheriff, 1722-1725; naval officer for the North Potomac District, 1727-1744; born circa 1683 (aged about 60 when deposed in 1743), died testate by Apr 1, 1744 (date of probate; Elizabeth Lee, widow). {Ref: BDML II:526; INAC 37B:83; MDWB 23:480; MDCB 82:1; MDEP:115}

LEE, RICHARD (Talbot County), captain by 1668. {Ref: ARMD 54:460}

LEE, RICHARD (Prince George's and Charles Counties), captain by 1734; naval officer of the Potomac District, 1744-1747; member of the Upper House (Maryland Council), 1745-1770, 1773-1774; born circa 1705-1706 (aged about 30 when deposed in 1735 and aged about 37 when deposed in 1743), died Jan 26, 1787. {Ref: BDML II:528-529; MDEP:115}

LEE, SEATHER (St. Mary's County), captain by 1695. {Ref: INAC 18:170}

LEE, THOMAS (Talbot County), captain before 1709 (estate of Capt. Thomas Lee was mentioned in an inventory of the estate of Edward Leeds on Jan 4, 1709/10). {Ref: INAC 30:32}

LEE, WILLIAM (Kent County), soldier (rank not stated) circa 1675; paid for his services in the late expedition against the Nanticoke Indians in 1678. {Ref: ARMD 7:94}
LEE, WILLIAM (county or port not indicated), captain and master of the brigantine *Betty* of Maryland in 1690. {Ref: ARMD 8:237}
LEECH, EDWARD (Kent County), captain by 1733. {Ref: INKC:178}
LEECH, JOHN, SR. (Calvert County), Protestant and probable soldier in the Revolution of 1689; signed an address and took a loyalty oath supporting the King of England and "to reestablish Lord Baltimore in his ancient power and government" on Nov 16, 1689. {Ref: ARMD 8:132}
LEECH, THOMAS (England and Talbot County), mariner and sailor on the ship *Relief* of New Castle commanded by Capt. John Anderson in 1692. {Ref: ARMD 13:334-335}
LEEDS (LEEADS, LEEDES), WILLIAM (England, and Kent and Talbot Counties), soldier (rank not stated) on Isle of Kent who swore allegiance to the Commonwealth of England on Apr 5, 1652; captain by 1661; member of the Lower House of the Maryland Assembly, 1661; paid for his services "for pouder and shott for 3 souldiers sent to the Susquahanakes" in 1661; died testate by Dec 1, 1688 (date of probate). See "John Emkson," q.v. {Ref: ARMD 3:411, 3:455, 54:225, 54:231; BDML II:531; TALR 9:132; INKC:101; MDWB 6:47; INAC 10:197}
LEGATT (LEGAT), JOHN (Anne Arundel County), soldier (rank not stated) who served under Governor Stone at the Battle of the Severn on Mar 25, 1655 and was subsequently executed (shot). {Ref: FAAH:26}
LEGER, PETER (county not indicted), colonel before 1702 (he was listed among many who received payment from the estate of Madam Henrietta Maria Lloyd, deceased, of Talbot County, on Jul 14, 1702). {Ref: INAC 22:44}
LEIGH, JOHN (St. Mary's County), captain by 1727. {Ref: MDAD 8:288}
LEONARD, JOHN (Baltimore County), soldier (rank not stated) circa 1675; paid for his services in the late expedition against the Nanticoke Indians in 1678; died intestate by Mar 1, 1678/9 (date of administration bond). {Ref: ARMD 7:95; BBCF:401}
LEROUNT, JOHN (England and Prince George's County), mariner, captain, and master of the pink *Richmond* of London in 1697. {Ref: PGLR A:109}
LESTER, SHADRACK (Annapolis and Patuxent), captain and commander of the ship *Hammond* riding in Severn River on Jun 14, 1721 and May 16, 1722; the ship *Friends Adventure* arrived in Patuxent around the first of May, 1729, but its master "Capt. Lester" had died at sea. {Ref: AALR CW#1:372, 494; MDAD 8:439; MDGZ, May 6, 1729}
LETHERSON, ---- (St. Mary's County), captain by 1695. {Ref: INAC 10:403}
LETORT, ---- (France and Cecil County), captain before 1686; "Protestant sent over with a considerable cargo and several French Protestants" by the West Jersey Company in 1686; "Frenchman who lived back in the woods where Peter

Basilion once lived, about 30 miles from any inhabitants, and traded with the Indians" in 1696. {Ref: ARMD 20:406, 20:470}

LETTON, GEORGE (Anne Arundel County), captain by 1722. {Ref: MDAD 5:13}

LEVENS (LEAVENS), RICHARD (England and St. Mary's County), seaman on the ship *Ruth* in 1676-1677. {Ref: ARMD 51:474, 66:301, 67:36}

LEVERSON, PETER (Cecil County), military officer (rank not stated) who swore allegiance to the King & Queen of England in 1696. {Ref: ARMD 20:546}

LEVING, JOSEPH (William and Mary Parish, Charles County), a seafaring man in 1697. {Ref: ARMD 25:597}

LEVYSON, WILLIAM (Baltimore County), lieutenant who swore allegiance to the King & Queen of England in 1696. {Ref: ARMD 20:544}

LEWGER, JOHN (Charles County), soldier (rank not stated) by 1666; signed a petition to the governor to "displace Capt. William Boreman whom was lately constituted captain of the militia" on Sep 12, 1666; possibly born in 1628, died testate by Dec 9, 1669 (date of probate; Martha Lewger, widow). {Ref: ARMD 3:556; BDML II:533; MDWB 1:356}

LEWIS, ---- (Dorchester County), corporal before 1678; paid for his services in the late expedition against the Nanticoke Indians in 1678. {Ref: ARMD 7:93}

LEWIS, ALEXANDER (Calvert County), Protestant and probable soldier in the Revolution of 1689; signed an address and took a loyalty oath supporting the King of England and "to reestablish Lord Baltimore in his ancient power and government" on Nov 16, 1689. {Ref: ARMD 8:132}

LEWIS, HENRY (St. Mary's County), Protestant and probable soldier in the Revolution of 1689; signed an address and took a loyalty oath (made his "H" mark) supporting the King of England and the reestablishment of Lord Baltimore into power on Nov 28, 1689; born circa 1641 (aged about 40 when deposed in 1681). {Ref: ARMD 8:147, 17:50}

LEWIS, JOHN (Kent County), soldier (rank not stated) circa 1675; paid for his services in the late expedition against the Nanticoke Indians in 1678. {Ref: ARMD 7:94}

LEWIS, JOHN (Anne Arundel County), waterman on South River before 1727; lot owner in London Town by 1727. {Ref: AALR SY#1:376-377}

LEWIS, RICHARD (Somerset County), soldier (rank not stated) circa 1675; paid for his services in the late expedition against the Nanticoke Indians in 1678. {Ref: ARMD 7:99}

LEWIS, URSULA, see "William Lewis," q.v.

LEWIS, WILLIAM (St. Mary's and Charles Counties), lieutenant by 1649; captain who served under Governor Stone at the Battle of the Severn on Mar 25, 1655 and was subsequently executed (Ursula Lewis, widow, later married George Goodrick or Goodericke, of Port Tobacco). {Ref: ARMD 4:514-515, 10:35, 10:363, 41:58, 41:230-231, 51:137, 51:350-351; FAAH:25-27; FMDP:233-234; CHLR A:3, A:6}

LEWIS, WILLIAM (Charles and/or Prince George's County), captain by 1718. {Ref: CHLR H#2:207}

LEWISON, LEWEE (county not indicated), Frenchman and interpreter who lived among the Susquehannah Indians in 1697. {Ref: ARMD 23:428-429}

LEYLER, JAMES (Prince George's County), soldier (rank not stated) under the command of Col. Ninian Beale from June, 1699 to May, 1700. {Ref: ARMD 24:121-122}

LIDDLE, DANIEL (Charles County), sailor by 1719. {Ref: MDAD 2:128}

LIGHT, JOSHUA (Somerset County), Protestant and probable soldier in the Revolution of 1689; signed an address and took a loyalty oath supporting the King of England and "for enabling us to defend ourselves against all invaders" on Nov 28, 1689. {Ref: ARMD 8:140}

LIGHTFOOT (LYTFOOT), THOMAS (Baltimore County), appointed Chief Ranger of Baltimore County on Apr 12, 1683; died testate by Jun 17, 1687 (date of probate; Rebecca Lytfoot, widow). {Ref: BBCF:403; MDWB 4:272}

LIGOTT, WILLIAM (England and Pocomoke District), captain and commander of the English ship *Endeavour* of Dublin in 1697. {Ref: ARMD 23:138}

LINCH, JOHN (county or port not indicated), captain and master of the ship *True Love* in 1668. {Ref: MDHM 5:341}

LINDON, ---- (Somerset County), major by 1679. {Ref: INAC 6:354}

LINDOW, JAMES (Somerset County), captain by 1724. {Ref: CESM:62}

LINDSEY (LENDSEY, LINDESEY), EDMOND (Charles County), soldier (rank not stated) in Capt. James Langworth's Company before 1661 (year of the captain's death, but his ammunition report was not filed until 1664 by Henry Adames); born circa 1625 (aged about 26 when deposed in 1651). {Ref: ARMD 10:118, 60:353; CHLR B:379; MDEP:116-117}

LINDSEY (LENDSEY, LINSEY), JAMES (Charles County), soldier (rank not stated) by 1647; sergeant, 1651; lieutenant, 1658; signed a petition to the governor to "displace Capt. William Boreman whom was lately constituted captain of the militia" on Sep 12, 1666; born circa 1626-1628 (aged about 30 or 32 when deposed twice in 1658), died testate by May 3, 1671 (date of probate; Mary Lindsey, widow). {Ref: ARMD 3:556, 3:561, 4:311, 10:134, 41:79, 41:84, 41:154, 53:376; CHLR B:379; MDWB 1:433; MDEP:116-117}

LINDSEY, MARY, see "James Lindsey," q.v.

LINGAN, GEORGE (Calvert County), member of the Lower House of the Maryland Assembly, 1686-1688, 1694-1696; Protestant and probable soldier in the Revolution of 1689; signed an address and took a loyalty oath supporting the King of England and "to reestablish Lord Baltimore in his ancient power and government" on Nov 16, 1689; sheriff, 1696-1698; died testate by May 17, 1708 (date of probate; Ann Lingan, widow). {Ref: ARMD 8:131; BDML II:533-534; MDWB 12:248}

LINGEART, THOMAS (Calvert County), Protestant and probable soldier in the Revolution of 1689; signed an address and took a loyalty oath supporting the King of England and "to reestablish Lord Baltimore in his ancient power and government" on Nov 16, 1689. {Ref: ARMD 8:132}

LINN, JOHN (county not indicated), mariner by 1696. {Ref: INAC 13B:140}

LIRYATT, JOHN (Calvert County), Protestant and probable soldier in the Revolution of 1689; signed an address and took a loyalty oath supporting the King of England and the reestablishment of Lord Baltimore into power on Nov 28, 1689. {Ref: ARMD 8:145}

LISBY, JACOB (Anne Arundel County), soldier (rank not stated) circa 1675; paid for his services in the late expedition against the Nanticoke Indians in 1678. {Ref: ARMD 7:96}

LISTER, EDMOND (England, Virginia and Maryland), captain and mariner before 1667; a deposition in London on Apr 16, 1667 stated "Edmond Lister, alias Francis Jackson, late of Thornton in Craven, Yorkshire, gentleman, now or late resident in Maryland" owed money to Capt. John Whitty, deceased (Sarah Whitty, administratrix); he acquired part of Devil's Island on Maryland's Eastern Shore in 1670. {Ref: LMCL:43; Land Patent ABH:312, 5:64, 16:83}

LISTER, JOHN (Baltimore County), captain of the ship *Francis and Rachell* in 1724. {Ref: BALR IS#G}

LITTLE, CHRISTOPHER (Somerset County), soldier (rank not stated) circa 1675; paid for his services in the late expedition against the Nanticoke Indians in 1678. {Ref: ARMD 7:98}

LITTLE, JOHN (St. Mary's County), soldier (rank not stated) circa 1675; paid for his services in the late expedition against the Nanticoke Indians in 1678; Protestant and probable soldier in the Revolution of 1689; signed an address and took a loyalty oath supporting the King of England and the reestablishment of Lord Baltimore into power on Nov 28, 1689; died testate on Dec 22, 1695 (date of recording and probate of nuncupative will; Mary Little, widow). {Ref: ARMD 7:103, 8:147; MDWB 7:137}

LITTLEPAGE, JAMES (Charles County), soldier (rank not stated) by 1682; paid for his services out of an assessment levied by the General Assembly for the public good in 1682. {Ref: ARMD 7:440; CHLR B:288}

LIVERMORE, WILLIAM (Patuxent District), captain of the sloop *Maryland* in 1729-1730. {Ref: MDGZ, Apr 8, 1729; CVPR:12}

LIVESEY (LEVESLY, LEIVSAY), GILBERT (England and Talbot County), captain and master of the ship *Reserve* of Liverpool and the ship *Lawrence* of Liverpool in 1690; mariner and lot owner in Williamstadt in 1702; captain, 1705. {Ref: ARMD 8:237; TALR 9:123; INAC 25:261}

LIZLANDE, JEREMIAH (Anne Arundel County), captain and commander of the frigate *Samuell* riding at anchor in Severn River on Jan 26, 1718/9. {Ref: AALR IB#2:528}

LLEWELLIN, JOHN (St. Mary's County), Protestant and probable soldier in the Revolution of 1689; signed an address and took a loyalty oath supporting the King of England and the reestablishment of Lord Baltimore into power on Nov 28, 1689; clerk to the Maryland Council by 1684; born circa 1652 (aged about 40 when deposed in 1692). {Ref: ARMD 8:146, 8:495, 17:329-331}

LLOYD, ANN, see "James Lloyd," q.v.
LLOYD, CORNELIUS (St. Mary's County), lieutenant colonel by 1654. {Ref: ARMD 10:381}
LLOYD, EDWARD (Wales, Virginia, Anne Arundel and Talbot Counties, and England), burgess in Lower Norfolk County, Virginia, 1644-1646; "commander of Annarundell County" in 1650-1652; Parliamentary Commission, 1654-1658; member of the Assembly of Providence in 1654; commander of the Puritan forces at the Battle of the Severn on Mar 25, 1655; member of the Lower House of Anne Arundel County in 1658; provincial court justice, 1654-1668; member of the Upper House (Maryland Council), 1659-1666; born circa 1620, died in 1696 in England. {Ref: ARMD 10:200; BDML II:534}
LLOYD, EDWARD (Talbot County), colonel by 1698; member of the Lower House of the Maryland Assembly, 1697-1701; major general of the Eastern Shore in 1707 (although referred to as colonel in a 1708 deposition); president of the Maryland Council and acting governor, 1709-1714; born circa 1670, died testate on Mar 20, 1718/9 (will probated on Apr 8, 1719; Sarah Lloyd, widow). {Ref: ARMD 24:112, 24:129, 25:130, 25:245, 27:377, 29:347; MDEP:118; BDML II:534-535; MDWB 15:80}
LLOYD, EDWARD (Kent County), colonel by 1733. {Ref: INKC:178}
LLOYD, HENRIETTA MARIA, see "Philemon Lloyd" and "Colonel Jacob" and "Captain Wellbourne" and "Peter Leger," q.v.
LLOYD (LOYD), JAMES (Anne Arundel County), military officer (rank not stated) who swore allegiance to the King & Queen of England in 1696. {Ref: ARMD 20:541}
LLOYD (LOYD), JAMES (Talbot County), colonel before 1723; member of the Lower House of the Maryland Assembly, 1712-1722; member of the Upper House (Maryland Council), 1722-1723; born on Mar 7, 1679/80, died intestate on Sep 27, 1723 (Mrs. Ann Lloyd, administratrix). {Ref: BDML II:539; MINV 10:309, 11:253; MDAD 7:260-272}
LLOYD (LOYD), JOHN (Kent County), military officer (rank not stated) who swore allegiance to the King & Queen of England in 1696. {Ref: ARMD 20:540}
LLOYD (LOYD), PHILEMON (Virginia and Anne Arundel, Kent and Talbot Counties), captain by 1667; member of the Talbot County Court, 1670-1685; member of the Lower House of the Maryland Assembly, 1671-1684; captain of the troop of horse in Chester and Wye Rivers, commissioned Jul 2, 1677; paid for his services in the late expedition against the Nanticoke Indians in 1678 and 1682; colonel by 1679; court justice (quorum), 1679; speaker of the General Assembly in 1681; colonel and Protestant in command of the horse troops of Talbot, Kent and Cecil Counties in 1681; Indian Agent for the Province of Maryland at the peace talks at Fort Albany in 1682; born circa 1646, died testate on Jun 22, 1685 (will probated on Jul 16, 1685; Henrietta Maria Lloyd, widow). See "Jacob Young," q.v. {Ref: ARMD 5:11, 5:310, 7:87, 7:88, 7:134, 7:443, 15:226-128, 15:254, 15:327, 17:68, 17:76, 17:113, 54:275, 54:502; BDML II:541; TALR 1:68; MDWB 4:186; INAC 13B:93}

LLOYD, REDERICK (St. Mary's County), military officer (rank not stated) who swore allegiance to the King & Queen of England in 1696. {Ref: ARMD 20:540}

LLOYD, SARAH, see "Edward Lloyd," q.v.

LOCKWOOD, ROBERT (England and Anne Arundel County), captain of a troop of horse "formerly raised in the Division of Herring Creek and elsewhere in the county" in 1694; military officer (captain) who swore allegiance to the King & Queen of England in 1696; "Robert Lockwood, of Anne Arundel County, son of Robert and Elizabeth Lockwood, of Aberford, Yorkshire, England" died testate by Apr 22, 1709 (date of probate; Elizabeth Lockwood, widow). {Ref: ARMD 29:64, 20:108, 20:541, 23:19; MDWB 12:75, pt. 2}

LODGE, THOMAS (Baltimore County), Protestant and probable soldier in the Revolution of 1689; signed an address and took a loyalty oath supporting the King of England and the reestablishment of Lord Baltimore into power on Nov 28, 1689. {Ref: ARMD 8:136}

LODGINGS, THOMAS (Talbot County), soldier (rank not stated) circa 1675; paid for his services in the late expedition against the Nanticoke Indians in 1678. {Ref: ARMD 7:89}

LOMAX, BLANCH, see "Cleybourn Lomax," q.v.

LOMAX, CLEYBOURN (Charles County), soldier (rank not stated) circa 1675; paid for his services in the late expedition against the Nanticoke Indians in 1678; paid again for his services in 1695 (name also listed as "Cleborn Lomax" and "Cleborne Lomax, Sr." and "Cleeburn Lomax"); born circa 1643 (aged about 55 when deposed in 1698), died by Dec 28, 1699 (date of inventory; Blanch Lomax, widow). {Ref: ARMD 7:101, 38:72; INAC 19½B:38, 20:193; MDEP:119}

LOMAX, OSBORNE (Charles County), Protestant and probable soldier in the Revolution of 1689; signed an address and took a loyalty oath supporting the King of England and the reestablishment of Lord Baltimore into power on Nov 28, 1689. {Ref: ARMD 8:138}

LONDON, AMBROSE (Northampton, Virginia, and Annamessex, Somerset County), major by 1678; paid for his services in the late expedition against the Nanticoke Indians in 1678; member of the Lower House of the Maryland Assembly, 1671-1675; county court justice, 1679-1783 (name misinterpreted once as "Ambrose Loudon"); died intestate by November, 1706. {Ref: ARMD 7:99, 7:100, 15:275, 15:328; OSES:284, 450; BDML II:545}

LONELY, DELL (Kent County), soldier (rank not stated) in Capt. William Leeds (Leeads) Company by May 23, 1662, at which time he signed a petition about the misuse of company money by Capt. Thomas Brednox (Bradnox), late of Isle of Kent, deceased. {Ref: ARMD 3:455}

LONG, ALEXANDER (Anne Arundel and Prince George's Counties), captain and master of the ship *Mary Ann* riding in the Eastern Branch of the Patuxent River on Apr 13, 1726; master of the ship *Mary and Ann* in Annapolis in 1731. {Ref: PGLR M:150; CVPR:12}

LONG, CURTICE (Kent County), soldier (rank not stated) circa 1675; paid for his services in the late expedition against the Nanticoke Indians in 1678. {Ref: ARMD 7:94}

LONG, EMANUELL (Patuxent District), captain and master of the ship *Mary* in 1730-1731. {Ref: CVPR:12}

LONG, THOMAS (Baltimore County), major by 1677 and in command of foot militia under Col. George Wells in 1678; sheriff, 1676-1679; one of the officers of "Middle Town in Middle River" circa 1676; justice of the peace, 1677-1691; quorum, 1679-1686; member of the Lower House of the Maryland Assembly, 1683-1684; died intestate by October, 1691. {Ref: ARMD 7:509, 7:611, 13:243, 15:38, 15:198, 15:232, 15:254, 15:327, 17:380; BDML II:545; BBCF:409; INAC 13A:226}

LONG, THOMAS (Dorchester County), soldier (rank not stated) circa 1675; paid for his services in the late expedition against the Nanticoke Indians in 1678; died testate by May 29, 1686 (date of probate). {Ref: ARMD 7:93; MDWB 4:215}

LONG, WILLIAM (Somerset or Dorchester County), captain and master of the ship *John and Benjamin* of Boston in 1677. {Ref: INAC 5:345}

LONGBOTHAM, EDMOND (Anne Arundel County), captain and master of the ship *Leviathin* riding in Beard's Creek in South River on Jul 16, 1708. {Ref: AALR WT#2:638}

LONGDEN, EPHRAIM (England and Cecil County), captain, mariner and master of the ship *Hopewell* in 1718. {Ref: CELR 3:185}

LONGHORN, THOMAS (Anne Arundel County), captain and master of the ship *Laywe* by 1722. {Ref: MDAD 5:13}

LONGSTONE, WILLIAM (county not indicated), probable soldier (rank not stated) before 1682; paid for his services out of an assessment levied by the General Assembly for the public good in 1682. {Ref: ARMD 7:443}

LOOCKERMAN (LOCKERMAN, LOOKERMAN), JACOB (New Amsterdam, and St. Mary's and Dorchester Counties), soldier (rank not stated) circa 1675; paid for his services in the late expedition against the Nanticoke Indians in 1678; paid for his services again in 1695; major by 1700; doctor and member of the Lower House of the Maryland Assembly, 1697-1704; lieutenant colonel, 1702; colonel, 1715; born circa 1652, died testate on Aug 17, 1730 (will probated on Oct 27, 1730; Dorothy Loockerman, widow). {Ref: ARMD 7:102, 7:612, 24:29, 24:129, 38:72; SOJR III:66; BDML II:547; MWDB 20:109; INAC 35B:10}

LOOKE, RICHARD (Calvert County), Protestant and probable soldier in the Revolution of 1689; signed an address and took a loyalty oath supporting the King of England and "to reestablish Lord Baltimore in his ancient power and government" on Nov 16, 1689. {Ref: ARMD 8:131}

LORD, WILLIAM (county or port not indicated), captain and master of the ketch *Adventure* of Boston in 1691. {Ref: ARMD 8:240}

LOUIS, JEREMIAH (Somerset County), captain and shipmaster by 1716. {Ref: INAC 37A:82}

LOUNSDELL, JOHN (Somerset County), carpenter and probable seaman by 1716. {Ref: INAC 37A:82}

LOVEDAY, WILLIAM (Charles County), soldier (rank not stated) circa 1675; paid for his services in the late expedition against the Nanticoke Indians in 1678. {Ref: ARMD 7:101}

LOVELL, WILLIAM (county or port not indicated), captain and master of the ship *John and Francis* in 1690. {Ref: ARMD 8:237}

LOVERING, JOHN (England and Annapolis), captain of the ship *Sophia* of Biddeford in 1731-1734. {Ref: MDGZ, Mar 16, 1732/3 and Aug 2, 1734; CVPR:12}

LOVETT, THOMAS (county or port not indicated), captain and master of the brigantine *Susannah* of Spanish Town in 1698. {Ref: ARMD 25:16-17}

LOWE, ELIZABETH, see "Vincent Lowe," q.v.

LOWE, HENRY (Kent County), colonel by 1733. {Ref: INKC:178}

LOWE, HENRY, SR. (England, and Calvert and St. Mary's Counties), naval officer of Patuxent District, 1684-1685; Protestant and soldier in the Revolution of 1689; signed an address and took a loyalty oath supporting the King of England and "to reestablish Lord Baltimore in his ancient power and government" on Nov 16, 1689; provincial court justice, 1694-1696; lieutenant colonel, 1697; member of the Lower House of the Maryland Assembly, 1701-1704; colonel by 1712; died testate by Nov 6, 1717 (date of probate). {Ref: ARMD 8:132, 24:128, 25:597; BDML II:548; MDWB 14:453; INAC 39C:162}

LOWE (LOW), JOHN (England and St. Mary's County), Protestant and soldier in the Revolution of 1689; signed an address and took a loyalty oath supporting the King of England and the reestablishment of Lord Baltimore into power on Nov 28, 1689 (name listed once as "John Loe"); major by 1697; member of the Lower House of the Maryland Assembly, 1697-1701; died testate by Jul 15, 1701 (date of probate; Rebecca Low or Lowe, widow, later married Thomas Mudd). {Ref: ARMD 8:147, 24:35, 24:128, 24:234, 25:597; BDML II:549; MDWB 11:175; INAC 21:208, 29:177, 29:300}

LOWE, NICHOLAS (England, and Calvert and Talbot Counties), military officer (rank not stated) who swore allegiance to the King & Queen of England in 1696; sheriff, Talbot County, 1696-1698; resident of the town and port of Oxford; captain by 1699; major by 1704; colonel by 1708; member of the Lower House of the Maryland Assembly, 1694-1711; born circa 1662 (aged about 49 when deposed in 1711), died intestate on Oct 22, 1714. {Ref: ARMD 20:542, 27:203; BDML II:549-550; TALR 12:314; INAC 19½A:108, 36B:76; MDEP:121}

LOWE, REBECCA, see "John Lowe," q.v.

LOWE, THOMAS (Baltimore County), soldier (rank not stated) circa 1675; paid for his services in the late expedition against the Nanticoke Indians in 1678. {Ref: ARMD 7:95}

LOWE (LOW), THOMAS (St. Mary's County), Protestant and probable soldier in the Revolution of 1689; signed an address and took a loyalty oath supporting the King of England and the reestablishment of Lord Baltimore into power on Nov 28, 1689. {Ref: ARMD 8:146}

LOWE (LOW), VINCENT (England, and Great Choptank Island, Talbot County), colonel by 1676; paid for his services in the late expedition against the Nanticoke Indians in 1678; court justice (quorum), 1679; provincial court justice, 1679-1689; Roman Catholic in command of the foot forces of Talbot County, 1681-1688; colonel and member of the Upper House (Maryland Council), 1681-1688; colonel and officer of the town of Oxford in 1686; died testate by Oct 20, 1692 (date of probate; Elizabeth Lowe, widow). See "Walter Taylor," q.v. {Ref: ARMD 5:309, 5:462, 5:502, 5:554, 7:92, 15:254, 17:68, 17:75; BDML II:551; TALR 5:108; MDWB 6:7; INAC 10:256}

LOWERY (LOWRY), WILLIAM (St. Mary's County), soldier (rank not stated) circa 1675; paid for his services in the late expedition against the Nanticoke Indians in 1678; died testate by Dec 9, 1698 (date of probate). {Ref: ARMD 7:103; MDWB 6:208}

LOWES, ESTHER, see "Henry Lowes," q.v.

LOWES, HENRY (Somerset County), captain and master of the ship *Leah* in 1731 (listed simply as "Capt. Lows" in the 1734 tax list for Wicomico Hundred); died testate by Jun 26, 1761 (date of probate; Esther Lowes, widow). {Ref: CVPR:12; SOTL:1734; MDWB 35:348}

LOWES, THOMAS (Baltimore County), Protestant and probable soldier in the Revolution of 1689; signed an address and took a loyalty oath supporting the King of England and the reestablishment of Lord Baltimore into power on Nov 28, 1689. {Ref: ARMD 8:137}

LOWRY, JOHN (Dorchester County), captain by 1702. {Ref: INAC 23:84}

LOWTHER, JOHN (England and Prince George's County), captain and commander of the galley *Lowther* in 1698-1699. {Ref: ARMD 23:466; PGLR A:169}

LUCAS, CHARLES (England and Anne Arundel County), captain and commander of the ship *Hopewell* riding in West River on Jan 5, 1720/1 and Mar 7, 1721/2; died testate on Apr 15, 1722 at the home of Alexander Warfield (nuncupative will probated on May 1, 1722). {Ref: AALR CW#1:293, 473; MDWB 17:262; MDAD 4:181, 193}

LUCAS, JOHN (Somerset County), Protestant and probable soldier in the Revolution of 1689; signed an address and took a loyalty oath supporting the King of England and "for enabling us to defend ourselves against all invaders" on Nov 28, 1689. {Ref: ARMD 8:140}

LUCAS, JOHN (Talbot County), soldier (rank not stated) circa 1675; paid for his services in the late expedition against the Nanticoke Indians in 1678; born circa 1654-1655 (adjudged to be about 13 years old when indentured to John Barke on Jan 21, 1667/8). {Ref: ARMD 7:89, 54:416}

LUCOMBE, JOHN (England and Calvert County), captain and commander of the ship *Connary Bird* or *Cannary Bird* in 1677. {Ref: ARMD 67:175}

LUDDINTON, ---- (St. Mary's County), soldier (rank not stated) in 1642. {Ref: ARMD 4:130-131}

LUDFORD, ARTHUR (St. Mary's County), soldier (rank not stated) circa 1675; paid for his services in the late expedition against the Nanticoke Indians in 1678. {Ref: ARMD 7:103}

LUFFE (LUFTE), STEPHEN (England and Somerset County), captain by 1687; supported the Revolution of 1689; member of the Lower House of the Maryland Assembly, 1686-1688; sheriff, 1690-1692; died in 1693. {Ref: BDML II:553-554}

LUKE, JOHN (England and Potomac District), captain and master of the ship *Resolution* of Plymouth in 1693 and master of the ship *Mercy* in 1697. {Ref: ARMD 20:182, 23:172; INAC 13B:107}

LUMBARD, FRANCIS (Kent County), soldier (rank not stated) on Isle of Kent who swore allegiance to the Commonwealth of England on Apr 5, 1652. {Ref: INKC:101}

LUNN (LUN), JOHN (Dorchester County), soldier (rank not stated) circa 1675; paid for his services in the late expedition against the Nanticoke Indians in 1678; born circa 1654 (aged about 55 when deposed in 1709). {Ref: ARMD 7:93; MDEP:121}

LUNN, THOMAS (Anne Arundel County), soldier (rank not stated) circa 1675; paid for his services in the late expedition against the Nanticoke Indians in 1678. {Ref: ARMD 7:96}

LURDEN, CORNELIUS (Dorchester County), soldier (rank not stated) circa 1675; paid for his services in the late expedition against the Nanticoke Indians in 1678. {Ref: ARMD 7:93}

LURTEN, ROBERT (county or port not indicated), captain and master of the ship *William ---- [sic]* in 1692. {Ref: ARMD 8:371}

LURTING, THOMAS (England and Annapolis), captain by 1696; commander of the ship *Josiah* in 1698. {Ref: ARMD 23:28, 23:434}

LURTING, WILLIAM (Cecil County), captain by 1695. {Ref: ARMD 23:289; INCC:134}

LUTWYDGE, JAMES (Charles County), captain by 1728. {Ref: MDAD 9:129}

LUX, ANN, see "Darby Lux," q.v.

LUX, DARBY (England, and Anne Arundel and Baltimore Counties), captain, mariner, and commander of the ship *Gilbert* in 1720-1722; mariner, of the Kingdom of Great Britain, on Jul 16, 1722 (date of deed in Anne Arundel County); commander of the ship *Jonathan* riding in Severn River on Apr 25, 1723; captain, of Anne Arundel County, in 1728; commander of the ship *Patapsico* or *Patapsco Merchant* of London in 1729-1734; commander of the galley *Genoa* in 1738; one of the commissioners of Baltimore Town; captain of militia by 1743 for Baltimore County; born Jun 15, 1695, died testate on Oct 14, 1750 (will probated Nov 2, 1750; Ann Lux, widow). See "John Lux" and "Francis Pilcar," q.v. {Ref: BDML II:554-555; AALR CW#1:297, 346, 483; AALR RCW#2:10, 142; HBCC:56; MDAD 9:199; MDGZ, Jun 24, 1729 and Jul 19, 1734; CVPR:12; BBCF:416}

LUX, JOHN (England, and Anne Arundel and Prince George's Counties), mariner and captain of the ship *Owners Good Will* in 1721; died by Jan 29, 1727/8 (date of inventory; Capt. Darby Lux, administrator). {Ref: BDML II:554; MINV 13:64; MDAD 9:199}

LUX, WILLIAM (England and Anne Arundel County), captain and commander of the ship *Concord* lying in Herring Bay on Feb 4, 1712/3, and riding at anchor in South River on Dec 28, 1715 and Jan 9, 1716/7 and Dec 7, 1717 and Feb 24, 1718/9 and Feb 4, 1724/5. See "William Lax," q.v. {Ref: BDML II:554; AALR IB#2:18, 261, 325, 416, 528, SY#1:70}

LYDSTONE (LYDSON), NICHOLAS (England and Annapolis District), captain of a ship (no name given) in 1696-1698. {Ref: ARMD 23:466, 25:588}

LYELL (LIELL), WILLIAM (England and Annapolis District), captain of the ship *Blossom* of Barnstaple (Barnstable) in 1729; captain and master of the ship *Blossom* of Biddeford in 1731. {Ref: CVPR:12; MDGZ, Apr 1, 1729}

LYLE, JOHN (Charles County), captain and master of the ship *Excise Merchant* in 1691; born circa 1646-1647 (servant of Mathias O'Brian who was adjudged by the county court to be about 17 years old on Mar 8, 1663/4). {Ref: ARMD 8:239, 53:451}

LYNE, GEORGE (county or port not stated), seaman and "one of the company taken upon the ship *St. George* in 1659. {Ref: ARMD 41:308}

LYNE, MR., see "John Harris," q.v.

LYNES, PHILLIP (England, and St. Mary's and Charles Counties), soldier (rank not stated) circa 1675; paid for his services in the late expedition against the Nanticoke Indians in 1678; paid for his services out of an assessment levied by the General Assembly for the public good in 1682; Protestant and probable soldier in the Revolution of 1689; signed an address and took a loyalty oath supporting the King of England and the reestablishment of Lord Baltimore into power on Nov 28, 1689; mayor of St. Mary's City, 1694; appointed Chief Ranger of Charles County by the governor of Maryland on Oct 20, 1706; born circa 1649 (aged about 49 when deposed in 1692), died testate in Annapolis before Aug 15, 1709 (date of probate in Charles County; Ann Lynes, widow). {Ref: ARMD 7:101, 7:440, 8:138, 8:433-434, 20:147; BDML II:558; CHLR C#2:38; MDWB 12:151, pt. 2}

LYON, JOHN (Somerset County), soldier (rank not stated) circa 1675; paid for his services in the late expedition against the Nanticoke Indians in 1678; one John Lyon died testate in Dorchester County by Jan 5, 1703/4 (date of probate; Mary Lyon, widow). {Ref: ARMD 7:98; MDWB 3:14}

LYTFOOT, REBECCA, see "Thomas Lightfoot," q.v.

MABB, WILLIAM (England and Patuxent District), captain and commander of the ship *Recovery* of London in 1697-1698. {Ref: ARMD 23:399}

MACALY, THOMAS (Anne Arundel County), military officer (rank not stated) who swore allegiance to the King & Queen of England in 1696. {Ref: ARMD 20:542}

MACAY, WILLIAM (England and St. Mary's), captain and commander of the ship *Providence* of London in 1692. {Ref: ARMD 13:320}

MACCORMECK, PATRICK (Kent County), soldier (rank not stated) circa 1675; paid for his services in the late expedition against the Nanticoke Indians in 1678. {Ref: ARMD 7:94}

MACFFENIN, WILLIAM (St. Mary's County), sergeant in 1642. "Will Mack Ffenin" was paid for one month's service as a sergeant under Capt. William Brainthwaite in November, 1642. {Ref: ARMD 3:119, 3:122}

MACKALL, JOHN (Calvert County), captain by 1708; lieutenant colonel by 1713; member of the Lower House of the Maryland Assembly between 1708 and 1734 (speaker, 1725-1734); colonel, 1713; provincial court justice, 1718-1725; born circa 1669, died testate by Dec 21, 1739 (date of probate; Susanna Mackall, widow). {Ref: ARMD 27:202, 29:218, 29:248, 29:391, 29:451, 30:158, 30:359, 33:161, 34:61, 34:199, 34:401, 39:55, 39:181; BDML II:563-564; HCCM:292-293; MDWB 22:113}

MACKBRIDE, JOHN (Somerset County), Protestant and probable soldier in the Revolution of 1689; signed an address and took a loyalty oath supporting the King of England and "for enabling us to defend ourselves against all invaders" on Nov 28, 1689. {Ref: ARMD 8:141}

MACKCLURE, RICHARD (Somerset County), Protestant and probable soldier in the Revolution of 1689; signed an address and took a loyalty oath supporting the King of England and "for enabling us to defend ourselves against all invaders" on Nov 28, 1689. {Ref: ARMD 8:140}

MACKCULLAH, ALEXANDER (Somerset County), Protestant and probable soldier in the Revolution of 1689; signed an address and took a loyalty oath supporting the King of England and "for enabling us to defend ourselves against all invaders" on Nov 28, 1689. {Ref: ARMD 8:140}

MACKDOWELL, PATRICK (Talbot County), soldier (rank not stated) circa 1675; paid for his services in the late expedition against the Nanticoke Indians in 1678. {Ref: ARMD 7:92}

MACKEELE (MACKEELL), JOHN (Dorchester County), lieutenant by 1678; paid for his services in the late expedition against the Nanticoke Indians in 1678; captain before 1694; he was probably the "John Mukel" (misinterpreted as "John Muket") who was a captain of foot soldiers in 1689; lieutenant colonel, commissioned Oct 9, 1694; died testate by Apr 16, 1696 (date of probate). {Ref: ARMD 7:93, 13:244, 20:153; MDWB 7:209; INAC 14:10}

MACKEELE, WILLIAM (Dorchester County), captain before 1702; died circa 1702 (undated inventory). {Ref: INAC 23:140}

MACKENRY, COLLEN (St. Mary's County), soldier (rank not stated) circa 1675; paid for his services in the late expedition against the Nanticoke Indians in 1678. {Ref: ARMD 7:102}

MACKFARLING, JOHN (Talbot County), soldier (rank not stated) circa 1675; paid for his services in the late expedition against the Nanticoke Indians in 1678. {Ref: ARMD 7:92}

MACKGRAW, OWEN, see "Owen Maragh," q.v.

MACKIE (McKEY), ANDREW (All Hallows Parish, Somerset County), mariner and sailor on the ship *Blessing* riding at anchor in Senepuxen Inlet on Apr 13, 1717. {Ref: SOJR III:194-196}

MACKLIN, RICHARD (Talbot County), Protestant and probable soldier in the Revolution of 1689; signed an address and took a loyalty oath supporting the King of England and the reestablishment of Lord Baltimore into power on Nov 18, 1689. {Ref: ARMD 8:134}

MACKLIN, ROBERT (Talbot County), Protestant and probable soldier in the Revolution of 1689; signed an address and took a loyalty oath supporting the King of England and the reestablishment of Lord Baltimore into power on Nov 18, 1689. {Ref: ARMD 8:134}

MACKNEW, JEREMIAH (Charles County), soldier (rank not stated) circa 1675; paid for his services in the late expedition against the Nanticoke Indians in 1678. {Ref: ARMD 7:101}

MACKNITT, JOHN (Somerset County), Protestant and probable soldier in the Revolution of 1689; signed an address and took a loyalty oath supporting the King of England and "for enabling us to defend ourselves against all invaders" on Nov 28, 1689. {Ref: ARMD 8:140}

MACKVEALL, DANIELL (Cecil County), military officer (rank not stated) who swore allegiance to the King & Queen of England in 1696. {Ref: ARMD 20:546}

MACKY, DANIELL (Baltimore County), soldier (rank not stated) circa 1675; paid for his services in the late expedition against the Nanticoke Indians in 1678. {Ref: ARMD 7:95}

MACKY, JOHN (Somerset County), soldier (rank not stated) circa 1675; paid for his services in the late expedition against the Nanticoke Indians in 1678. {Ref: ARMD 7:97}

MACLOUGHLIN, KENELM (Charles County), soldier (rank not stated) circa 1675; paid for his services in the late expedition against the Nanticoke Indians in 1678. {Ref: ARMD 7:101}

MACNEMARA, THOMAS (Anne Arundel County), naval officer of the Patuxent District in 1718; died intestate by May 17, 1721 (date of administration account; Margaret Macnemara, widow). {Ref: ARMD 33:159; MDAD 3:429}

MACONICK, JOHN (Kent County), soldier (rank not stated) on Isle of Kent who swore allegiance to the Commonwealth of England on Apr 5, 1652. {Ref: INKC:101}

MACRAH, OWEN, see "Owen Maragh," q.v.

MACRINNON, JOHN (Kent County), soldier (rank not stated) in Capt. William Leeds (Leeads) Company by May 23, 1662, at which time he signed a petition about the misuse of company money by Capt. Thomas Brednox (Bradnox), late of Isle of Kent, deceased. {Ref: ARMD 3:455}

MADAM, EDWARD (England and Annapolis), seaman on the ship *Hartwell* of London commanded by Capt. Nicholas Humphries in March, 1697/8. {Ref: ARMD 23:397}

MADBURY, JOHN (Talbot County), soldier (rank not stated) circa 1675; paid for his services in the late expedition against the Nanticoke Indians in 1678. {Ref: ARMD 7:90}

MADDOX (MADDUX, MATTUX), ALEXANDER (Somerset County), soldier (rank not stated) circa 1675; paid for his services in the late expedition against the Nanticoke Indians in 1678; Protestant and probable soldier in the Revolution of 1689; signed an address and took a loyalty oath supporting the King of England and "for enabling us to defend ourselves against all invaders" on Nov 28, 1689. {Ref: ARMD 7:97, 8:141}

MADDOX (MADDUX), LAZARUS (Somerset County), Protestant and probable soldier in the Revolution of 1689; signed an address and took a loyalty oath supporting the King of England and "for enabling us to defend ourselves against all invaders" on Nov 28, 1689; died intestate by Sep 25, 1718 (date of administration account; Sarah Maddox, widow). {Ref: ARMD 8:141; MDAD 1:251}

MADDOX, SAMUELL (St. Mary's County), lieutenant by 1678; paid for his services in the late expedition against the Nanticoke Indians in 1678; died testate by Mar 9, 1684/5 (date of probate). {Ref: ARMD 7:102; MDWB 4:93}

MAGERIDGS, GILBERT (county or port not indicated), captain and master of the ship *Crowne* of Topsham in 1691. {Ref: ARMD 8:238}

MAGIER, JOHN (England, Queen Anne's County and Potomac District), captain and master of the ship *Rebecca* of London in 1729; commander of the ship *Lee* riding at anchor in Wye River on Mar 24, 1730 and in the Potomac District in 1731. {Ref: QALR RT#A:47; MDGZ, Apr 22, 1729; CVPR:12}

MAGRUDER (MACGREGOR), ALEXANDER (Scotland and Calvert County), colonel in the Royal Army who was captured by Oliver Cromwell's forces at the Battle of Worcester in 1651 and indentured to service in Maryland in 1652; born circa 1610, died testate by Jul 25, 1677 (date of probate; Elizabeth Magruder, widow). {Ref: BMDL II:570; HCCM:294; RMHF I:254; MDWB 5:261}

MAGRUDER, ELIZABETH, see "Alexander Magruder," q.v.

MAGRUDER, SAMUEL (Calvert and Prince George's Counties), military officer (rank not stated) who swore allegiance to the King & Queen of England in 1696 (name misinterpreted once as "Samuel Mageador"); captain, 1698; member of the Lower House of the Maryland Assembly, 1704-1707; born 1654, died testate by Apr 16, 1711 (date of probate; Sarah Magruder, widow). {Ref: ARMD 20:546; BDML II:570; MDWB 13:210}

MAGRUDER, SARAH, see "Samuel Magruder," q.v.

MAIN, ROBERT (Annapolis District), captain and master of the *Globe* in 1731. See "Robert Mayne," q.v. {Ref: CVPR:12}

MALDEN, FRANCIS (Talbot County), soldier (rank not stated) circa 1675; paid for his services in the late expedition against the Nanticoke Indians in 1678. {Ref: ARMD 7:87}

MALLETT, JOHN (Somerset County), probable soldier (rank not stated) before 1682; paid for his services out of an assessment levied by the General Assembly for the public good in 1682; assistant Indian interpreter by 1687. {Ref: ARMD 5:555, 7:442}

MAN (MANN), EDWARD (England, Virginia, and Talbot County), soldier (rank not stated) circa 1675; paid for his services in the late expedition against the Nanticoke Indians in 1678; court justice (quorum), 1679-1689; Protestant and probable soldier in the Revolution of 1689; signed an address and took a loyalty oath supporting the King of England and the reestablishment of Lord Baltimore into power on Nov 28, 1689; died testate by Dec 1, 1696 (date of probate). {Ref: ARMD 7:89, 8:144, 8:159, 15:254, 15:327, 17:380, 69:310; BDML II:609; MDWB 7:273}

MAN, HENRY (Anne Arundel County), captain and commander of the ship *Mary and Elizabeth* riding at anchor in South River on Jun 15, 1720. {Ref: AALR CW#1:172}

MANARY, RICHARD (Cecil County), military officer (rank not stated) who swore allegiance to the King & Queen of England in 1696. {Ref: ARMD 20:546}

MANGLES, ABRAHAM (Potomac District), captain and master of the ships *George* and *Perle* in 1697. {Ref: ARMD 23:172}

MANKIN, MICHAEL (Ireland and Talbot County), captain and commander of the ship *Friendship* of Belfast by 1716. {Ref: TALR 12:287}

MANKIN, STEPHEN (Charles County), Protestant and probable soldier in the Revolution of 1689; signed an address and took a loyalty oath supporting the King of England and the reestablishment of Lord Baltimore into power on Nov 28, 1689. {Ref: ARMD 8:138}

MANLOVE, THOMAS (Somerset County), soldier (rank not stated) circa 1675; paid for his services in the late expedition against the Nanticoke Indians in 1678; paid for his services out of an assessment levied by the General Assembly for the public good in 1682 (name listed once as "Thomas Manloe"). {Ref: ARMD 7:99, 7:441}

MANLOVE, WILLIAM (Somerset County), soldier (rank not stated) circa 1675; paid for his services in the late expedition against the Nanticoke Indians in 1678. {Ref: ARMD 7:99}

MANNING, BENJAMIN (Patuxent District), captain and master of the ship *Intent* in 1730-1731. {Ref: CVPR:12}

MANNING, ELLINOR, see "John Manning," q.v.

MANNING, JOHN (Calvert County), Protestant and probable soldier in the Revolution of 1689; signed an address and took a loyalty oath supporting the King of England and "to reestablish Lord Baltimore in his ancient power and government" on Nov 16, 1689; died intestate by Jul 15, 1725 (date of administration account; Ellinor Manning, widow). {Ref: ARMD 8:132; MDAD 7:26}

MANNING, JOSEPH (Charles County), soldier (rank not stated) circa 1675; paid for his services in the late expedition against the Nanticoke Indians in 1678; Protestant and probable soldier in the Revolution of 1689; signed an address and took a loyalty oath supporting the King of England and the reestablishment of Lord Baltimore into power on Nov 28, 1689; died testate by Feb 4, 1717/8 (date of probate). {Ref: ARMD 7:101, 8:138; MDWB 14:447}

MANNING, MR., see "Sampson Waring," q.v.

MANNING (MANNYING), NATHANIEL (Calvert County), Protestant and probable soldier in the Revolution of 1689; signed an address and took a loyalty oath supporting the King of England and "to reestablish Lord Baltimore in his ancient power and government" on Nov 16, 1689. {Ref: ARMD 8:132}

MANNING, NICHOLAS (Calvert County), captain by 1678. {Ref: INAC 5:382}

MANNING (MANING), THOMAS (Somerset County), captain and land owner by 1677. {Ref: ARMD 67:448}

MANNING (MANNYNG), THOMAS (England and Calvert County), Puritan and captain by 1660; member of the Lower House of the Maryland Assembly, 1661-1662; died testate by Mar 8, 1670/1 (date of probate). {Ref: ARMD 3:401, 49:3, 49:246, 49:408; HCCM:295; BDML II:571}

MANSELL, ROBERT (England and St. Mary's County), captain and commander of the ship *Orion and Ann* in 1692; "Robert Mansell, taylor" died testate in St. Mary's County by Oct 5, 1717 (date of probate) and mentioned his cousin Robert Mansell of Hatherly in Devonshire, England. {Ref: ARMD 8:314; MDWB 14:403}

MANSELL, VINCENT (St. Mary's County), Indian interpreter by 1681. {Ref: ARMD 15:364}

MANSFIELD, PAUL (Potomac District), captain and master of the ship *Endeavour* in 1730-1731. {Ref: CVPR:12}

MANSFIELD, VINCENT (St. Mary's County), ranger by 1675; his horse was taken by the Indians at the Susquehannough fort in 1675. {Ref: ARMD 15:56, 66:268}

MARAGH (MARRAH, MACRAH, MACKGRAW), OWEN (Manokin Hundred, Somerset County), probable soldier (rank not stated) before 1682; paid for his services out of an assessment levied by the General Assembly for the public good in 1682; Protestant and soldier in the Revolution of 1689; signed an address and took a loyalty oath supporting the King of England and "for enabling us to defend ourselves against all invaders" on Nov 28, 1689; died testate by Mar 14, 1692/3 (date of probate; Mary Maragh, widow). {Ref: ARMD 7:443, 8:140; OSES:450; MDWB 6:45}

MARCH, CAPTAIN, see "Thomas Marsh," q.v.

MARCH, MATHIAS (Queen Anne's County), captain by 1719. {Ref: MDAD 2:325}

MARCHANT (MERCHANT), WILLIAM (Dorchester County), soldier (rank not stated) circa 1675; paid for his services in the late expedition against the Nanticoke Indians in 1678; died testate by Sep 23, 1717 (date of probate). {Ref: ARMD 7:93; MDWB 14:325}

MARIARTE (MARIARTEE), DANIEL (Anne Arundel County), military officer (rank not stated) who swore allegiance to the King & Queen of England in 1696 (name misspelled once as "Daniell Marsharte"); member of the Lower House of the Maryland Assembly, 1708-1724; captain by 1711; sheriff, 1726; born circa 1676, died testate by Feb 26, 1726/7 (date of probate; Elinor Mariarte, widow). {Ref: ARMD 20:541, 27:200, 27:202, 27:410, 29:33, 29:391, 30:107, 30:360, 33:158, 34:61, 34:199; BDML II:574; MDWB 19:270; MINV 12:437}

MARIARTE, NINIAN (Anne Arundel County), probable soldier by the 1730's; commissioned Ranger of Prince George's County on Mar 15, 1736/7; son of Daniel Mariarte, *q.v.* {Ref: MDCB 82:47}

MARKEHORNE, ROBERT (Talbot County), soldier (rank not stated) circa 1675; paid for his services in the late expedition against the Nanticoke Indians in 1678. {Ref: ARMD 7:92}

MARKENSON, HANCE (Cecil County), soldier (rank not stated) circa 1675; paid for his services in the late expedition against the Nanticoke Indians in 1678. {Ref: ARMD 7:95}

MARKIN, THOMAS (Prince George's County), captain by 1705. {Ref: INAC 25:48}

MARKLAND, EDWARD (England and Talbot County), captain and mariner by 1717; commander of the ship *Peggy* of Liverpool in 1717; captain, 1725. {Ref: TALR 12:317; MDAD 6:384}

MARRAH, JAMES (Somerset County), Protestant and probable soldier in the Revolution of 1689; signed an address and took a loyalty oath supporting the King of England and "for enabling us to defend ourselves against all invaders" on Nov 28, 1689. {Ref: ARMD 8:140}

MARRETT, JOHN (Somerset County), soldier (rank not stated) circa 1675; paid for his services in the late expedition against the Nanticoke Indians in 1678. {Ref: ARMD 7:98}

MARROW, AUGUSTINE (Somerset County), soldier (rank not stated) circa 1675; paid for his services in the late expedition against the Nanticoke Indians in 1678. {Ref: ARMD 7:98}

MARROW, JAMES (Oxford District), captain and master of the ship *Betty and Lydia* in 1730. {Ref: CVPR:12}

MARRUM, THOMAS (St. Mary's County), Protestant and probable soldier in the Revolution of 1689; signed an address and took a loyalty oath supporting the King of England and the reestablishment of Lord Baltimore into power on Nov 28, 1689. {Ref: ARMD 8:147}

MARSH, GILBERT (Baltimore and Prince George's Counties), probable soldier (rank not stated) before 1682; paid for his services out of an assessment levied by the General Assembly for the public good in 1682; died testate by Feb 19, 1724/5 (date of probate). {Ref: ARMD 7:440; BBCF:422; MDWB 18:344; MDAD 7:274}

MARSH, JANE, see "Thomas Marsh," q.v.

MARSH, MATHEW (England and Annapolis), captain of the ship *Faulcon* of Biddeford in 1734. {Ref: MDGZ, Jul 19, 1734}

MARSH, PAUL (England, and Anne Arundel and Somerset Counties, and Sussex County, Delaware), commissioned "captain of foot from Nantecoke to Manaokin" on Feb 9, 1669; member of the Lower House of the Maryland Assembly, 1671-1675; died in Delaware in 1684. {Ref: ARMD 5:61, 5:111; BDML II:574}

MARSH, THOMAS (England, Virginia, and Anne Arundel County), signer of a treaty with Susquehanna Indians on July 5, 1652; provincial court justice before 1655; soldier (rank not stated) who "apparently died of wounds received in the battle against the proprietor's forces at Providence, Anne Arundel County, March 25, 1655" and an administration bond was granted to Sarah Marsh (widow) on Mar 20, 1655/6. {Ref: BDML II:574-575}

MARSH, THOMAS (Virginia, and Anne Arundel and Kent Counties), soldier (rank not stated) circa 1675; paid for his services in the late expedition against the Nanticoke Indians in 1678; member of the Lower House of the Maryland Assembly, 1676-1679; mentioned in Col. Henry Coursey's letter to the Maryland Council as "Capt. March of the Island of Kent is dead and there is no captain in that place" in 1681; born circa 1643, died testate by Oct 28, 1679 (date of probate; Jane Marsh, widow). {Ref: ARMD 7:94, 7:134; 15:93, 17:76; FAAH:43; BDML II:575; INAC 6:380; MDWB 10:82}

MARSH, THOMAS (Queen Anne's County), captain and master of the schooner *Nancy* (built in Talbot County) in 1733; master and part owner of the schooner *Swallow* (built at Wye River) in 1734. {Ref: MDCB 82:7, 21}

MARSHALL, JOHN (county or port not indicated), captain and master of the ship *Burdochs Factor* of London in 1691. {Ref: ARMD 8:239, 23:10}

MARSHALL, THOMAS (Somerset County), soldier (rank not stated) circa 1675; paid for his services in the late expedition against the Nanticoke Indians in 1678. {Ref: ARMD 7:99}

MARSHALL, THOMAS (Baltimore County), soldier (rank not stated) circa 1675; paid for his services in the late expedition against the Nanticoke Indians in 1678. {Ref: ARMD 7:95}

MARSHALL, THOMAS (England, and Talbot and Queen's Anne Counties), seaman on the ship *Ruth* in 1676; captain and master of the ship *Loyalty* of Bydeford in 1690; commander of the ship *Sarah Hawke* in 1702 and land owner in Talbot County; mariner, of Abbotsham, County Devon, died by 1720. {Ref: ARMD 8:238, 51:474, 66:301; TALR 9:116; QALR IK#B:12}

MARSHALL, WILLIAM (Charles County), soldier (rank not stated) by 1666; signed a petition to the governor to "displace Capt. William Boreman whom was lately constituted captain of the militia" on Sep 12, 1666; died testate by Jun 28, 1698 (date of probate). {Ref: ARMD 3:556, 3:561; MDWB 6:152}

MARTIN, ---- (St. Mary's County), soldier (rank not stated) circa 1675; for whom Ann Martin was paid for his services in the late expedition against the Nanticoke Indians in 1678. {Ref: ARMD 7:102}

MARTIN, ANTHONY (Anne Arundel County), captain and commander of the frigate *Mansell* riding at anchor in South River on Jul 8, 1708. {Ref: AALR WT#2:637}

MARTIN, FRANCIS (Somerset County), soldier (rank not stated) circa 1675; paid for his services in the late expedition against the Nanticoke Indians in 1678; died testate by Aug 3, 1699 (date of probate; Mary Martin, widow, later married William Brittingham). {Ref: ARMD 7:97; MDWB 6:320; Rent Rolls}

MARTIN, GEORGE (Ireland and St. Mary's County), captain and commander of the ship *Adventure* of Dublin in 1688; captain and master of the sloop *John and Robert* in 1690 and the ship *William and Mary* in 1693. {Ref: ARMD 8:237, 20:183, 23:59}

MARTIN, GEORGE (Annapolis District), captain and master of the sloop *Agnes* in 1729; master of the ship *Rover* in 1730. {Ref: MDGZ, May 27, 1729; CVPR:12}

MARTIN, HENRY (Potomac District), captain and master of the ship *Rebekah* in 1697. {Ref: ARMD 23:172}

MARTIN, JAMES (Scotland, and Somerset and Worcester Counties), captain by 1734; colonel by 1740; member of the Lower House of the Maryland Assembly, 1742, representing Somerset County; sheriff, Worcester County, 1742-1745; died testate by Mar 3, 1747/8 (date of probate; Mary Martin, widow). {Ref: BDML II:576-577; MDWB 25:242}

MARTIN, JANE, see "Thomas Martin," q.v.

MARTIN (MARTEN, MARTYNE), JOHN (Charles County), Protestant and probable soldier in the Revolution of 1689; signed an address and took a loyalty oath supporting the King of England and the reestablishment of Lord Baltimore into power on Nov 28, 1689; born circa 1641 (aged about 40 when deposed in 1681). {Ref: ARMD 8:138, 15:406}

MARTIN, LODWICK (Spesutia Hundred, Baltimore County), Protestant and probable soldier in the Revolution of 1689; signed an address and took a loyalty oath supporting the King of England and the reestablishment of Lord Baltimore into power on Nov 28, 1689. {Ref: ARMD 8:137; BBCF:425}

MARTIN, MARY, see "James Martin" and "Francis Martin," q.v.

MARTIN, MICHAEL (Annapolis District), captain and master of the snow *Mary* in 1728-1729. {Ref: MDGZ, Mar 11, 1728/9}

MARTIN, ROBERT (Kent County), soldier (rank not stated) on Isle of Kent who swore allegiance to the Commonwealth of England on Apr 5, 1652. {Ref: INKC:101}

MARTIN, THOMAS (Talbot County), soldier (rank not stated) circa 1675; paid for his services in the late expedition against the Nanticoke Indians in 1678; "Thomas Martin, Sr." wrote his will on Aug 27, 1690 and died by Aug 2, 1705 (date of probate; Jane Martin, widow, later married Solomon Robinson, as noted in a 1721 account). See "Isaac Hetson," q.v. {Ref: ARMD 7:90; MDWB 3:667; MDAD 3:473}

MARTINDELL, SAMUELL (Talbot County), ensign who swore allegiance to the King & Queen of England in 1696. {Ref: ARMD 20:542}

MARTYN, RICHARD (county or port not indicated), mariner in the 1730's; captain and master of the schooner *Annapolis*, formerly called *Adventure*, in 1739 (built at Newbury in New England in 1733 and called *Patuxent* when "condemned by Admiralty court"). {Ref: MDCB 82:77}

MASDIN, FRANCIS (Calvert County), Protestant and probable soldier in the Revolution of 1689; signed an address and took a loyalty oath supporting the King of England and "to reestablish Lord Baltimore in his ancient power and government" on Nov 16, 1689. {Ref: ARMD 8:132}

MASON, EDWARD (Anne Arundel County), soldier (rank not stated) circa 1675; paid for his services in the late expedition against the Nanticoke Indians in 1678. {Ref: ARMD 7:96}

MASON, GEORGE (Virginia and Charles County), captain in Stafford County by 1705; land owner in Charles County in 1705. {Ref: CHLR Z:203}

MASON, LAWRENCE (Annapolis District), mariner by 1734; captain of the sloop *Mulberry* in 1734; captain and master of the sloop *Betty* (built in Somerset County) in 1737. {Ref: MDGZ, Nov 29, 1734; MDCB 82:51}

MASON, LEMUEL (Dorchester County), colonel by 1672. {Ref: DOLR 4 Old 6}

MASON (MASSON), WILLIAM (Cecil County), mariner and land owner on Bohemia River in Cecil County by 1723; captain and master of the brigantine *Thomas and Sarah* of Boston in 1728-1731. {Ref: MDGZ, Dec 17, 1728 and Jun 3, 1729; CELR 4:39-40; CVPR:12}

MASTIN, WILLIAM (Prince George's County), captain and commander of the ship *Friend's Adventure* in 1722. {Ref: PGLR I:465}

MATHENA, DANIEL, see "Thomas Clark," q.v.

MATHERS, ROGER, see "Roger Mothers," q.v.

MATHIAS, THOMAS (county not indicated), private in the Maryland troops "raised to strengthen Albany, New York and resist the French and Indian enemies" in 1690. {Ref: SHMD I:355}

MATSON (MATSONE), MATTHIAS (Cecil County), soldier (rank not stated) circa 1675; paid for his services in the late expedition against the Nanticoke Indians in 1678. {Ref: ARMD 7:95}

MATTHEWS (MATHEWS), MAURICE (Dorchester County), cornet before 1678; paid for his services in the late expedition against the Nanticoke Indians in 1678; "Morrice Matthews" died testate by Apr 28, 1707 (date of probate). {Ref: ARMD 7:92; MDWB 12:298}

MATTHEWS (MATHEWS), ROGER (England, and St. George's Parish, Baltimore County), Protestant and soldier in the Revolution of 1689; signed an address and took a loyalty oath supporting the King of England and the reestablishment of Lord Baltimore into power on Nov 28, 1689 (name listed once as "Rogers Mathews"); lieutenant by 1696; swore allegiance to the King & Queen of England in 1696; born circa 1651, died testate in December, 1709 (will probated on Mar 7, 1709/10). See "Roger Mothers," q.v. {Ref: ARMD 8:137, 20:544, 23:20; BDML II:582; BBCF:427; MDWB 13:205}

MATTHEWS (MATHEWS), SAMUEL (St. Mary's County), colonel, 1656. {Ref: ARMD 3:331}

MATTHEWS (MATHEWS), THOMAS (St. Mary's County), probable soldier and officer by 1665; ordered by the Maryland Council "that Thomas Mathews doe send to the Emperour of Pascuttoway and the rest of the Indian Kings in Potomoke river to send out partyes to search for the Enemy Indians now abroad" on Jul 26, 1665. {Ref: ARMD 3:532}

MATTINGLY (MATTINGLEY), EDWARD (county or port not indicated), mariner by 1734; captain and master of the sloop *James* in 1737 (built in Accomack County, Virginia in 1731); master and part owner of the sloop *Pembroke* in 1739 (built at Pembroke in New England in 1735). {Ref: MDCB 82:48, 75}

MATTOCKS, HENRY (England and St. Mary's County), captain and master of the ship *Robert and Andrew* of Weymouth in 1693. {Ref: ARMD 20:182}

MAUD (MAUDE), DANIEL (England, and Talbot and Anne Arundel Counties), captain and master of the ship *Mary Ann* of London in 1705; mariner, of London, and land owner in Talbot County in 1712; captain and commander of the ship *Hopewell* riding at anchor in West River on Jan 31, 1716/7 and Jan 30, 1717/8 (name misinterpreted once as "Daniel Mande"); captain and merchant in London in 1728. {Ref: ARMD 25:351; TALR 12:97; AALR WT#2:325, AALR IB#2:334, 426; MDAD 9:44}

MAULDIN, BRIDGET, see "Francis Mauldin (Cecil County)," q.v.

MAULDIN, ELIZABETH, see "Francis Mauldin (Calvert County)," q.v.

MAULDIN, FRANCIS (Cecil County), court justice, 1708-1729; member of the Lower House of the Maryland Assembly, 1715, 1722-1727; major by 1725; died Jan 30, 1734/5 (will probated on Feb 20, 1734/5; Bridget Mauldin, widow). {Ref: ARMD 20:543; BDML II:583-584; MDWB 21:330}

MAULDIN, FRANCIS (Calvert County), military officer (rank not stated) who swore allegiance to the King & Queen of England in 1696; died testate by Mar 19, 1710/1 (date of probate; Elizabeth Mauldin, widow). {Ref: MDWB 13:175}

MAWMAN, THOMAS (Talbot County), soldier (rank not stated) circa 1675; paid for his services in the late expedition against the Nanticoke Indians in 1678. {Ref: ARMD 7:92}

MAXFIELD, JOSEPH (Talbot County), soldier (rank not stated) circa 1675; paid for his services in the late expedition against the Nanticoke Indians in 1678; he may have been the Col. Maxfield who died by 1753 in Kent County. {Ref: ARMD 7:90; KELR JS#27:254; CFES 2:88}

MAXWELL, JAMES (Anne Arundel and St. John's Parish, Baltimore Counties), captain by 1691; captain of rangers "from the Falls of Potapsicoe to Susquhanno River with 6 men" in 1692; captain of foot troops by 1694; major, commissioned Oct 9, 1694; swore allegiance to the King & Queen of England in 1696 (name listed as "Maj. James Maxfeild" in 1701); colonel by 1706;

member of the Lower House of the Maryland Assembly, 1694-1727; born circa 1662, died testate on Jan 5, 1727/8 (will probated on Mar 8, 1727/8; Anne Maxwell, widow, later married William Savory). {Ref: ARMD 8:339, 8:398, 20:109-110, 20:153, 20:544, 23:411, 25:337, 27:202, 29:452, 30:360, 34:61, 38:72; HBCC:44; INAC 21:203; BDML II:584-585; BBCF:430; MINV 15:446; MDAD 12:130}

MAY, JOHN (Cecil County), soldier (rank not stated) circa 1675; paid for his services in the late expedition against the Nanticoke Indians in 1678. {Ref: ARMD 7:95}

MAYDOWE, JOHN (Calvert County), Protestant and probable soldier in the Revolution of 1689; signed an address and took a loyalty oath (made his "T" mark) supporting the King of England and "to reestablish Lord Baltimore in his ancient power and government" on Nov 16, 1689. {Ref: ARMD 8:131}

MAYLE (MAILE), ANTHONY (Talbot County), soldier (rank not stated) circa 1675; paid for his services in the late expedition against the Nanticoke Indians in 1678; court justice, 1679 (name mistakenly listed once as "Anthony Magle"). {Ref: ARMD 7:88, 15:254, 15:327}

MAYNARD, EDWARD (county or port not stated), captain and commander of the ship *William* of Dover in 1669. {Ref: ARMD 57:549}

MAYNE (MAIN), ROBERT (England and Annapolis), captain of the ship *Juliana* of Biddeford in 1729 and of the ship *Crown* of Biddeford in 1732-1733. {Ref: MDGZ, Apr 8, 1729 and Mar 16, 1732/3}

MAYOE, SAMUELL (Coventry Parish, Somerset County), mariner by 1716. {Ref: SOJR III:103}

MAYPHES, ROBERT (St. Mary's or Charles County), mariner who served on the bark *Mayflower* under Capt. Daniel Hutt in 1659. {Ref: ARMD 41:287}

McCLESTER, DANIEL (Somerset County), mariner before 1720; died testate by Oct 4, 1743 (date of probate; wrote his will on Sep 1, 1720 before starting on a voyage to Bardadoes). {Ref: BDML II:587; MDWB 23:189}

McCLESTER, JOHN (Stepney Parish, Somerset County), military officer (rank not stated) who swore allegiance to the King & Queen of England in 1696; member of the Lower House of the Maryland Assembly, 1704-1707; captain by 1709; born circa 1672, died testate by Dec 3, 1742 (date of probate). {Ref: ARMD 20:544; BDML II:587-588; SOJR II:54; MDWB 22:521}

McCLESTER, JOSEPH (Somerset County), captain by 1724. {Ref: CESM:62}

McKARTER, ALEXANDER (Charles County), Protestant and probable soldier in the Revolution of 1689; signed an address and took a loyalty oath supporting the King of England and the reestablishment of Lord Baltimore into power on Nov 28, 1689; "Alexander McCottor" was born circa 1660 (aged about 54 when deposed in 1714 in Talbot County) and "Alexander Mecotter" died intestate by Jul 24, 1721 (date of administration account). Additional research will be necessary before drawing conclusions. {Ref: ARMD 8:138; MDEP:127; MDAD 3:498}

MEAD, WILLIAM (Somerset County), Protestant and probable soldier in the Revolution of 1689; signed an address and took a loyalty oath supporting the

King of England and "for enabling us to defend ourselves against all invaders" on Nov 28, 1689. {Ref: ARMD 8:141}

MEALES, JOHN, see "Francis Pilcar," q.v.

MEASON, WILLIAM (Cecil County), probable officer in the 1730's; captain before 1741; died intestate by Feb 16, 1741/2 (date of inventory). {Ref: MINV 26:578}

MEATEAG, CORNELIUS (Kent County), soldier (rank not stated) in Capt. William Leeds (Leeads) Company by May 23, 1662, at which time he signed a petition about the misuse of company money by Capt. Thomas Brednox (Bradnox), late of Isle of Kent, deceased. {Ref: ARMD 3:455}

MECKO, SAMUEL (St. Mary's County), soldier before 1708; petitioned the Maryland Council (no date given) "setting forth he was one of the Guard and lost his Eye-Sight by Attendance in the Night" and he was granted 2000 lbs. of tobacco on Dec 7, 1708. {Ref: ARMD 27:290}

MECOMY (MECONNY), MACOM (Kent County), soldier (rank not stated) in Capt. William Leeds (Leeads) Company by May 23, 1662, at which time he signed a petition about the misuse of company money by Capt. Thomas Brednox (Bradnox), late of Isle of Kent, deceased; "Macume Meconny" was born circa 1637 (aged about 23 when deposed in 1660). {Ref: ARMD 3:455, 45:191}

MEECH, THOMAS (England and St. Mary's County), captain by 1692; he was charged in England with trading between Virginia and Scotland with forged and counterfeited certificates (of which he freely confessed his guilt and then engaged in discovering and bringing to punishment other such offenders) in 1692-1693; commander of the sloop *Speedwell* of Maryland by 1694; appointed by the governor "to cruise upon the Coasts of Maryland and Pensilvania with power to examine all Ships trading to and from those parts ... for preventing frauds on that Coast" on Aug 9, 1694; died by Mar 28, 1696 (date of inventory); on Sep 7, 1698 his widow submitted a bill to the Maryland Council for payment of the services rendered by her late husband. {Ref: ARMD 20:124, 20:263, 25:1; INAC 13B:96}

MEEKINS, RICHARD (Talbot County), soldier (rank not stated) circa 1675; paid for his services in the late expedition against the Nanticoke Indians in 1678; born circa 1642 (aged about 62 when deposed in 1704 in Dorchester County); "Richard Meekins, Sr." died testate by Jun 3, 1710 (date of probate; Mary Meekins, widow). {Ref: ARMD 7:92; MDEP:129; MDWB 13:68}

MEERES (MEERS, MEARS), THOMAS (Virginia and Anne Arundel County), soldier (rank not stated) who served under Captain Fuller at the Battle of the Severn on Mar 25, 1655 and served on a Council of War after the battle; county justice, 1657; died testate by Sep 9, 1674 (date of probate; Elizabeth Meers, widow). See "John Homewood," q.v. {Ref: MDWB 2:3; FAAH:26, 44}

MEIRES, JAMES (Talbot County), captain by 1699. {Ref: INAC 19½A:159}

MELTON, JOHN (county not indicated), probable soldier (rank not stated) before 1682; paid for his services out of an assessment levied by the General Assembly for the public good in 1682. {Ref: ARMD 7:441}

MELVELL, WILLIAM (Somerset County), Protestant and probable soldier in the Revolution of 1689; signed an address and took a loyalty oath supporting the King of England and "for enabling us to defend ourselves against all invaders" on Nov 28, 1689. {Ref: ARMD 8:140}

MERCHANT, WILLIAM, see "William Marchant," q.v.

MEREDITH (MERIDETH), JOHN (Kent County), military officer (rank not stated) who swore allegiance to the King & Queen of England in 1696. {Ref: ARMD 20:541}

MEREDITH (MERIDITH), JOHN (Charles County), captain by 1728; master of the ship *William* in 1730-1731. {Ref: MDAD 9:50, 12:114; CVPR:12}

MEREDITH, ROGER (county not indicated), probable soldier (rank not stated) before 1682; paid for his services out of an assessment levied by the General Assembly for the public good in 1682. {Ref: ARMD 7:441}

MEREDITH, WILLIAM (Queen Anne's County), proposed for ensign in the Second Company of Foot on Jun 30, 1732, but refused to serve. {Ref: MDHR 1:11}

MEREY, ---- (Charles County), captain by 1722. {Ref: MDAD 4:224}

MERIDAY (MIRIDY), HENRY (Baltimore County), soldier (rank not stated) circa 1675; paid for his services in the late expedition against the Nanticoke Indians in 1678; died intestate by Sep 14, 1725 (date of administration account). {Ref: ARMD 7:96; MDAD 7:86}

MERIX, RICHARD (Talbot County), soldier (rank not stated) circa 1675; paid for his services in the late expedition against the Nanticoke Indians in 1678. {Ref: ARMD 7:90}

MERRIKIN, HUGH (Anne Arundel County), military officer (rank not stated) who swore allegiance to the King & Queen of England in 1696 (name also listed as "Hugh Merrikeine" and "Hugh Merriken"); born circa 1653 (aged about 26 when deposed in 1679), died intestate before May 3, 1699 (date of administration account). {Ref: ARMD 20:541; MDEP:129; INAC 18:118}

MERRIKIN, JOHN (Anne Arundel County), captain by 1734; born circa 1689 (aged about 45 when deposed in 1734). {Ref: MDEP:129}

MERRIOTT (MERIOT), WILLIAM (Annapolis District), captain and master of the sloop *Molly* of Maryland in 1730; master of the ship *St. Andrew* in 1731. {Ref: MDGZ, May 26, 1730; CVPR:12}

MERRYMAN (MERRIMAN), CHARLES, SR. (Virginia and Baltimore County), captain before 1696; swore allegiance to the King & Queen of England in 1696; captain on the north side of the Patapsco in 1703; born circa 1660, died testate on Dec 22, 1725 (will probated on Jan 14, 1725/6; Mary Merryman, widow). {Ref: ARMD 20:544; BCTL:36; BBCF:444; RMHF II:188; MDWB 18:431}

MESS, JULIAN (Somerset County), soldier (rank not stated) circa 1675; paid for his services in the late expedition against the Nanticoke Indians in 1678. {Ref: ARMD 7:98}

MESSERVEY, ALLEXANDER (Potomac District), captain and master of the ship *Abigail* in 1730-1731. {Ref: CVPR:12}

MESSHIER, WILLIAM (Dorchester County), soldier (rank not stated) circa 1675; paid for his services in the late expedition against the Nanticoke Indians in 1678. {Ref: ARMD 7:93}

MEWORTH, JOHN (Somerset County), soldier (rank not stated) circa 1675; paid for his services in the late expedition against the Nanticoke Indians in 1678. {Ref: ARMD 7:98}

MICHELL, HENRY (county not indicated), captain by 1696. {Ref: INAC 13B:140}

MICHELL, JOHN, see "John Mitchell," q.v.

MIDDLETON, EDWARD (Charles County), Protestant and probable soldier in the Revolution of 1689; signed an address and took a loyalty oath supporting the King of England and the reestablishment of Lord Baltimore into power on Nov 28, 1689. {Ref: ARMD 8:138}

MIDDLETON, JOHN (Prince George's County), captain by 1716; born circa 1673 (aged about 52 when deposed in 1725 and aged about 55 when deposed in 1728). {Ref: PGLR I:696, M:346, Q:386; INAC 37C:127}

MIDDLETON (MIDLETON), JOHN (Somerset County), soldier (rank not stated) circa 1675; paid for his services in the late expedition against the Nanticoke Indians in 1678. {Ref: ARMD 7:97}

MIDDLETON (MIDLETON), ROBERT (England and Talbot County), captain of the ship *Barbadoes Merchant* of Liverpool at Williamstadt, Maryland in 1697. {Ref: ARMD 23:137}

MIDDLETON (MIDLETON), ROBERT (Charles County), soldier (rank not stated) circa 1675; paid for his services in the late expedition against the Nanticoke Indians in 1678; born circa 1651 (aged about 30 when deposed in 1681). {Ref: ARMD 7:100, 15:403-404}

MIDGLEY, THOMAS (Somerset County), Protestant and probable soldier in the Revolution of 1689; signed an address and took a loyalty oath supporting the King of England and "for enabling us to defend ourselves against all invaders" on Nov 28, 1689. {Ref: ARMD 8:139}

MILBOURNE, RALPH (Somerset County), Protestant and probable soldier in the Revolution of 1689; signed an address and took a loyalty oath supporting the King of England and "for enabling us to defend ourselves against all invaders" on Nov 28, 1689; captain by 1715 (name also listed as "Ralph Milbourn" and "Ralphe Milborne"). {Ref: ARMD 8:140; SOJR III:38, 46}

MILBURNE, WILLIAM (St. Mary's County), soldier (rank not stated) circa 1675; paid for his services in the late expedition against the Nanticoke Indians in 1678. {Ref: ARMD 7:103}

MILES, HENRY (Annamessex, Somerset County), ensign before 1678; paid for his services in the late expedition against the Nanticoke Indians in 1678; died testate by Feb 20, 1696/7 (date of probate). {Ref: ARMD 7:97, 7:99; OSES:279; MDWB 7:296}

MILES, JOHN (St. Mary's County), probable soldier (rank not stated) before 1682; paid for his services out of an assessment levied by the General Assembly for the public good in 1682; died testate by Mar 16, 1697/8 (date of probate). {Ref: ARMD 7:441; MDWB 7:343}

MILES, ROBERT (Talbot County), soldier (rank not stated) circa 1675; paid for his services in the late expedition against the Nanticoke Indians in 1678. {Ref: ARMD 7:92}

MILES, WILLIAM (Kent County), "seaman within the said county" and a "sailor belonging to the *Factor* of Bediford" in 1697; captain by 1726. {Ref: ARMD 25:599; MINV 11:701}

MILL, WILLIAM (England and Annapolis District), captain of the ship *Triton* in 1734; mariner, of Biddeford, and master and owner of the ship *Bohemia* (built in Cecil County) in 1735. {Ref: MDGZ, Aug 2, 1734; MDCB 82:30}

MILLARETS, JOHN (St. Mary's County), Protestant and probable soldier in the Revolution of 1689; signed an address and took a loyalty oath (made his "R" mark) supporting the King of England and the reestablishment of Lord Baltimore into power on Nov 28, 1689. {Ref: ARMD 8:147}

MILLER, ANDREW (Somerset County), Protestant and probable soldier in the Revolution of 1689; signed an address and took a loyalty oath supporting the King of England and "for enabling us to defend ourselves against all invaders" on Nov 28, 1689. {Ref: ARMD 8:140}

MILLER, CHRISTOPHER (county or port not indicated), captain of the ship *Friendship* of London in 1668. {Ref: MDHM 5:339}

MILLER, JOHN (Somerset County), Protestant and probable soldier in the Revolution of 1689; signed an address and took a loyalty oath supporting the King of England and "for enabling us to defend ourselves against all invaders" on Nov 28, 1689. {Ref: ARMD 8:139}

MILLER, JOHN (England and Talbot County), captain and master of the ship *John and Susannah* of Bristol in 1691; master of the ship *Sarah* of Bristol in 1694; mariner of Bristol, England and land owner in Talbot County in 1694. {Ref: ARMD 8:239, 20:146, 25:600; TALR 7:144}

MILLER, WILLIAM (Kent County), military officer (rank not stated) who swore allegiance to the King & Queen of England in 1696. {Ref: ARMD 20:540}

MILLINGTON, ALLEMBY (Oxford District), captain and master of the ship *Henny* in 1731. {Ref: CVPR:12}

MILLINGTONE, OLIVER (Talbot County), soldier (rank not stated) circa 1675; paid for his services in the late expedition against the Nanticoke Indians in 1678. {Ref: ARMD 7:87}

MILLS, DAVID (Talbot County), a seafaring man in 1697; mariner and lot owner in the town and port of Oxford, 1708-1710. {Ref: ARMD 25:601; TALR 12:21}

MILLS, HENRY (Somerset County), Protestant and probable soldier in the Revolution of 1689; signed an address and took a loyalty oath supporting the King of England and "for enabling us to defend ourselves against all invaders" on Nov 28, 1689. {Ref: ARMD 8:141}

MILLS, JAMES (England, and Somerset and Baltimore Counties), soldier (rank not stated) circa 1675; paid for his services in the late expedition against the Nanticoke Indians in 1678; member of the Lower House of the Maryland Assembly, 1681-1682; paid for his services out of an assessment levied by the General Assembly for the public good in 1682; returned to England by 1689. {Ref: ARMD 7:96, 7:441; BBCF:450; BDML II:597}

MILLS, WILLIAM (England and Annapolis), captain by 1728; master of the ship *Swan* of Biddiford in 1728-1729; mariner, born circa 1700 (aged about 40 when deposed in 1740). {Ref: MDGZ, Feb 4, 1728/9 and Jun 17, 1729; MDAD 12:90; MDEP:132}

MILLS, WILLIAM (Dorchester County), soldier (rank not stated) circa 1675; paid for his services in the late expedition against the Nanticoke Indians in 1678. {Ref: ARMD 7:93}

MILLY, GILBERT (Kent County), captain by 1722. {Ref: MINV 7:93}

MILNER, JOHN (Patuxent District), captain and master of the ship *Gawen* in 1731. {Ref: CVPR:12}

MILSON (MILSONE), THOMAS (Talbot County), soldier (rank not stated) circa 1675; paid for his services in the late expedition against the Nanticoke Indians in 1678. {Ref: ARMD 7:89}

MINNOCK, JOHN (Prince George's County), captain by 1717. {Ref: INAC 37B:208}

MITCHELL (MICHELL), ANN, see "John Mitchell," q.v.

MITCHELL, GEORGE (Somerset County), soldier (rank not stated) circa 1675; paid for his services in the late expedition against the Nanticoke Indians in 1678; died intestate by Apr 6, 1702 (date of inventory). {Ref: ARMD 7:99; INAC 1:602}

MITCHELL, HENRY (England and Calvert County), ensign, 1661; captain of "a company of foot to be raised on the Clifts" in 1689; county commissioner by 1694; lieutenant colonel, commissioned Oct 9, 1694; colonel of Calvert County, appointed Aug 17, 1695; military officer who swore allegiance to the King & Queen of England in 1696; died by Jun 10, 1701 (date of inventory). {Ref: ARMD 3:435, 8:472, 13:242, 13:253, 20:108, 20:153, 20:281, 20:543, 23:284, 23:442, 25:59, 30:112; BDML II:598; INAC 20:247}

MITCHELL, JAMES (England, and Kent and Anne Arundel Counties), captain and commander of the ship *Adventure* of London in 1697; mariner, 1699; captain and master of the ship *Owner Adventure* riding at anchor in South River on Mar 28, 1703. {Ref: ARMD 23:393, 25:141-142; AALR WT#2:124; KELR M:94}

MITCHELL, JOHN (Talbot County), soldier (rank not stated) circa 1675; paid for his services in the late expedition against the Nanticoke Indians in 1678; "John

Michell" died testate by Sep 18, 1688 (date of probate; Ann Michell, widow). {Ref: ARMD 7:88; MDWB 6:40}

MITCHELL, MARKE (Dorchester County), soldier (rank not stated) circa 1675; paid for his services in the late expedition against the Nanticoke Indians in 1678. {Ref: ARMD 7:93}

MITCHELL, THOMAS (St. Mary's or Charles County), mariner who served on the bark *Mayflower* under Capt. Daniel Hutt in 1659; born circa 1621 (aged about 38 when deposed on Apr 23, 1659). {Ref: ARMD 41:288}

MITCHELL, THOMAS (Dorchester County), probable probable soldier (rank not stated) before 1682; paid for his services out of an assessment levied by the General Assembly for the public good in 1682. {Ref: ARMD 7:440}

MITCHELL, WILLIAM (England, and St. Mary's and Anne Arundel Counties), captain by 1650; member of the Upper House (Maryland Council), 1649-1651; George Howes stated that he was "servant for Capt. William Mitchell on board the ship *Thomas and John* at Debtford" in 1652; died intestate circa January, 1657. {Ref: ARMD 3:294, 10:72, 10:148, 10:179, 10:226, 10:451, 41:1, 41:10, 41:86; BDML II:599}

MOATS, JONAS (England and Potomac District), captain and master of the ship *Intelligence* in 1696. {Ref: ARMD 20:489}

MOLDER, JOHN (Talbot County), soldier (rank not stated) circa 1675; paid for his services in the late expedition against the Nanticoke Indians in 1678. {Ref: ARMD 7:90}

MOLREYNE, CORNELIUS (Talbot County), soldier (rank not stated) circa 1675; paid for his services in the late expedition against the Nanticoke Indians in 1678. {Ref: ARMD 7:89, 7:92}

MONDAY, HENRY, see "Henry Munday," q.v.

MONEY, ROBERT (Cecil County), soldier (rank not stated) circa 1675; paid for his services in the late expedition against the Nanticoke Indians in 1678. {Ref: ARMD 7:95}

MONSIEUR, TIMOTHY (Talbot County), soldier (rank not stated) circa 1675; paid for his services in the late expedition against the Nanticoke Indians in 1678. {Ref: ARMD 7:92}

MONTGOMERY, ROBERT, see "Thomas Smith," q.v.

MOODY, JAMES (St. Mary's County), soldier (rank not stated) circa 1675; paid for his services in the late expedition against the Nanticoke Indians in 1678. {Ref: ARMD 7:102}

MOODY, JAMES (Cecil County), captain and commander of Her Majesty's Ship the *Southhampton* in 1702; died intestate by Mar 18, 1733/4 (date of inventory; Sarah Moody, widow). {Ref: ARMD 25:145; MINV 18:371}

MOODY, JOHN (Talbot County), soldier (rank not stated) circa 1675; paid for his services in the late expedition against the Nanticoke Indians in 1678. {Ref: ARMD 7:88}

MOORE, GEORGE (Talbot County), sailor by 1720. {Ref: MDAD 2:518}

MOORE (MOOR), HENRY (Charles and Prince George's Counties), Indian interpreter by 1697; appointed by the Maryland Council and "empower'd to be General Interpreter for this Government upon any Treaty to be made with the Indians on the Western Shore" on Oct 20, 1697; born circa 1663 (aged about 67 when deposed on Aug 26, 1730). {Ref: ARMD 23:251-252; PGLR Q:68}

MOORE, JAMES (Kent County), captain and shipmaster by 1722. {Ref: MINV 7:93}

MOORE (MORE), JOHN (Somerset County), probable soldier (rank not stated) before 1682; paid for his services out of an assessment levied by the General Assembly for the public good in 1682; Protestant and soldier in the Revolution of 1689; signed an address and took a loyalty oath supporting the King of England and "for enabling us to defend ourselves against all invaders" on Nov 28, 1689. {Ref: ARMD 7:443, 8:140}

MOORE, JOS. (Kent County), captain and master of the ship *Parradox* in 1723. {Ref: MDAD 5:148}

MOORE (MORE), THOMAS (Kent County), soldier (rank not stated) circa 1675; paid for his services in the late expedition against the Nanticoke Indians in 1678. {Ref: ARMD 7:94}

MOORE (MORE), WILLIAM (Talbot County), soldier (rank not stated) circa 1675; paid for his services in the late expedition against the Nanticoke Indians in 1678. {Ref: ARMD 7:88}

MOORE (MOOR), WILLIAM (England and Annapolis), captain and master of the ship *Hopewell* of London in 1728. {Ref: MDGZ, Mar 11, 1728/9}

MOORESHEAD (MORESHEAD, MOORSHEAD), BENJAMIN (England and Anne Arundel County), captain and commander of the ship *Hopewell* riding in West River on Mar 13, 1723/4 and Mar 19, 1724/5; mariner, of London, bound for Maryland on Dec 12, 1724 (name misinterpeted once as "Benjamin Moreship, parish of Stepney, mariner" in 1725); commander of the ship *Hopewell* riding in West River on Apr 14, 1726; commander of the ship *Samuel and John* riding in South River on Feb 7, 1727/8; master of the ship *William and Isaac* in 1730. {Ref: AALR RCW#2:225, AALR SY#1:78, 122, 124, 185, 334; CVPR:12}

MORATT, JOHN (county not indicated), probable soldier (rank not stated) before 1682; paid for his services out of an assessment levied by the General Assembly for the public good in 1682. {Ref: ARMD 7:443}

MORELAND, JACOB (England, and Calvert and St. Mary's Counties), captain by 1697; member of the Lower House of the Maryland Assembly, 1697-1700; lieutenant colonel, 1701. {Ref: ARMD 25:117; BDML II:603}

MORGAN, ABRAHAM (Talbot County), Protestant and probable soldier in the Revolution of 1689; signed an address and took a loyalty oath supporting the King of England and the reestablishment of Lord Baltimore into power on Nov 28, 1689; born circa 1665 (aged about 46 when deposed in 1711 in Dorchester County). {Ref: ARMD 8:144; MDEP:133}

MORGAN, CHARLES (Dorchester County), soldier (rank not stated) circa 1675; paid for his services in the late expedition against the Nanticoke Indians in 1678. {Ref: ARMD 7:93}

MORGAN, HENRY (Kent County), soldier (rank not stated) on Isle of Kent who swore allegiance to the Commonwealth of England on Apr 5, 1652; assistant commander (commissioner) of Kent County, 1654; born circa 1614-1618 (aged about 30 when deposed in 1648 and aged about 42 when deposed on Feb 1, 1655/6; name listed once as "Henerie Morgan"). {Ref: ARMD 54:50-51; INKC:101, 103, 107}

MORGAN, HENRY (St. Mary's County), Protestant and probable soldier in the Revolution of 1689; signed an address and took a loyalty oath supporting the King of England and the reestablishment of Lord Baltimore into power on Nov 28, 1689. {Ref: ARMD 8:147}

MORGAN, HENRY (Baltimore County), soldier and probable officer in the 1730's; captain before 1745; born circa 1699 (aged about 46 when deposed in 1745). {Ref: MDEP:133}

MORGAN, JOHN (Kent County), soldier (rank not stated) in Capt. William Leeds (Leeads) Company by May 23, 1662, at which time he signed a petition about the misuse of company money by Capt. Thomas Brednox (Bradnox), late of Isle of Kent, deceased; born circa 1634 (aged about 27 when deposed in 1661). {Ref: ARMD 3:455, 54:230}

MORGAN, PHILLIP (Calvert County), Puritan leader and captain by 1656; commissioned "Captain over and to Exercise all the Inhabitants upon the Bay Side from the Plantation of Henry Cox upwards to the highest Extent of the County of Putuxent" on Mar 23, 1656/7 (name listed once as "Philip Morgin"); member of the Maryland Assembly in 1657. {Ref: ARMD 3:320, 3:359, 10:519; FAAH:27; HCCM:297; BDML II:603}

MORGAN, ROWLAND (Dorchester County), soldier (rank not stated) circa 1675; paid for his services in the late expedition against the Nanticoke Indians in 1678. {Ref: ARMD 7:92}

MORGAN, THOMAS (Somerset County), Protestant and probable soldier in the Revolution of 1689; signed an address and took a loyalty oath supporting the King of England and "for enabling us to defend ourselves against all invaders" on Nov 28, 1689. {Ref: ARMD 8:141}

MORGAN, THOMAS (Anne Arundel County), captain by 1693. {Ref: ARMD 20:201}

MORPAS, ANDREW (England and Potomac District), captain and master of a ship (no name given) of Liverpool in 1697. {Ref: ARMD 23:138}

MORRIS, ISAAC (Somerset County), Quaker who was a captain, master and part owner of the sloop *John Williams* in 1734-1735 (built in Maryland in 1734). {Ref: MDCB 82:26}

MORRIS (MORRICE), JACOB (St. Mary's County), soldier (rank not stated) circa 1675; paid for his services in the late expedition against the Nanticoke Indians in 1678. {Ref: ARMD 7:102}

MORRIS (MORRICE), MANUS (Somerset County), soldier (rank not stated) circa 1675; "Manus Morrice" was paid for his services in the late expedition against the Nanticoke Indians in 1678; "Manas Morris" died intestate by Aug 11, 1718 (date of administration account; Mary Morris, widow). {Ref: ARMD 7:98; MDAD 1:272}

MORRIS, MARY, see "Manus Morris," q.v.

MORRIS, ROBERT (England and Talbot County), mariner of Ratcliffe who served on the ship *Golden Fortune* commanded by Capt. Samuel Tilghman in 1653; mate who served on the ship *Golden Lyon* and participated in the Battle of the Severn on Mar 25, 1655; captain by 1657 and at least to 1669. {Ref: FAAH:24; ARMD 2:165-166, 10:567, 41:214, 54:437}

MORRIS, STEPHEN (Charles County), probable probable soldier (rank not stated) before 1682; paid for his services out of an assessment levied by the General Assembly for the public good in 1682; died intestate by May 30, 1719 (date of administration account). {Ref: ARMD 7:440; MDAD 2:70}

MORRIS (MORRICE), THOMAS (Baltimore County), soldier (rank not stated) circa 1675; paid for his services in the late expedition against the Nanticoke Indians in 1678. {Ref: ARMD 7:96}

MORRISON (MORRSON?), HENRY (England and St. Mary's County), captain and master of the ship *Elizabeth* of Londonderry in 1694. {Ref: ARMD 20:147}

MORTEMORE, ROBERT (Prince George's County), captain and master of the ship *Welcome* riding in the Patuxent River on Dec 28, 1723. {Ref: PGLR M:148}

MORTON, RICHARD (England and Calvert County), mariner, late of Wapping, County Middlesex, England "and seafaring in the ship commanded by Capt. Ralph Story" in 1662; died Mar 14, 1662/3 (shot to death by Patrick Due, of Bromall, St. Leonard's Hundred, Calvert County). {Ref: ARMD 49:10-14}

MOSELEY, JAMES (Dorchester County), soldier (rank not stated) circa 1675; paid for his services in the late expedition against the Nanticoke Indians in 1678. {Ref: ARMD 7:92}

MOSELEY, JOSEPH (Talbot County), soldier (rank not stated) circa 1675; paid for his services in the late expedition against the Nanticoke Indians in 1678. {Ref: ARMD 7:91}

MOSS, ELIZABETH, see "Richard Moss," q.v.

MOSS, JOHN (Kent County), soldier (rank not stated) circa 1675; paid for his services in the late expedition against the Nanticoke Indians in 1678. {Ref: ARMD 7:94}

MOSS, RICHARD (Magothy River, Anne Arundel County), Quaker who was assigned to a foot company of Capt. John Norwood in 1662, but refused to serve for religious reasons and was fined accordingly; died testate by Jan 30, 1700/1 (date of probate; Elizabeth Moss, widow). {Ref: AAGE:558; MDWB 11:15}

MOTHERS (MATHERS?), ROGER (county not indicated), probable soldier (rank not stated) before 1682; paid for his services out of an assessment levied by the General Assembly for the public good in 1682. {Ref: ARMD 7:441}

MOTLEY, JOHN (Prince George's County), mariner by 1734; captain and master of the shallop *Henry and Mocky* in 1736 (built in Prince George's County). {Ref: MDCB 82:43}

MOTTLEY, THOMAS (St. Mary's County), soldier (rank not stated) at the Susquehannough fort in 1675. {Ref: ARMD 66:268}

MOULD, JOHN (Baltimore County), probable soldier (rank not stated) before 1682; paid for his services out of an assessment levied by the General Assembly for the public good in 1682; died intestate by Jul 2, 1687 (date of inventory). {Ref: ARMD 7:441; BBCF:459}

MOUNTEGUE, WILLIAM (Talbot County), soldier (rank not stated) circa 1675; paid for his services in the late expedition against the Nanticoke Indians in 1678. {Ref: ARMD 7:88}

MOUNTJOY, JAMES (county or port not indicated), captain and master of the ship *Mayflower* by 1659; "one of the company taken upon the ship *St. George*" in 1659. {Ref: 41:306-309}

MOUNTS (MOUNCE), CHRISTOPHER (Cecil County), Indian interpreter by 1700; died testate by Dec 18, 1738 (date of probate). {Ref: ARMD 25:104; MDWB 22:24}

MUDD, THOMAS (St. Mary's County), court justice, 1679-1685; Indian interpreter before 1700; born circa 1647 (aged about 34 when deposed in 1681). See "John Lowe," q.v. {Ref: ARMD 15:256, 15:326, 17:55, 17:181-183, 17:379, 24:118}

MUDGE, WILLIAM (England, and Anne Arundel and Prince George's Counties), captain and commander of the ship *Ann Arundell* riding at anchor in Herring Bay on May 7, 1719; commander of the ship *Joseph and Mary* riding at anchor in Herring Bay on May 20, 1720 (name misspelled once as "William Midge"); commander of the ship *Charles* of London riding at anchor in Herring Bay on Dec 29, 1720; captain and commander of the ship *Tristan* in 1722-1723; commander of the ship *Charles* riding at anchor in Herring Bay on Dec 25, 1724 and Feb 9, 1725/6 and Jan 25, 1726/7 and Feb 7, 1727/8 and June 16, 1729. {Ref: AALR IB#2:544; AALR CW#1:167, 288; AALR SY#1:53, 163, 236, 334; MDGZ, Jun 17, 1729; PGLR I:465, M:148}

MUKEL (MUKET?), JOHN (Dorchester County), captain of a foot company in 1689. See "John Mackeele," q.v. {Ref: ARMD 13:234}

MULLEN, CHARLES (Somerset County), Protestant and probable soldier in the Revolution of 1689; signed an address and took a loyalty oath supporting the King of England and "for enabling us to defend ourselves against all invaders" on Nov 28, 1689. {Ref: ARMD 8:140}

MUNDAY (MONDAY), HENRY (England and St. Mary's), captain and master of a ship (no name given) riding at anchor at the mouth of the Patuxent River on

Jul 1, 1695 (date of petition); captain and master of the ship *John Hopewell* of London which was pirated by Capt. Henry King off the coast of Guinea in November, 1699; captain and mariner, of London, by 1716. See "Nicholas Gillebrand" and "John Burton" and "Leonard Rawlins" and "Edward Atterbury" and "John Sanders" and "William Parker" and "John Harris" and "Francis Brown," q.v. {Ref: ARMD 20:306, 25:94, 25:588; AALR CW#1:38}

MUNNES (MINNUS), THOMAS (St. Mary's County), seaman on a ship (no name given) commanded by Capt. Richard Husbands in 1649. {Ref: ARMD 10:9; FMDP:238}

MURDOCK (MOREDOCK), JOHN (Prince George's County), captain before 1709 and to at least 1722 (made payment before Apr 14, 1722 to the estate of Edward Butler, deceased, of Calvert County). {Ref: ARMD 27:392; BDML II:606; PGLR F Old 5:121; MDAD 4:203}

MURDOCK, JOHN (England and Annapolis), captain and master of the ship *Hope* of Liverpool in 1729. {Ref: MDGZ, Jul 22, 1729}

MURPHY (MURPHEY, MURFEY), JAMES (St. Michael's Parish, Talbot County), captain of a foot company before 1689; Protestant and soldier in the Revolution of 1689; signed an address and took a loyalty oath supporting the King of England and the reestablishment of Lord Baltimore into power on Nov 18, 1689; captain and owner of a sloop (no name given) in Talbot County in 1693; county justice, 1684-1698; died testate by May 9, 1699 (date of probate). {Ref: ARMD 8:134, 13:243, 15:327, 17:380, 20:138, 23:22, 25:600; CELR 2:81; INAC 12:116; BDML II:860; MDWB 6:258}

MURPHY, JOHN (Somerset County), soldier (rank not stated) circa 1675; paid for his services in the late expedition against the Nanticoke Indians in 1678. {Ref: ARMD 7:97, 7:99}

MURPHY (MURPHEY), PATRICK (Magothy River, Anne Arundel County), soldier (rank not stated) circa 1675; paid for his services in the late expedition against the Nanticoke Indians in 1678; died testate by Feb 10, 1702/3 (date of probate). {Ref: ARMD 7:97; MDWB 11:297}

MURRAY, DUNCAN (Annapolis and Pocomoke Districts), captain and master of the ship *Catherine and Ann* in 1730-1731; owner and master of the schooner *Isaac and Murray* (built in Somerset County) in 1735; master of the sloop *Catherine and Ann* in 1739 (built in Somerset County in 1738); his first name was spelled four different ways: Duncan, Dunkan, Dunkin, and Dunken. {Ref: CVPR:12; MDCB 82:30, 72}

MURRAY, JAMES (Charles County), captain by 1734; born circa 1704 (aged about 37 when deposed in 1741). {Ref: CHLR 39:288-289}

MURRAY (MURRY, MORRY), PHILIMON (St. Mary's or Calvert County), captain by 1684; accused (along with Hugh Raily) of assisting Col. George Talbott to escape in 1684, but then received a commission to be commander of the Christina fort (which had been previously commanded by said Talbott) in 1685; Maryland Council "ordered that the ffort at Christina Bridge and the guard there under the command of Capt. Philim. Murry be still continued and maintained for the preservation and defence of those parts from all forreigne Incroachments" on Mar 5, 1685/6; captain and commander of the fort at Christina Bridge ordered by the Maryland Council on May 26, 1686 "with the four men under his Command formerly appointed to keepe and maintaine the Fort at Christina Bridge for and in the right of the Right honorable the Lord Proprietor, doe still remaine and continue there to the end until further order from this board." {Ref: ARMD 5:459, 5:485, 17:370-371, 17:388-389, 17:465}

MURRAY, WILLIAM (county or port not indicated), mariner by 1734; captain and master of the brigantine *Leah* in 1737 (built in Somerset County in 1736). {Ref: MDCB 82:49}

MURRLIN, THOMAS (Annapolis District), captain of the sloop *Dolphin* in 1734. {Ref: MDGZ, Nov 29, 1734}

MURROW, ANDREW (St. Mary's County), soldier (rank not stated) before 1668; paid for his services in the last expedition against the Indians in 1668. {Ref: ARMD 5:35}

MURROW, JOHN (Kent County), "seaman within the said county" and a "sailor belonging to the *Factor* of Bediford" in 1697. {Ref: ARMD 25:599}

MURTHLAND, SAMUEL (Somerset County), captain and master of the ship *Helena* "lately seized and condemned in the Pocomoke District" in 1696. {Ref: ARMD 20:403}

MURTY (MURTEE), STEPHEN (Ireland and St. Mary's County), soldier (rank not stated) circa 1675; paid for his services in the late expedition against the Nanticoke Indians in 1678; died testate by Jun 4, 1684 (date of probate; Elizabeth Murty, widow). {Ref: ARMD 7:101-102; MDWB 4:41}

MUSTIAM, THOMAS (Charles County), soldier by 1665; "prest in the last indian Martch up the bay" and paid for his services on Dec 7, 1665. {Ref: ARMD 53:618-619}

MYNOCK, MICHAELL (Charles County), Protestant and probable soldier in the Revolution of 1689; signed an address and took a loyalty oath supporting the King of England and the reestablishment of Lord Baltimore into power on Nov 28, 1689. {Ref: ARMD 8:138}

NABB, JOHN (Talbot County), Protestant and probable soldier in the Revolution of 1689; signed an address and took a loyalty oath supporting the King of England and the reestablishment of Lord Baltimore into power on Nov 18, 1689; died testate by Feb 24, 1707/8 (date of probate; Elizabeth Nabb, widow). {Ref: ARMD 8:134; MDWB 12:233}

NALL, JOHN (county not indicated), captain by 1696. {Ref: ARMD 23:168}

NASH, ALLEXANDER (Kent County), soldier (rank not stated) in Capt. William Leeds (Leeads) Company by May 23, 1662, at which time he signed a petition about the misuse of company money by Capt. Thomas Brednox (Bradnox), late of Isle of Kent, deceased; died testate by May 1, 1681 (date of probate). {Ref: ARMD 3:455; MDWB 4:83}

NAYLOR, WILLIAM (Talbot County), soldier (rank not stated) circa 1675; paid for his services in the late expedition against the Nanticoke Indians in 1678. {Ref: ARMD 7:87}

NEALE, ANNE, see "James Neale," q.v.

NEALE, ANTHONY (Charles County), soldier (rank not stated) circa 1675; paid for his services in the late expedition against the Nanticoke Indians in 1678. {Ref: ARMD 7:101}

NEALE (NEALL), JAMES (England, and St. Mary's and Charles Counties), captain by 1659; member of the Upper House (Maryland Council) in 1662 and Lower House (Maryland Assembly) in 1666; captain, 1675; paid for his services in the late expedition against the Nanticoke Indians in 1678; born circa 1615, died testate by Mar 29, 1684 (date of probate; Anne Neale, widow). {Ref: ARMD 2:75, 3:434, 7:101, 7:611, 49:15, 49:177, 53:373; BDML II:609; RMHF I:269; CHLR A:3, A:61; INAC 1:520, 26:193; MDWB 4:40}

NEALL, JONATHAN (Anne Arundel County), military officer (rank not stated) who swore allegiance to the King & Queen of England in 1696. {Ref: ARMD 20:541}

NEAME, ROBERT (Somerset County), Protestant and probable soldier in the Revolution of 1689; signed an address and took a loyalty oath supporting the King of England and "for enabling us to defend ourselves against all invaders" on Nov 28, 1689. {Ref: ARMD 8:141}

NECK, JOHN (Kent County), soldier (rank not stated) circa 1675; paid for his services in the late expedition against the Nanticoke Indians in 1678; died testate by Jan 10, 1681/2 (date of probate). {Ref: ARMD 7:94; MDWB 2:183}

NEEDHAM, WALTER (England and Annapolis), seaman on the ship *Jefferyes* commanded by Capt. William Cooper on Feb 23, 1697/8 and who was "employed to bring John Sheffield's shallop from Patuxent to West River about a fortnight or three weeks ago." {Ref: ARMD 23:387}

NEEDHAM, WILLIAM (Calvert County), Protestant and probable soldier in the Revolution of 1689; signed an address and took a loyalty oath (made his "W" mark) supporting the King of England and "to reestablish Lord Baltimore in his ancient power and government" on Nov 16, 1689. {Ref: ARMD 8:132}

NEEDLES (NEDELLS), JOHN (Virginia and Talbot County), military officer (rank not stated) who swore allegiance to the King & Queen of England in 1696; captain before 1723 (year of death). {Ref: ARMD 20:542; BDML II:609; TALR 13:592}

NELSON, JOHN (Somerset County), Protestant and probable soldier in the Revolution of 1689; signed an address and took a loyalty oath supporting the King of England and "for enabling us to defend ourselves against all invaders" on Nov 28, 1689. {Ref: ARMD 8:140}

NELSON, WILLIAM (Somerset County), Protestant and probable soldier in the Revolution of 1689; signed an address and took a loyalty oath supporting the King of England and "for enabling us to defend ourselves against all invaders" on Nov 28, 1689. {Ref: ARMD 8:140}

NEUBY, JOHN (Prince George's County), soldier (trooper) under the command of Capt. Richard Owen in June, 1699. {Ref: ARMD 24:121}

NEVILL, JOHN (Charles County), seaman by 1643; born circa 1616-1619 (aged about 44 when deposed in 1660 and aged about 41 when deposed in 1660), died testate by Feb 4, 1664/5 (date of probate; Johanna Nevill, widow). {Ref: ARMD 4:223, 53:84, 53:134; CHLR A:100; FMDP:239-241; MDWB 1:222}

NEW, RICHARD (Charles County), soldier (rank not stated) circa 1675; paid for his services in the late expedition against the Nanticoke Indians in 1678. {Ref: ARMD 7:101}

NEWBEE, HENRY (Dorchester County), soldier (rank not stated) circa 1675; paid for his services in the late expedition against the Nanticoke Indians in 1678. {Ref: ARMD 7:93}

NEWBOLD, JANE, see "Thomas Newbold," q.v.

NEWBOLD, JOHN (Pocomoke District), captain and master of the ship *John and Elizabeth* in 1731. {Ref: CVPR:12}

NEWBOLD, THOMAS (Pocomoke River, Somerset County), soldier (rank not stated) circa 1675; paid for his services in the late expedition against the Nanticoke Indians in 1678 (name listed once as "Thomas Newbald"); court justice, 1679-1680; lieutenant in the horse troops, commissioned Dec 2, 1687; Protestant and soldier in the Revolution of 1689; signed an address and took a loyalty oath supporting the King of England and "for enabling us to defend ourselves against all invaders" on Nov 28, 1689; died testate by Jun 5, 1713 (date of probate; Jane Newbold, widow). {Ref: ARMD 5:568, 7:99, 8:141, 15:275, 15:328; MDWB 13:533}

NEWEN, OWEN (Charles County), soldier (rank not stated) circa 1675; paid for his services in the late expedition against the Nanticoke Indians in 1678. {Ref: ARMD 7:101}

NEWMAN, GEORGE (Charles County), Protestant and probable soldier in the Revolution of 1689; signed an address and took a loyalty oath supporting the King of England and the reestablishment of Lord Baltimore into power on Nov 28, 1689; born circa 1659 (aged about 53 when deposed in 1712), died intestate by September, 1724 (date of administration account). {Ref: ARMD 8:138; MDEP:138; MDAD 6:139}

NEWMAN, JOHN (Talbot County), soldier (rank not stated) circa 1675; paid for his services in the late expedition against the Nanticoke Indians in 1678 (name listed once as "John Numan"); Protestant and probable soldier in the Revolution of 1689; signed an address and took a loyalty oath supporting the King of England and the reestablishment of Lord Baltimore into power on Nov 18, 1689; born circa 1643-1644 (aged about 66 when deposed in 1709 and aged about 71 when deposed in 1715), died intestate by Nov 12, 1719 (date of administration account; Mary Newman, widow). {Ref: ARMD 7:90, 8:134; MDEP:139; MDAD 2:481}

NEWMAN, JOSEPH (Kent County), soldier (rank not stated) in Capt. William Leeds (Leeads) Company by May 23, 1662, at which time he signed a petition

about the misuse of company money by Capt. Thomas Brednox (Bradnox), late of Isle of Kent, deceased. {Ref: ARMD 3:455, 54:224}
NEWMAN, MARY, see "John Newman," q.v.
NEWMAN, RWA. (Charles County), Protestant and probable soldier in the Revolution of 1689; signed an address and took a loyalty oath supporting the King of England and the reestablishment of Lord Baltimore into power on Nov 28, 1689. {Ref: ARMD 8:138}
NEWTON (NEWTOWN), EDWARD (Dorchester County), soldier (rank not stated) circa 1675; paid for his services in the late expedition against the Nanticoke Indians in 1678; died testate by Mar 6, 1693/4 (date of probate; Margaret Newton, widow). {Ref: ARMD 7:93; MDWB 2:295}
NEWTON, JOHN (St. Mary's County), mariner by 1675. {Ref: ARMD 15:49}
NEWTON, JOHN (Dorchester County), soldier (rank not stated) circa 1675; paid for his services in the late expedition against the Nanticoke Indians in 1678. {Ref: ARMD 7:93}
NEWTON, MARGARET, see "Edward Newton (Newtown)," q.v.
NEWTON, RICHARD (Charles County), Protestant and probable soldier in the Revolution of 1689; signed an address and took a loyalty oath supporting the King of England and the reestablishment of Lord Baltimore into power on Nov 28, 1689. {Ref: ARMD 8:138}
NIBB, EDWARD (county not indicated), probable soldier (rank not stated) before 1682; paid for his services out of an assessment levied by the General Assembly for the public good in 1682. {Ref: ARMD 7:441}
NICHOLAS, JOHN (Dorchester County), soldier (rank not stated) circa 1675; paid for his services in the late expedition against the Nanticoke Indians in 1678. {Ref: ARMD 7:92}
NICHOLLS, ---- (Cecil County), captain by 1693. {Ref: INAC 10:282}
NICHOLS, AMOS, see "Cornelius Comegys," q.v.
NICHOLSON (NICHOLESON), ANTHONY (Charles County), captain by 1728. {Ref: MDAD 9:129}
NICHOLSON, FRANCIS (England, and St. Mary's and Annapolis), military officer and colonial bureaucrat; ensign, King Holland Regiment by 1678 in Tangiers (where he was promoted to captain, 1680-1684); captain under Edmund Andros in New York, 1686-1687; lieutenant governor of New York, 1689-1690; lieutenant governor of Virginia, 1690-1692; captain general, commander-in-chief, and governor of Maryland, 1693-1699; captain general and governor of Virginia, 1699-1705; general who led an expedition to the northern colonies, 1708-1711; governor and lieutenant general of Nova Scotia, 1712-1715; born 1655 in Yorkshire, died Mar 5, 1727/8 in London. {Ref: ARMD 20:100, 25:7; BDML II:613-614}
NICHOLSON, JOHN (Talbot County), soldier (rank not stated) circa 1675; paid for his services in the late expedition against the Nanticoke Indians in 1678. {Ref: ARMD 7:91}

NICHOLSON, JOSEPH (Kent County), soldier and probable officer in the 1730's; captain by 1740; colonel by the time of his death; born circa 1709, died circa 1787 in Chestertown. {Ref: CFES 2:239; BDML II:614}

NIXON, RALPH (Talbot County), soldier (rank not stated) circa 1675; paid for his services in the late expedition against the Nanticoke Indians in 1678. {Ref: ARMD 7:90}

NOBLE, ELIZABETH, see "William Noble," q.v.

NOBLE (NOBELL), GEORGE (Somerset County), Protestant and probable soldier in the Revolution of 1689; signed an address and took a loyalty oath supporting the King of England and "for enabling us to defend ourselves against all invaders" on Nov 28, 1689. {Ref: ARMD 8:141}

NOBLE, ISAAC (Somerset County), probable soldier (rank not stated) before 1682; paid for his services out of an assessment levied by the General Assembly for the public good in 1682. {Ref: ARMD 7:443}

NOBLE, ROBERT (Anne Arundel County), captain and commander of the ship *Gawin* riding at anchor in South River on Jan 28, 1716/7 and Jan 30, 1717/8. {Ref: AALR IB#2:333, 426}

NOBLE (NOBELL), WILLIAM (Somerset County), Protestant and probable soldier in the Revolution of 1689; signed an address and took a loyalty oath supporting the King of England and "for enabling us to defend ourselves against all invaders" on Nov 28, 1689; died testate by Jun 7, 1709 (date of probate; Elizabeth Noble, widow). {Ref: ARMD 8:141; MDWB 12:167, pt. 2}

NOBLES, ROBERT (Talbot County), soldier (rank not stated) circa 1675; paid for his services in the late expedition against the Nanticoke Indians in 1678. {Ref: ARMD 7:91}

NOERSTALLMAN, JOHN, see "John Vansaelsmans," q.v.

NORCOTT, THOMAS (England and St. Mary's), boatswain on the ship *Globe* of London commanded by Capt. Bartholomew Watts in 1682. {Ref: ARMD 7:281}

NOREST, ROBERT (Talbot County), Protestant and probable soldier in the Revolution of 1689; signed an address and took a loyalty oath supporting the King of England and the reestablishment of Lord Baltimore into power on Nov 18, 1689. {Ref: ARMD 8:134}

NORMAN, JOHN (St. Mary's County), soldier (rank not stated) circa 1675; paid for his services in the late expedition against the Nanticoke Indians in 1678; born circa 1638 (aged about 28 when deposed in 1661 in Charles County). {Ref: ARMD 7:103, 53:203}

NORMAN, WILLIAM (England and St. Mary's County), chirurgeon on the ship *Ruth* in 1676. {Ref: ARMD 66:301}

NORRIS, GILBERT (Annapolis District), captain of a ship (no name given) in 1698. {Ref: ARMD 23:404}

NORTH, CATHERINE, see "Robert North," q.v.

NORTH, EDWARD (Somerset County), captain by 1730; master of the ship *Sarah* or *Sarra* in 1730-1731 (noted as "left the province" in an administration account for the estate of Alexander Carlyle, deceased, in Somerset County on Jun 3, 1731); died intestate by Oct 2, 1733 (date of inventory). {Ref: CVPR:12; MDAD 11:67; MINV 18:71}

NORTH, JOHN (Somerset County), mariner by 1734; captain and master of the sloop *Valentine* in 1736 (built in Somerset County in 1735). {Ref: MDCB 82:42}

NORTH, ROBERT (England and Baltimore County), captain and mariner, of London, by 1724; land owner in Baltimore County on Jun 3, 1724; captain of the ship *Three Sisters* in 1729; listed on tax list for Patapsco Lower Hundred in 1737 (he also had quarters in Back River Upper Hundred); born by 1698 (baptized Oct 29, 1698 at Whittington, England), died testate on Mar 21, 1748/9 (will probated on Apr 5, 1749; Catherine North, widow). {Ref: BALR IS#G; MDGZ, Apr 1, 1729; HBCC:55; INBC:20, 24; BBCF:475; MDWB 25:561}

NORTH, THOMAS (Talbot County), sailor by 1720. {Ref: MDAD 2:518}

NORTH, WILLIAM (Kent County), soldier (rank not stated) circa 1675; paid for his services in the late expedition against the Nanticoke Indians in 1678. {Ref: ARMD 7:94}

NORTON, ROBERT (Baltimore County), captain of the ship *Content* in 1724. {Ref: BALR US#G}

NORTON, WALTER (England and Annapolis), captain and master of the ship *Ann Arundall* riding in the River Thames on Oct 13, 1701. {Ref: AALR WT#2:376}

NORWOOD, ANDREW (Anne Arundel County), soldier (rank not stated) circa 1675; paid for his services in the late expedition against the Nanticoke Indians in 1678; born circa 1634, died testate by Mar 7, 1701/2 (date of probate; Elizabeth Norwood, widow, later married Andrew Wellplay by 1706 and Charles Kilbourne after 1708). {Ref: ARMD 7:96; MDWB 11:174; Dorsey and Nimmo's *The Dorsey Family* (1947), pp. 203-205}

NORWOOD, ANN, see "John Norwood," q.v.

NORWOOD, ELIZABETH, see "Andrew Norwood," q.v.

NORWOOD, JOHN (Virginia and Anne Arundel County), captain by 1655; sheriff, 1655-1664; commissioned "to command all the forces from the head of Anne Arrundell River on the north side thereof to the south side of Patapsco River" on Dec 9, 1661; commissioner, 1664; chief justice, 1662-1672; born circa 1610, died intestate by Jun 19, 1672 (date of administration bond; Ann Norwood, widow, later married James Boyd). {Ref: ARMD 3:318, 3:348, 3:444, 3:449, 49:41, 49:304, 49:347; FAAH:28-29, 161; AALR RCW#2:39; AAGE:558; BBCF:476; INAC 1:159, 5:383}

NORWOOD, JOSEPH (Anne Arundel County), probable soldier (rank not stated) before 1682; paid for his services out of an assessment levied by the General Assembly for the public good in 1682. {Ref: ARMD 7:443}

NOTLEY, THOMAS (England, and Charles and St. Mary's Counties), deputy lieutenant and deputy governor of Maryland, 1676-1679; lieutenant general and chief justice, 1678; member of the Lower House (Maryland Assembly), 1663-1676, and Upper House (Maryland Council), 1678-1679; born circa 1634 (aged

about 28 when deposed in 1662), died testate by Apr 6, 1679 (date of probate).
{Ref: ARMD 15:118, 51:505; BDML II:616; MDEP:140; MDWB 10:7}

NOWELL, JAMES (Dorchester County), soldier (rank not stated) circa 1675; paid for his services in the late expedition against the Nanticoke Indians in 1678; died testate by Jun 11, 1718 (date of probate; Margaret Nowell, widow). {Ref: ARMD 7:93; MDWB 14:582}

NOWELL, LEWIS (Talbot County), soldier (rank not stated) circa 1675; paid for his services in the late expedition against the Nanticoke Indians in 1678. {Ref: ARMD 7:92}

NOWELL, WILLIAM (Cecil County), Protestant and probable soldier in the Revolution of 1689; signed an address and took a loyalty oath supporting the King of England and the reestablishment of Lord Baltimore into power on Nov 18, 1689. {Ref: ARMD 8:135}

NUGENT, CHRISTOPHER (Somerset County), soldier (rank not stated) circa 1675; paid for his services in the late expedition against the Nanticoke Indians in 1678. {Ref: ARMD 7:98}

NUTTER, CHARLES (Dorchester County), captain in the 1730's; died testate by May 11, 1738 (date of probate). {Ref: MDWB 21:881; MINV 23:162}

NUTTER, CHRISTOPHER (Northampton County, Virginia and Manokin Hundred, Somerset County), soldier (rank not stated) circa 1675; paid for his services in the late expedition against the Nanticoke Indians in 1678; paid again in 1682; Indian interpreter by 1693; born circa 1636, died testate by Mar 22, 1702/3 (date of probate). {Ref: ARMD 7:97-98, 7:442-443, 14:532; OSES:280, 453; MDWB 11:311}

NUTTHALL, JOHN (Calvert County), Protestant and probable soldier in the Revolution of 1689; signed an address and took a loyalty oath supporting the King of England and "to reestablish Lord Baltimore in his ancient power and government" on Nov 16, 1689. {Ref: ARMD 8:131; RMHF I:280-281}

O'CANE (O'KEINE), ROGER (Somerset County), soldier (rank not stated) circa 1675; paid for his services in the late expedition against the Nanticoke Indians in 1678; died testate by Jun 6, 1688 (date of probate). {Ref: ARMD 7:97; MDWB 6:23}

OCKMAN (OAKMAN), ---- (county or port not indicated), lieutenant on a ship (no name given) commanded by Capt. Charles Wager in 1696. {Ref: ARMD 23:5, 23:9}

ODBER (ODBUR), JOHN (Calvert County and Manokin Hundred, Somerset County), captain, commissioned in 1658 "to command all the forces from St. Leonard's Creek to the Coves on the north side of Patuxent River and from George Reade's to Cedar Point on the south side;" commissioned again on Feb 11, 1660; Commissioner of the Peace for the Eastern Shore below Choptank in February, 1663/4; born circa 1622 (aged about 36 when deposed in 1658) and killed in 1667 as reported to the Maryland Council on Aug 6, 1667 that "Captain John Odber and his servant being lately murdered by some of the Wiccomeses Indians" (in May, 1669 the murderer was proved to be an Indian named Anatchcomo). {Ref: ARMD 3:347, 3:402, 3:434, 5:195, 41:84; OSES:279, 314; MDEP:140}

ODCOCKE, HENRY (Talbot County), Protestant and probable soldier in the Revolution of 1689; signed an address and took a loyalty oath supporting the King of England and the reestablishment of Lord Baltimore into power on Nov 18, 1689. {Ref: ARMD 8:134}

ODELL, THOMAS (Anne Arundel County), military officer (rank not stated) who swore allegiance to the King & Queen of England in 1696; died testate by Apr 11, 1721 (date of probate; Sarah Odell, widow). {Ref: ARMD 20:542; MDWB 17:152}

OFFLEY, JOHN (Kent and Queen Anne's Counties), military officer (rank not stated) who swore allegiance to the King & Queen of England in 1696; died testate by Apr 20, 1709 (date of probate; Dorothy Offley, widow). {Ref: ARMD 20:541; MDWB 12:28, pt. 2}

OGDIN, JOHN (county not indicated), private in the Maryland troops "raised to strengthen Albany, New York and resist the French and Indian enemies" in 1690. {Ref: SHMD I:355}

OGILVY, GEORGE (All Hallows Parish, Somerset County), mariner and sailor on the ship *Blessing* riding at anchor in Senepuxen Inlet on Apr 13, 1717. {Ref: SOJR III:195-196}

OGLE, SAMUEL (England and Annapolis), captain of cavalry before 1731; lieutenant general, governor, and commander-in-chief of Maryland, 1731-1732; governor, 1733-1742, 1746-1752; born circa 1694, died May 3, 1752. {Ref: ARMD 28:12; BDML II:618-619}

O'KEINE, ROGER, see "Roger O'Cane," q.v.

OKELEY, EDWARD (Kent County), soldier (rank not stated) circa 1675; paid for his services in the late expedition against the Nanticoke Indians in 1678. {Ref: ARMD 7:94}

OLDFIELD, GEORGE (Elk River, Cecil County), Protestant and probable soldier in the Revolution of 1689; signed an address and took a loyalty oath supporting the King of England and the reestablishment of Lord Baltimore into power on Nov 18, 1689; born circa 1649 (aged about 46 when deposed in 1695). {Ref: ARMD 8:135; MDEP:141}

OLDSON, JOHN (Talbot County), sergeant who swore allegiance to the King & Queen of England in 1696. {Ref: ARMD 20:542}

OLDSON, PETER (England and Talbot County), captain and commander of the ship *Richard and Sarah* of London in 1696. {Ref: ARMD 25:558}

OLDTON, JOHN (Baltimore County), captain and commander of a party of rangers, 1694-1696; captain who swore allegiance to the King & Queen of England in 1696; captain and "commander of the Rangers in Baltimore County att the Garrison there" in 1697-1698; born circa 1669 (aged about 38 when deposed in 1707), died testate by Jun 30, 1709 (date of probate; Mary Oldton, widow). See "Thomas Roberts," q.v. {Ref: ARMD 20:204-205, 20:395, 20:423, 20:544, 23:103, 23:285, 23:404, 38:74; MDWB 12:105, pt. 2; INAC 32A:95; BBCF:480; MDEP:141}

OLFORD, JOHN, see "John Alford," q.v.

OLIVER, ROBERT (Annapolis District), captain and master of the ship *Adventure* in 1730. {Ref: CVPR:12}

OLIVER, ROGER (St. Mary's County), captain and mariner, 1637. {Ref: ARMD 1:6}

O'MEALY (O'MALE), BRYAN (Talbot County), soldier (rank not stated) circa 1675; paid for his services in the late expedition against the Nanticoke Indians in 1678; died testate by Mar 24, 1684/5 (date of probate; Mary O'Mealy, widow). {Ref: ARMD 7:87; MDWB 4:114}

O'NEALE (O'NEALL), HUGH (Charles and/or St. Mary's County), captain by 1661 and to at least 1675. {Ref: ARMD 49:177, 529; CHLR B:72; INAC 1:519}

OPY, THOMAS (England and Anne Arundel County), captain and commander of the ship *Richard and James* of Bristol in 1682. {Ref: INAC 7C:151}

ORAM, ROBERT (Pocomoke District), captain and master of the ship *Nonesuch* in 1731. {Ref: CVPR:12}

ORCHARD, GEORGE (county or port not indicated), captain and master of the ship *John and Francis* of London in 1691. {Ref: ARMD 8:239}

ORCHARD, RICHARD (England and St. Mary's), captain and master of the ship *Dove* which brought the first colonists (along with the ship *Ark*) to Maryland and arrived on Mar 25, 1634. {Ref: FMDP:48-52}

ORDE, MARK (England and Patuxent District), captain and commander of the pink *Reward* of London in 1707. {Ref: ARMD 27:8}

ORSON (ORSONE), BRYAN (Charles County), soldier (rank not stated) circa 1675; paid for his services in the late expedition against the Nanticoke Indians in 1678. *Note:* He may be the "Bearer Orson" who was born circa 1656 (servant to Robert Clarke who was adjudged to be about aged 13 by the county court on Jan 12, 1668/9). Additional research will be necessary before drawing conclusions. {Ref: ARMD 7:101, 60:179}

ORTIE, ---- (Anne Arundel County), colonel by 1675. {Ref: INAC 1:279}

ORTON, HENRY (Calvert County), Protestant and probable soldier in the Revolution of 1689; signed an address and took a loyalty oath supporting the King of England and "to reestablish Lord Baltimore in his ancient power and government" on Nov 16, 1689. {Ref: ARMD 8:131}

ORTON, THOMAS (Calvert and Prince George's Counties), ranger under the command of Capt. Richard Brightwell in 1692; soldier (rank not stated) under the command of Col. Ninian Beale from June, 1699 to May, 1700. {Ref: ARMD 8:445, 24:121-122}

OSBORNE, ATTALANTA, see "John Osborne," q.v.

OSBORNE, JOHN (England and Somerset County), captain by 1682; court justice, 1679-1680; member of the Lower House of the Maryland Assembly, 1682-1684; deputy surveyor, 1683-1684 (name also listed as "John Osborn" and "John Osbourne"); died testate by Jun 16, 1687 (date of probate; Attalanta Osborne, widow). {Ref: ARMD 7:360, 7:442, 7:611, 13:244, 15:275, 15:328, 17:363, 17:390; BDML II:624; MDWB 4:266}

OSBORNE, MARGARET, see "William Osborne," q.v.

OSBORNE, THOMAS (Kent County), soldier (rank not stated) in Capt. William Leeds (Leeads) Company by May 23, 1662, at which time he signed a petition about the misuse of company money by Capt. Thomas Brednox (Bradnox), late of Isle of Kent, deceased. {Ref: ARMD 3:455}

OSBORNE, WILLIAM (Bush River, Baltimore County), soldier (rank not stated) circa 1675; paid for his services in the late expedition against the Nanticoke Indians in 1678; paid for his services out of an assessment levied by the General Assembly for the public good in 1682 (name also listed as "William Orsborne" and "William Asborne"); born circa 1627 (aged about 76 when deposed in 1703), died testate by Mar 7, 1704/5 (date of probate; Margaret Osborne, widow). See "John Wallston," q.v. {Ref: ARMD 7:95, 7:441; BBCF:483-484; MDEP:141; MDWB 3:433}

OSTHMOTHERLY, JOHN (Kent County), "seaman within the said county" and a "sailor belonging to the *Loves Increase* of Whitehaven" in 1697. {Ref: ARMD 25:600}

OSWELL, WILLIAM (Somerset County), Protestant and probable soldier in the Revolution of 1689; signed an address and took a loyalty oath supporting the King of England and "for enabling us to defend ourselves against all invaders" on Nov 28, 1689. {Ref: ARMD 8:140}

OTTAWAY, THOMAS, see "Thomas Attoway," q.v.

OUCHTERLONEY (OUKTERLONY), PATRICK (Scotland and Calvert County), mariner (possibly in the 1730's and 1740's) of Arbroath, Angus, Scotland; settled in Calvert County (no date given), married Elizabeth (no last name given) and died testate between May 18, 1753 and Jun 28, 1754 in Calvert County (will probated in Edinburgh, Scotland in 1758). {Ref: SCOT:120; MDWB 29:170}

OUGHTERBRIDGE, BOWER (Pocomoke District), captain and master of the ship *Mulberry* in 1730-1731. {Ref: CVPR:12}

OUGHTERBRIDGE, JOHN (Pocomoke District), captain and master of the ship *Charming Betty* in 1730-1731. {Ref: CVPR:12}

OVERZEE, SYMON, see "William Cornelius," q.v.

OWEN, ANSON (Annapolis District), captain of the sloop *Mary* in 1734. {Ref: MDGZ, Nov 29, 1734}

OWEN, GEORGE (Kent County), "seaman within the said county" and a "sailor belonging to the *Factor* of Bediford" in 1697. {Ref: ARMD 25:599}

OWEN, JOHN (county not indicated), private in the Maryland troops "raised to strengthen Albany, New York and resist the French and Indian enemies" in 1690. {Ref: SHMD I:355}

OWEN (OWING), RICHARD (Dorchester County), soldier (rank not stated) circa 1675; paid for his services in the late expedition against the Nanticoke Indians in 1678; died testate by Dec 3, 1713 (date of probate; Jane Owing, widow). {Ref: ARMD 7:93; MDWB 13:616}

OWEN, WILLIAM (Somerset County), Protestant and probable soldier in the Revolution of 1689; signed an address and took a loyalty oath supporting the King of England and "for enabling us to defend ourselves against all invaders" on Nov 28, 1689. {Ref: ARMD 8:140}

OWING, JANE, see "Richard Owen (Owing)," q.v.

OWINGS, RACHEL, see "Richard Owings (Owen)," q.v.

OWINGS (OWEN), RICHARD (Anne Arundel and Baltimore Counties), captain, 1697; Maryland Council ordered "fifteen men shall be raised that are to strengthen the Garrison and ffrontiers at Potomock ... that Richard Owen of Ann Arrundell County be Captain over the said men and Gyles Hill of St. Maries County the Lieutenant" on Oct 16, 1697; captain of a party of rangers "upon Potomack" in 1698; captain under the command of Col. Ninian Beale from Jun 18, 1699 to May 6, 1700; "Richard Owings" was a captain on the north side of the Patapsco by 1702; died intestate by Nov 14, 1716 (date of administration bond; Rachel Owings, widow). {Ref: ARMD 23:246, 23:406, 24:121-122; BCTL:27, 35; INAC 36B:288; BBCF:486; PFMD:77}

OWINGS, RICHARD (Baltimore County), probable soldier in the 1730's; captain by 1737 (listed on tax list for Soldier's Delight Hundred); born circa 1711, died after 1750 (owned land in Maryland at that time and later moved his family to South Carolina). {Ref: BBCF:487; INBC:26}

OWINS, OWIN (Talbot County), corporal who swore allegiance to the King & Queen of England in 1696. {Ref: ARMD 20:542}

OXFORD, THOMAS (Somerset County), soldier (rank not stated) circa 1675; paid for his services in the late expedition against the Nanticoke Indians in 1678; Protestant and soldier in the Revolution of 1689; signed an address and took a loyalty oath supporting the King of England and "for enabling us to defend ourselves against all invaders" on Nov 28, 1689; died testate by May 26, 1721 (date of probate; Hannah Oxford, widow). {Ref: ARMD 7:99, 8:140; MDWB 16:433; MDAD 4:121}

PACA, AQUILA (St. George's Parish, Baltimore County), captain by the 1730's; name listed as "Capt. Aq'a Peca" in the Spesutia Lower Hundred tax list of 1737; member of the Lower House of the Maryland Assembly, 1741-1743; major before 1743; born circa 1703, died testate on Feb 8, 1743/4 (will probated on Mar 13, 1743/4; Rachel Paca, widow). {Ref: BDML II:630; BBCF:488-489; INBC:15; MDWB 23:566, 22:192; MINV 37:240}

PACE, THOMAS, see "Thomas Peace," q.v.

PACY (PACEY), SAMUELL (England, and Annapolis and Prince George's County), mariner, captain, and commander of the ship *Colchester Adventure* in 1698; land owner in Prince George's County in 1701. {Ref: ARMD 23:434, 23:474; PGLR A:417}

PADDISON (PADDISONE, PADASON), JOHN (Talbot County), soldier (rank not stated) circa 1675; paid for his services in the late expedition against the Nanticoke Indians in 1678; paid for his services out of an assessment levied by the General Assembly for the public good in 1682; ensign who swore allegiance to the King & Queen of England in 1696; died testate by Jan 22, 1700/1 (date of probate; Elizabeth Padason, widow). {Ref: ARMD 7:88, 7:439, 20:542; MDWB 11:42}

PAGAN (PAGGEN), PETER (England and Annapolis), captain by 1695; he was "remitted in the first ffleet out of the Publick Revenue ... being sent to purchase publick Arms for the defence of this Province" on Aug 24, 1695; captain and merchant, of London, 1698. {Ref: ARMD 20:299, 20:460, 23:434}

PAGE, JONATHAN (Kent County), mariner, of Chestertown, in the 1730's. {Ref: CFES 1:289; KELR JS#18:213}

PAGE, STEPHEN (Somerset County), Protestant and probable soldier in the Revolution of 1689; signed an address and took a loyalty oath supporting the King of England and "for enabling us to defend ourselves against all invaders" on Nov 28, 1689. {Ref: ARMD 8:140}

PAINE, JANE, see "Thomas Paine," q.v.

PAINE, MATTHEW (county or port not indicated), captain by 1698. {Ref: INAC 18:219}

PAINE, THOMAS (St. Mary's County), lieutenant, commissioned Apr 1, 1668; "Thomas Paine, of St. Jerome's" died testate by May 23, 1673 (date of probate; Jane Paine, widow). {Ref: ARMD 5:28; MDWB 1:531}

PAINTER (PAYNTER), NICHOLAS (St. Mary's and Anne Arundel Counties), soldier (rank not stated) circa 1675; paid for his services in the late expedition against the Nanticoke Indians in 1678; died testate by Dec 27, 1684 (date of probate; administration account filed in Anne Arundel County on May 8, 1686 by Col. William Burges, executor). {Ref: ARMD 5:465, 7:102; INAC 10:156; MDWB 4:56}

PAINTER, JOHN (Pocomoke District), captain and master of the ship *Speedwell* in 1730-1731. {Ref: CVPR:12}

PALBORTT, GEORGE (St. Mary's County), colonel by 1687 (his name appeared on a list payments received from the estate of Denis Hurley, deceased). *Note:* His name may have been misinterpreted and this could actually be Col. George Talbott, *q.v.* {Ref: INAC 9:324}

PALLEX, JOHN (Anne Arundel County), military officer (rank not stated) who swore allegiance to the King & Queen of England in 1696. {Ref: ARMD 20:542}

PALMER, CHARLES (Somerset County), mariner by 1734; captain and master of the sloop *Flying Fish* in 1736 (built at Bohemia River in 1730); master and part owner of the brigantine *Hercules* in 1738 (built in Somerset County in 1736). {Ref: MDCB 82:44, 65}

PALMER, DANIEL (Baltimore County), ensign before 1696; swore allegiance to the King & Queen of England in 1696 (name listed once as "Daniell Parmer"); died intestate by May 12, 1698 (date of administration bond). {Ref: ARMD 20:544; BBCF:490}

PALMER, JOSEPH (Annapolis District), captain and master of the ship *Constant Mary* in 1703. {Ref: ARMD 24:315}

PALMER, WILLIAM (Somerset County), soldier (rank not stated) circa 1675; paid for his services in the late expedition against the Nanticoke Indians in 1678. {Ref: ARMD 7:99}

PANDER, EDWARD (Dorchester County), ensign before 1678; paid for his services in the late expedition against the Nanticoke Indians in 1678. {Ref: ARMD 7:93}

PANNIWELL, THOMAS (Anne Arundel County), captain by 1728. {Ref: MDGZ, Mar 4, 1728/9}

PANTER (PAINTER), JOHN (Monie, Somerset County), soldier (rank not stated) circa 1675; paid for his services in the late expedition against the Nanticoke Indians in 1678 (name listed once as "John Panther"); paid for his services out of an assessment levied by the General Assembly for the public good in 1682; died testate by Aug 2, 1714 (date of probate; Dorothy Panter, widow). {Ref: ARMD 7:98, 7:442, 23:22; OSES:280; MDWB 13:738}

PARAMOUR, ---- (Anne Arundel County), captain by 1705. {Ref: INAC 25:208}

PARDON, JAMES (Annapolis District), captain and master of the ship *Juliana* in 1731. {Ref: CVPR:12}

PARDUE, STEPHEN (Dorchester County), soldier (rank not stated) circa 1675; paid for his services in the late expedition against the Nanticoke Indians in 1678. {Ref: ARMD 7:93}

PARK, GEORGE (Somerset County), Protestant and probable soldier in the Revolution of 1689; signed an address and took a loyalty oath supporting the King of England and "for enabling us to defend ourselves against all invaders" on Nov 28, 1689. {Ref: ARMD 8:140}

PARKER, ABRAHAM (county not indicated), probable soldier (rank not stated) before 1682; paid for his services out of an assessment levied by the General Assembly for the public good in 1682. {Ref: ARMD 7:439}

PARKER, HENRY (Talbot County), soldier (rank not stated) circa 1675; paid for his services in the late expedition against the Nanticoke Indians in 1678; died testate by Jul 12, 1687 (date of probate). {Ref: ARMD 7:92; MDWB 4:259}

PARKER, JOHN, see "Thomas Smith," q.v.

PARKER, MARY, see "William Parker," q.v.

PARKER, ROBERT (county not indicated), probable soldier (rank not stated) before 1682; paid for his services out of an assessment levied by the General Assembly for the public good in 1682. {Ref: ARMD 7:440}

PARKER, THOMAS (Charles County), Protestant and probable soldier in the Revolution of 1689; signed an address and took a loyalty oath supporting the King of England and the reestablishment of Lord Baltimore into power on Nov 28, 1689. {Ref: ARMD 8:138}

PARKER, WILLIAM (St. Mary's County), soldier (rank not stated) circa 1675; paid for his services in the late expedition against the Nanticoke Indians in 1678. {Ref: ARMD 7:103}

PARKER, WILLIAM (Calvert County), captain by 1696; military officer (rank not stated) who swore allegiance to the King & Queen of England in 1696; member of the Lower House of the Maryland Assembly, 1700-1704; major before 1710; died testate by Mar 7, 1710/1 (date of probate; Mary Parker, widow). {Ref: ARMD 20:543; BDML II:635; MDWB 13:174}

PARKER, WILLIAM (county or port not indicated), seaman on the ship *John Hopewell* of London under Capt. Henry Munday in 1699 who ran away to the pirate Capt. Henry King; reported by the Maryland Council that he "may happen to come into these American parts" in 1700. {Ref: ARMD 25:100}

PARKS, CHARLES (England and Charles County), mariner of London before 1682 and Charles County by 1682. {Ref: INAC 7C:131}

PARKS, MATHEW (Charles County), sailor by 1719. {Ref: MDAD 2:128}

PARKS, NATHANIEL (England and Charles County), captain and master of the ship *Mary* of Liverpool in 1719. {Ref: CHLR H#2:280}

PARMER, DANIELL, see "Daniel Palmer," q.v.

PARNES, RICHARD (Talbot and Kent Counties), soldier (rank not stated) circa 1675; paid for his services in the late expedition against the Nanticoke Indians in 1678; Protestant and soldier in the Revolution of 1689; signed an address and took a loyalty oath supporting the King of England and the reestablishment of Lord Baltimore into power on Nov 18, 1689; military officer (rank not stated) who swore allegiance to the King & Queen of England in 1696. {Ref: ARMD 7:87, 8:134, 20:541}

PARNEY, JAMES (Anne Arundel County), military officer (rank not stated) who swore allegiance to the King & Queen of England in 1696. {Ref: ARMD 20:542}

PARRAMORE (PARRAMOUR), JOHN (Virginia and Somerset County), soldier (rank not stated) circa 1675; paid for his services in the late expedition against the Nanticoke Indians in 1678; paid for his services out of an assessment levied by the General Assembly for the public good in 1682. {Ref: ARMD 7:98, 7:442, 7:443}

PARRISH, EDWARD (Anne Arundel County), soldier (rank not stated) circa 1675; paid for his services in the late expedition against the Nanticoke Indians in 1678. {Ref: ARMD 7:96}

PARRISH, ROBERT (Talbot County), soldier (rank not stated) circa 1675; paid for his services in the late expedition against the Nanticoke Indians in 1678. {Ref: ARMD 7:89}

PARRON, ---- (England and Cecil County), captain and commander of the ship *Elizabeth and Katherine* in 1679-1680. {Ref: CELR 1:123}

PARROTT, ELIZABETH, see "Gabriell Parrott," q.v.

PARROTT, GABRIELL (Anne Arundel County), soldier (rank not stated) circa 1675; paid for his services in the late expedition against the Nanticoke Indians in 1678; "Gabriell Parrott, Jr." died testate by May 17, 1698 (date of probate; Elizabeth Parrott, widow) and "Gabriell Parrott" died testate by Dec 19, 1704 (date of probate). Additional research will be necessary before drawing conclusions. {Ref: ARMD 7:96; MDWB 6:100, 3:440}

PARROTT, GEORGE (Talbot County), soldier (rank not stated) circa 1675; paid for his services in the late expedition against the Nanticoke Indians in 1678. {Ref: ARMD 7:89}

PARROTT, HENRY (Talbot County), soldier (rank not stated) circa 1675; paid for his services in the late expedition against the Nanticoke Indians in 1678 (name listed once as "Henry Parrat"); died testate by Oct 22, 1685 (date of probate; Mary Parrott, widow). {Ref: ARMD 7:89; MDWB 4:199}

PARROTT, MARY, see "Henry Parrott," q.v.

PARROTT, WILLIAM (Talbot County), soldier (rank not stated) circa 1675; paid for his services in the late expedition against the Nanticoke Indians in 1678; died testate by Mar 18, 1696/7 (date of probate). {Ref: ARMD 7:89; MDWB 7:271}

PARSLOW, THOMAS (Calvert County), captain before 1694; died testate by May 10, 1694 (date of probate; Helen Parslow, widow). {Ref: ARMD 20:108; MDWB 2:280}

PARSLOW, THOMAS (Calvert County), Protestant and probable soldier in the Revolution of 1689; signed an address and took a loyalty oath supporting the King of England and the reestablishment of Lord Baltimore into power on Nov 28, 1689. {Ref: ARMD 8:145}

PARSONS, AMOSS (Somerset County), soldier (rank not stated) circa 1675; paid for his services in the late expedition against the Nanticoke Indians in 1678. {Ref: ARMD 7:97}

PARSONS, EDWARD (St. Mary's County), seaman whose name appeared on "a list of men that goe by water when employed" in 1697; died testate by Apr 21, 1716 (date of probate; Mary Parsons, widow; mentioned land in St. Mary's County and on the Kenebuck River in New England). {Ref: ARMD 25:597; MDWB 14:228}

PARSONS, JOHN (Somerset County), soldier (rank not stated) circa 1675; paid for his services in the late expedition against the Nanticoke Indians in 1678; Protestant and probable soldier in the Revolution of 1689 (name listed once as "John Parsones"); signed an address and took a loyalty oath supporting the King of England and "for enabling us to defend ourselves against all invaders" on Nov 28, 1689; "John Persons, of Wiccocomico in Somerset County" died testate by Apr 1, 1712 (date of probate). {Ref: ARMD 7:98, 8:139; MDWB 13:424}

PARSONS, JOHN (Baltimore County), sergeant before 1678; paid for his services in the late expedition against the Nanticoke Indians in 1678. {Ref: ARMD 7:95}

PARSONS, MARY, see "Peter Parsons," q.v.

PARSONS (PARSONE), PETER (Somerset County), soldier (rank not stated) circa 1675; paid for his services in the late expedition against the Nanticoke Indians in 1678; died testate by Mar 28, 1687 (date of probate; Mary Parsons, widow). {Ref: ARMD 7:98; MDWB 4:246}

PARTIS, CHARLES (England, St. Mary's County and Patuxent District), captain by 1688; master of the ship *Ann* of Newcastle in 1692. {Ref: ARMD 13:272; INAC 10:177}

PARTIS, FRANCIS (England, and Charles and Calvert Counties), captain of the ship *Prosperous* of Newcastle in 1674; captain and commander of the ship *Merchant's Consent* of London in 1678-1679. See "Peter Hughes," q.v. {Ref: ARMD 15:244; INAC 9:421; MDHM 5:340}

PASCO, THOMAS (Annapolis District), captain and master of the ship *Ann* in 1731. {Ref: CVPR:12}

PASSEY, JOHN (Charles County), soldier (rank not stated) circa 1675; paid for his services in the late expedition against the Nanticoke Indians in 1678. {Ref: ARMD 7:101}

PATERSON, DAVID (Potomac District), captain and master of the ship *Ann and Jane* in 1730-1731. {Ref: CVPR:12}

PATRICK, JOHN (Talbot County), soldier (rank not stated) circa 1675; paid for his services in the late expedition against the Nanticoke Indians in 1678. {Ref: ARMD 7:90}

PATRICK, JOHN (Kent County), soldier (rank not stated) circa 1675; paid for his services in the late expedition against the Nanticoke Indians in 1678. {Ref: ARMD 7:94}

PAWMAN, JOHN (Calvert County), Protestant and probable soldier in the Revolution of 1689; signed an address and took a loyalty oath supporting the King of England and "to reestablish Lord Baltimore in his ancient power and government" on Nov 16, 1689. {Ref: ARMD 8:131}

PAYNE, EDMUND (Charles County), captain by 1684 and to at least 1698. {Ref: ARMD 23:442; INAC 8:221}

PAYNE, JOHN (Talbot County), soldier (rank not stated) circa 1675; paid for his services in the late expedition against the Nanticoke Indians in 1678. {Ref: ARMD 7:88}

PAYNE, JOHN (St. Mary's County), captain of a ship (no name given) in 1694. {Ref: ARMD 20:139}

PAYNE, JOHN (Calvert County), Protestant and probable soldier in the Revolution of 1689; signed an address and took a loyalty oath supporting the King of England and the reestablishment of Lord Baltimore into power on Nov 28, 1689. {Ref: ARMD 8:145}

PAYNE (PAINE), JOHN (St. Mary's County), soldier (rank not stated) before 1682; paid for his services out of an assessment levied by the General Assembly for the public good in 1682; captain of a company of foot troops "to be raised betweene Mr. Henry Brent's house in Pattuxent river and the mouth of the said river" in 1689; port collector who was "murdered in the execution of his Office by some Papists confederate under Major Seawell a late popish Governor there on board a yacht belonging to the said Seawell" on Jan 3, 1690 (brother of Dr. William Payne). See "Richard Sewall" and "George Talbott" and "John Woodcock," q.v. {Ref: ARMD 7:441, 13:242, 8:173-176}

PAYNE (PAYN), JOHN (Charles County), Protestant and probable soldier in the Revolution of 1689; signed an address and took a loyalty oath supporting the King of England and the reestablishment of Lord Baltimore into power on Nov 28, 1689; one "John Paynes" was born circa 1669 (aged about 76 when deposed in 1745 in Charles County). {Ref: ARMD 8:138; MDEP:145}

PAYNE, JOSEPH (county of port not indicated), captain and master of the ship *Globe* in 1686. {Ref: INAC 8:467}

PAYNE, THOMAS (St. Mary's or Charles County), sailor who served on the bark *Mayflower* under Capt. Daniel Hutt in 1659. {Ref: ARMD 41:287}

PAYNE, WILLIAM, see "John Payne," q.v.

PEACE (PACE), THOMAS (St. Mary's County), captain before 1698; died by May 16, 1698 (date of inventory). {Ref: INAC 16:205}

PEACK, JANE, see "Joseph Peake (Peack)," q.v.

PEACOCK (PEACOCKE), JAMES (England and Talbot County), master and mariner of Stockton upon Tease, County Durham, England, before 1685; land owner in Talbot County by 1685. {Ref: TALR 5:49}

PEACOCK (PEACOK), JOHN (St. Mary's County), soldier (rank not stated) circa 1675; paid for his services in the late expedition against the Nanticoke Indians in 1678. {Ref: ARMD 7:102}

PEACOCK (PEECOCK), JOHN (Calvert County), Protestant and probable soldier in the Revolution of 1689; signed an address and took a loyalty oath (made his "E" mark) supporting the King of England and "to reestablish Lord Baltimore in his ancient power and government" on Nov 16, 1689. {Ref: ARMD 8:132}

PEAKE (PEACK), JOSEPH (Back River, Baltimore County), Protestant and probable soldier in the Revolution of 1689; signed an address and took a loyalty oath supporting the King of England and the reestablishment of Lord Baltimore into power on Nov 28, 1689; died testate by Oct 27, 1700 (date of probate; Jane Peack, widow). {Ref: ARMD 8:137; BBCF:496; MDWB 11:7}

PEAKE, RICHARD (Somerset County), soldier (rank not stated) circa 1675; paid for his services in the late expedition against the Nanticoke Indians in 1678. {Ref: ARMD 7:98, 7:100}

PEAL, RICHARD (St. Mary's County), Protestant and probable soldier in the Revolution of 1689; signed an address and took a loyalty oath supporting the King of England and the reestablishment of Lord Baltimore into power on Nov 28, 1689. {Ref: ARMD 8:147}

PEARCE, BENJAMIN (Cecil County), colonel by 1723; born circa 1681-1685 (aged about 34 when deposed in 1719 and aged about 50 when deposed in 1731), died testate by Apr 22, 1734 (date of probate; Mary Pearce, widow). {Ref: ARMD 34:742; BDML II:639; CELR 4:234; INCC:135; MDEP:145; MDWB 21:189}

PEARCE, DANIEL (Kent and Cecil Counties), captain by 1718; member of the Lower House of the Maryland Assembly, 1708-1714; land owner on the east side of Elk River; born circa 1678 (aged about 44 when deposed in 1722), died testate by Jan 4, 1727/8 (date of probate; Mary Pearce, widow). {Ref: BDML II:640; CELR 2:282; INKC:157; MDEP:145; MDWB 19:361}

PEARCE (PEERCE), EDWARD (county or port not indicated), captain of the ship *Golden Fortune* of London in 1668-1670. {Ref: ARMD 51:39; MDHM 5:340}

PEARCE, GIDEON (Kent and Cecil Counties), mariner and vestryman in Shrewsbury Parish by 1713; captain of the sloop *John and Mary* in 1734; born circa 1678 (aged about 58 when deposed in 1736). {Ref: MDGZ, Sep 27, 1734; MDEP:145}

PEARCE, ISABELLA, see "William Pearce," q.v.

PEARCE, MARY, see "Benjamin Pearce" and "Daniel Pearce," q.v.

PEARCE (PEARSE), RICHARD (England and Talbot County), captain, commander and master of the pinke *Lemon* of Falmouth in 1691-1693. {Ref: ARMD 8:240; TALR 7:103}

PEARCE (PIERCE), WILLIAM (England, and Cecil and Kent Counties), captain by 1678; paid for his services in the late expedition against the Nanticoke Indians in 1678; court justice, 1679; he was possibly the William Peerce who was recommended for captain of a company of foot by Col. Henry Coursey in 1681; sheriff, 1685-1686; captain of a foot company, 1689 (name misspelled once as "William Peace"); lieutenant colonel, commissioned Oct 9, 1694; appointed naval officer in Cecil County at the head of the Bay on Oct 18, 1694; colonel by 1696; military officer who swore allegiance to the King & Queen of England in 1696; member of the Lower House of the Maryland Assembly between 1676 and 1707; justice of the peace by 1714; born circa 1643-1644 (aged about 56 when deposed in 1699 and aged about 70 when deposed in 1714), died testate by Mar 5, 1720/1 (date of probate; Isabella Pearce, widow). {Ref: ARMD 5:470, 7:95, 13:244, 15:255, 15:326, 17:76, 17:381, 20:139, 20:153, 20:160, 20:213, 20:545, 23:20, 24:25, 24:71; BDML II:641; CELR 2:302; INCC:134; MDEP:145; MDWB 16:333; MINV 6:155}

PEARCE, WILLIAM (Kent County), colonel by 1733. {Ref: INKC:178}

PEARK, ANNE, see "Robert Perke," q.v.

PEARSON, RICHARD (Oxford District), captain and master of the ship *Globe* in 1731. {Ref: CVPR:12}

PEASLY, JOHN (Anne Arundel County), military officer (rank not stated) who swore allegiance to the King & Queen of England in 1696; captain; died testate by Jan 29, 1708/9 (date of probate). {Ref: ARMD 20:541; AAGE:561-562; MDWB 12:321}

PECK, JOHN (Kent County), soldier (rank not stated) circa 1675; paid for his services in the late expedition against the Nanticoke Indians in 1678. {Ref: ARMD 7:94}

PECKET, ELIZABETH, see "William Pickett," q.v.

PEDRO, JOHN (Anne Arundel County), soldier (rank not stated) who served under Governor Stone at the Battle of the Severn on Mar 25, 1655 and was subsequently executed (shot). {Ref: FAAH:26}

PEERCE (PEIRCE), JOHN (St. Mary's County), lieutenant by 1676; commissioned "Captain of the Guard of the house at Mattapenny Sewall and that he have six horsemen and two files of ffoott under his command with a Sergeant and a Corporall" on Aug 5, 1676; Maryland Council ordered "that Capt. John Peerce (for the Safety of his Lordship's house at Mattapenny) have under his Command twelve horsemen, fowre & twenty ffootmen, two Sergeants, and a Corporall" on Aug 17, 1676; captain, paid for his services in the late expedition against the Nanticoke Indians in 1678. {Ref: ARMD 7:104, 15:118, 15:125}

PEGG, STEVEN (Talbot County), soldier (rank not stated) circa 1675; paid for his services in the late expedition against the Nanticoke Indians in 1678. {Ref: ARMD 7:92}

PEIGHEN, THOMAS (England and Anne Arundel County), captain and commander of the frigate *Coleman* riding at anchor in Severn River on Apr 17, 1712 and Apr 30, 1713 and Feb 13, 1715/6. {Ref: AALR PK:446, IB#2:26, 265}

PEIGHIN (PIEGHEN), THOMAS (England and St. Mary's County), captain and master of the ship *Supply* of Whitt in 1669; captain of the ship *Ruth* in 1676-1677; captain, 1679. {Ref: MDHM 5:340; ARMD 51:474, 66:301, 67:36; INAC 6:512}

PEIRCE, JOHN (Somerset County), soldier (rank not stated) circa 1675; paid for his services in the late expedition against the Nanticoke Indians in 1678. {Ref: ARMD 7:98}

PEIRCEFALL, JOHN (Kent County), soldier (rank not stated) circa 1675; paid for his services in the late expedition against the Nanticoke Indians in 1678. {Ref: ARMD 7:94}

PEIRCY (PIERCY), CHEESEMAN (Prince George's and Anne Arundel Counties), captain and commander of the ship *William and Martha* in 1722-1726, riding in the mouth of Severn River on Apr 28, 1725 and riding in Patuxent River on Apr 16, 1726 (name mistakenly listed once as "Cheesman Pierey"). {Ref: AALR SY#1:83; PGLR I:465, M:149}

PEIRPOINT, AMOS (Anne Arundel County), military officer (rank not stated) who swore allegiance to the King & Queen of England in 1696; died testate by Jun 24, 1718 (date of probate). {Ref: ARMD 20:541; MDWB 14:680; MDAD 2:354}

PEIRSON, JOHN (Dorchester County), soldier (rank not stated) circa 1675; paid for his services in the late expedition against the Nanticoke Indians in 1678. {Ref: ARMD 7:93}

PELLEW, HUMPHREY (England and Annapolis), captain by 1696; commander of the ship *Braggett* in 1698. {Ref: ARMD 20:460, 23:434}

PELLEY, RICHARD (St. Mary's County), soldier (rank not stated) circa 1675; paid for his services in the late expedition against the Nanticoke Indians in 1678. {Ref: ARMD 7:103}

PEMBROOKE, JOHN (Calvert County), probable soldier (rank not stated) before 1682; paid for his services out of an assessment levied by the General Assembly for the public good in 1682. {Ref: ARMD 7:440}

PENN, WILLIAM (England and St. Mary's County), captain and master of the ship *Amity* of London in 1690; captain and master of a ship (no name given) riding at anchor at the mouth of the Patuxent River on Jul 1, 1695 (date of petition); died by Nov 3, 1696 (date of inventory). {Ref: ARMD 8:237, 20:306; INAC 15:52}

PENSAX, DANIELL (Somerset County), captain by 1688. {Ref: INAC 10:65}

PENURY, WILLIAM (Cecil County), probable soldier (rank not stated) before 1682; paid for his services out of an assessment levied by the General Assembly for the public good in 1682. {Ref: ARMD 7:440}

PENY, ROBERT (Somerset County), Protestant and probable soldier in the Revolution of 1689; signed an address and took a loyalty oath supporting the King of England and "for enabling us to defend ourselves against all invaders" on Nov 28, 1689. {Ref: ARMD 8:141}

PEOPLE, JOHN (Dorchester County), soldier (rank not stated) circa 1675; paid for his services in the late expedition against the Nanticoke Indians in 1678. {Ref: ARMD 7:93}

PEPPER, RICHARD (Somerset County), Protestant and probable soldier in the Revolution of 1689; signed an address and took a loyalty oath supporting the King of England and "for enabling us to defend ourselves against all invaders" on Nov 28, 1689. {Ref: ARMD 8:140}

PEPPER, TOBIAS (Somerset County), Protestant and probable soldier in the Revolution of 1689; signed an address and took a loyalty oath supporting the King of England and "for enabling us to defend ourselves against all invaders" on Nov 28, 1689; died intestate by Mar 22, 1721/2 (date of administration account). {Ref: ARMD 8:140; MDAD 4:119}

PERCE, EDWARD (England and St. Mary's), captain, mariner, and commander of the ship *Goulden Ffortune* riding at anchor in St. George's River on Jan 26, 1664/5. {Ref: ARMD 49:359}

PERICE, SAMUEL (Charles County), captain by 1722. {Ref: MDAD 4:224}

PERKE, ROBERT (Kent County), soldier (rank not stated) circa 1675; paid for his services in the late expedition against the Nanticoke Indians in 1678; "Robert Peark" died testate after Dec 19, 1706 (date will was written; no date of probate was given; Anne Peark, widow). {Ref: ARMD 7:94; MDWB 12:260}

PERKINS, BENJAMIN (Pocomoke District), captain and master of the ship *Rebecca* in 1730-1731. {Ref: CVPR:12}

PERKINS, JOHN (Somerset County), soldier (rank not stated) circa 1675; paid for his services in the late expedition against the Nanticoke Indians in 1678; born circa 1643 (aged about 70 when deposed in 1713). {Ref: ARMD 7:97; MDEP:147}

PERLE, JAMES (Dorchester County), soldier (rank not stated) circa 1675; paid for his services in the late expedition against the Nanticoke Indians in 1678; one "James Pearle" died testate by Mar 14, 1686/7 (date of probate). {Ref: ARMD 7:93; MDWB 4:238}

PERLE, JOHN (Talbot County), soldier (rank not stated) circa 1675; paid for his services in the late expedition against the Nanticoke Indians in 1678. {Ref: ARMD 7:88}

PERREY, WILLIAM (Talbot County), soldier (rank not stated) circa 1675; paid for his services in the late expedition against the Nanticoke Indians in 1678. {Ref: ARMD 7:87}

PERRIE, NICHOLAS (England and St. Mary's), helper on the ship *Dove* in 1633-1634. {Ref: FMDP:343}

PERRIE (PERRY), SAMUEL (Prince George's County), captain and mariner by 1712; commander of the ship *Generous Jenny* in 1714; captain of the galley *Hope* in 1723; major by 1724; member of the Lower House of the Maryland Assembly, 1728; died intestate by Dec 16, 1729 (date of inventory; Sarah Perrie, widow, later married Patrick Andrew). {Ref: ARMD 25:501; BDML II:643-644; PGLR Q:225; MINV 15:296; MDAD 11:130}

PERRIE, SARAH, see "Samuel Perrie," q.v.

PERRIS, ---- (Calvert County), captain by 1686. {Ref: INAC 9:263}

PERRY, RICHARD (England and Calvert County), captain by 1672; member of the Lower House of the Maryland Assembly in 1671; an early land owner in what is now Prince George's County, he returned to England in 1672. {Ref: ARMD 51:87; BDML II:644; PGLR A:161}

PERRY (PAREY), RICHARD (Prince George's County), captain before 1712. {Ref: PGLR F Old 5:213, 5:588}

PERRYMAN (PERRIMAN), JOHN (Anne Arundel County), captain and commander of the ship *Alentego* riding at anchor in South River on Sep 24, 1720; commander of the ship *Ruby* riding in South River on May 20, 1723. {Ref: AALR CW#1:256, RCW#2:151}

PERSONS, JOHN, see "John Parsons," q.v.

PETELL, JOHN (Patuxent District), captain and master of the ship *Greyhound* in 1730-1731. {Ref: CVPR:12}

PETER, JOHN (Somerset County), soldier (rank not stated) circa 1675; paid for his services in the late expedition against the Nanticoke Indians in 1678. {Ref: ARMD 7:97}

PETER, SAMUEL (Calvert County), ranger under the command of Capt. Richard Brightwell in 1692. {Ref: ARMD 8:445}

PETERFRANCK, JOHN (Somerset County), Protestant and probable soldier in the Revolution of 1689; signed an address and took a loyalty oath supporting the King of England and "for enabling us to defend ourselves against all invaders" on Nov 28, 1689. {Ref: ARMD 8:140}

PETERKIN, JAMES (Dorchester County), soldier (rank not stated) circa 1675; paid for his services in the late expedition against the Nanticoke Indians in 1678. {Ref: ARMD 7:93}

PETERS, EDWARD (Anne Arundel County), captain by 1721. {Ref: MDAD 4:32}

PETERSON, ARCHIBALD (Anne Arundel County), captain and commander of the ship *George* riding at anchor in South River on Jun 6, 1718. {Ref: AALR IB#2:464}

PETERSON, HENDRICK (Cecil or Kent County), Indian interpreter by 1697-1698. {Ref: ARMD 23:428}

PETERSON, JACOB (Charles County), mariner by 1677. {Ref: CHLR G:162}

PETERSON, JEFFRY (Cecil County), corporal before 1678; paid for his services in the late expedition against the Nanticoke Indians in 1678; died testate by Nov 21, 1709 (date of probate). {Ref: ARMD 7:95; MDWB 13:234}

PETERSON, THOMAS (Talbot County), soldier (rank not stated) circa 1675; paid for his services in the late expedition against the Nanticoke Indians in 1678. {Ref: ARMD 7:92}

PETT, THOMAS (Kent County), soldier (rank not stated) on Isle of Kent who swore allegiance to the Commonwealth of England on Apr 5, 1652. {Ref: INKC:101}

PEVERELL (PEVERALL, PEVERILL), DANIELL (Spesutie Hundred, Baltimore County), soldier (rank not stated) circa 1675; paid for his services in the late expedition against the Nanticoke Indians in 1678; Protestant and probable soldier in the Revolution of 1689; signed an address and took a loyalty oath supporting the King of England and the reestablishment of Lord Baltimore into power on Nov 28, 1689; died testate by May 2, 1692 (date of probate; Hannah Peverell, widow, later married George Smith). {Ref: ARMD 7:95, 8:137; BBCF:502-503; Land Office HS#1:350}

PEY, JOHN (Kent County), soldier (rank not stated) circa 1675; paid for his services in the late expedition against the Nanticoke Indians in 1678. {Ref: ARMD 7:94}

PHEBUS, GEORGE (Somerset County), soldier (rank not stated) circa 1675; paid for his services in the late expedition against the Nanticoke Indians in 1678; Protestant and probable soldier in the Revolution of 1689; signed an address and took a loyalty oath supporting the King of England and "for enabling us to defend ourselves against all invaders" on Nov 28, 1689. {Ref: ARMD 7:100, 8:140}

PHELPS, CUTHBERT (Talbot County), soldier (rank not stated) circa 1675; paid for his services in the late expedition against the Nanticoke Indians in 1678. {Ref: ARMD 7:91}

PHELPS, DARBY (Talbot County), soldier (rank not stated) circa 1675; paid for his services in the late expedition against the Nanticoke Indians in 1678. {Ref: ARMD 7:92}

PHELPS, JOHN (St. Mary's County), naval officer for the Potomac District in 1712. {Ref: ARMD 29:86}

PHEYPO, MARKS (St. Mary's County), sergeant by 1647 under Capt. John Price at the fort at St. Inego's (listed as "Serjt. Mark's Pheipo" in 1652); "Mark Pheypo" was born circa 1617 (aged about 35 when deposed in 1652, but another deposition in 1658 listed his age as about 58, thus born circa 1600);

"Marke Phepo" died testate by Feb 8, 1669 (date of probate). {Ref: ARMD 4:313, 4:514, 10:134, 10:239, 41:161; MDEP:148; MDWB 1:370}

PHIBBARD (PHIPHEARD, PHIPPELD), PETER (Calvert County), captain and mariner by 1687; died by November, 1688 (date of inventory). {Ref: INAC 10:16, 10:135, 10:282}

PHILLIPS, BENJAMIN (Anne Arundel County), captain and commander of the ship *John and Margrett* riding at South River on Sep 6, 1705. {Ref: AALR WT#2:249}

PHILLIPS, EDWARD (England and Anne Arundel County), captain and commander of the ship *Cheswick* or *Chiswick* of London riding at anchor in South River on May 1, 1712. {Ref: AALR PK:448; CHLR D#2:80}

PHILLIPS, GEORGE (St. Mary's County), captain and master of the ship *John* in 1692-1695. {Ref: ARMD 8:371; INAC 10:403}

PHILLIPS (PHILIPS), HENRY (Somerset County), Protestant and probable soldier in the Revolution of 1689; signed an address and took a loyalty oath supporting the King of England and "for enabling us to defend ourselves against all invaders" on Nov 28, 1689. {Ref: ARMD 8:139}

PHILLIPS, JAMES (England and Baltimore County), soldier (rank not stated) circa 1675; paid for his services in the late expedition against the Nanticoke Indians in 1678; paid for his services out of an assessment levied by the General Assembly for the public good in 1682; officer of the town of Baltimore in 1686; baptized Dec 11, 1642 (at Sedgeley, Staffordshire), died testate by Jun 4, 1689 (date of probate; Susanna Phillips, widow, later married Benjamin Arnold). {Ref: ARMD 5:503, 7:95, 7:441, 7:611, 20:64, 20:109-110; BBCF:503}

PHILLIPS, JAMES (Baltimore County), Protestant and probable soldier in the Revolution of 1689; signed an address and took a loyalty oath supporting the King of England and the reestablishment of Lord Baltimore into power on Nov 28, 1689; captain of a "company of foot to be raised as formerly in Spesutia Hundred, within Baltimore County" in 1694; major, 1708-1714; member of the Lower House of the Maryland Assembly, 1699-1720; colonel, 1715-1720; died testate on Mar 30, 1720 (will probated on Apr 30, 1720; Johanna Phillips, widow, later married Aquila Hall). {Ref: ARMD 8:136, 27:202, 29:35, 30:107, 30:129, 33:566; BDML II:646; MDWB 16:18; MINV 10:174; BBCF:504; MDAD 10:274}

PHILLIPS, JOHANNA, see "James Phillips," q.v.

PHILLIPS (PHILIPS), JOHN (Kent County), soldier (rank not stated) on Isle of Kent who swore allegiance to the Commonwealth of England on Apr 5, 1652. {Ref: INKC:101}

PHILLIPS (PHILLIP), JOHN (Prince George's County), captain of a ship (no name given) riding in the Patuxent River on Dec 28, 1723 and Jan 24, 1724/5. {Ref: PGLR M:148-149}

PHILLIPS (PHILIPS), LOELING (county not indicated), private in the Maryland troops "raised to strengthen Albany, New York and resist the French and Indian enemies" in 1690. {Ref: SHMD I:355}

PHILLIPS, OWEN (England and Patuxent District), captain of a ship *Samuel and John* of London in 1696-1697. See "James White" and "George Bliss" and "Robert Pullman," q.v. {Ref: ARMD 23:28, 23:137, 25:556-557}

PHILLIPS, ROGER (Somerset County), Protestant and probable soldier in the Revolution of 1689; signed an address and took a loyalty oath supporting the King of England and "for enabling us to defend ourselves against all invaders" on Nov 28, 1689. {Ref: ARMD 8:141}

PHILLIPS, SAMUEL (Anne Arundel County), captain by 1680. {Ref: FAAH:490; INAC 7A:172}

PHILLIPS, SAMUEL, JR. (England, and Anne Arundel and St. Mary's Counties), captain, commander and master of the ship *Baltimore* of London, 1692-1698; captain and master of a ship (no name given) riding at anchor at the mouth of the Patuxent River on Jul 1, 1695 (date of petition); captain of a ship (no name given) in 1702; name listed at times without the "Jr." {Ref: ARMD 8:371, 20:306, 23:405, 23:466, 24:303, 25:588, 38:72; INAC 10:351}

PHILLIPS, SUSANNA, see "James Phillips," q.v.

PHILLIPS, THOMAS (Dorchester County), soldier (rank not stated) circa 1675; paid for his services in the late expedition against the Nanticoke Indians in 1678; one Thomas Phillips died testate by Jun 4, 1704 and another Thomas Phillips died testate by Aug 14, 1711. Additional research will be necessary before drawing conclusions. {Ref: ARMD 7:93; MDWB 13:350; Testamentary Proceedings 18:35, Div. B}

PHILLIPS, WILLIAM (New England and Annapolis), captain of the ship *Content* of New England in 1732-1733. {Ref: MDGZ, Mar 16, 1732/3}

PHILLIPS, WILLIAM (Talbot County), soldier (rank not stated) circa 1675; paid for his services in the late expedition against the Nanticoke Indians in 1678; born circa 1634 (aged about 19 when deposed in 1653). {Ref: ARMD 7:87, 10:288}

PHILPOTT, EDWARD (Charles County), Protestant and probable soldier in the Revolution of 1689; signed an address and took a loyalty oath supporting the King of England and the reestablishment of Lord Baltimore into power on Nov 28, 1689. See "William Smallwood," q.v. {Ref: ARMD 8:138}

PHILPOTT, ELEANOR, see "William Smallwood," q.v.

PHILPOTT, GEORGE (Anne Arundel County), captain and commander of the ship *Cinqueport* riding in West River on Feb 20, 1722/3. {Ref: AALR RCW#2:103}

PHILPOTT (PHILPOT), ROBERT (England and Kent Island), commander of the Isle of Kent, 1637; member of Assembly, Kent Isle, 1637; soldier (rank not stated) in 1642; born circa 1600, died by 1651. {Ref: ARMD 4:131-132; BDML II:646; INKC:178}

PHIPPEN, JOSEPH (Patuxent District), captain and master of the ship *John and Benjamin* in 1730-1731. {Ref: CVPR:12}

PICKARD (PICURD), NICHOLAS (Kent County), soldier (rank not stated) on Isle of Kent who swore allegiance to the Commonwealth of England on Apr 5,

1652; born circa 1610 (aged about 46 when deposed in 1656). {Ref: ARMD 54:70; INKC:101, 106}

PICKERIN, THOMAS (St. Mary's County), captain by 1679. {Ref: INAC 6:512}

PICKETT, WILLIAM (England, and Kent and Baltimore Counties), soldier (rank not stated) circa 1675; paid for his services in the late expedition against the Nanticoke Indians in 1678; member of the Lower House of the Maryland Assembly in 1708; "William Pecket" died testate by Jul 18, 1710 (date of probate; Elizabeth Pecket, widow, later married John Taylor). {Ref: ARMD 7:94, BDML II:647; BBCF:505; MDWB 13:122}

PIERCE (PEIRCE), JOHN, see "John Peerce," q.v.

PIHALL, PEETER (Kent County), soldier (rank not stated) in Capt. William Leeds (Leeads) Company by May 23, 1662, at which time he signed a petition about the misuse of company money by Capt. Thomas Brednox (Bradnox), late of Isle of Kent, deceased. {Ref: ARMD 3:455}

PIKE, STEPHEN (England and Annapolis), captain of the ship *Arabella* of London in 1731-1733. {Ref: MDGZ, Mar 16, 1732/3. {Ref: CVPR:12}

PILCAR, FRANCIS (Baltimore County), a sailor on the ship *Patapsco Merchant* lying in Patapsco River in October, 1734 and commanded by Darby Lux; he was reportedly a sailor and runaway servant of John Meales at Patapsco Ferry and "a Frenchman who speaks broken English." {Ref: MDGZ, Nov 1, 1734}

PILE (PILES), JOSEPH (St. Mary's County), court justice, 1679-1683 (quorum, 1685); captain and officer of the town of Newport in 1686; member of the Lower House of the Maryland Assembly, 1686-1688; died testate by Nov 8, 1692 (date of probate). {Ref: ARMD 5:502, 15:256, 15:326, 17:181-183, 17:379; BDML II:647; MDWB 6:64; INAC 10LC:22}

PILES, PHILEMON (Kent County), "seaman within the said county" and a "sailor belonging to the *Factor* of Bediford" in 1697. {Ref: ARMD 25:599}

PINDAR, EDWARD (England and Dorchester County), captain by 1691; elected to the Lower House of the Maryland Assembly in 1686, but resigned to become sheriff; died in February, 1692/3. {Ref: BDML II:648}

PINE, JOHN (Anne Arundel County), captain and commander of the ship *Prosperous Anne* riding at anchor at Beard's Creek in South River on Jun 30, 1708 and in South River on Mar 15, 1719/20 and Apr 25, 1721. {Ref: AALR WT#2:637, CW#1:131, 357}

PINEY, ALLEXANDER (England and St. Mary's County), captain and master of the ship *Nathaniell* of Bristol in 1693. {Ref: ARMD 20:182}

PINNELL, JOHN (England, and Anne Arundel and Talbot Counties), captain and master of the brigantine *Providence* riding at the port of Annapolis on Aug 22, 1706; commander of the ship *Rachell* riding at anchor in the Great Choptank River on Jun 15, 1715. {Ref: AALR WT#2:385, IB#2:216}

PINNER, RICHARD (Virginia and St. Mary's County), mariner by 1651; born circa 1615 (aged about 36 when deposed in 1651). {Ref: ARMD 10:103-104}

PIPER, JOHN (Charles County), soldier (rank not stated) who was issued a "gun or fowling piece" by Col. Warren on Sep 15, 1694; born circa 1628 (aged about 30 when deposed in 1657 and 1658, and aged about 34 when deposed in 1662). {Ref: ARMD 20:206, 20:208, 41:26, 53:22, 53:239}

PIPER, WILLIAM (Somerset County), captain by 1692; died by Apr 7, 1703 (date of inventory; name listed once as "Capt. William Pipper"). {Ref: OSES:153, ARMD 23:404, 25:598; INAC 24:112, 27:33; SOJR I:101}

PITT, JOHN (Dorchester County), captain by 1728. {Ref: MDAD 9:216}

PITT (PITTS), JOHN (Talbot County), soldier (rank not stated) circa 1675; paid for his services in the late expedition against the Nanticoke Indians in 1678; born circa 1648 (aged about 60 when deposed in 1708). {Ref: ARMD 7:89; MDEP:150}

PITT (PITTS), THOMAS (England and Patuxent District), captain, commander, and master of the ship *Francis and Mary* of London, 1691-1694; captain and commander of the ship *Providence* of London in 1697. {Ref: ARMD 8:238, 20:147, 23:137}

PITTS, ---- (Baltimore County), captain by 1697. {Ref: INAC 15:151}

PITTS, JOHN (Dorchester County), soldier and probable officer in the 1730's; captain before 1740 (wife Mary, aged about 50, deposed in 1741). {Ref: DOLR 12 Old 124}

PLANNER (PLANER), WILLIAM, JR. (Annamessex Hundred, Somerset County), Protestant and soldier in the Revolution of 1689; signed an address and took a loyalty oath supporting the King of England and "for enabling us to defend ourselves against all invaders" on Nov 28, 1689; captain before 1715; county commissioner in 1715; named as one of the guardians of the children of Capt. William Bolithoe, deceased, in March, 1721/2; died testate by Oct 1, 1734 (date of probate). {Ref: ARMD 8:141; SOJR III:1; CESM:6; MDWB 17:120, 21:226; MINV 20:319}

PLANNER (PLANER), WILLIAM, SR. (Annamessex Hundred, Somerset County), soldier (rank not stated) circa 1675; paid for his services in the late expedition against the Nanticoke Indians in 1678; Protestant and soldier in the Revolution of 1689; signed an address and took a loyalty oath supporting the King of England and "for enabling us to defend ourselves against all invaders" on Nov 28, 1689; major by 1696. {Ref: ARMD 7:100, 8:141, 23:22; OSES:289}

PLATER, GEORGE (England, and St. Mary's and Calvert Counties), Protestant and probable soldier in the Revolution of 1689; signed an address and took a loyalty oath supporting the King of England and the reestablishment of Lord Baltimore into power on Nov 28, 1689; naval officer of Patuxent District, 1693-1694; acting attorney general, 1691-1692; born circa 1664 (aged about 30 when deposed in 1694), died before Jan 1, 1707/8 (date of inventory). {Ref: ARMD 8:146, 20:179; MDEP:150; BDML II:649-650; INAC 28:26}

PLATER, GEORGE (Annapolis and St. Mary's County), naval officer for the port of Patuxent, 1729-1755; soldier and probable officer in the 1730's; colonel by 1748; member of the Upper House of the Maryland Assembly, 1732-1755;

born circa 1695 (son of George Plater, *q.v.*), died May 17, 1755 (will probated on Jun 6, 1755). {Ref: BDML II:649-650; MDWB 29:466-468; MDCB 82:1}

PLEBE, GEORGE (Charles County), Protestant and probable soldier in the Revolution of 1689; signed an address and took a loyalty oath supporting the King of England and the reestablishment of Lord Baltimore into power on Nov 28, 1689. {Ref: ARMD 8:138}

PLESTO (PLESTOE), EDWARD (Kent County), captain before 1717; died testate by Jun 18, 1718 (date of probate). {Ref: MDWB 14:638; MINV 1:236; MDAD 3:267}

PLOVEY, WILLIAM (Dorchester County), soldier (rank not stated) circa 1675; paid for his services in the late expedition against the Nanticoke Indians in 1678. {Ref: ARMD 7:93}

PLUMMER, HENRY (Dorchester County), soldier (rank not stated) circa 1675; paid for his services in the late expedition against the Nanticoke Indians in 1678. {Ref: ARMD 7:93}

PLUMMER, JOHN (Dorchester County), soldier (rank not stated) circa 1675; paid for his services in the late expedition against the Nanticoke Indians in 1678. {Ref: ARMD 7:93}

POINTER, THOMAS, see "Thomas Poynter," q.v.

POLANTINE, NICOLAS (St. Mary's County), soldier (rank not stated) in 1642. {Ref: ARMD 4:130-131}

POLK, ROBERT (Somerset County), Protestant and probable soldier in the Revolution of 1689; signed an address and took a loyalty oath supporting the King of England and "for enabling us to defend ourselves against all invaders" on Nov 28, 1689. {Ref: ARMD 8:140}

POLK, WILLIAM (Somerset County), Protestant and probable soldier in the Revolution of 1689; signed an address and took a loyalty oath supporting the King of England and "for enabling us to defend ourselves against all invaders" on Nov 28, 1689. {Ref: ARMD 8:140}

POLLARD, TOBIAS (Dorchester County), captain by 1728; major by 1740; member of the Lower House of the Maryland Assembly, 1716-1718; born circa 1669 (possibly in Calvert County), died testate by Sep 11, 1749 (date of probate in Dorchester County). {Ref: BDML II:655-656; MDWB 27:290}

POLLETT, THOMAS (Somerset County), Protestant and probable soldier in the Revolution of 1689; signed an address and took a loyalty oath supporting the King of England and "for enabling us to defend ourselves against all invaders" on Nov 28, 1689. {Ref: ARMD 8:140}

POLLINGTON, JOHN (Dorchester County), soldier (rank not stated) circa 1675; paid for his services in the late expedition against the Nanticoke Indians in 1678. {Ref: ARMD 7:93}

PONTINGALL, WILLIAM (Nanjemy Parish, Charles County), a seafaring man in 1697. {Ref: ARMD 25:597}

POOLE, THOMAS (Somerset County), Protestant and probable soldier in the Revolution of 1689; signed an address and took a loyalty oath supporting the

King of England and "for enabling us to defend ourselves against all invaders" on Nov 28, 1689. {Ref: ARMD 8:141}

POOR, THOMAS (county not indicated), private in the Maryland troops "raised to strengthen Albany, New York and resist the French and Indian enemies" in 1690. {Ref: SHMD I:355}

POORE, JOHN (Talbot County), soldier (rank not stated) circa 1675; paid for his services in the late expedition against the Nanticoke Indians in 1678. {Ref: ARMD 7:91}

POPE, FRANCIS (Charles County), soldier (rank not stated) before 1664; signed a petition to the governor to "displace Capt. William Boreman whom was lately constituted captain of the militia" on Sep 12, 1666; born circa 1610 (aged about 38 when deposed in 1648), died testate by Jan 27, 1671/2 (date of probate). {Ref: ARMD 3:556, 3:561, 4:372; CHLR B:379; MDWB 1:470}

POPE, JOHN (Dorchester County), soldier (rank not stated) circa 1675; paid for his services in the late expedition against the Nanticoke Indians in 1678; paid for his services out of an assessment levied by the General Assembly for the public good in 1682. {Ref: ARMD 7:92, 7:440}

POPE, JOHN (Somerset County), Protestant and probable soldier in the Revolution of 1689; signed an address and took a loyalty oath supporting the King of England and "for enabling us to defend ourselves against all invaders" on Nov 28, 1689; died testate by Apr 10, 1721/2 (date of probate; Mary Pope, widow). {Ref: ARMD 8:140; MDWB 16:430; MDAD 4:280}

POPE, MARY, see "John Pope," q.v.

POPE, NATHANIEL (Kent and St. Mary's Counties, and Virginia), member of the Maryland Assembly in 1637; officer "entrusted by Gov. Calvert with the task of pacifying Kent Island" in 1646; settled permanently in Virginia by 1654; lieutenant colonel, Westmoreland Troops, 1655; court justice by 1657; died in 1660 in Virginia. {Ref: BMDL II:656; RMHF I:299; CHLR B:44}

POPELEY, RICHARD (Charles River, Virginia and Kent Island), captain before 1640; born circa 1601 (aged about 39 when deposed in 1640). {Ref: ARMD 5:225-227}

POPELY, THOMAS (Kent County), soldier (rank not stated) circa 1675; paid for his services in the late expedition against the Nanticoke Indians in 1678. {Ref: ARMD 7:94}

POPLESTONE, PHILL. (county or port not indicated), captain and master of the ship *Encrease* which "came out of Ireland" in 1678. {Ref: MDHM 5:339}

PORTER, ELIZABETH, see "John Porter," q.v.

PORTER, HENRY (St. Mary's County), Protestant and probable soldier in the Revolution of 1689; signed an address and took a loyalty oath supporting the King of England and the reestablishment of Lord Baltimore into power on Nov 28, 1689 (name listed as "Henry Portter"). {Ref: ARMD 8:146}

PORTER, JOHN (Somerset County), Protestant and probable soldier in the Revolution of 1689; signed an address and took a loyalty oath supporting the

King of England and "for enabling us to defend ourselves against all invaders" on Nov 28, 1689; died testate by May 24, 1709 (date of probate; Elizabeth Porter, widow). {Ref: ARMD 8:141; MDWB 12:173, pt. 2}

PORTER, JOHN (Kent County), soldier (rank not stated) circa 1675; paid for his services in the late expedition against the Nanticoke Indians in 1678. {Ref: ARMD 7:94}

PORTER, PETER, JR. (Virginia and Anne Arundel County), probable soldier by 1675; born in 1640, killed by Indians before Aug 1, 1676 (date of inventory). {Ref: RMHF II:293; INAC 3:87}

PORTER, PETER, SR. (England, Virginia, and Anne Arundel County), soldier (rank not stated) in Capt. Eppes' Company of Indian Fighters in 1623-1624 along the Eastern Shore of Virginia; removed to Anne Arundel County in 1649; born in 1602, died intestate in 1658. {Ref: RMHF II:293}

PORTER, WILLIAM (St. Mary's County), soldier (rank not stated) circa 1675; paid for his services in the late expedition against the Nanticoke Indians in 1678; captain by 1694. {Ref: ARMD 7:102, 20:228}

PORTWOOD, MARTIN (Charles County), soldier (rank not stated) who was issued a "gun or fowling piece" by Col. Warren on Sep 15, 1694. {Ref: ARMD 20:206, 20:208}

POSEY, BENJAMEN (Charles County), Protestant and probable soldier in the Revolution of 1689; signed an address and took a loyalty oath supporting the King of England and the reestablishment of Lord Baltimore into power on Nov 28, 1689. {Ref: ARMD 8:138}

POTT, FRANCE (St. Mary's County), captain by 1646. {Ref: ARMD 3:179}

POTT, MARTHA, see "Hans Hanson," q.v.

POTT (POTTS), WILLIAM (Kent County), captain by 1703; justice by 1707; major before 1716; died by Sep 27, 1716 (date of probate). See "Hans Hanson," q.v. {Ref: CMSP 1:7 - The Black Books; MDWB 14:158; INAC 37B:191; INKC:150}

POTT (POTTS), WILLIAM (Kent County), captain by 1733 and to at least 1742. {Ref: INKC:178}

POTTER, MARTIN (Kent County), mariner by 1734; captain and master of the brigantine *Charming Sally* (built in 1733) in 1737. {Ref: INKC:178; MDCB 82:47}

POULSON (POWLSON), GILBERT (Anne Arundel County), captain before 1722; captain, mariner and master of the ship *Dolphin* in 1724-1725. {Ref: ARMD 25:426; MDAD 5:74; AALR SY#1:291}

POW, ---- (Prince George's County), captain by 1719. {Ref: MDAD 2:1}

POWELL, BERNARD (Talbot County), soldier (rank not stated) circa 1675; paid for his services in the late expedition against the Nanticoke Indians in 1678. {Ref: ARMD 7:88}

POWELL, CHRISTOPHER (Talbot County), probable soldier (rank not stated) before 1682; paid for his services out of an assessment levied by the General Assembly for the public good in 1682. {Ref: ARMD 7:439}

POWELL, GEORGE (Talbot County), soldier (rank not stated) circa 1675; paid for his services in the late expedition against the Nanticoke Indians in 1678; paid for his services out of an assessment levied by the General Assembly for the public good in 1682. {Ref: ARMD 7:90, 7:440}

POWELL, HOWELL (Talbot County), soldier (rank not stated) circa 1675; paid for his services in the late expedition against the Nanticoke Indians in 1678. {Ref: ARMD 7:89}

POWELL, JAMES, see "Richard Colegate," q.v.

POWELL, JOHN (Anne Arundel County), probable soldier (rank not stated) before 1682; paid for his services out of an assessment levied by the General Assembly for the public good in 1682; "John Powell, Jr., son of John Powell, deceased, of Anne Arundel County" died testate by Apr 6, 1716 (date of probate). {Ref: ARMD 7:440; MDWB 14:227}

POWELL, ROBERT (Charles County), probable soldier (rank not stated) before 1682; paid for his services out of an assessment levied by the General Assembly for the public good in 1682; Protestant and probable soldier in the Revolution of 1689; signed an address and took a loyalty oath supporting the King of England and the reestablishment of Lord Baltimore into power on Nov 28, 1689 (name was listed twice: once as "Robert Powell" and once as "Robert Powel"). {Ref: ARMD 7:440, 8:138}

POWELL, STEWART (England and Queen Anne's County), captain and commander of the ship *Adventure* riding at anchor in Chester River on Jun 24, 1728. {Ref: QALR IK#C:186}

POWELL, WALTER (Somerset County), possible soldier (rank not stated) circa 1675; paid for his services in the late expedition against the Nanticoke Indians in 1678; died testate by Feb 4, 1696/7 (date of probate). {Ref: ARMD 7:99; MDWB 7:151}

POWELL, WILLIAM (Kent County), military officer (rank not stated) who swore allegiance to the King & Queen of England in 1696. {Ref: ARMD 20:541}

POWERS, MR., see "Daniel Haynes," q.v.

POYNTER (POINTER), THOMAS (Virginia and Somerset County), Protestant and soldier in the Revolution of 1689; signed an address and took a loyalty oath supporting the King of England and "for enabling us to defend ourselves against all invaders" on Nov 28, 1689; military officer (rank not stated) who swore allegiance to the King & Queen of England in 1696; captain by 1698; died testate by Dec 3, 1705 (date of probate; Elizabeth Poynter, widow). {Ref: ARMD 8:140, 20:544; INAC 17:125; MDWB 12:9}

PRATT, THOMAS (Anne Arundel County), soldier (rank not stated) circa 1675; paid for his services in the late expedition against the Nanticoke Indians in 1678; died testate by Jul 11, 1711 (date of probate; Jane Pratt, widow). {Ref: ARMD 7:96; MDWB 13:337}

PREIND, JAMES (county or port not indicated), captain and master of the ship *Richard and James* of Bristol in 1690. {Ref: ARMD 8:238}

PRENTICE, J. (Annapolis District), captain of the ship *Sea Flower* in 1734. {Ref: MDGZ, Aug 2, 1734}

PRENTICE, WILLIAM (Somerset County), soldier (rank not stated) circa 1675; paid for his services in the late expedition against the Nanticoke Indians in 1678. {Ref: ARMD 7:99}

PRESSLY, PETTER (St. Mary's County), colonel by 1720. {Ref: MDAD 3:76}

PRESSON, BENJAMIN (Potomac District), captain and master of the ship *Tryall* in 1730-1731. {Ref: CVPR:12}

PRESTON, JAMES (Baltimore County), soldier (rank not stated) by 1711; Maryland Assembly noted that "upon his Petition setting forth that he was Windbound & could not come to the muster is dismissed on promise to do his Duty" on Oct 26, 1711; died testate by Nov 5, 1729 (date of probate; Sarah Preston, widow). {Ref: ARMD 29:11; BBCF:518-519; MDWB 19:778}

PRESTON, MARY, see "Thomas Preston," q.v.

PRESTON, RICHARD (England, Virginia, and Calvert County), Puritan leader in Virginia before 1650; colonel and commander on the north side of the Patuxent River in Maryland by 1651; parliamentary commissioner in 1652; participated in the Battle of the Severn on Mar 25, 1655; temporary secretary of the province in 1665-1666; member of the Lower House of the Maryland Assembly in 1654-1666 (representing Calvert County) and in 1669 (representing Dorchester County); prominent leader of the Puritan forces in Maryland during the commonwealth period; died testate by Jan 8, 1669/70 (date of probate in Calvert County). {Ref: BDML II:660; HCCM:34, 303-304; FAAH:22, 37, 112-113; MDWB 1:357; LMCL:83}

PRESTON, SARAH, see "James Preston," q.v.

PRESTON, THOMAS (Baltimore County), soldier (rank not stated) circa 1675; paid for his services in the late expedition against the Nanticoke Indians in 1678; cornet before 1682; paid for his services out of an assessment levied by the General Assembly for the public good in 1682; captain who swore allegiance to the King & Queen of England in 1696; captain on north side of the Gunpowder, 1702-1703 (name listed once as "Thomas Prestone"); born circa 1646 (aged about 58 when deposed in 1704), died testate by Dec 30, 1710 (date of probate; Mary Preston, widow). {Ref: ARMD 7:95, 7:441, 20:544, 23:20; INAC 21:233; MDEP:152; BBCF:518; BCTL:24, 33; MDWB 13:155}

PRETTIMAN, JOHN (St. Mary's County), soldier (rank not stated) before 1642 who was hired to go on Capt. Mathias De Sousa's pinnace for two months service in 1642; "Jac: Preteman" was paid for 3 weeks' service under Capt. William Brainthwaite in November, 1642. {Ref: ARMD 3:119, 3:122, 4:138}

PRICE, ABRAHAM (St. Mary's County), soldier (rank not stated) circa 1675; paid for his services in the late expedition against the Nanticoke Indians in 1678; Protestant and probable soldier in the Revolution of 1689; signed an address and took a loyalty oath supporting the King of England and the reestablishment of Lord Baltimore into power on Nov 28, 1689. {Ref: ARMD 7:102, 8:146}

PRICE, ANDREW (Talbot County), soldier (rank not stated) circa 1675; paid for his services in the late expedition against the Nanticoke Indians in 1678; died testate by Oct 28, 1700 (date of probate; Mary Price, widow). {Ref: ARMD 7:88, 7:90; MDWB 6:404}

PRICE, ANDREW (Queen Anne's County), captain and justice of the peace by 1724; captain of the Fourth Company of Foot on Jun 30, 1732. {Ref: QALR IK#B:267; MDHR 1:11}

PRICE, ANDREW (Talbot County), mariner by 1717; captain and master of the sloop *Adventure* in 1734-1735 (formerly the *Patuxent*, built at Newbury, Massachusetts in 1733); captain and master of the brigantine *Rebecca* in 1736 (built at the Choptank River in 1735). {Ref: QALR IK#A:124; MDCB 82:26, 82:42}

PRICE, EDWARD (Charles County), corporal before 1678; paid for his services in the late expedition against the Nanticoke Indians in 1678. {Ref: ARMD 7:100}

PRICE, ELIZABETH, see "John Price," q.v.

PRICE, EVAN (St. Mary's County), soldier (rank not stated) circa 1675; paid for his services in the late expedition against the Nanticoke Indians in 1678. {Ref: ARMD 7:103}

PRICE, HENRY (Queen Anne's County), mariner by 1716. {Ref: QALR IK#A:88}

PRICE, HENRY (Talbot County), Protestant and probable soldier in the Revolution of 1689; signed an address and took a loyalty oath supporting the King of England and the reestablishment of Lord Baltimore into power on Nov 18, 1689. {Ref: ARMD 8:134}

PRICE, JACOB (Annapolis District), captain and master of the sloop *Pilgrim* in 1728. {Ref: MDGZ, Dec 31, 1728}

PRICE, JOHN (county not indicated), captain by 1657. {Ref: ARMD 10:552}

PRICE, JOHN (St. George's Hundred, St. Mary's County), captain of the fort at St. Inego's, 1646-1652; mustermaster general, 1648; member of the Upper House (Maryland Council), 1648-1660; provincial court justice, 1648-1654, 1658-1660; colonel who served under Governor Stone at the Battle of the Severn on Mar 25, 1655; councellor, 1659; born circa 1607-1608 (aged about 40 when deposed on Jan 4, 1647/8), died testate by Mar 11, 1660/1 (date of probate). {Ref: ARMD 1:214, 1:382, 4:312, 4:358, 10:72, 10:246, 41:51, 41:141; BDML II:660-661; FAAH:26; MDWB 1:141}

PRICE, JOHN (Talbot County), soldier (rank not stated) circa 1675; paid for his services in the late expedition against the Nanticoke Indians in 1678; colonel and land owner on Chester River before 1694; one John Price, of Bullenbrooke, died testate by Nov 21, 1702 (date of probate; Margery Price, widow) and another John Price died testate by May 23, 1713 (date of probate; Elizabeth Price, widow). Additional research will be necessary before drawing conclusions. {Ref: ARMD 7:90; TALR 7:105; MDWB 11:257, 13:562}

PRICE, JOHN (Somerset County), soldier (rank not stated) circa 1675; paid for his services in the late expedition against the Nanticoke Indians in 1678; died testate by Oct 19, 1703 (date of probate; Elizabeth Price, widow). {Ref: ARMD 7:99; MDWB 3:260}

PRICE, JOHN (Scotland, Boston, and Maryland, port not indicated), captain and master of the English built pink *Providence* in 1695. {Ref: ARMD 20:340}

PRICE, MARGERY, see "John Price," q.v.
PRICE, MARY, see "Andrew Price," q.v.
PRICE, THOMAS (Somerset County), soldier (rank not stated) circa 1675; paid for his services in the late expedition against the Nanticoke Indians in 1678. {Ref: ARMD 7:100}
PRICE, THOMAS (St. Mary's County), soldier (rank not stated) circa 1675; paid for his services in the late expedition against the Nanticoke Indians in 1678; captain by 1689. {Ref: ARMD 7:103; INAC 10:230}
PRICE, THOMAS, JR. (St. Mary's County), Protestant and probable soldier in the Revolution of 1689; signed an address and took a loyalty oath supporting the King of England and the reestablishment of Lord Baltimore into power on Nov 28, 1689. {Ref: ARMD 8:147}
PRICE, WILLIAM (Kent County), soldier (rank not stated) on Isle of Kent who swore allegiance to the Commonwealth of England on Apr 5, 1652; soldier (rank not stated) in Capt. William Leeds (Leeads) Company by May 23, 1662, at which time he signed a petition about the misuse of company money by Capt. Thomas Brednox (Bradnox), late of Isle of Kent, deceased; born circa 1625 (aged about 30 when deposed in 1655 and aged about 30 or 31 when deposed in 1656). {Ref: ARMD 3:455, 54:62-64, 54:71; INKC:101, 108}
PRICE, WILLIAM (Kent County), military officer (rank not stated) who swore allegiance to the King & Queen of England in 1696. {Ref: ARMD 20:540}
PRICHARD (PRITCHARD), JOHN (England and Prince George's County), gentleman, merchant, and captain by the 1730's; died testate by Oct 30, 1741 (date of probate; Katherine Prichard, widow). {Ref: MDWB 22:398; MINV 26:462, 27:430; MDAD 19:179}
PRISE, PHILIP (county not indicated), private in the Maryland troops "raised to strengthen Albany, New York and resist the French and Indian enemies" in 1690. {Ref: SHMD I:355}
PRISWICK, CHRISTOPHER (Prince George's County and Patuxent District), captain by 1730; master of the ship *Charming Sukey* in 1731. {Ref: CVPR:12; MDAD 10:692}
PRITTY, ISAAC (Somerset County), mariner by 1726. {Ref: MDAD 8:48}
PRIVIT, ---- (county or port not indicated), captain by 1693. {Ref: ARMD 20:186}
PROBATE, JOHN (county not indicated), probable soldier (rank not stated) before 1682; paid for his services out of an assessment levied by the General Assembly for the public good in 1682. {Ref: ARMD 7:441}
PROBE, EDWARD (St. Mary's County), Protestant and probable soldier in the Revolution of 1689; signed an address and took a loyalty oath supporting the King of England and the reestablishment of Lord Baltimore into power on Nov 28, 1689. {Ref: ARMD 8:147}
PROCTER, ALEXANDER (Somerset County), Protestant and probable soldier in the Revolution of 1689; signed an address and took a loyalty oath supporting

the King of England and "for enabling us to defend ourselves against all invaders" on Nov 28, 1689. {Ref: ARMD 8:139}

PROCTER, ROBERT (Anne Arundel County), soldier (rank not stated) circa 1675; paid for his services in the late expedition against the Nanticoke Indians in 1678; submitted a request for payment for "boat and shallop services" to the Maryland Council on Sep 3, 1681; died intestate by Feb 6, 1698/9 (date of administration account). {Ref: ARMD 7:96, 7:149; INAC 17:176}

PROFFITT, THOMAS (Somerset County), soldier (rank not stated) circa 1675; paid for his services in the late expedition against the Nanticoke Indians in 1678. {Ref: ARMD 7:99}

PROUT, TIMOTHY (New England and Somerset County), captain of the ship *Providence* of Boston in 1681; apparently he visited, but did not live in Maryland. {Ref: INAC 7B:98; HCCM:471}

PROW (TROW?), JOSEPH (Potomac District), captain and master of the ship *Mary* in 1730-1731. {Ref: CVPR:12}

PRUETT, ANDREW (Dorchester County), soldier (rank not stated) circa 1675; paid for his services in the late expedition against the Nanticoke Indians in 1678. {Ref: ARMD 7:93}

PRYOR, WILLIAM (Kent and Queen Anne's Counties), probable soldier (rank not stated) before 1682; paid for his services out of an assessment levied by the General Assembly for the public good in 1682. {Ref: ARMD 7:439}

PUCKER, NATHANIEL (Talbot County), Protestant and probable soldier in the Revolution of 1689; signed an address and took a loyalty oath supporting the King of England and the reestablishment of Lord Baltimore into power on Nov 18, 1689. {Ref: ARMD 8:134}

PUDDINGTON, GEORGE (England, Virginia, and South River, Anne Arundel County), captain by 1650; member of the Lower House of the Maryland Assembly, 1650-1651, 1663-1664; died testate by Sep 24, 1674 (date of probate; Jane Puddington, widow). {Ref: BDML II:662; FAAH:45; MDWB 2:6}

PULLEN, RICHARD (Anne Arundel County), Quaker who was assigned to a foot company of Capt. John Norwood in 1662, but refused to serve for religious reasons and was fined accordingly. {Ref: AAGE:558}

PULLMAN, JOSEPH (England and Anne Arundel County), captain and master of a ship *Hunter*, of London, riding at anchor in the Severn River in April, 1704. {Ref: AALR WT#2:332; TALR 9:381}

PULLMAN, ROBERT (county or port not indicated), sailor on board the ship *Samuel and John* commanded by Capt. Phillips in 1696. {Ref: ARMD 25:557}

PULSIFER, DAVID (Patuxent District), captain of a ship (no name given) in 1718. {Ref: ARMD 33:159}

PULTON, ALEXIUS (St. Mary's County), surgeon in 1642; paid for one month's service in Capt. William Brainthwaite's Company in November, 1642. {Ref: ARMD 3:119}

PURCELL, JOHN (Talbot County), soldier (rank not stated) circa 1675; paid for his services in the late expedition against the Nanticoke Indians in 1678. {Ref: ARMD 7:92}

PURLIVANT, ---- (St. Mary's County), soldier (rank not stated) in 1642. {Ref: ARMD 4:130-131}

PURNALL, KATHARINE, see "Thomas Purnell," q.v.

PURNALL, RICHARD (St. Mary's County), soldier (rank not stated) circa 1675; paid for his services in the late expedition against the Nanticoke Indians in 1678. {Ref: ARMD 7:103}

PURNALL, WILLIAM (St. Mary's County), soldier (rank not stated) circa 1675; paid for his services in the late expedition against the Nanticoke Indians in 1678. {Ref: ARMD 7:103}

PURNELL, JOHN (Somerset County), constable, Mattapony Hundred, 1694-1695; captain by 1722; member of the Lower House of the Maryland Assembly, 1712-1718; sheriff, 1728-1731; died testate by Mar 3, 1742/3 (date of probate; Martha Purnell, widow). {Ref: BDML II:662; MDWB 23:177}

PURNELL, MARTHA, see "John Purnell," q.v.

PURNELL (PURNALL), THOMAS (Somerset County), captain by 1713; died testate by Apr 2, 1723 (date of probate; Katherine Purnall, widow). See "Edward Hammond," q.v. {Ref: INAC 35A:284; MDWB 18:91}

PURNHAM, JOHN (Somerset County), mariner by 1734; captain, master and owner of the sloop *Ganett* (built in Somerset County) in 1735. {Ref: MDCB 82:38}

PUSEY, CALEB (England and Calvert County), associate master on the ship *Assurance* under the command of Capt. Isaac Bromwell in 1635. {Ref: RMHF II:100}

PUSSER, JOHN (Kent County), soldier (rank not stated) in Capt. William Leeds (Leeads) Company by May 23, 1662, at which time he signed a petition about the misuse of company money by Capt. Thomas Brednox (Bradnox), late of Isle of Kent, deceased. {Ref: ARMD 3:455}

PYE, EDWARD (England and Charles County), colonel and commander of the militia of foot, 1685; provincial court justice, 1683-1689; colonel and officer of the town of Bristoll and Chandler Town, 1686; colonel and member of the Maryland Council, 1687-1689; died intestate by Jan 8, 1696/7 (date of inventory). {Ref: ARMD 5:457, 5:503, 5:527, 5:554, 8:39, 13:242, 17:390; BDML II:669; INAC 15:44}

QUARRY (QUARY), ROBERT (England, Pennsylvania, West Jersey, South Carolina, and Annapolis, Maryland, but was never permanently a resident), colonel and colonial bureaucrat; acquired a seat member in the Upper House (Maryland Council) "to enhance his authority as a customs official and to observe local politics for the Crown" between 1704 and 1714, but seldom attended; served as "Surveyour General of her Majesty's Customs on the Continent of America" from 1702 to 1714; born circa 1644, died in 1714 (place not stated). {Ref: ARMD 23:512, 27:384, 27:392; BDML II:670}

QUIGLEY, JOHN (England, St. Mary's City, Talbot County, and Virginia), captain, gentleman, and merchant in St. Mary's before 1673; in Talbot County by 1676; paid for his services in the late expedition against the Nanticoke Indians in 1678; captain and master of the ship *St. George* of London which came to Maryland in 1678; reportedly in Virginia by 1679, but noted as "Capt. John Quigley of Maryland" in a deposition taken on Jul 7, 1679 in London; one John Quigley died in Dorchester County in 1682. Additional research will be necessary before drawing conclusions. {Ref: ARMD 2:551, 7:103, 15:39, 15:47, 15:61, 15:264, 51:516, 65:181, 67:421; INAC 2:179, 7C:313; LMCL:57; Land Patent 15:553}

QUINTON, WALTER (Talbot and Dorchester Counties), soldier (rank not stated) circa 1675; paid for his services in the late expedition against the Nanticoke Indians in 1678; Protestant and probable soldier in the Revolution of 1689; signed an address and took a loyalty oath supporting the King of England and the reestablishment of Lord Baltimore into power on Nov 28, 1689 (name listed once as "Warlter Quinton"); died testate by May 17, 1728 (date of probate). {Ref: ARMD 7:88, 8:144; MDWB 19:427; MDAD 10:78}

RABNETT, FRANCIS (St. Mary's County), soldier (rank not stated) in 1642. {Ref: ARMD 4:130-131}

RACE, JOHN (Anne Arundel County), captain and commander of the ship *South River Merchant* riding at anchor in South River on Sep 12, 1705. {Ref: AALR WT#2:249}

RACHDALE, EDWARD (Talbot County), captain by 1710. {Ref: INAC 32A:15}

RACKFORD, HERIOT (Annapolis District), captain and master of the ship *Princess Carolina* in 1731. {Ref: CVPR:12}

RACKLIFF (RACKLIFFE), CHARLES (Somerset County), captain lieutenant in the horse troops of Somerset County, commissioned Dec 2, 1687; captain of a company of foot in 1689; Protestant and soldier in the Revolution of 1689; signed an address and took a loyalty oath supporting the King of England and "for enabling us to defend ourselves against all invaders" on Nov 28, 1689 (name also listed as "Charles Ractlife" and "Charles Ratcliff" and "Charles Ratliff"); captain of horse troops in 1694; died testate by May 20, 1696 (date of probate; Elizabeth Rackliff, widow). {Ref: ARMD 5:568, 8:140, 13:244, 20:110; INAC 13B:145; MDWB 7:152}

RAILY, HUGH, see "Philim Murray," q.v.

RAINER, GEORGE (Jamaica and Annapolis), captain of a private man of war ship (no name given) out of Jamaica in 1690 and which returned to Maryland in 1692. {Ref: ARMD 23:473}

RAKE, RICHARD (Calvert County), Protestant and probable soldier in the Revolution of 1689; signed an address and took a loyalty oath supporting the King of England and "to reestablish Lord Baltimore in his ancient power and government" on Nov 16, 1689. {Ref: ARMD 8:131}

RAMSEY, HENRY (Anne Arundel County), captain and commander of the ship *Experiment* riding at anchor in Severn River on Nov 4, 1717. {Ref: AALR IB#2:395}

RANDALL, CHRISTOPHER (Baltimore County), soldier (rank not stated) circa 1675; paid for his services in the late expedition against the Nanticoke Indians in 1678; died intestate by Feb 25, 1684/5 (date of administration bond; Johanna Randall, widow, later married John Gadsby). {Ref: ARMD 7:96; BBCF:528}

RANDALL (RANDELL, RENDALL), JOHN (England, and Baltimore and Anne Arundel Counties), captain of the ship *Elizabeth* in 1724; captain of the ship *Supply* of London in 1729-1730; master of the ship *Elizabeth* in 1731; captain of the ship *Success* in 1734. {Ref: MDGZ, Apr 8, 1729 and Sep 27, 1734; BALR IS#G; CVPR:12; FAAH:130}

RANDALL, JOHANNA, see "Christopher Randall," q.v.

RANDALL, MATHEW (county not indicated), private in the Maryland troops "raised to strengthen Albany, New York and resist the French and Indian enemies" in 1690 (name listed as "Matha Randall"). {Ref: SHMD I:355}

RANDFORD (RANFORD), WILLIAM (Charles County), corporal before 1682; paid for his services out of an assessment levied by the General Assembly for the public good in 1682; born circa 1660 (servant to John Clarke when his age was adjudged to be about 13 by the county court in 1673). {Ref: ARMD 7:439, 7:442, 60:498}

RANDLE, SAMUELL (Talbot County), soldier (rank not stated) circa 1675; paid for his services in the late expedition against the Nanticoke Indians in 1678. {Ref: ARMD 7:92}

RANDOLL, ROBERT (Cecil County), Protestant and probable soldier in the Revolution of 1689; signed an address and took a loyalty oath supporting the King of England and the reestablishment of Lord Baltimore into power on Nov 18, 1689. {Ref: ARMD 8:135}

RANKIN, ---- (St. Mary's County), captain by 1709. {Ref: INAC 29:177}

RANSMAN, WILLIAM (St. Mary's County), soldier (rank not stated) circa 1675; paid for his services in the late expedition against the Nanticoke Indians in 1678. {Ref: ARMD 7:102}

RANSOME, WILLIAM (Baltimore County), soldier (rank not stated) circa 1675; paid for his services in the late expedition against the Nanticoke Indians in 1678; a "William Ransom" died testate in Prince George's County by Aug 9, 1718 (date of probate). Additional research will be necessary before drawing conclusions. {Ref: ARMD 7:96}

RAPPE, ---- (Cecil County), captain by 1698. {Ref: INAC 18:229}

RASEN, PHILIP (Cecil County), military officer (rank not stated) who swore allegiance to the King & Queen of England in 1696. {Ref: ARMD 20:546}

RATCHDALE, EDWARD (England and Talbot County), captain and mariner before 1713; master and co-owner of the ship *Elizabeth* of Liverpool and of a settlement and factory at Oxford on Treadhaven Creek in Choptank River in Talbot County before 1714. {Ref: TALR 12:173, 229}

RATCLIFF, JOHN (Charles County), Protestant and probable soldier in the Revolution of 1689; signed an address and took a loyalty oath supporting the

King of England and the reestablishment of Lord Baltimore into power on Nov 28, 1689. {Ref: ARMD 8:138}

RATHBORNE, WILLIAM (Talbot County), soldier (rank not stated) circa 1675; paid for his services in the late expedition against the Nanticoke Indians in 1678. {Ref: ARMD 7:88}

RAVENS, ABRAHAM (county or port not indicated), captain and master of the ship *Hopewell* in 1691. {Ref: ARMD 8:239}

RAWLE, JOSEPH (Anne Arundel County), mariner by 1734; captain, master and owner of the schooner *Hawke* (built at Herring Bay) in 1735. {Ref: MDCB 82:39}

RAWLEY, JOHN (Somerset County), Protestant and probable soldier in the Revolution of 1689; signed an address and took a loyalty oath supporting the King of England and "for enabling us to defend ourselves against all invaders" on Nov 28, 1689. {Ref: ARMD 8:140}

RAWLINGS, DANN. (Charles and Calvert Counties), Protestant and probable soldier in the Revolution of 1689; signed an address and took a loyalty oath supporting the King of England and "to reestablish Lord Baltimore in his ancient power and government" on Nov 16, 1689. {Ref: ARMD 8:131; FAAH:134}

RAWLINS, LEONARD (county or port not indicated), seaman on the ship *John Hopewell* of London under Capt. Henry Munday in 1699 who ran away to the pirate Capt. Henry King; reported by the Maryland Council that he "may happen to come into these American parts" in 1700. {Ref: ARMD 25:100}

RAWLINSON (RAWLISON), CHARLES (St. Mary's County), soldier by 1648; "received a cow in partial payment for his services at the fort" in 1649 {Ref: ARMD 4:384, 10:6}

RAY, THOMAS (Calvert County), captain by 1705. {Ref: INAC 25:138}

RAZOLINI, ONORIO (Anne Arundel County), commissioned master gunner, storekeeper, and Keeper of the Council Chambers in Annapolis on Jun 4, 1734. {Ref: MDCB 82:18}

REACE, JOHN (Annapolis District), captain and commander of the ship *South River* in 1706. {Ref: AALR WT#2:335}

READ (READE, REED), GEORGE (St. Mary's and Calvert Counties), ensign, commissioned May 8, 1658; captain, commissioned Jun 6, 1665 to command all the forces about St. Leonard's Creek; born circa 1631 (aged about 27 when deposed on Dec 29, 1658), died before Jul 28, 1674 (date of account filed by Joane Tyler, relict). See "Henry Hooper" and "Thomas Brooke" and "John Odber," q.v. {Ref: ARMD 3:344, 3:523, 41:219; INAC 1:54}

READ (READE), GEORGE (Talbot County), soldier (rank not stated) circa 1675; paid for his services in the late expedition against the Nanticoke Indians in 1678; died testate by Mar 23, 1683/4 (date of probate; Mary Reade, widow). {Ref: ARMD 7:83; MDWB 4:10}

READ, GEORGE (Annapolis District), captain and master of the ship *Gloucester* of Virginia in 1729. {Ref: MDGZ, Apr 1, 1729}

READ, HUMPHREY (Somerset County), Protestant and probable soldier in the Revolution of 1689; signed an address and took a loyalty oath supporting the King of England and "for enabling us to defend ourselves against all invaders" on Nov 28, 1689. {Ref: ARMD 8:141}

READ (READE), JOHN (Calvert County), Protestant and probable soldier in the Revolution of 1689; signed an address and took a loyalty oath supporting the King of England and "to reestablish Lord Baltimore in his ancient power and government" on Nov 16, 1689. {Ref: ARMD 8:132}

READ, JOHN (Anne Arundel County), captain by 1699. {Ref: INAC 19½B:75}

READ, MARY, see "Richard Read" and "George Read," q.v.

READ, MATHEW (Kent County), soldier (rank not stated) on Isle of Kent who swore allegiance to the Commonwealth of England on Apr 5, 1652; soldier (rank not stated) in Capt. William Leeds (Leeads) Company by May 23, 1662, at which time he signed a petition about the misuse of company money by Capt. Thomas Brednox (Bradnox), late of Isle of Kent, deceased. {Ref: ARMD 3:455; INKC:101}

READ, RICHARD (England and Prince George's County), captain and mariner by 1719; "Richard Read, mariner, Deptford, County of Kent" died testate by Feb 24, 1730/1 (date of inventory in Maryland); will was written and witnessed in England on May 14, 1711, witnessed again in Maryland on Jun 18, 1723, and probated on May 23, 1732 (Mary Read, widow). {Ref: PGLR F Old 5:275; PGLR I:602; MDAD 10:285; MDWB 20:376; MINV 17:498}

READ, SAMUEL (Anne Arundel County), captain and commander of the ship *Susannah and Sarah* riding at anchor in South River on Feb 24, 1718/9. {Ref: AALR IB#2:528}

READ (REED), THOMAS (England and Anne Arundel County), captain and commander of the brigantine *Boneta* of London riding in Herring Bay on Jan 3, 1723/4 and Mar 22, 1724/5 and Apr 19, 1726 and Mar 1, 1728/9 (ship listed incorrectly once as *Bonsta Brigint*); master of the ship *Caleb and John* in 1731. {Ref: AALR RCW#2:213, SY#1:79, 188; MDGZ, Mar 11, 1728/9; CVPR:12}

READ, WALTER (Somerset County), Protestant and probable soldier in the Revolution of 1689; signed an address and took a loyalty oath supporting the King of England and "for enabling us to defend ourselves against all invaders" on Nov 28, 1689 (name listed once as "Waller Read"); died intestate by May 24, 1721 (date of administration account). {Ref: ARMD 8:140; MDAD 3:391}

REANS, THOMAS (St. Mary's County), military officer (rank not stated) who swore allegiance to the King & Queen of England in 1696. {Ref: ARMD 20:540}

REAS, JOHN (England and Anne Arundel County), captain by 1707; commander of the ship *South River Merchant* riding at anchor at the mouth of South River on Jan 3, 1707/8 and Mar 13, 1711/2 and Apr 30, 1713; died by April, 1715 (date of inventory); captain and mariner of the City of London (account filed in Anne Arundel County on Apr 30, 1717 by Capt. Stephen Yoakley, administrator). See "John Reece," q.v. {Ref: AALR WT#2:564, PK:441, IB#2:26; INAC 36B:165, 38A:72}

REDHALE, WALTER (Talbot County), soldier (rank not stated) circa 1675; paid for his services in the late expedition against the Nanticoke Indians in 1678. {Ref: ARMD 7:90}

REDICH, JOHN (Charles County), lieutenant, 1681. {Ref: ARMD 15:404}

REDMAN, EDWARD (St. Mary's County), Protestant and probable soldier in the Revolution of 1689; signed an address and took a loyalty oath supporting the King of England and the reestablishment of Lord Baltimore into power on Nov 28, 1689. {Ref: ARMD 8:146}

REDMAN, JOHN (St. Mary's County), Protestant and probable soldier in the Revolution of 1689; signed an address and took a loyalty oath (made his "I R" mark) supporting the King of England and the reestablishment of Lord Baltimore into power on Nov 28, 1689. {Ref: ARMD 8:147}

REECE, JOHN (England and Anne Arundel County), mariner, of London, by Aug 1, 1713. See "John Reas," q.v. {Ref: AALR IB#2:95}

REED, PATRICK (Somerset County), Protestant and probable soldier in the Revolution of 1689; signed an address and took a loyalty oath supporting the King of England and "for enabling us to defend ourselves against all invaders" on Nov 28, 1689. {Ref: ARMD 8:140}

REED, RALPH (Anne Arundel County), captain and master of the frigate *Thomas Coleman* riding in Severn River on Apr 30, 1707, and commander of the frigate *Coleman* riding at anchor in Herring Bay on Mar 10, 1707/8. {Ref: AALR WT#2:160, 589}

REED, ROBERT (Dorchester County), mariner, 1698. {Ref: ARMD 25:19}

REERELY, JOHN (St. Mary's County), Protestant and probable soldier in the Revolution of 1689; signed an address and took a loyalty oath supporting the King of England and the reestablishment of Lord Baltimore into power on Nov 28, 1689. {Ref: ARMD 8:147}

REEVE, JOSEPH (Dorchester County), soldier (rank not stated) circa 1675; paid for his services in the late expedition against the Nanticoke Indians in 1678. {Ref: ARMD 7:93}

REEVES, JANE, see "Upgate Reeves," q.v.

REEVES, MARY, see "Thomas Reeves," q.v.

REEVES (REEVE), PETER (England and Annapolis), captain of a ship (no name given) in 1696-1698. {Ref: ARMD 23:466, 25:588}

REEVES (REVES), THOMAS (St. Mary's County), soldier (rank not stated) circa 1675; paid for his services in the late expedition against the Nanticoke Indians in 1678; born circa 1644 (aged about 70 when deposed in 1714), died testate by Jun 7, 1719 (date of probate; Mary Reves, widow). {Ref: ARMD 7:102; MDEP:157; MDWB 15:323}

REEVES, UPGATE (St. Mary's County), Protestant and probable soldier in the Revolution of 1689; signed an address and took a loyalty oath supporting the

King of England and the reestablishment of Lord Baltimore into power on Nov 28, 1689 (name also listed as "Upgate Reves" and "Ubgat Reeves" and "Ubgatt Reaves"); born circa 1669 (aged about 57 when deposed in 1726 and aged about 69 when deposed in 1738), died testate by Feb 6, 1738/9 (date of probate; Jane Reeves, widow). {Ref: ARMD 8:146; MDEP:156; MDWB 22:40}

REID, RICHARD (England and Prince George's County), captain and master of the ship *Ardam* or *Arden* of London riding at anchor in Patuxent River on Jul 3, 1710 and May 9, 1711. {Ref: PGLR F Old 5:121, 178}

RENCHER (RENSHAW, REMSHAW), JOHN (Somerset County), soldier (rank not stated) circa 1675; paid for his services in the late expedition against the Nanticoke Indians in 1678; Protestant and probable soldier in the Revolution of 1689; signed an address and took a loyalty oath supporting the King of England and "for enabling us to defend ourselves against all invaders" on Nov 28, 1689; died testate by Dec 1, 1711 (date of probate; Frances Rencher, widow). {Ref: ARMD 7:98, 8:139; MDWB 13:369}

RENDALL, JOHN, see "John Randall," q.v.

REVECLIPP, CHRISTOPHER (Kent County), "seaman within the said county" and a "sailor belonging to Mr. Powers ship in the stocks" in 1697. {Ref: ARMD 25:599}

REVELL, RANDALL (Manokin Hundred, Somerset County), probable soldier (rank not stated) before 1682; paid for his services out of an assessment levied by the General Assembly for the public good in 1682 (name listed once as "Jr."); Protestant and soldier in the Revolution of 1689; signed an address and took a loyalty oath supporting the King of England and "for enabling us to defend ourselves against all invaders" on Nov 28, 1689; "Randall Reavell (Revell), yeoman," born circa 1661, died testate by Jun 18, 1718 (date of probate). {Ref: ARMD 7:442, 8:139; OSES:279, 456; BDML II:676; MDWB 14:622; LMCL:64}

REVES, MARY, see "Thomas Reeves," q.v.

REVETT, THOMAS (Patuxent District), captain and master of the ship *Baltimore* riding in the Patuxent River on Apr 30, 1726; master of the ship *Regard* in 1730-1731. {Ref: PGLR M:149; CVPR:12}

REXLY, WILLIAM (Talbot County), soldier (rank not stated) circa 1675; paid for his services in the late expedition against the Nanticoke Indians in 1678. {Ref: ARMD 7:89}

REYLEY, THOMAS (Prince George's County), soldier (trooper) under the command of Capt. Richard Owen in June, 1699. {Ref: ARMD 24:121}

REYNES, JOHN (Charles County), soldier (rank not stated) circa 1675; paid for his services in the late expedition against the Nanticoke Indians in 1678. {Ref: ARMD 7:101}

REYNOLDS, THOMAS (Potomac District), captain and master of the ship *Sarah* in 1730-1731. {Ref: CVPR:12}

REYNOLDS, THOMAS (St. Mary's County), Protestant and probable soldier in the Revolution of 1689; signed an address and took a loyalty oath (made his "I" mark) supporting the King of England and the reestablishment of Lord Baltimore into power on Nov 28, 1689. {Ref: ARMD 8:147}

REYNOLDS (REYNALDS), THOMAS (England and St. Mary's County), captain and master of the ship *Loyalty* of Liverpool in 1693. {Ref: ARMD 20:182}

REYNOLDS (RAYNOLDS, RENNOLLS), WILLIAM (England and Anne Arundel County), captain and commander of the ship *Adventure* riding in West River on Feb 13, 1720/1, and riding in South River on Mar 7, 1721/2 and Apr 15, 1723 and Mar 27, 1724; mariner, of London, on Aug 6, 1724 (date of appointment of attorney in Annapolis); commander of the ship *Adventure* riding in South River on Feb 19, 1725/6; commander of the *Indeavor* riding in South River on Jun 17, 1728; master of the *Endeavour* of London in 1729; master of the ship *William and Catherine* in Annapolis in 1731. {Ref: AALR CW#1:319, 481; AALR RCW#2:136, 225; AALR SY#1:27, 168, 424; MDGZ, Apr 22, 1729; CVPR:12; MDAD 10:125}

RHODES, ---- (county not indicated), captain by 1696. {Ref: ARMD 23:5}

RICAUD (RICAD, RICOD), THOMAS (Kent County), military officer (rank not stated) who swore allegiance to the King & Queen of England in 1696; died testate by Jun 3, 1722 (date of probate; Mary Ricaud, widow). {Ref: ARMD 20:540; MDWB 17:174}

RICCARD, SAMUELL (England and Charles County), captain and commander of the pink *Joshua* of London in 1704. {Ref: CHLR Z:275}

RICE, ROGER (St. Mary's County), soldier (rank not stated) circa 1675; paid for his services in the late expedition against the Nanticoke Indians in 1678. {Ref: ARMD 7:103}

RICHARDS, EDWARD (Charles County), soldier by 1665; "prest in the last indian Martch up the bay" and paid for his services on Dec 7, 1665. {Ref: ARMD 53:618-619}

RICHARDS, JOHN (Somerset County), soldier (rank not stated) circa 1675; paid for his services in the late expedition against the Nanticoke Indians in 1678. {Ref: ARMD 7:98}

RICHARDSON, ELIZABETH, see "William Richardson" and "John Richardson," q.v.

RICHARDSON, GEORGE (Talbot County), commissioned "captain of all that troop of horse that shall march out of Choptanck and St. Miles Rivers upon any expedition against any Indian enemy whatsoever" on Jul 2, 1667. {Ref: ARMD 5:10}

RICHARDSON, JOHN (county or port not indicated), captain and master of the ship *Endeavour* of London in 1691. {Ref: ARMD 8:238}

RICHARDSON, JOHN (Dorchester County), soldier (rank not stated) circa 1675; paid for his services in the late expedition against the Nanticoke Indians in 1678 (name listed once as "John Richardsone"); paid for his services out of an assessment levied by the General Assembly for the public good in 1682; died testate by Apr 27, 1723 (date of probate; Elizabeth Richardson, widow). {Ref: ARMD 7:92, 7:94, 7:442; MDWB 18:79}

RICHARDSON, MARK (Baltimore County), probable soldier (rank not stated) before 1682; paid for his services out of an assessment levied by the General Assembly for the public good in 1682; Protestant and probable soldier in the Revolution of 1689; signed an address and took a loyalty oath supporting the King of England and the reestablishment of Lord Baltimore into power on Nov 28, 1689; died testate by Feb 27, 1704/5 (date of probate; Susanna Richardson, widow). {Ref: ARMD 7:441, 7:611, 8:136; BBCF:540; MDWB 12:6}

RICHARDSON, SAMUEL (Kent County), captain by 1733. {Ref: INKC:178}

RICHARDSON, SAMUEL (Annapolis District), captain and commander of the ship *Faulkoner* or *Falconer* in 1705 and which ship was riding at anchor in Severn River on Mar 5, 1707; captain, 1715. {Ref: AALR WT#2:316, 587; CELR 1:483; INAC 36B:69}

RICHARDSON, SUSANNA, see "Thomas Richardson" and "Mark Richardson," q.v.

RICHARDSON, THOMAS (Pocomoke District), captain and master of the ship *Sommersett* in 1731. {Ref: CVPR:12}

RICHARDSON, THOMAS (Baltimore County), captain on the south side of Gunpowder Hundred in 1694 and 1700. {Ref: INBC:4; BCTL:9}

RICHARDSON, THOMAS (Baltimore County), captain of horse troops in 1689; Maryland Council ordered that "Capt. Thomas Richardson at request is appointed Chief Ranger for part of Baltimore County (to wit) from the falls of Back River upward to the extent of said county" on Aug 16, 1692; Maryland Council ordered "Capt. Thomas Richardson with twelve men under his command be appointed to range in the frontiers of Baltimore County" on Aug 17, 1692; appointed ranger by the Maryland Council "for the ensuing year from the Freshes of Pottuxen to the falls of Potapsicoe" on Oct 14, 1692; commissioned lieutenant colonel on Oct 9, 1694; military officer (lieutenant colonel) who swore allegiance to the King & Queen of England in 1696; colonel by 1699; colonel on the south side of Gunpowder Hundred in 1695-1701; died by Apr 24, 1702 (date of probate; Susanna Richardson, widow). {Ref: ARMD 8:339, 8:354, 8:398, 13:243, 20:109-110, 20:153, 20:544, 23:428; BCTL:16; BALR IS#IK:92-94; INAC 11B:32, 21:395; INBC:8; MDWB 11:201}

RICHARDSON, WILLIAM (Anne Arundel County), Quaker who was assigned to a foot company of Capt. John Norwood in 1662, but refused to serve for religious reasons and was fined accordingly; died testate by May 28, 1698 (date of probate; Elizabeth Richardson, widow). {Ref: AAGE:558; FAAH:174-175; MDWB 7:388}

RICHARDSON, WILLIAM (Prince George's County and Patuxent District), captain and commander of the ship *Goodwill* in 1722-1725 and riding in the Patuxent River on Jan 24, 1724/5 and Jan 29, 1725/6; master of the ship *Champion* in 1731. {Ref: PGLR I:465; PGLR M:148-150; CVPR:12; MDAD 10:125}

RICHARDSON, WILLIAM, JR. (Anne Arundel County), captain and commander of the ship *West River Merchant* riding at anchor in West River on Mar 2, 1718/9 and Apr 30, 1720. {Ref: AALR IB#2:530, CW#1:167}

RICHESON, JOHN (Kent County), soldier (rank not stated) on Isle of Kent who swore allegiance to the Commonwealth of England on Apr 5, 1652. {Ref: INKC:101}

RICHFORD, PAUL (England and Prince George's County), captain and master of the ship *William and Mary* "now riding at anchor in the river of Patuxon and God's Grace bound for London" on Oct 4, 1709. {Ref: PGLR F Old 5:147}

RICHINS, RICHARD (Somerset County), soldier (rank not stated) circa 1675; paid for his services in the late expedition against the Nanticoke Indians in 1678. {Ref: ARMD 7:98}

RICHMOND, ANDREW (Anne Arundel County), master gunner, store keeper and armorer for the town and port of Annapolis in 1704. {Ref: ARMD 25:183}

RIDER (RYDAR), CHARLES (Dorchester County), probable soldier and officer in the 1730's; captain before 1740 (executor of "Col. John Ryder," *q.v.*). {Ref: MINV 25:218}

RIDER (RYDER), JOHN (England and Dorchester County), captain by 1708 (name mistakenly listed once as "Capt. John Tryder"); member of the Lower House of the Maryland Assembly, 1719-1722, 1725-1727; colonel by 1728; member of the Maryland Council, 1729-1739; born on Oct 30, 1686, died testate on Feb 16, 1739/40 (will probated on Apr 9, 1740; Mary Rider, widow). See "Charles Rider," q.v. {Ref: ARMD 25:419, 25:512, 33:159, 34:61, 34:65; BDML II:680-681; SOJR III:66; DOLR 8 Old 200; MDWB 22:157; MINV 40:27}

RIDER, JOHN (Oxford District and Dorchester County), captain by 1713; captain and master of the ship *Content* in 1731. {Ref: INAC 35A:195; CVPR:12}

RIDER, MARY, see "John Rider (Ryder)," q.v.

RIDGAWAY, WILLIAM (Talbot County), Protestant and probable soldier in the Revolution of 1689; signed an address and took a loyalty oath supporting the King of England and the reestablishment of Lord Baltimore into power on Nov 28, 1689. {Ref: ARMD 8:144}

RIDGELY, ELIZABETH, see "Henry Ridgely," q.v.

RIDGELY (RIDGELEY), HENRY (England, Virginia, and Anne Arundel and Prince George's Counties), captain of foot troops in the Revolution of 1689; major by 1692; court justice, 1692; member of the Lower House of the Maryland Assembly, 1692-1694; major of foot troops in 1694; lieutenant colonel, commissioned Jul 30, 1694; colonel, paid for his services by the Maryland Assembly in 1695; reported by the Maryland Council that he was "very Antient & desirous to lay down his Commission of Colonel of this County of Ann Arundel County" on Oct 4, 1699; colonel, merchant and gentleman by 1703; born circa 1625, died testate by Jul 13, 1710 (date of probate; Mary Ridgely, widow). {Ref: ARMD 8:324, 13:242, 20:108, 20:130, 20:153, 23:171, 23:419, 25:80, 38:72; FAAH:40, 77-78, 190; BDML II:687; RMHF II:293; MDWB 13:89; AALR WT#2:58}

RIDGELY (RIDGLEY), HENRY (Prince George's and Anne Arundel Counties), captain of a company in Prince George's County before 1709; Maryland Council reported "Capt. Henry Ridgley being removed out of Prince George's County into Ann Arundel" on Nov 10, 1709; colonel by 1711; died testate by Mar 14, 1749/50 (date of probate; Elizabeth Ridgely, widow). See "Thomas Claggett," q.v. {Ref: ARMD 27:403; FAAH:351-352; MDWB 27:160}

RIDGELY, MARY, see "Henry Ridgely," q.v.

RIDGELY (RIDGELEY), ROBERT (Talbot County), soldier (rank not stated) circa 1675; paid for his services in the late expedition against the Nanticoke Indians in 1678. {Ref: ARMD 7:89}

RIDGELY, WILLIAM (Anne Arundel County), soldier (rank not stated) circa 1675; paid for his services in the late expedition against the Nanticoke Indians in 1678; died intestate in 1716. {Ref: ARMD 7:96; FAAH:81-82}

RIGBY, LEWIS (England and Somerset County), mate on the ship *Betty Gally* of Liverpool riding at anchor in Monocan River on Jan 16, 1716/7. {Ref: SOJR III:186}

RIGBY, NATHANIEL (Baltimore County), probable soldier and officer in the 1720's and 1730's; colonel by 1737 (name shown as "Col. Nat Rigbie" on Deer Creek Hundred tax list); born Apr 28, 1695, died by Aug 29, 1752 (date of administration bond; Sabina Rigby, widow). {Ref: BBCF:543; INBC:11}

RIGBY, SABINA, see "Nathan Rigby," q.v.

RIGGIN, HENRY (Cecil County), captain by 1725. {Ref: MDAD 7:59}

RIGGS, JOHN (England and Anne Arundel County), ensign by 1689. {Ref: FAAH:354}

RIMMER, HUGH (Dorchester County), captain in the 1730's and 1740's; died intestate by Aug 12, 1745 (date inventory approved by Mary Rimmer, administratrix). *Note:* Since his name does not appear on any extant militia lists between 1732 and 1745, his service was either prior to 1732 or he was a sea captain. Additional research will be necessary before drawing conclusions. {Ref: MINV 32:132}

RINGGOLD, ---- (Kent County), major by 1694. {Ref: ARMD 20:205}

RINGGOLD, FRANCES, see "Thomas Ringgold," q.v.

RINGGOLD, JAMES (Kent County), major by 1674; paid for his services in the late expedition against the Nanticoke Indians in 1678; court justice, 1674-1680; born circa 1637 (aged about 23 when deposed on Dec 20, 1660), died testate by Sep 28, 1686 (date of probate; Mary Ringgold, widow). {Ref: ARMD 7:94, 15:38, 15:67, 15:328, 17:169, 54:190; CFES 2:268; INKC:125; INAC 9:224; MDWB 4:232}

RINGGOLD, JOHN (Kent County), soldier (rank not stated) on Isle of Kent who swore allegiance to the Commonwealth of England on Apr 5, 1652; "John Ringold, of Hunting Field" died testate by Sep 17, 1672 (date of probate). {Ref: INKC:101; MDWB 1:497}

RINGGOLD, MARY, see "James Ringgold," q.v.

RINGGOLD, REBECCA, see "Thomas Ringgold," q.v.

RINGGOLD, THOMAS (Kent County), soldier (rank not stated) on Isle of Kent who swore allegiance to the Commonwealth of England on Apr 5, 1652; assistant commander (commissioner) of Kent County, 1654; born circa 1609-1611 (aged about 43 when deposed in 1652 and aged about 44 when deposed in 1655). {Ref: ARMD 54:10, 54:33; INKC:101-104}

RINGGOLD, THOMAS (Kent County), military officer (rank not stated) who swore allegiance to the King & Queen of England in 1696; captain and member of the Commission of the Peace in 1697; major by 1705; member of the Lower House of the Maryland Assembly in 1710; born circa 1665, died testate by Oct 16, 1711 (date of probate; Frances Ringgold, widow). {Ref: ARMD 20:540, 23:198, 27:495; BDML II:693-694; CFES 2:269; MDWB 13:394; CELR 1:290; INKC:150; MDWB 13:394}

RINGGOLD, THOMAS (Kent County), captain before 1728; died intestate in August, 1728 (inventory dated Dec 17, 1728; Rebecca Ringgold, administratrix). {Ref: CFES 2:273; MINV 14:73}

RIPPINGTON, FRANCIS (Talbot County), soldier (rank not stated) circa 1675; paid for his services in the late expedition against the Nanticoke Indians in 1678. {Ref: ARMD 7:88}

RIPPON (RIPPIN, RIPPEN), HENRY (Cecil and Kent Counties), mariner of Cecil County by 1731; land owner on the Chester River in 1731; appeared in Kent County debt books in 1733. {Ref: QALR RT#A:111; INKC:178; CELR 5:47}

RISBROOK, WILLIAM (St. Mary's County), soldier (rank not stated) in 1642. {Ref: ARMD 4:130-131}

RISTEAU, JOHN (France and Baltimore County), captain and commander of a militia fort on his plantation *Risteau's Garrison* circa 1718-1741; court justice, 1736-1743; sheriff, 1743-1746; died testate by May 12, 1760 (date of probate; Katherine Risteau, widow). {Ref: BDML II:697; MDWB 30:858}

RITSON, ISAAC (Talbot County), captain by 1725. {Ref: MDAD 7:10}

RIVERS, CHRISTOPHER (Charles County), soldier (rank not stated) in Capt. James Langworth's Company before 1661 (year of the captain's death, but his ammunition report was not filed until 1664 by Henry Adames). {Ref: CHLR B:379}

RIVIER, PETER (France and Annapolis), captain and commander of the pink *John* of Bordeaux in 1695. {Ref: ARMD 20:338}

ROACH, JOHN (Somerset County), Protestant and probable soldier in the Revolution of 1689; signed an address and took a loyalty oath supporting the King of England and "for enabling us to defend ourselves against all invaders" on Nov 28, 1689; died intestate by Aug 15, 1720 (date of administration account; Sarah Roach, widow). {Ref: ARMD 8:140; MDAD 3:237}

ROBARDS, THOMAS, see "Thomas Roberts," q.v.

ROBBISON, JOHN (Talbot County), soldier (rank not stated) circa 1675; paid for his services in the late expedition against the Nanticoke Indians in 1678. {Ref: ARMD 7:88}

ROBENSONE, JOHN (Kent County), soldier (rank not stated) circa 1675; paid for his services in the late expedition against the Nanticoke Indians in 1678. {Ref: ARMD 7:94}

ROBERSON, JOHN (Kent County), military officer (rank not stated) who swore allegiance to the King & Queen of England in 1696. {Ref: ARMD 20:540}

ROBERSONE, RICHARD (St. Mary's County), soldier (rank not stated) circa 1675; paid for his services in the late expedition against the Nanticoke Indians in 1678. {Ref: ARMD 7:103}

ROBERTS, ELIZABETH, see "Thomas Roberts," q.v.

ROBERTS, STANNOP (St. Mary's County), soldier (rank not stated) in 1647. {Ref: ARMD 1:226, 4:323}

ROBERTS, THOMAS (Bear Creek, Patapsco River, Baltimore County), ranger, appointed by Capt. John Oldton as a "well quallified person & good woods man & fit to be Imployed in Ranging for the Publick Service of this Province" on Mar 23, 1694/5; lieutenant who swore allegiance to the King & Queen of England in 1696; deposition on Jul 3, 1696 stated "that Capt. Oldton's party of Rangers being at one time in, and the Lieutenant's party out upon Ranging, he did not goe out to Relieve the Lieutenant's party according to appointment, Whereupon the Lieutenant's party came in, and so both parties were in at one time. That the said Rangers do not live at the place Setled beyond the inhabitants, but that they Come in among the inhabitants" (name listed once as "Thomas Robards"); born circa 1656 (aged about 40 when deposed in 1696), died testate by Feb 1, 1709/10 (date of probate; Elizabeth Roberts, widow). {Ref: ARMD 20:205, 20:452, 20:544; BBCF:547; MDWB 13:31}

ROBERTS, WILLIAM (county not indicated), probable soldier (rank not stated) before 1682; paid for his services out of an assessment levied by the General Assembly for the public good in 1682. {Ref: ARMD 7:439}

ROBERTS, WILLIAM (England and St. Mary's County), captain and master of the ship *Reserve* of Bristoll in 1693. {Ref: ARMD 20:182}

ROBERTSON, ANDREW (All Hallows Parish, Somerset County), mariner and sailor on the ship *Blessing* riding at anchor in Senepuxen Inlet on Apr 13, 1717. {Ref: MGSB 36:4, p. 645; SOJR III:192-193, 195-196}

ROBERTSON (ROBERTSONE), ROBERT (Dorchester County), soldier (rank not stated) circa 1675; paid for his services in the late expedition against the Nanticoke Indians in 1678; a Robert Robertson died testate in Talbot County by Oct 3, 1706 (date of probate). {Ref: ARMD 7:93; MDWB 12:95}

ROBERTSON (ROBISON), ROBERT (All Hallows Parish, Somerset County), mariner and sailor on the ship *Blessing* riding at anchor in Senepuxen Inlet on Apr 13, 1717. {Ref: MGSB 36:4, p. 645; SOJR III:192-196}

ROBINS, ARRALANTER, see "Thomas Robins," q.v.

ROBINS (ROBBINS), GEORGE (Talbot County), soldier (rank not stated) circa 1675; paid for his services in the late expedition against the Nanticoke Indians in 1678; born 1635, died testate by Jun 11, 1694 (date of probate; Margaret Robins, widow). {Ref: ARMD 7:90; BDML II:701; MDWB 7:90}

ROBINS, JAMES (Pocomoke District), captain and master of the ship *Friends of Virginia* in 1731. {Ref: CVPR:12}

ROBINS (ROBBINS), JOHN (Somerset County), captain by 1678. See "Thomas Robins," q.v. {Ref: INAC 5:377}

ROBINS, MARGARET, see "George Robins," q.v.

ROBINS, OBEDIENCE, see "Thomas Robins," q.v.

ROBINS, RICHARD (England and Maryland, port not indicated), captain and master of the ship *Speedwell* of London in 1690; captain and master of the ship *Olive Branch* of London in 1691. {Ref: ARMD 8:237, 8:240}

ROBINS, STEPHEN (England, and Anne Arundel and Cecil Counties), mariner, of London, by Sep 30, 1703 (date of power of attorney to his friend James Willson, of Cecil County); captain and commander of the ship *Josiah* riding at anchor in South River on Jun 11, 1714. {Ref: AALR IB#2:140; CELR 1:336}

ROBINS, THOMAS (Worcester County), probable soldier in the 1730's (his grandfather John Robins and great-grandfather Obedience Robins had both been colonels in Virginia); styled "captain" by 1749; member of the Lower House of the Maryland Assembly, 1742-1751; born circa 1702, died testate by Jun 20, 1766 (date of probate; Arralanter Robins, widow). {Ref: BDML II:702; MDWB 34:172}

ROBINS, THOMAS (St. Peter's Parish, Talbot County), military officer (rank not stated) who swore allegiance to the King & Queen of England in 1696; member of the Lower House of the Maryland Assembly, 1708-1718; major by 1717; born 1672, died intestate on Dec 29, 1721. {Ref: ARMD 20:542, 27:203; BDML II:701-702; MINV 8:22}

ROBINSON, ---- (Dorchester County), captain of a ship (no name given) in 1723. {Ref: MDAD 5:279}

ROBINSON, CHARLES (Talbot County), Protestant and probable soldier in the Revolution of 1689; signed an address and took a loyalty oath supporting the King of England and the reestablishment of Lord Baltimore into power on Nov 18, 1689. {Ref: ARMD 8:134}

ROBINSON, HENDIGE (county or port not indicated), captain of the ship *Edward and Dudley* in 1697. {Ref: ARMD 23:169}

ROBINSON, JOHN (Kent County), military officer (rank not stated) who swore allegiance to the King & Queen of England in 1696. {Ref: ARMD 20:540}

ROBINSON, RICHARD (England and Charles County), captain and commander of the ship *John* of Hull in 1675. {Ref: ARMD 15:56}

ROBINSON, SOLOMON, see "Thomas Martin," q.v.

ROBINSON, THOMAS (Cecil County), captain of a shallop (no name given) in 1697; captain of a ship (no name given) in 1702. {Ref: ARMD 24:303, 25:599; INAC 20:273}

ROBINSON (ROBISSON), WILLIAM (Charles County), soldier (rank not stated) by 1664; paid for his services out of an assessment levied by the General Assembly for the public good in 1682; born circa 1631-1634 (aged about 24 when deposed in 1658 and aged about 29 when deposed in 1660), died by Feb 13, 1696/7 (date of probate; nuncupative will was given on Jan 28, 1696/7). {Ref: ARMD 7:442-443, 41:165, 53:85; CHLR A:100, B:379; MDWB 6:370}

ROBOTHAM (ROBBOTHAM), GEORGE (England, and Calvert, Dorchester and Talbot Counties), soldier (rank not stated) circa 1675; paid for his services in the late expedition against the Nanticoke Indians in 1678; member of the Lower House of the Maryland Assembly, 1681-1688; officer of King's Creek Town in 1686; Protestant and probable soldier in the Revolution of 1689; signed an address and took a loyalty oath supporting the King of England and the reestablishment of Lord Baltimore into power on Nov 28, 1689; colonel by 1691; member of the Maryland Council, 1691-1698; provincial court justice, 1691-1694; appointed Judge of the Court of Admiralty for the Eastern Shore on Oct 18, 1694; one of the commissioners of the Port of Williamstadt in 1695; military officer who swore allegiance to the King & Queen of England in 1696; died testate by April 20, 1698 (date of inventory; will probated on Apr 26, 1698). {Ref: ARMD 5:502, 7:89, 8:144, 8:280, 17:380, 20:153, 20:161, 20:379, 20:542, 23:33, 23:234, 25:558, 38:73; BDML II:702-703; TALR 5:319; MDWB 7:358; INAC 16:77}

ROBSONE, ROWLAND (Talbot County), soldier (rank not stated) circa 1675; paid for his services in the late expedition against the Nanticoke Indians in 1678. {Ref: ARMD 7:90}

ROBSONE (ROBSON), WILLIAM (Dorchester County), soldier (rank not stated) circa 1675; paid for his services in the late expedition against the Nanticoke Indians in 1678; born circa 1642 (aged about 70 when deposed in 1712). {Ref: ARMD 7:92-93; MDEP:160}

ROBYSON, ANDREW (Anne Arundel County), soldier (rank not stated) circa 1675; paid for his services in the late expedition against the Nanticoke Indians in 1678. {Ref: ARMD 7:96}

ROBYSON, THOMAS (St. Mary's County), soldier (rank not stated) circa 1675; paid for his services in the late expedition against the Nanticoke Indians in 1678. {Ref: ARMD 7:102}

ROCHE, JOHN (Somerset County), soldier (rank not stated) circa 1675; paid for his services in the late expedition against the Nanticoke Indians in 1678. {Ref: ARMD 7:99}

ROCHEFORT (ROCHFORD), LAWRENCE (Charles County), Protestant and probable soldier in the Revolution of 1689; signed an address and took a loyalty oath supporting the King of England and the reestablishment of Lord Baltimore into power on Nov 28, 1689; born circa 1634 (aged about 63 when deposed in 1697). {Ref: ARMD 8:138; MDEP:160}

ROCK, ---- (Kent County), captain of a ship (no name given) on Worton Creek circa 1718 (mentioned in the deposition of William Beck on Oct 20, 1743). {Ref: CFES 1:29; KELR JS#25:197}

ROCK, JOHN (England and Annapolis), captain, commander and master of the ship *Happy Return* of Bideford in 1691-1696. {Ref: ARMD 8:240, 23:137}

ROCK, WILLIAM (England and Anne Arundel County), captain, mariner, and master of the ship *Tant* of Bytheford in 1702; captain to at least 1724. {Ref: AALR WT#2:54; INAC 36B:173; MDAD 6:156}

RODDRY, JOHN (Kent County), "seaman within the said county" and a "sailor belonging to the *Loves Increase* of Whitehaven" in 1697. {Ref: ARMD 25:600}

ROE, EDWARD (Talbot County), captain before 1676; soldier (rank and first name not stated) whose widow Mary Roe was paid in 1678 for his services in the late expedition against the Nanticoke Indians in 1678; died by Jul 3, 1676 (date of inventory). {Ref: ARMD 7:88, 7:89; INAC 2:177}

ROE, MARY, see "Edward Roe," q.v.

ROE, THOMAS (Talbot County), soldier (rank not stated) circa 1675; paid for his services in the late expedition against the Nanticoke Indians in 1678; one "Thomas Roe, Sr., planter" died testate in Queen Anne's County by May 7, 1712 (date of probate; Frances Roe, widow). {Ref: ARMD 7:87; MDWB 13:408}

ROGERS, DAVID (Talbot County), soldier (rank not stated) circa 1675; paid for his services in the late expedition against the Nanticoke Indians in 1678; died testate by Sep 22, 1698 (date of probate). {Ref: ARMD 7:87; MDWB 6:168}

ROGERS, EDWARD (Kent County), military officer (rank not stated) who swore allegiance to the King & Queen of England in 1696. {Ref: ARMD 20:541}

ROGERS, ELIZABETH, see "John Rogers," q.v.

ROGERS, JOHN (England and Pocomoke District), captain and master of the bark *Mermaid* in 1698. {Ref: ARMD 23:402}

ROGERS, JOHN (Charles Counties), naval officer of the Potomac District in 1711; died testate by Jan 13, 1717/8 (date of probate; Elizabeth Rogers, widow). {Ref: ARMD 29:11; MDWB 14:521}

ROGERS, WILLIAM (New England and Anne Arundel County), captain by 1729; chief clerk and register of the Prerogative Court, 1736-1749; born circa 1699, died intestate by Feb 15, 1749/50 (date of inventory). {Ref: BDML II:703; MDGZ, Jan 14, 1728/9; MINV 15:73, 43:75; MDAD 11:125}

ROLAND, ROBERT (Charles County), soldier (rank not stated) circa 1675; paid for his services in the late expedition against the Nanticoke Indians in 1678. {Ref: ARMD 7:101}

ROLPH, THOMAS (Somerset County), soldier (rank not stated) circa 1675; paid for his services in the late expedition against the Nanticoke Indians in 1678 (name listed once as "Thomas Ralph"); died testate by Mar 3, 1743/4 (date of probate). {Ref: ARMD 7:98; MDWB 23:405}

ROOKE, EDWARD (Somerset County), mariner by 1734 (and land owner in Queen Anne's County in 1735). {Ref: QALR RT#A:372}

ROOKEWOOD, EDWARD (Charles County), Protestant and probable soldier in the Revolution of 1689; signed an address and took a loyalty oath supporting the King of England and the reestablishment of Lord Baltimore into power on Nov 28, 1689. {Ref: ARMD 8:138}

ROOKINS, THOMAS (England and Talbot County), mariner and sailor on the ship *Relief* of New Castle commanded by Capt. John Anderson in 1692. {Ref: ARMD 13:334-335}

ROPER, WILLIAM (St. Mary's County), captain by 1644. {Ref: ARMD 10:212}

ROSE, JOHN (St. Mary's County), Protestant and probable soldier in the Revolution of 1689; signed an address and took a loyalty oath supporting the King of England and the reestablishment of Lord Baltimore into power on Nov 28, 1689. {Ref: ARMD 8:146}

ROSIER, MR., see "Humphrey Howell," q.v.

ROSMONDSON, HANCE (Kent County), soldier (rank not stated) circa 1675; paid for his services in the late expedition against the Nanticoke Indians in 1678. {Ref: ARMD 7:94}

ROSS, ALLEN (Somerset County), Protestant and probable soldier in the Revolution of 1689; signed an address and took a loyalty oath supporting the King of England and "for enabling us to defend ourselves against all invaders" on Nov 28, 1689. {Ref: ARMD 8:141}

ROSS, JAMES (Talbot County), Protestant and probable soldier in the Revolution of 1689; signed an address and took a loyalty oath supporting the King of England and the reestablishment of Lord Baltimore into power on Nov 28, 1689. {Ref: ARMD 8:144}

ROSS, JOHN (St. Mary's County), soldier (rank not stated) circa 1675; paid for his services in the late expedition against the Nanticoke Indians in 1678. {Ref: ARMD 7:102}

ROSS, JOHN (Dorchester County), lieutenant by 1678; paid for his services in the late expedition against the Nanticoke Indians in 1678; died testate by Apr 22, 1695 (date of probate; Mabella Ross, widow, later married Anthony Talle). {Ref: ARMD 7:92; MDWB 7:177}

ROSS, MABELLA, see "John Ross," q.v.

ROUND, JAMES (Somerset County), Protestant and probable soldier in the Revolution of 1689; signed an address and took a loyalty oath supporting the King of England and "for enabling us to defend ourselves against all invaders" on Nov 28, 1689. {Ref: ARMD 8:141}

ROUND, WILLIAM (Somerset County), Protestant and probable soldier in the Revolution of 1689; signed an address and took a loyalty oath supporting the King of England and "for enabling us to defend ourselves against all invaders" on Nov 28, 1689. {Ref: ARMD 8:140}

ROUND (ROWND), WILLIAM (Snow Hill, Somerset County), captain and mariner by 1711; died testate by Feb 26, 1718/9 (date of probate; Mary Round, widow). See "William Rownd," q.v. {Ref: MGSB 36:4, pp. 645-647; SOJR III:39; INAC 32C:122; MINV 3:249; MDWB 15:25}

ROUS, ROBERT (St. Mary's County), soldier (rank not stated) circa 1675; paid for his services in the late expedition against the Nanticoke Indians in 1678. {Ref: ARMD 7:103}

ROUSBY, CHRISTOPHER, see "George Talbott" and "Thomas Allen," q.v.

ROUSBY, JOHN (Calvert County), colonel by 1707; naval officer for Patuxent District, 1707-1717; member of the Lower House of the Maryland Assembly, 1712-1721; member of the Upper House (Maryland Council), 1721-1737; born 1685, died by Oct 8, 1744 (date of probate). {Ref: ARMD 29:40; HCCM:307; RMHF II:323; BDML II:705-706}

ROW, HENRY (New York, and Kent or Queen Anne's County), mariner by Aug 18, 1721 (date a power of attorney was granted to William Trew of Kent County). {Ref: QALR IK#B:245}

ROWE, THOMAS (Queen Anne's County), proposed for ensign in the Fourth Company of Foot on Jun 30, 1732. {Ref: MDHR 1:11}

ROWELL, JOHN (Somerset County), soldier (rank not stated) circa 1675; paid for his services in the late expedition against the Nanticoke Indians in 1678; Protestant and probable soldier in the Revolution of 1689; signed an address and took a loyalty oath supporting the King of England and "for enabling us to defend ourselves against all invaders" on Nov 28, 1689. {Ref: ARMD 7:99, 8:140}

ROWLEDGE, EDWARD, see "Edward Rutledge," q.v.

ROWND, WILLIAM (Somerset County), captain by 1721 (received payment from the estate of David Nienburge, deceased, on Feb 15, 1721/2). See "William Round," q.v. {Ref: MDAD 4:102}

ROYSTON, RICHARD (Talbot County), soldier (rank not stated) circa 1675; paid for his services in the late expedition against the Nanticoke Indians in 1678. {Ref: ARMD 5:81, 7:90}

ROZER, BENJAMIN (Virginia and Charles County), high sheriff of Charles County, 1667-1677; major by 1677; provincial court justice, 1677-1681; paid for his services in the late expedition against the Nanticoke Indians in 1678; colonel by 1679; Protestant member of the Upper House (Maryland Council), 1678-1681; died intestate by May 25, 1681 (date of inventory). {Ref: ARMD 5:4, 5:309, 7:101, 15:57, 15:269, 51:321, 57:34; BDML II:707; CHLR H:304; INAC 5:393, 7C:98; LMCL:59}

RUMBALL, ANTHONY (Talbot County), Protestant and probable soldier in the Revolution of 1689; signed an address and took a loyalty oath supporting the King of England and the reestablishment of Lord Baltimore into power on Nov 28, 1689. {Ref: ARMD 8:144; MDEP:161}

RUMSEY, ISAAC (county not indicated), private in the Maryland troops "raised to strengthen Albany, New York and resist the French and Indian enemies" in 1690. {Ref: SHMD I:355}

RUMSEY, JOSEPH (county not indicated), sergeant in the Maryland troops "raised to strengthen Albany, New York and resist the French and Indian enemies" in 1690. {Ref: SHMD I:355}

RUMSEY, SABINA, see "William Rumsey," q.v.

RUMSEY, WILLIAM (Cecil County), naval officer for the district of Cecil County, 1733-1742; styled "captain" by the time of his death; member of the Lower House of the Maryland Assembly, 1738-1741; born Apr 1, 1698, died testate by Mar 1, 1742/3 (date of probate; Sabina Rumsey, widow). {Ref: BDML II:709; MDWB 23:41; MDCB 82:2}

RUSH, EDWARD (Kent County), military officer (rank not stated) who swore allegiance to the King & Queen of England in 1696. {Ref: ARMD 20:541}

RUSH, JOHN (Annapolis District), captain and master of the ship *Concord* in 1734. {Ref: MDGZ, Jul 19, 1734}

RUSSELL, CHRISTOPHER (Charles County), captain, commissioned Feb 7, 1660; born circa 1614 (aged about 45 when deposed on Jan 26, 1658/9), died by 1662. {Ref: ARMD 3:402, 49:72; CHLR A:35, A:219-220, B:30; MDEP:161}

RUSSELL, DANIELL (Anne Arundel County), captain and commander of the ship *Forward* riding in Severn River on Feb 8, 1722/3 and Jan 1, 1724/5 and Dec 31, 1725; master of the ship *Hume* in 1731. {Ref: AALR RCW#2:98, SY#1:54, 154; CVPR:12}

RUSSELL, EDWARD (St. Mary's County), captain by 1694. {Ref: ARMD 20:209}

RUSSELL, ELIZABETH, see "Michaell Russell," q.v.

RUSSELL, JOHN (England, Virginia, Kent Island and Kent County), soldier (rank not stated) on Isle of Kent who swore allegiance to the Commonwealth of England on Apr 5, 1652; assistant commander (commissioner) of Kent County, 1654; captain by 1655; member of the Lower House of the Maryland Assembly, 1659; born circa 1621-1622 (aged about 34 when deposed on Feb 1, 1655/6), died testate by Jan 18, 1660/1 (date of probate; Juliana Russell, widow). {Ref: ARMD 54:52; BDML II:710; INKC:101, 103, 107; MDWB 1:122}

RUSSELL, JULIANA, see "John Russell," q.v.

RUSSELL, MICHAELL (Talbot County), soldier (rank not stated) circa 1675; paid for his services in the late expedition against the Nanticoke Indians in 1678; died testate by Feb 3, 1704/5 (date of probate; Elizabeth Russell, widow). {Ref: ARMD 7:88; MDWB 3:663}

RUSSELL (RUSSEL), PAUL (England and Annapolis), seaman on the ship *Hartwell* of London commanded by Capt. Nicholas Humphries in March, 1697/8. {Ref: ARMD 23:397}

RUSSELL, WILLIAM (Anne Arundel County), soldier (rank not stated) circa 1675; paid for his services in the late expedition against the Nanticoke Indians in 1678. {Ref: ARMD 7:96}

RUSSELL, WILLIAM (Dorchester County), captain by 1723. {Ref: MDAD 5:377}

RUST, JOHN (Somerset County), Protestant and probable soldier in the Revolution of 1689; signed an address and took a loyalty oath supporting the King of

England and "for enabling us to defend ourselves against all invaders" on Nov 28, 1689. {Ref: ARMD 8:140}

RUTLEDGE (ROWLEDGE), EDWARD (Baltimore County), soldier (rank not stated) circa 1675; paid for his services in the late expedition against the Nanticoke Indians in 1678. {Ref: ARMD 7:95; BBCF:561}

RUTTY, DAVID (Talbot County), soldier (rank not stated) circa 1675; paid for his services in the late expedition against the Nanticoke Indians in 1678. {Ref: ARMD 7:92}

RUXTONE (RUXTON), NICHOLAS (Baltimore County), soldier (rank not stated) circa 1675; paid for his services in the late expedition against the Nanticoke Indians in 1678; one "Nicholas Ruxton" died intestate by Mar 30, 1680 (date of inventory) and a "Nicholas Ruxtone, of Patapsco River" died testate by Dec 8, 1700 (date of probate; Mary Ruxtone, widow). Additional research will be necessary before drawing conclusions. {Ref: ARMD 7:95; INAC 7A:95; MDWB 6:401}

RYAN, CORNELIUS (Kent County), military officer (rank not stated) who swore allegiance to the King & Queen of England in 1696; died testate by Aug 6, 1711 (date of probate). {Ref: ARMD 20:540; MDWB 13:313}

RYCROFT, WILLIAM (Prince George's County), captain before 1699; died by Feb 14, 1699/1700 (date of inventory). {Ref: INAC 19½B:24}

RYDAR, CHARLES, see "Charles Rider," q.v.

RYE, CHARLES, see "Thomas Blake," q.v.

RYE, JANE, see "Thomas Blake," q.v.

RYLANDS, WILLIAM (St. Mary's County), Protestant and probable soldier in the Revolution of 1689; signed an address and took a loyalty oath supporting the King of England and the reestablishment of Lord Baltimore into power on Nov 28, 1689. {Ref: ARMD 8:147}

RYMOUR (RYMER), JOHN (England and Potomac District), captain and master of the ship *Planter* of Liverpool in 1697. {Ref: ARMD 23:138, 23:172}

SADD, RICHARD (Baltimore County), soldier (rank not stated) circa 1675; paid for his services in the late expedition against the Nanticoke Indians in 1678. {Ref: ARMD 7:96}

SADLER, JOHN (Barbadoes and Somerset County), captain and mariner by 1697 and at least to 1708. {Ref: SOJR I:196}

SADLER, MICAYAH (Somerset County), Protestant and probable soldier in the Revolution of 1689; signed an address and took a loyalty oath supporting the King of England and "for enabling us to defend ourselves against all invaders" on Nov 28, 1689. {Ref: ARMD 8:139}

SALES, CLEMENT (Talbot County), soldier (rank not stated) circa 1675; paid for his services in the late expedition against the Nanticoke Indians in 1678. {Ref: ARMD 7:88}

SALLERS, JOHN, see "John Sollers," q.v.

SALLEY, JOHN (St. Mary's County), captain and master of the ship brigantine *Hopewell* of Maryland in 1694. {Ref: ARMD 20:146}

SALMON, JAMES (Baltimore County), Protestant and probable soldier in the Revolution of 1689; signed an address and took a loyalty oath supporting the King of England and the reestablishment of Lord Baltimore into power on Nov 28, 1689. {Ref: ARMD 8:136}

SALMON (SAMON), JOHN (county or port not indicated), captain and master of the ship *Sara and Elizabeth* of Maryland in 1691. {Ref: ARMD 8:239}

SALMON, NICHOLAS (county or port not indicated), seaman on the ship *George* in 1659. {Ref: ARMD 41:307}

SALMON, THOMAS (England and Talbot County), captain before 1696; commander of the ship *Habitation* of London riding in the Choptank River on Oct 5, 1696 and at which time an inquiry was made into the circumstances of his death by the Maryland Council. {Ref: ARMD 20:512, 23:168}

SALSBURY, ANN, see "John Salisbury," q.v.

SALWAY, ANTHONY, see "Richard Ewen," q.v.

SAMPSON, ELIZABETH, see "Richard Sampson," q.v.

SAMPSON, HENRY (Anne Arundel County), captain and commander of the ship *Experiment* riding at anchor in Severn River on Aug 19, 1718, at Annapolis on Nov 4, 1720, and riding in Severn River on Aug 18, 1721. {Ref: AALR CW#1:52, 261, 414}

SAMPSON, JEREMIAH (England, and Prince George's and Anne Arundel Counties), captain and master of the ship *Colchester Adventer* "riding in the freshes of the Patuxen" on Jun 18, 1706; commander of the ship *Colchester Adventure* riding at anchor in South River on Feb 16, 1710/1; commander of the ship *Colchester* riding at anchor in Severn River on May 1, 1714 and May 5, 1716 (name listed once as "Jeremiah Samson"); mariner and lot owner in Annapolis on Duke of Gloucester Street on Jun 28, 1715; mariner and land owner in Prince George's County by 1717; "Jeremiah Sampson, St. Mary's Parish, London, late of Rotherhith in County of Surry, mariner" died testate by Feb 2, 1717/8 (date of probate in Maryland). {Ref: AALR WT#2:479, PK:436, IB#2:197, 276, CW#1:198, 298; PGLR F Old 5:624; MDWB 14:493; MDAD 3:191}

SAMPSON, RICHARD (Baltimore County), soldier (rank not stated) circa 1675; paid for his services in the late expedition against the Nanticoke Indians in 1678 (name listed once as "Richard Sampsone"); died intestate by Jul 4, 1709 (date of administration bond; Elizabeth Sampson, widow, later married Thomas Stone). {Ref: ARMD 7:95, 23:20; BBCF:564; MDAD 3:117}

SANDERS, JOHN (Potomac District and Cecil County), captain and master of the ship *Rogers* in 1697; captain of a sloop (no name given) on Sep 10, 1703 (date of letter at Bohemia in Cecil County). {Ref: ARMD 23:171; CELR 1:334}

SANDERS, ROBERT, see "John Ball" and "Samuell Bowman" and "John Gardiner," q.v.

SANDERS, WILLIAM (Talbot County), corporal who swore allegiance to the King & Queen of England in 1696. {Ref: ARMD 20:542}

SANDS, JOHN, see "John Fullwood," q.v.

SANDS, THOMAS (Charles County), captain by 1691. {Ref: INAC 12:21}

SANGSTER, JAMES (Somerset County), Protestant and probable soldier in the Revolution of 1689; signed an address and took a loyalty oath supporting the King of England and "for enabling us to defend ourselves against all invaders" on Nov 28, 1689. {Ref: ARMD 8:141}

SARGENT, JOHN (Anne Arundel County), captain and commander of the ship *Dove* on Apr 21, 1724. {Ref: AALR RCW#2:235}

SAUNDERS (SANDERS), EDWARD (England, and Anne Arundel and Queen Anne's Counties), captain by 1724; master of the ship *Sophia* of Biddeford, 1726-1729. {Ref: MDAD 6:320; QALR IK#C:117-118; MDGZ, Feb 4, 1728/9}

SAUNDERS, JOHN (Somerset County), Protestant and probable soldier in the Revolution of 1689; signed an address and took a loyalty oath supporting the King of England and "for enabling us to defend ourselves against all invaders" on Nov 28, 1689. {Ref: ARMD 8:140}

SAUNDERS, THOMAS (Talbot County), soldier (rank not stated) circa 1675; paid for his services in the late expedition against the Nanticoke Indians in 1678. {Ref: ARMD 7:92}

SAUSER (SAWSER, SAUCER), BENJAMIN (Somerset County), soldier by 1678 and probably the "Sergeant Sawser" who was paid for his services in the late expedition against the Nanticoke Indians in 1678; "Capt. Benj: Saucer" was captain of foot troops by 1694; "Benjamin Sawser" (misinterpreted once as "Benjn. Lawser") was a military officer (rank not stated) who swore allegiance to the King & Queen of England in 1696; "Benjamin Sauser (Saser), Sr." died testate by Jun 20, 1716 (date of probate). {Ref: ARMD 7:97, 20:110, 20:544}

SAVAGE, JOHN (St. Mary's County), seaman whose name appeared on "a list of men that goe by water when employed" in 1697. {Ref: ARMD 25:597}

SAVAGE, JOHN (Dorchester County), soldier (rank not stated) circa 1675; paid for his services in the late expedition against the Nanticoke Indians in 1678. {Ref: ARMD 7:92}

SAWYER, PETER, see "Peter Sayer," q.v.

SAXFIELD, JAMES (Talbot County), soldier (rank not stated) circa 1675; paid for his services in the late expedition against the Nanticoke Indians in 1678. {Ref: ARMD 7:90}

SAYER (SAWYER), PETER (Talbot County), captain by 1678; paid for his services in the late expedition against the Nanticoke Indians in 1678; captain and court justice, 1681; major by 1683; sheriff, 1685; major in command of troops in Talbot County, 1686 (name listed once as "Maj. Sawer"); Maryland Council recorded on Apr 10, 1688 that "Major Peter Sayer present Sheriff of Talbot County being intended for England as he himself gives it out whereby there will be a Vacancy of the Sher: Place" in this county; colonel by 1693 (listed as "Col. Sayer" and "Col. Sayers" in 1697); died testate by Nov 2, 1697 (date of probate; Frances Sayer, widow). See "William Combes," q.v. {Ref:

ARMD 5:460, 5:470, 7:88, 7:91, 8:22, 8:560, 15:346, 17:177, 17:380, 25:600; INAC 5:400, 9:263, 17:78; MDWB 7:334}

SCARBOROUGH (SCARBROUGH), JOHN (Somerset and Worcester Counties), probable soldier and officer in 1730's since he was a colonel in the militia by 1745; member of the Lower House of the Maryland Assembly, 1745-1761; born circa 1694, died testate by Sep 19, 1775 (date of probate). {Ref: BDML II:711-712; MDWB 40:462}

SCARBURGH, CHARLES (Somerset County), major by 1688. {Ref: INAC 10:66}

SCARBURGH, EDMUND (Virginia and Somerset County), colonel by 1661; a prominent colonial figure on the Eastern Shore and surveyor general of Virginia; born circa 1618, died after 1671. {Ref: ARMD 3:436; BDML II:711}

SCARBUROW, EDMUND (Somerset County), captain by 1680. {Ref: INAC 7B:110}

SCARTH, ISAAC (Anne Arundel and Calvert Counties), captain and commander of the ship *Jonathan and Ann* riding at anchor in South River on May 25, 1714 and riding at anchor in Herring Bay on Apr 16, 1716; captain and commander of the ship *Sea Horse* in 1722 and master of said ship riding in the Patuxent River on Feb 24, 1723/4 (name misinterpreted once as "Isaac Searth"). {Ref: AALR IB#2:137, 273; PGLR I:465, M:148}

SCARTH, JONATHAN (England and Anne Arundel County), captain by 1699 and to at least 1729; "Jonathon Scarth & Son (merchants in London)" before 1730. {Ref: INAC 19:86; MDAD 9:487, 10:558}

SCEEL, EDWARD (Somerset County), boatswain by 1716. {Ref: INAC 37A:82}

SCHEE, HARMANUS (Kent County), captain by 1717. {Ref: INAC 37C:138}

SCHOLLING, JONATHAN (Kent County), military officer (rank not stated) who swore allegiance to the King & Queen of England in 1696. {Ref: ARMD 20:541}

SCOFFIN, JOHN (St. Mary's County), soldier (rank not stated) in 1642; paid for 3 weeks' service under Capt. William Brainthwaite in November, 1642. {Ref: ARMD 3:119, 3:122}

SCOT, ANDREW (Anne Arundel County), captain and commander of the galley *Jonathan* riding at anchor in South River on Sep 15, 1715. {Ref: AALR IB#2:243}

SCOTT, CHRISTIAN, see "John Scott," q.v.

SCOTT, CUTHBERT, see "John Jordaine," q.v.

SCOTT, DANIEL (Baltimore County), ensign before 1696; military officer who swore allegiance to the King & Queen of England in 1696; died intestate by Jun 4, 1725 (date of administration bond); inventory of "Daniel Scott the Elder" was taken on Jun 9, 1725 (Jane Scott, widow, later married John Watson). {Ref: ARMD 20:544, 23:20; BDML II:714-715; BBCF:567; MINV 10:402; MDAD 6:406}

SCOTT, DAY (Somerset County), captain and master of the sloop *Eleanor* in 1734 (built in Somerset County in 1730); born circa 1706 (aged about 45 when deposed in 1745), died testate by Aug 17, 1757 (date of probate). {Ref: MDCB 82:20; MDEP:164; MDWB 30:356}

SCOTT, EDWARD (Chester Hundred, Kent County), captain by 1707; member of the Lower House of the Maryland Assembly, 1710-1718; lieutenant colonel by 1715; colonel by 1717; died testate by Nov 15, 1725 (date of probate;

Rachel Scott, widow). {Ref: ARMD 27:495, 29:204, 29:401, 30:389, 33:156, 34:741; BDML II:715; CESM:1; KELR JS#X:110; CFES 1:312; INKC:150; INAC 39B:33; MDWB 18:420; MINV 11:289; MDEP:163}

SCOTT, ELIZABETH, see "John Scott" and "John Jordain," q.v.

SCOTT (SCOT), GEORGE (county not indicated), private in the Maryland troops "raised to strengthen Albany, New York and resist the French and Indian enemies" in 1690. {Ref: SHMD I:355}

SCOTT, JAMES (Talbot County), soldier (rank not stated) circa 1675; paid for his services in the late expedition against the Nanticoke Indians in 1678; died testate by Feb 4, 1681/2 (date of probate; Mary Scott, widow). {Ref: ARMD 7:91; MDWB 4:72}

SCOTT, JAMES (county or port not indicated), captain and master of the brigantine *Mayflower* in 1696. {Ref: ARMD 23:12}

SCOTT, JANE, see "Daniel Scott," q.v.

SCOTT, JOHN (England and Patuxent District), captain of the brigantine *Katherine* in 1694-1695; one John Scott died testate in Calvert County by Mar 4, 1699/1700 (date of probate; Christian Scott, widow). {Ref: ARMD 23:317; MDWB 6:342}

SCOTT, JOHN (Somerset and Worcester Counties), captain by 1724; died testate by Jul 8, 1763 (date of probate; Elizabeth Scott, widow). {Ref: CESM:62; MDEP:164; MDWB 31:965}

SCOTT (SCOT), JOHN (Calvert County), Protestant and probable soldier in the Revolution of 1689; signed an address and took a loyalty oath supporting the King of England and "to reestablish Lord Baltimore in his ancient power and government" on Nov 16, 1689. {Ref: ARMD 8:132}

SCOTT, MARY, see "James Talbott," q.v.

SCOTT, RACHEL, see "Edward Scott," q.v.

SCOTT, WILLIAM (St. Mary's County), captain and mariner by 1652. {Ref: ARMD 10:187, 10:343}

SCOTTING, JOSEPH (England and St. Mary's County), captain and master of the ship *John and Thomas* of London in 1691; captain and master of a ship (no name given) riding at anchor at the mouth of the Patuxent River on Jul 1, 1695 (date of petition). {Ref: ARMD 8:239, 20:306}

SCOUGALL, ALEXANDER (Annapolis District), captain and master of the ship *Benedict* in 1730-1731; captain and master of the snow *London Town* of Maryland in 1732; captain and master of the ship *Frederick* in 1734; master of the sloop *Charming Molly* in 1738 (built at Herring Creek in 1733). {Ref: MDGZ, Mar 16, 1732/3 and Sep 27, 1734; CVPR:12; MDCB 82:49, 82:57}

SCOVELL, GEORGE, see "William Claiborne," q.v.

SCRIVAN, WILLIAM (Kent County), soldier (rank not stated) circa 1675; paid for his services in the late expedition against the Nanticoke Indians in 1678. {Ref: ARMD 7:94}

SCURFFIELD, EDWARD (St. Mary's County), captain and mariner, 1650. {Ref: ARMD 10:53}

SCURY, SAMUEL (Potomac District), captain and master of the ship *Swann* in 1697. {Ref: ARMD 23:172}
SEALEY, DANIELL (Somerset County), soldier (rank not stated) circa 1675; paid for his services in the late expedition against the Nanticoke Indians in 1678. {Ref: ARMD 7:98}
SEALING, GEORGE (Calvert County), Protestant and probable soldier in the Revolution of 1689; signed an address and took a loyalty oath (made his "X" mark) supporting the King of England and "to reestablish Lord Baltimore in his ancient power and government" on Nov 16, 1689. {Ref: ARMD 8:132}
SEALY, WILLIAM (Somerset County), sergeant before 1682; paid for his services out of an assessment levied by the General Assembly for the public good in 1682. {Ref: ARMD 7:439}
SEAMAN, JAMES (St. Mary's County), military officer (rank not stated) who swore allegiance to the King & Queen of England in 1696. {Ref: ARMD 20:540}
SEARELL, ROBERT (St. Mary's County), boatswain by 1665. {Ref: ARMD 49:434}
SEARRA, GEORGE (St. Mary's County), soldier (rank not stated) circa 1675; paid for his services in the late expedition against the Nanticoke Indians in 1678. {Ref: ARMD 7:103}
SEATON, JOHN (county or port not indicated), captain and master of the ship *Good Hope* of London in 1691. {Ref: ARMD 8:240}
SEAWARD, JOSEPH (Somerset County), soldier (rank not stated) circa 1675; paid for his services in the late expedition against the Nanticoke Indians in 1678. {Ref: ARMD 7:97}
SEDDEMAN, RICHARD (Talbot County), Protestant and probable soldier in the Revolution of 1689; signed an address and took a loyalty oath supporting the King of England and the reestablishment of Lord Baltimore into power on Nov 18, 1689. {Ref: ARMD 8:134}
SEDGWICK, JAMES (Talbot County), soldier (rank not stated) circa 1675; paid for his services in the late expedition against the Nanticoke Indians in 1678; Protestant and probable soldier in the Revolution of 1689; signed an address and took a loyalty oath supporting the King of England and the reestablishment of Lord Baltimore into power on Nov 28, 1689; died testate by Sep 11, 1694 (date of probate). {Ref: ARMD 7:90, 8:144; MDWB 7:77}
SEDWICK, BENJAMIN, see "John Godsgrace," q.v.
SEGAR, EDWARD (Talbot County), soldier (rank not stated) circa 1675; paid for his services in the late expedition against the Nanticoke Indians in 1678. {Ref: ARMD 7:88}
SEGARR, WILLIAM (Kent County), soldier (rank not stated) circa 1675; paid for his services in the late expedition against the Nanticoke Indians in 1678. {Ref: ARMD 7:94}
SELBE, MARY, see "Daniell Selby," q.v.
SELBY (SELBE), DANIELL (Somerset County), soldier (rank not stated) circa 1675; paid for his services in the late expedition against the Nanticoke Indians

in 1678; died testate by May 16, 1696 (date of probate; Mary Selbe, widow). {Ref: ARMD 7:99; MDWB 7:244}

SELBY, EDWARD (Anne Arundel County), captain before Nov 1, 1693 (date of deed). {Ref: AALR WH#4:229}

SELBY, JOHN (Anne Arundel County), military officer (rank not stated) who swore allegiance to the King & Queen of England in 1696. {Ref: ARMD 20:541}

SELWOOD, WILLIAM (Talbot County), captain by 1706. {Ref: INAC 25:246}

SEMON, WILLIAM (Prince George's County), soldier (trooper) under the command of Capt. Richard Owen in June, 1699. {Ref: ARMD 24:121}

SENHOUSE, ANDREW (Oxford District), captain and master of the ship *Tryall* in 1731. {Ref: CVPR:12}

SENHOUSE, ANDREW (Annapolis District), captain and commander of a ship (no name given) in 1698. {Ref: ARMD 23:466}

SENNET, GARRARD (Charles County), soldier (rank not stated) in Capt. James Langworth's Company before 1661 (year of the captain's death, but his ammunition report was not filed until 1664 by Henry Adames); name listed once as "Garrat Sennet." {Ref: ARMD 53:118; CHLR B:379}

SEPSEN, JOHN (Kent County), soldier (rank not stated) on Isle of Kent who swore allegiance to the Commonwealth of England on Apr 5, 1652. {Ref: INKC:101}

SERGEANT (SERGENT), JOHN (Talbot County), soldier (rank not stated) circa 1675; paid for his services in the late expedition against the Nanticoke Indians in 1678; died by Nov 30, 1698 (date of inventory). {Ref: ARMD 7:90; INAC 18:233}

SERLE, WILLIAM (Talbot County), soldier (rank not stated) circa 1675; paid for his services in the late expedition against the Nanticoke Indians in 1678. {Ref: ARMD 7:89}

SEWALL, HENRY (England and Calvert County), colonel, 1661-1665; member of the Upper House (Maryland Council), 1662-1664; provincial court justice, 1661-1665; died testate by Apr 17, 1665 (date of probate; Jane Sewall, widow). See "Nicholas Sewall," q.v. {Ref: BDML II:724; HCCM:309; MDWB 1:225}

SEWALL, JANE, see "Henry Sewall," q.v.

SEWALL (SEWELL, SEAWALL), NICHOLAS (England and St. Mary's County), major by 1682; member of the Upper House (Maryland Council), 1682-1689; on May 31, 1692 "Major Nicholas Sewall by his petition prays allowance for three Horses prest from him in the time of the late Revolution for his Majestys Service and made use of for some Considerable time one of them the best and his own Particular Riding Horse so Grossly abused that soon after he was Returned home died, his Family Provisions and his Hay Oates and Straw Fodder for his Cattle and other Creatures all destroyed and devoured by the Guards quartered upon him and by that means his stock also died;" major, son, and heir of Henry Sewall, deceased, *q.v.* (as noted in General Assembly proceedings on Jul 22, 1721); born circa 1655 (aged about 67 when deposed in 1722), died testate by May 9, 1737 (date of probate). {Ref: ARMD 5:462, 13:324-

325, 17:365, 20:201, 34:132; MDAD 2:411; BDML II:724-725; MDEP:165; PGLR A:417, Q:571; MDWB 21:775}

SEWALL (SEAWALL), RICHARD (St. Mary's County), major by 1690; noted in a letter from John Coode to the Secretary of State on Mar 14, 1690 that "Major Richard Seawall sonn to the Lady Baltemore one of the late deputy Governors and secretaries of this Province (with others whom wee have sufficient to accuse of tyranack and treasonable practices) fled with a small yacht with armes and ammunition into Virginia from whence returned suddenly againe into this Province, upon his returne came to shore. In the interim Mr. Paine, Collector, in a small boat with four men went on board ..." and demanded their reason for entering without clearance and "was immediately shott dead ... Seawell was then a shore when the fact was committed but suddenly fled back allsoe into Virginia where he is still at libertie." {Ref: ARMD 8:171}

SEWALL, SAMUELL (Somerset County), lieutenant before 1678; paid for his services in the late expedition against the Nanticoke Indians in 1678. {Ref: ARMD 7:99}

SEWALL (SEWELL), THOMAS (Somerset County), soldier (rank not stated) circa 1675; paid for his services in the late expedition against the Nanticoke Indians in 1678; born circa 1634 (aged about 29 when deposed in 1663), died testate by Mar 14, 1692/3 (date of probate; Jane Sewell, widow). {Ref: ARMD 7:100, 49:140; MDWB 6:33}

SEWELL, ELIZABETH, see "Henry Sewell," q.v.

SEWELL, HENRY (St. Mary's and/or Anne Arundel County), colonel by 1686 (his name appeared on a list of debts in an estate account filed in St. Mary's County in 1686); one Henry Sewell died testate in Anne Arundel County by Dec 5, 1700 (date of probate; Elizabeth Sewell, widow) and another Henry Sewell died testate in St. Mary's County by May 7, 1722 (date of probate; mentioned his brother Nicholas and their father Major Nicholas Sewell). Additional research will be necessary before drawing conclusions. {Ref: FAAH:136-138; INAC 8:479; MDWB 11:16, 17:142}

SEWELL, JANE, see "Thomas Sewall," q.v.

SEWELL, WILLIAM (Prince George's County), foot soldier (rank not stated) under the command of Capt. Richard Owen in June, 1699. {Ref: ARMD 24:122}

SEWER, FRANCIS (Patuxent District), captain and master of the ship *Chance* in 1731. {Ref: CVPR:12}

SEXTONE, PATRICK (Kent County), soldier (rank not stated) circa 1675; paid for his services in the late expedition against the Nanticoke Indians in 1678. {Ref: ARMD 7:94}

SEYMOUR, JOHN (England and Annapolis), military officer and colonial bureaucrat; captain by 1667; lieutenant colonel of Life Guards in 1687; participated in the French campaigns of William III and in the Spanish campaigns of 1702; colonel by 1702; commissioned captain general and governor of Maryland in 1702 and "personally assumed office" on Apr 12, 1704, having arrived in this province after 36 years in the British Army; born

1649, died testate on Jul 30, 1709 (will probated on Sep 17, 1709; Hester Seymour, present wife and widow). {Ref: ARMD 24:355, 25:163, 25:243, 29:358; BDML II:726; CHLR C#2:38; MDWB 12:155, pt. 2}

SHADWELL, CHRISTOPHER (Charles and Somerset Counties), soldier (rank not stated) circa 1675; paid for his services in Charles County in the late expedition against the Nanticoke Indians in 1678; paid for his services in Somerset County out of an assessment levied by the General Assembly for the public good in 1682. {Ref: ARMD 7:101, 7:442}

SHANK (SHANKS, SHANKES), JOHN (St. Mary's County), Indian interpreter by 1681; died testate by Feb 16, 1684/5 (date of probate; Abigall Shank, widow). {Ref: ARMD 15:364; MDWB 4:91}

SHANKLAND, WILLIAM (Somerset County), Protestant and probable soldier in the Revolution of 1689; signed an address and took a loyalty oath supporting the King of England and "for enabling us to defend ourselves against all invaders" on Nov 28, 1689. {Ref: ARMD 8:141}

SHANKS (SHANKE), JOHN (St. Mary's County), Protestant and probable soldier in the Revolution of 1689; signed an address and took a loyalty oath supporting the King of England and the reestablishment of Lord Baltimore into power on Nov 28, 1689; died intestate by Mar 3, 1720/1 (date of administrtation account). {Ref: ARMD 8:147, 23:442; MDAD 2:433}

SHANNADIN, JEREMIAH (Calvert County), military officer (rank not stated) who swore allegiance to the King & Queen of England in 1696. {Ref: ARMD 20:543}

SHARP, JOHN (Annapolis District), captain and master of the ship *David and Sarah* riding in Severn River on Jun 12, 1706. {Ref: AALR WT#2:346; INAC 35A:259}

SHARP, ROBERT (Annapolis District), captain and master of the sloop *Phoenix* in 1734. {Ref: MDGZ, May 24, 1734}

SHARPE, ELIZABETH, see "William Sharpe," q.v.

SHARPE, ROBERT (Somerset County), ensign before 1678; paid for his services in the late expedition against the Nanticoke Indians in 1678. {Ref: ARMD 7:97}

SHARPE (SHARP), WILLIAM (Calvert and Talbot Counties), probable soldier (rank not stated) by 1678; paid for his services in the late expedition against the Nanticoke Indians in 1678; he supported the Revolution of 1689 (signed an address and took a loyalty oath supporting the King of England and the reestablishment of Lord Baltimore into power on Nov 28, 1689), but his Quakerism excluded him from office after 1692; born circa 1655, died testate by Sep 7, 1699 (date of probate; Elizabeth Sharpe, widow). {Ref: ARMD 7:89, 8:144, 17:380; BDML II:728; MDWB 6:289}

SHARPLESS, CUTHBERT (St. Mary's County), captain and master of the ship *Barbados Merchant* in 1693. {Ref: ARMD 20:183}

SHARTEE, MARTINE (county not indicated), Frenchman and Indian interpreter who married among the Shawanole Indians before 1697. {Ref: ARMD 23:428-429}

SHAW (SHAWE), RALPH (Charles County), probable soldier (rank not stated) before 1682; paid for his services out of an assessment levied by the General Assembly for the public good in 1682; Protestant and probable soldier in the Revolution of 1689; signed an address and took a loyalty oath supporting the King of England and the reestablishment of Lord Baltimore into power on Nov 28, 1689. {Ref: ARMD 7:440, 8:138}

SHEELES, JOHN (Charles County), soldier (rank not stated) who was issued a "gun or fowling piece" by Col. Warren on Sep 15, 1694. {Ref: ARMD 20:206, 20:208}

SHEFIELD, FRANCIS (St. Mary's County), soldier (rank not stated) circa 1675; paid for his services in the late expedition against the Nanticoke Indians in 1678. {Ref: ARMD 7:102}

SHEFFIELD, FRANCIS (William and Mary Parish, Charles County), a seafaring man in 1697. {Ref: ARMD 25:597}

SHEFFIELD, JOHN, see "Isaac Hammerton" and "Walter Needham," q.v.

SHELLDRAKE, HENRY (Cecil County), soldier (rank not stated) circa 1675; paid for his services in the late expedition against the Nanticoke Indians in 1678. {Ref: ARMD 7:95}

SHEPHERD, CHARLES (Charles County), Protestant and probable soldier in the Revolution of 1689; signed an address and took a loyalty oath supporting the King of England and the reestablishment of Lord Baltimore into power on Nov 28, 1689. {Ref: ARMD 8:138}

SHEPHERD (SHEPHARD), FRANCIS (Talbot County), Protestant and probable soldier in the Revolution of 1689; signed an address and took a loyalty oath supporting the King of England and the reestablishment of Lord Baltimore into power on Nov 18, 1689; died testate by Mar 21, 1691/2 (date of probate). {Ref: ARMD 8:134; MDWB 7:29}

SHEPHERD (SHEEPARD), JOHN (Kent County), military officer (rank not stated) who swore allegiance to the King & Queen of England in 1696. {Ref: ARMD 20:540}

SHEPHERD (SHEPPARD, SHEPPART), JOHN (New England and St. Mary's County), mariner by 1664; "John Shepheard, of New England" died testate in Maryland by Mar 15, 1676/7 (date of probate). {Ref: ARMD 49:191, 49:210; MINV 3:123; MDWB 5:171}

SHEPHERD, RICHARD (St. Mary's County), captain and master of the ship *St. George* in 1681. {Ref: ARMD 5:301}

SHEPHERD (SHEPHEARD), ROBERT (Calvert County), Protestant and probable soldier in the Revolution of 1689; signed an address and took a loyalty oath supporting the King of England and "to reestablish Lord Baltimore in his ancient power and government" on Nov 16, 1689. {Ref: ARMD 8:131}

SHERCLIFFE, MILDRED, see "William Shirtliffe," q.v.

SHERED, SAMUEL (county not indicated), private in the Maryland troops "raised to strengthen Albany, New York and resist the French and Indian enemies" in 1690. {Ref: SHMD I:355}

SHEREDINE, THOMAS (Calvert and Baltimore Counties), captain by 1724; sheriff, Baltimore County, 1727-1730, 1750-1752; major by 1744; member of the Lower House of the Maryland Assembly, 1732-1750; born circa 1699 (aged about 35 when deposed in 1734, aged about 45 when deposed in 1744, and aged about 46 when deposed in 1745), died intestate on May 28, 1752 (Tabitha Sheredine, widow). {Ref: BDML II:730-731; BALR IS#G; BBCF:576; HBCC:45, 311; MDEP:166; MDGZ, Apr 26, 1745}

SHERLY, RICHARD (St. Mary's County), seaman whose name appeared on "a list of men that goe by water when employed" in 1697. {Ref: ARMD 25:597}

SHERRIFFE, ALEXANDER (Cecil County), soldier (rank not stated) circa 1675; paid for his services in the late expedition against the Nanticoke Indians in 1678. {Ref: ARMD 7:95}

SHERWOOD, HUGH (Talbot County), Protestant and probable soldier in the Revolution of 1689; signed an address and took a loyalty oath supporting the King of England and the reestablishment of Lord Baltimore into power on Nov 18, 1689. {Ref: ARMD 8:134}

SHILD, THOMAS (Somerset County), Protestant and probable soldier in the Revolution of 1689; signed an address and took a loyalty oath supporting the King of England and "for enabling us to defend ourselves against all invaders" on Nov 28, 1689; a "Thomas Shiles" died intestate by Mar 25, 1721/2 (date of administration account; Naomy Shiles, widow). Additional research will be necessary before drawing conclusions. {Ref: ARMD 8:139; MDAD 3:380}

SHIPWAY, JOHN (Somerset County), soldier (rank not stated) circa 1675; paid for his services in the late expedition against the Nanticoke Indians in 1678; died testate by Sep 24, 1687 (date of probate). {Ref: ARMD 7:100; MDWB 4:273}

SHIRLEY, JAMES (Pocomoke District), captain and master of the ship *John and Anna* in 1731. {Ref: CVPR:12}

SHIRTLIFFE (SHERCLIFFE), WILLIAM (St. Mary's County), soldier (rank not stated) circa 1675; paid for his services in the late expedition against the Nanticoke Indians in 1678; died testate by Jul 1, 1707 (date of probate; Mildred Shercliffe, widow). {Ref: ARMD 7:102; MDWB 12:157}

SHLEVINGTONE, RICHARD (Talbot County), soldier (rank not stated) circa 1675; paid for his services in the late expedition against the Nanticoke Indians in 1678. {Ref: ARMD 7:92}

SHORTER, JOHN (Anne Arundel County), captain and commander of the ship *Hopewell* riding in West River on Feb 13, 1727/8. {Ref: AALR SY#1:339}

SHOVEBOTTOM, RICHARD (St. Mary's County), seaman whose name appeared on "a list of men that goe by water when employed" in 1697. {Ref: ARMD 25:597}

SHOWELL, SAMUEL (Somerset County), Protestant and probable soldier in the Revolution of 1689; signed an address and took a loyalty oath supporting the

King of England and "for enabling us to defend ourselves against all invaders" on Nov 28, 1689. {Ref: ARMD 8:140}

SHUTTLEWORTH, BARNABAS (England and Talbot County), mariner, of Bristol, by 1677. {Ref: ARMD 66:472, 67:223}

SHUTTLEWORTH, THOMAS (Charles County), soldier (rank not stated) circa 1675; paid for his services in the late expedition against the Nanticoke Indians in 1678. {Ref: ARMD 7:101}

SICKLEMORE, SAMUEL (Baltimore County), lieutenant by 1696; swore allegiance to the King & Queen of England in 1696 (name listed as "Samuell Sycklemore"); member of the Lower House of the Maryland Assembly, 1701-1704; born circa 1659 (aged about 46 when deposed in 1705), died circa 1714. {Ref: ARMD 20:544; BDML II:736; BBCF:579; MDEP:167}

SIDBURRY, EDWARD (Somerset County), soldier (rank not stated) circa 1675; paid for his services in the late expedition against the Nanticoke Indians in 1678. {Ref: ARMD 7:99}

SIDWELL, ROGER, see "Thomas Todd," q.v.

SIKES, THOMAS (St. Mary's County), Protestant and probable soldier in the Revolution of 1689; signed an address and took a loyalty oath supporting the King of England and the reestablishment of Lord Baltimore into power on Nov 28, 1689. {Ref: ARMD 8:146}

SILIVANE (SILVANE), JAMES (Somerset County), soldier (rank not stated) circa 1675; paid for his services in the late expedition against the Nanticoke Indians in 1678. {Ref: ARMD 7:98}

SIMMES, IGNATIUS (Charles County), mariner by 1734; captain and master of the schooner *Eleanor* in May, 1736 (built at the Potomac River in 1735) and master of the schooner *Polly* in August, 1736 (built at Pamunkie in 1736). {Ref: MDCB 82:44-45}

SIMMES, JAMES (St. Mary's County), Protestant and probable soldier in the Revolution of 1689; signed an address and took a loyalty oath supporting the King of England and the reestablishment of Lord Baltimore into power on Nov 28, 1689. {Ref: ARMD 8:146}

SIMMONS, THOMAS, JR. (Calvert County), Protestant and probable soldier in the Revolution of 1689; signed an address and took a loyalty oath supporting the King of England and "to reestablish Lord Baltimore in his ancient power and government" on Nov 16, 1689. {Ref: ARMD 8:132}

SIMONDS, JAMES (county not indicated), probable soldier (rank not stated) before 1682; paid for his services out of an assessment levied by the General Assembly for the public good in 1682. {Ref: ARMD 7:440}

SIMPSON, ALEXANDER (Charles County), soldier (rank not stated) in Capt. James Langworth's Company before 1661 (year of the captain's death, but his ammunition report was not filed until 1664 by Henry Adames); died testate by Apr 12, 1670 (date of probate). {Ref: CHLR B:379; MDWB 1:379}

SIMPSON, JEREMIAH (Talbot County), a seafaring man in 1697. {Ref: ARMD 25:601}

SIMPSON, PAUL (St. Mary's County), captain and mariner by 1649; born circa 1590 (aged about 60 when deposed on Jun 28, 1650 and Sep 24, 1650). {Ref: ARMD 4:512, 10:20, 10:73, 10:190; FMDP:221}

SIMS, RICHARD (Charles County), soldier (rank not stated) in Capt. James Langworth's Company before 1661 (year of the captain's death, but his ammunition report was not filed until 1664 by Henry Adames). {Ref: CHLR B:379}

SIMSON, ROBERT (Somerset County), Protestant and probable soldier in the Revolution of 1689; signed an address and took a loyalty oath supporting the King of England and "for enabling us to defend ourselves against all invaders" on Nov 28, 1689. {Ref: ARMD 8:139}

SINCLEARE, JAMES, JR. (Scotland, England, and Maryland, port not indicated), captain by 1696; master of the ship *James and John* in 1696. {Ref: ARMD 20:340-341}

SINCLEARE (SINCKLARE), ROBERT (England and Maryland, port not indicated), captain by 1688; captain and master of the ship *Elizabeth* in 1695. {Ref: ARMD 20:340; INAC 10:117}

SINGLETON, JOHN (St. Mary's County), soldier (rank not stated) circa 1675; paid for his services in the late expedition against the Nanticoke Indians in 1678. {Ref: ARMD 7:102}

SINKLAR, MICHAELL, see "Charles Greenbury," q.v.

SINNS, THOMAS (Talbot County), soldier (rank not stated) circa 1675; paid for his services in the late expedition against the Nanticoke Indians in 1678. {Ref: ARMD 7:88}

SINUES, ---- (county or port not indicated), captain of a ship (no name given) in 1696. {Ref: ARMD 23:10}

SISSORS, EDWARD (St. Mary's County), Protestant and probable soldier in the Revolution of 1689; signed an address and took a loyalty oath supporting the King of England and the reestablishment of Lord Baltimore into power on Nov 28, 1689. {Ref: ARMD 8:147}

SKIME, ROGER (Calvert County), Protestant and probable soldier in the Revolution of 1689; signed an address and took a loyalty oath supporting the King of England and "to reestablish Lord Baltimore in his ancient power and government" on Nov 16, 1689. {Ref: ARMD 8:131}

SKINNER, ADDERTON (Calvert County), major by 1732; member of the Lower House of the Maryland Assembly, 1725-1737; colonel by 1752; born circa 1677-1678 (aged about 60 when deposed in 1737 and aged about 68 when deposed in 1747), died testate by Nov 20, 1756 (date of probate). {Ref: ARMD 39:55, 39:151, 39:220; BDML II:738; HCCM:311; MDEP:168; MDWB 30:208}

SKINNER, ANDREW (Anne Arundel County), ensign, commissioned Dec 9, 1661. {Ref: ARMD 3:444}

SKINNER, ANDREW (Talbot County), soldier (rank not stated) circa 1675; paid for his services in the late expedition against the Nanticoke Indians in 1678; mariner by 1711; "Andrew Skinner, gentleman" died testate by Jul 28, 1717 (date of probate; Elizabeth Skinner, widow). {Ref: ARMD 7:87, 7:91; TALR 12:379; MDWB 14:557}

SKINNER, ANNE (ANN), see "Robert Skinner," q.v.

SKINNER, CLARKE (Calvert County), military officer (rank not stated) who swore allegiance to the King & Queen of England in 1696. {Ref: ARMD 20:543}

SKINNER, ELIZABETH, see "Andrew Skinner," q.v.

SKINNER, JOHN (St. Mary's County), captain and mariner by 1643. {Ref: ARMD 4:189}

SKINNER, ROBERT (England and Calvert County), soldier (rank not stated) circa 1675; paid for his services in the late expedition against the Nanticoke Indians in 1678; died testate by Dec 13, 1686 (date of probate; Anne Storer Truman Skinner, widow). {Ref: ARMD 7:103; BDML II:738; HCCM:311; MDWB 4:230}

SKINNER, ROBERT (Calvert County), military officer (rank not stated) who swore allegiance to the King & Queen of England in 1696; member of the Lower House of the Maryland Assembly, 1704-1711; died intestate by Jan 26, 1712/3 (date of administration bond; Ann Tannihill Skinner, widow). {Ref: ARMD 20:543; BDML II:738}

SKINNER, THOMAS (Somerset County), soldier (rank not stated) circa 1675; paid for his services in the late expedition against the Nanticoke Indians in 1678. {Ref: ARMD 7:99}

SKIPPER, JOHN (St. Mary's County), Protestant and probable soldier in the Revolution of 1689; signed an address and took a loyalty oath supporting the King of England and the reestablishment of Lord Baltimore into power on Nov 28, 1689. {Ref: ARMD 8:147}

SLADE, WILLIAM (Baltimore County), lieutenant by 1696; swore allegiance to the King & Queen of England in 1696; "Capt. William Slayd" witnessed the will of George Hope in 1721; "William Slade" died testate by May 19, 1731 (date of probate). {Ref: ARMD 20:544; MDWB 16:480, 20:276; BBCF:585}

SLATER, JOHN (Talbot County), soldier (rank not stated) circa 1675; paid for services in late expedition against Nanticoke Indians in 1678. {ARMD 7:92}

SLATER, RICHARD (Kent County), soldier (rank not stated) on Isle of Kent who swore allegiance to the Commonwealth of England in 1652. {INKC:101}

SLEICOME, GEORGE (Dorchester County), sailor before 1725; died testate by Nov 26, 1725 (date of probate; Sarah Sleicome, widow). {MDWB 18:414}

SLYE, CHARLES (St. Mary's County), soldier circa 1702 to 1732; adjutant, 1732-1734; petitioned the governor in August, 1732, stating he "is a Native of this Province and has served the Crowns of Great Britain as a Souldier for the space of thirty years and upwards; and being qualified in military Discipline for handling of Arms for Horse and foot with great Dexterity and hopes that upon Tryall he shall give your Excellency full Satisfaction of his Capacity in that

Affair; May it therefore please your Excellency to appoint your Petitioner Adjutant over the Militia of this his Lordships Province with a Competency for his Support such as to your Excellency shall seem meet." On Aug 8, 1732 he was appointed Adjutant of this Province with an annual allowance of £40 sterling. {Ref: ARMD 28:12-13, 28:70}

SLYE (SLY), GERRARD (England and St. Mary's County), captain by 1675; captain of a party of rangers ordered on Nov 3, 1675 "to Range the woods about Pascattoway & the Susquahanough ffort, to take upp all such horses as they shall finde that were lost by the Souldiers in the late Expedition against the Susquahanough Indians" in 1675; captain on the Council of War in July, 1676; paid for his services in the late expedition against the Nanticoke Indians in 1678; captain and high sheriff of St. Mary's County, 1678; court justice (quorum), 1679; captain and merchant, 1697-1703; died by May 4, 1703 (date of first inventory). See "Edward Evans," q.v. {Ref: ARMD 7:102, 15:56, 15:99, 15:190, 15:255, 15:326, 23:293, 24:113; INAC 24:147; LMCL:65}

SLYE (SLY), JOHN (St. Mary's County), captain by 1654; commissioned captain of militia "in St. Maries and Patomock River from Clements Bay upwards and all the forces in those parts" on Apr 24, 1655. {Ref: ARMD 10:413}

SLYE (SLY, SLEY), ROBERT (England and St. Clement's Manor, St. Mary's County), captain by 1655; member of the Lower House of the Maryland Assembly, 1657-1669; born circa 1628 (aged about 30 when deposed in 1658 and aged about 38 when deposed in 1666), died testate by Mar 13, 1670/1 (date of probate; Susannah Slye, widow). {Ref: ARMD 1:359, 41:145, 57:33; FAAH:27; BDML II:739; MDWB 1:422}

SLYE, SUSANNAH, see "Robert Slye," q.v.

SMALLPAGE, ROBERT (Charles County), probable soldier (rank not stated) before 1682; paid for his services out of an assessment levied by the General Assembly for the public good in 1682; died testate by Apr 2, 1698 (date of probate). {Ref: ARMD 7:439; MDWB 6:75}

SMALLWOOD, ELEANOR, see "William Smallwood," q.v.

SMALLWOOD, JAMES, SR. (England and Charles County), ranger, 1675; member of George Godfrey's troop of soldiers in 1681; probable soldier (rank not stated) before 1682; paid for his services out of an assessment levied by the General Assembly for the public good in 1682; major of foot troops in 1689; Protestant and soldier in the Revolution of 1689; signed an address and took a loyalty oath supporting the King of England and the reestablishment of Lord Baltimore into power on Nov 28, 1689; member of the Lower House of the Maryland Assembly, 1692-1714; military officer who swore allegiance to the King & Queen of England in 1696; major, paid "for his trouble, horse higher & other Charges aboute the Indians affairs" on May 8, 1700; lieutenant colonel by 1701; colonel by 1704; died testate by Jan 12, 1714/5 (date of probate; Mary Smallwood, widow); his death was also noted in a petition by his son Ledstone Smallwood and grandson John Smallwood on May 5, 1715. {Ref: ARMD 7:439,

8:138, 8:404, 13:242, 13:351, 15:56, 20:109, 20:130, 20:153, 20:543, 23:252, 24:35, 24:118, 24:128, 27:202, 29:204, 29:391, 30:114; BDML II:740; CHLR C#2:135; MDWB 14:31}

SMALLWOOD, LEDSTONE, see "James Smallwood," q.v.

SMALLWOOD, MARY, see "James Smallwood, Sr.," q.v.

SMALLWOOD, WILLIAM (Charles County), capatin before 1706; died testate by Jun 12, 1706 (date of probate; Eleanor Smallwood, widow); account filed Jun 23, 1708 by Eleanor Philpott (wife of Edward). {Ref: MDWB 12:27; INAC 28:129, 29:376}

SMART, JOHN (county or port not indicated), captain and master of the ship *Ogle* in 1734-1735 (formerly the *Success*, built at Boston in 1733). {Ref: MDCB 82:27}

SMART, RICHARD (Dorchester County), mariner by 1706; captain and master of the sloop *Speedwell* riding at anchor in West River on Jun 13, 1706; died testate by Jun 21, 1729 (date of probate; Elizabeth Smart, widow) {Ref: AALR WT#2:346; MDWB 19:714; MINV 15:132; MDAD 2:518, 10:148}

SMETH, ROBERT (Talbot County), Protestant and probable soldier in the Revolution of 1689; signed an address and took a loyalty oath supporting the King of England and the reestablishment of Lord Baltimore into power on Nov 28, 1689. {Ref: ARMD 8:144}

SMITH, ALICE, see "Thomas Smith," q.v.

SMITH, ANN, see "Henry Smith" and "Edward Smith," q.v.

SMITH, BENJAMIN (England and Cecil County), mariner, of Biddeford, by 1684; land owner on Guerdin's Creek and Elk River in Cecil County in 1685; died testate by Feb 15, 1687/8 (date of probate; Rebecca Smith, widow). {Ref: CELR 2:245-246; MDWB 4:290}

SMITH, BERNARD (Kent County), soldier (rank not stated) circa 1675; paid for his services in the late expedition against the Nanticoke Indians in 1678. {Ref: ARMD 7:94}

SMITH, CHARLES SOMERSET (Charles County), captain before 1733; born circa 1698 (aged about 20 when deposed in 1718), died testate by Feb 20, 1738/9 (date of probate; Margaret Smith, widow). {Ref: MDWB 22:23; MINV 24:183; MDAD 12:17; MDEP:170}

SMITH, DANIEL (St. Mary's County), Protestant and probable soldier in the Revolution of 1689; signed an address and took a loyalty oath (made his "X" mark) supporting the King of England and the reestablishment of Lord Baltimore into power on Nov 28, 1689; captain by 1696; "Daniel Smith, shipwright" died testate by Feb 1, 1719/20 (date of probate; Elizabeth Smith, widow). {Ref: ARMD 8:147; INAC 13B:141; MDWB 16:238}

SMITH, DANIEL (Cecil County), Protestant and probable soldier in the Revolution of 1689; signed an address and took a loyalty oath supporting the King of England and the reestablishment of Lord Baltimore into power on Nov 18, 1689. {Ref: ARMD 8:135}

SMITH, DOROTHY, see "John Smith," q.v.

SMITH, EDWARD (Talbot County), soldier (rank not stated) circa 1675; paid for his services in the late expedition against the Nanticoke Indians in 1678; died testate by Feb 26, 1687/8 (date of probate; Ann Smith, widow). {Ref: ARMD 7:87; MDWB 4:292}

SMITH, ELIZABETH, see "George Smith" and "Daniel Smith," q.v.

SMITH, GEORGE (Kent County), military officer (rank not stated) who swore allegiance to the King & Queen of England in 1696; died testate by Jan 1, 1710/1 (date of probate; Elizabeth Smith, widow). {Ref: ARMD 20:540; MDWB 13:190}

SMITH, GEORGE (Calvert County), ranger under the command of Capt. Richard Brightwell in 1692. {Ref: ARMD 8:445}

SMITH, GEORGE, see "Daniell Peverell," q.v.

SMITH, GERRARD (Kent County), military officer (rank not stated) who swore allegiance to the King & Queen of England in 1696. {Ref: ARMD 20:541}

SMITH, HADDOCK (Prince George's County), captain by 1717. {Ref: INAC 37B:208}

SMITH, HENRY (Somerset County), mariner by 1734; captain and master of the brigantine *Brereton* (built in Somerset County) in 1737; master of the brigantine *Middleham* in 1738 (built in Somerset County in 1737). {Ref: MDCB 82:52, 61}

SMITH, HENRY (England, Virginia, and Somerset County), captain by 1679; gentleman and justice of the peace, 1679; member of the Lower House of the Maryland Assembly, 1681-1684; Protestant and probable soldier in the Revolution of 1689; signed an address and took a loyalty oath supporting the King of England and "for enabling us to defend ourselves against all invaders" on Nov 28, 1689; born circa 1634 (aged about 58 when deposed on Dec 24, 1692), died before Oct 28, 1703 (date of legislative meeting). {Ref: ARMD 7:337, 7:360, 7:442, 7:611, 8:141, 8:504, 15:275, 15:328, 24:318; SOJR I:53; BDML II:743; INAC 7B:98, 25:290, 31:132}

SMITH, HENRY (England and St. Mary's County), captain by 1683; member of the Lower House of the Maryland Assembly, 1697; died testate by Feb 7, 1712/3 (date of probate; Ann Smith, widow). {Ref: BDML II:743; INAC 8:223; MDWB 13:495}

SMITH, JAMES (Somerset County), Protestant and probable soldier in the Revolution of 1689; signed an address and took a loyalty oath supporting the King of England and "for enabling us to defend ourselves against all invaders" on Nov 28, 1689. {Ref: ARMD 8:139}

SMITH, JAMES (Talbot County), soldier (rank not stated) circa 1675; paid for his services in the late expedition against the Nanticoke Indians in 1678; Protestant and probable soldier in the Revolution of 1689; signed an address and took a loyalty oath supporting the King of England and the reestablishment of Lord Baltimore into power on Nov 18, 1689 and Nov 28, 1689; captain by 1693; born circa 1645-1646 (aged about 26 when deposed in 1672 and aged about 28 when deposed in 1673). {Ref: ARMD 7:88, 8:134, 8:144, 54:553, 54:583; TALR 7:42}

SMITH, JAMES (Kent County), military officer (rank not stated) who swore allegiance to the King & Queen of England in 1696; captain and member of the

Commission of the Peace in 1697; captain and owner of a deck sloop (no name given) in 1697; died by May 11, 1700 (date of inventory). {Ref: ARMD 20:540, 23:198, 25:599-600; INAC 21:54}

SMITH, JAMES (Kent County), styled "captain" by 1722; member of the Lower House of the Maryland Assembly, 1719-1722; born circa 1683 (aged about 48 when deposed in 1731 and aged about 60 when deposed in 1743), died testate by Mar 22, 1760 (date of probate). {Ref: BMDL II:744; MDEP:171; MDWB 30:808}

SMITH, JAMES, see "Michael Jenifer," q.v.

SMITH, JNO. (Calvert County), Protestant and probable soldier in the Revolution of 1689; signed an address and took a loyalty oath supporting the King of England and "to reestablish Lord Baltimore in his ancient power and government" on Nov 16, 1689. {Ref: ARMD 8:131}

SMITH, JOHN (Kent County), soldier (rank not stated) on Isle of Kent who swore allegiance to the Commonwealth of England on Apr 5, 1652; soldier (rank not stated) in Capt. William Leeds (Leeads) Company by May 23, 1662, at which time he signed a petition about the misuse of company money by Capt. Thomas Brednox (Bradnox), late of Isle of Kent, deceased. {Ref: INKC:101; ARMD 3:455}

SMITH, JOHN (Annapolis District), captain of the ship *Charles* in 1734. {Ref: MDGZ, Aug 2, 1734}

SMITH, JOHN (England and Calvert County), soldier (rank not stated) in 1642; captain by 1654; commissioned a captain of militia on Apr 24, 1655 "in Putuxent County from Leonard's Creek downwards including both sides of the river at Putuxent ... and that Capt. John Smith the Muster Master Generall shall be Superintendent and Captain in Cheife over the said companies;" commander of Patuxent [now Calvert] County in 1655; died intestate by Dec 25, 1655. {Ref: ARMD 3:315, 4:130-131, 10:404, 10:412-413, 10:417; BDML II:745}

SMITH, JOHN (Calvert County), probable soldier (rank not stated) before 1682; paid for his services out of an assessment levied by the General Assembly for the public good in 1682; Protestant and probable soldier in the Revolution of 1689; signed an address and took a loyalty oath supporting the King of England and "to reestablish Lord Baltimore in his ancient power and government" on Nov 16, 1689; born circa 1649 (aged about 24 when deposed in 1673), died testate by Mar 19, 1717/8 (date of probate; Dorothy Smith, widow). {Ref: ARMD 7:442-443, 8:131; MDEP:171; MDWB 14:539}

SMITH, JOHN (Calvert County), captain before 1712; member of the Lower House of the Maryland Assembly, 1701-1704; sheriff, 1712-1713; major by 1718; colonel by 1722; provincial court justice, 1726-1735; died testate by Apr 25, 1738 (date of probate; Sarah Smith, widow). {Ref: ARMD 29:254; BDML II:745; PGLR M:128; MDAD 1:289; MDWB 21:873}

SMITH, JOHN (England and Prince George's County), mariner, of Lymhouse, County Middlesex, before 1709; land owner in Prince George's County by 1709. {Ref: PGLR F Old 5:104}

SMITH, JOHN (Somerset County), captain in the 1730's; died intestate by May 28, 1740 (date of inventory). {Ref: MINV 25:142}

SMITH, JONATHAN (Calvert County), Protestant and probable soldier in the Revolution of 1689; signed an address and took a loyalty oath (made his "X" mark) supporting the King of England and "to reestablish Lord Baltimore in his ancient power and government" on Nov 16, 1689. {Ref: ARMD 8:132}

SMITH, MARGARET, see "Charles Somerset Smith," q.v.

SMITH, MARY, see "Mathew Smith" and "Thomas Smith," q.v.

SMITH, MATHEW (Talbot County), soldier (rank not stated) circa 1675; paid for his services in the late expedition against the Nanticoke Indians in 1678. {Ref: ARMD 7:90; MDEP:171}

SMITH, MATHEW (Kent and Queen Anne's County), soldier (rank not stated) circa 1675; paid for his services in the late expedition against the Nanticoke Indians in 1678; died testate by Sep 13, 1709 (date of probate; Mary Smith, widow). {Ref: ARMD 7:94; MDWB 12:203, pt. 2}

SMITH, NATHAN (Anne Arundel County), a seafaring apprentice in 1697, "borne and belonging to this county, son of Nathan Smith." {Ref: ARMD 25:596; MDWB 4:50}

SMITH, NATHANIELL (county not indicated), probable soldier (rank not stated) before 1682; paid for his services out of an assessment levied by the General Assembly for the public good in 1682. {Ref: ARMD 7:440}

SMITH, NICHOLAS (England and Annapolis), mariner and master of the ship *Hopewell* in 1688; captain and master of the ship *N W Hopwell Nil--- [sic]*, of London, in 1690; commander of the ship *Hopewell* in 1694; captain of a ship (no name given) in 1696-1698; captain, 1703. {Ref: ARMD 8:40, 8:237, 5:588, 23:10, 23:466; AALR WT#2:181; INAC 13A:239}

SMITH, PHILIP (Annapolis District), captain of a ship (no name given) in 1729. {Ref: MDGZ, Apr 15, 1729}

SMITH, RACHEL, see "Walter Smith," q.v.

SMITH, RALPH, see "John Douglas," q.v.

SMITH, REBECCA, see "Benjamin Smith," q.v.

SMITH, RICHARD (Calvert County), captain by 1720 (received payment from the estate of Thomas Holdsworth, deceased, on Jul 9, 1720). {Ref: MDAD 3:101}

SMITH, RICHARD (Kent County), captain by 1733. {Ref: INKC:178}

SMITH, RICHARD (Cecil County), military officer (rank not stated) who swore allegiance to the King & Queen of England in 1696. {Ref: ARMD 20:546}

SMITH, RICHARD, JR. (St. Leonard's Creek, Calvert County), captain of a company of foot before 1689; Protestant and soldier in the Revolution of 1689; signed an address and took a loyalty oath supporting the King of England and "to reestablish Lord Baltimore in his ancient power and government" on Nov 16, 1689; he gave the Maryland Council "an account of what Arms the Soldiers under his Command delivered in his presence unto Col. Ninian Beale, at Mattapany house, upon the surrender of that Garrison (in the time of the

Revolution) to his Majesty" on Mar 3, 1695/6; noted as "Capt. Richard Smith of St. Leonard's Creek" in 1713; died testate by Mar 19, 1714/5 (date of probate). {Ref: ARMD 8:131, 8:147, 13:242, 20:369, 23:463, 29:253; PGLR M:479; MDWB 14:83}

SMITH, RICHARD, SR. (England and Calvert County), lieutenant who served under Captain Fuller at the Battle of the Severn on Mar 25, 1655 and served on a Council of War after the battle; member of the Lower House of the Maryland Assembly, 1658-1666; attorney general, 1657-1661; soldier (rank not stated) paid for his services in the late expedition against the Nanticoke Indians in 1678; opposed the Revolution of 1689; died circa 1690. {Ref: ARMD 7:103; FAAH:26; HCCM:312; BDML II:748}

SMITH, ROBERT (Talbot County), captain before 1695; master of the sloop *Robert and Ann* of Chester River in 1695. {Ref: ARMD 20:309}

SMITH, ROBERT (county or port not indicated), captain and master of the ship *Rotherdam Merchant* of Exon in 1691. {Ref: ARMD 8:238}

SMITH, SAMUEL (Charles County), mariner "sometymes in the Province of Maryland" before 1661; died by 1662. {Ref: ARMD 41:600, 49:63-65}

SMITH, SARAH, see "John Smith," q.v.

SMITH, THOMAS (Somerset County), Protestant and probable soldier in the Revolution of 1689; signed an address and took a loyalty oath supporting the King of England and "for enabling us to defend ourselves against all invaders" on Nov 28, 1689. {Ref: ARMD 8:139}

SMITH, THOMAS (St. Mary's County), mariner and sloopman by 1677; captain and master of the brigantine *Betty* of Maryland in 1690. {Ref: ARMD 8:237, 51:224, 67:59, 67:164; INAC 5:383}

SMITH, THOMAS (Manokin Hundred, Somerset County), sailor by 1733. {Ref: SOTL:1733}

SMITH, THOMAS (Baltimore County), soldier (rank not stated) circa 1675; paid for his services in the late expedition against the Nanticoke Indians in 1678; one Thomas Smith died intestate by Jan 29, 1699/1700 (date of inventory; Isabella Smith, widow, later married John Parker), another Thomas Smith died testate by March, 1717/8 (date of probate; Alice Smith, widow, later married Robert Montgomery), and another Thomas Smith died intestate by Aug 24, 1715/6 (date of administration bond; Mary Smith, widow). Additional research will be necessary before drawing conclusions. {Ref: ARMD 7:95; MDWB 14:542; BBCF:587, 593}

SMITH (SMYTH), THOMAS (England, and Talbot and Kent Counties), captain by 1681; major, commissioned Oct 9, 1694, and paid for his services in 1695; military officer who swore allegiance to the King & Queen of England in 1696; major and member of the Commission of the Peace in 1697; lieutenant colonel, 1699; member of the Lower House of the Maryland Assembly, 1681-1682, 1694-1707; colonel by 1703; provincial court judge, 1702-1719; member of the Maryland Council, 1716-1718; born circa 1656, died testate in May, 1719 (will probated on Aug 4, 1719; Martha Smyth, widow, was listed as Martha Smith, Quaker, in a 1721 account). {Ref: ARMD 7:236, 20:152, 20:541, 23:198, 24:6, 24:108, 24:128, 25:189, 29:224, 30:371, 38:75; BDML II:750; CFES 2:297; MDWB 15:159; MINV 4:11; INKC:150; MDAD 3:333}

SMITH (SMYTH), THOMAS (Kent County), soldier and probable officer in the 1730's; captain by 1738; member of the Lower House of the Maryland Assembly, 1738; born on Feb 21, 1710/1, died testate by Jan 9, 1741/2 (date of probate; Mary Smith, widow). {Ref: BDML II:750-751; CFES 2:299; MDWB 22:458; MINV 27:11}

SMITH, THOMAS, JR. (Anne Arundel County), military officer (rank not stated) who swore allegiance to the King & Queen of England in 1696; major by 1700. {Ref: ARMD 20:541, 24:35}

SMITH, WALTER (Kent County), soldier (rank not stated) circa 1675; paid for his services in the late expedition against the Nanticoke Indians in 1678. {Ref: ARMD 7:94}

SMITH, WALTER (Calvert County), captain of a company of foot troops in 1689; major, appointed Aug 17, 1695; military officer who swore allegiance to the King & Queen of England in 1696; member of the Lower House of the Maryland Assembly, 1696-1711; Protestant and soldier in the Revolution of 1689; signed an address and took a loyalty oath supporting the King of England and "to reestablish Lord Baltimore in his ancient power and government" on Nov 16, 1689; county court judge, 1699; member of the Maryland Assembly, 1701; lieutenant colonel, 1702; styled "colonel" after 1706; died testate by Jun 4, 1711 (date of probate; Rachel Smith, widow). {Ref: ARMD 8:131, 13:242, 20:281, 20:543, 23:469, 24:28, 24:108, 24:128, 25:75, 27:202, 29:35; BDML II:751; RMHF II:84; HCCM:313-314; PGLR A:357; MDWB 13:244; INAC 33A:50, 36B:229}

SMITH, WILLIAM (Somerset County), soldier (rank not stated) circa 1675; paid for his services in the late expedition against the Nanticoke Indians in 1678; Protestant and probable soldier in the Revolution of 1689; signed an address and took a loyalty oath supporting the King of England and "for enabling us to defend ourselves against all invaders" on Nov 28, 1689; died testate by Oct 10, 1720 (date of probate). {Ref: ARMD 7:98, 8:140; MDWB 16:323}

SMITH (SMYTH), WILLIAM (St. Mary's County), lieutenant, 1665; captain lieutenant, commissioned Sep 7, 1667. {Ref: ARMD 3:539, 3:556, 5:12-13}

SMITHERS, RICHARD, see "John Carvile," q.v.

SMITHSON (SMYTHSON), THOMAS (England and Talbot County), soldier (rank not stated) circa 1675; paid for his services in the late expedition against the Nanticoke Indians in 1678; court justice, 1685; Protestant and probable soldier in the Revolution of 1689; signed an address and took a loyalty oath supporting the King of England and the reestablishment of Lord Baltimore into power on Nov 18, 1689 and Nov 28, 1689; major, commissioned Oct 9, 1694; appointed naval officer at Oxford Towne in Talbot County on Oct 18, 1694; major who was paid for his services in 1695; major who swore allegiance to the King & Queen of England in 1696; lieutenant colonel by 1699; member of the

Lower House of the Maryland Assembly, 1694-1711; chief justice of the Provincial Court, 1702; colonel by 1706; Treasurer of the Eastern Shore, 1695-1713; died by Apr 9, 1714 (date of probate; Mary Smithson, widow). {Ref: ARMD 7:88, 8:134, 8:144, 20:153, 20:160, 20:542, 23:234, 23:285, 24:29, 24:108, 24:129, 25:120, 25:189, 27:203, 29:180, 29:386, 38:74; BDML II:753-754; MDWB 13:649}

SMOCHE, JOHN (Somerset County), Protestant and probable soldier in the Revolution of 1689; signed an address and took a loyalty oath supporting the King of England and "for enabling us to defend ourselves against all invaders" on Nov 28, 1689. {Ref: ARMD 8:139}

SMOOT, ANNE, see "Barton Smoot," q.v.

SMOOT, BARTON (Pickawaxon Hundred, Charles County), captain before 1731; born circa 1687-1688 (aged about 43 or 44 when deposed twice in 1731), died testate by Jan 16, 1744/5 (date of probate; Anne Smoot, widow). {Ref: MDEP:173; MDWB 23:662}

SMOOT, THOMAS (Charles County), military officer (rank not stated) who swore allegiance to the King & Queen of England in 1696; captain by 1703; sheriff, 1703 (name listed once as "Thomas Smoote"); born circa 1658, died testate by Jan 30, 1704/5 (date of probate). {Ref: ARMD 20:543, 25:150; CHLR Z:256; MDWB 3:486; INAC 26:125}

SMOOT, THOMAS (Port Tobacco Parish, Charles County), probable soldier in the 1730's; commissioned Ranger of Charles County on Apr 14, 1738; born circa 1707 (aged about 45 when deposed in 1752 and aged about 60 when deposed in 1767; son of Barton Smoot, q.v., but called himself "Thomas Smoot, Jr." to distinguish himself from a cousin "Thomas Smoot, Sr." who was about 10 years older); died testate by July 5, 1777 (date of probate). {Ref: MDCB 82:57; MDEP:173; Harry W. Newman's *The Smoots of Maryland and Virginia*, p. 60}

SMYTH, JOHN (Kent County), soldier (rank not stated) on Isle of Kent who swore allegiance to the Commonwealth of England on Apr 5, 1652. {Ref: INKC:101}

SMYTH, MARTHA, see "Thomas Smith (Smyth)," q.v.

SMYTH, THOMAS (St. Mary's County), captain and master of the ship *Accomacke Merchant* riding in St. George's River on Apr 25, 1665. {Ref: ARMD 49:434, 49:439}

SNELSON, JOHN (Dorchester County), captain before 1701; died by Apr 12, 1701 (date of inventory). {Ref: INAC 21:42, 38B:5; MDAD 1:110}

SNOOKE, JOHN (Dorchester County), soldier (rank not stated) circa 1675; paid for his services in the late expedition against the Nanticoke Indians in 1678. {Ref: ARMD 7:93}

SNOW, JOHN (St. Mary's County), captain and mariner by 1644. {Ref: ARMD 4:300}

SNOW, JOHN (Somerset County), Protestant and probable soldier in the Revolution of 1689; signed an address and took a loyalty oath supporting the King of England and "for enabling us to defend ourselves against all invaders" on Nov 28, 1689. {Ref: ARMD 8:140}

SNOWDEN, MR., see "Thomas Brown" and "Job Evans," q.v.

SNOWDEN, RICHARD (Wales and Anne Arundel County), held a major's commission under Oliver Cromwell circa 1650 before immigrating to Maryland; major circa 1660. {Ref: FAAH:361; RMHF I:159, 333}

SNOWDEN, RICHARD (Anne Arundel County), military officer (rank not stated) who swore allegiance to the King & Queen of England in 1696 (listed as "Sr."); captain by 1697 (listed as "Jr."). {Ref: ARMD 20:541, 23:283}

SNOWHILL, CHR. (county not indicated), probable soldier (rank not stated) before 1682; paid for his services out of an assessment levied by the General Assembly for the public good in 1682. {Ref: ARMD 7:442}

SOAMES, STEPHEN (Kent County), soldier (rank not stated) circa 1675; paid for his services in the late expedition against the Nanticoke Indians in 1678. {Ref: ARMD 7:94}

SOARE, JOHN (county or port not indicated), captain and master of the schooner *Elizabeth* in 1734 (formerly the *Mary*, built in New England in 1729). {Ref: MDCB 82:25}

SOCKERS(?), ---- (Kent County), captain by 1723. {Ref: MINV 8:166}

SOLLERS (SALLERS), JOHN (Anne Arundel and Calvert Counties), soldier (rank not stated) circa 1675; paid for his services in the late expedition against the Nanticoke Indians in 1678; court justice, 1679-1685; Protestant and probable soldier in the Revolution of 1689; signed an address and took a loyalty oath supporting the King of England and "to reestablish Lord Baltimore in his ancient power and government" on Nov 16, 1689; "John Sallers" died testate after Feb 15, 1699/1700 (date his will was written, but date of probate not given; Ann Sallers, widow). {Ref: ARMD 7:96, 8:132, 15:253, 17:379; HCCM:315, 471-473; RMHF I:335; MDWB 6:353}

SOMERLAND, JOHN (Anne Arundel County), military officer (rank not stated) who swore allegiance to the King & Queen of England in 1696. {Ref: ARMD 20:542}

SOMERS, SAMUEL (Somerset County), captain, 1677. {Ref: RMHF I:211}

SOMERVELL (SOMERVILLE), JAMES (Scotland and Calvert County), physician and soldier in the army of Bonnie Prince Charlie in 1715; captured by the English forces at the Battle of Sheriff Muir and indentured to service in the American colonies; settled on the Lower Cliffs of Calvert County about 1719; county justice, 1741-1750; high sheriff, 1744-1747; born circa 1693 (aged about 44 when deposed in 1737), died in 1754. {Ref: HCCM:316-317; MDEP:174}

SOTHERON, ELIZABETH, see "John Johnson Southeron," q.v.

SOTHORON, JOHN (Charles County), captain by 1734; died before 1764. See "John Johnson Sotheron," q.v. {Ref: CHLR N#3:63}

SOUSA, MATHIAS, see "Mathias de Sousa," q.v.

SOUTH, THOMAS (Kent County), soldier (rank not stated) on Isle of Kent who swore allegiance to the Commonwealth of England on Apr 5, 1652; born circa 1618 (aged about 36 when deposed in 1655, age about 38 when deposed in

1656, and aged about 40 when deposed in 1658), died testate by Oct 26, 1674 (date of probate; when he wrote his will on Oct 13, 1673 he "renounced Grace South, formerly called his wife." {Ref: ARMD 54:68, 131, 165; INKC:101, 108; MDWB 2:19}

SOUTHERBY, WILLIAM (Talbot County), soldier (rank not stated) circa 1675; paid for his services in the late expedition against the Nanticoke Indians in 1678. {Ref: ARMD 7:89}

SOUTHERON (SOUTHERN), RICHARD (Calvert and St. Mary's Counties), captain by the 1670's; born circa 1643 (aged about 50 when deposed in 1693), died by Sep 28, 1702 (date of inventory). {Ref: ARMD 8:557; INAC 23:173, 24:167}

SOUTHERON (SOTHERON), JOHN JOHNSON (St. Mary's County), captain by 1732; major before 1744; died testate by Dec 5, 1744 (date of probate; Elizabeth Sotheron, widow). {Ref: MDWB 24:4; MINV 31:71; CHLR N#3:63}

SPALDING, ALLOT (Somerset County), captain and mariner by 1734; owner and master of the sloop *Molly* (built in Somerset County) in 1735. {Ref: MDCB 82:30}

SPARK, MARY, wee "William Sparks," q.v.

SPARKS (SPARKES), WILLIAM (England, and Kent and Queen Anne's Counties), military officer (rank not stated) who swore allegiance to the King & Queen of England in 1696; "William Spark" died testate by Oct 24, 1709 (date of probate; Mary Spark, widow). {Ref: ARMD 20:540, 41:573; MDWB 13:4; *Chesapeake Cousins* 19:2, p. 39}

SPARKS (SPARKES), WILLIAM, JR. (Kent and Queen Anne's Counties), military officer (rank not stated) who swore allegiance to the King & Queen of England in 1696. {Ref: ARMD 20:540}

SPAVEN (SPEVIN), WILLIAM (Prince George's County), captain by 1723; master of the ship *Tobias* riding in the Patuxent River on Feb 24, 1723/4 and Jan 24, 1724/5; master of the ship *Enterprise* in 1731. {Ref: PGLR M:148-149; MDAD 8:337; CVPR:12}

SPEAK, THOMAS (St. Mary's County), soldier (rank not stated) in 1642; paid for 3 weeks' service under Capt. William Brainthwaite in November, 1642; died testate by Aug 6, 1681 (date of probate; Elizabeth Speak, widow). {Ref: ARMD 3:122; MDWB 2:160}

SPEDDEN, HUGH (Talbot County), mariner by 1704. {Ref: TALR 9:235}

SPENCE, ADAM (Somerset County), Protestant and probable soldier in the Revolution of 1689; signed an address and took a loyalty oath supporting the King of England and "for enabling us to defend ourselves against all invaders" on Nov 28, 1689. {Ref: ARMD 8:139}

SPENCE, DAVID (Wicomico, Somerset County), soldier (rank not stated) circa 1675; paid for his services in the late expedition against the Nanticoke Indians in 1678. {Ref: ARMD 7:98; OSES:280}

SPENCER, T. (England and Annapolis), captain of the ship *Peace* of Biddeford in 1734. {Ref: MDGZ, Jul 19, 1734}

SPENCER, THOMAS (Prince George's County), captain and commander of the ship *Orford* or *Oxford* in 1722. {Ref: PGLR I:465}
SPENCER, WILLIAM (Patuxent District), captain and master of the ship *John and Elizabeth* in 1731. {Ref: CVPR:12}
SPEVAN, NATHAN (Prince George's County), captain and commander of the ship *Unity* in 1722. {Ref: PGLR I:465}
SPICER, JOHN (Somerset County), soldier (rank not stated) circa 1675; paid for his services in the late expedition against the Nanticoke Indians in 1678. {Ref: ARMD 7:98}
SPIKEMAN, WILLIAM (Charles County), Protestant and probable soldier in the Revolution of 1689; signed an address and took a loyalty oath supporting the King of England and the reestablishment of Lord Baltimore into power on Nov 28, 1689. {Ref: ARMD 8:138}
SPINK (SPINKE), HENRY (St. Mary's County), soldier (rank not stated) by 1648; served under the command of Capt. Thomas Baldridge and his "company of rebells" in 1648; born circa 1621 (aged about 26 when deposed in 1647), died testate by Oct 26, 1695 (date of probate). {Ref: ARMD 4:324, 4:453; MDWB 7:138; INAC 14:6; MDEP:175}
SPINKS, ENOCH, see "Tobias Stansbury," q.v.
SPONDINES, HUGH (Talbot County), a seafaring man in 1697. {Ref: ARMD 25:601}
SPOONER, CHARLES (Somerset County), soldier (rank not stated) circa 1675; paid for his services in the late expedition against the Nanticoke Indians in 1678. {Ref: ARMD 7:98}
SPOORE (SPOUR), EDWARD (Virginia and Prince George's County, Patuxent and Potomac Districts), captain and master of the ship *Howlaste Moreti* riding in the Patuxent River on Apr 15, 1726; captain of a ship (no name given) riding in the Patuxent River in April, 1729; master of the ship *Harrard* in the Potomac District in 1730-1731; master and owner of the sloop *Ann* in 1738 (built in Maryland in 1737). {Ref: PGLR M:150; MDGZ, Apr 29, 1729; CVPR:12; MDCB 82:64}
SPRACKLING, RICHARD (Anne Arundel County), captain and commander of the ship *Debtford* riding at anchor in Severn River on Feb 26, 1707. {Ref: AALR WT#2:587}
SPRIGG, EDWARD (Queen Anne Parish, Prince George's County), captain by 1727; major by 1732; provincial court justice, 1732; member of the Lower House of the Maryland Assembly, 1729-1751; colonel by 1743; born circa 1696-1698 (aged about 50 when deposed in 1748, aged about 52 or 53 when deposed again in 1748, and aged about 53 when deposed in 1750), died testate by Feb 21, 1751/2 (date of probate; Mary Sprigg, widow). {Ref: ARMD 39:13, 39:55, 39:151, 39:220; BDML II:760; MDGZ, Apr 26, 1745; PGLR M:380, Q:694; MDEP:175; MDWB 28:231}
SPRIGG, MARY, see "Edward Sprigg," q.v.
SPRIGG, THOMAS (England, Virginia, and St. Mary's and Calvert Counties), served as an officer in the Royal Lancers in England; migrated first to Virginia

and then to Maryland; sheriff and a justice of Calvert County between 1661-1674; soldier (rank not stated) circa 1675; paid for his services in the late expedition against the Nanticoke Indians in 1678; born circa 1630 (aged about 35 when deposed in 1665, and aged about 64 when deposed in 1694), died testate by Dec 29, 1704 (date of probate; name listed as "Thomas Sprigg, Sr." in his will). {Ref: ARMD 7:104, 49:508; RMHF I:338, II:313, 316; MDEP:175; MDWB 3:443}

SPRIGG, THOMAS (England, and Calvert and Prince George's Counties), major by 1711; member of the Lower House of the Maryland Assembly, 1712-1715; lieutenant colonel by 1715; colonel by 1719; moved to London in 1722 and died after 1728. {Ref: ARMD 29:227, 29:391, 30:107; BDML II:756; PGLR F Old 5:207}

SPRIGG, THOMAS, JR. (Calvert County), colonel of militia, 1697-1704; born 1670, died 1739. *Note:* There appears to be discrepancies in the information contained in some sources about this Thomas and the two others listed above. Additional research will be necessary before drawing conclusions. {Ref: RMHF I:338, II:313, 316}

SPROUCE, GEORGE (Dorchester County), soldier (rank not stated) circa 1675; paid for his services in the late expedition against the Nanticoke Indians in 1678. {Ref: ARMD 7:93}

SPRY, FRANCIS (Prince George's County), mariner by 1699. {Ref: PGLR A:160}

SPRY, JOHN (Anne Arundel County), captain and skipper of the sloop *Margrett's Industry* in 1707. {Ref: ARMD 27:31, 27:33, 27:118}

SPURRAWAY, WILLIAM (Dorchester County), soldier (rank not stated) circa 1675; paid for his services in the late expedition against the Nanticoke Indians in 1678. {Ref: ARMD 7:93}

SQUIRE, JOHN (Talbot County), soldier (rank not stated) circa 1675; paid for his services in the late expedition against the Nanticoke Indians in 1678; Indian interpreter by 1681. {Ref: ARMD 7:88, 15:413}

STACY, JOHN (county not indicated), probable soldier (rank not stated) before 1682; paid for his services out of an assessment levied by the General Assembly for the public good in 1682. {Ref: ARMD 7:440}

STAMMARD, JOHN (Dorchester County), soldier (rank not stated) circa 1675; paid for his services in the late expedition against the Nanticoke Indians in 1678. {Ref: ARMD 7:93}

STAMPER, ROBERT (Prince George's County), mariner in the 1730's, perhaps earlier; captain and master of the brigantine *Revenge* in 1739 (built in the colony of Virginia); died intestate by Apr 30, 1744 (date of inventory). {Ref: MDCB 82:78; MINV 29:156}

STANBURY, JOHN (Charles County), soldier (rank not stated) circa 1675; paid for his services in the late expedition against the Nanticoke Indians in 1678. {Ref: ARMD 7:101}

STANFORD, JAMES (Talbot County), lieutenant who swore allegiance to the King & Queen of England in 1696. {Ref: ARMD 20:542}

STANLEY (STANDLEY), JOHN (Talbot County), soldier (rank not stated) circa 1675; paid for his services in the late expedition against the Nanticoke Indians in 1678; captain by 1684; captain of a troop of horse in 1689; Protestant and soldier in the Revolution of 1689; signed an address and took a loyalty oath supporting the King of England and the reestablishment of Lord Baltimore into power on Nov 28, 1689; major by 1696; died by May 20, 1696 (date of administration account). {Ref: ARMD 7:88, 8:144, 13:243; BDML II:701; INAC 8:206, 13B:11}

STANLEY (STANDLEY), ROBERT (county or port not indicated), seaman by 1698. {Ref: INAC 13A:44}

STANNER, RICHARD (St. Mary's County), soldier (rank not stated) circa 1675; paid for his services in the late expedition against the Nanticoke Indians in 1678. {Ref: ARMD 7:103}

STANSBURY (STANSBERRY), TOBIAS (Baltimore County), ranger appointed by Capt. John Oldton as a "well quallified person & good woods man & fit to be Imployed in Ranging for the Publick Service of this Province" on Mar 23, 1694/5; born before 1658, died intestate by Apr 23, 1709 (date of administration bond; Sarah Stansbury, widow, later married Enoch Spinks). {Ref: ARMD 20:205; BBCF:601}

STANSBY (STANESBY, STANDSBY), JOHN (Baltimore County), captain by 1676; paid for his services in the late expedition against the Nanticoke Indians in 1678; member of the Lower House of the Maryland Assembly, 1676-1679; sheriff, 1679-1681; died intestate by Feb 6, 1682/3 (date of administration). See "Godefrid Harmer," q.v. {Ref: ARMD 7:95, 15:251, 15:253, 15:327; BDML II:769; INAC 7B:84, 8:190}

STAPLEFORT (STAPELFORT), RAYMOND (Dorchester County), sheriff, 1668; soldier (rank not stated) circa 1675; paid for his services in the late expedition against the Nanticoke Indians in 1678; born circa 1623 (aged about 45 when deposed in 1668), died testate by Sep 3, 1687 (date of probate). {Ref: ARMD 7:94, 51:321, 57:319; MDWB 4:265}

STAPLES (STAPELL), MICHAEL (England and Anne Arundel County), captain and commander of the ship *Edward and Mary* of London in 1690; captain and master of the ship *Sara and Mary Hopewell* riding at anchor in Severn River on May 19, 1705. {Ref: AALR WT#2:323; ARMD 8:210, 8:371}

STARK, CHRISTOPHER (Somerset County), mariner by 1726. {Ref: MDAD 8:48}

STARKEY, ROBERT (Potomac District), captain and master of the sloop *Albemarle* in 1697. {Ref: ARMD 23:171-172}

STARRET, JOHN (Somerset County), Protestant and probable soldier in the Revolution of 1689; signed an address and took a loyalty oath supporting the King of England and "for enabling us to defend ourselves against all invaders" on Nov 28, 1689. {Ref: ARMD 8:141}

STEELL, JOHN (Somerset County), Protestant and probable soldier in the Revolution of 1689; signed an address and took a loyalty oath supporting the

King of England and "for enabling us to defend ourselves against all invaders" on Nov 28, 1689. {Ref: ARMD 8:140}

STEELMAN, JOHN HANS (Prince George's County), captain by Feb 17, 1721/2 when the proceedings of the Maryland Council with regards to the murder of an Indian about ten days earlier indicated "that Capt. John Hans Steelman is Come to Monocasey and hath sent for his Son [i.e., John Hans Steelman, Jr.] who is gone back to him from the Sugar lands whether he is fled for fear of the Indians the Frontier Inhabitants are altogether uncapable of making any defence having neither Powder nor Ball." {Ref: ARMD 25:380}

STEETMAN (STEELMAN), HANS (county not indicated), captain and "Interpreter in Chiefe for the Northern Parts of this Province" in 1697. See "John Hans Tilman" and "John Hans Steelman," q.v. {Ref: ARMD 23:428}

STEGOLL, MOSES (Kent County), soldier (rank not stated) in Capt. William Leeds (Leeads) Company by May 23, 1662, at which time he signed a petition about the misuse of company money by Capt. Thomas Brednox (Bradnox), late of Isle of Kent, deceased. {Ref: ARMD 3:455}

STEPHENS, CHARLES (Anne Arundel County), soldier (rank not stated) circa 1675; paid for his services in the late expedition against the Nanticoke Indians in 1678. {Ref: ARMD 7:96}

STEPHENS, DOROTHY, see "John Stevens (Stephens)," q.v.

STEPHENS, EDWARD (Talbot County), soldier (rank not stated) circa 1675; paid for his services in the late expedition against the Nanticoke Indians in 1678. {Ref: ARMD 7:91}

STEPHENS, JOSEPH (St. Mary's County), captain by 1695. {Ref: INAC 10:403}

STEPHENS, RICHARD (Talbot County), soldier (rank not stated) circa 1675; paid for his services in the late expedition against the Nanticoke Indians in 1678. {Ref: ARMD 7:88}

STEPHENSON, PHILLIP (Talbot County), soldier (rank not stated) circa 1675; paid for his services in the late expedition against the Nanticoke Indians in 1678. {Ref: ARMD 7:91}

STEPHYNS, EPHRAIM (Anne Arundel County), captain and master of the pink *Thomas and Sarah* lying in South River on Oct 18, 1708. {Ref: AALR WT#2:658}

STEPTOWE, PHILLIP (Baltimore County), soldier (rank not stated) circa 1675; paid for his services in the late expedition against the Nanticoke Indians in 1678. {Ref: ARMD 7:96}

STERLING, JOHN (Somerset County), captain by 1677. {Ref: RMHF I:211, II:256}

STERNBROUGH, DODMAN (Baltimore County), soldier (rank not stated) circa 1675; paid for his services in the late expedition against the Nanticoke Indians in 1678. {Ref: ARMD 7:96}

STEVENS, ELIZABETH, see "William Stevens," q.v.

STEVENS, GEORGE (Cecil County), Protestant and probable soldier in the Revolution of 1689; signed an address and took a loyalty oath supporting the

King of England and the reestablishment of Lord Baltimore into power on Nov 18, 1689. {Ref: ARMD 8:135}

STEVENS (STEPHENS), JOHN (Dorchester County), probable soldier (rank not stated) before 1682; paid for his services out of an assessment levied by the General Assembly for the public good in 1682; coroner, 1678; died testate by Nov 7, 1692 (date of probate; Dorothy Stephens, widow). {Ref: ARMD 7:443, 51:223; MDWB 2:285}

STEVENS (STEVINS), JOSEPH (England, and St. Mary's County), captain and commander of the ship *Ruth* of London in 1692. {Ref: ARMD 13:323}

STEVENS, RICHARD (Kent County), soldier (rank not stated) in Capt. William Leeds (Leeads) Company by May 23, 1662, at which time he signed a petition about the misuse of company money by Capt. Thomas Brednox (Bradnox), late of Isle of Kent, deceased. {Ref: ARMD 3:455}

STEVENS, SYMON (Talbot County), soldier (rank not stated) circa 1675; paid for his services in the late expedition against the Nanticoke Indians in 1678. {Ref: ARMD 7:88, 7:91}

STEVENS, THOMAS (Kent County), "seaman within the said county" and a "sailor belonging to the *Factor* of Bediford" in 1697. {Ref: ARMD 25:599}

STEVENS (STEPHENS), WILLIAM (England, Virginia, and Rehoboth, Pocomoke, Somerset County), colonel by 1678; paid for his services in the late expedition against the Nanticoke Indians in 1678; member of the Lower House of the Maryland Assembly, 1669, 1676-1678; court justice (quorum), 1679; colonel "sworne one of his Lordshipps privy Councell" on Oct 7, 1679; provincial court justice, 1679-1687; Protestant member of the Upper House (Maryland Council), 1681-1686; colonel in command of the horse troops in Somerset and Dorchester Counties in 1681; paid for his services out of an assessment levied by the General Assembly for the public good in 1682; colonel in command of troops in Somerset County and officer of the town of Rehoboth in 1686; colonel in command of the militia in Somerset County, 1687; born circa 1630, died testate on Dec 23, 1687 (will probated on Mar 26, 1688; Elizabeth Stevens, widow). {Ref: ARMD 5:309, 5:310, 5:460, 5:503, 5:527, 5:554, 7:93-94, 7:112, 7:443, 7:611, 15:260, 15:275, 17:68, 17:75, 17:380, 51:223; OSES:284, 461; BDML II:776-777; INAC 10:61; MDWB 4:296}

STEVENSON, ROBERT (St. Mary's County), captain and master of a ship (no name given) riding at anchor at the mouth of the Patuxent River on Jul 1, 1695 (date of petition). {Ref: ARMD 20:306}

STEVENSON (STIVENSON), THOMAS (Somerset County), Protestant and probable soldier in the Revolution of 1689; signed an address and took a loyalty oath supporting the King of England and "for enabling us to defend ourselves against all invaders" on Nov 28, 1689. {Ref: ARMD 8:139}

STEVENSON, WILLIAM (Somerset County), Protestant and probable soldier in the Revolution of 1689; signed an address and took a loyalty oath supporting

the King of England and "for enabling us to defend ourselves against all invaders" on Nov 28, 1689. {Ref: ARMD 8:140}

STEVERNSON, THOMAS (Talbot County), soldier (rank not stated) circa 1675; paid for his services in the late expedition against the Nanticoke Indians in 1678. {Ref: ARMD 7:91}

STEWARD, DAVID (Anne Arundel County), lieutenant, commissioned Dec 9, 1661; born circa 1616 (aged about 80 when he wrote his will on Oct 11, 1696), died testate by May 21, 1697 (date of probate; Margaret Steward, widow). {Ref: ARMD 3:444; MDWB 7:281}

STEWARD, JOHN (Talbot County), soldier (rank not stated) circa 1675; paid for his services in the late expedition against the Nanticoke Indians in 1678. {Ref: ARMD 7:92}

STEWARD, JOHN (Dorchester County), soldier (rank not stated) circa 1675; paid for his services in the late expedition against the Nanticoke Indians in 1678. {Ref: ARMD 7:94}

STEWARD, MARGARET, see "David Steward," q.v.

STEWART, JAMES (Pocomoke District), captain and master of the galley *Cathcart* or *Cath Cart* in 1731. {Ref: CVPR:12}

STILDEN, CHARLES, see "Charles Tilden," q.v.

STILES, ROBERT (Baltimore County), soldier (rank not stated) circa 1675; paid for his services in the late expedition against the Nanticoke Indians in 1678. {Ref: ARMD 7:96}

STIMSON, WILLIAM (St. Mary's County), Protestant and probable soldier in the Revolution of 1689; signed an address and took a loyalty oath supporting the King of England and the reestablishment of Lord Baltimore into power on Nov 28, 1689. {Ref: ARMD 8:147}

STINCHCOMB, HANNAH, see "Nathaniel Stinchcomb," q.v.

STINCHCOMB, JOHN (Baltimore County), soldier and probable officer by the 1730's; born circa 1700 (captain, aged about 67 when deposed in 1767), son of Nathaniel Stinchcomb, q.v. {Ref: BBCF:611; MDEP:177}

STINCHCOMB, NATHANIEL (Anne Arundel and Baltimore Counties), captain before 1710; born circa 1671, died intestate by Jun 13, 1710 (date of inventory; Hannah Stinchcomb, widow, later married Edward Teal). {Ref: BBCF:611; INAC 32A:98; PFMD:77}

STOAKLEY, WOODMAN, see "Woodman Stockley," q.v.

STOCKER, JOHN (Talbot County), soldier (rank not stated) circa 1675; paid for his services in the late expedition against the Nanticoke Indians in 1678. {Ref: ARMD 7:90}

STOCKETT, FRANCIS (England, and Baltimore and Anne Arundel Counties), militia company chirurgeon (physician), 1661; member of the Lower House of the Maryland Assembly, 1659-1660; born circa 1634 (aged about 31 when deposed in 1665), died intestate by Sep 1, 1687 (date of inventory). {Ref: ARMD 3:411, 49:490; BDML II:779; INAC 9:445}

STOCKETT, LEWIS (England, and Baltimore and Anne Arundel Counties), colonel of foot troops by 1664; Maryland Council ordered "that the Souldiers now all ready raised be sent forthwith to the Frontire, That is to say that the partyes drawn out of St. Marys, Charles & Kent County's be sent into Baltemore County there to secure that County as well on the Easterne as on the westerne side of the bay & to be Commanded by Coll. Lewis Stockett or some other fitt person of an abler body to Endure the hardship of the Woods living in that County and to be Appoynted by him" and further ordered "that Coll. Stockett send Order to presse Twenty soldiers well provided as aforesaid in Talbott County & on the south-side of Choptancke river in case he doe find he hath not force Enough to resist the Enemy" on Jul 26, 1665; Lewis had "immigrated by 1664 but apparently did not remain long in Maryland" and he was the brother of Francis Stockett, *q.v.* and Thomas Stockett, *q.v.* {Ref: ARMD 3:530-533; BDML II:779; FAAH:93; INCC:133}

STOCKETT, MARY, see "Thomas Stockett," q.v.

STOCKETT, THOMAS (England, and Baltimore and Anne Arundel Counties), captain by 1661; burgess (member of the General Assembly), representing Baltimore County, 1661-1664; sheriff, Anne Arundel County, 1666-1670; died testate by May 4, 1671 (date of probate; Mary Stockett, widow, later married George Yate, *q.v.*). "Col. Thomas Stockett" was mentioned in a deed in Baltimore County on Aug 20, 1686. Additional research will be necessary before drawing conclusions. {Ref: ARMD 1:426, 5:4, 5:29, 51:321; BDML II:779-780; FAAH:93; BALR RR#HS; MDWB 1:430; BBCF:710}

STOCKLEY (STOAKLEY), WOODMAN (England and Hunting Creek, Calvert County), Puritan leader and captain, commissioned Mar 23, 1656/7 in what was then Patuxent County; member of the Lower House of the Maryland Assembly, 1658; died testate by Oct 30, 1663 (date of probate; America Stockley, widow). {Ref: ARMD 3:320; BDML II:780; HCCM:320; MDWB 1:181}

STOCKWELL, WILLIAM (Talbot County), soldier (rank not stated) circa 1675; paid for his services in the late expedition against the Nanticoke Indians in 1678; died testate by Oct 21, 1701 (date of probate). {Ref: ARMD 7:89; MDWB 11:222}

STODDARD, SAMSON (St. Mary's County), captain by 1696. {Ref: INAC 14:80}

STODDERT, ELIZABETH, see "James Stoddert," q.v.

STODDERT (STODDART), JAMES (Scotland and Prince George's County), major by 1714; member of the Lower House of the Maryland Assembly, 1714-1726; provincial court justice, 1717-1726; born circa 1667 (aged about 57 when deposed on Feb 23, 1724/5 and aged about 58 when deposed on Aug 9, 1725), died testate by May 31, 1726 (date of probate; Elizabeth Stoddert, widow). {Ref: BDML II:782; PGLR I:626, 678; MDWB 19:61}

STODDERT (STODART), JOHN (Prince George's and Charles Counties), probable soldier in the 1730's and 1740's since he was a captain by 1748 of a company of foot soldiers that was originally part of the Prince George's County militia that was later annexed to Charles County; member of the Lower House of the Maryland Assembly, 1734-1738, 1745-1757; born circa 1705, died testate by May 18, 1767 (date of probate). {Ref: BDML II:782-783; MDWB 35:328}

STOKES, JOHN (England and Baltimore County), captain, formerly of London, was in Baltimore County before 1723; died testate by Sep 5, 1732 (date of probate; Susanna Stokes, widow). {Ref: LMCL:67; BALR IS#G; BBCF:613; MDWB 20:444}

STONE, ELLINOR, see "John Stone," q.v.

STONE, JOHN (Virginia and Charles County), probable soldier (rank not stated) by 1678; Indian interpreter by 1679; paid for his services out of an assessment levied by the General Assembly for the public good in 1682; court justice, 1674-1685 (quorum, 1675, 1685); member of the Lower House of the Maryland Assembly, 1678-1682, 1686-1688; born circa 1648, died testate by Aug 10, 1698 (date of probate; Ellinor Stone, widow). {Ref: ARMD 7:440, 15:68, 15:327, 17:380; BDML II:783-784; MDWB 6:153}

STONE, KATHERINE, see "Thomas Stone," q.v.

STONE, MATHUSALEM (county not indicated), probable soldier (rank not stated) before 1682; paid for his services out of an assessment levied by the General Assembly for the public good in 1682. {Ref: ARMD 7:439}

STONE, THEODOSIA, see "William Stone," q.v.

STONE, THOMAS (Nanjemy Parish, Charles County), captain before 1721; member of the Lower House of the Maryland Assemblyin 1715; born circa 1677 (aged about 44 when deposed in 1721), died testate by Nov 7, 1727 (date of probate; Katherine Stone, widow). {Ref: MDEP:178; BDML II:786; MDWB 19:254}

STONE, THOMAS, see "Richard Sampson," q.v.

STONE, VERLINDA, see "William Stone," q.v.

STONE, WILLIAM (England, Virginia, and St. Mary's County), captain by 1645; first Protestant governor, 1648-1656, and leader of Lord Baltimore's forces at the Battle of the Severn on Mar 25, 1655 (wounded and captured); councellor, 1656-1659; provincial court justice, 1657-1659; born circa 1603, died testate by Dec 21, 1660 (date of probate; Verlinda Stone, widow). See "Thomas Greene," q.v. {Ref: ARMD 1:382, 10:213, 10:219, 13:15, 41:39; FAAH:26; BDML II:788; RMHF II:159; MDWB 1:89}

STONE, WILLIAM (Charles County), Protestant and probable soldier in the Revolution of 1689; signed an address and took a loyalty oath supporting the King of England and the reestablishment of Lord Baltimore into power on Nov 28, 1689; born circa 1667 (aged about 52 when deposed in 1719, aged about 60 when deposed in 1727, and aged about 61 when deposed in 1728), died testate by Aug 12, 1731 (date of probate; Theodosia Stone, widow). {Ref: ARMD 8:138; MDEP:178; MDWB 20:221}

STONEMAN, SAMUEL (England and Annapolis District), captain and master of the galley *Sasafrax* of Truro in 1728-1731. {Ref: MDGZ, Mar 11, 1728/9; CVPR:12}

STONES, ROBERT (England and Annapolis District), captain and master of the ship *Mainwaring* of Liverpool in 1728-1729. {Ref: MDGZ, Feb 4, 1728/9}

STONEY, RALPH (county or port not indicated), captain and commander of the ship *Friendship* of London in 1666. {Ref: MDHM 5:339}

STORY, ANN, see "Walter Story," q.v.

STORY, AVIE, see "Ralph Story," q.v.

STORY, FRANCIS (Talbot County), soldier (rank not stated) circa 1675; paid for his services in the late expedition against the Nanticoke Indians in 1678. {Ref: ARMD 7:87}

STORY, RALPH (Calvert County), captain and master of a ship (no name given) in 1663; died testate by Jan 6, 1663/4 (date of probate; Avie Story, widow). See "Richard Morton" and "John Adams" and "Elias Chandler" and "Tobias Dunkin," q.v. {Ref: ARMD 49:10, 49:204; MDWB 1:195}

STORY (STOREY), WALTER (Charles County), captain by 1705; sheriff, 1705-1708; major by 1707; member of the Lower House of the Maryland Assembly, 1708-1714; colonel by 1718; born circa 1666-1667 (aged about 56 when deposed in 1722 and aged about 58 when deposed in 1725), died testate by Apr 4, 1726 (date of probate; Ann Story, widow). {Ref: ARMD 29:204, 29:454, 29:467; BDML II:790; CHLR C#2:83, H#2:219; MDEP:179; MDWB 18:498}

STOWARD, CHARLES (Kent County), soldier (rank not stated) in Capt. William Leeds (Leeads) Company by May 23, 1662, at which time he signed a petition about the misuse of company money by Capt. Thomas Brednox (Bradnox), late of Isle of Kent, deceased. {Ref: ARMD 3:455}

STRADFORD, JOSEPH (St. Mary's County), soldier (rank not stated) circa 1675; paid for his services in the late expedition against the Nanticoke Indians in 1678. {Ref: ARMD 7:102}

STRANGE, JONATHAN (Cecil County), mariner by 1734; captain and owner of the brigantine *Union* (built in Cecil County) in 1737. {Ref: MDCB 82:49}

STRATON, JAMES (Annapolis District), captain and master of the ship *Mary* of Montross in 1729. {Ref: MDGZ, Apr 29, 1729}

STRAWBRIDGE, JOHN (Somerset County), Protestant and probable soldier in the Revolution of 1689; signed an address and took a loyalty oath supporting the King of England and "for enabling us to defend ourselves against all invaders" on Nov 28, 1689. {Ref: ARMD 8:140}

STREETER, EDWARD (St. Mary's County), captain by 1656; he married the relict of Col. Thomas Burbage, *q.v.* {Ref: ARMD 10:469, 41:126}

STRINGER, JOHN (county not indicated), colonel by 1688. {Ref: INAC 10:67}

STRINGER, THOMAS (Prince George's County), captain and commander of the ship *Welcome George* in 1723-1725 and riding in the Patuxent River on Apr 20, 1725. {Ref: PGLR I:465, M:149}

STRINGFELLOW, ELISHA (Kent and Queen Anne's Counties), captain by 1726; commander of the ship *Rose* riding at anchor in Chester River on Apr 20, 1726 and Jun 8, 1727 and Jun 26, 1728; commander of the ship *Peregrine* riding at anchor in Wye River on Feb 7, 1732; mariner and resident on Wye River by 1733; appeared in Kent County debt books, 1733-1747. {Ref: QALR IK#C:47, 118, 186; QALR RT#A:182, 239; MDAD 11:452; INKC:178}

STRONG, JAMES (Talbot County), captain before 1684; died testate after Jan 7, 1684/5 (date he wrote his will; exact date of probate not indicted; Mary Strong, widow). {Ref: MDWB 4:149; INAC 10:324; MDAD 10:324}

STRONG, JOHN (St. Mary's County), soldier (rank not stated) by 1677; paid for his services in the late expedition against the Nanticoke Indians in 1678; probably the "Capt. Strong" mentioned in the administration account of Roger Thorpe, deceased, in St. Mary's County in 1677 and possibly the "Capt. Strong" mentioned in Col. Henry Coursey's letter to the Maryland Council in 1681. {Ref: ARMD 7:103, 17:76-77; INAC 5:80}

STRONG, LEONARD (Calvert County), Puritan leader and officer (rank not stated) who served under Captain Fuller at the Battle of the Severn on Mar 25, 1655; served on a Council of War after the battle (and wrote an eyewitness account of the battle in which he gloated over the utter defeat of Lord Baltimore's men). {Ref: FAAH:26; HCCM:320}

STRONG, MARY, see "James Strong," q.v.

STROTTAN, ---- (England and Anne Arundel County), captain, of London, by 1698. {Ref: INAC 16:58}

STROUD, JOSEPH (Patuxent District), captain and master of the brigantine *Daniell* in 1730. {Ref: CVPR:12}

STUBBORNE, JOHN (St. Mary's County), soldier (rank not stated) in 1642; paid for 3 weeks' service under Capt. William Brainthwaite in November, 1642. {Ref: ARMD 3:119, 3:122}

STUDBOY, JAMES (Prince George's County), captain and master of the ship *John* riding in the Patuxent River on Apr 27, 1726. {Ref: PGLR M:150}

STURDICA, THOMAS (St. Mary's County), soldier (rank not stated) circa 1675; paid for his services in the late expedition against the Nanticoke Indians in 1678. {Ref: ARMD 7:103}

STURGESS, GEORGE (Somerset County), soldier (rank not stated) circa 1675; paid for his services in the late expedition against the Nanticoke Indians in 1678. {Ref: ARMD 7:98}

STURGIS, THOMAS (county not indicated), sergeant in the Maryland troops "raised to strengthen Albany, New York and resist the French and Indian enemies" in 1690. {Ref: SHMD I:355}

STURMAN, MR., see "John Greenold," q.v.

STURNE, MICHAELL (Talbot County), soldier (rank not stated) circa 1675; paid for his services in the late expedition against the Nanticoke Indians in 1678. {Ref: ARMD 7:92}

SUFF, STEPHEN (Somerset County), Protestant and probable soldier in the Revolution of 1689; signed an address and took a loyalty oath supporting the

King of England and "for enabling us to defend ourselves against all invaders" on Nov 28, 1689. {Ref: ARMD 8:141}

SULLIVAN (SULLIVAINE), OWEN (Talbot County), a seafaring man in 1697 (name listed as "Owen Silivant"); born circa 1681, "Owen Sullivant" was adjudged to be 17 years old by the county court in 1698; "Owen Sullivaine" died testate by Mar 8, 1708/9 (date of probate; Mary Sullivaine, widow). {Ref: ARMD 25:601; MDWB 12:4, pt. 2; Talbot County Judgments AB8:573}

SUMMERS, ROGER (Talbot County), soldier (rank not stated) circa 1675; paid for his services in the late expedition against the Nanticoke Indians in 1678. {Ref: ARMD 7:88, 90}

SUMNER, JOHN (Prince George's County), captain and commander of the ship *Restoration* in 1722. {Ref: PGLR I:465}

SUMNER, ROBERT, see "John Sunderland," q.v.

SUNDERLAND, EDWARD (Annapolis District), captain of the sloop *Beginning* in 1734. {Ref: MDGZ, Nov 1, 1734}

SUNDERLAND, JOHN (England and Calvert County), Protestant and probable soldier in the Revolution of 1689; signed an address and took a loyalty oath supporting the King of England and "to reestablish Lord Baltimore in his ancient power and government" on Nov 16, 1689; born 1652, died intestate by Aug 14, 1695 (date of administration account; Margaret Sunderland, widow, had married Robert Sumner before that date). {Ref: ARMD 8:132; HCCM:320-321, 474-475; INAC 10:432, 14:64}

SURNAM, EDWARD (Somerset County), Protestant and probable soldier in the Revolution of 1689; signed an address and took a loyalty oath supporting the King of England and "for enabling us to defend ourselves against all invaders" on Nov 28, 1689. {Ref: ARMD 8:140}

SURTING, WILLIAM (Cecil County), captain by 1696. {Ref: INCC:134}

SUTTON, ASHBURY (Annapolis District), captain and master of the ship *Samuel* of Maryland in 1729 (owner in 1733); master of the ship *Two Sisters* in 1730. {Ref: MDGZ, Apr 15, 1729; CVPR:12; MDCB 82:2}

SUTTON, CAESAR (England and Kent County), chirurgeon on the ship *King Solomon* in 1670. {Ref: INKC:140}

SUTTON, FRANCIS (Talbot County), corporal who swore allegiance to the King & Queen of England in 1696; died testate by Jan 22, 1706/7 (date of probate). {Ref: ARMD 20:542; MDWB 12:103; INAC 26:197}

SUTTON, HENRY (Talbot County), captain and owner of a vessel (no name given) in 1697. {Ref: ARMD 23:169, 25:600}

SUTTON, PHILLIP (Dorchester County), soldier (rank not stated) circa 1675; paid for his services in the late expedition against the Nanticoke Indians in 1678. {Ref: ARMD 7:93}

SUTTON, RICHARD (Anne Arundel County), captain and commander of the ship *John and Richard* riding at anchor in South River on Jan 3, 1705. {Ref: AALR WT#2:293}

SUTTON, THOMAS (Talbot County), captain and master of the pinke *Concord* of Maryland in 1691; captain, 1702. {Ref: ARMD 8:239; INAC 23:111}

SWADDLE, CUTHBERT (Anne Arundel County), captain by 1721. {Ref: MDAD 4:32}

SWAIN, THOMAS (England and Kent Island), captain of a ship (no name given) of Bristol in 1698. {Ref: ARMD 23:401}

SWAINE, JOHN (Somerset County), Protestant and probable soldier in the Revolution of 1689; signed an address and took a loyalty oath supporting the King of England and "for enabling us to defend ourselves against all invaders" on Nov 28, 1689. {Ref: ARMD 8:140}

SWAINE, JOHN (Talbot County), Protestant and probable soldier in the Revolution of 1689; signed an address and took a loyalty oath supporting the King of England and the reestablishment of Lord Baltimore into power on Nov 18, 1689. {Ref: ARMD 8:134}

SWANN (SWAN), JAMES (St. Mary's County), Protestant and soldier in the Revolution of 1689; signed an address and took a loyalty oath supporting the King of England and the reestablishment of Lord Baltimore into power on Nov 28, 1689; captain by 1703; died by May 26, 1708 (date of administration account; Judith Swann, widow). {Ref: ARMD 8:146; INAC 24:32, 28:217}

SWAYSBURY, JOHN (Talbot County), soldier (rank not stated) circa 1675; paid for his services in the late expedition against the Nanticoke Indians in 1678. {Ref: ARMD 7:87}

SWEATNAM (SWEETNAM, SWETNAM, SWETTMAN, SWETTNOM), EDWARD (Kent County), soldier (rank not stated) circa 1675; paid for his services in the late expedition against the Nanticoke Indians in 1678; lieutenant in a company of foot, commissioned Feb 28, 1681; county sheriff and officer of the town of New Yarmouth in 1686; captain of a foot company, 1689; military officer (rank not stated) who swore allegiance to the King & Queen of England in 1696; born circa 1650 (aged about 34 when deposed in 1684), died testate by Mar 20, 1698/9 (date of probate). {Ref: ARMD 5:470, 5:502, 7:94, 13:243, 17:78, 17:292, 20:540; TALR 6:21; INAC 16:149, 27:185; MDWB 6:249}

SWEATNAM (SWETNAM, SWEATMAN), RICHARD (Talbot County), soldier (rank not stated) circa 1675; paid for his services in the late expedition against the Nanticoke Indians in 1678; Protestant and probable soldier in the Revolution of 1689; signed an address and took a loyalty oath supporting the King of England and the reestablishment of Lord Baltimore into power on Nov 28, 1689 (name listed once as "Dick Sweatnam" and once as "Ritchard Sweatman"); captain by 1696; military officer who swore allegiance to the King & Queen of England in 1696; died testate by Jul 21, 1697 (date of probate; Jane Sweatnam, widow). {Ref: ARMD 7:102, 8:144, 8:159, 20:542; MDWB 7:304}

SWEATNAM, JANE, see "Edward Sweatnam," q.v.

SWIFT, HUMPHREY (Calvert County), Protestant and probable soldier in the Revolution of 1689; signed an address and took a loyalty oath supporting the King of England and "to reestablish Lord Baltimore in his ancient power and government" on Nov 16, 1689. {Ref: ARMD 8:132}

SWIFT, RALPH (Talbot County), soldier (rank not stated) circa 1675; paid for his services in the late expedition against the Nanticoke Indians in 1678. {Ref: ARMD 7:88}

SWITT, JOHN (England and Talbot County), mariner of London and land owner in Talbot County by 1688. {Ref: TALR 5:270}

SYBREY (SIBREY), JONATHAN (Kent, Cecil and Talbot Counties), captain, 1665-1684; sheriff, Cecil County, 1676-1678; paid for his services in the late expedition against the Nanticoke Indians in 1678; court justice (quorum), 1679; member of the Lower House of the Maryland Assembly, 1676-1682; sheriff, Talbot County, 1683-1684; accidentally drowned in June, 1684. {Ref: ARMD 3:528, 7:95, 7:265, 15:77, 15:135, 15:232, 15:255, 17:76, 17:142; BDML II:796}

SYMMONDS, JOHN (Talbot County), soldier (rank not stated) circa 1675; paid for his services in the late expedition against the Nanticoke Indians in 1678. {Ref: ARMD 7:88}

SYMMONDS, THOMAS (Dorchester County), soldier (rank not stated) circa 1675; paid for his services in the late expedition against the Nanticoke Indians in 1678. {Ref: ARMD 7:93}

SYMPSON, PATRICK (Anne Arundel County), captain and master of the brigantine *Batchelor's Club* in 1733 (formerly the *Monokin*, built in Somerset County in 1725). {Ref: MDWB 20:807; MDCB 82:8}

SYMPSON, RICHARD (Anne Arundel County), captain by 1733. {Ref: MINV 20:113}

TAILLOR (TAILLER), THOMAS (England and Anne Arundel County), lieutenant colonel on the Council of War in 1676; member of the Lower House of the Maryland Assembly, 1659, 1669-1673, and Upper House, 1674-1688; colonel and Protestant member of the Maryland Council, 1677-1681; colonel in command of the horse troops of Baltimore, Anne Arundel, and part of Calvert County, 1681-1688; returned to England in 1688; one "Thomas Taillor, of Maryland, then in London" was still living in February, 1711/2. Additional research will be necessary before drawing conclusions. {Ref: ARMD 2:507, 5:309, 5:310, 7:112, 15:99, 15:198, 15:253, 17:74-75; BDML II:796-797; LMCL:89}

TAILLOR, THOMAS (Dorchester County), captain by 1679; court justice (quorum), 1679. See "Thomas Taylor" and the other "Thomas Taillor," q.v. Additional research will be necessary before drawing conclusions. {Ref: ARMD 15:254}

TALBOTT (TALBOT), GEORGE (Ireland and Cecil County), colonel, 1679-1684; provincial court justice, 1679-1684; member of the Upper House, 1681-1683; petitioned the Maryland Council "for pay to be allowed the Souldiers placed at the ffort at Christina Bridge to keepe guard there by his Lordship's order" in 1684; John Coode's letter to the Secretary of State in 1690 noted that

Christopher Rousby had been the collector before John Paine and he (Rousby) had been murdered after a violent argument on the king's ship *Quaker Ketch* by "one Coll. Geo: Talbot an Irish papist and Chiefe Governor" on Oct 31, 1684 (One version is that Talbot escaped to Virginia, but later surrendered to Maryland authorities; he was then released to Virginia for trial and was found guilty in April, 1686, but was pardoned by King James II later that year; he subsequently served in the army of King James II and was outlawed in England for treason. Another version is that Talbot killed Rousby in an impromptu duel which was illegal in Maryland, so he took refuge in Virginia where dueling was legal; when the full circumstances were revealed, charges were withdrawn and Talbot returned to Maryland and eventually to England). See "Thomas Allen" and "Philim Murray" and "George Palbortt," q.v. {Ref: ARMD 7:459, 7:612, 8:172, 17:284, 17:299-307, 17:355-357, 17:371; BDML II:797; HCCM:25, 475}

TALBOTT, MARGARETT, see "William Talbott," q.v.

TALBOTT, WILLIAM (England and Baltimore County), soldier (rank not stated) circa 1675; paid for his services in the late expedition against the Nanticoke Indians in 1678; served in the Lower House of the Maryland Assembly, 1712-1713; died testate by Nov 16, 1713 (date of probate; Margarett Talbott, widow). {Ref: ARMD 7:95; BDML II:798; MDWB 13:642; INAC 38A:40}

TALLE, ANTHONY, see "John Ross," q.v.

TALMER, OLIVER (Cecil County), military officer (rank not stated) who swore allegiance to the King & Queen of England in 1696. {Ref: ARMD 20:546}

TANNER, JOHN (Anne Arundel and Calvert Counties), commander of a ship (no name given) in 1698; captain by 1698 and to at least 1716. {Ref: ARMD 23:466; INAC 25:364, 37A:115}

TANNER, NATHANIEL (Anne Arundel County), captain and commander of the ship *Towns End* riding in Severn River on Jan 18, 1725/6. {Ref: AALR SY#1:157}

TANNETT, EDWARD (Annapolis District), captain of the ship *Phoenix* of Maryland in 1734. {Ref: MDGZ, Jul 19, 1734}

TAPTICOE, WILLIAM (Dorchester County), soldier (rank not stated) circa 1675; paid for his services in the late expedition against the Nanticoke Indians in 1678. {Ref: ARMD 7:93}

TARBULL, WILLIAM (Queen Anne's County), major in the Second Company of Foot on Jun 30, 1732. {Ref: MDHR 1:11}

TARCELL, FRANCIS (Dorchester County), soldier (rank not stated) circa 1675; paid for his services in the late expedition against the Nanticoke Indians in 1678. {Ref: ARMD 7:93}

TARLETON (TARLETONE), EDWARD (England and St. Mary's County), captain of the ship *Dublin Merchant* in 1675; captain and master of the ship *Oake* of Liverpoole in 1694. {Ref: ARMD 20:147; INAC 1:272, 4:1}

TARLING, ANDREW (Cecil County), soldier (rank not stated) circa 1675; paid for his services in the late expedition against the Nanticoke Indians in 1678. {Ref: ARMD 7:95}

TARR, JOHN (Bogerternorton Hundred, Somerset County), Protestant and probable soldier in the Revolution of 1689; signed an address and took a loyalty oath supporting the King of England and "for enabling us to defend ourselves against all invaders" on Nov 28, 1689; died testate by Aug 20, 1695 (date of probate; Mary Tarr, widow). {Ref: ARMD 8:141; PFMD:90; OSES:464; MDWB 7:131}

TASKER, BENJAMIN (Calvert, Anne Arundel, and Prince George's Counties), colonel and naval officer for the port of Annapolis by 1719; sheriff, 1717-1720; provincial court justice, 1726-1753; mayor of Annapolis for four terms; re-commissioned naval officer, 1733-1742; commissary general, 1733-1734, 1754-1756; president of the Maryland Council and acting governor, 1752-1753; born circa 1690-1691 (aged about 45 when deposed in 1736 and aged about 51 when deposed in 1741), died testate on Jun 19, 1768. {Ref: BDML II:799-801; HCCM:325; MDCB 82:1; MDEP:181; MDWB 36:482}

TASKER, THOMAS (England and Calvert County), captain of a company of foot troops in 1689; Protestant, justice of the peace, and soldier during the Revolution of 1689 (commanded a company of infantry which took part in the capture of St. Mary's City and Mattapany); signed an address and took a loyalty oath supporting the King of England and the reestablishment of Lord Baltimore into power on Nov 28, 1689; colonel by 1698 (succeeded Colonel Jowles as commander of the county militia); member of the Lower House of the Maryland Assembly, 1692-1699, and Upper House, 1699-1700; died testate by Aug 31, 1700 (date of probate). {Ref: ARMD 8:145, 13:242, 23:6, 23:278, 23:406; BDML II:802; HCCM:325; MDWB 11:137}

TAW, JOHN (St. Mary's County), Protestant and probable soldier in the Revolution of 1689; signed an address and took a loyalty oath supporting the King of England and the reestablishment of Lord Baltimore into power on Nov 28, 1689. See "John Touch (Tauh?)," q.v. {Ref: ARMD 8:147}

TAYLARD, WILLIAM (St. Mary's and Calvert County), Protestant and probable soldier in the Revolution of 1689; signed an address and took a loyalty oath supporting the King of England and the reestablishment of Lord Baltimore into power on Nov 28, 1689 (name listed only as "W. Taylard"); clerk of the provincial court by 1693; captain by 1702; born circa 1662 (aged about 47 when deposed in 1709), died testate by Jan 26, 1711/2 (date of probate; Audry Taylard, widow, died testate in 1721). {Ref: ARMD 8:147, 8:494; MDEP:181; MDWB 13:338, 17:4; INAC 23:104}

TAYLOR, ABRAHAM (Oxford District), captain and master of the ship *Swallow* in 1731. {Ref: CVPR:12}

TAYLOR, ANN, see "William Taylor," q.v.

TAYLOR, DOROTHY, see "John Taylor" and "Lawrence Taylor," q.v.

TAYLOR, EDWARD (Dorchester County), lieutenant before 1678; paid for his services in the late expedition against the Nanticoke Indians in 1678. {Ref: ARMD 7:93}

TAYLOR, ELIZABETH, see "Thomas Taylor," q.v.

TAYLOR, GEORGE (Anne Arundel County), captain and master of the ship *Maryland* in 1682. {Ref: INAC 7C:151}

TAYLOR, HENRY (Kent County), soldier (rank not stated) on Isle of Kent who swore allegiance to the Commonwealth of England on Apr 5, 1652; born circa 1629 (aged about 26 when deposed in 1655; name listed once as "Henerie Telior"). {Ref: INKC:101, 106}

TAYLOR, HENRY (Calvert County), probable soldier (rank not stated) before 1682; paid for his services out of an assessment levied by the General Assembly for the public good in 1682; ranger under the command of Capt. Richard Brightwell in 1692. {Ref: ARMD 7:439, 8:445}

TAYLOR, JAMES, see "Isaac Kilson," q.v.

TAYLOR, JOHN (Baltimore County), captain by 1724; member of the Lower House of the Maryland Assembly, 1722-1724; died by 1737, possibly in North Carolina. {Ref: BDML II:804; HBCC:44}

TAYLOR, JOHN (Dorchester County), captain by 1700; sheriff, 1684-1686; member of the Lower House of the Maryland Assembly, 1704-1705; born circa 1662 (aged about 34 when deposed in 1696), died testate by Feb 4, 1705/6 (date of probate; Dorothy Taylor, widow). {Ref: ARMD 24:8, 25:559; BDML II:804; MDWB 3:736}

TAYLOR, JOHN (Dorchester County), captain by 1728; born circa 1684-1688 (aged about 40 and 42 when deposed twice in 1728 and aged about 54 when deposed in 1738; son of John Taylor). {Ref: MDEP:181}

TAYLOR (TAYLER), JOHN (Somerset County), Protestant and probable soldier in the Revolution of 1689; signed an address and took a loyalty oath supporting the King of England and "for enabling us to defend ourselves against all invaders" on Nov 28, 1689. {Ref: ARMD 8:141}

TAYLOR, JOHN, see "William Pickett," q.v.

TAYLOR, LAWRENCE (Spesutia Hundred, Baltimore County), soldier (rank not stated) circa 1675; paid for his services in the late expedition against the Nanticoke Indians in 1678; also paid for his services out of an assessment levied by the General Assembly for the public good in 1682; died testate by Nov 25, 1701 (date of probate; Dorothy Taylor, widow). {Ref: ARMD 7:95, 7:441; BBCF:624; MDWB 11:177}

TAYLOR, PETER, see "Thomas Taylor," q.v.

TAYLOR, PHILIP (Dorchester County), captain before 1649; born circa 1610, died circa 1649. {Ref: BDML II:804}

TAYLOR, RICHARD (Talbot County), soldier (rank not stated) circa 1675; paid for his services in the late expedition against the Nanticoke Indians in 1678. {Ref: ARMD 7:88}

TAYLOR, SAMUEL (Talbot County), soldier (rank not stated) circa 1675; paid for his services in the late expedition against the Nanticoke Indians in 1678 (name listed once as "Samuell Taylour"); Protestant and probable soldier in the Revolution of 1689; signed an address and took a loyalty oath supporting the

King of England and the reestablishment of Lord Baltimore into power on Nov 18, 1689. {Ref: ARMD 7:92, 8:134}

TAYLOR, THOMAS (Talbot County), soldier (rank not stated) circa 1675; paid for his services in the late expedition against the Nanticoke Indians in 1678; died testate by Mar 25, 1685 (date of probate; Elizabeth Taylor, widow). {Ref: ARMD 7:87, 7:89; MDWB 4:92}

TAYLOR, THOMAS (St. Mary's County), colonel by 1685. See "Thomas Taillor," q.v. {Ref: INAC 8:519}

TAYLOR, THOMAS (Dorchester County), captain before 1678; paid for his services in the late expedition against the Nanticoke Indians in 1678; major and court justice, 1680-1685; authorized by the Maryland Council "to range with his troope (when and as often as occasion shall require) in any part of the said County [Dorchester] for the discovery of any Enemy that may attempt or Designe any violence or injury to the Inhabitants there" in 1681; major in command of troops in Dorchester County, 1686; major and officer of the town of Cambridge, 1686; major in command of the militia in Dorchester County, 1687; major, 1703 (mentioned his son Peter Taylor); one Thomas Taylor died testate by June, 1709 (date of probate; Jane Taylor, widow). See "Thomas Taillor," q.v. {Ref: ARMD 5:460, 5:503, 5:554, 7:92-93, 7:612, 13:244, 15:326, 15:363, 17:381, 25:150; DOLR 8 Old 90, 247; DOLR 9 Old 138; MDWB 12:113, pt. 2}

TAYLOR, THOMAS (Kent County), soldier (rank not stated) on Isle of Kent who swore allegiance to the Commonwealth of England on Apr 5, 1652. {Ref: INKC:101}

TAYLOR, WALTER (Talbot County), possible soldier by 1694 when he was paid for his services by the Maryland Assembly; born circa 1663 (adjudged to be about 12 years old by the county court in 1675 when he was a servant to Vincent Lowe). {Ref: ARMD 38:55, 66:126}

TAYLOR, WILLIAM (Talbot County), soldier (rank not stated) circa 1675; paid for his services in the late expedition against the Nanticoke Indians in 1678. {Ref: ARMD 7:88, 91}

TAYLOR (TAYLER), WILLIAM (Charles County), Protestant and probable soldier in the Revolution of 1689; signed an address and took a loyalty oath supporting the King of England and the reestablishment of Lord Baltimore into power on Nov 28, 1689. {Ref: ARMD 8:138}

TAYLOR (TAYLER), WILLIAM (St. Mary's County), soldier (rank not stated) circa 1675; paid for his services in the late expedition against the Nanticoke Indians in 1678; Protestant and probable soldier in the Revolution of 1689; signed an address and took a loyalty oath supporting the King of England and the reestablishment of Lord Baltimore into power on Nov 28, 1689; died testate by Jun 5, 1714 (date of probate; Ann Taylor, widow). {Ref: ARMD 7:102, 8:147; MDWB 14:4}

TEAGLE, NATHANIELL (Talbot County), soldier (rank not stated) circa 1675; paid for his services in the late expedition against the Nanticoke Indians in

1678; died testate by Dec 20, 1708 (date of probate). {Ref: ARMD 7:87; MDWB 12:22, pt. 2}

TEAL, EDWARD, see "Nathaniel Stinchcomb," q.v.

TELIOR, HENERIE, see "Henry Taylor," q.v.

TENER, WILLIAM (Cecil County), mariner by Aug 1, 1720 (date of deed of gift to his daughter Elizabeth Tener "for his natural love and affection and because he is moving"). {Ref: CELR 3:312}

TENNANT (TENNENT), JOHN (Kent County), captain, mariner, and master of the ship *Chester* in 1730-1731; master of the sloop *Two Brothers* in 1736 (built at Chester River in 1730); master of the schooner *Tryall* in 1738 (built in Maryland in 1735); died testate by Jun 16, 1744 (date of probate; Elizabeth Tennant, widow). {Ref: CFES 1:328; MDWB 23:593; INKC:178; CVPR:12; MDWB 23:593; MDCB 82:46, 65}

TENNISON, ABSOLON (St. Mary's County), Protestant and probable soldier in the Revolution of 1689; signed an address and took a loyalty oath supporting the King of England and the reestablishment of Lord Baltimore into power on Nov 28, 1689. {Ref: ARMD 8:146}

TENNISON, JUSTINIAN (St. Mary's County), soldier (rank not stated) circa 1675; paid for his services in the late expedition against the Nanticoke Indians in 1678. {Ref: ARMD 7:102}

TETHERTON, WILLIAM (St. Mary's County), soldier (rank not stated) circa 1675; paid for his services in the late expedition against the Nanticoke Indians in 1678. {Ref: ARMD 7:102}

TEUXBURY, ---- (Anne Arundel County), captain by 1705. {Ref: INAC 25:208}

THARPES, WILLIAM (Talbot County), soldier (rank not stated) circa 1675; paid for his services in the late expedition against the Nanticoke Indians in 1678. {Ref: ARMD 7:91}

THEAMES, RICHARD (Kent County), soldier (rank not stated) circa 1675; paid for his services in the late expedition against the Nanticoke Indians in 1678. {Ref: ARMD 7:94}

THEOBALLS, CLEMENT (Charles County), soldier (rank not stated) in Capt. James Langworth's Company before 1661 (year of the captain's death, but his ammunition report was not filed until 1664 by Henry Adames). {Ref: CHLR B:379}

THEXTON (THEAKSTON), THOMAS (Kent and Cecil Counties), soldier (rank not stated) circa 1675; paid for his services in the late expedition against the Nanticoke Indians in 1678; member of the Lower House of the Maryland Assembly, 1692-1693; died intestate in 1698. {Ref: ARMD 7:94; BDML II:807}

THOMAS, ---- (Anne Arundel or Calvert County), soldier (rank not stated) who served under Captain Fuller at the Battle of the Severn on Mar 25, 1655 and was probably the "one Thomas" *[sic]* who served on a Council of War after the battle. {Ref: FAAH:26}

THOMAS, ALEXANDER (Somerset County), soldier (rank not stated) circa 1675; paid for his services in the late expedition against the Nanticoke Indians in 1678; Protestant and probable soldier in the Revolution of 1689; signed an address and took a loyalty oath supporting the King of England and "for enabling us to defend ourselves against all invaders" on Nov 28, 1689; died testate by Jan 14, 1695/6 (date of probate). {Ref: ARMD 7:98, 8:141; MDWB 7:179}

THOMAS, ANNE, see "Thristram Thomas," q.v.

THOMAS, BENJAMIN (Charles County), captain by 1705 (date of accounting on the disbursement of his estate). {Ref: CHLR Z:268}

THOMAS, BENONI (Charles County), captain before 1713; died testate by Feb 25, 1713/4 (date of probate; Katharine Thomas, widow). {Ref: INAC 36A:62; MDWB 13:678}

THOMAS, ELIZABETH, see "William Thomas," q.v.

THOMAS, GRIFFITH (Talbot County), soldier (rank not stated) circa 1675; paid for his services in the late expedition against the Nanticoke Indians in 1678. {Ref: ARMD 7:88}

THOMAS, HUGH (Charles County), soldier (rank not stated) circa 1675; paid for his services in the late expedition against the Nanticoke Indians in 1678; born circa 1638 (aged about 24 when deposed on October 1, 1662). {Ref: ARMD 7:102, 53:255; CHLR A:247}

THOMAS, JAMES (county not indicated), captain by 1706. {Ref: ARMD 25:203}

THOMAS, JANE, see "Robert Thomas," q.v.

THOMAS, JOHN (Dorchester County), soldier (rank not stated) circa 1675; paid for his services in the late expedition against the Nanticoke Indians in 1678. {Ref: ARMD 7:92}

THOMAS, JOHN (Talbot County), soldier (rank not stated) circa 1675; paid for his services in the late expedition against the Nanticoke Indians in 1678. {Ref: ARMD 7:90}

THOMAS, JOHN (Charles County), a seafaring man in 1697. {Ref: ARMD 25:597}

THOMAS, JOHN (Baltimore County), captain by 1689; county court justice, 1689; major of foot troops, 1690; sheriff, 1694-1696; colonel, commissioned Oct 9, 1694 and swore allegiance to the King & Queen of England in 1696; colonel on the north side of the Patapsco, 1695-1703; Maryland Council "ordered that Colonel John Thomas of Baltimore County for his late irregularitys be left out of the Commission of the peace in Baltimore County" on Oct 11, 1700; died by Jan 3, 1717/8 (date of administration bond; Sarah Thomas, widow). See "Charles Whitehead," q.v. {Ref: ARMD 20:77, 20:109-110, 20:153, 20:202, 20:544, 23:15, 23:285, 25:108; BBCF:633; BCTL:5, 27, 34; INBC:9; AAGE:568-569; BDML II:808; MINV 1:18}

THOMAS, KATHARINE, see "Benoni Thomas," q.v.

THOMAS, PHILIP (England, and Calvert and Anne Arundel Counties), lieutenant by 1655; Puritan leader against the supporters of Lord Baltimore in the Battle of the Severn on Mar 25, 1655 and served on the Council of War after the battle; provincial court commissioner, 1656/1657; died testate by Jul 10, 1675 (date of probate; Sarah Thomas, widow). {Ref: RMHF II:199; MDWB 2:350}

THOMAS, ROBERT (Anne Arundel County), boatman, late of Annapolis, died before Nov 9, 1720 (date of deed by Jane Thomas, widow). {Ref: AALR CW#1:298}

THOMAS, SAMUEL (Kent County), military officer (rank not stated) who swore allegiance to the King & Queen of England in 1696; captain by 1722; colonel by 1733. {Ref: ARMD 20:541; CESM:56; MINV 10:375; INKC:178}

THOMAS, SAMUELL (Kent County), sailor by 1723. {Ref: MDAD 5:148}

THOMAS, SARAH, see "John Thomas" and "Philip Thomas," q.v.

THOMAS, TRISTRAM (England and Talbot County), soldier (rank not stated) circa 1675 (name listed as "Thristram Thomas"); paid for his services in the late expedition against the Nanticoke Indians in 1678; "Trustam Thomas" died testate by May 22, 1686 (date of probate; Anne Thomas, widow). {Ref: ARMD 7:88-90; RMHF II:162-163; MDWB 4:226}

THOMAS, WILLIAM (St. Mary's County), captain before 1685; died testate by Mar 26, 1685 (date of probate; Elizabeth Thomas, widow). See "William Barton, Sr.," q.v. {Ref: INAC 8:523; MDWB 4:107}

THOMASINE, RICHARD (Dorchester County), soldier (rank not stated) circa 1675; paid for his services in the late expedition against the Nanticoke Indians in 1678. {Ref: ARMD 7:93}

THOMLINS, EDWARD (Talbot County), soldier (rank not stated) circa 1675; paid for his services in the late expedition against the Nanticoke Indians in 1678. {Ref: ARMD 7:88}

THOMPSON, AUGUSTINE (Cecil and Queen Anne's Counties), captain of the militia in the Upper Chester and Choptank Rivers area in 1732; member of the Lower House of the Maryland Assembly, 1728-1731; born circa 1691 (aged about 41 when deposed in 1732), died on Feb 26, 1738/9 (will probated on Apr 24, 1739; Elizabeth Thompson, widow). {Ref: MDHR 1:11; BDML II:815; MDEP:184; MDWB 22:85}

THOMPSON, ELIZABETH, see "Augustine Thompson," q.v.

THOMPSON, GEORGE (St. Mary's County), captain before 1702; born circa 1637 (aged about 65 when deposed in 1702), died by Mar 17, 1712/3 (date of inventory). {Ref: INAC 35A:13; MDEP:184}

THOMPSON, GEORGE (Charles County), soldier (rank not stated) in Capt. James Langworth's Company before 1661 (year of the captain's death, but his ammunition report was not filed until 1664 by Henry Adames). {Ref: CHLR B:379}

THOMPSON, HERBERT (county not indicated), probable soldier by 1694 when paid for his services by the Maryland Assembly. {Ref: ARMD 38:55}

THOMPSON, JOHN (England and Cecil County), captain by 1694; major, commissioned Oct 9, 1694; appointed "naval officer of the limits and precincts of Cecil County" on Nov 17, 1694; military officer who swore allegiance to the

King & Queen of England in 1696; "navall officer of Caecill County" in 1695; colonel, 1697; "naval officer of the head of the Bay" in 1700; member of the Lower House of the Maryland Assembly, 1695-1701; died testate by Jul 4, 1702 (date of probate; Judith Thompson, widow). {Ref: ARMD 20:111, 20:153, 20:213, 20:261, 20:545, 23:20, 23:94, 23:278-279, 24:6, 24:35, 24:129, 24:234, 25:107; BDML II:815-816; INAC 25:83; MDWB 11:233}

THOMPSON, JOHN BAPTIST (Anne Arundel County), mariner in the 1730's; captain and master of the sloop *Tryal* by 1739 (built in Herring Bay in 1733). {Ref: MDCB 82:79}

THOMPSON, JUDITH, see "John Thompson," q.v.

THOMPSON, RICHARD (Cecil County and Delaware), captain by 1723; commissioned Ranger of the Woods in Cecil County on Apr 25, 1735; born circa 1680 (aged about 80 when deposed in 1760), died testate by Nov 23, 1775 (date of probate) in New Castle County. {Ref: BDML II:817; MDEP:185; MDCB 82:28; DE Wills K:273}

THOMPSON, RICHARD (Baltimore County), ensign before 1696; swore allegiance to the King & Queen of England in 1696; died testate by Jun 30, 1698 (date of probate). {Ref: ARMD 20:544; MDWB 6:140}

THOMPSON, ROBERT (St. Mary's County), boatswain on Mr. Wright's ship (no name given) in 1659. {Ref: ARMD 41:341}

THOMPSON, ROBERT (Charles County), Protestant and probable soldier in the Revolution of 1689; signed an address and took a loyalty oath supporting the King of England and the reestablishment of Lord Baltimore into power on Nov 28, 1689. {Ref: ARMD 8:138}

THOMPSON, WILLIAM (Prince George's County), soldier (rank not stated) under the command of Col. Ninian Beale from June, 1699 to May, 1700; born circa 1649 (aged about 80 when deposed on Aug 22, 1729; mentioned Col. Beale about 46 years ago). {Ref: ARMD 24:121-122; PGLR M:488}

THOMPSON, WILLIAM (Anne Arundel County), captain and commander of the ship *Prudent Mary*, rising at anchor in South River on Jan 11, 1715/6. {Ref: AALR IB#2:262}

THOMSON, JAMES (England and Charles County), "sailorman of Shatsbury, County Dorsett" before 1695; land owner in Charles County by 1695. {Ref: PGLR A:18}

THOMSON, JAMES (Charles County), Protestant and probable soldier in the Revolution of 1689; signed an address and took a loyalty oath supporting the King of England and the reestablishment of Lord Baltimore into power on Nov 28, 1689. {Ref: ARMD 8:138}

THOMSON, JOHN (Isle of Kent), soldier (rank not stated) who was captured along with Sergeant Vaughan in 1635 near Palmer's Island and held prisoner by William Clayborne on Kent Island; died testate by May 7, 1649 (date of probate). {Ref: ARMD 3:174; FMDP:265; MDWB 1:12}

THORNBOROUGH, ROWLAND (Baltimore County), soldier (rank not stated) circa 1675; paid for his services in the late expedition against the Nanticoke

Indians in 1678 (name mistakenly listed as "Rowland Thornebridge"); "Rouland Thornborough" died testate at Back River in Baltimore County by Jun 23, 1696 (date of probate; Ann Thornborough, widow). {Ref: ARMD 7:95; RMHF I:355; MDWB 7:200}

THORNE, WILLIAM (Virginia and Somerset County), commissioned "to bee captain at Monoakin and Anamesick" on May 2, 1662; member of the Somerset County Court, 1665; commissioned "to Command all the fforces (as Captain) on the Easterne Shore of this Province from Wiccocomoco that Joynes upon Mannij to that part of Pocamoke on the said Easterne Shore, that is or shall be inhabited, within this said province of Maryland, them to muster Exercise &c." on Sep 2, 1665; died in 1669/70 (exact date of probate not indicated; will written on Feb 12, 1665/6; Winifred Thorne, widow). {Ref: ARMD 3:453, 3:533, 54:616; OSES:73, 69, 279, 285, 312; MDWB 1:368}

THORNHILL, ROBERT (Dorchester County), soldier (rank not stated) circa 1675; paid for his services in the late expedition against the Nanticoke Indians in 1678. {Ref: ARMD 7:92}

THORNTON, POSTHUMUS (Prince George's County and Patuxent District), captain and commander of the ship *Ann* or *Anne* in 1722-1724, riding in the Patuxent River on Jan 11, 1723/4 and Jan 24, 1724/5, and the ship *Richard and Ann* riding in the Patuxent River on Feb 1, 1725/6; master of the ship *Mary* in 1731; died testate by Oct 10, 1738 (date of probate; Eleanor Thornton, widow). {Ref: PGLR I:465, M:148-140; CVPR:12; MDWB 22:1; MDAD 35:246}

THORPE, THOMAS (Anne Arundel County), captain and commander of the galley *Finch* riding in Severn River on Apr 24, 1723. {Ref: AALR RCW#2:141}

THRIFT, JOHN (Talbot County), military officer (rank not stated) who swore allegiance to the King & Queen of England in 1696. {Ref: ARMD 20:542}

THURBER, JOHN (county or port not indicated), captain and commander of the ship *Philip* of New York, sailing from Maryland, in 1684. {Ref: ARMD 8:564, 20:369}

THURSTON, CHARLES (St. Mary's County), captain and mariner, 1653. {Ref: ARMD 10:355}

THURSTON, MARY, see "Thomas Thurston," q.v.

THURSTON, RICHARD (St. Mary's County), captain and mariner, 1653. {Ref: ARMD 10:355}

THURSTON, THOMAS (England, Virginia, and Baltimore County), member of the Lower House of the Maryland Assembly, 1686-1688; attended the Associators Convention, 1689-1692; colonel between 1690-1692 (considered a "renegade Quaker" in 1690); born circa 1622, died testate by Apr 13, 1693 (date of probate; Mary Thurston, widow). {Ref: BDML II:818; BBCF:639-640; MDWB 6:31}

TIBALDS, JOHN (Talbot County), soldier (rank not stated) circa 1675; paid for his services in the late expedition against the Nanticoke Indians in 1678. {Ref: ARMD 7:87}

TILDEN, CHARLES (Kent County), court justice, 1685; military officer (rank not stated) who swore allegiance to the King & Queen of England in 1696 (name mistakenly listed once as "Stilden"). {Ref: ARMD 17:379, 20:540}

TILDEN, JOHN (Kent County), captain by 1733. {Ref: INKC:178}

TILDEN, MARMADUKE (Kent County), styled "captain" by 1726; member of the Lower House of the Maryland Assembly, 1725-1726; died testate on Jun 20, 1726 (will probated on Oct 19, 1726). {Ref: BDML II:819; MDWB 19:20; MINV 12:467; MDAD 9:265}

TILGHMAN, ANNA MARIA, see "Richard Tilghman," q.v.

TILGHMAN (TILMAN, TILLMAN), GIDEON (Manokin Hundred, Somerset County), soldier (rank not stated) circa 1675; paid for his services in the late expedition against the Nanticoke Indians in 1678; "Giddeon Tilman (Tillman), planter" died testate by May 19, 1720 (date of probate). {Ref: ARMD 7:99; OSES:280; SOJR II:59; MDWB 16:244}

TILGHMAN, RICHARD (Talbot, Kent, and Queen Anne's Counties), captain by 1706; member of the Lower House of the Maryland Assembly, representing Talbot County, 1697-1704; lieutenant colonel, 1707; sheriff, Queen Anne's County, 1709-1710; member of the Maryland Council, 1711-1738; referred to as colonel in 1713, lieutenant colonel in 1714, and colonel in 1716; colonel of a troop of horse on Jun 30, 1732; born Feb 23, 1672/3 (aged about 60 when deposed in 1732), died testate on Jan 23, 1738/9 (will probated on Feb 14, 1738/9; Anna Maria Tilghman, widow). {Ref: ARMD 25:277, 25:377, 25:512, 28:12, 29:4, 29:321, 29:347, 33:156, 34:5; CESM:56; MDHR 1:11; BDML II:830; MDWB 22:35-36}

TILGHMAN, RICHARD (Talbot County), Protestant and probable soldier in the Revolution of 1689; signed an address and took a loyalty oath supporting the King of England and the reestablishment of Lord Baltimore into power on Nov 18, 1689. {Ref: ARMD 8:134}

TILGHMAN (TILLMAN), SAMUEL (England and St. Mary's County), mariner, of Ratcliffe, County of Middlesex, by 1653; captain and commander of the ship *Golden Fortune*, 1653-1664; born after 1620 (aged "40 plus years" when deposed in 1660). See "John Winbridge" and "Robert Morris," q.v. {Ref: ARMD 3:387, 10:395, 41:92, 41:214-215, 41:276, 41:358, 49:18, 49:27, 49:247; CHLR B:368; MDEP:185}

TILGHMAN, WILLIAM (Talbot County), soldier (rank not stated) circa 1675; paid for his services in the late expedition against the Nanticoke Indians in 1678; born on Feb 16, 1658/9, died in 1682 (unmarried). {Ref: ARMD 7:88; BDML II:830}

TILLY, CALEB (county or port not indicated), captain and master of the ship *Pac* of Plymouth in 1690. {Ref: ARMD 8:237}

TILMAN, GIDEON, see "Gideon Tilghman," q.v.

TILMAN, JOHN HANS (Cecil County), captain and Indian trader "at the head of the bay" in 1698 (subsequently referred to once as simply "Capt. Hans"). See "Hans Steetman (Steelman)," q.v. {Ref: ARMD 23:444}

TIRKILL, THOMAS (St. Mary's County), soldier (rank not stated) circa 1675; paid for his services in the late expedition against the Nanticoke Indians in 1678. {Ref: ARMD 7:102}

TOCKFIELD, SAMUELL (Somerset County), soldier (rank not stated) circa 1675; paid for his services in the late expedition against the Nanticoke Indians in 1678. {Ref: ARMD 7:98}

TODD, LANCELOT (Baltimore and Anne Arundel Counties), captain, appointed in 1723 (name also listed as "Lance Todd" and "Lancellott Todd"); justice, Baltimore County, 1724, and Anne Arundel County, 1727-1732; born circa 1674, died testate by Jun 16, 1735 (date of probate). {Ref: MDAD 6:179; MDWB 2:368; Dorsey and Nimmo's *The Dorsey Family* (1947), pp. 194-195}

TODD, THOMAS (England, Virginia, and Anne Arundel and Baltimore Counties), captain before 1669; member of the Lower House of the Maryland Assembly, 1674-1675; baptized on Sep 12, 1619, wrote his will on Feb 26, 1675/6, and died after Apr 11, 1676 (probably died on a ship bound for England or shortly after reaching England); will was probated on May 30, 1677 in Baltimore County; Ann Todd or Todde, widow). *Note:* The name of Capt. Thomas Todd appeared among those who were to receive payment from the estate of Roger Sidwell, deceased, Baltimore County, on Sep 22, 1679. Additional research will be necessary before drawing conclusions. {Ref: BDML II:835-836; BBCF:643; FAAH:48; HBCC:55; MDWB 5:227; INAC 1:279, 6:423}

TODD, THOMAS (Baltimore County), soldier in the 1730's; captain by 1737 in Back River Upper Hundred; born circa 1706, died testate by Apr 2, 1739 (date of probate; Eleanor Todd, widow). {Ref: BBCF:644; INBC:20; MDWB 22:37}

TOMKYNS, EDWIN (Anne Arundel County), captain and commander of the ship *Worisster* "riding at anchor in Seavern River" on Jun 8, 1719. {Ref: AALR CW#1:17}

TOMSON, EDWARD (St. Mary's County), soldier (rank not stated) in 1642. {Ref: ARMD 4:130-131}

TOMSON, RICHARD (St. Mary's County), soldier (rank not stated) in 1642. {Ref: ARMD 4:130-131}

TONGE (TONG), JOHN (St. Clement's Manor, St. Mary's County), probable soldier (rank not stated) before 1682; paid for his services out of an assessment levied by the General Assembly for the public good in 1682; born circa 1658 (aged about 25 when deposed in 1683), died testate by Sep 1, 1688 (date of probate). {Ref: ARMD 7:441; MDEP:186; MDWB 6:9}

TONGE, WILLIAM (Talbot County), Protestant and probable soldier in the Revolution of 1689; signed an address and took a loyalty oath supporting the King of England and the reestablishment of Lord Baltimore into power on Nov 18, 1689. {Ref: ARMD 8:134}

TORVER, WILLIAM (England and Anne Arundel County), captain and commander of the ship *Recovery* riding at anchor in Severn River on Nov 25, 1717 and Feb 10, 1717/8 and Jan 6, 1718/9 and May 1, 1719 and Jan 25,

1719/20; mariner, of Ratcliff, Parish of St. Dunstain, Stepney, in 1721. {Ref: AALR IB#2:402, 428, 524, 544, CW#1:118, 351}

TOUCH (TAUH?), JOHN (county or port not indicated), captain and master of the ship *Edward and Sarah* of Maryland, 1690-1691. {Ref: ARMD 8:238, 8:240}

TOURNER, JAMES (county not indicated), probable soldier (rank not stated) before 1682; paid for his services out of an assessment levied by the General Assembly for the public good in 1682. {Ref: ARMD 7:439}

TOWERSON, EDWARD (England and Pocomoke District), captain and commander of the English pink *Dauphin* of Whitehaven in 1697. {Ref: ARMD 23:138}

TOWGOOD, JOSIAS (Prince George's and Anne Arundel Counties), gentleman by 1697; major by 1724; colonel before 1734; died testate by Mar 5, 1734/5 (date of probate; Mary Towgood, widow). {Ref: AALR RCW#2:250; PGLR A:91; MDWB 21:459}

TOWLES, WILLIAM (Baltimore County), captain by 1717. {Ref: INAC 38A:40}

TOWNSEND, BERNARD (Prince George's County), captain and commander of the ship *Molly* in 1723. {Ref: PGLR I:465}

TOWNSEND, ELIZABETH, see "John Townsend, Sr." q.v.

TOWNSEND, JOHN (Pocomoke District), captain and master of the ship *Endeavour* in 1731. {Ref: CVPR:12}

TOWNSEND, JOHN, SR. (Northampton, Virginia and Morumsco, Somerset County), soldier (rank not stated) circa 1675; paid for his services in the late expedition against the Nanticoke Indians in 1678; died testate by Sep 30, 1698 (date of probate; Elizabeth Townsend, widow). {Ref: ARMD 7:99; OSES:280, 459; MDWB 6:179}

TOWNSEND, THOMAS (Somerset County), soldier (rank not stated) circa 1675; paid for his services in the late expedition against the Nanticoke Indians in 1678; one "Thomas Townsing" died testate in Anne Arundel County by Jan 3, 1699/1700 (date of probate). {Ref: ARMD 7:97; MDWB 6:334}

TOWSON, GABRIEL (county not indicated), captain of the Maryland troops "raised to strengthen Albany, New York and resist the French and Indian enemies" in 1690. {Ref: SHMD I:355}

TRACEY, CHARLES (Calvert County), Protestant and probable soldier in the Revolution of 1689; signed an address and took a loyalty oath supporting the King of England and the reestablishment of Lord Baltimore into power on Nov 28, 1689. {Ref: ARMD 8:145}

TRAFFORD, FRANCIS (England and St. Mary's County), arrived in this province in high status (esquire and colonel) in 1642; member of the Maryland Council in 1642; sent by Gov. Leonard Calvert to Virginia in August, 1642, to request the aid of 100 men to fight Indians; left Maryland in 1643. {Ref: ARMD 1:169; BDML II:839}

TRAILE, WILLIAM (Somerset County), Protestant and probable soldier in the Revolution of 1689; signed an address and took a loyalty oath supporting the

King of England and "for enabling us to defend ourselves against all invaders" on Nov 28, 1689. {Ref: ARMD 8:141}

TRAVERS, THOMAS (Dorchester County), soldier and probable officer in the early 1700's; captain before 1764; born circa 1686 (aged about 78 when deposed in 1764), died intestate by Sep 25, 1772 (date of inventory). {Ref: MDEP:187; MINV 109:423}

TRAVIS (TRAUIS), PHILIP (county not indicated), private in the Maryland troops "raised to strengthen Albany, New York and resist the French and Indian enemies" in 1690. {Ref: SHMD I:355}

TRAYMAN, WILLIAM (Talbot County), soldier (rank not stated) circa 1675; paid for his services in the late expedition against the Nanticoke Indians in 1678. {Ref: ARMD 7:92}

TREGANY (TREGENY), HENRY (England and St. Mary's), captain and master of the ship *Canterberry* of London in 1694. {Ref: ARMD 20:147, 20:299}

TREGIAN, RICHARD (England and St. Mary's County), captain and master of the barque *Katherine* of Poole in 1693. {Ref: ARMD 20:182}

TREGO, WILLIAM (England, and St. Mary's and/or Calvert County), captain and master of the ship *Patience* of Bristol in 1671 (name also listed as "Trigo" and "Treago" and was most likely the "Capt. Tregoe" who appeared on a list of debts in the estates of George and Frances Beckwith, deceased, in Calvert County in 1676). {Ref: ARMD 5:100; INAC 2:179}

TREMANCE, JOHN (county not indicated), probable soldier (rank not stated) before 1682; paid for his services out of an assessment levied by the General Assembly for the public good in 1682. {Ref: ARMD 7:440}

TRESTRAN(?), RICHARD (county not indicated), captain by 1696; a "Richard Trensham" died intestate in Anne Arundel County by Sep 2, 1727 (date of administration account). Additional research will be necessary before drawing conclusions. {Ref: INAC 14:82; MDAD 8:319}

TREVET, JOHN (St. Mary's County), captain before 1694; master of the sloop *Johannis* in 1694. {Ref: ARMD 20:155, 20:185}

TREW, WILLIAM, see "Henry Row," q.v.

TREWHITT, ROBERT (Annapolis District), captain of the ship *Content* in 1734. {Ref: MDGZ, Nov 29, 1734}

TRICE, JOHN (Prince George's County), captain and master of the ship *Welcome* riding in the Eastern Branch of Patuxent River in January, 1724. {Ref: PGLR M:148}

TRICKETT (TRICKET), ABRAHAM (Kent County), captain and master of the ship *Margarett* in the Potomac District in 1697; died by Jun 7, 1700 (date of inventory). {Ref: ARMD 23:172; INAC 20:126}

TRIGGS, NATHANIEL (Annapolis District), mariner by 1734; captain and master of the schooner *Baltimore* in 1735 (built at Annapolis in 1734). {Ref: MDCB 82:38}

TRIPPE, ELIZABETH, see "Henry Trippe (Tripp)," q.v.

TRIPPE (TRIPP), HENRY (England and Dorchester County), captain of foot soldiers in 1676; paid for his services in the late expedition against the Nanticoke Indians in 1678; captain of "a party of foote" in 1681; captain and court justice in 1685; major of horse troops in 1689; member of the Lower House of the Maryland Assembly at various times between 1671 and 1692; Maryland Council indicated that "if it should please God that Major Tripp should Returne into the Countery he is to be Lieutenant Collonell" on Oct 9, 1694; born 1632, died testate by Mar 21, 1697/8 (date of probate; Elizabeth Trippe, widow). {Ref: ARMD 7:93, 7:612, 13:244, 13:253, 13:351, 15:124, 15:363, 17:381, 20:153; BDML II:840-841; MDWB 7:324}

TRIPPE, HENRY (Dorchester County), soldier and probable officer in the 1730's; captain by 1737; sheriff, 1731-1734; member of the Lower House of the Maryland Assembly, 1734-1740; major by 1744; died in December, 1744. {Ref: BDML II:841-842; MDGZ, Jan 17, 1745}

TRIPPE, HENRY (Dorchester County), captain by 1712; member of the Lower House of the Maryland Assembly, 1712-1715; died testate by Jan 17, 1723/4 (date of probate; Susannah Trippe, widow). {Ref: ARMD 29:353, 30:107; BDML II:841; DOLR 12 Old 215; SOJR III:66; MDWB 18:214; MINV 9:341, 10:331}

TRIPPE, SUSANNAH, see "Henry Trippe," q.v.

TROOPE (TROOP), ROBERT (Scotland and Charles County), lieutenant by 1660; captain by 1662; born circa 1635 (aged about 28 when deposed in 1663), died testate by Aug 1, 1666 (date of probate). {Ref: SCOT:157; ARMD 3:411, 53:119, 53:415; CHLR A:121, A:248, B:379, C:247; MDEP:187; MDWB 1:260}

TROTH, WILLIAM (Talbot County), Protestant and probable soldier in the Revolution of 1689; signed an address and took a loyalty oath supporting the King of England and the reestablishment of Lord Baltimore into power on Nov 28, 1689. {Ref: ARMD 8:144}

TROUGH, WILLIAM (Talbot County), soldier (rank not stated) circa 1675; paid for his services in the late expedition against the Nanticoke Indians in 1678. {Ref: ARMD 7:89}

TROW, JOSEPH, see "Joseph Prow," q.v.

TRUMAN (TRUEMAN), HENRY (Calvert County), Protestant and probable soldier in the Revolution of 1689; signed an address and took a loyalty oath supporting the King of England and the reestablishment of Lord Baltimore into power on Nov 28, 1689. {Ref: ARMD 8:145}

TRUMAN (TRUEMAN), THOMAS (England, and Calvert and St. Mary's Counties), participant and probable soldier in the Battle of the Severn on Mar 25, 1655 who was imprisoned for his role in Gov. William Stone's Rebellion against the Puritan government; lost all of his property, but after being released in 1656 he was rewarded with over 1,000 acres for his faithfulness to Lord Baltimore; lieutenant by 1658; captain by 1660; burgess (member of the General Assembly), 1661-1662; member of the Upper House at various times between 1666 and 1684; major by Sep 14, 1675 at which time he was appointed commander over Maryland forces to be raised in an expedition against the Susquehannock Indians and in cooperation with Virginia troops under Col. John Washington; Truman defeated the Indians and blockaded them in a fort which they had constructed near the Potomac River; infuriated by the many murders of white settlers he slaughtered all the Indians captives which he had taken; his act was contrary to Lord Baltimore's policy toward the Indians and he was charged with insubordination and treason; on May 27, 1676, after a trial by the Maryland Assembly, Major Truman was deemed "guilty of the First Article of the Impeachment for Commanding five of the Susquehannoughs that came out to treat With him to be put To death contrary to the Law of Nations and the Second Article of his Instructions by Which he was ordered to entertaine any Treaty with the Susquehannoughs;" on Jun 2, 1676 it was ruled that "Major Truman for his crime does not deserve death ... the very Indians that were there killed being proved to be murderers ... the said crime was not maliciously perpetrated or out of any designe to Prejudice the province, But meerely out of ignorance and to prevent a mutiny of the Whole Army as well Virginians as Marylanders;" he relinquished his military office and was dismissed from the Council as a compromise; he was released from his bond for good behavior in 1678; Major Truman served as a provincial court justice and on the Maryland Council again in 1683-1685; born circa 1628 (aged about 29 when deposed in 1657), died testate on Dec 6, 1685 (will probated on Dec 10, 1685; Mary Truman, widow), and buried at "Trent Hall" on the Patuxent River in St. Mary's County. {Ref: ARMD 1:426, 2:494, 2:501, 7:459, 15:49, 15:59, 17:168, 41:19, 41:277; FAAH:27; BDML II:842; HCCM:26-27, 326-327; INAC 9:160; MDWB 4:165}

TRUPSHAN, JOHN (Somerset County), Protestant and probable soldier in the Revolution of 1689; signed an address and took a loyalty oath supporting the King of England and "for enabling us to defend ourselves against all invaders" on Nov 28, 1689. {Ref: ARMD 8:141}

TRYDER, JOHN (Dorchester County), captain by 1715. See "John Ryder," q.v. {Ref: SOJR III:66}

TUBB, PETER (Charles County), soldier (rank not stated) circa 1675; paid for his services in the late expedition against the Nanticoke Indians in 1678. {Ref: ARMD 7:101}

TUBMAN, RICHARD (Dorchester County), soldier (rank not stated) circa 1675; paid for his services in the late expedition against the Nanticoke Indians in 1678. {Ref: ARMD 7:92}

TUCKER, ---- (Charles County), captain by 1714. {Ref: INAC 36B:30}

TUCKER, ---- (St. Mary's County), captain by 1718. {Ref: MDAD 1:325}

TUCKER, JOHN (Oxford District), captain and master of the ship *Experience* in 1731. {Ref: CVPR:12}

TUCKER, NATHANIELL (Talbot County), soldier (rank not stated) circa 1675; paid for his services in the late expedition against the Nanticoke Indians in 1678. {Ref: ARMD 7:90}

TUCKER, RICHARD (Dorchester County), soldier (rank not stated) circa 1675; paid for his services in the late expedition against the Nanticoke Indians in 1678. {Ref: ARMD 7:93}

TUCKER, STEPHEN (Anne Arundel County), captain and commander of a ship riding in South River and referred to as the *Young Princes Carolina* on Mar 21, 1720/1, the *Young Princess Caroline* on Mar 27, 1722, and the *Young Princes of Carolina* on Apr 17, 1723. {Ref: AALR CW#1:339, CW#1:483, RCW#2:136}

TUCKER, THOMAS (Kent County), "seaman within the said county" and a "sailor belonging to the *Factor* of Bediford" in 1697. {Ref: ARMD 25:599}

TUE, ---- (county not indicated), colonel before 1676. {Ref: INAC 2:179}

TULL, ANN, see "Thomas Tull," q.v.

TULL, ELIZABETH, see "Richard Tull," q.v.

TULL, RICHARD (Virginia and Annamessex, Somerset County), soldier (rank not stated) circa 1675; paid for his services in the late expedition against the Nanticoke Indians in 1678; Protestant and probable soldier in the Revolution of 1689; signed an address and took a loyalty oath supporting the King of England and "for enabling us to defend ourselves against all invaders" on Nov 28, 1689; one Richard Tull died testate by Aug 2, 1710 (date of probate; Elizabeth Tull, widow) and another Richard Tull died testate by Jun 5, 1711 (date of probate). Additional research will be necessary before drawing conclusions. {Ref: ARMD 7:100, 8:141; OSES:279, 460; MDWB 13:134, 258}

TULL, THOMAS (Virginia and Annamessex, Somerset County), soldier (rank not stated) circa 1675; paid for his services in the late expedition against the Nanticoke Indians in 1678; Protestant and probable soldier in the Revolution of 1689; signed an address and took a loyalty oath supporting the King of England and "for enabling us to defend ourselves against all invaders" on Nov 28, 1689; "Thomas Tull, Sr." died testate by Jun 28, 1720 (date of probate; Ann Tull, widow). {Ref: ARMD 7:99, 8:141; OSES:279, 460}

TULLY, ---- (Anne Arundel or Calvert County), captain by 1674. {Ref: INAC 1:158; ARMD 67:245}

TULLY (TULLEY), JOHN, SR. (England and Talbot County), captain by 1663; land owner in Chester River on Coursey's Creek in 1663. {Ref: ARMD 49:110, 49:335}

TUNNELL, THOMAS (St. Mary's County), lieutenant, 1655; born circa 1629-1630 (aged about 27 when deposed in January, 1656/7). {Ref: ARMD 3:326, 10:414, 10:496}

TUNSTALL, JOHN (Manokin Hundred, Somerset County), mariner before 1706; captain of the ship *Expedition* in 1706; master of the brigantine *Aspinwell* on 1709 (also listed as "Capt. John Tunstall, Jr." and "John Tunstoll" in 1709); master and owner of the schooner *Providence* (built in Somerset County) in 1733. {Ref: SOJR I:159, 203, II:10, 46, 132, III:10; MDCB 82:37; CESM:9}

TURBERVILE, GILBERT (St. Mary's County), possible probable soldier (rank not stated) before 1682; paid for his services out of an assessment levied by the

General Assembly for the public good in 1682; born circa 1647-1648 (aged about 45 or 46 when deposed in 1693), died testate by Jun 15, 1719 (date of probate; name listed once as "Mr. Gilbert Turbifield"). {Ref: ARMD 7:441, 8:512; MDWB 15:122; MDAD 3:225}

TURBUTT, MICHAEL (Talbot County), Protestant and probable soldier in the Revolution of 1689; signed an address and took a loyalty oath supporting the King of England and the reestablishment of Lord Baltimore into power on Nov 18 and Nov 28, 1689. {Ref: ARMD 8:134, 8:144}

TURBUTT, WILLIAM (Kent, Talbot, and Queen Anne's Counties), major of Queen Anne's County militia by 1728; member of the Lower House of the Maryland Assembly, 1716-1722, 1728-1731; provincial court justice, 1732; born on Feb 18, 1683/4 (aged about 45 when deposed in 1729), died testate by Nov 8, 1739 (date of probate). {Ref: BDML II:843-844; INKC:178; MDEP:188; MDWB 22:111}

TURKE, WILLIAM (Talbot County), soldier (rank not stated) circa 1675; paid for his services in the late expedition against the Nanticoke Indians in 1678. {Ref: ARMD 7:92}

TURLING, JOHN (St. Mary's and/or Charles County), Protestant and probable soldier in the Revolution of 1689; signed an address and took a loyalty oath supporting the King of England and the reestablishment of Lord Baltimore into power on Nov 28, 1689; soldier (rank not stated) who was issued a "gun or fowling piece" by Colonel Warren on Sep 15, 1694. {Ref: ARMD 8:146, 20:206, 20:208}

TURLOE (TURLO), WILLIAM (Queen Anne's County), major by 1709; court justice by 1714; died testate by Apr 8, 1719 (date of probate). {Ref: ARMD 27:384; QALR IK#A:1; MDWB 15:59}

TURNER, ANNE, see "Nicholas Turner," q.v.

TURNER, EDWARD (Charles County), Protestant and probable soldier in the Revolution of 1689; signed an address and took a loyalty oath supporting the King of England and the reestablishment of Lord Baltimore into power on Nov 28, 1689. {Ref: ARMD 8:138}

TURNER, GEORGE (Charles County), soldier (rank not stated) circa 1675; paid for his services in the late expedition against the Nanticoke Indians in 1678. {Ref: ARMD 7:101}

TURNER, HENRY (Dorchester County), soldier (rank not stated) circa 1675; paid for his services in the late expedition against the Nanticoke Indians in 1678. {Ref: ARMD 7:94}

TURNER, JAMES (Cecil County), mariner by 1734; captain and master of the sloop *Squirrel* in 1735 (built at North East River in 1734). {Ref: MDCB 82:32}

TURNER, JAMES (Charles County), Protestant and probable soldier in the Revolution of 1689; signed an address and took a loyalty oath supporting the King of England and the reestablishment of Lord Baltimore into power on Nov 28, 1689. {Ref: ARMD 8:138}

TURNER, JOHANNA, see "John Turner," q.v.

TURNER, JOHN (Cecil County), soldier (rank not stated) circa 1675; paid for his services in the late expedition against the Nanticoke Indians in 1678. {Ref: ARMD 7:95}

TURNER, JOHN (Calvert County), Protestant and probable soldier in the Revolution of 1689; signed an address and took a loyalty oath supporting the King of England and "to reestablish Lord Baltimore in his ancient power and government" on Nov 16, 1689 (name listed once as "John Terner"); died testate by Jul 28, 1716 (date of probate; Johanna Turner, widow). {Ref: ARMD 8:132; HCCM:328, 477; MDWB 14:205}

TURNER, NICHOLAS (Talbot County), soldier (rank not stated) circa 1675; paid for his services in the late expedition against the Nanticoke Indians in 1678; died testate by Apr 24, 1680 (date of probate; Anne Turner, widow and sole legatee). {Ref: ARMD 7:89; MDWB 2:88}

TURNER, NICHOLAS (St. Mary's County), soldier (rank not stated) circa 1675; paid for his services in the late expedition against the Nanticoke Indians in 1678. {Ref: ARMD 7:103}

TURNER, THOMAS (Anne Arundel County), Quaker who was assigned to a foot company of Capt. John Norwood in 1662, but refused to serve for religious reasons and was fined accordingly. {Ref: AAGE:558}

TURNER, WILLIAM (Calvert County), Protestant and probable soldier in the Revolution of 1689; signed an address and took a loyalty oath supporting the King of England and "to reestablish Lord Baltimore in his ancient power and government" on Nov 16, 1689. {Ref: ARMD 8:131; HCCM:477}

TWITT, JOHN (county or port not indicated), captain and master of the ship *Charles* of Plymouth in 1690. {Ref: ARMD 8:237}

TYER (TYRE), JAMES (Charles County), soldier (rank not stated) circa 1675; paid for his services in the late expedition against the Nanticoke Indians in 1678; court justice, 1680; paid for his services out of an assessment levied by the General Assembly for the public good in 1682; died testate by May 20, 1712 (date of probate; Margarett Tyer, widow). {Ref: ARMD 7:101, 7:441, 15:327; MDWB 13:400}

TYLER, JOANE, see "George Read (Reade)," q.v.

TYLER, JOHN (Baltimore County), probable soldier (rank not stated) before 1682; paid for his services out of an assessment levied by the General Assembly for the public good in 1682. {Ref: ARMD 7:441}

TYLER, JOHN (Somerset County), soldier (rank not stated) circa 1675; paid for his services in the late expedition against the Nanticoke Indians in 1678. {Ref: ARMD 7:97}

TYT, ---- (county not indicated), captain by 1688. {Ref: INAC 10:117}

UMBRESS, DENNIS (Cecil County), soldier (rank not stated) circa 1675; paid for his services in the late expedition against the Nanticoke Indians in 1678. {Ref: ARMD 7:95}

UNDERHILL, JOHN (St. Mary's County), soldier (rank not stated) by 1657; wounded (lame) and paid for his services in September, 1657. {Ref: ARMD 1:364}

UNGLE, ROBERT (Talbot County), naval officer at Oxford, 1719-1726; sheriff, 1704-1707, 1716-1718; member of the Lower House of the Maryland Assembly, 1708-1726; born Jan 23, 1670/1, died by Nov 17, 1726 (date of inventory; Frances Ungle, widow). {Ref: ARMD 33:180, 33:365; BDML II:846-847; MINV 11:792}

UPPINGTON, WALTER (county or port not indicated), captain and master of the ship *Maryland Merchant* of Bristoll in 1691. {Ref: ARMD 8:240}

UPTON, WILLIAM (St. Mary's County), captain and mariner, 1637. {Ref: ARMD 4:15}

URIEL (URIELL), GEORGE (England and Anne Arundel County), captain and master of the ship *William* of London in 1729-1734; died intestate by Dec 19, 1738 (date of inventory; his name was misinterpreted once as "Capt. George Wriel" and once as "Capt. George Unill"). {Ref: MDGZ, Apr 29, 1729 and Aug 2, 1734; CVPR:12; MINV 24:69, 25:393}

URSWOOD, ANDREW (Kent County), soldier (rank not stated) circa 1675; paid for his services in the late expedition against the Nanticoke Indians in 1678. {Ref: ARMD 7:94}

URUARD, JOHN (county or port not indicated), captain and master of the ship *Hopewell* of Exon in 1691. {Ref: ARMD 8:239}

UTIE (UTYE), NATHANIEL (England, Virginia, and Baltimore and Cecil Counties), colonel by 1652; commissioned Jul 20, 1658 as "commander in chief of all the forces to be raised between the Coves of Patuxent River and the seaven mountains" and also upon the Isle of Kent; member of the Upper House, 1658, and councellor, 1659; provincial court justice, 1658-1660, 1674-1675; burgess (member of the General Assembly), 1666, 1669; died intestate by Feb 25, 1675/6 (date of inventory; name listed once as "Col. Nathaniell Uty"). *Note:* In April, 1677 Utie's former servant Edward Inglish became a servant to Henry Johnson who had married Utie's widow (as noted in a petition by Inglish to the Maryland Council in 1682 in which he requested his freedom from Johnson since he had served for 5 years as agreed in 1677). It is interesting that on a list of debts and payments in 1688 for the estate of William Stevens, deceased, of Somerset County, the name of "Col. Nathaniell Utie, alias Nathaniell Johnson" appears. See "Francis Wright," q.v. {Ref: ARMD 1:382, 2:75, 3:349-351, 17:96, 41:157, 49:48; FAAH:29; BDML II:848; INCC:134; INAC 1:580, 10:68, 12:143; BBCF:655-656}

VALLIANT, JOHN, see "John Cooke," q.v.

VANBURKELOO, ABELL (Cecil County), captain by 1719. {Ref: CELR 3:247}

VANDER, JOHN (St. Mary's County), soldier (rank not stated) circa 1675; paid for his services in the late expedition against the Nanticoke Indians in 1678. {Ref: ARMD 7:102}

VANDERHEYDEN (VANDERHADEN), MATTHIAS (New Amsterdam, Delaware, and Cecil County), military officer (rank not stated) who swore allegiance to the King & Queen of England in 1696 (name listed once as "M:

361

V: Hayden"); naval officer of Cecil County, 1701-1711; member of the Lower House of the Maryland Assembly, 1708-1713; court justice, 1715; died testate by Jun 10, 1729 (date of probate; Anna Margaretta Vanderheyden, widow). {Ref: ARMD 20:111, 20:545, 23:21, 27:202, 29:205; BDML II:848-849; MDWB 19:776}

VANDERNORT, GEORGE (Talbot County), soldier (rank not stated) circa 1675; paid for his services in the late expedition against the Nanticoke Indians in 1678. {Ref: ARMD 7:88}

VANPELT, JOHN, JR. (Annapolis District), captain and master of the sloop *Mary* of New York in 1728. {Ref: MDGZ, Mar 11, 1728/9}

VANSAELSMANS, JOHN (Cecil County), Indian interpreter by 1697; name also listed as "John Vrans Saelsmans" and "Jno. Noerstallman." {Ref: ARMD 23:428, 23:431}

VANSWERINGEN, GARRETT (St. Mary's City), soldier (rank not stated) circa 1675; paid for his services in the late expedition against the Nanticoke Indians in 1678; alderman by 1684; paid for his services again in 1695; born circa 1636 (aged about 48 when deposed in 1684 and aged about 57 when deposed in 1693; name listed as "Garret Vansweeringen"), died testate by Feb 4, 1698/9 (date of probate; Mary Vansweringen, widow; petition filed by executors Joseph and Mary Vansweringen on May 3, 1700). {Ref: ARMD 5:417, 7:103, 8:511, 17:300, 24:18, 38:7; MDEP:190; MDWB 6:209}

VAUGHAN, ROBERT (England, and St. Mary's and Kent Counties), sergeant in joint charge of a pinnace captured by the forces of William Claiborne who held him prisoner on Kent Island in 1635; sergeant and high constable of St. George's Hundred, 1637; played an important part in the capture of Kent Island for the proprietor in 1638; lieutenant, 1640; member of the Maryland Assembly at various times between 1637 and 1647; captain and commander of the Isle of Kent, 1645-1660; swore allegiance to the Commonwealth of England on Apr 5, 1652; Kent County court justice, 1642-1668; born circa 1597 (aged about 62 when deposed on Apr 27, 1659), died intestate by January, 1668/9. See "John Thomson," q.v. {Ref: ARMD 1:2, 1:214, 1:359, 3:95, 4:502, 4:517, 5:172, 10:75, 41:113, 41:395, 54:2, 54:142; BDML II:849-850; INKC:101, 125, 178; FMDP:266-269; MDEP:190}

VAUGHAN, ROWLAND (Dorchester County), soldier (rank not stated) circa 1675; paid for his services in the late expedition against the Nanticoke Indians in 1678. {Ref: ARMD 7:93}

VAUGHAN, THOMAS (Talbot County), cornet before 1678; paid for his services in the late expedition against the Nanticoke Indians in 1678. {Ref: ARMD 7:88, 7:90}

VAUGHAN, WILLIAM (Somerset County), soldier (rank not stated) circa 1675; paid for his services in the late expedition against the Nanticoke Indians in 1678. {Ref: ARMD 7:98}

VAUGHAN, WILLIAM (Kent County), soldier (rank not stated) circa 1675; paid for his services in the late expedition against the Nanticoke Indians in 1678; died testate by Oct 20, 1684 (date of probate). {Ref: ARMD 7:94; MDWB 4:64}

VAUGHDREY (VOYDERY), JOHN (Charles County), soldier by 1665; "prest in the last indian Martch up the bay" and paid for his services on Dec 7, 1665; Indian interpreter by 1700. {Ref: ARMD 24:118, 53:618-619}

VAUX, DAVID (Talbot County), soldier (rank not stated) circa 1675; paid for his services in the late expedition against the Nanticoke Indians in 1678. {Ref: ARMD 7:88}

VEAZEY, JOHN (Cecil County), captain by 1734-1736; naval officer of Cecil County, 1743-1754; major, 1748; colonel, 1756; commander of county militia, 1758; member of the Lower House of the Maryland Assembly, 1761, 1768-1774; born Feb 12, 1701, died May 4, 1777. {Ref: BDML II:850}

VEITCH, ANN, see "Nathaniel Veitch," q.v.

VEITCH, JAMES (Calvert County), Puritan and lieutenant in the militia under Capt. Peter Johnson circa 1652-1655; sheriff, 1655; died by Sep 6, 1686 (date of administration account; Mary Veitch and John Veitch, administrators). {Ref: HCCM:35, 328; INAC 9:74}

VEITCH (VEATCH), JAMES (Calvert County), Protestant and probable soldier in the Revolution of 1689; signed an address and took a loyalty oath supporting the King of England and "to reestablish Lord Baltimore in his ancient power and government" on Nov 16, 1689. {Ref: ARMD 8:131}

VEITCH (VETCH), JOHN (Calvert County), Protestant and probable soldier in the Revolution of 1689; signed an address and took a loyalty oath supporting the King of England and "to reestablish Lord Baltimore in his ancient power and government" on Nov 16, 1689; "John Vetch" died intestate by Sep 25, 1696 (date of administration account; Nathan Vetch, administrator and brother). See "James Veitch," q.v. {Ref: ARMD 8:131; INAC 14:51}

VEITCH, MARY, see "James Veitch," q.v.

VEITCH, NATHANIEL (Calvert County), Protestant and probable soldier in the Revolution of 1689; signed an address and took a loyalty oath supporting the King of England and "to reestablish Lord Baltimore in his ancient power and government" on Nov 16, 1689; one "Nathan Veitch" died intestate in Prince George's County by Nov 3, 1705 (date of administration account; Ann Veitch, widow). See "John Veitch," q.v. {Ref: ARMD 8:131; INAC 25:114}

VEITCH, THOMAS (Dorchester County), soldier (rank not stated) circa 1675; paid for his services in the late expedition against the Nanticoke Indians in 1678. {Ref: ARMD 7:93}

VENABLE (VENABLES), JOSEPH (Somerset County), military officer (rank not stated), 1696, who swore allegiance to the King & Queen of England (name listed as "Joseph Venalles" in 1696, "Joseph Venables" in 1699 and 1717, and "Joseph Venable" in 1733); justice of the peace, 1707; died by Sep 24, 1733 (date of inventory). {Ref: ARMD 20:544; OSES:178; MGSB 36:4, p. 646; SOJR I:17; MINV 17:706}

VENNER, JOHN (Talbot County), soldier (rank not stated) circa 1675; paid for his services in the late expedition against the Nanticoke Indians in 1678. {Ref: ARMD 7:92}

VESEY, NATHANIEL (Somerset County), Protestant and probable soldier in the Revolution of 1689; signed an address and took a loyalty oath supporting the King of England and "for enabling us to defend ourselves against all invaders" on Nov 28, 1689. {Ref: ARMD 8:140}

VICARIS, JOHN (Kent County), captain of all the forces in Kent County, commissioned Jun 5, 1668; county court justice, 1668-1669; died intestate on Oct 24, 1669. {Ref: ARMD 5:30, 54:188, 54:248, 54:271, 54:282; INKC:124}

VICKERS, JOHN (Anne Arundel and Prince George's Counties), captain and commander of the ship *Robert* riding in Severn River on Jan 21, 1724/5 and the ship *John and Robert* riding in the Patuxent River on Jan 24, 1724/5; captain and master of the ship *Susannah and Elizabeth* riding in the Patuxent River on Feb 2, 1725/6. {Ref: AALR SY#1:68; PGLR M:149}

VIGOROUS, JOHN (Somerset County), soldier (rank not stated) circa 1675; paid for his services in the late expedition against the Nanticoke Indians in 1678. {Ref: ARMD 7:99}

VILLENEUFFE, GEORGE (Potomac District), captain and master of the ship *Phoenix* in 1730-1731. {Ref: CVPR:12}

VINCENT, JOHN (England and Annapolis District), captain by 1714; master of the ship *Mary* of London in 1729. {Ref: INAC 36B:24; MDGZ, Jul 22, 1729}

VINCENT, WILLIAM (Talbot County), soldier (rank not stated) circa 1675; paid for his services in the late expedition against the Nanticoke Indians in 1678. {Ref: ARMD 7:92}

VINCING, ---- (St. Mary's County), captain by 1719. {Ref: MDAD 1:426}

VINSON, GEORGE (Talbot County), corporal who swore allegiance to the King & Queen of England in 1696. {Ref: ARMD 20:542}

VOYDERY, JOHN, see "John Vaughdrey," q.v.

WADE, ELIZABETH, see "Robert Wade," q.v.

WADE, RICHARD (Charles County), Protestant and probable soldier in the Revolution of 1689; signed an address and took a loyalty oath supporting the King of England and the reestablishment of Lord Baltimore into power on Nov 28, 1689. {Ref: ARMD 8:138}

WADE, ROBERT (Charles and Prince George's Counties), captain of horse troops in Piscattoway Parish, 1695/1696; died testate by Feb 2, 1713/4 (date of probate; Elizabeth Wade, widow). {Ref: ARMD 20:379; INAC 35A:212; MDWB 13:612; PFMD:99}

WADE, ZACHARY (England, and St. Mary's and Charles Counties), soldier (rank not stated) by 1666; signed a petition to the governor to "displace Capt. William Boreman whom was lately constituted captain of the militia" on Sep 12, 1666; member of the Lower House of the Maryland Assembly, representing St. Mary's County in 1658 and Charles County in 1659-1662; sheriff, 1664-1665;

born circa 1627 (aged about 34 when deposed in 1661), died testate by May 25, 1677 (date of probate). {Ref: ARMD 3:556, 3:560; BDML II:851; MDEP:191; MDWB 9:16; PFMD:99}

WADSWORTH, WILLIAM (Calvert County), Protestant and probable soldier in the Revolution of 1689; signed an address and took a loyalty oath supporting the King of England and "to reestablish Lord Baltimore in his ancient power and government" on Nov 16, 1689. {Ref: ARMD 8:132; HCCM:329}

WAGER, CHARLES (Potomac District), captain and commodore of the Virginia and Maryland fleet in 1696. {Ref: ARMD 23:4-5}

WAIL, SAMUEL (county not indicated), private in the Maryland troops "raised to strengthen Albany, New York and resist the French and Indian enemies" in 1690. {Ref: SHMD I:355}

WAITE, JONATHAN (Dorchester County), soldier (rank not stated) circa 1675; paid for his services in the late expedition against the Nanticoke Indians in 1678. {Ref: ARMD 7:92}

WAKEFIELD, THOMAS (Charles County), soldier (rank not stated) circa 1675; paid for his services in the late expedition against the Nanticoke Indians in 1678; Protestant and probable soldier in the Revolution of 1689; signed an address and took a loyalty oath supporting the King of England and the reestablishment of Lord Baltimore into power on Nov 28, 1689; died testate by Feb 19, 1699/1700 (date of probate; Ann Wakefield, widow). {Ref: ARMD 7:101, 8:138; MDWB 6:335}

WAKEMAN, EBENNAZAR (county not indicated), ensign in the Maryland troops "raised to strengthen Albany, New York and resist the French and Indian enemies" in 1690. {Ref: SHMD I:355}

WALDIE, JAMES (Anne Arundel County), captain by 1699. {Ref: INAC 19½B:75}

WALKER, JANE, see "Thomas Walker," q.v.

WALKER, JOHN (Somerset County), soldier (rank not stated) circa 1675; paid for his services in the late expedition against the Nanticoke Indians in 1678. {Ref: ARMD 7:97}

WALKER, KATHARINE, see "William Walker," q.v.

WALKER, RICHARD (Potomac District), captain and master of the ship *Fradsham* in 1730-1731. {Ref: CVPR:12}

WALKER, ROBERT (Annapolis District), captain and master of the ship *Henry and Mary* in 1731. {Ref: CVPR:12}

WALKER, THOMAS (Wicomico Hundred, Somerset County), captain by 1677; high sheriff, 1677-1678; paid for his services in the late expedition against the Nanticoke Indians in 1678; justice of the peace, 1679; died testate by Mar 10, 1680/1 (date of probate; Jane Walker, widow). {Ref: ARMD 7:100, 15:162, 15:232, 15:275, 51:301; OSES:288; MDWB 2:128; INAC 6:354, 7B:98, 9:279}

WALKER, THOMAS (Somerset County), captain before 1680; assignor of lands in Somerset County in August, 1680; son of Capt. Thomas Walker, deceased, q.v. {Ref: Peter W. Coldham's *Settlers of Maryland, 1679-1700*, p. 178}

WALKER, THOMAS (county or port not indicated), captain and master of the ship *Thomas and Mary* of Bristol in 1689. {Ref: ARMD 8:236}

WALKER, THOMAS (Kent County), sailor by 1723. {Ref: MDAD 5:148}

WALKER, WILLIAM (Kent County), "seaman within the said county" and a "sailor belonging to the *Loves Increase* of Whitehaven" in 1697. {Ref: ARMD 25:600}

WALKER, WILLIAM (Dorchester County), soldier (rank not stated) circa 1675; paid for his services in the late expedition against the Nanticoke Indians in 1678; paid for his services out of an assessment levied by the General Assembly for the public good in 1682; died testate by Apr 30, 1711 (date of probate; Katharine Walker, widow). {Ref: ARMD 7:93, 7:442; MDWB 13:267}

WALKINSTON, EDWARD (Somerset County), captain by 1685. {Ref: INAC 8:417}

WALKS, JOHN (county or port not indicated), captain and master of the ship *Thomas and Mary* of Bristol in 1690. {Ref: ARMD 8:238}

WALLACE, JAMES (Prince George's County), captain, appointed Nov 10, 1709 to command the troops in Piscattaway Hundred; Maryland Council reported "That Commission issued to P. Georges County appointing Mr. John Bradford a Justice in the place of Mr. James Wallace gone for England" on Oct 26, 1710 (name misspelled once as "James Vallace"). {Ref: ARMD 27:403, 27:495}

WALLACE, JAMES (Annapolis District), captain and master of the schooner *Sarah and Rebecca* in 1734 (built at Elk River in 1733). {Ref: MDGZ, Sep 27, 1734; MDCB 82:47}

WALLER, THOMAS (Somerset County), Protestant and probable soldier in the Revolution of 1689; signed an address and took a loyalty oath supporting the King of England and "for enabling us to defend ourselves against all invaders" on Nov 28, 1689. {Ref: ARMD 8:139}

WALLER, WILLIAM (Somerset County), Protestant and probable soldier in the Revolution of 1689; signed an address and took a loyalty oath supporting the King of England and "for enabling us to defend ourselves against all invaders" on Nov 28, 1689. {Ref: ARMD 8:140}

WALLICE, JOHN (Dorchester County), soldier (rank not stated) circa 1675; paid for his services in the late expedition against the Nanticoke Indians in 1678. {Ref: ARMD 7:92}

WALLICE, THOMAS (Talbot County), soldier (rank not stated) circa 1675; paid for his services in the late expedition against the Nanticoke Indians in 1678. {Ref: ARMD 7:88}

WALLICE, WILLIAM (Baltimore County), lieutenant before 1678; paid for his services in the late expedition against the Nanticoke Indians in 1678. {Ref: ARMD 7:95}

WALLIS, ADAM (county or port not indicated), captain and master of the schooner *Sarah* in 1733 (formerly the *Ann of Virginia*, built in Salisbury, Massachusetts in 1728). {Ref: MDCB 82:9}

WALLSTON (WALSTON), JOHN (Baltimore County), soldier (rank not stated) circa 1675; paid for his services in the late expedition against the Nanticoke Indians in 1678; Protestant and probable soldier in the Revolution of 1689; signed an address and took a loyalty oath supporting the King of England and the reestablishment of Lord Baltimore into power on Nov 28, 1689; died by Apr 17, 1693 (date of probate; Margaret Wallston, widow, later married William Osborne). {Ref: ARMD 7:95, 8:136; BBCF:661-662; MDWB 6:49}

WALNER, JOHN (Talbot County), soldier (rank not stated) circa 1675; paid for his services in the late expedition against the Nanticoke Indians in 1678. {Ref: ARMD 7:92}

WALSTONE, SAMUELL (Somerset County), soldier (rank not stated) circa 1675; paid for his services in the late expedition against the Nanticoke Indians in 1678. {Ref: ARMD 7:97}

WALSTONE, THOMAS (Somerset County), soldier (rank not stated) circa 1675; paid for his services in the late expedition against the Nanticoke Indians in 1678. {Ref: ARMD 7:100}

WALSTONE, WILLIAM (Somerset County), soldier (rank not stated) circa 1675; paid for his services in the late expedition against the Nanticoke Indians in 1678. {Ref: ARMD 7:100}

WALTERS, WILLIAM (Charles County), major by 1662. {Ref: ARMD 3:455}

WALTON, JOHN (Somerset County), soldier (rank not stated) circa 1675; paid for his services in the late expedition against the Nanticoke Indians in 1678; one John Walton died testate by Feb 5, 1716/7 (date of probate) and he had a son named John. Additional research will be necessary before drawing conclusions. {Ref: ARMD 7:97; MDWB 14:371}

WALTON, JOHN (Baltimore County), cornet before 1678; paid for his services in the late expedition against the Nanticoke Indians in 1678. {Ref: ARMD 7:95}

WALTON, REBECCA, see "William Walton," q.v.

WALTON (WALLTON), WILLIAM (Somerset County), soldier (rank not stated) circa 1675; paid for his services in the late expedition against the Nanticoke Indians in 1678; died testate by Aug 25, 1686 (date of probate; Rebecca Walton, widow). {Ref: ARMD 7:99; MDWB 4:224}

WAMLESS, JAMES (Calvert County), Protestant and probable soldier in the Revolution of 1689; signed an address and took a loyalty oath supporting the King of England and "to reestablish Lord Baltimore in his ancient power and government" on Nov 16, 1689. {Ref: ARMD 8:131}

WAPLE (WAPPLE), JAMES (Charles and/or Prince George's Counties), soldier and ranger under the command of Capt. Richard Brightwell, 1692-1697; born circa 1657 (aged about 40 when deposed on Oct 12, 1697 regarding the murder of John Baker, q.v., a fellow soldier). {Ref: ARMD 8:445, 23:75, 23:325}

WAPLES, PETER, see "Peter Whaples," q.v.

WARD, BENJAMIN (Potomac District), captain and master of the ship *Endeavour* in 1730-1731. {Ref: CVPR:12}

WARD, HENRY (Delaware and Cecil County), soldier (rank not stated) circa 1675; paid for his services in the late expedition against the Nanticoke Indians in 1678; member of the Lower House of the Maryland Assembly, 1674-1675; captain of a company of foot, commissioned Feb 28, 1681; died intestate by Feb 10, 1683/4 (inventory taken on Apr 29, 1684). {Ref: ARMD 7:95, 15:38, 15:69, 17:78; BDML II:858; TALR 5:280; INAC 8:163}

WARD, JOHN (England, and Somerset and Cecil Counties), soldier (rank not stated) circa 1675; paid for his services in the late expedition against the Nanticoke Indians in 1678; paid for his services out of an assessment levied by the General Assembly for the public good in 1682; major by 1712; member of the Lower House of the Maryland Assembly, 1708-1737; lieutenant colonel by 1715; colonel by 1719; born circa 1671 (aged about 50 when deposed in 1721), died testate by Mar 13, 1747/8 (date of probate; Mary Ward, widow). {Ref: ARMD 7:98, 7:440, 30:129, 30:389, 33:157, 34:278, 34:401, 34:742, 39:55, 39:151; BDML II:859; TALR 12:392; CELR 2:172; INCC:134; MDEP:193; MDWB 25:284; MINV 36:66}

WARD, JOHN (Anne Arundel and Calvert Counties), Puritan and soldier (rank not stated) in the militia circa 1668. {Ref: HCCM:329}

WARD, MARGARET, see "Matthew Tilghman Ward," q.v.

WARD, MARY, see "John Ward" and "William Ward," q.v.

WARD, MATTHEW (Kent County), military officer (rank not stated) who swore allegiance to the King & Queen of England in 1696. {Ref: ARMD 20:540}

WARD, MATTHEW TILGHMAN (Bay Hundred, Talbot County), lieutenant colonel by 1712; colonel by 1721; member of the Lower House of the Maryland Assembly, 1712-1718 (listed once as "Col. Tilghman Ward" in 1713 and as "Lt. Col. Tilghman Ward" and "Col. Matthew Tilghman Ward" in 1714); member of the Upper House (Maryland Council), 1719-1740; major general by 1739; born circa 1676, died testate by Jun 22, 1741 (date of probate; Margaret Ward, widow). {Ref: ARMD 25:339, 25:377, 25:504, 287:65, 29:212, 29:269, 29:391, 30:129, 30:360, 34:278, 39:11; BDML II:860; CESM:21; MDWB 22:363}

WARD, REBECCA, see "Robert Ward," q.v.

WARD, ROBERT (Anne Arundel County), soldier (rank not stated) circa 1675; paid for his services in the late expedition against the Nanticoke Indians in 1678; one Robert Ward died testate by Nov 3, 1709 (date of probate) and another Robert Ward died testate by May 19, 1720 (date of probate; Rebecca Ward, widow). Additional research will be necessary before drawing conclusions. {Ref: ARMD 7:97; MDWB 12:193, pt. 2; MDWB 16:59}

WARD, THOMAS (Kent County), soldier (rank not stated) on Isle of Kent who swore allegiance to the Commonwealth of England on Apr 5, 1652; born circa 1606 (aged about 49 when deposed on Oct 29, 1655). {Ref: INKC:101, 104}

WARD, WILLIAM (Charles County), soldier (rank not stated) circa 1675; paid for his services in the late expedition against the Nanticoke Indians in 1678; paid for his services out of an assessment levied by the General Assembly for the public good in 1682; died testate by May 21, 1685 (date of probate; Mary Ward, widow). {Ref: ARMD 7:101, 7:440; MDWB 4:155}

WARFIELD, ALEXANDER (Middle Neck Hundred, Anne Arundel County), constable, 1708-1709; probable militia officer in 1730's; captain by 1740; member of the Lower House of the Maryland Assembly, 1714-1718; born circa 1678 (aged about 44 when deposed in 1722, aged "near 52" when deposed in 1729, and aged about 53 when deposed in 1731), died testate by Jun 11, 1740 (date of probate; Sarah Warfield, widow). See "Charles Lucas," q.v. {Ref: BDML II:861-862; FAAH:86; MDEP:193; MDWB 22:272; MINV 25:430}

WARFIELD (WAUFILD), RICHARD (England and Anne Arundel County), military officer (rank not stated) who swore allegiance to the King & Queen of England in 1696; born circa 1640, died testate by Feb 11, 1703/4 (date of probate). {Ref: ARMD 20:541-542; FAAH:83-84; BDML II:862; RMHF II:293; MDWB 11:409}

WARFIELD, SARAH, see "Alexander Warfield," q.v.

WARING, BASIL (Calvert and Prince George's Counties), captain of dragoons, commissioned Jul 14, 1715; born 1683, died intestate by Jul 25, 1733 (date of inventory; Martha Waring, widow). {Ref: RMHF II:334-335; MINV 17:363}

WARING, MARTHA, see "Basil Waring," q.v.

WARING (WARRING, WARREN), SAMPSON (England, Virginia, and Calvert County), Puritan and captain circa 1651; participated in the Battle of the Severn on Mar 25, 1655 and served on a Council of War after the battle; commissioned "to be commander of all the Military forces & Soldiers being and residing on Herringe Creeke Including all the Plantations about Mr. Ayres his Creek and from them Downwards taking in Capt. Carter's and Mr. Richard Wells his plantations, & Extending down the Bay to the Land Seated by Mr. Manning and So downwards According to an Act of Assembly in that Case Provided" on Apr 24, 1655; paid for his services in September, 1657; member of the Lower House of the Maryland Assembly in 1660; captain, 1664-1670; born circa 1618 (aged about 39 when deposed in 1657 and aged about 43 when deposed in 1661), died testate by Mar 18, 1670/1 (date of probate; Sarah Waring, widow). {Ref: ARMD 1:365, 3:317, 10:413, 10:553, 41:11, 41:164, 41:520, 49:185, 49:444; FAAH:26; BDML II:864; RMHF II:334; HCCM:330; MDWB 1:233, 1:421}

WARNER, FRANCIS (Calvert County), ranger under the command of Capt. Richard Brightwell in 1692. {Ref: ARMD 8:445}

WARNER, GEORGE (Cecil County), Protestant and probable soldier in the Revolution of 1689; signed an address and took a loyalty oath supporting the King of England and the reestablishment of Lord Baltimore into power on Nov 18, 1689. {Ref: ARMD 8:135}

WARNER, JOHN (Somerset County), soldier (rank not stated) circa 1675; paid for his services in the late expedition against the Nanticoke Indians in 1678. {Ref: ARMD 7:98}

WARNER, SAMUEL (Calvert County), Protestant and probable soldier in the Revolution of 1689; signed an address and took a loyalty oath supporting the King of England and the reestablishment of Lord Baltimore into power on Nov 28, 1689. {Ref: ARMD 8:145}

WARRELOE, ---- (England and St. Mary's), mate on the ship *Dove* in 1633-1634. {Ref: FMDP:343}

WARREN, ELIZABETH, see "Thomas Warren," q.v.

WARREN, HENRY (Charles County), captain by 1697. {Ref: INAC 14:128}

WARREN, HUMPHREY, JR. (England and Charles County), captain by 1682; court justice, 1676-1691; lieutenant colonel by 1689; Protestant and soldier in the Revolution of 1689; signed an address and took a loyalty oath supporting the King of England and the reestablishment of Lord Baltimore into power on Nov 28, 1689; sheriff, 1691-1694; colonel of foot troops, 1694-1695; born circa 1655, died testate by Feb 25, 1694/5 (date of probate; Margery Warren, widow, later married Thomas Buford). See "John Turling," q.v. {Ref: ARMD 7:611, 8:138, 8:404, 15:327, 17:380, 20:109, 20:153, 20:206-207; BDML II:865; RMHF I:373, II:319; INAC 7C:131, 10:376; MDWB 7:65}

WARREN, JONATHAN (Anne Arundel County), military officer (rank not stated) who swore allegiance to the King & Queen of England in 1696. {Ref: ARMD 20:542}

WARREN, MARGERY, see "Humphrey Warren, Jr.," q.v.

WARREN, RICHARD (Somerset County), soldier (rank not stated) circa 1675; paid for his services in the late expedition against the Nanticoke Indians in 1678; Protestant and soldier in the Revolution of 1689; signed an address and took a loyalty oath supporting the King of England and "for enabling us to defend ourselves against all invaders" on Nov 28, 1689. {Ref: ARMD 7:97, 8:139}

WARREN, THOMAS (Kent County), lieutenant by 1678; paid for his services in the late expedition against the Nanticoke Indians in 1678; died testate by Mar 28, 1685 (date of probate; Elizabeth Warren, widow). {Ref: ARMD 7:94; MDWB 4:99}

WASHINGTON, JOHN, see "Thomas Truman," q.v.

WASHINGTON, LAWRENCE, see "Ninian Beale" and "Captain Bourne," q.v.

WASON, MARY, see "Francis Wasson," q.v.

WASSE, JAMES (Talbot County), soldier (rank not stated) circa 1675; paid for his services in the late expedition against the Nanticoke Indians in 1678. {Ref: ARMD 7:87}

WASSON (WASON), FRANCIS (England and Anne Arundel County), captain and commander of the ship *West River Merchant* riding at anchor in West River on Jun 19, 1708; mariner, late of Tottenham, County of Middlesex, died testate by Sep 23, 1723 (appointment of attorney by Mary Wason, widow). {Ref: AALR WT#2:636, RCW#2:237}

WATERHOUSE, ARTHUR (Pocomoke District), captain and master of the ship *John and Elizabeth* in 1731. {Ref: CVPR:12}

WATERHOUSE, SAMUELL (Pocomoke District), captain and master of the ship *Seaflower* in 1730-1731. {Ref: CVPR:12}

WATERLING, WALTER (St. Mary's County), seaman by 1654. {Ref: ARMD 10:395}

WATERLY, JOHN (Dorchester County), soldier (rank not stated) circa 1675; paid for his services in the late expedition against the Nanticoke Indians in 1678. {Ref: ARMD 7:93}

WATERS, ALLEXANDER (Kent County), soldier (rank not stated) in Capt. William Leeds (Leeads) Company by May 23, 1662, at which time he signed a petition about the misuse of company money by Capt. Thomas Brednox (Bradnox), late of Isle of Kent, deceased. {Ref: ARMD 3:455}

WATERS, CHRISTOPHER (Anne Arundel County), military officer (rank not stated) who swore allegiance to the King & Queen of England in 1696. {Ref: ARMD 20:542}

WATERS, GEORGE (St. Mary's County), colonel by 1663. {Ref: ARMD 49:15}

WATERS, JOHN (Anne Arundel County), soldier (rank not stated) circa 1675; paid for his services in the late expedition against the Nanticoke Indians in 1678. {Ref: ARMD 7:96}

WATERS, WILLIAM (Virginia and Somerset County), colonel before 1678; paid for his services in the late expedition against the Nanticoke Indians in 1678; burgess and justice in Northampton County, Virginia in the 1650's (a revision of colonial boundaries apparently put some of his Virginia land in Maryland); died circa 1685. {Ref: ARMD 7:100; BDML II:865}

WATERSON, ROBERT (St. Mary's County), soldier (rank not stated) before 1668; paid for his services in the last expedition against the Indians in 1668. {Ref: ARMD 5:35}

WATERTON, JOHN (England and Baltimore County), member of the Lower House of the Maryland Assembly, 1671-1674, 1676-1682; captain, 1678-1682; justice of the peace, 1674-1682; died testate by Jul 20, 1682 (date of probate). {Ref: ARMD 15:198, 15:254, 15:327; BDML II:868-869; INAC 7C:244; MDWB 4:85}

WATH, ---- (St. Mary's County), captain by 1718. {Ref: MDAD 1:322}

WATHEN, WILLIAM (county or port not indicated), captain and master of the ship *Francis and Mary* in 1668. {Ref: MDHM 5:339}

WATKINS, ---- (Baltimore County), ensign before 1678; paid for his services in the late expedition against the Nanticoke Indians in 1678. {Ref: ARMD 7:95}

WATKINS, ANN, see "Samuel Watkins," q.v.

WATKINS, EDWARD (England, and Somerset, St. Mary's and Calvert Counties), mariner, of Bristol, 1680; captain and commander of the ship *Margarett* of London "rideing at anchor in Pottomock River within this Province" in 1684; died by Sep 17, 1688 (date of inventory filed in Somerset County). {Ref: ARMD 17:272; INAC 7A:135, 8:320, 10:97}

WATKINS, JOHN (Talbot County), soldier (rank not stated) circa 1675; paid for his services in the late expedition against the Nanticoke Indians in 1678. {Ref: ARMD 7:91}

WATKINS, JOHN (Anne Arundel County), soldier (rank not stated) circa 1675; paid for his services in the late expedition against the Nanticoke Indians in 1678. {Ref: ARMD 7:96}

WATKINS, SAMUEL (England, and St. Mary's and Anne Arundel Counties), naval officer for the Patuxent District, 1695-1698; member of the Lower House of the Maryland Assembly, 1696; died testate by Sep 11, 1700 (date of probate; Ann Watkins, widow). {Ref: ARMD 23:109; BDML II:869; MDWB 6:377}

WATKINS, WALTER (St. Mary's County), Protestant and probable soldier in the Revolution of 1689; signed an address and took a loyalty oath supporting the King of England and the reestablishment of Lord Baltimore into power on Nov 28, 1689. {Ref: ARMD 8:147}

WATKYNS, THOMAS (Dorchester County), mariner by 1734; captain and master of the sloop *Mary Anna* (built in Dorchester County) in 1737. {Ref: MDCB 82:50}

WATSON, ANDREW (Charles County), soldier (rank not stated) in Capt. James Langworth's Company before 1661 (year of the captain's death, but his ammunition report was not filed until 1664 by Henry Adames); born circa 1629 (aged about 30 when deposed in 1659). {Ref: ARMD 53:46; CHLR B:379}

WATSON (WATTSON), DAVID (Talbot County), soldier (rank not stated) circa 1675; paid for his services in the late expedition against the Nanticoke Indians in 1678. {Ref: ARMD 7:92}

WATSON, FRANCIS (Annapolis District), captain and commander of the ship *West River* on Nov 5, 1705; commander of the ship *Richard and Margaret* riding at anchor in West River on Apr 27, 1712. {Ref: AALR WT#2:258, PK:446}

WATSON, JACOB (Pocomoke District), captain and master of the sloop *Countrey* in 1731. {Ref: CVPR:12}

WATSON, JAMES (Kent County), military officer (rank not stated) who swore allegiance to the King & Queen of England in 1696. {Ref: ARMD 20:540}

WATSON, JO. (St. Mary's County), Protestant and probable soldier in the Revolution of 1689; signed an address and took a loyalty oath supporting the King of England and the reestablishment of Lord Baltimore into power on Nov 28, 1689 (name listed as "Jo. Watson"); a John Watson was born circa 1649 (aged about 35 when deposed in 1684 in St. Mary's County). Additional research may be necessary before drawing conclusions. {Ref: ARMD 8:146, 17:307}

WATSON, JOHN (Annapolis District), captain of the ship *Robert and Mary* in 1734. {Ref: MDGZ, Nov 29, 1734}

WATSON, JOHN, see "Daniel Scott," q.v.

WATSON, ROBERT (Annapolis District), captain of the sloop *John and Mary* of Maryland in 1734. {Ref: MDGZ, Jul 19, 1734}

WATSON, WILLIAM (Dorchester County), soldier (rank not stated) circa 1675; paid for his services in the late expedition against the Nanticoke Indians in 1678; "William Wattson (Whatson)" died testate by Jan 10, 1715/6 (date of probate). {Ref: ARMD 7:93; MDWB 14:182}

WATT, JOHN (Somerset County), Protestant and probable soldier in the Revolution of 1689; signed an address and took a loyalty oath supporting the King of England and "for enabling us to defend ourselves against all invaders" on Nov 28, 1689. {Ref: ARMD 8:141}

WATT, JOHN (Prince George's County), captain and master of the ship *Anne* riding in the Eastern Branch of the Patuxent River on Jun 7, 1726. {Ref: PGLR M:150}

WATT, ROBERT (Prince George's County), captain and master of the ship *Berkley* riding in the Patuxent River on Apr 30, 1726. {Ref: PGLR M:149}

WATTS, BARTHOLOMEW (England and St. Mary's), captain and commander of the ship *Globe* of London, 1682-1692; captain, 1695. See "Francis French" and "Thomas Norcott," q.v. {Ref: ARMD 7:281, 8:371, 20:306}

WATTS, DANIEL (England, and Anne Arundel and Prince George's Counties, Potomac and Patuxent Districts), captain and master of a ship (no name given) riding at anchor at the mouth of the Patuxent River on Jul 1, 1695; captain and commander of the ship *Annarundell* "now lying in Putuxent River" on Jun 28, 1707; captain and commander of the ship *Globe* "at anchor in Purtuxen River in Prince George's County" on Apr 2, 1717; commander of the ship *Globe* in 1722-1724, riding in the Potomac River on Jan 24, 1724/5 and "lately arrived at Pattowmack" in February, 1728/9; master of the ship *Baltimore* in the Potomac District in 1730-1731; mariner, of London, and captain of the schooner *Eleanor and Elizabeth* in 1734 (built in Maryland in 1732). {Ref: ARMD 20:306, 23:466; AALR WT#2:511, IB#2:345; MDGZ, Feb 18, 1728/9; PGLR I:465, M:149; CVPR:12; MDCB 82:13}

WATTS, GEORGE (Talbot County), soldier (rank not stated) circa 1675; paid for his services in the late expedition against the Nanticoke Indians in 1678. {Ref: ARMD 7:91}

WATTS, GEORGE, JR. (Talbot County), soldier (rank not stated) circa 1675; paid for his services in the late expedition against the Nanticoke Indians in 1678. {Ref: ARMD 7:92}

WATTS, HENRY (Prince George's County), captain and master of the ship *Hazzard* riding in the Potomac River on Mar 30, 1726. {Ref: PGLR M:150}

WATTS, JOHN (Annapolis District), captain and master of the ship *William and John* of Maryland in 1730. {Ref: MDGZ, May 26, 1730}

WATTS, MARGARET, see "William Watts," q.v.

WATTS, PETER (St. Mary's County), Protestant and probable soldier in the Revolution of 1689; signed an address and took a loyalty oath (made his "P" mark) supporting the King of England and the reestablishment of Lord Baltimore into power on Nov 28, 1689; born circa 1669 (aged about 47 when deposed in 1716). {Ref: ARMD 8:147; MDEP:196}

WATTS, WILLIAM (St. Mary's County), ensign by 1678; paid for his services in the late expedition against the Nanticoke Indians in 1678; died testate by Jan 25, 1699/1700 (date of probate; Margaret Watts, widow). {Ref: ARMD 7;102, 34:401; MDWB 6:324}

WATTS, WILLIAM (St. Mary's County), captain by 1704; member of the Lower House of the Maryland Assembly, 1701-1723; major by 1716; colonel by 1721; born circa 1660 (aged about 61 when deposed in 1721), died testate by Jan 22, 1723/4 (date of probate). {Ref: BDML II:870; MDEP:196; MDAD 4:42; MDWB 18:211; MINV 9:322}

WAUGHOP, KATHERINE, see "Thomas Waughop," q.v.

WAUGHOP (WAUGHOB), THOMAS (St. Mary's County), Protestant and soldier in the Revolution of 1689; signed an address and took a loyalty oath supporting the King of England and the reestablishment of Lord Baltimore into power on Nov 28, 1689 (name listed once as "Thomas Waughou"); captain of horse troops by 1694; coroner and member of the Commission of the Peace in 1694; military officer who swore allegiance to the King & Queen of England in 1696; member of the Lower House of the Maryland Assembly, 1694-1700; died intestate in December, 1700. {Ref: ARMD 8:147, 20:64, 20:72, 20:106, 20:540, 24:40, 24:108, 38:72; BDML II:871}

WAUGHOP, THOMAS (St. Mary's County), captain by 1727; member of the Lower House of the Maryland Assembly, 1716-1735; died testate by Apr 17, 1735 (date of probate; Katherine Waughop, widow). {Ref: ARMD 39:55, 39:151, 39:220; BDML II:871; MDWB 21:370}

WAYMAN, LEYNOARD (Anne Arundel County), military officer (rank not stated) who swore allegiance to the King & Queen of England in 1696; "Leonard Wayman, Sr." died testate by Apr 6, 1721 (date of probate). {Ref: ARMD 20:541; MDWB 16:441}

WEARE, JOHN (St. Mary's County), soldier (rank not stated) circa 1675; paid for his services in the late expedition against the Nanticoke Indians in 1678. {Ref: ARMD 7:102}

WEARE, PHILIP (England and Cecil County), captain and master of the ship *Reformation* in 1723. {Ref: CELR 4:182}

WEATHERLY (WETHERLY), JAMES (Wicomico, Somerset County), soldier (rank not stated) circa 1675; paid for his services in the late expedition against the Nanticoke Indians in 1678; died by Jun 7, 1711 (date of administration account). {Ref: ARMD 7:97, 7:98; OSES:153; INAC 36A:41}

WEAVER, ARCHER (Anne Arundel County), captain and commander of the ship *Tower Hill* riding in Shipping Creek of South River on Apr 25, 1726. {Ref: AALR SY#1:188}

WEAVER, JOHN, see "John Copson," q.v.

WEBB, EDMUND (Kent and Talbot Counties), soldier (rank not stated) circa 1675; paid for his services in the late expedition against the Nanticoke Indians (name listed once as "Edmt. Weebe"); paid for his services out of an assessment levied by the General Assembly for the public good in 1682; son of "Edward Webb," q.v. {Ref: ARMD 7:92, 7:440}

WEBB, EDWARD (Kent and Talbot Counties), soldier (rank not stated) on Isle of Kent who swore allegiance to the Commonwealth of England on Apr 5, 1652; died testate by Jan 1, 1685/6 (date of probate). {Ref: INKC:101; MDWB 4:203}

WEBB, JOHN (Somerset County), soldier (rank not stated) circa 1675; paid for his services in the late expedition against the Nanticoke Indians in 1678. {Ref: ARMD 7:99}

WEBB, KATHERINE, see "William Webb," q.v.

WEBB, MICHAELL (Charles County), soldier (rank not stated) circa 1675; paid for his services in the late expedition against the Nanticoke Indians in 1678. {Ref: ARMD 7:101}

WEBB, REBECCA, see "Richard Webb," q.v.

WEBB, RICHARD (Talbot County), soldier (rank not stated) circa 1675; paid for his services in the late expedition against the Nanticoke Indians in 1678; one "Richard Webb, planter" died testate by Jun 16, 1719 (date of probate; Rebecca Webb, widow) and he was a Quaker at the time of his death; therefore, additional research will be necessary before drawing conclusions about military service. {Ref: ARMD 7:88; MDWB 15:119}

WEBB, SARAH, see "William Webb," q.v.

WEBB, THOMAS (St. Mary's County), Protestant and probable soldier in the Revolution of 1689; signed an address and took a loyalty oath supporting the King of England and the reestablishment of Lord Baltimore into power on Nov 28, 1689. {Ref: ARMD 8:147}

WEBB, WILLIAM (Talbot County), soldier (rank not stated) circa 1675; paid for his services in the late expedition against the Nanticoke Indians in 1678; sergeant who swore allegiance to the King & Queen of England in 1696; died testate by Jan 23, 1704/5 (date of probate; Katherine Webb, present wife and widow). {Ref: ARMD 7:90, 7:92, 20:542; MDWB 3:467}

WEBB, WILLIAM (England and Anne Arundel County), captain and mariner, of Bristol, before 1710; died testate by Nov 24, 1710 (date of probate in Anne Arundel County; Sarah Webb, widow). {Ref: MDWB 13:144; INAC 32A:97, 33A:70}

WEBBER, LEONARD (Calvert County), captain of the ship *Golden Lyon* in 1675-1677. {Ref: INAC 1:297, 4:175}

WEBBER, THOMAS (St. Mary's County), mariner before 1653; captain and master of a ship (no name given) "then lying in St. George's River in the province of Maryland" in February, 1654; captain, 1658. {Ref: ARMD 3:297, 10:317, 41:125, 41:147}

WEBBES, THOMAS (county or port not indicated), captain and master of the ship *Merchant Adventure* of London in 1691. {Ref: ARMD 8:240}

WEBSTER, EDWARD (St. Mary's County), probable soldier (rank not stated) before 1682; paid for his services out of an assessment levied by the General Assembly for the public good in 1682. {Ref: ARMD 7:440}

WEDILL, ROGER, see "Roger Wheedle," q.v.

WEEKES, JOHN (county not indicated), probable soldier by 1694 when paid for his services by the Maryland Assembly. {Ref: ARMD 38:55}

WEEKS (WEEKES), JOSEPH, see "Joseph Wicks," q.v.

WEEST, HENRY (Kent County), soldier (rank not stated) on Isle of Kent who swore allegiance to the Commonwealth of England on Apr 5, 1652. {Ref: INKC:101}

WEEST, THOMAS (Kent County), soldier (rank not stated) on Isle of Kent who swore allegiance to the Commonwealth of England on Apr 5, 1652. {Ref: INKC:101}

WEIGHBURNE, JOHN (Kent County), soldier (rank not stated) circa 1675; paid for his services in the late expedition against the Nanticoke Indians in 1678. {Ref: ARMD 7:94}

WELCH, DANIEL, see "Daniell Welsh," q.v.

WELCH, MORRICE (St. Mary's County), soldier (rank not stated) circa 1675; paid for his services in the late expedition against the Nanticoke Indians in 1678. {Ref: ARMD 7:103}

WELCH, SILVESTER (Anne Arundel County), captain by 1707. {Ref: ARMD 25:218}

WELLBOURNE, ---- (county not indicated), captain by 1702; he was listed among many who received payment from the estate of Madam Henrietta Maria Lloyd, deceased, of Talbot County, on May 2, 1702. {Ref: INAC 21:339}

WELLPLAY, ANDREW, see "Andrew Norwood," q.v.

WELLS, BLANCH, see "George Wells," q.v.

WELLS, DANIELL (county or port not indicated), sailor by 1707. {Ref: ARMD 27:34}

WELLS, FRANCIS, see "Richard Barry," q.v.

WELLS, GEORGE (Virginia, and Anne Arundel and Baltimore Counties), captain by 1667; county court justice, 1672-1689; member of the Lower House of the Maryland Assembly, 1674-1682; captain on the Council of War in July, 1676; colonel and commander-in-chief of all foot militia in Baltimore County by 1678; paid for his services in the late expedition against the Nanticoke Indians in 1678; colonel and Protestant in command of the foot forces of Baltimore County, 1681; member of the Lower House, 1686-1688; colonel in command of the militia in Baltimore County, 1687-1689; Protestant and soldier in the Revolution of 1689; signed an address and took a loyalty oath supporting the King of England and the reestablishment of Lord Baltimore into power on Nov 28, 1689; provincial court justice, 1694-1695; died testate by Jul 19, 1696 (date of burial; will dated Feb 20, 1695/6; Blanch Wells, widow, was a daughter of Samuel Goldsmith, q.v.). See "Thomas Long" and "---- Dockings," q.v. {Ref: ARMD 5:10, 5:309, 5:460, 5:527, 5:554, 7:96, 7:611, 8:136, 13:243, 15:38, 15:99, 15:198, 15:254, 15:327, 17:76, 17:381; BDML II:876-877; BBCF:674; INAC 15:8; MDWB 7:192}

WELLS, HENRY (Patuxent and Potomac Districts), captain and master of the ship *Ann* in 1731. {Ref: CVPR:12}

WELLS, JANE, see "John Wells," q.v.

WELLS, JOHN (Kent, Talbot, and Queen Anne's Counties), soldier (rank not stated) circa 1675; paid for his services in the late expedition against the Nanticoke Indians in 1678; captain by 1703; member of the Lower House of the Maryland Assembly, 1704-1714; born circa 1655, died by Nov 15, 1714 (date of probate; Jane Wells, widow). {Ref: ARMD 7:90, 29:468; BDML II:877; INKC:150; MDWB 14:1}

WELLS, JOHN (Potomac District), captain and master of the ship *Content* in 1730-1731. {Ref: CVPR:12}

WELLS, RICHARD (Anne Arundel County), soldier (rank not stated) circa 1675; paid for his services in the late expedition against the Nanticoke Indians in 1678. See "Sampson Waring," q.v. {Ref: ARMD 7:96}

WELLS, WILLIAM (Charles County), soldier (rank not stated) circa 1675; paid for his services in the late expedition against the Nanticoke Indians in 1678. {Ref: ARMD 7:101}

WELLS, ZERUBABLE (Talbot County), Protestant and probable soldier in the Revolution of 1689; signed an address and took a loyalty oath supporting the King of England and the reestablishment of Lord Baltimore into power on Nov 18, 1689. {Ref: ARMD 8:134}

WELSE, JOHN (Talbot County), ensign who swore allegiance to the King & Queen of England in 1696. {Ref: ARMD 20:542}

WELSH (WELCH), DANIELL (Patapsco Hundred, Baltimore County), ranger, appointed Mar 23, 1694/5 by Capt. John Oldton as a "well quallified person & good woods man & fit to be Imployed in Ranging for the Publick Service of this Province." {Ref: ARMD 20:205; BBCF:672}

WELSH, JOHN (Anne Arundel County), captain and commander of the ship *Hope for Betty* riding at anchor in South River on Apr 9, 1708. {Ref: AALR WT#2:610}

WELSH, JOHN (Anne Arundel County), captain by 1674; justice of the peace, 1674-1679; sheriff, 1677-1679; major by 1680; died testate by Mar 3, 1683/4 (date of probate; Mary Welsh, widow). {Ref: ARMD 7:515, 15:38, 15:253; FAAH:91-92; RMHF I:388; INAC 7A:172; MDWB 4:35}

WELSH, JOHN (St. Mary's County), captain by 1719. {Ref: MDAD 2:221}

WELSH, MARY, see "John Welsh," q.v.

WENTWORTH, THOMAS (Charles County), soldier (rank not stated) in Capt. James Langworth's Company before 1661 (year of the captain's death, but his ammunition report was not filed until 1664 by Henry Adames). {Ref: CHLR B:379}

WEST, CATHARINE, see "John West," q.v.

WEST, HENRY, see "Henry Weest," q.v.

WEST, JOHN (Annapolis District), captain of the snow *Molly* (or *Charming Molly*) of Maryland in 1729-1734. {Ref: MDGZ, Apr 1, 1729 and Nov 29, 1734; CVPR:12}

WEST, JOHN (Somerset County), Protestant and probable soldier in the Revolution of 1689; signed an address and took a loyalty oath supporting the King of England and "for enabling us to defend ourselves against all invaders" on Nov 28, 1689. {Ref: ARMD 8:141}

WEST, JOHN, SR. (Virginia and Manokin Hundred, Somerset County), naval officer of Pocomoke District, 1697-1698; sheriff, 1698-1701; captain by 1701;

justice of the peace, 1707; member of the Lower House of the Maryland Assembly, 1708-1711; died testate by Jun 9, 1716 (date of probate; Catoron or Catharine West, widow). See "Captain Bourne," q.v. {Ref: ARMD 23:135, 23:287, 24:422, 27:202; CMSP 1:7 - The Black Books; BDML II:878; MDWB 14:120; SOJR I:1, III:38-40; INAC 38A:175}

WESTBURY, WILLIAM (Anne Arundel and Baltimore Counties), probable soldier (rank not stated) before 1682; paid for his services out of an assessment levied by the General Assembly for the public good in 1682; died intestate by Mar 3, 1690/1 (date of administration bond; Jane Westbury, widow). {Ref: ARMD 7:441; BBCF:677}

WESTCOTT (WESTCOATE), JOHN (England and St. Mary's County), chief mate on the ship *Ruth* in 1676-1677. {Ref: ARMD 51:474, 66:301-302, 67:36}

WESTGARTH, GEORGE (England and Anne Arundel County), captain and commander of the ship *West River Merchant* riding at anchor in West River on May 1, 1712 and again on May 2, 1713; mariner, of London, by 1715; captain and commander of the ship *Susannah* riding at anchor in West River on Dec 23, 1715 and Jan 31, 1716/7 and Jan 30, 1717/8 and Jan 26, 1718/9 and May 1, 1719 (name listed once as "George Westgirth"). {Ref: ARMD 25:351; AALR PK:446, IB#2:26, 206, 261, 333, 426, 526, 544}

WETHERBY, THOMAS (Talbot County), Protestant and probable soldier in the Revolution of 1689; signed an address and took a loyalty oath supporting the King of England and the reestablishment of Lord Baltimore into power on Nov 18, 1689. {Ref: ARMD 8:134}

WETHERELL, THOMAS (Kent County), soldier (rank not stated) on Isle of Kent who swore allegiance to the Commonwealth of England on Apr 5, 1652; lieutenant, commissioned Jul 20, 1658; born circa 1607-1609 (aged about 47 when deposed in 1656 and aged about 53 when deposed in 1660). {Ref: ARMD 3:349, 3:351, 41:503; INKC:101, 108}

WETHERLY, RICHARD (St. Mary's County), captain and mariner by 1642. {Ref: ARMD 4:153}

WHALE, CHARLES (England and Anne Arundel County), captain and mariner, formerly of London, died testate in Anne Arundel County by Jul 4, 1733 (date of probate). {Ref: MDWB 20:807; MINV 20:113}

WHAPLES, PETER (Somerset County), Protestant and probable soldier in the Revolution of 1689; signed an address and took a loyalty oath supporting the King of England and "for enabling us to defend ourselves against all invaders" on Nov 28, 1689. {Ref: ARMD 8:141}

WHARLORY, ---- (Dorchester County), captain by 1695. {Ref: INAC 10:435}

WHARTON, ---- (Talbot County), captain of the ship *John and Jacob* in 1671. {Ref: ARMD 54:520}

WHARTON, JESSE (England, Barbadoes, and St. Mary's County), colonel by 1675; member of the Upper House (Maryland Council), 1672-1676; died in July, 1676. {Ref: ARMD 2:507, 15:57-58, 15:91; BDML II:880}

WHARTON, THOMAS (England and Talbot County), mariner and captain by 1698; merchant in London by 1701. {Ref: TALR 9:104; INAC 13B:36}

WHARTON (WARTON), THOMAS (Charles County), soldier (rank not stated) by 1664; paid for his services out of an assessment levied by the General Assembly for the public good in 1682. {Ref: ARMD 7:440; CHLR B:379}

WHEATLY, DANIELL (Talbot County), soldier (rank not stated) circa 1675; paid for his services in the late expedition against the Nanticoke Indians in 1678. {Ref: ARMD 7:88}

WHEATLY, WILLIAM (Anne Arundel County), captain by 1674. {Ref: INAC 1:158}

WHEEDLE, ROGER (Talbot County), soldier (rank not stated) circa 1675; paid for his services in the late expedition against the Nanticoke Indians in 1678; "Roger Wedill" died testate by Mar 31, 1686 (date of probate). {Ref: ARMD 7:90; MDWB 4:300}

WHEELE, CHARLES (Anne Arundel County), captain and commander of the ship *Gilbert* riding at anchor in South River on Dec 27, 1715. {Ref: AALR IB#2:261}

WHEELER, JAMES (Charles County), trooper in Capt. Randolph Brandt's Company, "they being the onely Roman Catholicks in the troope" in 1681. {Ref: ARMD 15:402}

WHEELER, JOHN (Charles County), ensign in Capt. James Langworth's Company circa 1659 to 1661 (year of his captain's death; name listed once as "John Wheller"); captain by 1676; major of foot troops, 1681-1689; court justice, 1685; born circa 1630 (aged about 61 when deposed on Oct 22, 1691), died testate by Jan 9, 1694/5 (date of probate; Mary Wheeler, widow). See "Thomas Colebourne," q.v. {Ref: ARMD 2:551, 7:251, 13:243, 17:79, 17:380, 53:119; CHLR A:121, B:379, Q:62, R#1:275; INAC 4:312; MDWB 7:70}

WHEELER, MARY, see "John Wheeler," q.v.

WHEELER, ROBERT (Prince George's County), captain by 1730. {Ref: MDAD 10:583, 10:590}

WHEELER, WILLIAM (St. Mary's County), captain by 1684. {Ref: ARMD 17:307}

WHERRETT, WILLIAM (St. Mary's County), Protestant and probable soldier in the Revolution of 1689; signed an address and took a loyalty oath supporting the King of England and the reestablishment of Lord Baltimore into power on Nov 28, 1689. {Ref: ARMD 8:147}

WHERRITT, WILLIAM, see "---- Hanse," q.v.

WHICHALEY, THOMAS (Charles County), Protestant and probable soldier in the Revolution of 1689; signed an address and took a loyalty oath supporting the King of England and the reestablishment of Lord Baltimore into power on Nov 28, 1689; born circa 1656 (aged about 45 when deposed in 1701). {Ref: ARMD 8:138; MDEP:199}

WHICHCOTE, PAUL (Baltimore County), captain and master of the brigantine *Baltimore* in 1734 (built in Baltimore in 1732). {Ref: MDGZ, Sep 27, 1734; MDCB 82:47}

WHIGHT, JOHN (Prince George's County), captain (nominated) who swore allegiance to the King & Queen of England in 1696. {Ref: ARMD 20:546}

WHISTON, JOHN (Annapolis District), captain and master of the ship *Exchange* of Instokey in 1730. {Ref: MDGZ, Jun 16, 1730}

WHITE, ALEXANDER (Somerset County), Protestant and probable soldier in the Revolution of 1689; signed an address and took a loyalty oath supporting the King of England and "for enabling us to defend ourselves against all invaders" on Nov 28, 1689. {Ref: ARMD 8:140}

WHITE, ELIZABETH, see "Richard White," q.v.

WHITE, JAMES (county or port not indicated), ship's carpenter on the ship *Samuel and John* commanded by Capt. Phillips by 1696 (as indicated in 1696 deposition). {Ref: ARMD 25:556-557}

WHITE, JOHN (Virginia and Pocomoke, Somerset County), commissioned captain of horse troops "for the whole county of Somerset" on Feb 9, 1669/70; member of the Lower House of the Maryland Assembly, 1676-1679; sheriff, 1679-1683; died testate on Jun 3, 1685 (will probated on Oct 3, 1685; Sarah White, widow, later married Lawrence Crawford of Kent County, Delaware). {Ref: ARMD 5:61, 15:275, 15:328; OSES:153, 283, 331; BDML II:882-883; MDWB 4:200}

WHITE, JOHN (Virginia and Somerset County), Protestant and probable soldier in the Revolution of 1689; signed an address and took a loyalty oath supporting the King of England and "for enabling us to defend ourselves against all invaders" on Nov 28, 1689; died testate by Jan 20, 1722/3 (date of probate). {Ref: ARMD 8:140; PFMD:109; MDWB 18:5}

WHITE, JOHN (Kent County), soldier (rank not stated) in Capt. William Leeds (Leeads) Company by May 23, 1662, at which time he signed a petition about the misuse of company money by Capt. Thomas Brednox (Bradnox), late of Isle of Kent, deceased; born circa 1638 (aged about 22 when deposed on Dec 20, 1660). {Ref: ARMD 3:455, 54:191; INKC:125}

WHITE (WIGHT), JOHN (England, and Calvert and Prince George's Counties), captain of foot troops, 1695/1696; member of the Lower House of the Maryland Assembly, 1697-1704; died intestate in 1705. {Ref: ARMD 20:379; BDML II:887-888}

WHITE, PHILIP (St. Mary's County), captain and mariner by 1643. {Ref: ARMD 4:257}

WHITE, RICHARD (Talbot County), soldier (rank not stated) circa 1675; paid for his services in the late expedition against the Nanticoke Indians in 1678; born circa 1633 (aged about 80 when deposed in 1713), died testate by Feb 23, 1719/20 (date of probate; Elizabeth White, widow). {Ref: ARMD 7:89, 7:92; MDEP:200; MDWB 15:302}

WHITE, ROBERT (Kent County), soldier (rank not stated) circa 1675; paid for his services in the late expedition against the Nanticoke Indians in 1678. {Ref: ARMD 7:94}

WHITE, SARAH, see "John White," q.v.

WHITEHEAD, CHARLES (Anne Arundel and Baltimore Counties), captain by 1717 (named as next of kin of Col. John Thomas, deceased, in March, 1718). {Ref: MINV 1:19; BBCF:689}

WHITEHEAD, JOHN (Anne Arundel County), probable soldier (rank not stated) before 1682; paid for his services out of an assessment levied by the General Assembly for the public good in 1682. {Ref: ARMD 7:440}

WHITESIDE, ---- (Somerset County), captain by 1702. {Ref: SOJR I:183}

WHITHALL, JOHN (Kent County), military officer (rank not stated) who swore allegiance to the King & Queen of England in 1696. {Ref: ARMD 20:540}

WHITHORN (WHITHORE, WHITEHORNE), BARTHOLOMEW (county or port not indicated), captain of a ship (no name given) between 1696 and 1702. {Ref: ARMD 23:28, 23:169, 24:303}

WHITING (WHITEING), JOSHUA (Potomac District), captain and master of the ship *John and Betty* in 1697. {Ref: ARMD 23:172}

WHITLOW, JOHN (St. Mary's County), captain and master of the ship *William and Betty* in 1730-1731. {Ref: CVPR:12; MDAD 10:233}

WHITSON, JOHN (Annapolis District), captain and master of the ship *Exchange* of Biddeford in 1731. {Ref: CVPR:12}

WHITSON, MARKE (England and St. Mary's), captain and commander of the bark *Maryland Merchant* of Bideford in 1690. {Ref: ARMD 8:171, 8:238}

WHITSON, WILLIAM (Talbot County), soldier (rank not stated) circa 1675; paid for his services in the late expedition against the Nanticoke Indians in 1678. {Ref: ARMD 7:90}

WHITTEWELL, JOHN (Talbot County), soldier (rank not stated) circa 1675; paid for his services in the late expedition against the Nanticoke Indians in 1678. {Ref: ARMD 7:91}

WHITTINGTON, ANDREW (Somerset County), soldier (rank not stated) circa 1675; paid for his services in the late expedition against the Nanticoke Indians in 1678; paid for his services out of an assessment levied by the General Assembly for the public good, 1682. {Ref: ARMD 7:99, 7:441}

WHITTINGTON, JANE, see "John Whittington," q.v.

WHITTINGTON, JOHN (England, and Kent, Talbot and Queen Anne's Counties), soldier (rank not stated) circa 1675; paid for his services in the late expedition against the Nanticoke Indians in Talbot County; Protestant and soldier in the Revolution of 1689; signed an address and took a loyalty oath supporting the King of England and the reestablishment of Lord Baltimore into power on Nov 18 and Nov 28, 1689; military officer (rank not stated) who swore allegiance to the King & Queen of England in 1696; major by 1697; member of the Lower House of the Maryland Assembly, 1697-1715; colonel by 1712; born circa 1654 (aged about 60 when deposed in 1714), died testate by May 15, 1722 (date of probate; Jane Whittington, widow). {Ref: ARMD 7:89, 8:134, 8:144, 20:540, 24:128; BDML II:884-885; MDEP:201; MDWB 17:202}

WHITTINGTON, THOMAS (St. Mary's County), soldier (rank not stated) circa 1675; paid for his services in the late expedition against the Nanticoke Indians in 1678. {Ref: ARMD 7:103}

WHITTINGTON, WILLIAM (Calvert County), Protestant and probable soldier in the Revolution of 1689; signed an address and took a loyalty oath (made his "W" mark) supporting the King of England and "to reestablish Lord Baltimore in his ancient power and government" on Nov 16, 1689. {Ref: ARMD 8:131}

WHITTINGTON, WILLIAM (Virginia and Coventry Parish, Somerset County), captain by 1686; member of the Lower House of the Maryland Assembly, 1692-1704; captain of foot troops in 1694; major, commissioned Oct 9, 1694; military officer who swore allegiance to the King & Queen of England in 1696; sheriff, 1697; lieutenant colonel by 1699; provincial court justice, 1701-1704; colonel by 1705; member of the Upper House (Maryland Council), 1709-1717; colonel and commander-in-chief of Somerset County requested by the Maryland Council "to procure a Great Gun to make an Alarm & to employ Persons to look out on the Sea side" on Nov 4, 1712; born circa 1649 (aged about 63 when deposed in 1712; name listed as "William Wittenton, Sr."), died testate by Apr 11, 1720 (date of probate). {Ref: ARMD 5:536, 13:355, 20:110, 20:153, 20:406, 20:544, 23:445, 24:129, 25:74, 25:245, 27:384, 29:81, 29:92, 38:74; CMSP 1:7 - The Black Books; BDML II:885-886; SOJR III:41; MDEP:206; MDWB 16:105; MINV 11:579}

WHITTLE, GEORGE (St. Mary's County), soldier (rank not stated), 1657; wounded and paid for his services in September, 1657. {Ref: ARMD 1:364}

WHITTLE, KATHERINE, see "William Whittle," q.v.

WHITTLE, WILLIAM (St. Mary's County), soldier (rank not stated) in 1647; died by Mar 13, 1673/4 (date of probate of nuncupative will which was given on Mar 12, 1673/4); Katherine Whittle, widow). {Ref: ARMD 1:226; MDWB 1:597}

WHITTY, DOROTHY, see "Richard Whitty," q.v.

WHITTY, JOHN (England and St. Mary's County), captain by 1657; deceased by 1667 (date of deposition in London; Sarah Whitty, administratrix). {Ref: LMCL:43; ARMD 41:434, 57:205}

WHITTY (WHITTIE, WHITTEE, WHITY), RICHARD (Somerset County), lieutenant before 1678; paid for his services in the late expedition against the Nanticoke Indians in 1678; captain by 1692; died testate by Mar 15, 1692/3 (date of probate; Dorothy Whitty, widow). {Ref: ARMD 7:97, 7:100; OSES:153, 280; MDWB 6:35; INAC 10:285}

WHITTY, SARAH, see "John Whitty," q.v.

WHORCON, JOHN (St. Mary's County), captain by 1694. {Ref: INAC 13A:120}

WHYT, ---- (county not indicated), captain by 1688. {Ref: INAC 10:117}

WIATT, JOHN (Kent County), military officer (rank not stated) who swore allegiance to the King & Queen of England in 1696. {Ref: ARMD 20:540}

WIATT, THOMAS (Kent County), military officer (rank not stated) who swore allegiance to the King & Queen of England in 1696. {Ref: ARMD 20:540}

WIAXALL, WILLIAM (county or port not indicated), captain and master of the ship *Sunflower* of Bristol in 1689. {Ref: ARMD 8:236}

WICKES (WICKS, WEEKES, WEECKES), JOSEPH (Virginia and Kent, Cecil, and Talbot Counties), soldier (rank not stated) on Isle of Kent who swore allegiance to the Commonwealth of England on Apr 5, 1652; assistant commander (commissioner) of Kent County, 1654; captain of militia by 1654; member of the Maryland Assembly in 1657; member of the Lower House, representing Kent County in 1659, Talbot County in 1671-1675, and Kent County in 1676-1684; major by 1662; soldier (rank not stated), paid for his services in the late expedition against the Nanticoke Indians in 1678; major and court justice, 1680-1683; born circa 1620 (aged about 37 when deposed in 1657), died by Feb 21, 1692/3 (date of inventory in Kent County). {Ref: ARMD 1:359, 7:94, 10:493, 15:38, 15:67, 15:70, 15:93, 15:328, 17:169, 54:10, 54:120; RMHF I:264; FAAH:27; BDML II:887; INKC 101, 103; INAC 12:4}

WICKETT, JOHN (Talbot County), soldier (rank not stated) circa 1675; paid for his services in the late expedition against the Nanticoke Indians in 1678. {Ref: ARMD 7:88}

WIGGENS, GILES (county or port not indicated), captain of a ship (no name given) in 1696. {Ref: ARMD 25:588}

WIGGENS, JOHN (Talbot County), soldier (rank not stated) circa 1675; paid for his services in the late expedition against the Nanticoke Indians in 1678. {Ref: ARMD 7:92}

WIGGINER, GILES (Annapolis District), captain and commander of a ship (no name given) in 1698. {Ref: ARMD 23:466}

WIGHT, JOHN, see "John White," q.v.

WIGHTMAN, ROBERT (All Hallows Parish, Somerset County), mariner and sailor on the ship *Blessing* riding at anchor in Senepuxen Inlet on Apr 13, 1717. {Ref: MGSB 36:4, p. 645; SOJR III:193, 195-196}

WILCOCK, JON. (Kent County), "seaman within the said county" and a "sailor belonging to Mr. Powers ship in the stocks" in 1697. {Ref: ARMD 25:599}

WILDE (WILD), ABRAHAM (England, and Baltimore and Cecil Counties), captain of a company of foot before 1681; court justice, Baltimore County, 1672-1674, and Cecil County, 1674-1676; land owner on south side of Elk River; county commissioner by 1683 and returned to England thereafter; captain and master of the ship *Avarilla* riding in Patuxent River on Nov 15, 1688; captain and master of the ship *Dilligence* of London in 1691; mariner, late of the Parish of Stepney, County Middlesex, died by November, 1701, probably in England. {Ref: ARMD 8:52, 8:239, 17:76, 17:78, 17:137; BDML II:888; CELR 2:29}

WILDE, ISAAC (Anne Arundel County), captain by 1698. {Ref: INAC 16:129}

WILDER, JOHN (Charles County), military officer (rank not stated) who swore allegiance to the King & Queen of England in 1696. {Ref: ARMD 20:543}

WILDGOOSE, JAMES (Kent County), soldier (rank not stated) circa 1675; paid for his services in the late expedition against the Nanticoke Indians in 1678. {Ref: ARMD 7:94}

WILDGOOSE, RICHARD (Somerset County), Protestant and probable soldier in the Revolution of 1689; signed an address and took a loyalty oath supporting

the King of England and "for enabling us to defend ourselves against all invaders" on Nov 28, 1689. {Ref: ARMD 8:140}

WILDING, HUGH (county not indicated), probable soldier (rank not stated) before 1682; paid for his services out of an assessment levied by the General Assembly for the public good in 1682. {Ref: ARMD 7:440}

WILKINSON, HENRY (Talbot County), soldier (rank not stated) circa 1675; paid for his services in the late expedition against the Nanticoke Indians in 1678. {Ref: ARMD 7:89}

WILKINSON, JOHN (Talbot County), probable soldier (rank not stated) before 1682; paid for his services out of an assessment levied by the General Assembly for the public good in 1682. {Ref: ARMD 7:440}

WILKINSON, JOSEPH (Calvert County), captain of the ship *Crown* in 1722; master of the ship *Judith* riding in Patuxent River on Feb 24, 1723/4 and Jan 24, 1724/5 and Feb 5, 1725/6 and Mar 30, 1726 (name mistakenly listed once as "Joseph Williamson"); commander of a ship (no name given) riding in Patuxent River in 1729; merchant by 1730; died testate by Jul 15, 1735 (date of probate; Mary Wilkinson, widow). {Ref: MDGZ, Apr 29, 1729; PGLR I:465, M:148-150, M:491, Q:230; MDWB 21:424; MINV 21:156}

WILKINSON, MARY, see "Joseph Wilkinson," q.v.

WILKINSON (WILKISON), PHILIP (England and Anne Arundel County), captain and commander of the ship *Jane* riding at anchor in South River on Apr 23, 1719 and Feb 19, 1719/20 and Dec 29, 1720 (name of ship was mistakenly listed as *James*) and Apr 21, 1724; commander of the ship *Cleavland* riding in South River on Feb 16, 1725/6; captain of the ship *Peach Blossom* of London in 1729. {Ref: AALR IB#2:541, CW#1:127, 288, RCW#2:235, SY#1:167; MDAD 5:13; MDGZ, Apr 29, 1729}

WILKINSON, TAMAR, see "William Wilkinson," q.v.

WILKINSON (WILKESON), WILLIAM (Calvert County), Protestant and probable soldier in the Revolution of 1689; signed an address and took a loyalty oath supporting the King of England and "to reestablish Lord Baltimore in his ancient power and government" on Nov 16, 1689. {Ref: ARMD 8:132}

WILKINSON (WILKESON), WILLIAM (Baltimore County), Protestant and probable soldier in the Revolution of 1689; signed an address and took a loyalty oath supporting the King of England and the reestablishment of Lord Baltimore into power on Nov 28, 1689; died testate by Jun 16, 1718 (date of probate; Tamar Wilkinson, widow). {Ref: ARMD 8:136; BBCF:690-691; MDWB 14:603}

WILL, GEORGE (Prince George's County), captain and master of the ship *Robert and Mary* riding in the Patuxent River on Apr 15, 1726. {Ref: PGLR M:150}

WILLEE, JOHN (St. Mary's County), soldier (rank not stated) circa 1675; paid for his services in the late expedition against the Nanticoke Indians in 1678. {Ref: ARMD 7:103}

WILLIAMS, ELISABETH, see "Hugh Williams," q.v.

WILLIAM, GILES (Talbot County), soldier (rank not stated) circa 1675; paid for his services in the late expedition against the Nanticoke Indians in 1678. {Ref: ARMD 7:88}

WILLIAM, THOMAS (Somerset County), soldier (rank not stated) circa 1675; paid for his services in the late expedition against the Nanticoke Indians in 1678. {Ref: ARMD 7:99}

WILLIAMS, BENJAMIN (Anne Arundel County), military officer (rank not stated) who swore allegiance to the King & Queen of England in 1696. {Ref: ARMD 20:541}

WILLIAMS, EDWARD (Somerset County), soldier (rank not stated) circa 1675; paid for his services in the late expedition against the Nanticoke Indians in 1678. {Ref: ARMD 7:97}

WILLIAMS, GEORGE (Potomac District), captain and master of the ship *Sea Flower* in 1730-1731. {Ref: CVPR:12}

WILLIAMS, HENRY (Oxford District), captain and master of the ship *Robert* in 1731. {Ref: CVPR:12}

WILLIAMS, HUGH (Calvert County), probable soldier (rank not stated) before 1682; paid for his services out of an assessment levied by the General Assembly for the public good in 1682; died intestate by Jul 22, 1721 (date of administration account; Elisabeth Williams, widow). {Ref: ARMD 7:439; MDAD 4:60}

WILLIAMS, JOHN (St. Mary's County), soldier (rank not stated) circa 1675; paid for his services in the late expedition against the Nanticoke Indians in 1678; also paid again in 1682 and 1694. {Ref: ARMD 7:102, 7:443, 38:55}

WILLIAMS, JOHN (Somerset County), Protestant and probable soldier in the Revolution of 1689; signed an address and took a loyalty oath supporting the King of England and "for enabling us to defend ourselves against all invaders" on Nov 28, 1689. {Ref: ARMD 8:141}

WILLIAMS, JOHN (Somerset County), mariner by 1734; captain and master of the sloop *Esther* (built in Somerset County) in 1735. {Ref: MDCB 82:38}

WILLIAMS, JOSEPH (Talbot County), soldier (rank not stated) circa 1675; paid for his services in the late expedition against the Nanticoke Indians in 1678. {Ref: ARMD 7:88, 7:103}

WILLIAMS, MICHAEL (Virginia and Annamessex, Somerset County), soldier (rank not stated) circa 1675; paid for his services in the late expedition against the Nanticoke Indians in 1678; died testate by Dec 1, 1699 (date of probate; Patience Williams, widow). {Ref: ARMD 7:100; OSES:463; MDWB 6:318}

WILLIAMS, PATIENCE, see "Michael Williams," q.v.

WILLIAMS, RICHARD (England and Annapolis), captain of the ship *Clapham* of London in 1729. {Ref: MDGZ, May 20, 1729}

WILLIAMS, RICHARD (Anne Arundel County), soldier (rank not stated) circa 1675; paid for his services in the late expedition against the Nanticoke Indians in 1678. {Ref: ARMD 7:97}

WILLIAMS, SUSAN, see "William Williams, Sr.," q.v.

WILLIAMS, THOMAS (Virginia and Annamessex, Somerset County), soldier (rank not stated) circa 1675; paid for his services in the late expedition against the Nanticoke Indians in 1678; died testate by May 5, 1720 (date of probate). {Ref: ARMD 7:100; OSES:463; MDWB 16:103}

WILLIAMS, WILLIAM, JR. (Calvert County), military officer (rank not stated) who swore allegiance to the King & Queen of England in 1696. {Ref: ARMD 20:543}

WILLIAMS, WILLIAM, SR. (Calvert County), captain by 1685; military officer (rank not stated) who swore allegiance to the King & Queen of England in 1696; a "William Williams" died testate by Mar 13, 1720/1 (date of probate; Susan Williams, widow). {Ref: ARMD 20:543; INAC 8:320; MDWB 16:403}

WILLIAMSON, RALPH (England, Potomac District, and Charles County), captain and master of the ship *Charity* of Liverpool in 1697; mariner of Liverpool and land owner in Charles County in March, 1703/4. {Ref: ARMD 23:138; CHLR Z:86}

WILLICE, RICHARD (Talbot County), soldier (rank not stated) circa 1675; paid for his services in the late expedition against the Nanticoke Indians in 1678. {Ref: ARMD 7:87}

WILLIS, RICHARD (Dorchester County), captain by 1730. {Ref: MDAD 10:437}

WILLOBY, ANNE, see "William Willoughby," q.v.

WILLOUGHBY (WILLOBY, WILLOWBY), JOHN (Anne Arundel County), military officer (rank not stated) who swore allegiance to the King & Queen of England in 1696; died testate by Mar 1, 1702/3 (date of probate; Sarah Willoughby, widow). See "Robert Franklin," q.v. {Ref: ARMD 20:542}

WILLOUGHBY, SARAH, see "John Willoughby" and "Robert Franklin," q.v.

WILLOUGHBY (WILLOBY), WILLIAM (England and Dorchester County), soldier (rank not stated) circa 1675; paid for his services in the late expedition against the Nanticoke Indians in 1678; born circa 1624 (aged about 86 when deposed in 1710), died testate in 1713 (will dated Sep 13, 1712; exact date of probate in 1713 was not indicated; Anne Willoby, widow). {Ref: ARMD 7:92, 7:94; MDWB 13:538}

WILLS, PETER (Anne Arundel County), captain and commander of the ship *Susannah and Sarah* riding at anchor in South River on Feb 7, 1712/3; captain and master of the frigate *Rappahannock* riding in South River on Jun 25, 1711; captain and commander of the ship *Susannah and Sarah* riding at anchor in South River on Apr 16, 1716 and Jan 22, 1716/7 and Nov 22, 1717 and Jan 26, 1719/20; commander of the ship *Booth* riding in South River on Apr 11, 1721 and Mar 10, 1721/2. {Ref: AALR IB#2:18, 216, 273, 333, 401, CW#1:119, 350, 481}

WILLS, THOMAS (England and St. Mary's County), captain and master of the ship *Friends Agreement* of Bristoll in 1693; captain, 1696. {Ref: ARMD 20:182, 23:28}

WILLSON, ABIGALL, see "Andrew Wilson (Willson)," q.v.

WILLSON, ELIZABETH, see "George Wilson (Willson)," q.v.

WILMORE, CHARLES (Anne Arundel County), soldier (rank not stated) circa 1675; paid for his services in the late expedition against the Nanticoke Indians in 1678. {Ref: ARMD 7:97}

WILMOT, WILLIAM (Somerset County), Protestant and probable soldier in the Revolution of 1689; signed an address and took a loyalty oath supporting the King of England and "for enabling us to defend ourselves against all invaders" on Nov 28, 1689. {Ref: ARMD 8:139}

WILSON, ABIGAIL, see "David Wilson," q.v.

WILSON (WILLSON, WILSONE), ANDREW (Somerset County), soldier (rank not stated) circa 1675; paid for his services in the late expedition against the Nanticoke Indians in 1678; died testate by Jun 10, 1715 (date of probate; Abigall Willson, widow). {Ref: ARMD 7:99}

WILSON, DAVID (Somerset County), probable soldier in the 1730's since he was a captain by 1737; member of the Lower House of the Maryland Assembly, 1744-1745; born 1704, died testate by Nov 26, 1750 (date of probate; Abigail Wilson, widow). {Ref: BDML II:897-898; MDWB 27:441}

WILSON, EPHRAIM (Back River, Manokin Hundred, Somerset County), Protestant and probable soldier in the Revolution of 1689; signed an address and took a loyalty oath supporting the King of England and "for enabling us to defend ourselves against all invaders" on Nov 28, 1689; captain before 1714; born circa 1667 (aged about 56 when deposed in 1723), died testate by Nov 26, 1732 (date of probate; Frances Wilson, widow). {Ref: ARMD 8:139; INAC 36B:343; MDEP:205; MDWB 20:526}

WILSON, FRANCES, see "Ephraim Wilson," q.v.

WILSON, GEORGE (Kent County), captain by 1733; member of the Lower House of the Maryland Assembly, 1728-1748; born circa 1696 (aged about 50 when deposed in 1746), died testate by Mar 4, 1748 (date of probate; Mary Wilson, widow). {Ref: ARMD 39:151, 39:220; BDML II:898; MDEP:205; MDWB 26:74}

WILSON (WILLSON), GEORGE (Somerset County), soldier (rank not stated) circa 1675; paid for his services in the late expedition against the Nanticoke Indians in 1678; died testate by Aug 2, 1709 (date of probate; Elizabeth Willson, widow). {Ref: ARMD 7:100; MDWB 12:175, pt. 2}

WILSON, JAMES (Talbot County), soldier (rank not stated) circa 1675; paid for his services in the late expedition against the Nanticoke Indians in 1678. {Ref: ARMD 7:92}

WILSON, JOHN (Pocomoke District), captain and master of the ship *Sommersett* in April, 1731. {Ref: CVPR:12}

WILSON, JOHN (St. Mary's County), soldier (rank not stated) circa 1675; paid for his services in the late expedition against the Nanticoke Indians in 1678. {Ref: ARMD 7:103}

WILSON, JOHN (Calvert County), military officer (rank not stated) who swore allegiance to the King & Queen of England in 1696; died intestate by Dec 9,

1720 (date of administration account; Sarah Wilson, widow). {Ref: ARMD 20:543; MDAD 3:181}

WILSON, JOHN (Annapolis District), captain and master of the ship *Rebecca* of Ayre in April, 1731. {Ref: CVPR:12}

WILSON, JOHN (Charles County), Protestant and probable soldier in the Revolution of 1689; signed an address and took a loyalty oath supporting the King of England and the reestablishment of Lord Baltimore into power on Nov 28, 1689. {Ref: ARMD 8:138}

WILSON, JOSEPH (Calvert County), Protestant and probable soldier in the Revolution of 1689; signed an address and took a loyalty oath supporting the King of England and "to reestablish Lord Baltimore in his ancient power and government" on Nov 16, 1689. {Ref: ARMD 8:132}

WILSON, JOSIAH (Calvert, Prince George's, and Anne Arundel Counties), Protestant and probable soldier in the Revolution of 1689; signed an address and took a loyalty oath supporting the King of England and "to reestablish Lord Baltimore in his ancient power and government" on Nov 16, 1689; captain by 1697; major by 1702; sheriff of Calvert County, 1698-1703, Prince George's County, 1704-1705, and Anne Arundel County, 1706-1708; sergeant at arms for the Maryland Council, 1708; member of the Lower House of the Maryland Assembly, 1715-1717 (name also listed as "Josiah Willson" and "Josias Wilson" and "Maj. Josias Willson" and "Maj. Josiah Wilson"); died testate by Dec 5, 1717 (date of probate). {Ref: ARMD 8:132, 23:419, 25:132, 25:150, 25:204, 25:240, 30:107; BDML II:899; HCCM:335; PGLR A:445; MDWB 14:381; MDAD 1:432}

WILSON, MARGARET, see "Daniel Dixon," q.v.

WILSON, MARY, see "George Wilson," q.v.

WILSON (WILLSON), MATHEW (Anne Arundel County), captain by 1719. {Ref: MINV 3:302}

WILSON, MICHAELL (Patuxent District), captain and master of the ship *Katherine and Elizabeth* in 1731. {Ref: CVPR:12}

WILSON (WILSONE), ROBERT (Somerset County), soldier (rank not stated) circa 1675; paid for his services in the late expedition against the Nanticoke Indians in 1678. {Ref: ARMD 7:98, 7:100}

WILSON, SAMUELL (Pocomoke District), captain and master of the ship *Betty* in 1730-1731. {Ref: CVPR:12}

WILSON (WILSONE), SAMUELL (county not indicated), captain by 1696. {Ref: INAC 13B:134}

WILSON, SARAH, see "John Wilson," q.v.

WILSON, THOMAS (Talbot County), soldier (rank not stated) circa 1675; paid for his services in the late expedition against the Nanticoke Indians in 1678. {Ref: ARMD 7:91}

WILSON, THOMAS (St. Mary's County), captain by 1654. {Ref: ARMD 10:382}

WILSON, THOMAS (Kent County), soldier (rank not stated) circa 1675; paid for his services in the late expedition against the Nanticoke Indians in 1678. {Ref: ARMD 7:94}

WILSON, THOMAS (Somerset County), Protestant and probable soldier in the Revolution of 1689; signed an address and took a loyalty oath supporting the King of England and "for enabling us to defend ourselves against all invaders" on Nov 28, 1689. {Ref: ARMD 8:139}

WILSON, WILLIAM (Somerset County), Protestant and probable soldier in the Revolution of 1689; signed an address and took a loyalty oath supporting the King of England and "for enabling us to defend ourselves against all invaders" on Nov 28, 1689. {Ref: ARMD 8:140}

WIMPLE, MINDERT (Oxford District), captain and master of the ship *Albany* in 1730. {Ref: CVPR:12}

WINBRIDGE, JOHN (St. Mary's County), quartermaster to Capt. Tillman in 1654. {Ref: ARMD 10:395}

WINCHESTER, JOHN (Kent County), soldier (rank not stated) on Isle of Kent who swore allegiance to the Commonwealth of England on Apr 5, 1652; soldier (rank not stated) in Capt. William Leeds (Leeads) Company by May 23, 1662, at which time he signed a petition about the misuse of company money by Capt. Thomas Brednox (Bradnox), late of Isle of Kent, deceased; born circa 1623-1626 (aged about 30 when deposed in 1653 and aged about 29 when deposed in 1655); "John Winchester, Sr." died Aug 22, 1669. {Ref: ARMD 3:455, 54:19, 54:188; INKC:101, 106}

WINCHOUGH, EDWARD (Kent County), soldier (rank not stated) circa 1675; paid for his services in the late expedition against the Nanticoke Indians in 1678. {Ref: ARMD 7:94}

WINCKLES, EDWARD (Talbot County), soldier (rank not stated) circa 1675; paid for his services in the late expedition against the Nanticoke Indians in 1678. {Ref: ARMD 7:87-91}

WINCOTT, JOHN (Charles County), Protestant and probable soldier in the Revolution of 1689; signed an address and took a loyalty oath supporting the King of England and the reestablishment of Lord Baltimore into power on Nov 28, 1689. {Ref: ARMD 8:138}

WINDELL, RICHARD (St. Mary's County), captain by 1678. {Ref: INAC 5:382}

WINDER, EDMUND (Anne Arundel County), captain by 1652; parliamentary commissioner in 1652. {Ref: FAAH:37}

WINDER, JOHN (Virginia and Wicomico Hundred, Somerset County), sergeant before 1678; paid for his services in the late expedition against the Nanticoke Indians in 1678; court justice, 1679-1680; lieutenant by 1680; captain by 1682; paid for his services out of an assessment levied by the General Assembly for the public good in 1682; captain in the horse troops of Somerset County, commissioned Dec 2, 1687; captain of a troop of horse in 1689; Protestant and soldier in the Revolution of 1689; signed an address and took a loyalty oath supporting the King of England and "for enabling us to defend ourselves against all invaders" on Nov 28, 1689; lieutenant colonel, commissioned Oct 9, 1694; military officer who swore allegiance to the King & Queen of England in 1696; lieutenant colonel, reported to the Maryland Council as being sick on Oct 4, 1697; died testate by Sep 23, 1698 (date of probate). {Ref: ARMD 5:555, 5:568, 7:98, 7:442-443, 7:611, 8:141, 13:244, 15:275, 15:328, 20:153, 20:544, 23:285; OSES:280, 283, 332; INAC 19:65; MDWB 6:276}

WINDER, JOHN (Charles County), sergeant by 1678; paid for his services in the late expedition against the Nanticoke Indians in 1678. {Ref: ARMD 7:101}

WINDER, THOMAS (Somerset County), soldier (rank not stated) circa 1675; paid for his services in the late expedition against the Nanticoke Indians in 1678; paid for his services out of an assessment levied by the General Assembly for the public good in 1682; cornet in the horse troops of Somerset County, commissioned Dec 2, 1687; military officer (rank not stated) who swore allegiance to the King & Queen of England in 1696 (name listed once as "Thomas Window"). {Ref: ARMD 5:568, 7:104, 7:443, 20:544}

WINDER, WILLIAM (Somerset County), mariner by 1743; captain and master of the sloop *Polly* in 1749 and co-owner of the schooner *Betty* in 1750; member of the Lower House of the Maryland Assembly, 1765-1766; subscription officer, Continental Loan Office, 1779; born Mar 16, 1714/5, died in 1792. {Ref: BDML II:903}

WINDHAM, EDWARD (Virginia, but no evidence he ever actually was a resident of Maryland), captain by 1651; appointed to the Maryland Council and Provincial Court in 1652, but no evidence of service (only man with this name in the Maryland-Virginia area at this time); born 1616, date of death not known (last mentioned in the land records of Lower Norfolk County in 1654). {Ref: BDML II:904-905}

WING, ROBERT (Dorchester County), mariner by 1726; captain by 1732; master of the sloop *Elizabeth* in 1735 (built at Amesbury, Massachusetts in 1734); died intestate by Jun 7, 1741 (date of inventory; Ann Wing, widow). {Ref: DOLR 8 Old 146; DOLR 12 Old 131; MDCB 82:32; MINV 26:187}

WINGFIELD, RICHARD (Baltimore County), captain of the ship *William and Jane* in 1724. {Ref: BALR IS#G}

WINN, JOHN (county or port not indicated), captain and master of the ship *Mary* of London in 1691. {Ref: ARMD 8:239}

WINNING, WILLIAM (Calvert County), Protestant and probable soldier in the Revolution of 1689; signed an address and took a loyalty oath supporting the King of England and "to reestablish Lord Baltimore in his ancient power and government" on Nov 16, 1689. {Ref: ARMD 8:131}

WINSLOW, JOSEPH, see "Richard Collett," q.v.

WINTELL, THOMAS (Dorchester County), "boatson" by 1676. {Ref: INAC 3:7}

WINTERSELL, WILLIAM (Talbot County), soldier (rank not stated) circa 1675; paid for his services in the late expedition against the Nanticoke Indians in 1678; died testate by Jan 15, 1716/7 (date of probate; Jane Wintersell, widow). {Ref: ARMD 7:90; MDWB 14:241}

WINTOUR (WINTER), FRANCIS (England and St. Mary's), lieutenant by 1634. {Ref: FMDP:179, 271}

WINTOUR (WINTER), ROBERT (England and St. Mary's), captain and commander of the ship *Ark* which brought the first colonists (along with the ship *Dove*) to Maryland and arrived on Mar 25, 1634; he returned to England and returned to Maryland with five servants in 1637; Catholic member of the Maryland Council, 1637-1638; died by Sep 4, 1638 (date of inventory). {Ref: FMDP:271-273; ARMD 1:2, 1:6, 4:26, 4:47, 4:85-88; BDML II:905}

WISE, CHRISTOPHER (Talbot County), soldier (rank not stated) circa 1675; paid for his services in the late expedition against the Nanticoke Indians in 1678. {Ref: ARMD 7:87}

WISE, SAMUEL (Somerset County), mariner by the 1730's; captain and master of the sloop *Royal Oak* (built in Somerset County) in 1739. {Ref: MDCB 82:78}

WISEMAN, EDMOND (county or port not indicated), captain and master of the ship *Elisabeth and Mary* in 1720. {Ref: MINV 4:258}

WITHERS, JOHN (Prince George's County), foot soldier (rank not stated) under the command of Capt. Richard Owen in June, 1699. {Ref: ARMD 24:121}

WITHERS, JOHN (Charles County), captain by 1697. {Ref: ARMD 23:294}

WITHERS, SAMUEL (Talbot County), Protestant and probable soldier in the Revolution of 1689; signed an address and took a loyalty oath supporting the King of England and the reestablishment of Lord Baltimore into power on Nov 28, 1689. {Ref: ARMD 8:144}

WITHINGTON, THOMAS (St. Mary's County), captain and master of a ship (no name given) riding at anchor at the mouth of the Patuxent River on Jul 1, 1695 (date of petition). {Ref: ARMD 20:306}

WITTER, THOMAS (Charles County), soldier (rank not stated) circa 1675; paid for his services in the late expedition against the Nanticoke Indians in 1678. {Ref: ARMD 7:101}

WITTICOMB, THOMAS (county or port not indicated), captain and master of the sloop *Elizabeth and Hannah* (built in Maryland) in 1733. {Ref: MDCB 82:14}

WOLLIS, ALEXANDER (county not indicated), probable soldier (rank not stated) before 1682; paid for his services out of an assessment levied by the General Assembly for the public good in 1682. {Ref: ARMD 7:441}

WOOD, EDWARD, JR. (Hunting Creek, Calvert County), Protestant and probable soldier in the Revolution of 1689; signed an address and took a loyalty oath supporting the King of England and "to reestablish Lord Baltimore in his ancient power and government" on Nov 16, 1689. {Ref: ARMD 8:132; HCCM:336}

WOOD, JOHN (Somerset County), soldier (rank not stated) circa 1675; paid for his services in the late expedition against the Nanticoke Indians in 1678. {Ref: ARMD 7:98}

WOOD, JOHN (Charles County), soldier (rank not stated) circa 1675; paid for his services in the late expedition against the Nanticoke Indians in 1678; "John Wood, Sr." died testate by Apr 6, 1716 (date of probate; Margaret Wood, widow). {Ref: ARMD 7:101; MDWB 14:106}

WOOD, MARGARET, see "John Wood," q.v.

WOOD, MATHIAS (Charles County), drummer in 1676. {Ref: ARMD 2:551}
WOOD, PETER (Charles County), captain by 1734. {Ref: CHLR Y#3:599}
WOOD, THOMAS (Talbot County), soldier (rank not stated) circa 1675; paid for his services in the late expedition against the Nanticoke Indians in 1678. {Ref: ARMD 7:87}
WOOD, WILLIAM (Calvert County), Protestant and probable soldier in the Revolution of 1689; signed an address and took a loyalty oath (made his "X" mark) supporting the King of England and "to reestablish Lord Baltimore in his ancient power and government" on Nov 16, 1689. {Ref: ARMD 8:131}
WOODARD, JOHN (Somerset County), soldier (rank not stated) circa 1675; paid for his services in the late expedition against the Nanticoke Indians in 1678. {Ref: ARMD 7:97}
WOODBERRY, BENJAMIN (Potomac District), captain and master of the ship *Intention* in 1730-1731. {Ref: CVPR:12}
WOODBERRY, ISAAC (Potomac District), captain and master of the ship *Elizabeth* in 1730-1731. {Ref: CVPR:12}
WOODBERRY, WILLIAM (county or port not indicated), captain and master of the sloop *Neptune* of Salin in 1690. {Ref: ARMD 8:237}
WOODCOCK, JOHN (St. Mary's County), sailor by 1690; he killed John Payne (Collector of Patuxent District) on board a yacht commanded by Major Seawall on Jan 3, 1690 and was subsequently executed for the murder. See "John Payne," q.v. {Ref: ARMD 8:516}
WOODCRAFT, RICHARD (Somerset County), Protestant and probable soldier in the Revolution of 1689; signed an address and took a loyalty oath supporting the King of England and "for enabling us to defend ourselves against all invaders" on Nov 28, 1689. {Ref: ARMD 8:140}
WOODFIELD (WOODFEILD), WALTER (Anne Arundel County), probable soldier (rank not stated) before 1682; paid for his services out of an assessment levied by the General Assembly for the public good in 1682. {Ref: ARMD 7:441}
WOODFIND (WOODVINE), JOHN (Baltimore County), soldier (rank not stated) circa 1675; paid for his services in the late expedition against the Nanticoke Indians in 1678; died without issue (no date given). {Ref: ARMD 7:96; BBCF:704}
WOODFORD, THOMAS (Dorchester County), captain by 1728. {Ref: MDAD 9:217}
WOODNETT, LAWRENCE (Dorchester County), soldier (rank not stated) circa 1675; paid for his services in the late expedition against the Nanticoke Indians in 1678. {Ref: ARMD 7:93}
WOODROFFE, J. (Calvert County), Protestant and probable soldier in the Revolution of 1689; signed an address and took a loyalty oath supporting the King of England and the reestablishment of Lord Baltimore into power on Nov 28, 1689. {Ref: ARMD 8:145}
WOODS, JEREMIAH (county not indicated), probable soldier (rank not stated) before 1682; paid for his services out of an assessment levied by the General Assembly for the public good in 1682. {Ref: ARMD 7:440}

WOODS, JOSEPH (Kent County), "seaman within the said county" and a "sailor belonging to the *Loves Increase* of Whitehaven" in 1697. {Ref: ARMD 25:600}

WOODWARD, SAMUEL (New England and Maryland, port not indicated), captain and master of the ketch *Mary* in 1686. {Ref: ARMD 5:488}

WOODWARD, THOMAS (Annapolis and Patuxent Districts), captain and master of the ship *Providence* of Virginia in 1730-1731. {Ref: MDGZ, May 26, 1730; CVPR:12}

WOOLAND, EDWARD (Dorchester County), captain before 1696; died by May 17, 1699 (date of inventory). {Ref: INAC 13B:135, 19:131}

WOOLCHURCH (WOLCHURCH, WOOLCHURGE), HENRY (Talbot County), soldier (rank not stated) circa 1675; paid for his services in the late expedition against the Nanticoke Indians in 1678; died testate by Sep 28, 1695 (date of probate). {Ref: ARMD 7:89; INAC 10:424-426; MDWB 7:120}

WOOLEN, JOHN (Dorchester County), captain by 1725. {Ref: MDAD 7:176}

WOOLFORD, ELIZABETH, see "Roger Woolford," q.v.

WOOLFORD (WOOLLFORD), JAMES (Dorchester County), captain by 1727; born circa 1679-1681 (aged about 51 when deposed in 1730, aged about 53 when deposed in 1733, and aged about 59 when deposed in 1740). {Ref: DOLR 8 Old 200, 9 Old 135, 12 Old 116; MDEP:206}

WOOLFORD (WOOLLFORD), ROGER (Virginia and Manokin Hundred, Somerset County), soldier (rank not stated) circa 1675; paid for his services in the late expedition against the Nanticoke Indians in 1678; member of the Lower House of the Maryland Assembly, 1671-1693; court justice, 1679-1680; died testate by Feb 26, 1702/3 (date of probate). {Ref: ARMD 7:100, 15:275, 15:328; BDML II:908; OSES:280, 464; MDWB 11:304}

WOOLFORD (WOOLLFORD), ROGER (Dorchester County and Manokin Hundred, Somerset County), sheriff, Dorchester County, 1702-1706, 1709-1711; major by 1714; member of the Lower House of the Maryland Assembly, 1707-1720; colonel by 1720; born circa 1673 (aged about 33 when deposed in 1706), died testate by Dec 8, 1730 (date of probate; Elizabeth Woolford, widow). {Ref: ARMD 27:203, 29:227, 29:248, 30:129, 33:365, 34:61; CESM:10; BDML II:908-909; MDEP:207; MDWB 20:119; MINV 16:257}

WOOLFORD (WOOLLFORD), THOMAS (Dorchester County), captain by 1728; member of the Lower House of the Maryland Assembly, 1732-1737; born circa 1699, died intestate in 1750/1751. {Ref: BDML II:909-910}

WOOLMAN (WOOLLMAN), RICHARD (Virginia, and Anne Arundel and Talbot Counties), lieutenant by 1657; provincial court justice, 1657-1658; burgess (member of the Lower House of the Maryland Assembly) from Anne Arundel County in 1659-1660; gentleman, lieutenant, and burgess from Talbot County in 1662-1681; captain by 1662; member of the Anne Arundel County Court, 1658, and Talbot County Court, 1661-1681; soldier (rank not stated) circa 1675; paid for his services in the late expedition against the Nanticoke Indians in 1678; died by Aug 26, 1681 (date vacancy filled in the General Assembly). {Ref: ARMD 1:382, 1:426, 7:91, 7:134, 15:70, 15:254, 15:327, 54:364; BDML II:910}

WORSLEY (WORSTLEY), GEORGE (Kent County), military officer (rank not stated) who swore allegiance to the King & Queen of England in 1696; died testate by Jan 15, 1721/2 (date of probate of nuncupative will). {Ref: ARMD 20:541; MDWB 17:77}

WORTHINGTON, ALICE, see "Samuel Worthington," q.v.

WORTHINGTON, JOHN (Anne Arundel County), captain by 1659; died by 1663 (widow Sarah Worthington mentioned in land conveyance). {Ref: AALR IH#1:145-146}

WORTHINGTON, JOHN (England and Anne Arundel County), captain by 1675; paid for his services in the late expedition against the Nanticoke Indians in 1678; captain and court justice in 1692; captain of horse troops and county coroner in 1694; military officer (rank not stated) who swore allegiance to the King & Queen of England in 1696; member of the Lower House of the Maryland Assembly, 1699-1700; born 1650, died testate on Apr 9, 1701 (will probated on May 7, 1701; Sarah Worthington, widow, later married Capt. John Brice, q.v.). {Ref: ARMD 7:96, 20:107-108, 20:541, 24:38; FAAH:145-147; RMHF II:291; AALR WT#1:124, WT#2:545; BDML II:913-914; AAGE:309-310; MDWB 11:63}

WORTHINGTON, SAMUEL (England and Somerset County), Protestant and soldier in the Revolution of 1689; signed an address and took a loyalty oath supporting the King of England and "for enabling us to defend ourselves against all invaders" on Nov 28, 1689; military officer (rank not stated) who swore allegiance to the King & Queen of England in 1696; member of the Lower House of the Maryland Assembly, 1708-1714; died testate by Jun 19, 1717 (date of probate; Alice Worthington, widow). {Ref: ARMD 8:141, 20:544, 27:202; BDML II:915; MDWB 14:406}

WORTHINGTON, SARAH, see "John Worthington," q.v.

WORTHINGTON, WILLIAM, see "John Cromwell," q.v.

WOTTERS, JOHN (Talbot County), soldier (rank not stated) circa 1675; paid for his services in the late expedition against the Nanticoke Indians in 1678. {Ref: ARMD 7:89}

WOTTON, EDWARD (Somerset County), soldier (rank not stated) circa 1675; paid for his services in the late expedition against the Nanticoke Indians in 1678. {Ref: ARMD 7:98}

WOULDHAVE, WILLIAM (Somerset County), Protestant and probable soldier in the Revolution of 1689; signed an address and took a loyalty oath supporting the King of England and "for enabling us to defend ourselves against all invaders" on Nov 28, 1689. {Ref: ARMD 8:140}

WRAXALL, PETER (county or port not indicated), captain and master of the ship *Maryland Merchant* in 1668. {Ref: MDHM 5:340}

WRIEL, GEORGE, see "George Uriel," q.v.

WRIGHT, ALICE, see "Edward Wright," q.v.

WRIGHT, CHARLES (Kent and Queen Anne's Counties), military officer (rank not stated) who swore allegiance to the King & Queen of England in 1696; died testate by Jul 4, 1720 (date of probate; Katherine Wright, widow). {Ref: ARMD 20:541; MDWB 16:131}

WRIGHT, EDWARD (Queen Anne's County), Indian interpreter by 1723; captain of the Third Company of Foot on Jun 30, 1732; member of the Lower House of the Maryland Assembly at various times between 1716 and 1740; died Jan 8, 1740/1 (will probated on Jan 14, 1740/1; Alice Wright, widow). {Ref: ARMD 25:419, 39:220; MDHR 1:11; BDML II:918-919; MDWB 22:288}

WRIGHT, EZEKIEL (Anne Arundel County), captain of the ship *Nightingale* before 1720. See "Edward Butler," q.v. {Ref: MDAD 3:278; MINV 15:60}

WRIGHT, FRANCIS (Wales and Baltimore County), sheriff, 1661; member of the Lower House of the Maryland Assembly, 1663-1664 (when the Council met in September, 1664, he had gone on a special service to the Susquehannock Fort to bring back accurate information to the Assembly and Col. Nathaniel Utie presented a petition asking that Wright be excused); captain lieutenant of foot troops, commissioned Oct 7, 1665; died testate by Mar 25, 1667 (date of probate). {Ref: ARMD 3:533; BDML II:919; BBCF:707; MDWB 1:298}

WRIGHT, JOHN (Baltimore County), probable soldier (rank not stated) before 1682; paid for his services out of an assessment levied by the General Assembly for the public good in 1682. {Ref: ARMD 7:441}

WRIGHT, JOSEPH (Calvert County), Protestant and probable soldier in the Revolution of 1689; signed an address and took a loyalty oath supporting the King of England and "to reestablish Lord Baltimore in his ancient power and government" on Nov 16, 1689. {Ref: ARMD 8:131}

WRIGHT, KATHERINE, see "Charles Wright," q.v.

WRIGHT, MR., see "Robert Thompson," q.v.

WRIGHT, NATHANIEL (England and Queen Anne's County), captain before 1700; born circa 1657, died testate by Apr 25, 1710 (date of probate; Sarah Wright, widow). {Ref: MDWB 13:1; INAC 31:382; INAC 36A:206-207; *Chesapeake Cousins* 19:2, p. 39}

WRIGHT, RACHEL, see "William Wright," q.v.

WRIGHT (WRITE), SAMUELL (Talbot County), soldier (rank not stated) circa 1675; paid for his services in the late expedition against the Nanticoke Indians in 1678. {Ref: ARMD 7:88}

WRIGHT, SARAH, see "Nathaniel Wright," q.v.

WRIGHT, SOLOMON (England, and Kent and Queen Anne's Counties), military officer (rank not stated) who swore allegiance to the King & Queen of England in 1696; member of the Lower House of the Maryland Assembly, representing Kent County in 1700, and Queen Anne's County in 1708-1714; born circa 1655 (aged about 60 when deposed in 1715), died testate by Apr 20, 1717 (date of probate). {Ref: ARMD 20:541, 27:202; BDML II:923; MDEP:208; MDWB 14:330}

WRIGHT, THOMAS HYNSON (Queen Anne's County), possible soldier in the early 1700's; commissioned Ranger of Queen Anne's County on Mar 21, 1738/9; born circa 1687 (aged about 42 when deposed in 1729, aged about 49 when deposed in 1736, and aged about 52 when deposed in 1739). {Ref: MDCB 82:71; MDEP:208}

WRIGHT, WILLIAM (St. Mary's County), probable soldier (rank not stated) before 1682; paid for his services out of an assessment levied by the General Assembly for the public good in 1682; died intestate by May 13, 1721 (date of administration account; Rachel Wright, widow). {Ref: ARMD 7:442; MDAD 5:93; MDAD 4:421}

WROTH, JOHN (England, and Cecil and Kent Counties), Protestant and probable soldier in the Revolution of 1689; signed an address and took a loyalty oath supporting the King of England and the reestablishment of Lord Baltimore into power on Nov 18, 1689 (name listed only as "J. Wroth"); military officer (rank not stated) who swore allegiance to the King & Queen of England in 1696; member of the Lower House of the Maryland Assembly, 1692-1693; died by November 21, 1706 (date of burial). {Ref: ARMD 8:135, 20:541; BDML II:927}

WYATT, JOHN (Kent Island), captain and commander of the Isle of Kent in 1644. {Ref: INKC:178}

WYATT, THOMAS, see "Thomas Wiatt," q.v.

WYE, WILLIAM, JR. (Somerset County), mariner by 1734; captain, master and owner of the sloop *Seahorse* in 1738 (built in Somerset County in 1733). {Ref: MDCB 82:60}

WYNN (WYNNE), JOHN (Poplar Hill, St. Mary's County), doctor and probable soldier (rank not stated) circa 1675; paid for his services in the late expedition against the Nanticoke Indians in 1678; died testate by Mar 10, 1684/5 (date of probate; Anne Wynne, widow). {Ref: ARMD 7:102; MDWB 4:58}

YARDLEY, FRANCIS (Virginia, and Anne Arundel, St. Mary's, and Charles Counties), soldier and officer who lived in Northampton County, Virginia in 1642 and was in Maryland by 1651 (registered his cattle marks); colonel by 1652; parliamentary commissioner and councillor of Anne Arundel County in 1652-1653; died by 1655 in Lower Norfolk County, Virginia (on Apr 26, 1658 his relict Mrs. Sarah Yardley was mentioned in a Maryland provincial court case). *Note:* One source stated that he was "of Portobacco, Maryland" while another source stated "he owned land on Portobacco Creek, but never settled permanently in Maryland." Additional research will be necessary before drawing conclusions. {Ref: ARMD 3:276, 10:186, 41:51, 41:82; FAAH:37; BDML II:927-928}

YARDNALL, RICHARD (Baltimore County), soldier (rank not stated) circa 1675; paid for his services in the late expedition against the Nanticoke Indians in 1678. {Ref: ARMD 7:96}

YATE, GEORGE (Anne Arundel and Baltimore Counties), soldier (rank not stated) circa 1675; paid for his services in the late expedition against the

Nanticoke Indians in 1678; one "George Yate" died circa 1691 and another "George Yeate" (son of George Yate) died testate by Nov 18, 1717 (date of probate; Ruth Yate, widow). Additional research will be necessary before drawing conclusions. See "Thomas Stockett," q.v. {Ref: ARMD 7:96, 7:611; MDWB 14:540; BBCF:710}

YATE, JOHN (Dorchester County), soldier (rank not stated) circa 1675; paid for his services in the late expedition against the Nanticoke Indians in 1678. {Ref: ARMD 7:93}

YATE, RUTH, see "George Yate," q.v.

YATE, THOMAS (Kent County), soldier (rank not stated) circa 1675; paid for his services in the late expedition against the Nanticoke Indians in 1678. {Ref: ARMD 7:94}

YATES, ROBERT (Charles County), captain by 1725; major by 1742; member of the Lower House of the Maryland Assembly in 1742; born circa 1685-1689 (aged about 30 when deposed in 1719, aged about 40 when deposed in 1725, and aged about 53 when deposed in 1742); died intestate by Jul 27, 1743 (date of inventory; Ann Yates, widow). {Ref: CHLR M#2:83; BDML II:928; MINV 28:239}

YEILDHALL, WILLIAM (Anne Arundel County), soldier (rank not stated) circa 1675; paid for his services in the late expedition against the Nanticoke Indians in 1678; died testate by Jul 26, 1684 (date of probate; Jane Yeildhall, widow). {Ref: ARMD 7:96; MDWB 4:44}

YEO, JOHN (Kent County), "seaman within the said county" and a "sailor (master) belonging to the *Factor* of Bediford" in 1697. {Ref: ARMD 25:599}

YEOMAN, CHRISTOPHER (Annapolis District), captain and master of the ship *Three Brothers* in 1731. {Ref: CVPR:12}

YEOMANS, THOMAS (Talbot County), soldier (rank not stated) circa 1675; paid for his services in the late expedition against the Nanticoke Indians in 1678. {Ref: ARMD 7:87}

YEWELL, THOMAS (Kent Island and Wye River, Talbot County), soldier (rank not stated) circa 1675; paid for his services in the late expedition against the Nanticoke Indians in 1678 (name listed once as "Thomas Youall" and misinterpreted once as "Thomas Yeovill"); born circa 1618 (aged about 22 when deposed in 1640), died testate by Jun 18, 1696 (date of probate; Sarah Yewell, widow). {Ref: ARMD 5:189-191, 7:91; MDWB 7:143}

YOAKLEY (YOAKLY), MICHAEL (Annapolis District), captain of a ship (no name given) in 1696; captain and master of the ship *Hopewell* riding at anchor in Severn River on Apr 5, 1701 and Jun 3, 1704. {Ref: ARMD 23:10; AALR WT#2:324-325}

YOAKLEY (YOAKLY), STEPHEN (Anne Arundel and Charles Counties), captain by 1714; commander of the ship *South River Merchant* riding at anchor in South River on Mar 9, 1714/5; master and commander of the ship *Coeur Fidelle* (also spelled *Cour Fidel* and *Coaurfidell*) riding in South River on Apr 30, 1724 and Feb 17, 1725/6 and Oct 4, 1726; mariner and land owner on the Western Branch of the Patuxent River by 1729; died by Jan 29, 1733/4 (date of inventory). See "John Reas," q.v. {Ref: AALR IB#2:197, AALR RCW#2:235, AALR SY#1:167, 273-274; PGLR M:508; MINV 18:33}

YONN, JOHN (Talbot County), Protestant and probable soldier in the Revolution of 1689; signed an address and took a loyalty oath supporting the King of England and the reestablishment of Lord Baltimore into power on Nov 18, 1689. {Ref: ARMD 8:134}

YORK (YORKE), WILLIAM (Bush River, Baltimore County), sergeant before 1682; paid for his services out of an assessment levied by the General Assembly for the public good in 1682; died testate by Feb 6, 1690/1 (date of probate; Mary Yorke, widow). {Ref: ARMD 7:441; BBCF:712; MDWB 6:71}

YORKSON, YORK (Cecil County), Protestant and probable soldier in the Revolution of 1689; signed an address and took a loyalty oath supporting the King of England and the reestablishment of Lord Baltimore into power on Nov 18, 1689. {Ref: ARMD 8:135}

YOUNG, DOROTHY, see "Richard Young," q.v.

YOUNG, ELIZABETH, see "George Young" and "Nicholas Young," q.v.

YOUNG, GEORGE (Anne Arundel and Calvert Counties), Protestant and probable soldier in the Revolution of 1689; signed an address and took a loyalty oath supporting the King of England and "to reestablish Lord Baltimore in his ancient power and government" on Nov 16, 1689; born circa 1651 (aged about 60 when deposed in 1711), died testate by Jun 7, 1718 (date of probate; Elizabeth Young, widow). See "Richard Young," q.v. {Ref: ARMD 8:132; HCCM:337; MDEP:209; MDWB 14:613}

YOUNG, JACOB (Delaware, and Baltimore and Cecil Counties), Indian interpreter in Maryland by 1672 and lived in Delaware until August, 1676; attended the peace talks with Col. Henry Coursey and Col. Philemon Lloyd at Fort Albany in 1682; died testate after Feb 22, 1696/7 (date he wrote his will). {Ref: ARMD 7:363, 7:386-392, 15:122, 15:358, 17:113, 51:87; MDWB 7:277}

YOUNG, JOHN (Anne Arundel County), captain by 1709; master gunner and storekeeper of the magazine at Annapolis in 1714; doorkeeper to the Maryland Council by 1723. {Ref: ARMD 25:295, 25:447, 27:451}

YOUNG, LAURENCE (Charles County), soldier (rank not stated) circa 1675; paid for his services in the late expedition against the Nanticoke Indians in 1678. {Ref: ARMD 7:101}

YOUNG, NICHOLAS (England and St. Mary's County), captain by 1665; member of the Lower House of the Maryland Assembly, 1666; captain, paid for his services on September 25, 1666; captain lieutenant, commissioned Sep 7, 1667; died testate by Jan 29, 1669/70 (date of probate; Elizabeth Young, widow). {Ref: ARMD 3:557, 5:13; BDML II:931; MDWB 1:365}

YOUNG, RICHARD (England, and Magothy River, Anne Arundel County), Puritan and captain by 1649; sheriff after 1650 (date of death not known; Dorothy Young, widow; sons Richard, George, and William Young were in Calvert County circa 1663). {Ref: HCCM:336-337; Land Patent 6:77-79}

YOUNG, SAMUEL (England and Anne Arundel County), burgess (member of Lower House of the General Assembly), 1698-1724; Treasurer of the Western Shore, 1700-1736; provincial court justice, 1705-1707, 1712-1725; lieutenant colonel by 1714; colonel by 1721; died testate on Jun 23, 1736 (will probated on Jul 7, 1736). {Ref: ARMD 25:39, 25:277, 25:377, 25:418, 29:347, 30:165, 34:741; BDML II:931; AALR RCW#2:59; MDWB 21:707; MINV 24:130}

YOUNG, WILLIAM, see "Richard Young," q.v.

YOUNG, WILLIAM (Talbot County), soldier (rank not stated) circa 1675; paid for his services in the late expedition against the Nanticoke Indians in 1678. {Ref: ARMD 7:91}

YOUNGER, JOHN (Potomac District), captain and master of the ship *Union* in 1730-1731. {Ref: CVPR:12}

YOUNGER, JOHN (Talbot County), soldier (rank not stated) circa 1675; paid for his services in the late expedition against the Nanticoke Indians in 1678. {Ref: ARMD 7:92}

YOUNGMAN, JOHN (Talbot County), soldier (rank not stated) circa 1675; paid for his services in the late expedition against the Nanticoke Indians in 1678. {Ref: ARMD 7:90}

Other books by the author:

A Closer Look at St. John's Parish Registers [Baltimore County, Maryland], 1701-1801

A Collection of Maryland Church Records

A Guide to Genealogical Research in Maryland: 5th Edition, Revised and Enlarged

Abstracts of the Ledgers and Accounts of the Bush Store and Rock Run Store, 1759-1771

Abstracts of the Orphans Court Proceedings of Harford County, 1778-1800

Abstracts of Wills, Harford County, Maryland, 1800-1805

Baltimore City [Maryland] Deaths and Burials, 1834-1840

Baltimore County, Maryland, Overseers of Roads, 1693-1793

Bastardy Cases in Baltimore County, Maryland, 1673-1783

Bastardy Cases in Harford County, Maryland, 1774-1844

Bible and Family Records of Harford County, Maryland Families: Volume V

Children of Harford County: Indentures and Guardianships, 1801-1830

Colonial Delaware Soldiers and Sailors, 1638-1776

*Colonial Families of the Eastern Shore of Maryland
Volumes 5, 6, 7, 8, 9, 11, 12, 13, 14, and 16*

Colonial Maryland Soldiers and Sailors, 1634-1734

Dr. John Archer's First Medical Ledger, 1767-1769, Annotated Abstracts

Early Anglican Records of Cecil County

*Early Harford Countians, Individuals Living in Harford County, Maryland in Its Formative Years
Volume 1: A to K, Volume 2: L to Z, and Volume 3: Supplement*

Harford County Taxpayers in 1870, 1872 and 1883

Harford County, Maryland Divorce Cases, 1827-1912: An Annotated Index

Heirs and Legatees of Harford County, Maryland, 1774-1802

Heirs and Legatees of Harford County, Maryland, 1802-1846

Inhabitants of Baltimore County, Maryland, 1763-1774

Inhabitants of Cecil County, Maryland, 1649-1774

Inhabitants of Harford County, Maryland, 1791-1800

Inhabitants of Kent County, Maryland, 1637-1787

*Joseph A. Pennington & Co., Havre De Grace, Maryland Funeral Home Records:
Volume II, 1877-1882, 1893-1900*

Maryland Bible Records, Volume 1: Baltimore and Harford Counties

Maryland Bible Records, Volume 2: Baltimore and Harford Counties

Maryland Bible Records, Volume 3: Carroll County

Maryland Bible Records, Volume 4: Eastern Shore

Maryland Deponents, 1634-1799

Maryland Deponents: Volume 3, 1634-1776

*Maryland Public Service Records, 1775-1783: A Compendium of Men and Women of
Maryland Who Rendered Aid in Support of the American Cause against
Great Britain during the Revolutionary War*

*Marylanders to Carolina: Migration of Marylanders to
North Carolina and South Carolina prior to 1800*

Marylanders to Kentucky, 1775-1825

Methodist Records of Baltimore City, Maryland: Volume 1, 1799-1829

Methodist Records of Baltimore City, Maryland: Volume 2, 1830-1839

Methodist Records of Baltimore City, Maryland: Volume 3, 1840-1850 (East City Station)

More Maryland Deponents, 1716-1799

More Marylanders to Carolina: Migration of Marylanders to North Carolina and South Carolina prior to 1800

More Marylanders to Kentucky, 1778-1828

Outpensioners of Harford County, Maryland, 1856-1896

Presbyterian Records of Baltimore City, Maryland, 1765-1840

Quaker Records of Baltimore and Harford Counties, Maryland, 1801-1825

Quaker Records of Northern Maryland, 1716-1800

Quaker Records of Southern Maryland, 1658-1800

Revolutionary Patriots of Anne Arundel County, Maryland

Revolutionary Patriots of Baltimore Town and Baltimore County, 1775-1783

Revolutionary Patriots of Calvert and St. Mary's Counties, Maryland, 1775-1783

Revolutionary Patriots of Caroline County, Maryland, 1775-1783

Revolutionary Patriots of Cecil County, Maryland

Revolutionary Patriots of Charles County, Maryland, 1775-1783

Revolutionary Patriots of Delaware, 1775-1783

Revolutionary Patriots of Dorchester County, Maryland, 1775-1783

Revolutionary Patriots of Frederick County, Maryland, 1775-1783

Revolutionary Patriots of Harford County, Maryland, 1775-1783

Revolutionary Patriots of Kent and Queen Anne's Counties

Revolutionary Patriots of Lancaster County, Pennsylvania

Revolutionary Patriots of Maryland, 1775-1783: A Supplement

Revolutionary Patriots of Maryland, 1775-1783: Second Supplement

Revolutionary Patriots of Montgomery County, Maryland, 1776-1783

Revolutionary Patriots of Prince George's County, Maryland, 1775-1783

Revolutionary Patriots of Talbot County, Maryland, 1775-1783

Revolutionary Patriots of Worcester and Somerset Counties, Maryland, 1775-1783

Revolutionary Patriots of Washington County, Maryland, 1776-1783

St. George's (Old Spesutia) Parish, Harford County, Maryland: Church and Cemetery Records, 1820-1920

St. John's and St. George's Parish Registers, 1696-1851

Survey Field Book of David and William Clark in Harford County, Maryland, 1770-1812

The Crenshaws of Kentucky, 1800-1995

The Delaware Militia in the War of 1812

Union Chapel United Methodist Church Cemetery Tombstone Inscriptions, Wilna, Harford County, Maryland